Ius Gentium: Comparative Perspectives on Law and Justice

Volume 66

More information about this series at http://www.springer.com/series/7888

Stefan Huygebaert · Georges Martyn
Vanessa Paumen · Eric Bousmar
Xavier Rousseaux
Editors

The Art of Law

Artistic Representations and Iconography of Law and Justice in Context, from the Middle Ages to the First World War

Springer

Editors
Stefan Huygebaert
Department of Art, Ghent Legal History Institute, FWO (Research Foundation Flanders)
Ghent University
Ghent, Belgium

Georges Martyn
Ghent Legal History Institute
Ghent University
Ghent, Belgium

Vanessa Paumen
Flemish research centre for the arts of the Burgundian Netherlands, Musea Brugge
Bruges, Belgium

Eric Bousmar
Centre de recherches en histoire du droit et des institutions
Université Saint-Louis
Brussels, Belgium

Xavier Rousseaux
Centre d'histoire du droit et de la justice
Université catholique de Louvain
Louvain-la-Neuve, Belgium

ISSN 1534-6781 ISSN 2214-9902 (electronic)
Ius Gentium: Comparative Perspectives on Law and Justice
ISBN 978-3-030-08100-3 ISBN 978-3-319-90787-1 (eBook)
https://doi.org/10.1007/978-3-319-90787-1

This Springer imprint is published by the registered company Springer Nature Switzerland AG
The registered company address is: Gewerbestrasse 11, 6330 Cham, Switzerland

Preface

This edited volume is the result of a fruitful cooperation between historians, jurists, art historians and legal historians, and assembles a selection of papers presented at the international conference *The Art of Law. Artistic Representations and Iconography of Law and Justice in Context, from the Middle Ages to the First World War*, held in Bruges (Belgium) from 16 to 18 January 2017. The academic meeting was organised by the Flemish research centre for the arts of the Burgundian Netherlands (Musea Brugge) and the Ghent Legal History Institute (Ghent University), and had its venue in the Groeningemuseum.

From 28 October 2016 through 5 February 2017, the museum hosted the exhibition *The Art of Law. Three Centuries of Justice depicted*. This art exhibition, curated by Vanessa Paumen and Tine Van Poucke, featured about 130 artworks from over 30 national and international museums, libraries and private collections and focused on themes related to justice as expressed in artworks of various media from about 1450 through 1750. The curators, together with Georges Martyn and Stefan Huygebaert from the Legal History Institute of Ghent University, aimed to demonstrate how strongly interconnected art and law were during this period. In the second chapter of this contributed volume, Vanessa Paumen, curator of the exhibition, briefly describes the objectives and particular features of the exhibition and highlights some exhibited artworks and objects.

Referring to the exhibition, an open call for papers was published via various history, art history and legal history networks. The scientific committee of the conference was composed of Prof. Marc Boone (Ghent University, Medieval History), Prof. Eric Bousmar (Université Saint-Louis Brussels, Centre de Recherches en Histoire du Droit et des Institutions), Prof. Bruno Dewever (Ghent University, Contemporary History), Drs. Stefan Huygebaert (Ghent University/ FWO, Art History), Prof. Samuel Mareel (Museum Hof van Busleyden Malines, Royal Museum of Fine Arts Antwerp, Ghent University), Prof. Georges Martyn (Ghent University, Faculty of Law and Criminology), Vanessa Paumen (Flemish research centre for the arts in the Burgundian Netherlands, Musea Brugge), Prof. Xavier Rousseaux (Université catholique de Louvain, Centre d'Histoire du Droit et de la Justice) and Prof. Nathalie Tousignant (Université Saint-Louis Brussels,

Centre de recherches en histoire du droit et des institutions). From the more than 50 proposals, the committee selected 25 researchers to present a paper on aspects of legal iconography and legal iconology. This list was completed by eight invited speakers, renowned scholars who have been publishing on the interdisciplinary subject of art and law in the past years. The interaction among the participants, younger and more experienced scholars, jurists, criminologists, anthropologists, art historians and general historians, led to innovative insights and attractive new hypotheses.

After the conference, the organisers invited a selection of the speakers to deliver a text for publication, asking them to take into account the discussions during the conference, and the remarks made by independent external reviewers. As a result, the present book does not contain the complete proceedings of the whole 3-day conference. Financial limitation obliged the editors to make a choice, based, on the one hand, on the quality of the presented papers, and, on the other, on the concern to make a relevant and coherent book (as some kind of second panel to the diptych constituted together with the catalogue of the exhibition mentioned above). Peer review by both art and legal historians guarantee the high level of the contributions. The editors wish to thank all speakers and participants for the thought-provoking discussions, and the contributors to this book for taking into account the remarks and suggestions made by the editors and the external reviewers.

Acknowledgements are also due to the subsidising institutions, who made both the conference and these proceedings possible: the Fonds National de la Recherche Scientifique FNRS, Research Foundation Flanders (FWO), Flemish research centre for the arts of the Burgundian Netherlands (Musea Brugge) and, most prominently, the Belgian Federal Science Policy Department's Interuniversity Attraction Pole 'Justice and Populations: The Belgian Experience in International Perspective, 1795–2015'. This inter-university research project includes both Belgian universities and other scientific institutions, as well as several international partners. The fourth work package of the Interuniversity Attraction Pole (P7/22) 'Long term (Self-) Representations of Justice' focuses on post-1795 legal iconography, which perfectly fits in the scope of the conference.

The first part of this contributed volume gives a general introduction to the subject of historical legal iconography and iconology, particularly focusing on the subject of justice administration. In the first chapter, the editors situate the overall theme and briefly introduce how the several contributors handle various aspects of the broad topic. Vanessa Paumen, curator of the aforementioned exhibition, shines light on how justice was depicted in the Early Modern Era, highlighting the main themes and artworks of the exhibition. Dr. Carolin Behrmann, keynote speaker at the conference, elaborates on early modern iconology.

Parts II–V contain various case studies from Western art. The second part deals with classical *exempla justitiae* as part of the decoration of courtrooms and justice places (incl. churches), while the third part concentrates on the representation of judges, lawyers, their work and their symbols. Part IV has chapters on artworks in criminal law and criminal justice administration in art. The last part is dedicated to courtroom decorations in the long nineteenth century. The very first chapter of the first part explicitly weaves threads between the various contributions: evolving iconography, shifting symbolism, analogies and antinomies and comparative remarks.

Ghent, Belgium Stefan Huygebaert
Ghent, Belgium Georges Martyn
Bruges, Belgium Vanessa Paumen
Brussels, Belgium Eric Bousmar
Louvain-la-Neuve, Belgium Xavier Rousseaux

Acknowledgements

This book has been published with the support of

- The Interuniversity Attraction Poles, programme initiated by the Belgian Science Policy Office (Interuniversity Attraction Pole '*Justice and Populations: The Belgian Experience in International Perspective, 1795–2015*')
- FWO—Research Foundation Flanders
- FNRS—Fund for Scientific Research Wallonia-Brussels Federation

Contents

Editors and Contributors

About the Editors

Stefan Huygebaert is an art historian (Ghent University, 2011). Since October 2012, he is preparing a Ph.D. thesis at the Ghent Legal History Institute/Department of Art History (Ghent University), entitled *Visual Idea(l)s of Law and Justice*. This Ph.D. research analyses the visual language of law and justice in Belgium during the nineteenth century. Since October 2015, he is a Research Foundation Flanders (FWO) Ph.D. fellow. Both in 2014–2015 and in 2016–2017, he was a Predoctoral Fellow at the Kunsthistorisches Institut in Florenz, within the Minerva Research Group 'The Nomos of Images: Manifestation and Iconology of Law'. He has published on legal and constitutional iconology and nineteenth-century art.

Georges Martyn studied Law (1984–1989) and Medieval Studies (1989–1991) and obtained a Ph.D. degree in Law at the Catholic University of Leuven in 1996, with a dissertation on private law legislation in the early modern Netherlands. He has been an '*advocaat*' (barrister/lawyer) between 1992 and 2008 at the bar of Kortrijk, is now honorary member of the Ghent bar and is a substitute justice of the peace in Kortrijk since 1999. He is Full Professor at the University of Ghent Law School since 1999, teaching mainly history of public law at bachelor level and Law and the Humanities at master level.

Vanessa Paumen is the Coordinator of The Flemish research centre for the arts in the Burgundian Netherlands (Musea Brugge). Its mission is to initiate, facilitate, stimulate and disseminate research related to Flemish art of the fifteenth and sixteenth centuries. At the centre, Vanessa co-develops and coordinates academic programmes, annual lectures series and the expansion of the library in the fields of fifteenth and sixteenth centuries art history and related areas. She is an art historian specialised in Northern Renaissance art and obtained her degrees in Art History from The University of Texas at Austin (USA). She is the Curator of the exhibition

'The art of law. Three centuries of justice depicted' at the Groeningemuseum (Bruges) and editor/author of its accompanying catalogue.

Eric Bousmar studied History (1991) and Medieval Studies (1992) in Louvain-la-Neuve and Leuven and obtained his Ph.D. in Louvain-la-Neuve (1997). He is at present a Full Professor at the Université Saint-Louis—Bruxelles, Faculty of Arts, and one of the three directors of this university's research centre in legal and political history (the *CRHiDI*). He focuses on the political and cultural history of the Low Countries under Burgundian and early Habsburg rule, as well as on matters of historiography, memory and medievalism. This includes an interest for visual materials, gender and historical anthropology.

Xavier Rousseaux is Research Director (FRS-FNRS) and Professor at the Université catholique de Louvain, Centre d'histoire du droit et de la justice. Working extensively on the history of crime and justice, he is coordinating the IAP Justice and Populations. The Belgian experience in international Perspective, 1795–1950. He co-edited with M. De Koster and D. Heirbaut *Tweehonderd Jaar Justitie. Historische Encyclopedie van de Belgische Justitie, Deux siècles de justice belge. Encyclopédie historique de la justice belge* (Bruges, La Charte-Die Keure, 2015) and with A. Hondeghem and F. Schoenaers *Modernisation of the Criminal Justice Chain and the Judicial System. New Insights on Trust, Cooperation and Human Capital* (Springer, 2015).

Contributors

Carolin Behrmann Minerva Research Group 'The Nomos of Images: Manifestation and Iconology of Law', Kunsthistorisches Institut in Florenz – Max-Planck-Institut, Florence, Italy

Jérôme de Brouwer Centre for Legal History and Legal Anthropology, Free University of Brussels (ULB), Brussels, Belgium

Amandine De Burchgraeve FRS-FNRS (Université catholique de Louvain, IUAP 9/22 Justice and Populations), Louvain, Belgium

Guy Delmarcel Department of Art History, University of Leuven, Louvain, Belgium

Brecht Deseure Institute of Philosophy, University of Leuven, Leuven, Belgium

Gaëlle Dubois FRS-FNRS (Université catholique de Louvain, IUAP 9/22 Justice and Populations), Louvain, Belgium

Jozefien Feyaerts Department of Art History, Ghent University, Ghent, Belgium

Tamara Golan History of Art Department, Johns Hopkins University, Baltimore, MD, USA

Valérie Hayaert Käte Hamburger Kolleg “Recht als Kultur”, Internationales Kolleg für Geisteswissenschaftliche Forschung/Center for Advanced Study in the Humanities “Law as Culture”, Bonn, Germany

Ann-Kathrin Hubrich Department of Art History, Graduate School Humanities, University of Hamburg, and Hamburger Kunsthalle, Hamburg, Germany

Stefan Huygebaert Department of Art History, Musicology and Theatre Studies, Ghent Legal History Institute, Ghent University and Research Foundation Flanders (FWO), Ghent, Belgium

Felix Jäger Minerva Research Group ‘The Nomos of Images: Manifestation and Iconology of Law’, Kunsthistorisches Institut in Florenz, Max-Planck-Institut, Florence, Italy

Gustav Kalm Department of Anthropology, Columbia University, New York, USA

Rahela Khorakiwala Centre for the Study of Law and Governance, Jawaharlal Nehru University, New Delhi, India

Mia Korpiola Faculty of Law, University of Turku, Turku, Finland

Georges Martyn Ghent Legal History Institute, Ghent University, Ghent, Belgium

Vanessa Paumen Flemish research centre for the arts in the Burgundian Netherlands (Musea Brugge), Bruges, Belgium

Xavier Rousseaux Fonds National de la Recherche Scientifique, Centre for Law and Justice History, Université catholique de Louvain, Louvain-La-Neuve, Belgium

Clare Sandford-Couch School of Law, Faculty of Business and Law, Northumbria University, Newcastle, UK

Raf Verstegen Law Faculty, University of Leuven, Leuven, Belgium

Alain Wijffels Faculteit Rechtsgeleerdheid, Universiteit Leiden, Leiden, The Netherlands; Faculteit Rechtsgeleerdheid, KU Leuven, Leuven, Belgium; Faculté de Droit, Université catholique de Louvain, Louvain-la-Neuve, Belgium; CNRS, Centre d’histoire judiciaire, Université de Lille 2, Lille, France

Paul De Win Formerly Legal History Institute, Ghent University, Ghent, Belgium; Federal Public Service of Foreign Affairs, Brussels, Belgium

Beatrijs Wolters van der Wey Royal Institute for Cultural Heritage (KIK-IRPA), Brussels, Belgium

Part I
Law, Justice and Art in Historical Perspective

Chapter 1
Twenty New Contributions to the Upcoming Research Field of Historical Legal Iconology

Georges Martyn and Stefan Huygebaert

Abstract In the general introduction to this contributed volume of selected conference proceedings, the title 'The Art of Law' is explained, particularly by situating the Bruges interdisciplinary conference in the 'Arts and Humanities' movement. A short overview of the *status quaestionis* of historical legal iconology is given, and suggestions are made on how art historians and legal historians can collaborate in a field of research that is very attractive for both disciplines. This introductory paper also identifies some methodological and material links between the various contributions to the volume.

1.1 Introduction

In 1405, court clerk Jan Matthijsen wrote an account on the judicial proceedings and the applicable law of his home town of Den Briel in Holland. In his *Rechtsboek van Den Briel*, he specified what a proper courtroom—or, more precisely, a 'deliberation room'—should look like. '[T]he room will be made clean inside and filled with paintings and inscribed with good old wise words, from which one can acquire wisdom and cleverness; as one says: to behold is to be aware, to think upon, to remember well…' (Paumen 2016, p. 81; and see the contribution by *Hubrich* in this volume). The phrase convincingly illustrates the link, in the late medieval and early modern Low Countries, between law and the visual arts in general, and the use of courtroom decorations in particular. From town hall decorations depicting the Last Judgment and so-called *exempla justitiae*, via the allegory of justice in the figure of a woman with scales and a sword on frontispieces of books, to the nineteenth-century

G. Martyn (✉)
Ghent Legal History Institute, Ghent University, Ghent, Belgium
e-mail: Georges.Martyn@UGent.be

S. Huygebaert
Flemish Research Fund (FWO), Ghent Legal History Institute, Ghent University, Ghent, Belgium
e-mail: Stefan.Huygebaert@UGent.be

S. Huygebaert et al. (eds.), *The Art of Law*, Ius Gentium: Comparative Perspectives on Law and Justice 66, https://doi.org/10.1007/978-3-319-90787-1_1

imposing architecture of palaces of justice, time and again it becomes clear that the practitioners of law used art in order to legitimate, explain and enlighten their judicial function, to perform their duty and to achieve their ideal of justice. This is the very heart of the subject of this contributed volume. It assembles a selection of papers presented at an international conference held in Bruges (Groeningemuseum) in January 2017, in the margin of the exhibition *The Art of Law. Three Centuries of Justice Depicted* (on which one can read more in Chap. 2 of this volume).

After some terminological remarks on the title *The Art of Law* (par. 2), this introductory chapter situates historical legal iconology in the wider context of the 'Law and the Humanities' movement and gives a short *status quaestionis* of this interdisciplinary research field (par. 3), before introducing the various contributions, comparing their methodology and content (par. 4). This chapter is concluded by some practical recommendations (par. 5).

1.2 The 'Art of Law' in the Sense of Historical Legal Iconology

Reading or hearing the exhibition and conference title *The Art of Law* might be a source of confusion, or at least raise more questions than it answers. 'Law' is already a terminological container for a range of broadly diverging concepts, going from Murphy's law over the laws of nature to juridical concepts such as general legislation, administrative deeds and case to case justice administration, and 'art' is probably a term whose meaning is even broader, as well as more vague.

The 'law' this book talks about is the set of rules and institutions used by the authorities (whose authority is based on legal—today more particularly constitutional—grounds) to order society. There is local, regional, national and international law, there are unwritten customary rules, statutory codes and legislation, there is theoretical jurisprudence, and there is day-to-day legal practice. Legal rules are age-old or brand new, created by a (legal or constitutional, or at the very least legitimate) authority. In Western countries, the legislator makes the law, and to a certain extent the judge, especially in the common law tradition. Rules, from the legislative branch as well as from other 'lawgivers', are applied by subjects and functionaries. And in case of dispute, judges—from the judiciary branch, but also private arbitrators and administrative courts—decide, declare void, annul, punish, condemn, etc. Law is the prominent institutional tool in all three branches of the *trias politica*. However, ask a man or woman in the street what law is, and he or she will most probably talk about courts, palaces of justice, the work of pleading lawyers wearing black gowns, inquiring public prosecutors and deciding judges. Although 'law' is more than 'justice administration', courtroom work is the most typical of all legal work, or at least the most recognisable to the broader public. No wonder that, through the centuries, artists too thought of court sessions when they were asked to portray law. 'Thinking of law' is 'thinking of courts applying rules', also for artists. *Three Centuries of Justice Depicted* was the subtitle of the Bruges exhibition (which focused solely on Ancien Régime art, whereas the conference expanded its scope to include the long nineteenth century as well). In both the exhibition and the conference, justice administration, in both civil and criminal cases, was the main point of interest. These practices revolve around the work of legal professionals such as judges, lawyers, proctors, registrars, in one word 'jurists'.

Art, on the other hand, is the work of 'artists'. And there are many kinds of them, just as there are many 'arts'. This book is not about literary art in prose and poetry, nor is it about the performing arts and music, cinema or comic books. The arts envisaged in the title of the conference are the classical visual arts. Contributions comment mostly on paintings (frescoes, canvasses and panels), but also on prints, drawings, reliefs, tapestries and sculptures. All of them could be independent works of art, but they are also decorative elements in a bigger whole, or even complete architectural *Gesammtkunstwerke*. As 'seeing' is a first step in 'understanding', illustrations (referred to in the texts by '*Fig. n.n*') in the various contributions show to the reader what the authors describe and analyse. The artworks under investigation are to be 'seen', to be 'looked at'. In the call for papers for the conference, the speakers were invited to provide not only a theoretical abstract, but also some images of concrete works of art, as examples or focus of their text. This is why each contribution is illustrated by images,[1] and why, in a certain sense, these proceedings form a diptych with the Bruges exhibition catalogue (Huygebaert et al. 2016).

So, what then is the 'art of law'? The title in no way refers to the skills trained jurists apply to solve legal problems: it is not the *ars boni et aequi*, the 'art of goodness and equity' that stands for legal science, i.e. the Roman *ius* as it was described in the preamble of Justinian's *Digest*. Neither is the art of law the—be it artistic, aesthetic, beautiful or not—result of law as such. Law does not generate anything. Jurists and institutions do. A statutory text might, and a judicial decision or (certainly) a doctrinal contribution can, be 'artistic'. But that is not what this book is about. This volume is about visual artworks, created by artists, and most often commissioned by jurists or legal, especially judicial, institutions (e.g. Block 1997).

The artworks discussed by the several scholars contributing to this volume 'represent', 'imagine', 'show', 'learn', 'instruct', or 'appeal'. They are created in a judicial or juridical context and echo legal concepts. 'Law' in its broadest sense gives meaning, or at least extra information, to what is represented. For example: left and right are compositional concepts but also the places of parties in a courtroom; Red is the colour of Christ's robe on Judgment Day, but also that of the magistrate's gown; Scales are a commercial object, but also a symbol for the equilibrium that stands for the judicial decision; A branch of a tree can also be the

[1]Unfortunately, it was not possible to obtain reproduction rights for all artworks mentioned in the contributions. The editors refer to *The Art of Law* exhibition catalogue for some of them, while most other images can easily be traced and found (be it not always in the most optimal quality) by simply entering the artist's name and the work's title in any internet search engine.

'rod of justice'; An iconographical—mostly pejorative—symbol such as the blindfold can become a positive sign of impartiality in a judicial context. And so on.

What *The Art of Law* is about, is investigating how, in Western culture, jurists and artists have interacted throughout the centuries. Jurists commissioned and inspired. Artists interpreted and created. This is why legal historians and art historians can help each other when studying these artworks. Knowledge of the law helps to understand the art, but knowledge of the art also contributes to a better understanding of law's original intent and social effects.

Most contributions to this volume describe specific artworks and subject them to an iconographical analysis. Iconography scrutinises signs, symbols, allegories and attributes, and tries to 'explain what one sees'. Many authors of the following contributions, however, go one step further, and also analyse the broader historical, institutional and social context, thus entering the field of iconology. Legal iconology in this sense studies the many interactions between the social networks of jurists and those of artists. Iconology studies how both law and art are socially embedded. The discussions following the presentations during the Bruges conference were at this point often very fruitful, and resulted in further and better elaborated texts.

The *The Art of Law* conference was, in sum, a feast of 'historical legal iconology': historical, because all contributions study art objects from—and contextualised in—a bygone age, from the Late Middle Ages to the outburst of the First World War. In these centuries, law and art, jurists and artists, seem to have been much closer to each other than today, in our specialised and professionalised world. Until the beginning of the twentieth century, for instance, top lawyers and magistrates were also leading figures in the world of art exhibitions, salons and artistic editions. Ancien Régime authorities nearly always used art to decorate courtrooms, while it is almost absent in the hieratic glass buildings of the twenty-first century. Unless of course one considers the architecture itself, transparent and open as it is nowadays, as an artistic statement.

The more one goes back towards the Middle Ages, the more art historians and legal historians seem to be able to understand each other. Latin was the *lingua franca*, and the common Christian roots were of paramount importance for the evolution of both art and law. Many early modern artworks cannot be understood fully without knowing the Bible, in the same way that early modern legal texts cannot be comprehended without knowing Roman (*ecclesia sub lege romana vivit*) and canon law. The Church engaged in education, both for artists and jurists. Law books, first in manuscript and later in print, spread throughout Europe (Dauchy et al. 2016), in the same way as artistic models were copied over and over again. There is a common European (and via the colonies 'Western') legal tradition as much as there is a common European artistic tradition. The crossroads of these traditions is what this contributed volume is about.

1.3 Law and Art in the Wider Field of Law and the Humanities

In recent years, we have witnessed a clear rise in scholarship on law and the visual (e.g. Douzinas and Nead 1999; Goodrich 2013, 2014; Goodrich and Hayaert 2015; Manchester and Becker-Moelands 1991; Manderson 2018; Resnik and Curtis 2011; Sherwin 2014), mostly originating in the wider field of 'Law and the Humanities' (Sarat et al. 2010). The Bruges conference wanted to contribute to this body of scholarship by focusing on imagery in its legal, historical and art-historical contexts.

'Law and the Humanities', just like 'Law and Economics', 'Law and Ethics' etc., is a way of looking at legal rules and institutions, and more in general, products of legal culture, from another point of view. Whereas most legal scholars research law and its history within the legal or juridical paradigm, 'Law and the Humanities' scholars take a step back, to look at law and its functioning from a distance, using the methods, definitions and paradigms of other social and cultural disciplines. 'Law and the Humanities' is essentially a cultural study of law, legal institutions, jurists and their writings, from the humanistic intellectual tradition of the liberal arts. The field(s) of study is (are) essentially interdisciplinary, exploring law's interaction with the world through the humanistic disciplines of classics, literature, philosophy, theology, and even poetry, music, cinema etc.

Looking at law from various points of view enriches the very idea of what law and legal science are, pretend to be, and often fail to be. The point of view from the field of Law and the Humanities is a critical one. Time and time again, it questions assumptions and aspirations ascribed to law. 'Law and Literature' is probably the oldest part of 'Law and the Humanities', and no one doubts the enriching experience literature can bring. Likewise, subjects such as 'Law and Cinema' or 'Law and Music' have found their way into conferences and academic education. 'Law and Art' is, at the moment, probably a somewhat less popular subject, even if it is certainly not untouched by international academic journals such as '*Law and Humanities*', '*Law, Culture and the Humanities*', '*Yale Journal of Law and the Humanities*', or '*Droit et Culture*'.

German-speaking scholarship has given rise to some more specialised journals on law and art: as a successor to *Forschungen zur Rechtsarchäologie und Rechtlichen Volkskunde* (1978–2007), there is *Signa Ivris. Beiträge zur Rechtsikonographie, Rechtsarchäologie und Rechtlichen Volkskunde* (2008–today). The fact that there are regular international conferences on (historical) legal iconography in Germanophone Europe (*Internationale Rechtsikonographie-Konferenze*) is without a doubt due to the fact that the founding fathers of this interdisciplinary field were Austrian, German and Swiss: Karl von Amira and Claudius von Schwerin (1943), and Hans Fehr (1923) and Luis Carlen. There is probably no other country with a legal archaeology and iconography museum as rich as the collection of the *Kriminalmuseum* in Rothenburg-ob-der-Tauber (Germany).

Although a basic introductory book to 'Law and Art' is still lacking, some major publications are of fundamental value. Both Wolfgang Schild (e.g. 1995) and Wolfgang Pleister have published various works on the subject, but the beautifully illustrated *Recht und Gerechtigkeit im Spiegel der europäischen Kunst* (1988) they have jointly edited is monumental. Robert Jacob's *Images de la Justice* (1994) is fundamental for French legal culture. These syntheses paved the way for the colossal work of Resnik and Curtis (2011).

While many of these fundamental works also pay attention to the role of the printed book, the most popular themes concern *exempla justitiae* and the evolution of allegories and symbols as part of courtroom decorations (e.g. De Ridder 1989 and Sutter 2008 for the Southern Netherlands; Lederle 1937 for Germany). Of law-related allegories, of course, the remarkable—and still not completely known[2]—birth and evolution of Lady Justice was the subject of numerous studies (e.g. Kissel 1984; Prosperi 2008; Robert 1993 and 1996; Rodríguez-López and Isabel 2003; Sbriccioli 2005). Additionally, the various ways in which other smaller images, gestures, utensils and symbols can refer to law, are very well presented in Kocher's (1992) collection. Printed matter, legal books and their frontispieces, titles and illustrations, but also emblem books, can be remarkable illustrations of law's history (Goodrich 2014; Röhl 2005), in the same way as their handwritten predecessors, Roman, canon and feudal law manuscripts, are of paramount importance for the emerging legal iconography (e.g. L'Engle and Gibbs 2001, or the many publications on the German *Sachsenspiegel*). Religious paintings, *Last Judgments*, but also painted martyrdom scenes, can be relevant as well for getting to know law and justice's past visually (Behrmann 2015).

Although the number of publications on historical legal iconography is growing, it is still a rather 'occasional' field of study. This book's conference was held in the margin of a temporary exhibition, just as it was the case in earlier times, for example at the celebration of the opening of a new judicial campus (Perez-Bustamante 2007, 2008), or an 'x-centennial' of a historical (Maes and Godenne 1949) or still functioning judicial institution (Dauchy and Demars-Sion 2001; Harju 2000; Moelands and De Smidt 1999). Some of these conferences and/or exhibitions usually drew attention to extreme subjects such as the horrible practice of the death penalty (Clair 2010) on the one hand, or satire and caricature on the other (Eichler et al. 2010, see also Chauvaud and Vernois 2004). It is nice to see that, recently, various legal history journals tend to have an iconographical article in each issue (e.g. the Dutch-Flemish journal *Pro Memorie*), or at least devote a special issue on the subject from time to time (e.g. *Rechtskultur*; see also Martyn et al. 2014). Furthermore, the legal iconography databases at Graz University (http://www-gewi.uni-graz.at/cocoon/rehi/), Yale Law School's Lillian Goldman Law Library Rare Book Collection (http://library.law.yale.edu/rarebooks; Widener and Weiner 2017), the legal images collection of the University of Modena (http://www.fondiantichi.

[2]See the contribution by Hayaert in this volume and the same author's paper for the Malines exhibition catalogue Call for Justice (Mareel 2018).

unimo.it/fa/giustizia/default.html), the Nomos (*cf. infra*) online exhibition (http://photothek.khi.fi.it/documents/oau/00000250?Language=en), and the project site on judicial images (http://judicialimages.org/) are inspiring as well.

As a complement to the abovementioned richly edited books, catalogues, journals and websites, the present contributed volume hopes to add value to the academic level of 'Law and Art'. The conference organisers and editors were happy to be able to collaborate with several top researchers. Dr. Carolin Behrmann, who was invited as keynote speaker, is the leader of one of the rare research groups specialised in legal iconology, at the Kunsthistorisches Institut in Florenz (*Nomos der Bilder. Manifestation und Ikonologie des Rechts. Minerva Forschungsgruppe*, see https://www.khi.fi.it/de/Nomos). *The Art of Law* wants to be more than just a collection of illustrations of legal history. This book's aim is not only to describe and analyse 'art on law', it also tries to take into account 'law on art'. There is, and always has been, a mutual interaction between the two. Although this volume is not a 'legal' book within the legal paradigm (i.e. it is not addressing juridical subjects as intellectual property rights, prohibited obscene art, problems with artistic use of private portraits, the conceptual definition of crimes such as art forgery or illegal citation etc.), it does acknowledge the importance of knowing what the law is or was at a certain moment in time, how jurists thought and worked, how justice was administrated etc. These things do matter in understanding many of the studied art objects. This is why this contributed volume is more about 'iconology' than only 'iconography', entering the larger field of how artists and jurists have interacted throughout Western history. Most of the research mentioned above was done by legal historians. One of the main goals of the Bruges conference was to invite art history scholars and enter into discussion with them in order to have a broader perspective on the role of images in law and justice administration.

'Law', 'scales', 'Lady Justice', 'judge' etc. are terms not unknown to art historians. Within the internationally used Iconclass classification system, they have found a place in category 44 (State, Law and Politics),[3] subcategory 44G (Law and Justice Administration). However, when using the publicly accessible thesaurus interface (www.iconclass.nl) one can find many other iconographical categories that deal with law and justice. Iconclass was created by art historians, and could be improved by starting a dialogue with legal historians. The editors hope to contribute to this objective.

---

[3]The field of 'political iconography' is close to that of 'legal iconography' and, at the moment, is probably being studied more thoroughly (e.g. Fleckner et al. 2011; Warnke 2010). Cultural historians especially have looked into official imagery as part of the symbolism of politics and power (e.g. Agulhon 1979; Hunt 1984), often confronting political with popular culture.

1.4 Twenty New Contributions to Historical Legal Iconology

1.4.1 General Thoughts

The conference program brought together original and interdisciplinary scholarship discussing the role of art in the practice of law, jurisprudence and justice administration from the Late Middle Ages through the long nineteenth century. Starting from the focus of the exhibition, the conference gave rise to discussions on artworks transgressing the geographical, chronological and practical boarders of the exhibition (see Chap. 2).

Geographically, the exhibition's and this volume's focus is on the historical Low Countries and parts of the German territory, but conference papers also dealt with the French (*Hayaert*), Indian (*Khorakiwala*), Italian (*Sandford-Couch*), Scandinavian (*Korpiola*) and Swiss (*Golan*) contexts. With the conference, the organisers wanted to give the floor to researchers who wanted to formulate answer (s) to some of the most pertinent questions regarding such issues as the theological origins of legal imagery and iconography, the use of art in the practice of law and jurisprudence, the impact of technological and genre evolutions (such as the printing press, frontispieces and/or emblemata on legal iconography), the presence and function of legal iconography in urban public space, the role of spectatorship in the relation between art and law, and imagery as a visual source for legal history. As the director of the aforementioned Nomos-project, dr. *Carolin Behrmann* was invited to elaborate on these and other questions in her keynote lecture. In the third chapter of this introductory part to the volume, she positions modern iconology within the broader fields of art and legal history, and explains how, until very recently, law and legal science seem to have been afraid of the 'ocular centrism' typical for so many other modern sciences. Referring to recent scholarship, she describes how understanding the law through the visual sphere has become a multifaceted enterprise with similar approaches and hypothetical assumptions just as in the humanities and science. Starting from the German word '*Bild*' and making a distinction between '(material) pictures' and '(mental) images', Behrmann shows how Anglo-American 'visual studies' have been looking at the interaction between art and law differently than the continental analysis building on the art historical foundations laid by scholars as Warburg and Panofsky. She further elaborates that art history as '*Bildgeschichte*' and legal culture, which deals with the pictures, objects, architecture and all other visual signs of legal contexts, are based on the methodological premise that images and objects 'reflect' the law. It brings her to the 'mirror axiom' of her paper's title. The mirror is an attribute of the personification of the virtue prudence, but in the Middle Ages, books as the *Saxon Mirror* were also some kind of codification of customary rules, some kind of 'reflection' of positive law. For ages, like a mirror of Princes was to the Prince, the *speculum iuris* was a specific genre that dealt with the education of the perfect jurist.

Carolin Behrmann further develops the mirror metaphor and raises questions on the 'reality' and the 'legal reality' of the mirrored images. 'A kind of "naive realism", that overrates the evidential value of pictures, tends to neglect varying interpretations of visual phenomena in law', she states. A challenging idea she proposes is that '(i)t should be asked why often studies about the legal visual realm consider the image as momentarily, as reflection and objectifying mirror of society rather than a complex organ of social memory that records and transmits far more than a hermeneutical reading of the verbal meanings of visual signs would disclose'. In order to elucidate, she takes a closer look, as so many historians, art historians and even legal historians have done before, at Jan Van Eyck's Arnolfini double portrait in the National Gallery in London. It is, to her, 'in many respects an insightful and early example of the dialogue between art history and legal history'. Some of the elements she studies in it are the expression of per fidem, as already 'discovered' by Panofsky, but especially the presence of the painter himself, seen in the mirror on the wall. Is his presence merely occasional, or is he a legally necessary witness, and does the painting only represent the marriage or does it play a role in the legal marriage procedure itself? Or was not a marriage, but only a betrothal represented here?

Starting from the well-known Van Eyck example, Carolin Behrmann more generally frames the contributions to this volume as investigations on how far visual images have effect, power, or become part of legal reasoning and the creation and institutionalisation of legal meaning. Assuming there is no 'golden wall' between the aesthetic realm and the legal one, one might induce that the analysis of form and even style of an artwork can unravel legal meaning. Just like 'mirror', also 'style' was, already in the Middle Ages, not only a general, but also a concrete legal term, referring to the customary rules of procedure of a particular court. Several of the Bruges conference's papers were incentives for the keynote speaker to elaborate on this new theme on art and law.

1.4.2 Moralising Law and Justice Representations in the Late Middle Ages and Early Modern Era

The second part of this volume addresses the most traditional theme of legal iconography, which was also at the heart of the Bruges exhibition: the decoration of places of justice. These include not only town halls, prisons and execution sites, but also sacred places such as church porches. Rooted in Christian faith, the almost omnipresent and most appealing representation of the ultimate example of justice, is the Last Judgment. *Clare Sandford-Couch* underlines that such images, in the medieval mind, could have both a religious and a civic meaning, allowing multiple and varying readings by viewers. She studies (preserved) representations of the Last Day in various cities of Northern Italy between 1300 and 1400, and argues that it is possible to see the emergence of a change in values and punishment practices in the iconography of these scenes. At first sight, one might think that, the more horrifying the images of hell become, the more punitive the legal system itself will be. However, her analysis suggests the opposite: around the same time, there seems to have been both a decline in the use of physical punishments in the secular courts and an increase of detailed representations of such punishments. The author investigates whether the artistic shift reveals a philosophy of law in a process of transition: from retributive to more utilitarian justice. The powerful visual effect of increasingly horrifying depictions of the punishment of sinners in the afterlife may have played an active role as some kind of 'visual trick', helping to address a gap between contemporary criminal justice practice and criminal justice rhetoric.

Finnish legal historian *Mia Korpiola* continues on this judicial-religious theme, and studies representations of the Last Judgment, as well as of other sacred themes, in Sweden and Finland. The examples she studies were created around the same time, but in a completely different legal and social context. Swedish lay judges, far away from the legal heart of Europe (i.e. Bologna and other centres of Roman and canon scholarship) had no university training at all. Public buildings and images were also scarcer. The only imagery that was seen and understood by all was ecclesiastical imagery in churches. The scope of their motifs, as far as law and justice are concerned, was limited: images of the Last Judgment and of Saint Michael weighing souls predominated. Few churches had murals with, for example, Moses receiving the Tables of the Law, Solomon's judgment, or truth- or justice-related Biblical verses in Latin. Like *Clare Sandford-Couch*, *Mia Korpiola* stresses the importance of the Last Judgment (and/or Saint Michael as some kind of *pars pro toto*), together with very often images of devils tempting people into sin and perdition. In Swedish legal culture, this kind of visualisations had a general moralising meaning, but also a practical judicial one, for example at the swearing of an oath.

Frescos and murals, in both Northern and Southern Europe, constituted a first generation of decorations for judicial spaces. Most originals are probably lost, but the ones that survived show a continuity with fifteenth and sixteenth century panel paintings, such as those exhibited in Bruges (cf. Chap. 1 of the catalogue for a general analysis). Around the same time, however, images were also spread by tapestries, an artistic and artisan product often forgotten by law and art historians. The conference organisers were very happy to welcome emeritus professor *Guy Delmarcel* to introduce the audience to the world of sixteenth century Flemish tapestries. Guy Delmarcel taught history of art at the University of Leuven, and was also curator of textiles at the Royal Museums of Art and History in Brussels. He has published extensively on the history of ancient Flemish tapestry. Legal iconography scholars have traditionally studied paintings, statues and engravings, but very little attention has been given to tapestries, a most expensive kind of decoration, commissioned particularly by the elite. It need not surprise us, for instance, that a tapestry centre such as the Flemish town of Oudenaarde ordered the example of the Chaste Susanne to be made for its own town hall. However, in his paper, Delmarcel draws our attention to some lesser known works of art, most of them commissioned by princely courts and on the one hand addressing justice as a virtue, but on the other also displaying several examples of enthroned judges and other court settings. The size of the commissioned works and the particular composition of tapestry cartoons resulted in some uncommon stories being represented, bringing together various allegories, personifications and *exempla justitiae* (more extensively described in Chap. 2 of the exhibition catalogue, to which Delmarcel's paper is a welcome addition).

A most peculiar *exemplum* is the story of the corrupt judge sentenced to be flayed alive by the Mesopotamian King Cambyses. Bruges' late-fifteenth century artist Gerard David's horrifying diptych depicting this 'evergreen' anti-corruption story was a central masterpiece of the Bruges exhibition (see Chap. 3 exh. cat.). Emeritus legal history professor *Raf Verstegen* situates it in a larger art-historical panorama. The iconographical tradition of the flaying of Saint Bartholomew was likely an inspiration for David, as well as for miniaturists of his time. However, the painter probably also diligently observed the flaying of animals, and not a judicial practice of human flaying, since the latter, although known to have happened in other times and places, is not documented to have occurred in the Netherlands. David was probably also inspired by the upcoming representations of anatomical lessons. After his Bruges panels (which focused on the flaying itself), the original bribery and the judge's arrest quickly disappeared as part of the traditional representation. Artists started concentrating on the installation of the young judge on his father's skin, often with the flaying scene in the background. The iconography of flaying moved to the Renaissance framings of the Marsyas legend. The Cambyses story itself ended in an emblematic empty skin, as represented for instance on frontispieces of legal books. However, both in print and in courtroom decorations, the judgment of Cambyses should surely be seen as a classical *exemplum justitiae*.

As the final chapter of the second part, *Ann-Kathrin Hubrich*'s paper treats both *exempla* and the Last Judgment in the context of the decorative programme of the *Niedergericht* (the Lower Court) of the German town of Lüneburg. In a sense, this paper summarises the essential content of the first part of this contributed volume, and is complementary to the three first chapters of the Bruges exhibition catalogue. The aim of all late medieval and early modern decorations of justice places (moralising the general public, but first and foremost the judges and the other actors of the courts), is beautifully illustrated in the example of Lüneburg. Hubrich's paper argues that the artistic programmes fulfilled a multi-layered function in their judicial surrounding: images, as both material and immaterial objects, have a metaphorical potential and at the same time function as agents in the process of administering justice. The Lüneburg Lower Court was equipped with several paintings, including a Last Judgment, coats of arms and exemplary judgments such as the ones of Solomon and Daniel (i.e. the Chaste Susanne). The Old and New Testament, but also allegorical figures are present, as in many other justice halls. What is particular about Lüneburg, however, is that some panels could be moved, so that various constellations were possible for various procedures. Lüneburg's *Niedergericht* is therefore at the same time a typical and an exceptional case of courtroom decoration.

1.4.3 Lawyers and Justices: Their Books, Their Work, Their Symbols

Part III of this contributed volume, still focusing on the Late Middle Ages and the Early Modern Era, looks at the people working in the courts: judges, jurists, and their acolytes. The reception of Roman and canon law especially has laid the basis of Western legal culture, with its learned terminology, its professionals, its 'styles' (procedures, uses and habits), all creating and/or using cultural objects.

In line with the *exempla* and other courtroom decorations discussed in part II, various courts, colleges of judges, or 'civic bodies' had their portraits hung in the neighbourhood of their working rooms. Starting from (a small set of) preserved works of Southern-Netherlandish art, art historian Beatrijs Wolters van der Wey studies this subgenre of portraiture in the Ancien Régime. Commissioners had themselves portrayed in combination with historical and allegorical motifs, or in scenes that were fitting for the group's judicial authority or legal privileges. The works considered in van der Wey's paper include famous specimens painted by Maarten de Vos (the Antwerp-based council of the Brabant Mint, painted in 1594) and Anthony van Dyck (the Brussels bench of aldermen in the company of Lady Justice, painted in 1634–1635, only known thanks to its *modello*). However, the author also describes and analyses other group portraits from Brussels, Malines, Namur and Ghent, some of them combined with a Last Judgment, or a judgment of Solomon or Cambyses, or with the allegorical figure of Lady Justice. What unites these majestic group portraits is the sense of authority and self-esteem they express, an image of 'the people of the law' so contrasting to the satirical and even mocking works by several critical artists around the same time (think for example of Pieter Bruegel the Younger's *The Village Lawyer*, discussed by *Gustav Kalm*).

The series *Litis abusus* by Hendrick Goltzius (reworked later on in different versions by Philips and Theodoor Galle), elucidated in this volume by legal historian *Alain Wijffels*, might at first glance also look like a critique of jurists and judges. On second glance, however, it is much more a critique of the (Romano-canonical) procedure itself, or even of judicial activity as such. The popular series of engravings expresses a strong moral criticism of, mostly civil, litigation. The series features litigation's traditional characteristics leading to an enormous number of written documents, to the excessive duration of processes and especially to enormous proceeding costs. Rather than legal professionals (present in most of the series' compositions), the litigant himself, as a private person, is the central character. The prints show greed and acrimony as the driving forces behind his procedural obstinacy, which ultimately leads to the exhaustion of his patrimonial, physical, mental and spiritual resources. The representation of civil litigation as a monstrous predator suggests that the system of civil procedure as such is flawed. Biblical quotes, at the bottom of each print, give religious force to the general moral message of the prints.

Satire, irony, and moral exhortations also played an essential role when, at the end of the fifteenth century in Sebastian Brant's *Ship of Fools*, Lady Justice, the allegorical female representation of justice with sword and scales originated in de Middle Ages, was blindfolded for the very first time. Chapter 5 of the Bruges exhibition catalogue addressed Lady Justice's history without going into the many possible reasons for her blindness or blindfold. Many scholars have been debating the issue, and art historian *Valérie Hayaert* adds a thought provoking chapter to that history in the present volume. She argues that the visual allegory of justice, as a civic theophany, excludes all kinds of contact between the figure (the embodiment) and the idea (divine justice). The blindfold is more than a semi-latent attribute. It is an *index animi*. It indicates that Lady Justice's body is meant to be perceived as a theophany. She elaborates her thesis by referring to Gaspard Heuvick's *Allegory of Justice*, addressed in the Bruges exhibition catalogue. However, she confronts her findings not only with jurist and satirist Sebastian Brant, but also with authors such as the French criminalist Pierre Ayrault. Both art and legal literature reveal how polysemic the blindfold was, and still is. Its nature is ambivalent: Justitia must see and, according to some Renaissance thinkers, the eye is the symbol of justice. Others, however, emphasise the glance of her eyes. The act of blindfolding Justitia is a paradoxical gesture: Is it a sign of blindness? A necessary avoidance of lucidity? A momentaneous disregard of the evidence put before the eyes? A mark of ecstasy? A shameful stigma? A trick? A game? A mark of derision? The list of questions demonstrates the many ways of reading this sign, dependent on its viewers, contexts, and intentions, of which Hayaert gives several examples, ranging from the sixteenth to eighteenth century, most of them 'explaining' the need for a symbol of impartiality.

With or without blindfold, Lady Justice was there to stay. She would never leave the courtrooms, town halls and legal books again. In printed books, she became a standard illustration or a decorative part of larger formats and designs. As was made clear in the Bruges exhibition (see Chap. 4 by Jos Monballyu in the exhibition catalogue), the practical handbooks (one on civil and one on criminal law) of the Flemish sixteenth-century jurist Joos de Damhouder are probably two of the most famous examples of illustrated doctrine, translated and edited in many places and times (Widener and Weiner 2017). Art historian *Felix Jäger* invites us to take a closer look at these books and their decorations, more particularly at their 'grotesques' and frames, up until now largely ignored by scholars. 'Usually understood as symptomatic of a general sense of crisis encapsulated in Mannerist art, the horror of the grotesque', he argues, 'proves to be functional to both political power and the administration of justice. The ambivalent characteristics of *furore* and *terribilità*, attributed to the artist by Italian art theory, however, in Northern Mannerism reappear as impersonal sensations exuding from the artwork itself. They subdue rather than liberate the fantasy of the viewer. Highlighted by the use of grotesques in legal imagery, this shift of emphasis from artistic freedom to political coercion and from imagination to horror mirrors a reversal in political theory that installed fear as medium of power.' Grotesques impart law with a visual force, directed towards the (learned) reader, but also at the public at large. Grotesques transcend the simple legal rational reasoning and emanate, irrationally, the violent basis of law. 'They do not appeal to rational deliberation or an abstract notion of justice',

Jäger writes, 'but address the viewer physically, enforcing his compliance. In other words, they do not work iconographically but iconically.'

With this daring hypothesis Jäger, like Hayaert, takes the step from iconographical analysis to iconology, and opens up the field of investigation in which law and art interact. *Gustav Kalm* continues on this path, and looks at the broader material context of legal work in the Early Modern Era. His contribution, more specifically, is about writing material as part of the material cult of notaries (a legal practitioner also present in the *Litis abusus* series discussed by *Wijffels*). *Kalm* treats the document as a social actor, as well as the transformation of the early modern 'administrative literacy' (*pratiques de l'écrit*). In essence, his essay is about the material culture of (university-trained) jurists and (practically-schooled) law practitioners as 'writing people'. As professionals producing written documents, notaries also needed to promote these documents and their own ability to be trusted. Hence, they needed to advertise themselves and their work as brokers of public trust. It is in the context of this trust-building economy that Kalm extensively studies various editions of the title page illustrations of the most popular German language notarial treatise from the sixteenth century: *Rhetoric und Teutsch Formular*. Its title page features woodcuts depicting an array of writing utensils, sometimes complemented with a writing notary and some further tools. 'Those pictures bare striking similarity to the imagery used to illustrate the booming genre of practical guidebooks for artisans of various sorts', Kalm explains, and 'as such they bring to the fore a peculiarly materialist understanding of legal work and offer thus a welcome counterpoint to most jurisprudence'.

Indeed, iconological analysis enables us, hundreds of years after date, to not only rationally 'understand' the law of the past, but also 'feel' its actual impact. Art and iconography give us a picture, a momentous photograph, better than written documents (legal as well as personal/biographical) do. If a source produces both written impressions and iconographical information at the same point in time, then we can really grasp the sense of the law and its context. This is the case for a huge manuscript, interspersed with around two hundred full-folio water colour drawings, that is now being preserved in the Royal Library of Belgium: *Tydsgebeurtenissen*. It is a rare example of an iconographic source that has recorded the reception of revolutionary iconography in the Southern Netherlands. Its author is the relatively obscure Antwerp aristocrat Pierre Antoine Joseph Goetsbloets. Historian *Brecht Deseure* describes and contextualises the iconography as far as it is related to law and justice. Goetsbloets made his own creative adaptation of the existing revolutionary iconography. The man was acquainted with revolutionary symbolism, which he not only copied into his chronicle, but also appropriated in a subversive way. Deseure looks at various illustrations from different points of view. He analyses their accuracy, their irony and the use of parody. His contribution beautifully concludes the third part of this contributed volume, by again taking up the idea of satire, which was also present in *Wijffels*' and *Hayaert*'s contributions, and by, like *Wolters van der Wey*, *Jäger* and *Kalm*, putting the impact of law and justice —or the lack of it—in a broader social context. Be it positive and/or negative, what is at stake in all of these is the general idea of justice: as an ideal, an activity, a burden or a profession.

1.4.4 Criminal Justice: Art, Object and Locus

The fourth part of this volume assembles some more specific essays, in at least a double sense. Its three contributions focus on criminal law, probably the most well-known branch of the law, or, to the broader public at least, the most intriguing. At the same time it is perhaps also the legal branch that is applied the least in everyday practice. Moreover, each of these three essays does not consist of a purely iconographical analysis, but also points at other interesting interactions between art and law. Nevertheless, in all three papers, particular artwork form the basis of the research (and are reproduced as illustrations).

The paintings, statues, stained-glass windows and other artistic objects which *Paul De Win* elaborates on, do not essentially 'represent' justice, the law or a juridical concept. They can be a statue of a saint or simply a bronze hand. However, each of these works of art is 'a result of the application of the law'. They are material relicts of ancient legal practice, or to use the erudite term: legal archaeology. Paul De Win, who has been active as a scholar since the 1980s (e.g. De Win 1992), could be called the father of legal archaeology in Belgium. He has thoroughly studied the country's pillories, invited renowned scholars from abroad to introduce the research field of legal archaeology in Belgium, and incited various public authorities and private organisations to make inventories of, and study, ancient legal objects. In his contribution to this volume he explains how it was not uncommon for early modern judicial sentences to force the convicted person to acquire, or finance, a work of art, or to have to provide specific objects. De Win distinguishes two types of objects: those that were only intended as decorations (for churches, town halls, public places…), and those that bore an explanatory text mentioning the crime and the name of the condemned, the 'defamatory' ones so to say. Often, explanatory plaques gave a description of the crime, the date of judgment and the name of the convicted person. One could call them 'shaming penalty pieces'. Their form was usually chosen in accordance with the misdeeds.

While the objects discussed by De Win were made by artists *after* a criminal sentence, *Tamara Golan*'s contribution is about the participation of an artist *during* a trial. She tells us how the Fribourg painter Hans Fries was summoned to Bern because, according to a trial document from 1508, he was best suited to verify whether or not the appearance of red tears on a sacred statue was brought about by human industry or art, or by means of a miracle. Hans Jetzer, a young novice in the Bern Dominican convent, had seen how a *pietà* sculpture on the altar had bloody tears rolling down the Virgin's face. The dispute between 'believers' and 'disbelievers' led to a trial. Fries' own participation as an expert witness in an 'inquisitional trial', a construction of the learned Romano-canonical law of the Late Middle Ages, might, according to Golan, have influenced the artist's thoughts on truth and justice. To make her point, she takes a close look at Fries' diptych of the *Kleiner Johannes Altar*. Featuring scenes of John the Evangelist's trial on Ephesus and his later visions of the Apocalypse on Patmos, this work is the artist's most 'juridical' work. The altar reveals his knowledge of the investigative mode of truth-seeking of the judicial *inquisition*. Golan's paper truly shows a remarkable interaction between 'art' and 'law', with an artist who, on the one hand functions as a judicial expert, and on the other hand uses his judicial experience as a basis for an artistic representation.

In their joint contribution, legal historians *Jérôme de Brouwer* and *Xavier Rousseaux* illustrate how changes in criminal law and its administration have changed the artistic representation of justice in the Early Modern Era and the nineteenth century. More particularly, they study the execution (and its representation) of the death penalty, a paramount expression of sovereign power and legitimate State violence, in the 'Belgian' territories. Many scholars have already studied the civilising tendencies of the late Ancien Régime, including the humanisation of criminal law under the influence of Enlightenment ideas. De Brouwer and Rousseaux add the 'artistic expression' of it to this body of work. From the 1770s to 1830s, in quickly succeeding political regimes, there was a decline in the execution of the death penalty and the public exposition of the executed. In nineteenth-century Belgium, this gradual disappearance correlated with a practically non-existent 'national iconography' of public executions. The authors enumerate the very few preserved iconographies of executions. They describe how legislative and judicial authorities tried to make capital execution less public in a context in which the criminal code inherited from the French Empire required it to take place in public. Whereas in earlier centuries, the few preserved representations showed scaffolding and public, in the nineteenth century artists mostly limited themselves to picture the 'result' of the '*simple privation de la vie*' by the guillotine. Some renowned artists painted nothing more than the severed heads, which, by the way, were also, in a context of quickly evolving science, sent to university for scientific research, a typical feature of 'modern' criminal policy. In this sense, this last contribution on criminal law administration bridges Ancien Régime and post-revolutionary justice, with its increasing importance of national codes and its exploding bureaucracy.

1.4.5 Justice Architecture and Decorations in the Long Nineteenth Century

This volume's final part is the most recent one, both in terms of its subject matter (it treats the most recent historical period), but also in terms of its authors: all are young scholars preparing a PhD. They are jurists, anthropologists, historians, art historians or architectural historians and most of them have already discussed their research among each other and with a larger audience of scholars during the past few years, among others in the framework of the Interuniversity Attraction Pole

Justice and Populations: The Belgian Experience in International Context, 1795–2015. Their methodology is interdisciplinary, based on archival sources, and they are well acquainted with the recent literature on 'Law and the Visual'. By focussing specifically on architecture and decoration, they continue the historical line of the courtroom iconography discussed in part II of this volume, but also take into account the criminal law evolution treated in part IV.

Architectural historian *Jozefien Feyaerts* studies Belgian examples of a late-eighteenth-century 'invention': the prison. Ancien Régime prisons were small, e.g. very often located in the towers of city gates, and served only to host so-called 'civil prisoners' (people locked up because of personal debts) on the one hand, and suspects who were temporarily kept in custody during their criminal trial on the other. The paramount role of imprisonment as a penalty is one of the results of the enlightened 'humanisation' of criminal law (see the contributions in part IV). Belgian prison reformer Édouard Ducpétiaux was an internationally important figure in the promotion of singular cell imprisonment. Feyaerts explains how his ideas were translated to architecture. Between 1850 and 1919, almost thirty new cellular prisons were built in Belgium to facilitate the strictly cellular regime. Architect Joseph-Jonas Dumont (1811–1859) introduced the English neo-Tudor style in his prison designs. Feyaerts explores the motives and meanings of his stylistic choice. Dumont was a pioneer of the neo-gothic style, which became a pre-eminent idiom to express national identity and was affiliated with the Catholic movement for a long time. Nevertheless, at the end of the century, it was also common in secular public building. Feyaerts elaborates on the examples of medieval city and Tudor castle gates that inspired the impressive outlook of the new prisons. The Belgian Ministry of Justice explicitly assigned Dumont to study the prison infrastructure in England, where, under the influence of the gothic revival movement, several penitentiaries were designed in neo-Tudor style too. By exploring criminal policy, architectural style, cultural foreign influences and social impact, Feyaerts draws a beautiful iconological picture of these late-nineteenth century prisons.

Policy (in a context of national State building), architectural style, foreign (French particularly) and historical influences, and social impact are also essential motives in the text by *Gaëlle Dubois* and *Amandine De Burchgraeve*. They study the *cour d'assises* of Brabant, one of Belgium's highest criminal courts, around 1900. The court was located in the Brussels iconic *Palais the Justice*, at that time one of the world's largest public buildings, with an impressive, eclectic style. The authors call the criminal court a 'place of education and entertainment', and do not only use architectural environment and anthropological analysis to come to their conclusions, but also rely on a close reading of contemporary news media. They describe how spectators see the judicial space as a theatre in which one attends a specific play: the judicial ritual. However, a visit to the *cour d'assises* was also an experience of education and warning. The authors describe and analyse the spectator's court visit trajectory, from the first steps into the court building, through the impressive *salle des pas perdus,* to the courtroom, and back again. 'By being present', the authors write, the spectator 'is confronted with the norms according to which society assesses behaviours, determines the limits of the tolerable, and punishes those who transgress them. He leaves trial with a message, as the initiatory architecture of the courthouse, the layout of the courtroom and the ritualised performance contribute to the expression and the transmission of a discourse on justice and, more broadly, on society'. This dissemination of societal and legal concepts is a beautiful expression of how legal iconology can contribute to a better understanding of law's impact.

Art historian *Stefan Huygebaert* continues in this line of thoughts, and concentrates on another *cour d'assises*, the one in Antwerp. More particularly, he studies the decoration programme of the historicising, moralising, and impressive murals realised between 1886 and 1893 by three traditionalist artists and a legal historian, and 'orchestrated' by a conservative Catholic judge. He reveals how different the art scenes of Brussels and Antwerp were, and how diverging the interactions between artists and jurists. Artistically, there were choices to be made between vanguard and traditionalism. Legally, in the last quarter of the nineteenth century, innovative Belgian criminal policy started to move towards a 'social defence' system under the influence of the international criminology movement. Conservative Catholics, however, held on to a moralising view on crime and criminality. Huygebaert argues that, in the Antwerp courtroom decoration commission, the leading magistrate demonstrated his combined artistic and legal conservatism and his opposition to recent legal changes in his choice of collaborators and iconography. The town archivist delivered a coloured reading of Antwerp's criminal history, and the executing artist deployed his characteristic historicising mode of depicting the 'old law' subject matter. This iconological study helps us to better understand both an iconography which in the judicial landscape of today's Belgium has become extraordinary, and an important turning point of the country's criminal legal history.

In an analogous way, the final contribution to this volume, by *Rahela Khorakiwala*, illustrates how law and culture (in this case of both Western and of Indian origin), history (and more particularly colonial history in this case) and architecture interact each time places of justice are to be designed. The author invites us to a visit of the Bombay High Court, and draws attention to the images of justice in the Colonial Courts of British India. Many refer to the old Western tradition, more particularly to the history of the *exempla* and Lady Justice studied in part II. Statues of justice and mercy were placed atop the High Court building. However, the visitor can also encounter carvings of a 'monkey judge' or a 'fox lawyer' on the pillars of the court. Khorakiwala explains how this iconography has played a role in the development of popular cultural imagery, and how it has its own folklore in the court today. With this late-nineteenth century eastern example, this contribution beautifully concludes the survey of the history and impact of Western legal iconography.

1.5 Illustrative Iconography, Elucidating Iconology, Indexes, New Horizons

As stated above, the pictures in the various contributions (as well as the images of other artworks mentioned, which should be easily consultable online) are part and parcel of the objective of this contributed volume: 'seeing is believing', 'seeing is beholding', 'seeing is understanding', 'seeing is wondering', 'seeing is remembering', 'seeing is fearing', 'seeing is learning', etc. The visual has an enormous impact on law, justice administration and public legal policy. This volume highlights some important and less important works of art as expressions of legal culture, which is always evolving over time and place. The editors have done their very best to arrange all intellectual property rights of the artists, the photographers and collection responsibles. In case there is any problem whatsoever at this point, please contact us through Georges.Martyn@UGent.be.

All of the artworks discussed in this volume are no longer mere illustrations of a historical period of law's history. All of our authors' iconographical and iconological analyses have turned these paintings, prints, tapestries and statues into vehicles for the understanding of law and justice, firstly as products of a cultural era, and secondly as visual expressions of legal theories and their social impact. The editors are very much indebted to the authors and thank each of them for having accepted to enter the enriching dialogue between scholars of various fields within the humanities. Almost all papers contain footnotes referring to other contributions, aimed at both elucidating certain points with analogies, and, in contrast, signalling differences and diverging evolutions.

Historical legal iconology is a young field of research, and the editors hope to have contributed to it. Without any doubt, much more is still to be said: about other works of the same artists, similar and diverging decorations of other courts, different artistic representations of the same legal concepts and doctrine, etc. In order to make this book as useful as possible, we added three indexes: one of the artists named in the various contributions, one of the (literary, philosophical and legal) authors mentioned (not, however, scholars of contemporary art and/or legal history, of whom reference lists at the end of each contribution are available), and, finally, an index of all cited quotes from the Bible. Given the enormous influence of this Holy Book for both the evolution of law and of art from the Christian Middle Ages onwards, this list may surely guide researchers to new horizons.

The editors hope to have paved the way for future interdisciplinary research. For Belgium, where both the *The Art of Law* exhibition and conference were held, it is in any case a pleasant omen to see that, in collaboration with the city festival *Op. Recht.Mechelen*, the Museum Hof van Busleyden in Malines hosted the exhibition *Call for Justice. Art and Law in the Burgundian Netherlands* (March–June 2018), curated by Samuel Mareel, Manfred Sellink, Ellen Goetstouwers and Elsje Janssen. Finally, as conference organizers we would like to express our gratitude towards the Research Foundation-Flanders (FWO), the *Fonds de la Recherche Scientifique* (F. R.S.-FNRS), the Interuniversity Attraction Pole '*Justice and Populations: The Belgian Experience in International Perspective, 1795-2015*', and the Flemish research centre for the arts in the Burgundian Netherlands (Musea Brugge).

References

Agulhon M (1979) Marianne au combat. L'imagerie et la symbolique républicaines de 1789 à 1880. Flammarion, Paris

Behrmann C (2015) Tyrann und Märtyrer: Bild und Ideengeschichte des Rechts um 1600. De Gruyter, Berlin

Block J (1997) The art of law: Le Jeune Barreau: patron of arts and letters. In: Block J (ed) Belgium. The golden decades. Peter Lang, New York

Chauvaud F, Vernois S (2004) Croquis, dessins et caricatures: La justice en images. In: Sociétés & représentations 18

Clair J (ed) (2010) Crime et châtiment. Musée d'Orsay & Gallimard, Paris

Dauchy S, Demars-Sion V (2001) La justice dans le Nord. Trois siècles d'histoire (1667–1967). Centre d'Histoire Judiciaire, Lille

Dauchy S, Martyn G, Musson A, Pihlajamäki H, Wijffels A (eds) (2016) The formation and transmission of western legal culture: 150 books that made the law in the age of printing. Springer, Cham

De Ridder JHA (1989) Gerechtigheidstaferelen voor schepenhuizen in de Zuidelijke Nederlanden in de 14de, 15de en 16de eeuw. Koninklijke Vlaamse Academie voor Wetenschappen, Letteren en Schone Kunsten van België, Brussels

De Win P (ed) (1992) Rechtsarcheologie en rechtsiconografie: een kennismaking. Handelingen van het Colloquium gehouden te Brussel op 27 April 1990. Rechtsarchäologie und Rechtsikonographie: eine Annäherung. Akten des Brüsselere Kolloquiums, 27. April 1990. Koninklijke Vlaamse Academie voor Wetenschappen, Letteren en Schone Kunsten van België, Brussels

Douzinas C, Nead L (eds) (1999) Law and the image. The authority of art and the aesthetics of law. University of Chicago Press, Chicago

Eichler A, Fußwinkel E, Löffler N (eds) (2010) Spott und Respekt. Die Justiz in der Kritik. Michael Imhof Verlag, Petersberg

Fehr H (1923) Das Recht im Bilde. Rentsch, Zürich

Fleckner U, Warnke M, Ziegler H (eds) (2011) Handbuch der politischen Ikonographie. C.H. Beck, Munich

Goodrich P (2013) On the futures of the fingerpost. Crit Inq 39:498–531

Goodrich P (2014) Legal emblems and the art of law: obiter depicta as the vision of governance. Cambridge University Press, Cambridge

Goodrich P, Hayaert V (eds) (2015) Genealogies of legal vision. Routledge, New York

Harju V (ed) (2000) Oikeuden kuva. Bilden av rätten och rättvisan. Riksdagbiblioteket, Helsinki

Hunt L (1984) Politics, culture and class in the French revolution. University of California Press, Berkeley

Huygebaert S, Martyn G, Paumen V, Van Poucke T (eds) (2016) The art of law. Three centuries of justice depicted (exh. cat. Bruges). Lannoo, Tielt

Jacob R (1994) Images de la justice. Essai sur l'iconographie judiciaire du Moyen Âge à l'âge classique. Le Léopard d'Or, Paris

Kissel OR (1984) Die Justitia. Reflexionen über ein Symbol und seine Darstellung in der bildenden Kunst. Beck, Munich

Kocher G (1992) Zeichen und Symbole des Rechts: Eine historische Ikonographie. Beck, Munich

Lederle U (1937) Gerechtigkeitsdarstellungen in deutschen und niederländischen Rathäusern. Kruse, Philippsburg

L'Engle S, Gibbs R (eds) (2001) Illuminating the law: legal manuscripts in Cambridge collections. Harvey Miller Publishers, London

Maes LT, Godenne W (eds) (1949) Catalogue de l'exposition internationale en souvenir du 475e anniversaire de l'établissement à Malines (1473/1474) du Grand Conseil tenue à l'Hôtel de Ville de Malines du 4 au 20 juin 1949 (exh. cat. Malines). Stad Mechelen, Malines

Manchester AH, Becker-Moelands MA (1991) An introduction to iconographical studies of legal history. In: Gordon WM, Fergus TD (eds) Legal history in the making. Proceedings of the ninth British legal history conference, Glasgow, 1989. Continnuum, London, pp 85–94
Manderson D (2018) Law and the visual: Representations, technologies, critique. University of Toronto Press, Toronto
Mareel S (ed) (2018) Call for justice. Art and law in the Low Countries (1450–1650). Hannibal, Mechelen
Martyn G, Brood P, Berkvens L (eds) (2014) Rechtsgeschiedenis verbeeld, special issue Pro Memorie. Bijdragen tot de rechtsgeschiedenis der Nederlanden 16
Moelands MA, de Smidt JT (eds) (1999) Weegschaal en zwaard. De verbeelding van recht en gerechtigheid in Nederland (exh. cat. The Hague). Jongbloed Juridische Boekhandel, Hague
Paumen V (2016) The skin of the judge: the judgment of Cambyses. In: Huygebaert et al. 2016, pp 81–91
Perez-Bustamante R (ed) (2007) Iustitia. La Justicia en las artes. Fundación Carlos de Amberes, Madrid
Perez-Bustamante R (ed) (2008) Campus. Imágenes de la Justicia. Real Fábrica de Tapices, Madrid
Pleister W, Schild W (1988) Recht und Gerechtigkeit im Spiegel der europäischen Kunst. DuMont, Cologne
Prosperi A (2008) Giustizia bendata: Percorsi storici di un'immagine. Einaudi, Turin
Resnik J, Curtis D (2011) Representing justice. Invention, controversy, and rights in city-states and democratic courtrooms. Yale University Press, New Haven (CT)
Robert C-N (1993) Une allégorie parfaite. La justice: vertu, courtisane et bourreau. Georg Éditeur, Genève
Robert C-N (1996) La justice dans ses décors (XVe-XVIe siècles). Droz, Genève
Rodríguez-López,, Isabel M (2003) La imagen de la justicia en las artes plásticas (desde la Antigüedad hasta las postrimerías del Medioevo). *Saberes Revista de estudios jurídicos, económicos y sociales* 1:1–26
Röhl KF (2005) Bilder in gedruckten Rechtsbüchern. In: KD Lerch (ed) Recht vermitteln: Strukturen, Formen und Medien des Kommunikation im Recht, vol III. Walter de Gruyter, Berlin, pp 267–347
Sarat A, Anderson M, Frank CO (2010) Law and the humanities: an introduction. Cambridge University Press, New York
Sbriccoli M (2005) La triade, le bandeau, le genou. Droit et procès pénal dans les allégories de la Justice du Moyen Âge à l'âge moderne. Crime, Histoire & Sociétés/Crime, History and Societies, vol IX(1), pp 33–78
Schild W (1995) Bilder von Recht und Gerechtigkeit. DuMont, Cologne
Sherwin RK (2014) Introduction: law, culture, and visual studies. In: Wagner A, Sherwin RK (eds) Law, culture and visual studies. Springer, London, pp xxxiii–xli
Sutter C (2008) Flämische Gerechtigkeitsbilder des 15. Jahrhunderts: die Visualisierung spätmittelalterlicher Auffassungen von Recht und Moral. VDM, Saarbrücken
von Amira K, von Schwerin C (1943) Rechtsarchäologie. Gegenstände, Formen und Symbole des Germanischen Rechts. Ahnenerbe Stiftung Verlag, Berlin
Warnke M (2010) Politische Ikonographie. In: Poeschel S (ed) Ikonographie. WBG, Darmstadt, pp 72–85
Widener M, Weiner MS (2017) Law's picture books: the Yale law library collection. Yale University, New York

Georges Martyn studied Law (1984–1989) and Medieval Studies (1989–1991) and obtained a Ph. D degree in Law at the Catholic University of Leuven in 1996, with a dissertation on private law legislation in the early modern Netherlands. He has been an '*advocaat*' (barrister/lawyer) between 1992 and 2008 at the bar of Kortrijk, is now honorary member of the Ghent bar, and is a substitute justice of the peace in Kortrijk since 1999. He is full professor at the University of Ghent Law School since 1999, teaching mainly history of public law at bachelor level and Law and the Humanities at master level.

Stefan Huygebaert is an art historian (Ghent University, 2011). Since October 2012, he is preparing a Ph.D thesis at the Ghent Legal History Institute/Department of Art History (Ghent University), entitled *Visual Ideals of Law and Justice*. This Ph.D research analyses the visual language of law & justice in Belgium during the nineteenth century. Since October 2015, he is a Research Foundation—Flanders (FWO) Ph.D fellow. Both in 2014–2015 and in 2016–2017, Stefan was a pre-doctoral fellow at the Kunsthistorisches Institut in Florenz, within the Minerva Research Group 'The Nomos of Images: Manifestation and Iconology of Law'. He has published on legal and constitutional iconology and nineteenth-century art.

Chapter 2
The Exhibition *The Art of Law. Three Centuries of Justice Depicted*

Vanessa Paumen

Abstract The impulse for the conference from which these proceedings are the result was formed by the exhibition '*The Art of Law. Three Centuries of Justice Depicted*', on view in the Groeningemuseum in Bruges from 27 October 2016 until 5 February 2017. The exhibition sought to highlight the development of the legal system and some of its judicial institutions in the Low Countries. The artworks in the exhibition were a testimony of the underlying values that guided justice and the practice of law during the period between around 1450 and 1750. The curators of the exhibition brought together over one hundred and twenty works within the theme of justice and courts of law. The works in the exhibition were approached not only from an art-historical perspective, but also from the context of law and justice. This supplementary perspective was meant to bring their original function to the fore. This section briefly discusses the most important themes of the exhibition (divine and worldly justice, *exempla justitiae*, the practice of justice, and Lady Justice), and focuses on some of the most important artworks within each theme.

2.1 A Thematic Approach

The curators of the exhibition, Vanessa Paumen and Tine Van Poucke (Groeningemuseum), brought together over one hundred and twenty works within the theme of justice and courts of law during the Ancien Régime. Professor Georges Martyn and PhD candidate Stefan Huygebaert (from the Ghent Institute for Legal History) adviced them on legal history. In line with the mission of the

---

The Art of Law. Three Centuries of Justice Depicted, Groeningemuseum, Bruges (27 October 2016–5 February 2017), curators Vanessa Paumen and Tine Van Poucke. Exhibition catalogue: Huygebaert et al. (2016a, b).

V. Paumen (✉)
Flemish research centre for the arts in the Burgundian Netherlands
(Musea Brugge), Bruges, Belgium
e-mail: Vanessa.Paumen@brugge.be

S. Huygebaert et al. (eds.), *The Art of Law*, Ius Gentium: Comparative Perspectives on Law and Justice 66, https://doi.org/10.1007/978-3-319-90787-1_2

Groeningemuseum, which aims to offer its visitors new perspectives by way of its temporary exhibitions, this major exhibition placed well-known works of art, as well as some lesser- known pieces, in the context of the history of law. The works in the exhibition were approached not only from an art-historical perspective, but also from the context of law and justice. This supplementary perspective was meant to bring their original function to the fore. The exhibition (Fig. 2.1) sought to highlight the development of the legal system, and some of its judicial institutions, in the Low Countries.

This interdisciplinary approach and the collaboration with academic institutions are part of the central mission of the Flemish research centre for the arts of the Burgundian Netherlands. The exhibition and the conference prove that such collaboration is not only *possible*, but leads to multi-dimensional results that are stimulating projects to work on for all parties involved. Even more importantly, they are also extremely beneficial to various audiences, from the museum visitor to the specialised scholar.

Nearly two years of exchanging ideas and intense coordination with the thirty-five lending institutions resulted in an exhibition that comprised more than one hundred artworks in nine galleries: paintings, prints, drawings, stained glass panels, manuscripts and early printed books as well as pieces of sculpture and other objects. All were related to justice, both in the sense of a political ideal and as the factual human act of justice administration by the courts of law during the Ancien Régime.

The works in the exhibition depicted Christ swaying the sword of justice, portrayed a wise judge about to have an innocent child chopped into two parts, and a father giving orders to have his son's eye gouged out. Visitors could encounter a vindictive woman submerging her enemy's head in a vessel of blood, and a judge tied to a wooden table having his skin stripped off. In various works, suspects of crimes were tortured in order to obtain confessions, a citizen of Bruges was shown hanging from the gallows for perjury, and several book illustrations depicted crimes and their gruesome punishments. The beautiful silver objects that were presented were actually part of a larger conviction. And the highest of all cardinal virtues—Justice—appeared in a print in the company of a fool. At first sight, these representations seem to be nothing more than horrible. And yet, they all fit within the theme of *justice*. How was justice understood, and what were the values that guided the practice of law during the Ancien Régime? Where can we situate the origin of the still ubiquitous Lady Justice, adorned with her attributes, sword, scales and blindfold?[1]

For this exhibition the curators started within the rich collections of Bruges, not only the Groeningemuseum, but also the Bruggemuseum, the Liberty of Bruges (*Brugse Vrije*) and Bruges' public library. These works were then supplemented with over one hundred relevant loans from museums, libraries, institutions, town halls and private collectors in Belgium and abroad. The works from the Bruges collections were presented in a new context, and placed in dialogue with artworks from other collections in the context of justice and law. Furthermore there were also

[1]Her enigmatic blindfold only appeared at the beginning of the Early Modern Era, as is clarified in the contribution by Valérie Hayaert in this volume.

several works in this exhibition that, up until then, had never or almost never been put on display in a museum.

For *The Art of Law,* several remarkable pieces were brought to the Groeningemuseum, including some that came straight from civic buildings. Thanks to the Maastricht authorities in the Netherlands, the large panel representing *Dual Justice* (Fig. 2.2), painted for the town around 1477 or 1499, could, for the very first time, be seen together with other major paintings of the same type. A fascinating painting from the Geraardsbergen town hall, reminiscent of Jheronimus Bosch, took pride of place alongside other works commissioned by town aldermen during the fifteenth and sixteenth centuries. These include, among others, Bruges' own *Last Judgment* paintings (1525 and 1551) by Jan Provoost (1465–1529) and Pieter Pourbus (ca. 1523–1584).

The town of Wesel in Germany contributed one of the most important pieces from its collection, while the Hanseatic city of Gdańsk in Poland sent one of seven pieces painted by Hans Vredeman de Vries (1527–1607) for its town hall, still in their original location. Private collections in Germany and Belgium contributed five fascinating stained-glass windows, a large painting and several very important printed items. Colijn de Coter (ca. 1450/1455-ca. 1539/1440), one of the so-called Flemish Primitives from the circle of Rogier van der Weyden (1400–1464), briefly returned to the Low Countries from a semi-private collection in the United States. In addition to this, the exhibition also included numerous valuable prints, drawings and objects from Dutch and Belgian collections, particularly from the Rijksmuseum in Amsterdam and the Royal Library of Belgium. The overwhelming number of positive responses to loan requests clearly demonstrated a readiness to take a fresh look at these artworks.

As is the case with all curatorial projects, ours as well faced certain limitations. The fact that justice-related artworks were often created specifically for public, governmental settings means that many of them are still in their original locations. For instance, the prime local example is the monumental mantelpiece in the manor house of the Liberty of Bruges, in which there is an alabaster sculpture of the story of *Susanna and the elders*. Then there are the paintings integrated into the walls of courtrooms as panels, or the statues of *Justitia* on the façades of governmental and court buildings. Of course, it was simply impossible to bring these to the museum to complete an exhibition.[2] Furthermore, many works were simply too large to be displayed in the Groeningemuseum.[3] Finally, there were also some important works that could not be moved due to conservation reasons.

---

[2]Some similar *in-situ* examples are addressed in the papers in these proceedings, such as the Italian frescoes studied by Clare Sandford-Couch, the paintings cycle for the Lüneburg lower court commented on by Ann-Kathrin Hubrich, or the decoration programs for palaces of justice in the nineteenth century discussed by Stefan Huygebaert and Rahela Khorakiwala.

[3]The exhibition was not able to host tapestry for example, but a paper by Belgian expert *par excellence* Guy Delmarcel on some wonderful examples of Flemish tapestries is included in this book. Another example which exceeded the wall space of the galleries, but still figures in Raf Verstegen's paper is *The Judgment of Cambyses*, painted in 1671 by Victor Bouquet for Nieuwpoort town hall.

2.2 Divine Judgment, Worldly Justice

Despite these limitations, the exhibition more than succeeded in achieving its goal: to highlight the most important aspects of the justice system as it existed during the Ancien Régime through artworks. The first gallery highlighted the Last Judgment and several paintings emphasising the duality between worldly and earthly justice. The Last Judgment was the most common subject used as decoration for courtrooms, and thus the primary example of an *exemplum justitiae*. Christ served as the judges' ultimate example for the performance of their important task on earth. Simultaneously, the Last Judgment was an explicit warning and reminder for the judges of the fact that they too would be submitted to Christ's final Judgment. The two aforementioned paintings from the Groeninge collection, by Jan Provoost (1525) and Pieter Pourbus (1551), commissioned for, respectively, the Town Hall and the Liberty of Bruges, were shown together with four other significant works commissioned for the decoration of courtrooms (Geraardsbergen, Graz, Maastricht and Wesel).

One alternative for the traditional Last Judgment paintings are works in which there is a clear link between heavenly and earthly justice in the courtroom. This was an expression of a typically medieval duality. Only four paintings of this type are still preserved, three of which could be seen together for the first time in this exhibition. The earliest work in the exhibition is the panel painting that once adorned the city hall of Graz in Austria. It dates back to 1478, and shows the town judge Nicolas Strobel—who commissioned the painting—seated in his function in a courtroom, at the moment of an oath-taking. Immediately above him, the heavenly Judgment is taking place. Strobel's red cloak mirrors that of Christ. By means of these visual connections, this painting makes a direct link between the heavenly and earthly judgment, and emphasises the importance of the judge's (nearly) divine task of pronouncing judgment on earth.

The highly detailed painting by Derick Baegert (1440–1515) dated to 1493–1494, from the German town of Wesel, provides us with an even wider view of the courtroom in session. Here too an oath is about to be taken. The judge, positioned high and dressed in a lavish attire of brocade and fur, makes a gesture with his right hand towards the painting of the Last Judgment on the wall. His left arm is directed downwards, to an intriguing scene in which an angel and a devil each whisper in one ear of the defendant as the oath is sworn. The judge's gesture over the head of the defendant makes a clear connection between a false oath and the punishment on Judgment Day of those who commit perjury on earth. The judge's position is identical to that of Christ in the painting on the wall and again emphasises the link between the role of Christ on Judgment Day and that of the earthly judge in court. This close connection between Christ and the judge, and by extension between religion and the administration of justice during this time period is of course one of the fundamental premises of the judicial system of this era. The Bible legitimised judicial power. Judges were required to fulfil the task as God's representatives on earth, and should therefore be God-fearing and incorruptible. Moreover, judges' judgments should not be human but divine. As a result, these judges were held to the highest standards, and were not to be influenced by corrupting emotions such as greed or partiality.

However, devilish temptation always lurks around the corner. It even hovers over the shoulders of the aldermen, as is very clearly visible in the painting from the Maastricht town hall (Fig. 2.2). That the aldermen—due to their position of power—were susceptible to corruption and the misuse of power is a theme that was present throughout the works in this exhibition. And while the Last Judgment continued to be the most prevalent subject of paintings used as decoration in courtrooms, by the fifteenth century it had become common practice to either add to, or replace it with paintings depicting other exemplary stories: *exempla justitiae*. The subject matter for these examples came from biblical, historical and legendary stories.

2.3 *Exempla Justitiae*: Inspiring Examples

The second gallery brought together a sampling of artworks, in various media, depicting the most-used inspirational themes that served as examples to aldermen judges. The Judgment of Solomon was, after the Last Judgment, the second most popular justice scene for the decoration of courtrooms. This biblical story (1 Kings 3:16–18) of the wise King Solomon who used his insight into human psychology to get to the truth, and thus to justice, was exemplified in the exhibition by the painting by Frans Floris I (1517–1570) that once adorned the city hall of Antwerp (Fig. 2.3).

Another well-known biblical narrative was that of the wise Daniel who intervened on Susanna's behalf by probing the elders for details to get to the truth. The story became a popular theme, especially in the sixteenth century, because it provided artists with the opportunity of depicting an erotic and voyeuristic scene of a young and beautiful bathing woman being spied on by old men. However, in a judicial context, it was the moment of Daniel's Judgment that was the most important. Another possibility was to depict the entire story in a series of separate scenes, as was often the case in prints or in sculpture, such as the elaborate alabaster frieze (1530) on the mantel in the courtroom of the *Brugse Vrije* in Bruges, sculpted by Guyot de Beaugrant (ca. 1500–1551). In the exhibition, the painting (from after 1625) a copy after a work by Valentin de Boulogne (1591–1632) shows a very young Daniel in the judge's seat, firmly point his finger at Susanna's accusers as a way to indicate the moment of his verdict. A court official in armour abruptly grabs one of the deceitful elders to lead him away, while the timid and chaste Susanna solemnly looks out of the painting, at the observer.

In addition to the Bible, subjects for *exempla justitiae* were also taken from historical and legendary tales. The bloody legend of King Zaleucus, set in the seventh century BC Greek colony of Locri (in Italy), featured in Valerius Maximus' *Factorum et dictorum memorabilium libri IX*. The King had installed very strict laws on adultery, which made the crime punishable by the removal of both eyes. When confronted with the adultery of his own son, Zaleucus adhered to impartiality and ordered the gruesome punishment to be carried out, as he would have done for any other citizen. However, when others pleaded for his leniency towards his only son and heir, he applied the law strictly yet creatively, and sacrificed his own eye as well as his son's, since he believed that his son's eyes were his as well. In the exhibition, a work from a private collection painted by Hans Vredeman de Vries shows a crowd of people gathered together in a typical Flemish town square, witnessing the execution of the punishment. The executioner, with a bare upper body, has already removed the king's eye and is about to gouge out one of the son's eyes. This vivid story was meant to serve as an inspiration for the aldermen not to be partial in their judgment. Nevertheless, it might have also inspired them to interpret some laws with a certain degree of creativity.

Exempla Justitiae did not only function as themes for large panel paintings such as the Vredeman de Vries' work. They also appeared as book illustrations as well as on smaller types of artworks, such as stained glass. The exhibition included ten stained-glass panels depicting themes related to justice. A preciously crafted stained glass roundel from about 1525 (Rijksmuseum, Amsterdam, Fig. 2.4) depicts both father and son at the horrible moment of the punishment while in the background, the son is caught in the bed of adultery.

Another theme that revolved around the subject of impartiality in judgment was the legendary story of the Roman emperor Trajan, who, upon hearing that one of his soldiers had trampled an innocent child to death, had him executed on the spot. In some medieval versions of the narrative, the man to be executed was not only the emperor's soldier, but his own son, which emphasised the element of impartiality even stronger. The print (1537) by Hans Sebald Beham (1500–1550) from the Rijksmusem that was shown in the exhibition 500–1550) clearly states (in its header) that the uncaring man was Trajan's '*filius ipsius*'. This legendary story was also one of the subjects of the famous large justice panels painting by Rogier van der Weyden for the Brussels town hall. In this case, it was depicted alongside the legend of Pope Gregorius, who discovered Trajan's skull with his tongue intact. The apocryphal addition to the story added a divine justification to the pagan emperor's judgment.

The justice panels from Brussels included another legendary story that also dealt with impartiality—an essential requirement for aldermen judges, and of which they clearly needed to be reminded. A paragon of impartiality was the fictional judge Herkinbald of Bourbon who, according to a twelfth century source,[4] was forgiven by divine intervention after having cut the throat of his nephew as an act of justice. Herkinbald, a count as well as judge, was aware that his nephew and heir had violated a servant girl and had not received due punishment for his crime. On his deathbed, the count was visited by his nephew. The sickly old man decides to take justice into his own hands, and cuts his nephew's throat. As a result, the bishop refused to administer the Holy Communion. However, the ciborium opens up and

[4]The *Illustrium miraculorum et historiarum memorabilium libri XII* by Caesarius of Heisterbach, a Cistercian monk who lived from about 1180 to 1240.

by divine intervention, the host floats into Herkinbald's mouth, as a sign of approval of his severe but just administration of justice.

This gallery also showcased the print series *Thronus Justitiae* by the Dutch engraver Willem van Swanenburg (1580–1612) (after designs by Joachim Wtewael, 1566–1638). Its title page (Fig. 2.5) is a visual summary of the hierarchy and origins of justice, with divine justice in the upper register and worldly justice in the lower. To the left and right of the cardinal virtue Justice (with scales and sword), we see Moses and Christ, who represent the Old and the New Covenant. In the niches in the middle register, we recognise Kings David and Solomon, bringers of divine justice on earth. Below, next to a female figure—probably *Prudentia* as the personification of wisdom—we see Otanes with his father's skin draped on his lap and Zaleucus having his eye gouged out. They represent the earthly judges who underwent personal experiences of good and just justice. These three registers are an introduction to the series with divine figures, divinely inspired rulers and worldly judges.

One of the works in this gallery, the story of the revenge of Tomyris (Fig. 2.6) was slightly *hors catégorie* as an *exemplum justitiae*, since it presents us with a non-example rather than an inspiring example. This work, part of the collection of Musea Brugge, was painted circa 1610 by Pieter Pieters (d. 1614), and adorned the courtroom of the Liberty of Bruges (*Brugse Vrije*). It depicts the story of a vengeful Tomyris, Queen of the Massagetae. The queen defeated her enemy Cyrus in an attack instigated by him in which she lost her own son, had Cyrus beheaded, and then drenched his head in a vessel of blood in order to symbolise his bloodlust. It is one of the only themes in justice paintings in which the protagonist is a woman. Tomyris and her cruel act exemplify revenge and judgment driven by emotions instead of reason—a type of behaviour the judges were to avoid at all cost. She became an example for judges of how not to practise law. The theme remained popular well into the seventeenth century.

2.4 The Judge's Skin: The Judgment of Cambyses

The tale of the judgment of Cambyses was another common theme for *exempla justitiae* paintings in the sixteenth and seventeenth centuries. Among the most important works of the Groeninge collection, and as far as we know, the very first large scale paintings of this story, are the justice panels painted by Gerard David (ca. 1450–1523) for the aldermen of Bruges. This diptych was also the starting point of the exhibition. The various questions raised by this work made the curators try to understand the various ways in which art played a role in late medieval views and concepts of justice and its application. The third gallery was devoted to the theme, and Gerard David's panels were grouped together with other works representing the same subject.

Usually on view in gallery one of the Groeningemuseum (which focuses on city commissions), the work—due to its very detailed depiction of a man being flayed alive—stops museum visitors in their tracks and usually leaves a lasting impression. It is often the work that visitors will remember the most after a visit to the museum. However, it lingers in the mind because of its detailed depiction of this gruesome act of skinning a living man, and much less so—or not at all—because of its function and the context in which the work was created. Nevertheless, Gerard David did not just paint something that is gruesome to look at. He left us with a work that embodies various aspects of fifteenth-century views on justice and judging.

The painting depicts the story of the King of Persia (who ruled from 529 to 522 BC), who came to know that one of his judges had accepted a bribe, and had thus tainted his noble profession with the vice of corruption. The King subsequently punished him by having him flayed alive. Sisamnes' skin then served a macabre purpose, as it was used as a cover for the seat of the new judge—Sisamnes' own son Otanes (already mentioned above when describing the *Thronus Iustitiae* title page)—as a tangible reminder of his father's objectionable behaviour. The Cambyses tale was recorded in Herodotus' *Historiae*, and reached Flanders through Latin versions such as Valerius Maximus' *Factorum et dictorum memorabilium libri IX* and the *Gesta Romanorum*. The story was often used as an admonition against corrupt judgment in a variety of moralising texts and anthologies.

Although the apocryphal tale is set in sixth-century BC Persia, David relocates the story to his own fifteenth-century Bruges. The protagonists and onlookers are dressed in contemporary attire and placed against the backdrop of the typical Flemish gothic architecture of Bruges. We recognise the Burgher's Lodge (*Poortersloge*), a gathering place of Bruges' upper crust, as well as the coats of arms of Bruges and Flanders above a portal. This doorway can be identified as the east façade of the city hall, where there may have been a loggia for open-air legal proceedings.

The painting opens up an array of questions.[5] Why did the aldermen of Bruges select this particular tale as the subject for their chamber? Were these large, impressive and memorable paintings conceived of as nothing more than a general *exemplum justitiae*? Or was it a more specific warning against the corrupt behaviour of judges? And was it perhaps specifically aimed at aldermen of Bruges, given the specific historical political context of the late-fifteenth-century uprising against Maximilan? Is there a reason why this gruesome punishment is depicted in such a prominent way? Why is, in David's painting, judge Sisamnes' arrest—signifying the loss of honour, reputation and status—so heavily emphasised? Is the painting perhaps a comment on Bruges' political disobedience during the time op upheaval (1487–1491)? Did the panels also serve as a professional group portrait of the new

[5]See, among many others, Raf Verstegen's contribution to this volume, as well as my contribution to the exhibition catalogue (The Skin of the Judge: The Judgment of Cambyses, in: Huygebaert et al. 2016a/b, 81–90) and Paumen 2016, and the references to Van Miegroet, van der Velden and others in these articles.

aldermen?[6] We might never know which of the aspects were deemed the most important by the aldermen. However, it is clear that the significance of the Gerard David paintings goes far beyond what meets the eye at first glance.

The story of Cambyses became a popular theme for courtrooms during the sixteenth and seventeenth centuries. The exhibition brought together various artworks, including a stained glass window from a private collection that can rarely be seen in a museum context, which show the various ways in which the story was depicted in the period after David had painted his large panels. In most of these works, the emphasis shifts away from the gruesome punishment, so accurately and vividly depicted by David, to the scene of Otanes taking seat as the new judge, trying to fulfil his heavy task in the ever-present reminder of his father's stripped-off skin. As far as we know, the subject was never again depicted in the way Gerard David did for his city hall commission.

2.5 The Practice of Justice Depicted

In several more intimate spaces, the exhibition highlighted aspects dealing with the practice and execution of law. Among the many smaller-sized works of art was the series of eight engravings after Philips Galle, entitled *Litis Abusus*. These prints show very clearly that, already in the sixteenth century, the process of litigation was a soul-wretching procedure that demanded time, patience and money.[7] In these prints, it was the procedure and the individual parties that were mocked, rather than the professionals involved. Many other works of art, however, criticised the actual 'men of law', very often portrayed as 'men of writing' and 'men of money'. Furthermore, the reception of the learned canon and Roman law paved the way for new professionals, such as solicitors, barristers, proctors, court clerks, bailiffs etc. They formed a new social group of self-conscientious men, many of whom were keen on commissioning artworks, representing both high ideals of justice and criticism of certain aspects of law and justice.

A print (from ca. 1521–1528) by Albrecht Dürer (1471–1528) and a stained glass panel (from about 1510) testify that corruption and bribery were just as much an issue in the Ancien Régime as they are today. Durer's woodcut shows a deceitful judge, seated on a bench and holding the rod of office. He openly admits his dishonesty by means of the banner over his head. It reads '*Ich bin die betrugnis*' (I am betrayal). To his left, three female figures are locked in the stocks with their legs, a well-known form of punishment at the time. They are Justice, Truth and

[6]On the representation of civic bodies and their identification with justice in Early Modern Flemish Portraiture, see Beatrijs Wolters van der Wey's contribution to this volume.

[7]The same series, but by a different designer, is the subject of the Alain Wijffels' paper in these proceedings.

Intellect. The message is clear: if a judge is dishonest, then justice, truth and intellect are incapacitated.

A similar message is expressed in a small stained glass panel from a private collection, in which Lady Justice is depicted with gold coins being poured over her head, resulting in a sword that was pointing to the ground. Next to her is truth, her lips sealed with a ring. When justice is corrupt, truth cannot speak out.

Several artworks focused on Bruges and the places where law was practised. The seventeenth-century painter Gillis van Tilborgh (ca. 1625–1678) depicted the interior of the Bruges aldermen's room of the Liberty of Bruges, including the Last Judgment painting by Pieter Pourbus we encountered in the first gallery of the exhibition.

Joos de Damhouder, a Bruges-rooted, internationally renowned lawyer, features in the exhibition through the display of various editions of his illustrated books, the *Praxis Rerum Civilium* and the *Praxis Rerum Criminalium*. These books had an international impact on the codification of legal practices. Of particular interest is the fact that Damhouder himself insisted that these books should be illustrated. These illustrations, woodcuts and engravings of varying quality, provide us with glimpses of the world of sixteenth-century legal practices. One of the many illustrations allows us to step back in time and enter a lawyer's office. Leather-bound books are placed on the shelf, the desk displays the tools of the writing trade,[8] while procedural bags are hung on the wall. A small stained-glass panel, like the ones in this exhibition, decorates the window. The caged bird, finally, may be an allusion to the lawyer's clients entering through the door, who will find themselves trapped in litigation.

A fascinating aspect of the execution of the law are several beautifully crafted silver objects. As 'penalty pieces',[9] they were part of a series of punishments. Some people convicted of slander or threats against judicial officials were forced to pay for the creation of a metal bust, or of a fist in cases of physical violence. Paying for the production of these pieces was usually only a part of the overall punishment. The convict often had to do public penance, and could be banished from the town as well. Objects such as these were on permanent display in the *vierschaar* (courtroom) or on the outside wall of the town hall. They were often accompanied by a plaque, explaining the reasons for the punitive measure, as could be seen in the examples from the town of Veurne on display in the exhibition. As such, they did not only function as a punishment, but also as a lasting reminder of the crime, a source of shame for his family and a deterring warning for others. They embody the exemplary nature of the justice system and emphasise that a properly working justice system was in place—like the gallows at the edge of town in Pieter Bruegel the Elder's (1525–1569) famous justice print. This brings us to the last theme of the exhibition.

[8]See Gustav Kalm's contribution in this volume.

[9]See Paul De Win,'s contribution in this volume.

2.6 Lady Justice

In the justice print of Bruegel's series on the seven virtues, Lady Justice is standing in the foreground against a city scape filled with various aspects of the practice and execution of justice taking place behind her. She is placed on a small podium, but seems unaware of the commotion surrounding her. She is blindfolded, and her scales and sword in place. Is she the same queen of all virtues reigning over all sins that Antonius Claeissens (ca. 1536–1613) depicted in the painting *Justice Conquers the Seven Deadly Sins*, or has she lost control over what the justice system had become in Bruegel's time? The exhibition ended with a closer look at Lady Justice, her attributes, and her evolution from one of the virtues to the iconic image with which we are all still familiar today, and which personifies the entire justice system.

During this period, the law was not yet codified, but written legislation and doctrine boomed nonetheless. The reason for this was the success of the printing press. At the same time, the image of Lady Justice developed as well. Around 1500, she steps to the fore as the most important of the four cardinal virtues. She starts to represent justice, both as an ideal and as a practice. The last gallery of the exhibition traced her development and iconography through paintings, prints, illuminations, emblem books and sculpture. A special place was reserved for one of the six panels from the city hall of Gdansk, painted by the Antwerp painter Hans Vredeman de Vries. *Justitia and Injustitia* combines many aspects that run through the exhibition. Here, good justice and bad justice—as part of a series of works highlighting good government—sit across each other. The former is blind (not merely blindfolded, as is often the case in representations of Lady Justice),[10] her sword resting on her shoulder and the scales in balance. The latter's sword is directed forward, as if ready for attack, her scales out of balance and her all-seeing eyes peering out. She seems to take in the ill advice from the figure next to her. The poor and needy are welcomed in Justitia's presence, and cast away on the opposite side. Rich and poor appeal for justice, but only *Injustitia* seems to make a distinction between the two, as gold coins are dropped into the open hands of the judge in front of her. Once again, the message is clear: only when there is impartiality, truth and the absence of corruption can justice, under divine sanction, truly reign. As such, she exalts a people, as shown in the painting (1656) painted for the Arnemuiden town hall by Dirck van Delen (1605–1671).

---

[10]Lady Justice is mostly blindfolded, but at times she is also depicted as being blind, without a cloth covering her seeing eyes, and with open eyes without sight. Unfortunately, in the English version of the exhibition catalogue a mistranslation regarding Vredeman De Vries' *Justitia and Injustitia* was not noticed by the editors. The Dutch '*zit de blinde Vrouwe Justitia*' should have been translated as '*a blind* Lady Justice chairs', and not, as is the case on page 154, '*a blindfolded* Lady Justice chairs' (Huygebaert et al. 2016a/b, p. 154). The editors hereby humbly apologise for this *erratum*.

2.7 A Stimulating Interdisciplinary Field of Study

Our anticipation that the exhibition would entice both a general and specialised audience was exceeded by the lauding reactions of its many visitors. For many specialists, an exhibition of this kind seemed to be long overdue. The curators' aim was that the exhibition would not only give the visitors a glimpse of the culture around law and justice during the Ancien Régime, but also stimulate thought and discussion about law and justice in our own society today. Furthermore, as art historians collaborating with legal historians on this exhibition and its conference, we wanted to emphasise the importance of a cross-pollination of these fields. This is particularly relevant in cases such as this, where the respective fields rarely ever cross over. The collaboration has not only proven to be a fruitful one but, as these papers make clear, one that needs to continue in order to yield results.

While the exhibition has been dismantled, the bigger story we wanted to tell continues to exist through the exhibition catalogue. It also served as an impetus for these proceedings. Furthermore, another exhibition on the intersection of art and law entitled *Call for Justice. Art and Law in the Burgundian Netherlands* was on view at the Hof van Busleyden in Malines, Belgium, from March through June 2018—further evidence that there is still much ground to be covered in this fascinating field of study.

References

Huygebaert S, Martyn G, Paumen V, Van Poucke T (ed) (2016a) The art of law. Three Centuries of Justice Depicted (exh. cat. Bruges). Lannoo, Tielt

Huygebaert S, Martyn G, Paumen V, Van Poucke T (ed) (2016b) De kunst van het recht. Drie eeuwen gerechtigheid in beeld (exh. cat. Bruges). Lannoo, Tielt

Paumen V (2016) De verbeelding van de rechtspraak. Of hoe een villing een rechtszaal sierde. Vind. Geschiedenis, archeologie, kunst en antiek 24:41–47

Vanessa Paumen is the coordinator of The Flemish research centre for the arts in the Burgundian Netherlands (Musea Brugge). Its mission is to initiate, facilitate, stimulate and disseminate research related to Flemish art of the 15th and 16th centuries. At the centre Vanessa co-develops and coordinates academic programs, annual lectures series and the expansion of the library in the fields of 15th and 16th century art history and related areas. She is an art historian specialised in Northern Renaissance art, and obtained her degrees in Art History from The University of Texas at Austin (USA). She is the curator of the exhibition 'The art of law. Three centuries of justice depicted' at the Groeningemuseum (Bruges) and editor/author of its accompanying catalogue.

Figures

Fig. 2.1 Exhibition poster, designed by PK Projects based on: Workshop of Jacob de Gheyn II, *Justice*, ca. 1591–1595, engraving, diam. 145 mm, Antwerp, Museum Plantin-Moretus. © Museum Plantin Moretus, Antwerp

Fig. 2.2 Jan van Brussel, *Dual Justice*, 1477 or 1499, oil on panel, 158 × 211.5 cm, Maastricht, Town of Maastricht, Huygebaert et al. (2016a, b), chap. 1, Fig. 1, cat. 6. © Stichting Restauratie Atelier Limburg (SRAL), Maastricht

Fig. 2.3 Frans Floris I, *The Judgment of Solomon*, 1547, oil on panel, 143 × 227 cm, Antwerp, Koninklijk Museum voor Schone Kunsten, Huygebaert et al. (2016a, b), chap. 2, Fig. 12, cat. 21. © www.lukasweb.be—Art in Flanders vzw, photo Hugo Maertens

Fig. 2.4 Anonymous, *The Judgment of Zaleucus*, ca. 1525, stained glass, diam. 22.5 cm, Amsterdam, Rijksmuseum, inv. BK-15119, Huygebaert et al. (2016a, b), p. 46–47, Fig. 17, cat. 28. © Rijksmuseum Amsterdam

Fig. 2.5 Willem Isaacsz. Van Swaneburg after Joachim Wtewael, *Thronus Iustitiae*, 1606, title page of a series of thirteen engravings, leaf ca. 300 × 400 mm, Brussels, Koninklijke Bibliotheek van België, Print room, Huygebaert et al. (2016a, b), p. 56–60, Fig. 21, cat. 7. © Koninklijke Bibliotheek van België, Brussels

Fig. 2.6 Pieter Pieters, *The Revenge of Tomyris*, 1610, oil on canvas, 184 × 175 cm, Bruges, Museum Brugse Vrije, nr. 2010. GRO0023.I, Huygebaert et al. (2016a, b), p. 53 and 64–67, Fig. 26, cat. 30. © www.lukasweb.be—Art in Flanders vzw, photo Dominique Provost

Chapter 3
The Mirror Axiom: Legal Iconology and The Lure of Reflection

Carolin Behrmann

> *The image in a mirror is merely the shadow arranged by the brilliance of the material receiving it.*
> Pliny, *Natural History*, IX, 97 (33–45)

Abstract The mirror metaphor bestrides and divides studies on images in law in two opposing factions, either confirming or dissenting the Law the notion of law by doubling or deferring its presence. Whereas legal history tends to read pictures and iconographies as depictions of a legal reality, art historical iconology interprets images beyond their conceptual historical evidence of the mirror surface, leaving it undecidable whether the reflection is real or present, or an event that is not assured and part of the artistic process. The paper explores the stability and abyssal structure of both formalising and revealing forces of the mirror axiom, asking how images reflect or constitute legal phenomena.

3.1 Pictorial Regimes

The history of research in the field of law and the image, of legal iconographies, or visual dimensions of judiciary practice, has brought forth contrasting approaches.[1] While the ubiquity of vision as master sense of the Modern Era has a long historical record, legal studies, however, discover the variety of the visual legacy of law only circumspectly and often with suspicion. Despite all tendencies of ocularcentrism

---

[1]An extensive bibliography would exceed a reasonable footnote. Some of the most recent titles are the exhibition catalogues Huygebaert et al. (2016), Widener et al. (2017), as well as the text volumes Del Mar and Goodrich (2014), Wagner and Sherwin (2014), Goodrich and Hayaert (2015), Goodrich (2017), and Manderson (2018).

C. Behrmann (✉)
Minerva Research Group 'The Nomos of Images: Manifestation and Iconology of Law', Kunsthistorisches Institut in Florenz – Max-Planck-Institut, Florence, Italy
e-mail: carolin.behrmann@khi.fi.it

S. Huygebaert et al. (eds.), *The Art of Law*, Ius Gentium: Comparative Perspectives on Law and Justice 66, https://doi.org/10.1007/978-3-319-90787-1_3

which prevailed since the early modern impact of the scientific revolution and continued to play a prominent role in a variety of ways for the notion of 'modernity', the field of law had been proven to be rather immune to the influence of visual phenomena until recently. The law, it has been believed, has to be kept blindfolded to secure the abstract logic of the institution.[2] There are many tropes contradicting this immunity that have found theoretical reception also in legal theory: as for example the 'mirror of nature' metaphor (Richard Rorty), the prevalence of surveillance and disciplinary strategies (Michel Foucault), the 'scopic field' as psychoanalytic dimension of the gaze (Maurice Merleau-Ponty, Jacques Lacan), or the idea of 'scopic regimes' (Martin Jay) that refer more generally to visual experiences mediated through technologies, such as photography, television, or the digital.[3] Especially during the course of the last two decades along with what has been called the 'pictorial' or 'iconic turn' researches about images and visual phenomena had a tendency to increase in all different disciplines.[4] Understanding the law through the visual sphere has become by now a multifaceted endeavour with similar approaches and hypothetical assumptions just as in the humanities and science.

Studies about art and law have been categorised in either legal rules that standardise images, or image-rules that shape the law.[5] The first category points to the using and regulating of images and art through political and legal systems. Images and symbols would give meaning to legal institutions and inspire people toward legislative aims and otherwise act to keep order. In contrast, image-rules refer to the representation of law, justice and legal themes in art through images. To review the complexity and tradition of these different approaches resulting from that distinction would take up a study in itself and exceeds the assignment of this paper.[6] However, the amount of research and interest cannot disguise the fact that basic assumptions in the visual legal dimension sometimes arise from scepticism, if not to say fear of the rift between language and the ambiguity of images. They are often regarded as overdetermined, ambiguous and polysemous, closer to the emotional or the unconscious realm than to legal logic and reasoning (Douzinas and Nead 1999, p. 15; Steinhauer 2003, p. 79–138). Along with such a mistrust there can be noted also a considerable neglect of the interpretation of historical contexts or studies about

---

[2]In numerous publications, Peter Goodrich (1996, 1997) elicited law's dependency on pictures and the visual, especially in his works on early modern legal emblems (recently Goodrich 2013, 2017).

[3]E.g. Jay's (1993) analysis of the ocularcentric discourse is a fundamental analytical survey of the history of visuality, that pronounced a paradigm shift to 'anti-ocularism' in the 1980s in Europe and the US. About the 'scopic regimes', see Jay (1988, p. 3–23).

[4]In the early 1990s W.J.T. Mitchell (1995, p. 11–13, and recently Mitchell 2015) related the 'pictorial turn' to Anglo-American and Continental post-structuralist philosophy. For a general synopsis and discussion see Boehme-Nessler (2011).

[5]Also termed as 'law's art' and 'art's law', see Douzinas and Nead (1999, p. 11) and Vismann (2007, p. 15).

[6]My forthcoming study *The Nomos of Images* analyses the history of methods and disciplinary intrications of art and legal history. See for a general description Behrmann (2013) and, Behrmann (2015, p. 37-51).

the cultural translation and diachronic continuity of form and style that go beyond mere juridical explanations. An exception have been works in the tradition of folklore studies, legal archaeology and legal iconography that have brought forward numerous key examples and interpretations of historical phenomena of legal culture (e.g. Maisel 1982, p. 279–286; Maisel 1993; Martyn et al. 2014). In general, the transparent quantity of historical approaches to legal images is striking when we consider that the discourses on legal images—as Pierre Legendre (1994) has pointed out—are themselves part of a process of institutionalisation, that not only determine juridical approaches to reality but also carry mythological meanings with them, producing images that constitute the individual and the collective, subjective and common knowledge of the law in general (Goodrich 1997).

3.2 Iconologies

One explanation for this neglect can be drawn from etymology and the notion of the word 'image' itself. The polysemantic meaning of the term refers to a broader aesthetic realm and embraces perception and sensation, as well as different phenomena such as painting, film, emblems, or simple patterns. The German word '*Bild*' is translated into English meaning 'image' as well as 'picture' or 'visual'. The disparity of these two terms is well known: image refers in general to optical appearances as well as mental representations, ideas or metaphors, that exist also without a medium, whereas pictures have a material basis and are bound to a medium. They are visible and destroyable. However, drawing a line between material pictures and mental images is virtually impossible.

Methodologically speaking there are thus two different approaches to images in law that should be distinguished: The more prevalent is influenced by the Anglo-American tradition of 'visual studies', referring to visual media in general. The other approach is rather associated with art historical methods and cultural theory, which is grounded in the idea of '*Bildwissenschaft*' and iconology.[7] Theoretical approaches to Visual Studies have criticised iconological investigation as being reduced to 'high' artworks, neglecting other types of modern visual media (Mitchell 2002, p. 231–250). Most prominently, it has been Panofsky's analysis of Renaissance humanistic symbolism and allegories, that was suspected to address only an elitist circle of art experts. However, contrariwise art history understood as '*Bildwissenschaft*' has included art as well as non-art in its frame of research from the early twentieth century on. Most prominently, this has been advanced methodologically in the works of intellectuals affiliated in the ambit of Aby M. Warburg's '*Kulturwissenschaftliche Bibliothek*' in Hamburg, such as Ernst

[7]A broader understanding of art history as '*Bildwissenschaft*' has been disregarded by visual studies, according to the critique of Bredekamp (2003, p. 418–428). For a more general survey see Davis (2011), as well as Moxey (2008, p. 131–146).

Cassirer, Erwin Panofsky and Edgar Wind (e.g. Holly 1984; Ferretti 1989). Through their forced exile during the Nazi Regime, that particular art historical method that was largely based on a broader concept of the image that was only underway to be discussed and formulated, was scattered and torn apart from its intellectual ambit (Ginzburg 2013, p. 17–59).

Central about Warburg's idea of iconography, coined 'iconology', is pursuing a diachronic line concerned with the afterlife of images ('*Nachleben der Bilder*') since Antiquity (Didi-Huberman 2002). Not understood as a structured synchronic narrative as in other cultural histories but as dissemination and re-composition of images and forms across time and space. Warburg emphasised moreover the unconscious charges that this migration of images carry with them.[8] This posed the problem of both conscious selection and cultural *translation* of forms as well as the unconscious inscription of tradition through coded visual signs (Johnson 2012). Thus, in visual images not only different types of motifs are to be identified, by attributing particular meaning to them, rather artefacts and objects are treated as sources with evidential value for the interpretation of political, cultural and social contexts.

Later, Panofsky went further in defining a 'visual logic' principle of manifestation according to which the principle of 'spatialisation' in the architectural hierarchical order of a gothic cathedral and the discursive order of the literary *manifestatio* would be conceived as being homologous.[9] Michel Foucault has underlined the most striking aspects of this method: 'Panofsky removes the privilege of discourse. Not in order to claim the autonomy of the plastic universe, but in order to describe the complexity of their interrelations: entwinement, isomorphism, transformation, translation, in short, this entire 'feston' of visible and speakable that characterises a culture in a moment of its history' (Foucault 2001, p. 649).

This idea of a complex visual logic leads to a fundamental but ambiguous point that lies at the core of the relationship between the disciplines of art history as '*Bildgeschichte*', and legal culture, which deals with the pictures, objects, architecture and all other visual signs of legal contexts. It is based on a methodological premise which presumes the evidential status of images and objects, that 'reflect' the law, herein after referred to as 'mirror axiom'.

3.3 Specular Dogma

Prudence's mirror, according to Cesare Ripa's *Iconologia*, leads mankind to a straight opinion and thus felicity. He calls Prudence the '*scienza del bene, e del male*', who would by virtue guide to the choice of good over evil. Hence, justice

[8]He defined them as 'engrams', which, in contrast to symbols, that are also transmitted by social memory, rather crystallise an emotional experience or energetic charge (Johnson 2012, 63).

[9]The *manifestatio* was aimed at the 'elucidation or clarification' of thought as it manifests itself within 'the completeness, self-sufficiency, and limitedness of a system of thought' (Panofsky 1951, p. 58).

would be the science of the right distribution of these two principles (Ripa 1777, p. 76). Since the early thirteenth century the mirror held in Prudence's hand, is a sign of self-reflection and shows her as able to align all actions to the norm of reason, which harmonises Prudence with the Divine will (Payer 1979, p. 55–70). The function of the mirror has been served since Greek Antiquity as model for the reflection of the cosmic rules in the normative apparatus of the *polis*. Numerous examples in town halls and courthouses show the two allegories inseparably together.[10] In a small engraving (after 1537) after Maarten van Heemskerck (1498–1574), we see blindfolded Justice who holds up a pair of scales and turns questioningly to Prudence who is reflecting her countenance in a mirror (Fig. 3.1).[11]

In legal practice, the 'speculum' has traditionally been a specific genre of treatise or handbook that deals with the education of the perfect jurist (Kelley 1988, p. 84–102). The *Speculum jurisconsultum, Rechtsspiegel, Mirror of lawyers* or *Lunette des avocats* reflected all legal rules in a large collection of judgments, but they also guided to ways of learning, teaching and practicing law (*methodus, modus, ratio, institutio*) as an image itself (Goodrich 1996, p. 95–97). In the foreword of the Saxon Mirror (*Sachsenspiegel*) the author explained that the Saxons should learn their law 'as a woman does her countenance in a mirror' (von Repgow and Schott 1984, p. 18). The origin and use of the specular metaphor in law has been analysed in length by Pierre Legendre (1994), who connects it to the broader discourse of the *Imago Dei*. Mirror and screen are of central significance as 'the law has to communicate itself in images in order to overcome its abstractness' (Vismann 2008, p. 1–9). Concerned with interrelations of the unconscious and the legal, Legendre (1997, p. 249) compares the process of seeing the own image in a mirror, far from a physical object as 'dogmatic universe of representational montages' that foredoom all common positivistic objectifications. He explains that in its strictest etymological sense, 'aesthetics' would be a 'term that refers to the sensory apprehension of thought' and is less abstract than it is commonly understood (Legendre 2008, p. 10). Also the 'dogmatic' would apply to a truth 'that is sanctioned by its staging: the mirror's truth or the emblem's, the legal truth which would be the exact opposite of a scientific demonstration', as it pertains to the acknowledgment of an aesthetic truth. The latter is defined as the 'truth of mirrors', the specular dogma: 'The mirror's truth is unquestionable. This is why the unquestionable authority of the presence that the mirror founds signals that the relation to images is intrinsically normative' (Legendre 2008, p. 16). The faith in images makes the aesthetic operation omnipotent, 'aesthetic truth is produced theatrically', in a scenic affirmation (Legendre 2008). As Prudence's mirror, the specular dogma reflected in art and aesthetics belongs to the foundational principles of legal dogmatics. Legendre deduces that legal authority is 'intrinsic to the symbolic dimension of social relations', just like a '"mirror" within which identity is constructed in the institution' (Legendre 1997, p. 1–36). The mirror in Prudence's

[10]On the mirror motif in art see Hartlaub (1951).

[11]For more examples see Curtis and Resnik (2011). This print was also part of the *The Art of Law* exhibition, see Huygebaert et al. (2016, p. 200), cat. 99.

hands refers thus to the operation of the law in general. Rather than being a reflection that duplicates reality, the mirror should be read as a *mise en abîme* (Derrida 1987, p. 17–36), as Prudence's self-reflection symbolizes the construction of identity in general, that lies at the core of the construction of identity, which lies at the core of legal dogmatics.

3.4 Distorted Reflexing

Notwithstanding the complexity of the mirror metaphor, images in law often are treated as figures of representational transparency that are connected rather to notions of realism, that promise to function as mirrors and 'reflect' legal reality.[12] The mirror is similar to the metaphor of a window that opens onto the world, and naturalises the artifice of the picture, claiming to be a perfect duplication of reality. Fixing a moment in time, and as such (legal) information, the mirror image signified an unmediated depiction of reality, that became relevant photographs, film and video. With the 'digital matrix of synthetic visual representations' the mirror has again gained momentum as a metaphor of images in law, at times when the legal world 'marches in lockstep with shared visual scripts and digital programs' (Sherwin 2014, p. xxxiv). Sherwin draws the comparison with 'a special kind of mirror that has been algorithmically encoded to reflect back other rooms and other faces, some of which may or may not be our own' (Sherwin 2014, p. xxxv).

A kind of 'naive realism', that overrates the evidential value of pictures, tends to neglect varying interpretations of visual phenomena in law, taking them as common sense (Feigenson 2014, p. 105–125). It should be asked why studies about the legal visual realm often consider the image as momentarily, as reflection and objectifying mirror of society rather than a complex organ of social memory that records and transmits far more than a hermeneutical reading of the verbal meanings of visual signs would disclose. The mirror metaphor has been a vehicle for divination and prophesy or creative imagination, and is more than an object to capture faithful representations. The value of reflection is not reduced to representational capacities. The mirror's reflective surface rather distorts reality (reversing the image) and yet provides other perspectives (as the self-portrait) and wider visual fields of vision (curved or convex mirrors) (Gasché 1986). Thus the mirror axiom becomes problematic when it acts on the assumption that images function as a mirror and reflect legal 'reality', rather than being regarded as generating this reality through its consistence and aesthetic operation.

One of the most well-known iconological examinations that is grounded in the assumption of a literal translation of the visual helps to understand the 'mirror axiom' that casts its shadow on the interpretation of legal artefacts and materiality.

---

[12]Rorty (1979) has drawn attention to the contingent character of the terms that are used to describe reality. The 'mirror' is the temptation to scientism and positivism, and one of the central metaphors of the myth that philosophy could reflect reality and the essence of nature like a mirror.

The interpretation of Jan van Eyck's Arnolfini double portrait in the National Gallery in London is in many respects an insightful and early example of an attempted dialogue between art history and legal history. The full-length portrait depicts the Italian merchant Giovanni Arnolfini, together with his wife, Giovanna Cenami, portrait, painted in 1434. The scene is set in their home in Bruges, showing the exquisitely dressed young couple, surrounded by various symbolical objects. In a short but seminal article published in the *Burlington Magazine* in 1934, Erwin Panofsky (1934, p. 117–119, 122–127) has interpreted the painting as picturing the act of a clandestine marriage.[13] This early iconological approach has become a widely received and debated reading of the picture. Apparently, the author did not expect at all the impact his new approach would have on further studies in early netherlandish art.[14] In 1932 he even complained to his friend Walter Friedländer about having an unproductive time, calling the article a 'stupid little essay for the Burl. Magazine'.[15] Nevertheless, he was very well aware that he has removed some of the mustiness that had misled art-historical interpretation about the meaning of the figuration. You could say that Panofsky's 'stupid little article' marked in a nutshell the initial ideas of iconological analysis as we understand it today. The article is well known for its description of Van Eyck's 'disguised symbolism', which takes seemingly accidental details such as the shoes, the candle, the fruits, or the embellishments of everyday objects and persuasively realistic domestic setting, and explains their 'hidden' symbolical meaning, conveying the sacramental nature of marriage. The interior and all its details are at the same time realistic and symbolical, and bear a complex universe of allegorical meanings (Bedaux 1986, p. 5–28).

Panofsky's legacy remains pervasive to this day (e.g. Postel 2016). However at the core of his analysis does not lie the visual form but rather the problem of historical shortcoming and shortsightedness, evolving from the expression '*per fidem*' in descriptions of the painting from the sixteenth and seventeenth century. Panofsky found it 'both amusing and instructive' to observe how an abstract legal term 'gradually developed into a living allegorical female figure' (Panofsky 1934, p. 118). Marc van Vaernewyck's *Spieghel der Nederlantscher Audtheyt* published in 1569 served as source for art-historical interpretations and led to quite a few misunderstandings. Panofsky assumed that Van Vaernewyck had never actually seen the picture. His misinterpretation was based on translating the expression '*per fidem*' as meaning the personification *fides*—while, in reality, as Panofsky (1934, p. 118) states: 'it was a law term'. Fides is neither embodied in the little Griffin Terrier at the couple's feet, nor is there any other allegorical figure accompanying the couple. Instead '*per fidem*' would identify the marital oath as a legal action itself. Panofsky explains that in medieval Latin, the word *fides* could be used as a

[13]He developed the argument further in Panofsky (1953).

[14]I am grateful to Eric Bousmar for indicating me his article (2009, p. 287–328) on the Arnolfini portrait with an extended *résumée* and current and thoroughly reconstructed overview of this vast field of research. See also more recently Postel (2016).

[15]He wrote the essay during a holiday on the island Bornholm '*wohin ich mich vor Hakenkreuz und Kunstgeschichte geflüchtet hatte*', see Wuttke (2001).

synonym for 'marital oath', more particularly the '*dextrarum iunctio*' the joining of (right) hands. Consequently, Jan van Eyck's portrait could not be described more briefly or more appropriately than by calling it the representation of a couple '*qui desponsari videbantur per fidem*', that is to say: 'who were contracting their marriage by a marital oath, more particularly by joining hands' (Panofsky 1934, p. 119). Panofsky called this case a 'lesson' for any art historian, 'not to attempt to use literary sources for the interpretation of pictures, before we have interpreted the literary sources themselves' (Panofsky 1934, p. 121).

The other aspect of Panofsky's iconological study was to pin down the legal significance of the artist's reflection in the mirror, showing him standing at the other end of the room evidencing his presence, and the artwork itself to the act of marriage. He turns the tables by examining the artist's signature in the picture to prove that, foremost, it is crucial to interpret the visual before it is possible to interpret the literary source. The most unusual reflective statement 'Jan van Eyck was here' ('*Johannes de eyck fuit hic*') (Fig. 3.2) written above the mirror evidences in Panofsky's interpretation that Van Eyck not only painted the picture but also witnessed the wedding. He thus concludes: 'Furthermore, the phrase makes perfectly good sense when we consider the legal situation as described in the preceding paragraphs. Since the two people portrayed were married merely '*per fidem*' the portrait meant no less than a 'pictorial marriage certificate' in which the statement that 'Jan van Eyck had been there' had the same importance and implied the same legal consequences as an 'affidavit' deposed by a witness at a modern registrar's office' (Panofsky 1934, p. 118). Further visual evidence is provided in the artist's presence reflected in the convex mirror which hangs at the wall: He stands in his blue robe in front of the couple, and raises his hand, just like Arnolfini himself. The convex surface of the mirror, that enhances the perception of objects and enables to observe otherwise imperceptible details, becomes a device for the manifestation of his authorial presence.

For Panofsky the documented role of the artist as witness of the marital oath, an oath that is merely given '*per fidem*', proves that the picture is not merely representing a legal event, but is rather inscribed into the legal process itself. The artist's signature on the painting's canvas is akin to the form and function of notarial calligraphy and authenticates the artist's.[16] Thus it is crucial to note that different dimensions of sign and representation testify to the marriage and mutually reinforce one another (Gaggi 1997, p. 4). Panofsky pointed at the fact that the herein expressed self-reference of the artist, who seems to institute the marital oath himself, is not just a simple counterfeiting gesture of the marital scene but, even more so, showing the artist as an essential and indispensable 'witness' according to canon law for the validity of the wedding. This kind of 'realistic' representation, the mirror reflection, and the notarial calligraphy are thus symptoms of the legal context. Notably in her analysis art historian Svetlana Alpers (1983, p. 70) has described this

[16]Following Panofsky's argument, Seidel (1989, p. 68–69) even argued that the mirror would be 'a seal-like object', and functioned as the artist's seal.

'coexistence' of both signs pointing to the presence of the artist as calling attention to the common function of verbal and visual signs, which are balanced in the Arnolfini portrait. However, as much evidential value the realism of Van Eyck seems to simulate, the portrait itself is far from being equal to any notarial document that is legalising the act of marriage.[17] The analogy between picture and legal certificate is alluring but unfortunately. Nevertheless, Panofsky's description of those multiple pictorial perspectives refers to the legal discourse and its dependence on dogmatic theatricality. Van Eyck stages the problem of marriage or marital oath as theatrical procedure, an institutional act in which he himself as witness in the convex mirror assumes a crucial role. In his portrayal of the Arnolfini couple the artist offers not only a vivid sense of their presence but demonstrates his knowledge about the legal act and institution, which has to be described as a concurrently fictive and constitutive process.

3.5 Luring Analogies

Other details of Van Eyck's portrait have raised similar questions about the legal status of the representation. Much has been written for example about the representation of the couple's hands (Fig. 3.3) as they join their right and left hand instead of both rights, while the female hand is open, as if receiving something. According to Panofsky, the combination of the groom's raised hand and this specific joining of hands is more likely to represent the speaking of an oath. For him, this inconsistency is explicable only through aspects of the pictorial composition and artistic license. From a formalistic point of view, 'Van Eyck took the liberty of joining the right hand of the bride with the left of the bridegroom, contrary to ritual and other representations of a marriage'. He wanted both to avoid the overlapping of the right arm, as well as a *contraposto* 'to contrive to build up the group symmetrically and to subdue the actual movement' (Panofsky 1934, p. 120). As crucial moment of this change in representation for Panofsky is the synergy between a religious and a legal gesture—the risen hand as a sign of '*fides levata*' that seems to be 'invested with the confident humility of a pious prayer'. It was this detail which led Edwin Hall to disagree with Panofsky's general assumption that the painting showed a wedding. Given the light touch and the composition of the picture, Hall contends that the touching of both hands would be more consistent with the entering into a betrothal agreement than a marriage ceremony (Hall 1994, p. 83).

Panofsky wrote his essay at a time of increasing interest in semiotics, the recognition of the importance of signs and signification and the relation of human self-identity within objects. The interest of the transformation of signs into a culturally meaningful world of objects is reflected in his definition of iconology, which bears striking resemblance to some ideas typical of semiology. This idea of

[17]See Hall's (1994, p. 161) critique of Seidel.

semiotics gave art history the instruments at hand to 'instill a painting with a richer historical, social, legal and political meaning' (Hasenmueller 1978, p. 289–301; see also Bal and Bryson 1991, p. 174–208). General issues were raised, such as the nature of representation, turning away from questions such as authorial intention, which is not per force congruent with the meaning of the picture. For instance, it was possible to interpret a painting beyond the mere narrative of the events depicted. Consequently, it was possible to detect in every detail a 'historically determinate sign of the culture that generated it' (Bal and Bryson 1991). Art does not simply 'express' a historical period that is bound to a horizontal, chronological reading of the events. Instead, according to Alpers, every artefact can be invested with a 'pictorial intelligence' that transcends the mere depiction of a historical scene and has a more diachronical (vertical) meaning.[18]

The most common art historical method of iconography was called into question, not because of its emphasis on motifs but because the interpretation in terms of moral messages disregarded their formal effect. Instead, iconological analysis, like Panofsky's interpretation of the Arnolfini wedding, promised a more contextual approach, without trying to 'unlock a painting or other representational form as a statement of explicit meanings' (Holly 1984, p. 14). Instead, iconology wanted to address underlying cultural principles of representation by primarily asking how meaning would be expressed in a specific visual order. However, the evidential value of these visual manifestations in art and the occurrence of underlying principles such as legal meanings have to be treated with caution. Panofsky himself expressed his doubts and difficulties with his methodology of 'disguised symbolism' and the interpretation of every detail as a meaningful metaphor and called it a 'danger that iconology will behave'. In a letter to his friend and iconologist William Heckscher he suggests scholarly discipline in three steps: 'There is, I am afraid, no other answer to this problem than the use of historical methods tempered, if possible, by common sense. We have to ask ourselves whether or not the symbolical significance of a given motif is a matter of established representational tradition;—whether or not a symbolical interpretation can be justified by definite texts or agrees with ideas demonstrably alive in the period and presumably familiar to its artists' (Holly 1984, p. 164).

Now we understand better the misapprehension Panofsky was mocking—the search for visual analogies for abstract legal terms cannot possibly stop at a simple analogy between legal institution and pictorial representation. This can be derived from the operation of signs in general. For semiotics, forms of signification in verbal and visual cannot be differentiated. The material side of artworks is less important than categories of narrative, textuality or realism.[19] The 'reality effect' of Early Netherlandish painting is rather to be conceived as conventional or symbolic,

[18]Alpers (1983) proposed the term 'pictorial intelligence' as alternative to visual narrative.

[19]Mieke Bal (1991) has defined artworks rather as 'effect' and 'set of all possible readings'. She defines signs as 'events' that have more than one meaning but are unstable, dependent on the way they are viewed. See also the comprehensive description in Hatt and Klonk (2006, p. 215).

with codes that suggest mimesis and manifest and create cultural values (Moxey 2001, p. 101). According to semiology every interpretation of a sign results in a new, more complex sign, which carries its reference along cumulatively, thereby adding something at each stage of interpretation to the reference (Hardwick 1977). The dog, the candle or the joining of hands—all these details—belong to the analysis of systematic associations of motif and literary content, the field of iconography. The interpretation of the artist as a witness and the painting itself as evidence or 'certificate' that proves the act of marriage or betrothal goes beyond the idea of a descriptive process that involves legal topoi and motives. The painting interpreted as 'evidence' and the painter as being a 'witness' to the legal act broadens the notion of the image, but it also insinuates the picture being an instrument of the legal act itself, which, however, remains speculative.

3.6 The Question of Style

Now, the question arises, and will be discussed at length in the contributions of this volume, as how far visual images have effect, power, or become part of legal reasoning or even of the institutionalisation of legal meaning. Can they—as Panofsky assumes—indeed be meaningful or practicable, purposeful for the law, or do they simply adorn, depict or illustrate it and belong rather to a pure aesthetical realm? Again it might be productive to critically question the notion and validity of the 'mirror axiom'. We know a lot about the sphere of visual artefacts and their complexity, beauty and also their anarchy and the ambivalent status they have in comparison to positivist facts. Therefore we are accustomed to separating the questions of aesthetics from the legal interpretation of artworks and fathom their historical value and meaning. Studies that described the interdependence of aesthetic form and legal content posed not only the question how law is depicted, but also vice versa how law might follow or respond to aethetic principles more generally (e.g. Kevelson 1992; Gearey 2001). For Desmond Manderson (2000, p. 27), legal aesthetics describe law's capacity to act normatively also outside the legal realm. The legal system is not 'merely the passive mirror of a worldview. The law is a kind of discourse whose outlook on the world takes its place as a way of perceiving events around us'.

The analysis of form and even style of an artwork can thus unravel legal meaning (Sauerländer 1983, p. 253–270). If we see 'style' exemplified in motifs and patterns as well as in 'some directly grasped quality of the artwork', that is not only seen as a 'symptomatic trait, like the non-aesthetic features of an artefact or sign', we also accept the style of an artwork in its own significance and important constituent of culture (Schapiro 1953, p. 287–312). 'Style' as a changing set of representational conventions that mediate the relationship between motif and nature can thus become relevant for the explanation of artworks in a legal context (Behrmann 2015). The origins of 'style' as a technical term can be found already in medieval legal doctrine, when the term *stilus* referred to either certain formal features of official legal documents or to customary procedural rules of specific courts.[20] The style can also refer to characteristic ways legislators, judges, law enforcement agencies talk and behave. As Erasmus has insisted in 1517, style (*stilus*) constitutes the character and quality—including appearance, voice, judgment, inventive power, control of material, and 'is manifest in speech even more than the likeness of the body is reflected in a mirror'.[21] Also, stylistic analysis can reveal how specific legal institutions operate and explain how legal systems express distinctive mentalities and cultural patterns.

In the example of the Arnolfini portrait, questions of style and form—which are connected to juridical notions of evidence,[22] proof, or the 'real world' etc.—come into play that are not explained by written sources or any other meaningful analogy. The art of this generation of Early Netherlandish painting is generally associated with a notion of 'realism' or 'naturalism', pictorial strategies that make the depicted vividly present and 'naturalistically' compelling through subtlety, nuance and verisimilitude. It is often said that the 'realism' of these new paintings would increase the sense of the beholder, making them almost believe that the scenes they witness were continuous with their own experience. Now, if we understand 'style' as 'a system of forms with a quality and a meaningful expression' within the legal world, through which 'certain values' can be communicated or even fixed, the visual signs—otherwise unrelated—can be understood as an image in which legal meaning becomes manifest.

Coming to a synthesis of what had been said, we can sum up three significant scores through which the mirror axiom in legal image studies might be tackled: Iconology has pointed to the problem that seeking visual analogy of juridical terms is disputable. Images work as signs adding up meaning from different contexts, discourses. The question of style enlarges the field of approaches toward the visual. The idea that images that would 'mirror' the real, the legal process etc. neglects their function as adjudicators and agents. Thus, a simple union between law and art cannot exclude other epistemes or cultural bonds, as the search for legitimation of legal operations could not be grasped.

In his book on 'Iconology' published in 1999, W.J.T. Mitchell has explored the nature of images and showed different ways in how the idea of imagery is discussed in relation to notions of picturing, imagining, perceiving, resembling or imitating in many different disciplines and discourses (Mitchell 1999, p. 92). He reminds us of Socrates' rejection of our cherished notion that truth is a matter of accurate imaging,

---

[20]Style, such as custom and usage are important categories that serve the law itself. '*Stilus*' (such as *stilus curie* or *stylus cancellarie*) refers to the manner of writing documents and acts for a specific purpose.

[21]Cited in Eden (2017), who refers to a brief appendix in Hans Georg Gadamer's *Truth and Method*, in which he associates the word 'style' with early modern French jurisprudence (a '*manuel de procéder*'), the way of conducting a trial. After the sixteenth century, the word would be used generally as to 'describe the manner in which something is presented in language' (Eden 2017, p. 88).

[22]See the contribution by Tamara Golan to this volume.

mirroring, or representing. Accordingly, all signs work through custom and convention, and all are imperfect, riddled with error. It is misleading to think that we can grasp the truth about things by knowing the right names, signs or representations of them. According to Socrates, the apprehension of beauty and goodness is only possible in an image that is 'provocative', meaning an imperfect picture or likeness that provokes reflection: 'To claim to have direct knowledge of the ideal, to claim that one possessed the perfect image of nature would be to commit idolatry, to mistake the image for what it represents' (Mitchell 1999, p. 93).

Now, as we know, the idolatrous notion of the image has not only become an important vehicle for natural sciences but also for epistemology in general to reflect and develop a more consistent idea of what is called the 'real' world. The analysis of the image itself, its form as such or stylistic appearance allows us to take a distance to what might otherwise lead to a holistic understanding of the relationship between the image and the subject matter. To understand the specific status and even 'force' (Fischer-Lescano 2016) of images, artefacts and objects in the juridical field (Bourdieu 1987), it might be conducive to go back to Plato's ideas about the knowledge of 'nature', the 'deep truth that lies beyond all appearances or images, which is not found to be a renunciation of the world of custom and convention, but by a dialogue within the world of convention that leads us to its limits' (Mitchell 1999, p. 94).

The idea of a 'nomology' of images in law refers not only to legal institutions or a system of rules, but also to a complex field of knowledge about rules and wider normative world of right and wrong, lawful and unlawful, which it cannot fully control even while attempting to do so. If we understand nomos as 'a present world constituted by a system of tension between reality and vision' (Cover 1993, p. 97), the constructive and destructive qualities of images, which have often also been described as 'power', should be analysed as belonging to the 'force' of law, or rather 'the mystical foundation of authority' (Derrida 1992). The notion of force considers also the external ideological, super-structural nature of law, which operates in the service of economic and political forces as well as the intrinsic relation between violence and law, which reflects upon the foundations and position of the law.

Bearing a differentiated notion of images, pictures, or 'Bild' in mind, proves that the artworks and artefacts studied are more than just illustrations of legal customs or purely decorative ornaments, but actively take part in juridical action and culture. Those manifestations defy the disciplinary boundaries of art history and visual culture in how they relate to form, content and style as well as tradition. It is not merely the 'legibility' of images (or their translatability to legal themes and reasoning), but also to a significant degree their general appearance as perceptible, outward and visible expressions that links the process of artistic conceptualisation to the framework of law. This shall contribute not only to an understanding of artefacts (pictures, objects) as an illustrative part of the law, but also to an understanding of law as a continuously evolving process that 'transforms concepts and notions within space and time'—equally taking into consideration that law at times is seeking visibility (representation, figuration) and stability through images.

References

Alpers S (1983) The art of describing: Dutch art in the seventeenth century. University of Chicago Press, Chicago
Bal M (1991) Reading Rembrandt: beyond the word-image opposition. Cambridge University Press, Cambridge
Bal M, Bryson N (1991) Semiotics and art history. Art Bull 73:174–208
Bedaux JB (1986) The reality of symbols: the question of disguised symbolism in Jan van Eyck's Arnolfini portrait. Simiolus 16:5–28
Behrmann C (2013) The authority of juridical objects. In: Ulrich Großmann G, Krutisch P (eds) The challenge of the object—33rd congress of the International Committee of the History of Art: congress proceedings. Germanisches Nationalmuseum, Nürnberg, pp 73–41
Behrmann C (2015) Tyrann und Märtyrer. Bild und Ideengeschichte des Rechts um 1600. De Gruyter, Berlin
Boehme-Nessler V (2011) Pictorial law modern law and the power of pictures. Springer, Berlin
Bourdieu P (1987) The force of law: toward a sociology in the juridical field. Hastings Law J 38:814–853
Bousmar E (2009) Le double portrait présumé des époux Arnolfini (1434) de Van Eyck. D'un mariage à l'italienne aux réseaux de la cour? In: Cauchies J-M (ed) Bourguignons en Italie, Italiens dans les pays bourguignons (XIVe-XVIe s.). Centre européen d'études bourguignonnes, Neuchâtelm, pp 287–328
Bredekamp H (2003) A neglected tradition? Art history as Bildwissenschaft. Crit Inq 29:418–428
Cover R (1993) Nomos and narrative. In: Minow M, Ryan M, Sarat A (eds) Narrative, violence, and the law: the essays of Robert Cover. University of Michigan Press, Ann Arbor, pp 95–172
Curtis D, Resnik J (2011) Representing justice: invention, controversy, and rights in city-states and democratic courtrooms. Yale University Press, New Haven
Davis W (2011) A general theory of visual culture. Princeton University Press, Princeton and Oxford
Del Mar M, Goodrich P (eds) (2014) Legal theory and the humanities. Ashgate, Farnham
Derrida J (1987) The truth in painting, trans Geoff Bennington. University of Chicago Press, Chicago
Derrida J (1992) Force of law: 'The mystical foundation of authority'. In: Cornell D, Rosenfeld M (eds) Deconstruction and the possibility of justice. Routledge, New York
Didi-Huberman G (2002) L'image survivante: histoire de l'art et temps des fantômes selon Aby Warburg. Minuit, Paris
Douzinas C, Nead L (eds) (1999) Law and the image: the authority of art and the aesthetics of law. University of Chicago Press, Chicago
Eden K (2017) Renaissance rediscovery of intimacy. University of Chicago Press, Chicago
Feigenson N (2014) Visual common sense. In: Wagner A, Sherwin R (eds) Law, culture and visual studies. Springer, Dordrecht, pp 105–125
Ferretti S (1989) Cassirer, Panofsky and Warburg: symbol, art and history. Yale University Press, New Haven
Fischer-Lescano A (2016) Sociological aesthetics of law. Law, Culture and the Humanities J 1–26
Foucault M (2001) Les mots et les images. In: Defert D, Ewald F (eds) Michel Foucault: Dits et écrits, tome I:1954–1975. Gallimard, Paris
Gaggi, S (1997) From text to hypertext: decentering the subject in fiction, film, the visual arts and electronic media. Pennsylvania Press, Philadelphia
Gasché R (1986) The tain of the mirror: Derrida and the philosophy of reflection. Harvard University Press, Cambridge
Gearey A (2001) Law and aesthetics. Hart Publishing, Oxford
Ginzburg C (2013) From Aby Warburg to E.H. Gombrich: a problem of methods. In: Ginzburg C (ed) Clues, myths, and the historical method. Johns Hopkins University Press, Baltimore, pp 17–59

Goodrich P (1996) Law in the court of love: literature and other minor jurisprudences. Routledge, London
Goodrich P (ed) (1997) Law and the unconscious-a Legendre reader. Macmillan, London
Goodrich P (2013) Legal emblems and the art of law: obiter depicta as the vision of governance. Cambridge University Press, New York
Goodrich P (2017) Imago decidendi: on the common law of images. Brill, Leiden
Goodrich P, Hayaert V (eds) (2015) Genealogies of legal vision. Routledge, London
Hall E (1994) The Arnolfini betrothal: mediaeval marriage and the enigma of Van Eyck's double portrait. University of California Press, Berkeley
Hardwick C (1977) Semiotics and significs: the correspondence between Charles S. Peirce and Lady Victoria Welby. Indiana University Press, Bloomington
Hartlaub GF (1951) Zauber des Spiegels: Geschichte und Bedeutung des Spiegels in der Kunst. Piper, Munich
Hasenmueller C (1978) Panofsky, iconography, and semiotics. J Aesthet Art Crit 36:289–301
Hatt M, Klonk C (2006) Art history: a critical introduction to its methods. Manchester University Press, Manchester
Holly MA (1984) Panofsky and the foundations of art history. Cornell University Press, Ithaca
Huygebaert S, Martyn G, Paumen V, Van Poucke T (eds) (2016) The art of law: three centuries of justice depicted. Lannoo, Tielt
Jay M (1988) Scopic regimes of modernity. In: Foster H (ed) Vision and visuality. Bay Press, Seattle, pp 3–23
Jay M (1993) Downcast eyes: the denigration of vision in the 20th century French thought. University of California Press, Berkeley
Johnson CD (2012) Memory, metaphor, and Aby Warburg's atlas of images. Cornell University Press, Ithaca
Kelley DR (1988) Jurisconsultus perfectus: the lawyer as renaissance man. J Warbg Court Inst 51:84–102
Kevelson R (1992) Law and aesthetics. Peter Lang, New York
Legendre P (1994) Dieu au Miroir: Étude sur l'institution des images. Paris, Fayard
Legendre P (1997) Introduction to the theory of the image: Narcissus and the other in the mirror. In: Goodrich P (ed) Law and the unconscious-a Legendre reader. Macmillan, London, pp 211–254
Legendre P (2008) The dogmatic value of aesthetics. Parallax 14:10–17
Maisel W (1982) L'archéologie juridique science auxiliaire de l'histoire des institutions et du droit. Revue Historique de Droit Français et Étranger 60:279–286
Maisel W (1993) Rechtsarchäologie Europas. Böhlau, Wien
Manderson D (2000) Songs without music. University of California Press, Berkeley
Manderson D (2018) Law and the visual: representations, technologies, and critique. University of Toronto Press, Toronto
Martyn G, Brood P, Berkvens AMJA (ed) (2014) Rechtsgeschiedenis verbeeld. Uitgeverij Verloren [special issue Pro Memorie 16.2], Hilversum
Mitchell WJT (1995) Picture theory. University of Chicago Press, Chicago
Mitchell WJT (1999) Iconology: image, text, ideology. University of Chicago Press, Chicago
Mitchell WJT (2002) Showing seeing: a critique of visual culture. In: Holly MA, Moxey K (eds) Art history, aesthetics, visual studies. Sterling and Francine Clark Art Institute, Williamstown
Mitchell WJT (2015) Image science: iconology, visual culture, and media aesthetics. The University of Chicago Press, Chicago
Moxey K (2001) The practice of persuasion: paradox and power in art history. Cornell University Press, Ithaca
Moxey K (2008) Visual studies and the iconic turn. J Vis Cult 7:131–146. https://doi.org/10.1177/1470412908091934
Panofsky E (1934) Jan van Eyck's Arnolfini portrait. Burlingt Mag Connoiss 64:117–119, 122–127

Panofsky E (1951) Gothic architecture and scholasticism. The Archabbey Press, Latrobe
Panofsky E (1953) Early Netherlandish paintings: its origins and character. Harvard University Press, Cambridge
Payer PJ (1979) Prudence and the principles of natural law: a medieval development. Speculum 54:55–70
Postel J-P (2016) L'affaire Arnolfini: enquête sur un tableau de Van Eyck. Actes Sud, Arles
Ripa C (1777) Iconologia. Piergiovanni Costantini, Perugia
Rorty R (1979) Philosophy and the mirror of nature. Princeton University Press, Princeton
Sauerländer W (1983) From stilus to style: reflections on the fate of a notion. Art Hist 6:253–270
Schapiro M (1953) Style. University of Chicago Press, Chicago
Seidel L (1989) Jan van Eyck's Arnolfini Portrait: business as usual? Crit Inq 16:55–86
Sherwin R (2014) Introduction: law, culture, and visual studies. In: Wagner A, Sherwin R (eds) Law, culture and visual studies. Springer, Dordrecht
Steinhauer F (2003) Who is afraid of black red and gold? Zur Geburt der Ikonophobie aus dem Geist des Kriegsrechts. In: Ernst WW (ed) Aufspaltung und Zerstörung durch disziplinäre Wissenschaften. Studien, Wien, pp 79–138
Vismann C (2007) Bildregime des Rechts-Rechtsregime des Bildes. In: Joly JB, Vismann C, Weitin T (eds) Bildregime des Rechts. Akademie Schloss Solitude, Stuttgart
Vismann C (2008) Image and law-a troubled relationship. Parallax 14:1–9
von Repgow E, Schott C (ed) (1984) Der Sachsenspiegel. Manesse, Zürich
Wagner A, Sherwin R (eds) (2014) Law, culture, and visual studies. Springer, Dordrecht
Widener M, Weiner MS, Talbot (eds) (2017) Law's picture books: the Yale Law Library collection. Lawbook Exchange Ltd., Clark
Wuttke D (ed) (2001) Erwin Panofsky. Korrespondenz 1: 1910–1936. Harrasowitz, Vienna

Carolin Behrmann has studied in Tübingen, Bologna and Berlin. From 2001 to 2011 she has worked and lectured at the Institute of Art and Visual Studies at Humboldt University, Berlin. In 2008 to 2009 she has been a predoctoral-fellow at the Getty Research Institute, Los Angeles. Her thesis *Tyrant and Martyr. Images and the History of Ideas of the Law around 1600* analyzes the correlation between Art and Law after the Council of Trent in the sixteenth and seventeenth century. In 2011 she has been a post-doctoral fellow and from 2012 to 2014 academic assistant at the Kunsthistorisches Institut in Florenz - Max-Planck-Institut. Since 2014 she is appointed by the Max-Planck-Gesellschaft to lead the international research group 'The Nomos of Images. Manifestation and Iconology of Law'.

Figures

Fig. 3.1 Cornelis Bos after Maarten van Heemskerck, *Prudentia (Prudence) and Justitia (Justice)*, 1537, engraving, 264 × 214 mm, © Brussels, Koninklijke Bibliotheek van België, Print Room, inv. nr. S.II 19159

Fig. 3.2 '*Johannes de eyck fuit hic 1434*', detail from: Jan Van Eyck, *Portrait of Giovanni Arnolfini and his Wife (The Arnolfini portrait)*, 1434, oil paint on panel, 82.2 × 60 cm, London, National Gallery, © Wikicommons

Fig. 3.3 Joined hands, detail from: Jan Van Eyck, *Portrait of Giovanni Arnolfini and his Wife (The Arnolfini portrait)*, 1434, oil paint on panel, 82.2 × 60 cm, London, National Gallery, © Wikicommons

Part II
Moralising Law and Justice Representations in the Late Middle Ages and Early Modern Era

Chapter 4
Changes in Late-Medieval Artistic Representations of Hell in the *Last Judgment* in North-Central Italy, ca. 1300–1400: A Visual Trick?

Clare Sandford-Couch

Abstract This chapter suggests that it is possible to see the emergence of changes in values and punishment practices—even the underlying philosophies—in the iconography of certain Last Judgment scenes commissioned and created in north-central Italy, 1300–1400. Increasingly horrifying images of hell featuring actual legal punishments might indicate an increasingly punitive legal system. However, analysis suggests that a decline in the use of physical punishments in the secular courts in this region seems to occur around the same time as an increase in detailed representations of such punishments in the Last Judgment images. The chapter explores the possibility that underlying this change in artistic representation is a philosophy of law in a process of transition; from retributive theories, to a more 'utilitarian' theory of punishment. Such a theory may suggest that, for the societies commissioning and viewing them, the powerful visual effect of increasingly horrifying depictions of the punishment of sinners in the afterlife may have played an active role in that society, a 'visual trick', helping to address a disconnect between contemporary criminal justice practice and criminal justice rhetoric.

4.1 Introduction

A substantial change in the artistic representation, in scenes of the Last Judgment, of the perceived fate awaiting those condemned to hell in the afterlife seems to appear between 1300 and 1400 in north-central Italy, what is now largely Tuscany. In addressing what could account for these changes, this chapter offers a new, legal perspective on a specific development in the representation of the torments of hell: increasingly horrifying images featuring actual legal punishments. Exploring possible connections between iconography and changing practices of the contemporary secular justice system, I suggest that for the societies commissioning and viewing

C. Sandford-Couch (✉)
School of Law, Faculty of Business and Law, Northumbria University, Newcastle, UK
e-mail: Clare@Sandford-Couch.com

S. Huygebaert et al. (eds.), *The Art of Law*, Ius Gentium: Comparative Perspectives on Law and Justice 66, https://doi.org/10.1007/978-3-319-90787-1_4

them, the images may have played an active role, addressing a 'disconnect' between contemporary criminal justice practice and criminal justice rhetoric.

Of course, any such interpretation must be speculative; we cannot know definitely how medieval viewers responded to these images, and the question of a possible 'function' of an artwork is complex. So, exploring how the medieval iconography of hell was deployed in communes and city-states in the region may well raise more questions than it answers. However, the iconography of the Last Judgment is multivalent: capable of conveying complex and different messages to different people at different times. Such images, in the medieval mind, could have both a religious and a civic meaning, allowing multiple and varying readings by viewers (Huygebaert et al. 2016, p. 15–34). By exploring changes to a long-established iconographic formula we may begin to glimpse some of the visual codes and embodied responses within the images.

An example of such an approach was Sbriccoli's (2005) exploration of a specific change in the iconography of the personification of Justice in Italy in the fourteenth century. He sought to explain Justitia acquiring a sword in addition to her scale in the context of the close relationship between criminal justice and iconography, attributing the change in artistic representation of the Virtue at least in part to certain changes to the administration of justice, including the newly acquired punishment power of the independent towns and cities, alongside the adoption into the secular justice system of the inquisitorial trial. The intention here is to focus on a further example of that close relationship between criminal justice and iconography, a development in the iconography of certain Last Judgment scenes commissioned and created in north-central Italy in that same period, ca. 1300–1400, to explore possible connections between artistic representation and the emergence of changes in values and punishment practices—even the underlying philosophies—in the administration of justice.

4.2 The Iconography of Hell

The basic elements of Last Judgment imagery derive from Biblical accounts, such as Matthew 25:31–46 and Revelation 20. Prior to circa 1250, depictions largely corresponded to an established iconographic formula: 'the arranged hierarchies of celestial beings, the time-honoured contrasts between the Saved and the Damned, the depiction of the infernal regions, the representation of Christ as the Judge of the World. Altogether it is overwhelming in the weight of its dogma' (Stubblebine 1969, p. 89–90). The hierarchical structure is most evident in those scenes featuring a strict demarcation of the registers, such as in Santa Maria Assunta in Torcello (twelfth/thirteenth century), Sant'Angelo in Formis (in Capua, Southern Italy, ca. 1180), and a panel, signed by Nicolaus and Johannes, now in the Pinacoteca Vaticana (possibly late eleventh century, or twelfth century). After circa 1270, there emerged a more complete Last Judgment scene, and generally more detailed representations began increasingly to focus on hell.

This can be explored through several key iconographic changes, although, as the dates of many *Last Judgments* remain the subject of academic debate, a precise chronological development is not possible. Firstly, some *Last Judgments* began to offer more detail in the depiction of hell than of paradise, for example, Guido da Siena's (1230–1290) *Last Judgment* (Grosetto, Museo Civico, ca. 1260/1270s). A second iconographic change was the development by the 1320/1330s of 'stand-alone' scenes of hell, separated from representations of heaven. The Magdalene Chapel (Cappella del Podestà) in the Bargello (Florence) arguably featured the first separated, independent images of heaven and hell (ca. 1320/1330s, although the dating of these frescoes, and the identity of the artist, is uncertain, Elliott 2000, p. 255). The Magdalene Chapel forms a sacred space in the Bargello, home of the machinery of civic justice. The fresco is badly damaged, but it appears to have featured opposing scenes of heaven and hell. Whether it also featured a Last Judgment is unclear. The image of hell occupies the entrance wall to the chapel. Alternatively, the separation of hell may have first appeared in Pisa, in the Campo Santo frescoes. This point is difficult to clarify, as the dating of these frescoes too is uncertain; most scholars now suggest a date circa 1330s.[1] The fresco cycle juxtaposes depictions of particular judgment—the *Triumph of Death*—and final judgment—the *Last Judgment* and *Hell*. This separation was developed, so that hell became decoupled from Last Judgment scenes and the subject instead of stand-alone images, as in the now-ruined fresco of hell in the Church of Santa Croce in Florence (ca. 1350; usually attributed to Andrea di Cione (Orcagna), 1308–1368), and the *Last Judgment* fresco in the Collegiate Church at San Gimignano (1393; Taddeo di Bartolo, 1362–1422).

A third iconographic change was a focus on the imagery of hell and greater specificity in the punishments inflicted upon the damned, many of which feature a certain symbolic logic. Some hells ascribe a particular punishment or reserve an area for those committing certain sins: adulterers hanged from sexual organs (Arena Chapel, ca. 1304–1310; Giotto di Bondone, 1266–1337), gluttons condemned to eat for eternity (San Gimignano), or sodomites impaled or roasted on a spit (Pisa *Camposanto*).[2] These indicate a belief in 'poetic justice' also evident in contemporary literature, most notably Dante's *Inferno*. The possible connection of several monumental *Last Judgments* to Dante's *Inferno* has provoked much speculation, but I suggest that what underpins Dante's work, as well as many contemporary artistic representations of hell, is a belief in the need for some form of 'proportion' between offence and punishment. This is evident, for example, in the Pisan *Camposanto* frescoes and the San Gimignano *Hell*.[3]

[1]The frescoes are variously attributed to Francesco Traini (1321–1365), the 'Master of the Triumph of Death', and Buonamico de Cristofano Buffalmacco (active 1315–1336).

[2]Mills (2005, p. 87) suggested the *Camposanto Hell* first clearly linked a punishment of roasting on a spit with sodomy.

[3]On the *Camposanto* frescoes as 'a supreme visualisation of the idea', see Mills (2005, p. 94).

The period may also have produced a fourth iconographic development, a 'secular' Last Judgment. Ambrogio Lorenzetti's (1290–1348) allegorical *Good and Bad Government* frescoes in the *Palazzo Pubblico*, Siena (1338–1340) can be interpreted in this light (Polzer 2002). This chapter will focus upon another iconographic change, arguably a further aspect of the secularisation of the Last Judgment scene and of the increased focus on the punishment of the damned.

4.3 The Punishment of Sinners

A significant development in the representation of hell in the fourteenth century was the appearance of the punishment of sinners in the context of actual punishments inflicted as part of the contemporary justice system.[4] This point has been made by several scholars, but with differing emphases. To summarise briefly what are often complex arguments, Edgerton (1985, p. 66–69) recognised in the scenes actual methods of contemporary punishment. Ariès (1985, p. 100–102) suggested that *Last Judgments* in this period shift from 'eschatology in favour of judicial machinery', which he attributed to an increase in legal consciousness. Baschet (1993, p. 278–285) suggested that rather than being representative of features of contemporary jurisprudence, these tortures were intended to recall literature of infernal visions. Link (1995, p. 119 and 136) interpreted this in context of the search for heretics by the inquisition. An alternative analysis is proposed here.

A point often overlooked or misinterpreted is that the focus of these scenes of hell is quite specific: they depict not torture, but punishment. Torture would be appropriate in a scene of particular judgment, that passed at the end of an individual's life, at point of death: sinners in purgatory awaited their final or last judgment at the end of the world, on Judgment Day, when they receive their due punishment or reward. Similarly, torture, in the contemporary justice system, tended to occur as a method of proof, forming part of the trial process before a verdict. The hell scenes represent the punishment of the damned after the final verdict of Divine Justice, after they are sent to hell, which perhaps makes it less surprising that scenes began to feature real contemporary after-verdict punishments.[5] These often graphic scenes reference aspects of secular justice practice, with a level of representational fidelity. This element of realistic punishment is not evident in earlier representations of hell, such as Torcello, or the Florentine Baptistery mosaic (second half thirteenth century), and there is speculation as to when it first appeared.

[4]Matters of crime, law and justice in late medieval Italy are the subject of a vast literature; for an overview, see the bibliographical note in the second edition of Dean (2007). The work of Italian historian Andrea Zorzi (1988, 1994) in particular offers valuable insights, focusing largely on fourteenth and fifteenth century Florence.

[5]Although often experiencing the same punishments, as these scenes depict, it is unlikely they were intended as re-enactments of the pain and suffering of martyrs.

The development in the representation of the Last Judgment scene to include a hell featuring punishments familiar to the contemporary justice system seems most clearly to appear circa 1320/1330s. It is not possible to correlate each punishment exactly to a specific image within the confines of this chapter, but some examples can be given. The focus here will be on frescoes which were largely accessible to the general population (not all can be illustrated here, and in several cases the poor condition of the frescoes leaves details unclear in reproduction. The fresco of hell in the Pisan *Camposanto* (ca. 1330s?), for example, was severely damaged during World War II).

The appearance in a depiction of hell of a particular punishment which may not feature in records of criminal justice practices from that same town or city is not overly problematic, as, 'for most of the period, the cities of the centre and north of Italy shared a roughly similar judicial structure and similar judicial procedures' (Dean 2007, p. 11). In part this must be attributable to the impact of Roman (and canon) law. In addition, punishment practice could be spread across the region, standardising the punishments awarded for particular offences. This was encouraged by the mobility of many officials of law enforcement, particularly the *podestà* and his judges, across the region, making conformity of practice more likely than not.[6] Also, cities achieving regional significance would seek to impose their punishment practices over areas that they dominated. In such circumstances, the appearance in the records of a specific punishment being meted out in one town for a particular offence, makes it almost certain that a similar outcome could be observed in others, even where contemporary records do not exist or may be silent upon the point. One must also consider the possibility of the movement of artists having a similar effect for the transmission of the iconography, as would an artist copying or incorporating elements from another's work. For example, the probable artist of the *Camposanto* fresco cycle, Buonamico di Cristofano Buffalmacco (active 1315–1336), was a Florentine working in Pisa. He may have seen the frescoes in the Magdalene Chapel in the Bargello, and his *Camposanto* frescoes were copied to a large extent in Bonaccorso di Cino's now fragmentary fresco in the *Ospedale della Misericordia* in Prato (1345).

A further note of caution before considering specific examples: primary sources for actual punishments carried out following conviction are relatively scarce. Surviving records, perhaps inevitably, are often incomplete. Although several thousand communal statutes survive from the thirteenth and fourteenth centuries, in some cases these may not prescribe a particular sentence to a specific crime; even where they do so, we cannot know that sentence was actually imposed (Ascheri 2013, p. 307–308). Even records of sentences do not reveal whether the punishment specified was carried out; it is possible many were never intended to be effected. The records would also not show where judges may have prescribed a more severe

[6]For a comprehensive analysis of the role of the podestà, (see Maire Vigueur 2000). Although there is no significant work in the English language on the role of the *podestà* in medieval Italy, (Chambers and Dean 1997) offers useful information.

or exemplary penalty for an absent defendant—many accused of crime would fail to appear in court—than the offence may have warranted to increase the deterrent effect. Social chronicles offer evidence of certain sentences and punishments being carried out, but these may be the exceptional, rather than the norm. However, some records do reveal actual punishments similar or even identical to certain of those appearing in certain Last Judgment scenes; the most serious were capital, while others would not inevitably result in death.

The most frequently used forms of capital punishment were decapitation or hanging; others appear more rarely, their use maybe more symbolic or dependent upon particular circumstance.[7] There were in addition different types of corporal punishment, having different physical (and mental) effects. Remember too that such punishments would be inflicted in public, which may have brought some element of shaming.

4.3.1 Beheading

Beheading—usually mercifully quick and relatively clean—was generally perceived as a 'better death' than being hanged. Several of the damned in the *Camposanto Hell* hold their severed heads (Fig. 4.1). Contemporary records confirm that many found guilty of murder were beheaded. This practice was widespread across the region and period. As a 'more honourable' death than being hanged, it was often used for noble offenders. Beheading was the specified punishment for vendetta causing death in the Florentine statutes of 1325, a crime often associated with young noble males (Dean 2007, p. 188). Beheading was also imposed for other serious crimes. In 1371 the *Cronica senesi* recorded that four men were beheaded in the Campo following social unrest (Dean 2007, p. 174). Also in 1371, two men in Lucca were beheaded in the Piazza San Michele for riot, according to the local chronicler Giovanni Sercambi (*Le croniche* vol. I).[8]

4.3.2 Hanging

Hanging was perceived as a degrading punishment (Mills 2005). It could be a long, painful and undignified death; in effect, the offender slowly suffocated in the noose. In the *Camposanto Hell* we see sinners hanging, some upside down (Fig. 4.1). This

[7]All images of Hell necessarily feature sinners being burned alive. Although this was a form of capital punishment in Roman law (regarded in Justinian's *Digest* as a secondary form of punishment to hanging and beheading), by the later medieval period it was particularly associated with the punishment of heresy, beyond the focus here on 'secular' punishments.

[8]G. Sercambi, *Le croniche di Giovanni Sercambi lucchese,* Salvatore Bongi (ed.), 3 vols. (Lucca: Tipografia Giusti 1892), volume 1, p. 204–5; for translation (see Dale et al. 2007, p. 163).

also appears in the *Last Judgment* in Viboldone Abbey, near Milan, for example (the fresco is often attributed to the Florentine artist Giusto de' Menabuoi (1320–1391) and dated to the 1350–1370s). The thirteenth century Chronicle of Salimbene relates how Modena hanged men deemed 'traitors' in 1287 (Coulton 1972, p. 209). The *Cronica senesi* records that in Siena in 1328, when several of the *podestà*'s men were killed attempting to quell food riots, six men accused of inciting the riots were publically hanged.

As a less 'honourable' punishment, hanging was deemed appropriate for thieves, possibly reflecting the contemporary conception of theft as 'infamous', meaning those who committed such offences were without honour (*fama*) and so deserving of a dishonourable treatment. Being hanged upside down was particularly shaming: this may stem from association with the hanging of Judas, or the lack of dignity in being inverted.[9] Giovanni Villani's (1276–1348) *Cronica* was written as year-to-year accounts, the last six volumes covering events affecting Florence from 1264 to 1346; as such it offers a near-contemporaneous report of Florence in 1343, when an official of the hated Duke of Athens was hanged by his feet (Porta 1991, volume 3, ca. 13–17, p. 336–340). The punishment may on occasion have been enhanced by disembowelling: in the *Camposanto Hell* several sinners with heads lolling after hanging feature innards spilling out from their bodies; one even observes his evisceration by a demon.

4.3.3 Boiling Alive

We see sinners in a pit (*bolgia*) in the *Camposanto Hell* (Fig. 4.2), but also in Santa Croce and San Gimignano frescoes. Whilst this might seem unlikely, images of being boiled alive could refer to a secular punishment. This could be used for serious crimes: the *Chronicon Parmense* recorded the communal authorities in Parma punishing a murderous cleric by boiling him in a pot on the *Piazza Communale* in 1236 (Thompson 2005, p. 45). This punishment may be attributed to a prohibition on the spilling of blood in sacred areas of Parma; Salimbene de Adam's *Cronica* reported that in Parma a communal statute of 1233 forbad 'shameful deeds' near the baptistery, on pain of being placed in chains in the main square (Jansen et al. 2009, p. 244). This too was contemporary reality: in Padua, a cleric thought to have committed twenty offences was imprisoned in an iron cage hanging from the tower of the *Palazzo Comunale* in 1301 (Cassidy 2004, p. 370).

[9]Hanging upside down is often associated with defaming images (*pittura infamante*) discussed in Edgerton 1985, p. 59–125.

4.3.4 Impaling

Several frescoes (*Camposanto* (Fig. 4.3), San Gimignano) feature sinners (sometimes identified as sodomites) being impaled, or others roasted on a spit. Whilst this is unlikely to have been effected in practice, there are similarities to an exemplary punishment of a youth convicted of being a 'public and notorious passive sodomite' in Florence in 1365: he was sentenced to be dragged by an ass to the 'place of justice', publicly castrated and punished by branding between the thighs with a hot iron (Mills 2005, p. 95).

4.3.5 Amputation

Some punishments, whilst physical and horrifying, would not have inevitably led to the death of the offender. The Magdalene Chapel in the Bargello (Florence) may have included scenes of amputations, although the state of the frescoes leaves this uncertain. In the *Camposanto* frescoes, demons devour limbs severed from sinners (Fig. 4.4). The amputation of limbs—usually hands—was deemed appropriate punishment for theft in an early-mid thirteenth century Parma communal statute: 'The *podestà* is to have men living within two miles of watercourses along which wood comes to the city (…) swear not to remove any wood (…) and the *podestà* is to set up gallows in two suitable places (…) and if anyone, male or female, is found stealing any of this wood, the *podestà* is to amputate one of their hands and hang it on the gallows, unless he or she redeems the hand at 100 s, and if he or she redeems the hand, he or she must carry the wood around his or her neck through the city and be whipped.'[10]

The loss of the right hand was the punishment imposed in Lucca in 1371 for a man involved in a riot, according to *Le chroniche di Giovanni Sercambi* (Dale et al. 2007, p. 163). Amputation was threatened by the *podestà* in Florence in 1344–1345, as an alternative if offenders failed to pay fines: in four cases hands, in another a foot, and in one case a tongue, would be removed (Cohn 2012, p. 111). In the *Camposanto* fresco of the *Triumph of Death*, one can see a possible victim of such a punishment, his right arm ending in a stump bound in a white cloth tied round his wrist with rope, a depiction clearly different to the unbound stumps of the leper behind him.

A punishment of having the tongue cut out can be seen in a *Last Judgment* at Campione d'Italia (1400). Those accused of treacherous activities could face having their tongues cut out; the fate of the sister of a man found guilty of betraying Bianello, Reggio Emilia, according to the *Cronica* of Salimbene (Coulton 1972, p. 209).

---

[10] *Statuta communis Parmae* (Parma 1855–6), p. 323, for translation (see Dean 2000, p. 126).

4.3.6 Skin Mutilation

A further category of corporal punishments included some form of mutilation of the skin. Although the *Camposanto* fresco is too badly damaged to allow us to make out fine details, such as a whip, skin mutilation by whipping too appears in Last Judgment scenes, in San Gimignano, for example. Whipping was a frequent punishment, often carried out in public. It may have been seen as a punishment for the infamous: a late thirteenth-century Florentine law provided that prostitutes could be whipped and their pimps fined (Jansen et al. 2009, p. 196–197).

The piercing or removal of skin seems to carry a particular symbolism, the removal of a protective barrier inspiring fear or repulsion (Mills 2005, p. 65–67). Many *Last Judgments* feature the integrity of the body being broken. In the *Camposanto Hell*, sinners are disembowelled, flesh is pierced by tridents or the claws of demons (Fig. 4.1); in the San Gimignano *Hell*, scorpions attack flesh; elsewhere demons stab with daggers. Punishment by piercing or puncturing skin appears often in Florentine territory. In Florence, in 1379, a female slave who had poisoned her master had her skin torn off with pincers, before she was burned to death (Dean 2007, p. 70). This may have been an exemplary punishment, possibly signifying opprobrium of a servant killing her master, but also because poisoning appears to have been regarded as a 'dishonourable' method of killing someone (Collard 2008). The pinching of flesh as exemplary punishment was again evident in Florence in 1390, when a rebel from San Miniato, in the Florentine territory, was paraded through the streets, gripped with iron pincers ripping away his flesh as he was led to the gallows (Cohn 2012, p. 113). Sentences could also be *attanagliato*, the flesh burned with red-hot tongs (Edgerton 1985, p. 141). In the San Gimignano *Hell*, demons approach sinners wielding iron pincers.

The appearance in the *Camposanto* fresco of a man being flayed (Fig. 4.4)—his skin removed by demons—is interesting, as there is no evidence of flaying used as a punishment in the later Middle Ages in north-central Italy, and *Last Judgments* rarely show people being flayed. However, the dissection of humans was not unknown around this time, with the first recorded autopsy on a human body in Italy taking place in 1286, in Cremona (Terry-Fritsch 2012, p. 26, note 69). The lack of anatomical detail here might suggest that the artist drew upon the skinning of animals, not humans.[11]

On this reading, these images from *Last Judgments* feature the torment of sinners in the context of actual contemporary punishments, the after-trial verdicts of secular justice. The didactic impact could be enhanced by 'labelling' to identify those guilty of particular behaviours or sins, so that those viewing the image could see the specific punishment being suffered. In several frescoes the sinners wear identifying labels, or a 'mitre', a form of paper hat bearing an inscription of the matter being punished, a feature of contemporary judicial practice. This is widespread and evident consistently across the *Trecento*: Giotto's Arena Chapel fresco in Padua (ca.

[11]On flaying, see Raf Verstegen's contribution in this volume.

1306), the Pisan *Camposanto* (ca. 1330s), the Church of Santa Croce in Florence (ca. 1350/60s), Viboldone Abbey near Milan (ca. 1350–1370s), and in San Gimignano (1393).

4.4 Why Depict Hell in the Context of Specific Contemporary Secular Punishments?

Having established that a correlation exists between certain images of hell and aspects of criminal justice practice, the obvious question is why this might be the case. The earliest of these horrifying hells appeared in buildings with a religious function: in baptisteries and *duomos*. Later frescoes appear also in locations with a funerary connection, such as the *Camposanto* in Pisa. This might suggest that religious patrons sought to utilise the deterrent effect of such images. Increasing awareness of the eternal consequences of certain behaviours—the Fourth Lateran Council (1215) appeared to make it clear that one's actions on earth would determine one's fate after death—might have concentrated the minds of those viewing *Last Judgments*. Elliott (2000, p. 183) suggested that 'the reappearance in the later thirteenth century of the "complete" Last Judgment scene, complete with vivid images of paradise and inferno, is most certainly related to the renewed interest in the fate of the soul after death'. The *Last Judgment* demonstrated—in a visual image understandable by all—the need to behave in an orthodox manner, a message clearly important to ecclesiastical authorities, particularly in the time of the papal inquisition.

But not all of these *Hells* were commissioned by or for religious authorities. One of the most artistically significant *Last Judgments* of the *Trecento* was commissioned by a private patron, Enrico Scrovegni. Some were commissioned by secular governmental authorities, such as the Magdalene Chapel in Florence. Others appear in buildings with a dual religious/secular function: baptisteries, for example, played a role in civic life as one could not be a citizen until baptised. In all cases, it is questionable whether so many images of contemporary secular punishments would have appeared in the communes without the approval and knowledge of the civic authorities. But this begs the question: why might civic authorities condone or even commission images of the punishments they inflicted through their administration of the justice system upon their own citizens? This was probably a deliberate and conscious choice, but why?

Around the early *Duecento* theories of criminal law developed which were based upon punishment being administered in this world, rather than being a matter for divine judgment in the next. As civic authorities assumed greater control of prosecution, they regarded themselves as having a duty to punish; adhering to the legal maxim, '*Rei publicae interest ne crimina remaneant impunita*' (It is in the public interest that crimes should not remain unpunished), required governing authorities of the city-states to prosecute and punish wrongdoing.[12] As communal authorities sought to secure social stability, civic harmony, or 'concord', they placed an increased and increasing emphasis on issues of law and order. The communes legislated on many matters. Statutes could define social and behavioural norms, to inspire or instil 'social discipline'. Many statutes referred to *publica utilitas*, a Roman law concept (Justinian's *Digest* 1.1.2), which could justify the steps taken by the authorities against their own citizens as part of the law-making and law-enforcing function.[13] Criminal behaviour and other wrongdoing threatened the common good: justice was vital to the preservation of a strong and peaceful society. Communal governments feared their hold on power could be threatened, particularly by a noble class unwilling or unable to accept a diminution of their authority. Inter-personal violence was also a potentially destabilising threat at this time; feuding or *vendetta* was eagerly pursued.

For Spierenburg (1984, p. 13), 'late medieval and early modern executions served especially to underline the power of the State. They were meant to be an exemplary manifestation of this power, precisely because it was not yet entirely taken for granted. The justice which the authorities displayed served to bolster up their precarious position'. Images of the infliction of punishment in Last Judgment scenes could achieve that same goal by visually expressing the consequences of wrongdoing. The eternal punishments inflicted on sinners in hell as a result of God's divine justice may have served as a justification for physical punishment following trial and sentence: human justice would merely (on a temporal level) be implementing the same or lesser torments as Divine Justice (in that case, for eternity). Viewing these scenes of hell left little doubt on these matters, the relevance of the message enhanced by the inclusion of contemporary and recognisable punishments.

4.5 Non-physical Punishments

If there was one area in which there was a clear, dramatic, and deeply-rooted dysfunction between the cultural formation and the practical execution of the law, it was precisely in that of penal repressions (Ascheri 2013, p. 341).

One might assume from the increasingly horrifying and realistic punishments featuring in some fourteenth century images of hell that civic authorities of the city-states demonstrably avoided any lightness in penalising wrongful behaviour, yet it is here we find an anomaly. It is around this time that they appear to have started to move away from physically destructive or disfiguring punishments, which were forever stigmatising and, offering offenders little or no possibility of

[12]Fraher (1984, 1989), amongst others, addresses the imperative to punish and its possible Roman law origins.

[13]For example, in the *Statuta lucensis civitatis,* IV.1, ca. 1322–1325.

reintegrating into society, seemed inevitably to lead to further criminality or a drain upon charitable resources. Evidence suggests an increasing willingness to utilise punishments which appeared significantly more lenient than those in the images of hell, ordering punishments not involving physical mutilation or execution for a wide variety of criminal activity. For example, the research of Cohn (2012, p. 111) indicates that of 63 individuals condemned to death by the *podestà* in Florence in 1344–1345—33 by beheading, 28 by hanging and two (intriguingly) by cremation—records indicate no special features to humiliate or harm the condemned: 'no instances of flogging, dragging, humiliating rides on donkeys faced backwards, no wearing of mitres or other special garments, no tortures with chains or pincers, and no punishment by mutilation'. So, what was happening instead? Again, only a brief overview is possible here.

4.5.1 Fines

An alternative to physical punishments was the use of monetary penalties.[14] The effectiveness or even the credibility of economic punishments such as fines would depend at least in part on how serious an economic loss the fine represented to the offender. Some statutes set a sliding scale of financial penalty, depending on the nature and severity of the offence; for example, increasing fines for assault where blood was drawn.[15] Many crimes, even murder, were punished by fines; advantageous for both offender and 'cash-strapped' communal authorities.[16] These are not compensatory payments made to the claimant or family of a victim, as under earlier forms of dispute resolution; these were 'State' controlled, imposed by communal authorities, and codified in their statutes. Fines were levied for violent crimes: Salimbene's *Cronica* noted one example from Modena where a son who 'grievously wounded and maimed' the man who had mocked his dead father was fined. Florentine statutes of 1325 provided as punishment in cases of vendetta causing 'disability of limb' or facial disfigurement, 'a fine double *what it would have been if the attack had not occurred as part of a vendetta*' [italics CSC]. This indicates that fines were normally levied for such attacks, but that fines were seen as suitable punishment in cases of vendetta is striking, given the extreme concern of the Florentine authorities at its socially destabilising effect.

[14]On fines, and sentencing practices, although not specific to late medieval Italy, (see Bourguignon and Rousseaux 2012).

[15]For example, the Statutes of Castellarquato, near Piacenza, ca. 1350, or the fourteenth century Roman statutes considered by Dean (2001, p. 131–132).

[16]For fines that included the financing of works of art, see Paul De Win in this volume.

4.5.2 Imprisonment

Similar trends towards non-violent punishment are evident in the new use of imprisonment as a punitive measure in the secular justice system from around the mid-thirteenth century.[17] Formal building programmes for municipal prisons appear from that time; Florence started in 1297, passing legislation for the building of the *Stinche* as a new prison. Other towns and cities soon followed, although the less wealthy may have eschewed the expense of building and maintaining prisons, and guarding prisoners.

Prisons were built at least in part as symbols of political authority and social control, indicating a preference for 'regulated interaction over social destruction' (Geltner 2008, p. 104–105). The development of punitive incarceration appears to indicate a significant shift away from notions of 'eye for an eye', or poetic justice, and towards something perhaps more socially useful. An ex-offender with physical mutilations was less likely to be able to reintegrate and successfully contribute to the common good of society than one sentenced to imprisonment, who, following his release, could become an economically viable citizen. Geltner's (2006, p. 3) dating of the emergence of municipal prisons to the late-thirteenth century, and research indicating the years circa 1250 to circa 1350 as 'a watershed period in the history of the prison', would seem to accord to the suggestions here linking these Last Judgment images of punishment to changes in communal authorities' prosecution practices.

4.5.3 Exile or Banishment

Exile or banishment was also a favoured option; in many cases the commune profited by confiscating the property of the exiled.[18] Much use was made of exile or the ban for political crimes, movingly addressed by Dante, but also by thirteenth century poets such as Guittone d'Arezzo. Banishment was considered an appropriate punishment in 1324 in Siena when a fist-fight erupted into mass violence, leaving four dead (*Cronica senese*). In Pistoia, a vendetta led to the murder of a judge in the palace of the *podestà* and in front of one of the *podestà*'s men; the murderer was fined and exiled (Dean 2000, p. 174 and 185–187).

[17]Dunbabin (2002) offers a general discussion on imprisonment in medieval society.

[18]On banishment see, for example, Starn 1982 and Nathalie Demaret, 'Du bannissement à la peine de mort, une même logique punitive?', in Bourguignon and Rousseaux (2012, p. 87–100).

4.5.4 Other Alternatives to Physical Punishment

Communal authorities could control who to prosecute, for what and how often; some offenders may never have been brought to trial. Many defendants would have been acquitted: Vallerani's (2012, Table 4.1) research into Perugia indicated around eighty to ninety percent of cases ended in acquittal in the late thirteenth century. Pardons may also have been granted in many cases, ensuring offenders would not receive physical punishment for their crimes. Offenders often benefitted from amnesties post-conviction. These frequently marked Easter or a patron saint's day. For example, a brothel-keeper in Florence, sent to the *Stinche* when unable to pay a fine ordered by the *podestà* in February 1346, was released as part of an Easter amnesty in 1347 (Jansen et al. 2009, p. 197–198). A vast, but unquantifiable, number of offenders would simply have voluntarily fled the jurisdiction pre-trial.

Civic authorities also sought to encourage peaceful dispute resolution alongside the legal system.[19] Peace agreements, amounting effectively to private justice, were not only condoned, but encouraged by communal authorities, often in an attempt to discourage violence and vendetta, and further the goal of a peaceful and stable society. Some had a public element, being formalised by a 'kiss of peace' in a church, for example. In Florence, in 1295, a ceremony of reconciliation was held in the church of San Pietro Scheraggio to end a feud between the Mannelli and Velluti clans; the ceremony culminated in a kiss on the mouth between the protagonists. *The Mystic Marriage of Saint Catherine* (ca. 1340), attributed to Barna da Siena (active 1330–1350), is thought to have been commissioned by Arigo di Neri Arighetti (named in an inscription) to celebrate the peaceful settlement of a feud, a visual form of peace agreement.[20] Even peace acts, which might appear a matter for agreement between those involved, provided an opportunity for social control. Florentine communal statutes of 1325 involved courts and judges in promoting negotiated agreements to resolve conflicts; in Bologna, lawyers and professors appear to have acted as arbitrators; for those entering a peace agreement to end a feud, the Sienese authorities offered to drop pending prosecutions or lift bans for acts related to the feud. Peace agreements stand as evidence for a less formal system of justice—and by implication the approval of non-physical punishment—operating outside the courts but with the approval and even encouragement of the communal authorities.

[19]Peace acts have been the subject of a number of studies, both in general and their use in certain cities; many focus on the role of the notary, drawing on surviving notarial acts.

[20]Now in the Museum of Fine Arts, Boston.

4.6 An Evolving Jurisprudence?

Certain Last Judgment scenes could suggest a 'just deserts' or retributive notion of justice—prevailed at this time. However—as we have seen—it is not clear that this was always the case. Concern at the imposition of physical punishment, particularly after the mid-thirteenth century, and the changes in justice system practice towards the use of lesser punishments might indicate a concomitant change in the philosophy of justice.

The social role or function of punishment in late medieval society has been much debated. As Joanna Carraway Vitiello has noted, "medieval public justice was characterised by its inherent tensions between a system designed for crime control and a society accustomed to self-help, and tensions between an ideal of public justice and a culture of private retribution" (Vitiello 2016, p. 1). There can be many justifications for punishments inflicted as part of a criminal justice system: the intention may be educative, revealing the punishment appropriate to the crime or sin, but also behaviours suitable for punishment, or punitive, or to pay back someone for harm they committed against others; or to prevent or reduce future harms, or indeed some combination of some or even all of those. While many such justifications have been considered, the philosophical debate has come to be largely dominated by two broad schools of thought, the retributive and the utilitarian.

In the former, someone who harms society by breaching its rules upsets the scales of justice: equilibrium is restored by punishing the perpetrator, in some way proportionate to the harm caused: punishment and wrongdoing are linked. An alternative theory of punishment seeks its justification in achieving some future goal—most often the prevention of future harm—by administering punishment.[21] Crime offended against society and so had to be punished: punishment was not only seen as a necessary response, but—significantly—as also having the potential to fulfil a wider social function of deterrence. The punishment inflicted should be just sufficient to prevent repetition of the harm, thereby incentivising individuals (whether the offender receiving the punishment, or others in society more generally who are aware of both offence and punishment) to act in accordance with normative behaviours. This theory of punishment suggests that members of society perform a type of 'cost-benefit-analysis' which may deter them from perpetrating harm, essentially a forward-looking process, much like encouraging people to engage with scenes of the punishments awaiting in hell for those who transgress.

Similarly, I suggest that the changing iconography of these scenes of hell too may be indicative of a different or evolving philosophy of justice prevailing in the communes. Images of punishment in *Last Judgments* could inhibit others within society from committing harm, encouraging citizens towards good behaviour, preserving the 'concord' or common good of the commune. Increasing the horror of images of hell by incorporating recognisable and realistic contemporary

---

[21]This utilitarian or consequentialist theory has come to be associated with the work of Bentham (1789).

punishments may well have had such an effect by conveying in unambiguous terms the dire consequences of particular transgressive behaviours (creating an association between behaviour and punishment) and providing people with an opportunity to dwell upon this. The issue of whether the deterrent impact of these images was intended for the individual or society more generally is unclear; either, or both, would serve the needs of the civic authorities.

If the intention behind commissioning horrifying representations of hell was didactic, to shape behaviour, to both deter and coerce, vivid and dynamic images of hell featuring punishments recognisably part of the contemporary justice system provided an ever-present reminder of the consequences of transgressive behaviour. Pain manifested 'the soul's sin and guilt, and its awareness of that guilt, of the ensuing retribution, and the fear thereof' (Cohen 2000, p. 45). A punishment that was both possible and real would carry a far greater deterrent effect; the desire to avoid such terrors could act as a considerable incentive to conform. Yet these images appear more severe than many contemporary realities; more like exemplary punishments. Perhaps this should not be surprising; spectacular executions were rare. But this leads to a new interpretative framework for the representation of violence in these *Last Judgment*s.

4.7 A 'Visual Trick'?

There were sound, often financial reasons for adopting restorative, non-punitive punishments, such as fine or imprisonment, exile or banishment. However, this is a precarious balance to strike: authorities that appear weak may encourage social and political violence threatening to their regime. Moves towards more lenient punishment were therefore potentially dangerous: civil authorities would have been alive to the possibility that any suggestion that offenders could expect to receive 'lighter' punishment (or none at all) might appear as though they were disregarding their duty to punish. Failure to punish would bring God's displeasure; crime, community and God were linked. This could work both ways. Edgerton (1985, p. 173) noted the belief that 'if the victim accepted physical torture and penance here on earth, he might then win eternal redemption for his soul in heaven'; the corollary being that a 'lighter' punishment could possibly deprive him of the possibility of salvation.

Many would have feared that changing punishment practices might act as an incentive to further criminality. It has been suggested that 'the two features of the judicial system that were blamed in this respect were the ease of obtaining pardon and the lightness of penalties' (Dean 2007, p. 89). Concerns that authorities might be inclined to make use of lesser punishments might remove an important deterrent, at a time when social unrest was an ever-present and active concern in many towns and cities.[22] Fines and other non-corporal or capital punishments could possibly appear less 'shaming' or 'stigmatising' than execution or punishment purposefully carried out in public. Public punishment rituals could act as propaganda, affording communal authorities opportunities to evidence their active commitment to justice in 'a display of judicial might' (Terry-Fritsch 2012, p. 21). Removing these public displays and their performative aspect removed this possibility. It is, perhaps, revealing that there is little evidence of prosecution practices based on fines or imprisonment in the punishments in representations of hell.

The problem is that the loss of dramatic corporal or capital punishment and the attendant public ritual could leave a lacuna—to be filled with doubt about criminal justice and those enforcing it, and fear at the possible consequences of failing to properly punish transgression. My suggestion is that visual representations of hell could serve an important function by 'bridging the gap'. This is where Esther Cohen's concept of the 'visual trick' may be relevant. Cohen (1990, p. 300) argued that medieval authorities (French, in her research) created a visual trick through their spectacular public executions. Even if infrequent, the public procession to the gallows and infliction of physical punishment was intended to make a lasting impression on the spectator, leading them to recall each individual execution. I suggest that certain *Last Judgments* were intended to perform a similar form of 'visual trick'.

These images draw on experiences shaped by medieval judicial spectacle and the complex performativity of legal punishment ritual. Viewers might have witnessed the infliction of corporal or capital punishment in their towns. The images may have encouraged them to recall what they had witnessed. The notion of 'recalling' an event is complex. In *The Book of Memory*, Mary Carruthers (1990) argued that medieval religious pictures could operate not as representations or replicas of something actual, but rather as signs to establish recollection. The question is whether these images of realistic corporal or capital punishments, often related to a specific crime or sin, were intended to encourage viewers to recall actual memories of witnessing such punishments being inflicted (a lived experience of criminal justice), or even to recall imagined images, pictures in the mind, drawing upon the 'social imaginary', recalling these punishments as what everyone in that society 'knew' would be meted out.

That the punishment was intended to be recognisable to a contemporary audience may be surmised from the appearance or non-appearance in representations of hell of sinners being tortured upon the wheel. The wheel was little used in north-central Italy, and this absence is evident in fourteenth-century representations of hell from these regions (Merback 1999, pp. 164–167). However, further north, its use was more widespread, particularly in Germany and Switzerland, and a representation of the *Last Judgment* from Campione d'Italia near Lake Lugano, shows a sinner in hell stretched on a wheel (1400). Its absence in regions which did not much use this form

[22]This concern appears to have remained during the fourteenth century, shared by commune or *signoria* alike.

of punishment, and its presence in areas that did, suggests that the images were intended to invoke a punishment that was relevant to a community, something that might actually have been witnessed or recalled by those viewing the image.

Yet not all those viewing these images would have experienced witnessing these punishments, and it was important to the communal authorities that the notion of such punishment was not remote or disconnected to their citizens. The punishments in effect had to form part of what we might now term the collective memory of the communes.[23] These images of hell could keep them in the collective conscious. In this sense, visual representations act as a means of preserving the memory of these corporal and capital punishments, and their connection to the crimes for which they could be inflicted. The iconography therefore helped to create and maintain collective memories, even while there was less opportunity to see these punishments inflicted in reality. In a sense, the images 'disguised' the realities of changing criminal justice practice, depicting something that was becoming less visible.

The question was 'not how the law worked, but how people saw it working' (Cohen 1990, p. 300). If justice is not seen to be done, can a community accept that it has been done at all? Punishments such as the ban or exile, even fines or imprisonment, are legally 'invisible'—there is no 'spectacle' of suffering for public consumption. 'Beholding the violence of the judicial process (…) served a ritual function that unified the community in its belief in the judicial process' (Terry-Fritsch 2012, p. 21). Rituals offer a 'reality' that creates, or contributes to, a sense of order: could removing criminal justice punishment rituals from the public gaze suggest an absence of order? This in turn might increase the likelihood or incidence of private vengeance, threatening the common good? Perhaps this created the need for some form of justice or punishment ritual for the public gaze. Terry-Fritsch (2012, p. 18) has argued that 'communal witnessing was critical to the entire judicial process (…) The efficacy of the punishment depended on the quality and quantity of its visualisation to the community'. Images communicate primarily through the visual sense—they are understood or appreciated by looking. So too punishment rituals require an audience, spectator or viewer. In this sense, images could help to bridge a 'perception gap' by offering up to the public gaze visual representations of the infliction of physical punishment. The bodily imagining of punishment could lead to satisfaction that justice was being done.

4.8 Conclusion

Changes in certain *Last Judgment* scenes towards more horrifying hells engage with changes in the justice system from the mid-thirteenth century; a system in transition, both in terms of changes in its practices but also its jurisprudence. A decline in

[23]For an introduction to the complex concept of the 'collective memory', see Gedi and Elam (1996), Wilson (2005, p. 53–62).

the use of physical punishments in the secular courts of towns and cities in north-central Italy seems to occur around the same time as an increase in detailed representations of such physical punishments in these Last Judgment images. It is arguable therefore that the decline in bodily punishments as legal sanction may have led to these artistic counterpoints. It is also arguable that the changing iconography was indicative or reflective of a changing philosophy of law, the images playing a 'visual trick', helping to address a disconnect between contemporary criminal justice practice and criminal justice rhetoric.

The 'visual trick' was that these images—whether in religious or civic buildings—could themselves act as public spectacles of punishment, conveying an impression far out of proportion to the actual and changing realities of criminal justice practice. Underlying the change in artistic representation is a change in punishment practice and a philosophy of law in a process of transition; from retributive theories, towards a more 'utilitarian' concept, and an awareness of the wider significance of punishment on the community as a whole. Gruesome depictions of hell featuring actual, recognisable corporal and capital punishments could play an active role in addressing this transition, keeping the concept and possibility of physical punishment fresh in peoples' minds, whilst practice and a developing jurisprudence urged limitations or restrictions on its use. As such, the images had of necessity to be spectacular. The density of visual information in these images is striking, the violence significant, encouraging the viewer to engage in affective interaction with scenes of bodily destruction. The location of these images was significant too: publically accessible, in effect the community could see justice being played out before their eyes—even as an evolving system for administering justice would reduce the possibility of witnessing such punishments in real life. For the societies commissioning and viewing them, the images may have played an active role helping communities to negotiate their shared lived experiences of changing criminal justice practice.

References

Ariès P (1985) Images of man and death, trans. Janet Lloyd. Harvard University Press, Cambridge (MA)

Ascheri M (2013) The laws of late Medieval Italy. Brill, Leiden

Baschet J (1993) Les justices de l'au delà. Les représentations de l'enfer en France et en Italie (XII-XV siècle). École française de Rome, Rome

Bentham J (1789) An introduction to the principles of morals and legislation. Payne & Son, London

Bourguignon M-A, Rousseaux X (ed) (2012) Amender, sanctionner et punir. Recherches sur l'histoire de la peine, du moyen-âge au XXe siècle. Presses universitaires de Louvain, Louvain-la-Neuve

Carraway Vitiello J (2016) Public justice and the criminal trial in late Medieval Italy. Brill, Leiden

Carruthers M (1990) The book of memory: a study of memory in Medieval culture. Cambridge University Press, New York

Cassidy B (2004) Laughing with Giotto at the Sinners in Hell. Viator Mediev Renaiss Stud 35:355–386

Chambers D, Dean T (1997) Clean hands and rough justice: an investigating magistrate in Renaissance Italy. University of Michigan Press, Ann Arbor

Cohen E (1990) To die a criminal for the public good: the execution ritual in Late Medieval Paris. In: Bachrach BS, Nicholas D (eds) Law, custom and the social fabric in Medieval Europe. Essays in Honor of Bryce Lyon. Medieval Institute Publications, Kalamazoo (MI), pp 285–304

Cohen E (2000) The animated pain of the body. Am Hist Rev 105:36–68

Collard F (2008) The crime of poison in the middle ages, trans. Deborah Nelson-Campbell. Praeger, London

Coulton GG (1972) From St Francis to Dante: translations from the chronicle of the Franciscan Salimbene (1221–1288). University of Pennsylvania Press, Philadelphia

Dale S, Williams Lewin A, Osheim DJ (2007) Chronicling history. Chroniclers and historians in Medieval and Renaissance Italy. Penn State University Press, University Park (PA)

Dean T (2000) The towns of Italy in the later middle ages. Manchester University Press, Manchester

Dean T (2001) Crime in Medieval Europe. Pearson Press, London

Dean T (2007) Crime and justice in late Medieval Italy. Cambridge University Press, Cambridge

Dunbabin J (2002) Captivity and imprisonment in Medieval Europe 1000–1300. Palgrave Macmillan, New York

Edgerton SY (1985) Pictures and punishment art and criminal prosecution during the Florentine Renaissance. Cornell University Press, Ithaca, New York

Elliott J (2000) The last judgment scene in central Italian painting, c. 1266–1343: the impact of Guelf politics, papal power and Angevin iconography. PhD thesis, University of Warwick

Fraher RM (1984) The theoretical justification for the new criminal law of the high middle ages: 'rei publicae interest, ne crimina remaneant impunita'. Illinois Law Review 577–595

Fraher RM (1989) Preventing crime in the high middle ages: the Medieval lawyers' search for deterrence. In: Sweeney JR, Chodorow S (eds) Popes, teachers, and canon law in the middle ages. Cornell University Press, Ithaca (NY), pp 212–233

Gedi N, Elam Y (1996) Collective memory. What is it? History and Memory 8(1):30–50

Geltner G (2006) Medieval prisons: between myth and purgatory. Hist Compass 4:1–13

Geltner G (2008) The Medieval prison: a social history. Princeton University Press, Princeton

Huygebaert S, Martyn G, Paumen V, Van Poucke T (eds) (2016) The art of law. three centuries of justice depicted (exh. cat. Bruges). Lannoo, Tielt

Jansen KL, Drell J, Andrews F (2009) Medieval Italy. University of Pennsylvania Press, Philadelphia

Cohn SK (2012) Repression of popular revolt in late Medieval and early Renaissance Italy. In SK Cohn, F Ricciardelli (eds) The culture of violence in Renaissance Italy: proceedings of the international conference, Georgetown University at Villa le Balze, 3–4 May 2010. Casa Editrice di Lettere, Florence, pp 99–121

Link L (1995) The devil: a mask without a face. Reaktion Books Ltd, London

Maire Vigueur J-C (ed) (2000) I podestà dell'Italia comunale. Parte I, Reclutamento e circolazione degli ufficiali forestieri (fine XII sec.-metà XIV sec.) (Collection de l'Ecole francaise de Rome, vol. CCLIVIII), 2 vol. (Rome: École Française de Rome)

Merback M (1999) The thief, the cross and the wheel: pain and the spectacle of punishment in Medieval and Renaissance Europe. Reaktion Books, London and Chicago

Mills R (2005) Suspended animation: pain, pleasure, and punishment in Medieval culture. Reaktion, London

Polzer J (2002) Ambrogio Lorenzetti's 'war and peace' murals revisited: contributions to the meaning of the 'good government allegory'. Artibus et Historiae 23(45):63–105

Giuseppe P (ed) (1991) Nuova cronica di Giovanni Villani. 3 volumes. Fondazione Pietro Bembo, Ugo Guanda Editore, Parma

Sbriccoli M (2005) La triade, le bandeau, le genou. Droit et procès pénal dans les allégories de la Justice du Moyen Âge à l'âge moderne, In: Crime, histoire & sociétés/crime, history and societies, vol 9, no 1, pp 33–78
Spierenburg, P (1984) The spectacle of suffering. Executions and the evolution of repression. From a pre-industrial metropolis to the European experience. Cambridge University Press, New York
Starn R (1982) Contrary commonwealth: the theme of exile in Medieval and Renaissance Italy. University of California Press, Berkeley
Stubblebine J (1969) Giotto: the Arena Chapel Frescoes. W.W. Norton & Co, New York
Terry-Firtsch A (2012) Proof in pierced flesh: Caravaggio's doubting Thomas and the beholder of wounds in early modern Italy. In Terry-Fritsch A, Felicia Labbie E (eds) Beholding violence in Medieval and early modern Europe. Ashgate, Farnham, pp 15–38
Thompson A (2005) Cities of God: the religion of the Italian communes 1125–1325. Pennsylvania State University Press, University Park, PA
Vallerani M (2012) Medieval public justice, trans. S.R. Blanshei. The Catholic University of America Press, Washington DC
Wilson JL (2005) Nostalgia: sanctuary of meaning. Bucknell University Press, Lewisburg
Zorzi A (1988) L'amministrazione della giustizia penale nella Repubblica fiorentina: Aspetti e problema. Leo S. Olschki, Florence
Zorzi A (1994) The judicial system in Florence. In Dean T, Lowe KJP (eds) Crime, society and the law in Renaissance Italy. Cambridge University Press, Cambridge

Clare Sandford-Couch graduated with a BA (Hons) in Jurisprudence from the University of Oxford and received her Ph.D. in Art History from the University of Edinburgh in 2014. After practising as a solicitor in London, she joined Northumbria University as a senior lecturer in law. She has published on legal history and the role of the arts and humanities in legal education. Her research interests largely address interactions of law and visual culture. Current ongoing research explores the last public execution in Newcastle upon Tyne, particularly in relation to the role of effigies.

Figures

Fig. 4.1 *Hell* (detail: sinners beheaded; sinners hanged upside down), attr. to Traini, 'Master of the Triumph of Death', or Buonamico Buffalmacco. *Last Judgment*, fresco, ca.1330s, Campo Santo, Pisa, © C. Sandford-Couch

Fig. 4.2 *Hell* (detail: sinners in pot or *bolgia*), attr. to Traini, 'Master of the Triumph of Death', or Buonamico Buffalmacco. *Last Judgment*, fresco, ca.1330s, Campo Santo, Pisa, © C. Sandford-Couch

Fig. 4.3 *Hell* (detail: sinners impaled), attr. to Traini, 'Master of the Triumph of Death', or Buonamico Buffalmacco. *Last Judgment*, fresco, ca.1330s, Campo Santo, Pisa, © C. Sandford-Couch

Fig. 4.4 *Hell* (detail: sinner flayed), attr. to Traini, 'Master of the Triumph of Death', or Buonamico Buffalmacco. *Last Judgment*, fresco, ca.1330s, Campo Santo, Pisa, © C. Sandford-Couch

Chapter 5
Medieval Iconography of Justice in a European Periphery: The Case of Sweden, ca. 1250–1550

Mia Korpiola

Abstract This chapter investigates medieval Sweden and its iconography of justice. The Swedish lay judges (noblemen, burghers and peasants) were without university education, and especially the commoners had few opportunities of seeing images of justice on artefacts or in secular buildings. Yet, the ecclesiastical imagery in churches was seen and understood by all, thanks to the Church's teaching. Based on surveys of justice-related iconography in medieval Swedish and Finnish (then part of Sweden) churches, the chapter argues that the scope of these motifs was very limited. Images of the Last Judgment and Saint Michael weighing souls predominate, while some churches had murals with Moses receiving the Tables of the Law, Solomon's justice, or truth- or justice-related Biblical verses in Latin. No images of Lady Justice (as one of the cardinal virtues) or other justice-related representations came up. Even only a fraction of the Finnish churches had a *Last Judgment* or *Saint Michael* to adorn them. However, these two images together, with images of devils tempting people to sin and perdition, were visualisations that had practical meaning in the Swedish legal culture. The practices of justice and judging were popular and daily reiterated, making each sworn oath a step towards either heaven or hell.

5.1 Introduction

In her recent study, Wartenberg (2015, p. 259) has highlighted that a new allegorical imagery of law and justice was created in the communal political, administrative, legal and judicial contexts of medieval Italy. It could be fitted to different local circumstances. Refined allegories and personifications based on Antiquity and history, as developed in late medieval Italy, came to replace the traditional ecclesiastical and courtly 'iconography of lordship' (*Herrschaftsikonographie*). In the Late Middle Ages and Early Renaissance, older Biblical images of justice, such as the Last Judgment or the judgment of Solomon were combined with images of the

M. Korpiola (✉)
Faculty of Law, University of Turku, Turku, Finland
e-mail: Mia.Korpiola@utu.fi

S. Huygebaert et al. (eds.), *The Art of Law*, Ius Gentium: Comparative Perspectives on Law and Justice 66, https://doi.org/10.1007/978-3-319-90787-1_5

virtues. Especially Justitia, the female personification of justice, increasingly became an omnipresent symbol of law and justice from the Late Middle Ages on. By the fifteenth and sixteenth centuries, images of justice were also decorating the town halls of urban centres in the Low Countries and Germany.[1]

In this paper, I will examine how this development is visible in late medieval Sweden, a European periphery. I will investigate the preserved range of medieval images of law and justice, without going into images of violence or crime. The iconography must be related to the special judicial context of medieval Sweden (which included present-day Finland). We have no information of justice-related imagery in medieval public buildings, and only a handful of surviving medieval Swedish law manuscripts—to which only a tiny elite had access—had images.

Medieval Sweden was a country in which practically all secular judges were laymen. Yet, the churches were the only places in which these laymen—noblemen, burghers and peasants—acting as judges, could behold images of law and justice, also available for bigger crowds. Although legal imagery (mostly the Last Judgment) can also be found in altarpieces, portals and tombs (Fig. 5.1), I will focus especially on church paintings.

My analysis and examples come mostly from Finnish medieval stone churches, on the one hand, and from the works of the most renowned of Swedish late-medieval church painters, Albertus Pictor (ca. 1440–1509), on the other. There were several groups of painters working in fifteenth- and early sixteenth-century Sweden, but the church paintings of his workshop have been recently the object of research and cataloguing.[2]

In the following, I argue that by and large medieval Swedes had access to legal iconography almost solely in churches. These were overwhelmingly focusing on the Last Judgment[3] and Christ as judge of the world (Mt. 25:31–46), while the archangel Michael weighing souls was also popular. Justitia seems to have been completely unknown and apparently only made her entry after the Reformation in the second half of the sixteenth century.

5.2 Late-Medieval and Sixteenth-Century Swedish Context: Images in Legal Manuscripts and Towns

In 1600, the population of the kingdom of Sweden (incl. Finland) comprised of ca. 1.2 million inhabitants. These consisted almost predominantly of mainly illiterate peasants, whereas the nobility, clergy and burghers formed under five percent of the

[1]See for several examples Huygebaert et al. (2016), *passim*, and the contributions by Hubrich and Verstegen in this volume.

[2]On the life of Albertus Pictor, see Svanberg and Öberg (2009), p. 11–16; on other masters and groups of painters: Lindblom (1944), p. 225–235 and 245–259.

[3]On the Last Judgment, see also the contributions of Hubrich and Sandford-Couch in this volume.

population. Medieval Sweden did not have feudalism, even if some feudal tendencies emerged particularly in the later 1400 s and early 1500 s. Communities were small, and, especially outside the heartlands of Sweden, situated far apart, some rather isolated by forests and big lakes. The country was strongly agricultural and autarkical. Sweden exported iron, butter, hides and leather, while mainly importing cloth, salt and hops (e.g. Heckscher 1935, p. 32–33, 39–40 and 55, and Appendix 5).

The Christianisation process started before 1000 in Southern and Central Sweden, while around 1200 the Catholic Church had been firmly established and organised in the whole realm. The Church was the main channel of continental cultural trends in the country. Higher learning was mostly acquired by high-ranking clerics who travelled abroad to study, first to Paris and Bologna, later also to Prague, Italian and German universities. Even if a university was established in Uppsala in 1477, its role in the higher education of medieval Sweden was small and short-lived.

In the field of law, the Church was the main conduit of the reception of learned law, in addition to German tradesmen and artisans, especially in towns. The reception of canon law is visible already in the twelfth century, while Roman legal influences were mostly a by-product of canon law. German town laws also influenced Swedish town laws. The judiciary was in the hands of non-learned laymen, including the King as the supreme secular judge of the country. In the countryside, noblemen (or their substitutes) acted as judge together with a jury (*nämnd*) of twelve peasant jurors. The provincial superior judge, the *lagman*, also adjudicated together with a jury of twelve local men. In the towns, the court was formed by the mayors and town councillors who were town burghers. The law of evidence was largely based on witnesses, oaths and oath-helpers.[4]

The provincial laws formed the first layer of codified law (ca. 1280–1350). However, in the mid-fourteenth century, these became largely replaced by King Magnus Eriksson's Law of the Realm and Town Law, commonly dated to ca. 1347–1360. Magnus Eriksson's laws became the dominant sources of law (customary law and jurisprudence being practically non-existent) for centuries. Apparently, late-medieval and sixteenth-century Swedish law manuscripts were locally written. To our day, dozens of them have survived. At least a number of such manuscripts were commissioned from scribes and clerics for the use of the small literate elite of noblemen, clerics, merchants and royal officials who were active in the administration of justice.

Relatively few medieval law manuscripts are illuminated. One of the best-known law manuscripts is B 172, Magnus Eriksson's Law for the Countryside, currently in the Royal Library of Sweden. It was first written, and then illuminated, in 1436–1437 for Bengt Jönsson [Oxenstierna] (d. 1450), a leading nobleman. He was since the 1420 s judge of the districts of Tierp and, later, Norunda, and in 1439–1440, as he became *lagman* of Uppland, one of the most important judges in the country

[4]For a standard overview on Swedish legal history, see Inger (2011). For an English overview on some aspects of Scandinavian legal history, see Korpiola forthcoming.

(Ferm 2006, p. 199–207; Myrdal 2006a, b).[5] This manuscript has only illuminated capital letters.

Manuscript B 68 of the Uppsala University Library is also a Magnus Eriksson's mid-fourteenth-century Law for the Countryside, written ca. 1430. Its images are fewer, but they are bigger in size (a page each) and they start each chapter. The first illustration at the beginning of the book represents Christ enthroned as a judge on a rainbow. Christ has the stigmata on his hands and feet as well as a halo with a cross, but he is alone, without intercessors, nor is he depicted with a lily and a sword, as was common elsewhere in Europe.[6]

In addition, the so-called Stockholm law book, a fifteenth-century town law manuscript, at the Royal Library in Stockholm, has a relatively large illustration of Christ judging the world, seated on a rainbow with a cruciform nimbus and the stigmata. The Virgin Mary stands on the right hand side of Christ as an intercessor, while a kneeling angel, probably archangel Michael, and a saint, possibly Saint John, are on his left. The human-faced bird on the angel's wing is thought to represent the human soul about to be weighed. The law text on the page discusses the election of the town officials. In the text scroll, the angel invites people to be judged by saying in Latin: '*Venite ad iudicium*', while the scroll upon the head of Christ advocates mercy ('*Misericordiam volo*').[7] These finest illustrated manuscripts and their law-related images were only accessible to a relatively small group of people from the elite (Fig. 5.2).

Late-medieval southern and central European towns are known to have commissioned paintings of justice for their meeting rooms. North of the Alps, these images were mainly religious up until the late sixteenth century, and they were placed in the immediate proximity of the judges. The Last Judgment was by far the most common subject of these. In glosses from 1330–1335 on Saxon law, it was observed that an image of 'the strict justice of our Lord' ('*daz strenge gerichte unsers herren*') was to be hung next to the judges in the town hall, and the first known record of the Last Judgment in such a context is from Hamburg in the 1340s (Janicka 2008, p. 71–73; Knust 2007, p. 33–47). Many late medieval and early modern town halls and courts were specifically designed to include a planned legal iconographical program.

Unfortunately, there is no information about this from late medieval urban Sweden. In Stockholm, the town hall building by the main marketplace was expanded in the Late Middle Ages and Early Modern Era by purchasing neighbouring houses. Consequently, the town hall was not a well-designed architectonic entity, but rather sprawling. It is assumed that the interior perished several times because of conflagrations in the course of the Middle Ages (in 1330, 1407, 1419, and even later). In 1472 and 1502, the council had glass windows installed (Schück

[5]On illustrated law manuscripts, see also Lindblom (1944), p. 228 and 298–299.

[6]Uppsala University Library, inv. B 68, f. 2v; referred image available online: http://www.alvin-portal.org/alvin/view.jsf?pid=alvin-record%3A73176&dswid=-4091.

[7]*Magnus Erikssons stadslag* (1966), plate 4 and accompanying caption.

1951, p. 169–180 and 468). There is no information in the Stockholm accounts that the town council would have commissioned panels or murals for its hall, also acting as a courtroom.[8] Theoretically, such commissions would not have been impossible, as for example Albertus Pictor is known to have resided in Stockholm for many decades. Moreover, several other painters (*malere*) are known to have lived in Stockholm for some time in the late 1510 s and early 1520 s. If so, no sources remain to tell the story. Instead, it is known that the town council had silverware, coins and a necklace destroyed in a fire recycled in order to have the great seal of the town and a reliquary made of them (*Stockholms stads skottebok 1460–1468*, p. 341–342, 345 and 349).

The Stockholm town councillors were patrons of two choirs, the choirs of the Mayors and of the Town Council, in the present-day *Storkyrkan* ('Great Church'), the main church of Stockholm, dedicated to Saint Nicholas. There is information on its interior decoration in an inventory from 1440, but no paintings are mentioned, rather books, textiles and liturgical silverware. Yet, it is known that at least the Choir of the Mayors had an altar painting as the town council decided to donate the painting (*thaffla*) that had formerly been at the altar to a monastery in Småland. However, unfortunately the painting or its subject are not described. Nor is there knowledge of whether it was replaced by another altar painting. Occasionally, legal acts taking place in the Choir of the Town Council in the presence of the councillors were recorded (De Brun and Roosval 1924–1928, p. 44, 49 and 360–363; *Stockholms stads skottebok 1460–1468*, p. 352–354; *Stockholms stads tänkeböcker 1483–1492*, p. 511 (14 February 1491); *Stockholms stads tänkeböcker 1474–1483*, p. 323–324 (26 November 1481)).

In short, apart from church paintings and law manuscripts, no artwork depicting justice is known to have been commissioned by Swedish medieval secular, ecclesiastical or town elites. Possibly, the small size of Swedish towns contributed to this. Stockholm, the capital of the Kingdom of Sweden, had only 4500–7000 inhabitants at the end of the Middle Ages, while most of the other medieval towns had less than one thousand (Lamberg 2001, p. 21).

5.3 Law- and Judgment-Related Motifs in Swedish Churches: Judgment of Solomon and Moses Receiving the Tables of the Law

In present-day Sweden about 2500 medieval churches still survive, about a dozen of which are wooden. Paintings have mainly survived in stone churches. In addition, the Swedish diocese of Turku, comprising much of present-day Finland, had 104

[8]I am greatly indebted to Dr. Marko Lamberg for sharing his deep knowledge of the history of Stockholm and for discussing the sources with me (e-mail from Marko Lamberg to Mia Korpiola, 13 January 2017).

medieval stone churches, built ca. 1270–1560. Church paintings have survived in Finnish churches from the thirteenth century on. 47 of these churches are known to have had whole series (65 all in all) of paintings. The rest had some or none. Law-related paintings were ordinarily part of such series (Hiekkanen 2014).[9] By contrast, many churches seem to have had no paintings or at least no paintings survive. In Sweden proper, paintings in churches were much more common. Of the 36 churches known to be painted by Albertus Pictor and his workshop in which paintings still survive to some extent, in 19 churches justice-related paintings still exist. As some paintings have been destroyed, the percentage (about 53) is likely to have been higher. Certain churches have several justice-related pictures.

The judgment of Solomon is one of the most classical images of justice in Europe. Yet, Albertus Pictor painted the topic of the judgment of Solomon in only four churches out of 36 (the churches of Härnevi, Täby, Vänge and Övergran, see Sandquist Öberg (2009), p. 201, 312, 351 and 401) (Fig. 5.3). By contrast, other topics related to Solomon—the queen of Sheba in front of Solomon and Solomon honouring his mother Bathsheba—appear in seven respectively six churches.[10] In the provinces around Lake Mälaren, the judgment of Solomon was also used in the churches of Knutby and Tortuna, while the topic seems to have been unpopular in Finnish churches (Nilsén 1986, p. 31, 43 and 297–294). This indicates that the famous *exemplum* of a wise judge was not deemed particularly important, nor commissioned frequently in medieval Sweden. Yet, the judgment of Solomon appears in connection with the Last Judgment in the *Biblia Pauperum* (*Biblia Pauperum* 2013, p. 92–93; Björndahl 2008, p. 94–95).

Another Biblical legal topic is the prophet Moses receiving the Tables of the Law from God's hands. The story is mostly based on Exodus 31:18 and 32:15–16. Moses conversed with God on Mount Sinai. At the end of the meeting, God gave Moses two tables of stone with his laws, written with God's own finger, for the Israelites to follow. This topic can be found in four of the churches painted by Albertus Pictor suggesting its relative rarity as a topic.[11] In Finnish churches, Moses and the Tables of the Law appear only a couple of times in connection with other Moses images.[12] Admittedly, Moses, divine law and the Ten Commandments became more important in Sweden after the Reformation, and the law of Moses (and God) was considered to be a binding legal source in the seventeenth century (Takala 1993). In post-Reformation church paintings, Moses was frequently

---

[9]On the legal connotation of imagery in religious places, see also the essay by Sandford-Couch in this volume.

[10]Solomon and the Queen of Sheba in Floda, Holy Trinity, Husby-Sjutolf, Härkeberga, Nederluleå, Odensala and Vaksala, and Solomon and Bathsheba in Danmark, Dingtuna, Holy Trinity, Odensala, Täby and Vänge, see Sandquist Öberg (2009), p. 408 and *passim*.

[11]These four churches are Almunge, Kalmar and Österunda in Uppland, and Kumla in Västmannaland (Sandquist Öberg 2009, p. 67 and 73, resp. p. 210, p. 383 and 386–387, and p. 218).

[12]E.g. in the churches of Hattula and Lohja (Sw. Lojo) (Hiekkanen 2014, p. 289 resp. p. 447).

depicted with the Tables of the Law in his hand. In the Church of Isokyrö (Sw. Storkyro), painted in 1560, the history of Moses is a major topic, and he is depicted twice receiving the Tables from God (Exodus 31:18 and 34:1) (Mielty and Mielty 2003, p. 38–39).

It is worth observing that certain traditional justice-related images seem not to have existed in late medieval Sweden. Apparently, there is no evidence of images of the seven Christian virtues, including the four cardinal virtues. In addition, there were no judgment scenes from classical history. More generally, personifications of the seven deadly sins or the Ten Commandments seem to have been relatively rare in Swedish churches.[13]

5.4 Truthfulness, (Divine) Justice and Judging in Text Scrolls

Text scrolls in connection to an image of a prophet (upper torso above waistline), with Bible verses in Latin related to truth and judging, can be found in certain Swedish late fifteenth- and early sixteenth-century churches. A unique example from the early sixteenth century comes from the church of Tensta in Uppland. A fashionable nobleman in Renaissance secular clothes possibly representing a secular judge—or alternatively a very unusual depiction of Saint Michael, without armour or angelic robes—is painted in the porch (Sw. *vapenhus*) of the church. He is surrounded by birds. His head is depicted in profile and he is stepping forward, grabbing with both hands a sword pointing down. On his side, there is a set of scales with two pans, in which small human figures (at least three all in all) can be seen. The accompanying scroll says in Latin: '*Nolite condemnare et non condemnabimini*' (Cornell and Wallin 1960, p. 21 and plate 27). The image of the judge thus refers to the beginning of the Biblical verse (Luke 6:37): '*Nolite judicare, et non judicabimini: nolite condemnare, et non condemnabimini. Dimitte, et dimittemini*'. In King James' Version of the Bible, this translates 'Judge not, and ye shall not be judged: condemn not, and ye shall not be condemned: forgive, and ye shall be forgiven'.

In the 36 churches painted by Albertus Pictor, we find text scrolls in eleven churches as discussed below in more detail. The most common of these are related to the importance of truthfulness and the condemning of duplicity. The verse of Isaiah 5:20, '*vae qui dicitis malum bonum et bonum malum*' ('Woe to you that call evil good, and good evil'), or in the form of '*Ve, qui dicunt malum bonum et bonum malum*', can be found in at least seven churches (Fig. 5.4).[14] Largely analogous is

---

[13]Searches in the database *Medeltidens bildvärld [The World of Medieval Images]*, http://medeltidbild.historiska.se/medeltidbild/sok/default.asp, conducted 16 May 2017.

[14]These seven churches are Almunge (Sandquist Öberg 2009, p. 73), Danmark (*ibidem*, p. 103), Håbo-Tibble (*ibidem*, p. 162), Härkeberga (Harlin and Norström 2003, p. 78; Sandquist Öberg

'*Qui vertit linguam incidit in malum*' ('He that hath a perverse tongue falleth into mischief', Prov. 17:20), only mentioned in the church of Danmark in Uppland (Sandquist Öberg 2009, p. 103).

Another citation which I have not been able to identify is '*Qui false narrat, nichil impetrat*' ('He who lies accomplishes nothing'). This citation can be found in the church of Almunge (Sandquist Öberg 2009, p. 74). Apparently, the quotation was relatively well-known. It appears ('*Qui male narrat, nihil impetrat*') in one of the sermons of Thomas à Kempis (ca. 1380–1471), a German cleric and theologian writer also active in the Netherlands. He refers to it as a *regula iuris*. However, it is not among the *Regulae iuris* published at the end of the *Liber Sextus* of 1298, nor in the title '*De diversis regulis iuris*' of the Digest.[15]

There were also several Biblical quotations on judgment and judging. Implying universal sentencing on the Day of Judgment, '*Justum et impium judicabit Dominus*' ('God shall judge both the just and the wicked', Ecclesiastes 3:17) appears in four churches.[16] The quotation '*Dominus iudicabit fines terrae*' ('The Lord shall judge the ends of the earth', 1 Sam. 2:10) sends the same message in the churches of Härkeberga (Harlin and Norström 2003, p. 69; Sandquist Öberg 2009, p. 184) and Storkyrka in Stockholm (Sandquist Öberg 2009, p. 286), while '*Iudicabit gentes at arguet populos multos*' ('He shall judge the gentiles, and rebuke many people', Isaiah 2:4) appears only in the church of Floda in Västmanland (Sandquist Öberg 2009, p. 136). In the same church also the verse '*Parata sunt derisoribus iudicia et mallei percutientes* [*stultorum corporibus*]' ('Judgments are prepared for scorners, and stripes for the back of fools', Prov. 19:29) can be found (Sandquist Öberg 2009, p. 133). Similarly, '*Accipere persona (m) impii in iudicio non est bonum*' ('It is not good to accept the person of the wicked when judging', Prov. 18:5) can only be found in Täby in Uppland (Sandquist Öberg 2009, p. 308). As the citation continues 'to overthrow the righteous in judgment', it is meant to discourage favouring the iniquitous when judging and deprive the innocent of justice.

Art historians are unanimous that at least various versions of the *Biblia Pauperum*, but possibly also of the *Speculum Humanae Salvationis* have been used as sources or models of at least some of the Swedish church paintings. Moreover, the *Biblia Pauperum* has been identified to have influenced church paintings in the German territories, England, France and Denmark (Bengtsson Melin 2013, p. 115–125; *Biblia Pauperum* 2008, p. 14–16; *Biblia Pauperum* 2013, p. 9–10). Thus, one immediately wonders whether the *Biblia Pauperum* and other model books lead the

2009, p. 174), Odensala (Sandquist Öberg 2009, p. 257), Täby (*ibidem*, p. 308) and Vänge (*ibidem*, p. 351).

[15]I would like to acknowledge the kind help of Lari Ahokas in finding the adage in one of Thomas à Kempis' sermons, printed e.g. in Thomas de Kempis (1568), p. 134 (*Sermonum secunda pars, De vana gloria vitanda, & humili obedientia sectanda*, Ser. VIII).

[16]Härnevi (Sandquist Öberg 2009, p. 201), Härkeberga (Harlin and Norström 2003, p. 68; Sandquist Öberg 2009, p. 184), Odensala (Sandquist Öberg 2009, p. 258) and Storkyrka in Stockholm (*ibidem*, p. 286), all situated in Uppland.

artists to use the verses appearing in the scrolls in the sample churches, instead of the many others found in the Bible.

Indeed, looking at the *Biblia Pauperum*, one finds all except one of the above-mentioned verses in the banderols. In its plate 21 [e.g. German edition from 1471] on Judas betraying Jesus by a kiss, we find the verse 'He that hath a perverse tongue falleth into mischief' (Prov. 17:20: '*Qui vertit linguam incidit in malum*', *Biblia Pauperum* 2013, p. 60–61). Plate 22 [e.g. German edition from 1471], Jesus in front of Pilate, has the verse of Isaiah 5:20 ('*Ve, qui dicunt malum bonum et bonum malum*') in a scene in which Queen Jezebel wanted to condemn and kill Eliah. The scene prophesised Pilate washing his hands, as does '*Accipere personam impii in iudicio non est bonum*' (Prov. 18:5), relating to the Babylonians wanting King Nebuchadnezzar to have David delivered into their hands (*Biblia Pauperum* 2013, p. 62–63; Harlin and Norström 2003, p. 78). In plate 23 [e.g. German edition from 1471] of the *Biblia Pauperum*, Jesus crowned with thorns and mocked by Jews has its parallel in prophet Elisha being mocked by boys. One of the accompanying scrolls is 'Judgments are prepared for scorners, and stripes for the back of fools' (Prov. 19:29) ('*Parata sunt derisoribus iudicia et mallei percuciencium*', *Biblia Pauperum* 2013, p. 64–65).

In the plate on the Last Judgment (37 in the German edition from 1471) in the *Biblia Pauperum*, we find three verses used in the sample churches. In relation to the judgment of Solomon, both the verses '*Iustum et impium iudicabit Dominus*' (Ecclesiastes 3:17) and '*Iudicabit gentes et arguet populos multos*' (Isaiah 2:4) can be found. In addition, King David judged and had executed the slayer of King Saul. Likened with Christ, King David was presented together with the text '*I Regum II: Dominus iudicabit fines terre*' (*Biblia Pauperum* 2013, p. 92–93). Although, at first sight, the *Biblia Pauperum* might seem to be in error as the verse can be found in 1 Samuel 2:10, it should be remembered that the books of Samuel (1 and 2) and Kings (1 and 2) (in the Protestant tradition) are often called First through Fourth Kings in the Catholic and Eastern Orthodox tradition. The scroll in the church of Härkeberga ('*I Regum ij—dominus iudicabit fines terre*') (Harlin and Norström 2003, p. 69 and Sandquist Öberg 2009, p. 184) in the sample follows the *Biblia Pauperum* in ascribing the text to 1 Kings instead of 1 Samuel, which makes clear that the *Biblia Pauperum* is to be situated in the Catholic tradition.

These Latin scrolls may have had a limited relevance for teaching the Swedish laity of the importance of justice and truthfulness. This may explain the relative scarcity of such verses. Moreover, while there were late-medieval *Biblia Pauperum* editions in the vernacular, such as the 1471 edition in German, the Biblical verses were in Latin in the sample churches even if the vernacular was occasionally used in the paintings even in a Biblical context (*Biblia Pauperum* 2008). This also indicates that educating the laity with the scrolls was not a major objective. Images of the Last Judgment and, to a lesser extent, Saint Michael weighing souls probably conveyed more efficient messages, unless such prophets and scrolls were used in sermons or other functions.

5.5 The Last Judgment and Saint Michael Weighing Souls

The weighing of the soul of the dead (*psychostasia*) was a topic known already in Ancient Egypt. In the underworld, the deeds of each person were judged in a process where the heart containing the soul of the deceased was weighed by the god Anubis against the feather of the goddess Maat, the personification of harmony, justice and truth. If found heavier than the feather of truth, the goddess Ammit was to devour the heart (Mark 2016). In the weighing process of souls adopted by Christianity, the role of Anubis came to be allotted to the Archangel Michael. However, in the early Middle Ages, Saint Michael was mostly depicted slaying a dragon. Michael and his scales became a more important topic in Christian art mainly due to influences of Byzantine art after 900, but the boom of imagery of the archangel with scales weighing souls took place in the thirteenth century (Schaller 2006, p. 259–261 and *passim*). Of the circa one hundred Finnish stone churches about ten to fifteen percent are known to have a Last Judgment or archangel Michael weighing souls motif.

Some scattered examples of the topic of the Last Judgment can already be found in Swedish churches as early as the twelfth century. One such example is a re-used frieze on the Last Judgment on the portal of the thirteenth-century church of Vänge in Gotland, apparently originating from an earlier twelfth-century church. The imagery has been considered to reflect Byzantine influences, and the anonymous artist has therefore been named Master Byzantios (Gustafsson 1967, p. 167–176; on Master Byzantios, see Lindblom 1944, p. 125–127). Another early example is a mid-twelfth century stone tomb in the form of a reliquary combining both Viking-Age and Romanesque styles as well as texts in Latin and Runic alphabets. The relief on one side depicts the Last Judgment. In similar tombs, also Saint Michael with his scales can be found (Lindblom 1944, p. 135–138).

In Finnish medieval churches, the last judgment was also the most common justice-related topic, appearing in at least twelve churches (Fig. 5.5).[17] Most of these wall paintings date from the period between 1450 and the 1520 s. The Last Judgment of the church of Finström, with a sword and lily (representing justice and mercy) coming out of Christ's mouth, dates from the mid-fifteenth century, while the paintings of Isokyrö—without the image of Christ as judge—have been dated to the 1560s (Fält 2012, p. 100–101; Mielty 2003, p. 80–81). In the churches painted by Albertus Pictor, the Last Judgment appears at least nine or ten times.[18] However, taking into account all the late medieval church paintings in the provinces around

[17]Laitila (Sw. Letala, Hiekkanen 2014, p. 78), Rymättylä (Sw. Rimito, *ibidem*, p. 163), Taivassalo (Sw. Tövsala, *ibidem*, p. 179), Hattula (*ibidem*, p. 287), Hollola (*ibidem*, p. 298–299), Finström (*ibidem*, p. 369), Jomala (*ibidem*, p. 389), Inkoo (Sw. Ingå, *ibidem*, p. 435), Lohja (Sw. Lojo, *ibidem*, p. 447 and 449), Espoo (Sw. Esbo, Fält 2012, p. 101), Siuntio (Sw. Sjundeå, Hiekkanen 2014, p. 479), and Isokyrö (Sw. Storkyro, *ibidem*, p. 501).

[18]According to Sandquist Öberg 2009, the churches are: probably Floda (p. 137), and Härkeberga (p. 184), Härnevi (p. 203), Sala (p. 272), Storkyrkan (p. 285), Torshälla (p. 292), Yttergran (p. 362), Ösmo (p. 374), Österunda (p. 387), and Övergran (p. 402).

Lake Mälaren—a central region in the country—the topic of the Last Judgment was the most frequent motif after the prophets. It appeared in 42 of the 97 series, making it 'a largely obligatory topic' in the churches (Nilsén 1986, p. 35, 45 and 372).

Regardless of what the special chosen themes of the church were, the Last Judgment was such a central topic that it was often included. For example, the fifteenth-century paintings of the former church of the Franciscan monastery in Arboga concentrate on the *vita* of Saint Francis as well as on Saint George; yet, the Last Judgment is even here one of the prominent topics (Kilström 1998, p. 10–11; Nisbeth 1995, p. 251).

In the Finnish churches, the placing (compass point) of the Last Judgment on the walls varies considerably. However, it was most commonly painted in the chancel. Painted in towering size on a central and visible location adjacent to the altar, the Last Judgment was to act as a collective reminder of the destiny of all souls (Fält 2012, p. 101). Anna Nilsén (1986, p. 372) also observes that the placing of the Last Judgment scenes varies, but that the common denominator is a desire for good visibility for the laity. This suggests a wish to have the dramatic scene of the doom guide the conduct of the church-goers.

The Archangel Michael in Swedish churches is sometimes shown killing a dragon or fighting demons and devils, not only with scales weighing souls (Melin 2009, p. 111–114; Nisbeth 1995, p. 162–163). In Finnish churches, Saint Michael weighs souls at least four times, but this figure is probably too low (Fig. 5.6).[19] In the churches painted by Albertus Pictor, Michael is depicted with scales weighing souls at least eleven times.[20] The sample of paintings by Albertus Pictor does not contain any images of the Virgin Mary participating in the weighing of souls, a topic especially prominent in England; by placing her rosary on the side of the soul, Mary helps the good deeds outweigh the bad (Oakes 2008, p. 119–121 and 129–166). However, in the rest of the late medieval churches of the Lake Mälaren region, Saint Michael weighing souls seems generally not to have been as popular a motive as for Albertus Pictor or in the Finnish churches (Nilsén 1986, p. 39 and 47).

As law-related wall paintings were not routinely included in the imagery of Swedish medieval churches, they may at least partly reflect individual preferences. Apparently, occasionally the church paintings were commissioned in accordance with a donor's or particular vicar's wishes. For example, the paintings of Saint Michael, the unusual motifs of the church and their central location in the Sala have been thought to reflect particular and conscious concerns for the salvation of the soul after death (Melin 2009, p. 114). Thus, they probably were especially commissioned. Another example is the church of Solna near Stockholm, with its unique *ars moriendi* theme, or the relatively few late-medieval churches with a Ten

[19]Hiekkanen (2014) mentions the following: Kumlinge (p. 394–395), Parainen (Sw. Pargas, p. 130), and Siuntio (Sw. Sjundeå, p. 479). For Kalanti (Sw. Kaland), see Tuominen and Salonen (1999), p. 98. In addition, Nilsén (1986, p. 49) adds Hattula and Taivassalo (Sw. Tövsala).

[20]According to Sandquist Öberg (2009), these churches are: Floda (p. 136), Härkeberga (p. 177), Härnevi (p. 200–201), Kumla (p. 223), Storkyrkan (p. 287), Täby (p. 312), Vänge (p. 350), Yttergran (p. 360), Ösmo (p. 378), Österunda (p. 387), and Övergran (p. 402).

Commandment scene, such as the churches of Litslena, Vendel and Ärentuna (Melin 2006, p. 112–122; Nilsén 1986, p. 256–258). However, the frequency of Last Judgment paintings, supplemented to a lesser degree by Archangel Michael with his scales, suggests a moralising tendency in teaching the laity. The concern for salvation was universal in medieval Europe, but in a lay-dominated legal system, with many members of the community acting in some capacity at the court (as jurors, surveyors, witnesses and oath-helpers) and serving the administration of justice, the souls and consciences of the laymen were central. Swedish oath formulas contained self-curses and certain even refer to the devil (Fig. 5.7).[21] In late medieval courtroom scenes from the German lands, oath-swearing was a key element and in some of them, a devil and an angel are fighting over the soul of the oath-taker (e.g. Huygebaert et al. 2016, p. 32; Jacob 1994, images 7 and 64). The weakness of the learned Romano-canonical procedure in medieval Sweden made oaths so central in legal proceedings. This, in turn, emphasised the role of conscience, individual responsibility and the necessity to speak the truth—all topics present in the medieval Swedish iconography of justice.

5.6 Conclusion

As Wartenberg (2015, p. 1–18 and 42–43) has described, the new allegorical imagery of justice, created in Italy and spreading north to Europe, was born in the distinct administrative, legal and judicial contexts of medieval Italy. Such contexts —reception of Roman law, emergence of universities and legal professionals, early Renaissance Humanism—were probably necessary for the development. However, these factors were lacking in medieval Sweden.

For most of the lay judges in Sweden, churches were the only places in which they saw legal imagery. By far the most common justice-related topic was—not unsurprisingly—Archangel Michael weighing souls. However, the Last Judgment also appeared, sometimes in connection with Saint Michael weighing souls. Moses

---

[21]Korpiola (2016): ' "So ask I that God and all the saints in heaven help me that this oath I am about to swear is true and not false. All the good God he created, both in the New and the Old Law, never benefit me, not by life nor by soul, if I swear this oath falsely.

[After putting the hand on the book:] All the good I have done in my life and will do in the future, all the goods I own both in mobiles and immobiles, may they never come to help, comfort, gladden or benefit me and my heirs neither in life nor soul in front of the face of Jesus Christ, if I swear this oath falsely.

All the good words and prayers that have come out and been said of the Christian congregation through their and my mouths after they and I could move their tongues and mouths to honour God, may they never be to my health or benefit, if I swear this oath falsely."

Conclusio: The man or woman who swears falsely on the book will endanger the soul, each time he blesses himself, he does it with the devil's hand, each time he eats, he puts food in his mouth with the devil's hand, each time he drinks, the same. And all he does, he does them with the devil's hand, until he has confessed, done public penance and been fined for perjury. *Finis*.'

receiving the Tables of the Law from heaven and prophets in connection with scrolls with Biblical citations related to judging or truthfulness also appear. Other justice-related motifs were infrequent, and especially the judgment of Solomon was strikingly rare. Patrons and commissioners of art (Church, parishioners, nobility, burghers) were obviously more interested in the lives of Jesus and Mary or other theological motifs.

However, the concern for people's consciences and salvation was a key factor for the righteous administration of justice in the non-learned and largely oral legal system, where simple people acted as co-judges. Justice was related to communal practices. It was participatory, inclusive and daily reiterated by practical and communal acts. In people's every-day life, the Devil constantly tempted them to commit sins and crimes as depicted on the walls of medieval churches. The individual decision between Paradise and Hell was represented in the oath formulas and images of justice alike, and nobody could escape the weighing of the soul on the Day of Judgment.

Justitia (and the other personifications of the main virtues) seem to have been totally unknown visual motifs in medieval Sweden, and the classical imagery of justice apparently only became more relevant in the Early Modern Era. For example, in the paintings of the church of Glanshammar from 1589, a winged Justitia with scales and a sword (but with her eyes uncovered) appears. The other cardinal virtues had replaced the saints in these rare murals (Curman et al. 1961, p. 426 and 445). However, even then its importance ought not to be exaggerated. Instead, the late apparition of Lady Justice in Sweden ought probably to be interpreted as one more sign of the influence of Humanist studies, the growing importance of Roman law and a more general cultural Europeanisation. The understanding of such non-religious iconography probably spread only slowly down from the elites to the judges of the commoner estates in early modern Sweden (e.g. Sunnqvist 2014).

References

Bengtsson Melin P (2013) Biblia pauperum och senmedeltida kyrkmålningar: Något om bildbruk och influenser. In Biblia Pauperum 2013:115–125

Biblia Pauperum med svensk text ur Bibel 2000, ed. Margareta Björndahl (2008) B4Press, Gothenburg

Biblia Pauperum: De fattigas bibel: En rik inspirationskälla för senmedeltiden: Ny edition med faksimil av blocktryck från 1400-talets mitt med svensk översättning och kommentarer, ed. Christina Sandquist Öberg (2013) Kungl. Vitterhets Historie och Antikvitets Akademien, Stockholm

Cornell H, Wallin S (1960) Uppsvenska kyrkomålningar på 1500-talet, vol II. Humanistiska sällsk, Stockholm

Curman S, Lundberg E, Mörner S, Waldén B (1961) Glanshammars härad, Sydvästra delen: Konsthistoriskt inventarium. Sveriges kyrkor, vol. XLII. Kungl. Stockholm: Vitterhets Historie och Antikvitets Akademien

De Brun F, Roosval J (1924–1928) S. Nikolai eller Storkyrkan i Stockholm: Konsthistoriskt inventarium, vol. A-B. Gunnar Tisells Tekniska Förlag, Stockholm
Fält K (2012) Wall Paintings, Workshops, and Visual Production in the Medieval Diocese of Turku from 1430 to 1540. Suomen muinaismuistoyhdistyksen aikakauskirja, vol. CXX. Suomen muinaismuistoyhdistys, Helsinki
Ferm O (2006) Bengt Jönsson (Oxenstierna): Vem var han? In Myrdal J, Melin P, Ferm O (eds) Den predikande räven: arbete, skämt och allvar i en medeltida illuminerad handskrift. Bokförlaget Signum, Lund, pp 199–207
Gustafsson E (1967) Yttersta domen i Vänge. In Nordisk medeltid: Konsthistoriska studier tillägnade Armin Tuulse, ed. Sten Karling, Erland Lagerlöf, and Jan Svanberg, 167–176. Acta Universitatis Stockholmiensis/Stockholm Studies in History of Art, vol. XIII. Stockholm University, Stockholm
Harlin T, Norström BZ (2003) The Pride of Härkeberga: Meet the Artist Albertus Pictor. Enköpings kyrkliga samfällighet, Enköping
Heckscher E (1935) Sveriges ekonomiska historia, vol. I.1. Albert Bonniers Förlag, Stockholm
Hiekkanen M (2014) Suomen keskiajan kivikirkot. Kirjokansi, vol. LXXXVII. Suomalaisen kirjallisuuden seura, Helsinki
Huygebaert S, Martyn G, Paumen V, Tine VP (eds) (2016) The Art of Law: three centuries of justice depicted [exh. Cat. Bruges]. Lannoo, Tielt
Inger G (2011) Svensk rättshistoria. Liber, Malmö
Jacob R (1994) Images de la justice: Essai sur l'iconographie judiciaire du Moyen Âge à l'âge classique. Éditions Le Léopard d'Or, Paris
Janicka D (2008) Die Rezeption des Sachsenspiegels und des Magdeburger Rechts am Beispiel von Thorn in Kulmer Land. In Rechts- und Sprachtransfer in Mittel- und Osteuropa: Sachsenspiegel und Magdeburger Recht, ed. Ernst Eichler, Heiner Lück, and Wieland Carls, 61–74. Ius Saxonico-Maidebvrgense in Oriente, vol. I. De Gruyter Recht, Berlin
Kilström B (1998) Heliga Trefaldighets kyrka i Arboga. Västerås Stifts kyrkobeskrivningskommitté, Västerås
Knust C (2007) Vorbild der Gerechtigkeit: Jan Provosts Gerichtsbild in Brügge mit einem Katalog seiner Werke. Vandenhoeck & Ruprecht, Göttingen
Korpiola M (2016) 'Signa sig med djävulens hand': Självförbannelser och edsformulär i den svenska förmoderna rättskulturen. In: Dahlén M, Nygren R (eds) Arbetslinjer och långa linjer: Vänbok till Mats Kumlien. Iustus Förlag, Uppsala, pp 249–271
Korpiola M [2018 - forthcoming]. High- and Late-Medieval Scandinavia: Codified Vernacular Law and Learned Legal Influences. In Oxford Handbook on Comparative Legal History, ed. Heikki Pihlajamäki, Mark Godfrey, and Markus D. Dubber. Oxford University Press, Oxford
Lamberg M (2001) Dannemännen i stadens råd: Rådmanskretsen i nordisks köpstäder under senmedeltiden. Monografier utgivna av Stockholms stad, vol. CLV. Stockholmia förlag, Stockholm
Lindblom A (1944) Sveriges konsthistoria från forntid till nutid, vol. I (Från stenåldern till Gustav Vasa). Nordisk rotogravyr, Stockholm
Magnus Erikssons stadslag i nusvensk tolkning, ed. Åke Holmbäck, and Elias Wessén (1966) Rättshistoriskt bibliotek, vol. VII. Lund
Mark JJ (2016) Egyptian Book of the Dead. In Ancient History Encyclopedia. http://www.ancient.eu/Egyptian_Book_of_the_Dead/. Accessed 31 Oct. 2017
Medeltidens bildvärld [The World of Medieval Images], database http://medeltidbild.historiska.se/medeltidbild/sok/default.asp
Melin P (2006) Fåfängans förgänglighet: allegorin som livs- och lärospegel hos Albertus Pictor. Stockholmia förlag, Stockholm
Melin P (2009) Sankt Mikael: Själarnas förkämpe i Sala. In: Melin P (ed) Albertus Pictor: Målare av sin tid, vol I. Kungl. Vitterhets historie och antikvitets akademien, Stockholm, pp 111–114
Mielty K, Mielty M-T (eds) (2003) Isonkyrön vanhan kirkon seinämaalaukset [The Wall-paintings of the Old Church of Isokyrö]. Isonkyrön seurakunta, Isokyrö

Myrdal J (2006a) Introduktion. In: Myrdal J, Melin P, Ferm O (eds) Den predikande räven. Bokförlaget Signum, Lund, pp 1–28
Myrdal J (2006b) En handskrifts bildvärld. In: Myrdal J, Melin P, Ferm O (eds) Den predikande räven. Bokförlaget Signum, Lund, pp 28–197
Nilsén A (1986) Program och funktion i senmedeltida kalkmåleri: Kyrkmålningar i Mälarlandskapen och Finland 1400-1534. Kungl. Vitterhets Historie och Antikvitets Akademien, Stockholm
Nisbeth Å (1995) Ordet som bild: Östgötskt kalkmåleri vid slutet av 1300-talet och början av 1400-talet. Sällskapet Runica et mediævalia, Stockholm
Oakes C (2008) Ora pro nobis: The Virgin as Intercessor in Medieval Art and Devotion. Harvey Miller Publishers, London
Öberg CS (2009) Albertus Pictor: Målare av sin tid 2: Samtliga bevarade motiv och språkband med kommentarer och analyser. Kungl. Vitterhets Historie och Antikvitets Akademien, Stockholm
Schaller A (2006) Der Erzengel Michael im frühen Mittelalter: Ikonographie und Verehrung eines Heiligen ohne Vita. Peter Lang, Bern
Schück H (1951) Stockholm vid 1400-talets slut. Hugo Gebers Förlag, Stockholm
Stockholms stads skottebok 1460–1468 samt strödda räkenskaper från 1430-talet och från åren 1460-1473, ed. Joh. Ax. Almquist. Stockholm: Kungl. Samfundet för utgifvande af handskrifter rörande Skandinaviens historia
Stockholms stads tänkeböcker 1474–1483 samt burspråk, ed. Emil Hildebrand. 1917. Stockholm: Kungl. Samfundet för utgifvande af handskrifter rörande Skandinaviens historia
Stockholms stads tänkeböcker 1483–1492, ed. Gottfrid Carlsson. 1944. Stockholm: Kungl. Samfundet för utgifvande af handskrifter rörande Skandinaviens historia
Sunnqvist, Martin. 2014. Insignia of Independence or Subordination? The Iconography of the Seals of the Svea Court of Appeal. In The Svea Court of Appeal in the Early Modern Period: Historical Reinterpretations and New Perspectives, ed. Mia Korpiola, 355–394. Rättshistoriska studier, vol. XXVI. The Olin Foundation, Stockholm
Svanberg J, Öberg J (2009) Albertus Pictor: En biografisk skiss. In: Melin P (ed) Albertus Pictor: Målare av sin tid, vol I. Kungl. Vitterhets historie och antikvitets akademien, Stockholm, pp 11–16
Takala M (1993) Lex Dei—Lex Politica Dei. Lex Politica Dei—teos ja Kaarle IX:n lainsäädäntö. Suomen Kirkkohistoriallisen Seuran Toimituksia, vol. CLX. Suomen Kirkkohistoriallinen Seura, Helsinki
Thomas a Kempis (1568) Opvscvla avrea, vereque; lucidissima, venerabilis Thoma e de Kempis, Canonici regvlaris. Apud Philippum Iuntam, & fratres, Venice
Tuominen LK, Salonen J (1999) Kalannin kirkko, vol I. Tuominen, Kalanti
Wartenberg I (2015) Bilder der Rechtsprechung: Spätmittelalterliche Wandmalereien in Regierungsräumen italienischer Kommunen. Ars et Scientia: Schriften von Kunstwissenschaft, vol. XI. Walter de Gruyter, Berlin

Mia Korpiola obtained a doctoral degree in Law at the University of Helsinki in 2004. She had various positions at the Faculty of Law of the University of Helsinki in 1997–2010 and 2013. She had post-doctoral funding from the Academy of Finland in 2007–2009, and in 2010–2013 she was fellow at the Helsinki Collegium for Advanced Studies. She became professor of legal history in Turku in 2014. She has authored Between Betrothal and Bedding: Marriage Formation in Sweden, 1200–1600 (2009) and edited several other books. Her bibliography lists dozens of articles on various topics.

Figures

Fig. 5.1 Detail from an altarpiece depicting the Last Judgment, originally from the Church of Björlanda (Hisingen, then in Norway), unknown artist, photo by Mia Korpiola with the permission of the Museum of Gothenburg, Sweden

Fig. 5.2 Jesus as Judge of the World, parchment manuscript of Magnus Eriksson's *Town Law*, unknown artist, fifteenth century, legal manuscript B 154, printed by kind permission of the National Library of Sweden

Fig. 5.3 Albertus Pictor and school, *Judgment of Solomon*, wall painting in the Church of Täby (Uppland), Sweden, photo by Lennart Karlsson, printed by kind permission of The Swedish History Museum

Fig. 5.4 Albertus Pictor and school, *Prophet holding a text scroll*, wall painting in the Church of Härkeberga (Uppland), Sweden, photo by Lennart Karlsson, printed by kind permission of The Swedish History Museum

Fig. 5.5 *Last Judgment*, wall painting in the Church of Lohja (Sw. Lojo), Finland, unknown artist, photo by Mia Korpiola

Fig. 5.6 *Saint Michael weighing souls*, wall painting in the Church of Siuntio (Sw. Sjundeå), unknown artist, Finland, photo by Mia Korpiola

Fig. 5.7 *Devils tempting eating and drinking people*, wall painting in the Church of Lohja (Sw. Lojo), Finland, unknown artist, photo by Mia Korpiola

Chapter 6
Justitia, Examples and Allegories of Justice, and Courts in Flemish Tapestry, 1450–1550

Guy Delmarcel

Abstract Between ca. 1450 and 1550, justice was a common theme in Flemish tapestry, usually in the form of allegorical scenes illustrated with examples from the Bible and world history. Furthermore, in moral or Biblical scenes, courts of justice were often depicted as well. There is one noticeable *exemplum justitiae* of the Roman Emperor Trajan which, up until now, has not been studied extensively. In this paper, an interpretation of this piece is offered by connecting it with the book *Ludus Scaccorum*.

6.1 Introduction

Since its inception in the early fourteenth century, tapestry has been the vehicle of numerous secular themes. Moral allegories, such as the virtue of justice, were represented either as personifications, or by means of examples from history. This essay examines some of the finest examples, woven in the heyday of Flemish tapestry, from the mid-fifteenth to the mid-sixteenth century.

6.2 Justitia

6.2.1 Justice, Highest Virtue of the Prince[1]

Administering justice is one of the public functions of the Prince: in doing so, he rewards the good and punishes the wicked. By administering justice, the ruler also

[1]*For this and the following paragraph, (see Delmarcel* 2000, *p. 115–124), where all the literary sources and bibliography are referred to in detail.*

G. Delmarcel (✉)
Department of Art History, University of Leuven, Louvain, Belgium
e-mail: Guy.Delmarcel@Outlook.be

S. Huygebaert et al. (eds.), *The Art of Law*, Ius Gentium: Comparative Perspectives on Law and Justice 66, https://doi.org/10.1007/978-3-319-90787-1_6

embodies social order. These ideas had been around in Western thought ever since Aristotle, for whom Justitia was the first requirement for holding public office. Cicero, in his *De officiis*, stresses the role of Justitia as the social driving force, giving everyone his due. This theme was taken up by medieval authors, such as the French scholastic philosopher William of Conches (ca. 1090–after 1154). Isidore of Seville (560–636), in his *Etymologiae*, derives the word *rex* from *recte facere*. Hence, in mirrors for Princes, from the Carolingians to Erasmus, justice became the very foundation of rule: the State itself could not survive without justice.[2]

In addition to this secular tradition, there is also a similar biblical and liturgical one on the same theme. In Psalms, numerous verses dealing with justice are ascribed to David, the model *par excellence* for the anointed King.[3] The liturgy of the coronation was centred around justice. The sceptre is the symbol of justice, the *virga virtutis atque aequitatis* (the rod of virtue and of equity), and King David is quoted as an example. One of the enamel plates of the octagonal Ottonian imperial crown, now in Vienna, shows David with the text '*Honor Regis iudicium diligit*' (Honour delights in the justice of the King). Dominican theologian Dirc van Delf (1365–1404) pertinently summarises the relationship between justice and the royal power in his description of the imperial throne, which is primarily a judge's throne. When the new ruler mounts his throne, he is told, at the moment of coronation: '*op een throen des rijcs so sitte glorioselic te doen recht ende rechtveerdicheit in alden landen*' ('to sit so gloriously on the kingdom's throne to do right and justice in all the lands'). In the subsequent sermon, he is told that he will govern himself through the other three cardinal virtues, but that justice will teach him '*hoe du die menschen selste voerstaen*' (how you will champion the people themselves). In the ethical system of the four cardinal virtues, *prudentia* or wisdom, as knowledge of our own nature, was most important. Then came two virtues that were remedies for the caprices of fate (*fortuna*), namely temperance in times of good fortune, and fortitude in times of adversity. The final one was justice, considered as the supreme virtue of the ruler (Huygebaert et al. 2016, p. 139–157).

6.2.2 Justice for the Good and the Evil

The most elaborate representation of justice in tapestry is a piece in the set of *Los Honores* (Delmarcel 2000, p. 115–124; Buchanan 2015, p. 120–121). It was woven in the manufacture of Peter van Edingen, alias van Aelst, (ca. 1465–1533) in Brussels between 1520 and 1525 to celebrate the coronation of Charles of Habsburg as Emperor of the Holy Roman Empire (Fig. 6.1). In this tapestry panel, Justice's personification is sitting in the middle of a pavilion. She is accompanied by

---

[2]Isidore, *Etymologiae*, ix, 3, 4: '*recte igitur faciendo regis nomen tenetur, peccando omittitur, (...) Rex eris si recte facies, si non facias, non eris*'.

[3]As in Psalms 89:14.

Fortitude and Temperance, while the Emperor Nero, as an example of injustice, is at her feet. The honest people are coming to her temple, and the upper corners show examples of great sinners. Justice's device is woven on top of the throne: '*justis remuneror, protego bonos, castigo nocentes*' ('I reward the righteous people, I protect the good, I punish the harmful'). The designers may have found inspiration for this text in the scene of Fortuna's downfall at the joyful entry of Charles of Habsburg into Bruges in 1515. There, the inscription about Justitia read: '*justos premio, bonos defendo, malos punio*', which the sixteenth century historiography Rémy du Puys translated as: '*Je remunère les iustes, je deffens les bons et punis les mauluais*'. The Latin text on the tapestry is a literal translation of Du Puys' version, so it is clear that his account was used here, whether or not he personally assisted in the creation of the tapestries.

The fact justice is regarded here as a royal virtue is proven by the emblem on her banners, borne by Tomyris and Scipio: a large queen bee, surrounded by her swarm. Since Antiquity, this was an image of the ideally constituted State. For Pliny, the 'King Bee'—it was thought that bees were governed by a male creature—either did not have a stinger, or made no use of it. The whole swarm always followed its ruler, and if he was captured, the whole nation was lost. The Renaissance picked up this allegory via Horapollo's *Hieroglyphica*. There, the swarm of bees became a symbol of the royal subjects, and the King himself, who did not use his stinger, illustrated the *clementia principis*.

At the feet of the principal virtues and in front of the semi-circular wall, we can see some women who, according to the inscriptions, represent the subsidiary virtues of Fortitudo and Temperantia. We can further identify Veritas, Observantia and Concordia on the left, and Verecundia, Fiducia and Misericordia on the right. Perhaps more important are the three personifications in the centre of the composition, which hand out gold chains to the just. On the left, we can see Reverentia with Rebecca, in the centre Gratia with David, and on the right Dignitas with Rachel and Esther at her feet.

On the cartouches next to the two side entrances, some inscriptions clarify the nature of the righteous who are rewarded here. On the left is woven: '*Nihil est profecto praestabilius quam plane intelligi nos ad Justiciam esse natos. Cicero*'. It is in fact taken from a longer phrase in Cicero's *De Legibus* (i, 28), which in translation reads: '[Of all matters discussed by scholars] none indeed is more important than the clear understanding that we were born for justice [and that law is not founded on common opinion, but on nature]'. In short, it is an apology for innate justice. On the right-hand side is its pendant: '*Beati qui custodiunt judicium et faciunt iustitiam omni tempore. Psal. CV*' ('Blessed are they that keep judgment, and he that doth righteousness at all times, Psalms 106:3'). Both nature and holy writ produce righteous men.

The examples from Antiquity were chosen rather arbitrarily. Most of them are virtuous figures who also appear elsewhere on the *Honores* tapestries, such as Antoninus Pius, Codrus, Camilla and Veturia. In the group on the right, there is a sturdy warrior, with a great plumed helmet, shield and battle-axe, who attracts special attention: Marcus Furius Camillus, who defeated the Gauls outside Rome and is held up by Valerius Maximus (*Facta et dicta memorabilia*, IV, 1, 2) as a model of temperance. In front of him is an old man,'Lytyrgvs', bent half over and talking to a lady named 'Placella'. Lycurgus, who gave Sparta its laws, was famous because of his strict legislation against unjust ownership of property. Vincent of Beauvais' *Speculum Historiale* praises Lycurgus, who gave to all equally and hence was a good example of distributive justice. The same medieval encyclopaedist also offers an explanation for the mysterious 'Placella': she is in fact Flaccilla or Placilla, the wife of the Emperor Theodosius the Great, and she was loved because she gave all her possessions to the poor, an example of royal *liberalitas*.

In the top corners of the tapestry, the vengeance wreaked by Justitia on the *nocentes*, the wicked, is illustrated by two scenes from classical mythology: on the left the fall of Phaeton, and on the right the classical torments of hell. At the left, the couplet in the top border explains: '*Motus ob audaces Phaetontis Juppiter ausus, Turbat in ultrices ora cadentis aquas*' ('Jupiter, moved by Phaeton's rash attempts, throws his countenance into confusion as he falls into the vengeful waters'). The exemplary value of this scene must have been clear to the observer, due to the long literary tradition associated with Ovid's text. In the *Ovidius Moralizatus*, a version in Latin prose of the *Ovide Moralisé*, Pierre Bersuire (ca. 1290–1362) turns Phaeton's fall into an allegory of ecclesiastical justice, with Apollo as the image of Christ, the *sol justitiae* (Huygebaert et al. 2016, p. 179–181, ill. 102 and cat. 112), and Phaeton as a prelate who must follow the right road of *justitia* and *aequitas*. Bersuire also uses the image of the king bee without a stinger, which is displayed on the banners. The *Ovide Moralisé* and Bersuire were put together in a printed compilation published in Bruges in 1484 and Paris in 1493. In it, there was, for the first time, a suggestion that the legend applied to the rulers of the world, who could not refrain their dynastic ambitions, and that the moral lesson was directed at their children. This example of royal *ambitio* and *temeritas* was very popular during the Renaissance. In his *Institutio principis christiani*, a mirror for Princes written for Charles of Habsburg, Erasmus quotes the story of Phaeton as an example of the Prince who no longer allows himself to be guided by reason, and consequently brings himself and his subjects to ruin. Shortly thereafter, the very same comparison was adopted by Alciato in his *Emblemata* as an illustration of the motto *In temerarios*. In his moralism on the theme, he associates the fall of Phaeton with the image of Fortuna's wheel, from which the reckless ruler falls.

In the top right corner, symmetrical to the fall of Phaeton and iconographically its complement, there is the punishment of some damned figures from classical mythology. The couplet above them emphasises the justness of their punishment: '*Sisyphus, Ixion, Tityus, Phineus, Danai grex/Seua luunt iustis crimina suppliciis*' ('Sisyphus, Ixion, Tityus, Phineus, and the flock of Danaids/Atone for their savage crimes with just penalties'). In the most familiar descriptions of the mythological underworld (Ovid and Virgil), the standard group of the damned consists of Tityus, Sisyphus, Ixion, the Danaids and Tantalus. The latter is missing here, and has been replaced by Phineus. This detail makes it plausible that a less familiar description of Hades was used here, particularly the one in Seneca's tragedy *Hercules furens* (vs. 750–759).

6.2.3 The Triumphal Chariot of Justice

Another Brussels tapestry set, woven around 1535–1540, is devoted to the triumphal *Cortege of the Seven Virtues*, of which Justice is one (Fig. 6.2) (Bennett 1992, p. 108–110; Delmarcel 1979). She holds a set of scales and a sword, while God the Father is giving her a second sword. Her triumphal chariot is moving to the left, drawn by two unicorns. Justice's emblematic bird, the crane, keeps his vigil at her feet. Here as well, several biblical heroes are used as examples, namely Noah, Sara, Rebecca, Joseph, Rachel and Jacob. However, examples from Antiquity are both more numerous and more obvious. The two warriors in armour who are walking in front of the unicorns are Scipio Africanus and Cato. At the foreground on the left, we see Trajan administrating justice to the widow for her dead son. Next to him, Charondas the lawgiver falls on his sword, having broken one of his own laws. He is followed by Zaleucus (Huygebaert et al. 2016, p. 46–47 and cat. 27–29 and 107), one eye covered, since he sacrificed an eye in order to save his son from total blindness, when the latter was condemned to lose his eyes for a crime. The designers' main source for these classical allusions was Valerius Maximus' *Facta et dicta memorabilia*, in his chapter *De Justitia*.

6.2.4 Justitia Among the Seven Virtues

One or two decades after this triumphal cortege of the virtues, around 1550, the theme of the Seven Virtues was taken up again in a tapestry set from Brussels, preserved today at the Kunsthistorisches Museum in Vienna (series XVII). Justice is now presiding over one large scene, namely the Judgment of Solomon (Fig. 6.3). The inscription on the cartouche in the upper border summarizes Justice' most important goal: '*Justitia est perpetua voluntas/Ius suum unicuique tribuens*', thus repeating the motto of the *justitia distributiva* illustrated in the older *Honores* piece. The side borders are ornated with elegant female figures, representing the positive and negative effects of Justice: Innocentia, Vindicta, Equitas, Negligentia, Crudelitas. The composition is attributed to Michiel Coxcie (1499–1592), one of the major tapestry designers of his time.

6.3 Courts of Justice

Courts of justice were represented in a rather uniform manner during the Early Modern Era. The judge sits on a throne on a central platform, surrounded by his assistants. In front of them, a clerk takes notes (Heinemann 1900). Such courts of Justice were also represented in Renaissance tapestry, mostly not for their own sake, but in a context of judgment scenes. A very early example is a late fifteenth century tapestry from a set of the *Life of Esther*, now in the Musée Lorrain in Nancy. The scene shows Ahasverus condemning Vasthi to be expelled from his palace. The clerk in front refers to a court scene (Franke 1998, plate 11).

The most illustrious depiction of a court of justice in the early sixteenth century can be found on the central piece of the already cited *Los Honores* series (Fig. 6.4). It is an allegory of imperial honour. Honour is on the judge's throne, surrounded by the court of virtuous men and women. A clerk is proclaiming the names of the honourable people, who get access to the temple of honour from the lateral pavilions. In the meantime, the dishonourable people from world history vainly try to climb to the temple in the front. The entire scene is related to an allegorical poem by Jean Lemaire de Belges (1473–1525), *Le Temple d'Honneur et de Vertus* (Buchanan 2015, p. 119; Delmarcel 2000, p. 91–101).

A less obvious example can be found in another contemporary tapestry series. In 1528 King Henry VIII of England bought a large ten-piece tapestry set depicting the *Story of David and Bathsheba*, which is now preserved in the Musée national de la Renaissance, at the castle of Écouen (Delmarcel 2008, p. 56–61 and 129–130). It tells the story of David and Bathsheba's adultery, their subsequent punishment, and David's final repentance. David sent Bathsheba's husband Uriah to die on the battlefield. According to the Book of Samuel, 'David then received Bathsheba in his palace'. In the tapestry set, this scene is apparently more a court of justice than a welcome. David is flanked by the two clerks, and Bathsheba is introduced by her lawyers. She apparently demands justice for her husband's death, while other lawyers or judges, the *gens de longue robe*, are entering at the right side (Fig. 6.5).

Scenes of justice could also be found outside the court buildings. On a late fifteenth-century piece, described in the Copenhagen museum's catalogue as *Peasants before a Judge*, a richly clad man sitting on a stone is holding a thin white stick, an attribute often identified as belonging to a figure of authority, particularly a judge. However, it could also refer to a landlord or a bailiff, collecting taxes from the countrymen (Woldbye 2006, p. 22–25).

6.4 *Exempla Justitiae*: The Emperor Trajan

As we have seen, allegories of justice in Flemish tapestry were always illustrated with historical examples. However, these classical stories themselves could also be used independently as models for good government. The most famous one is undoubtedly the tapestry with the well-known stories of the *Justice of Trajan and Herkinbald*, dated around 1460, and now at the Historisches Museum in Bern. It is a woven copy of four paintings (now lost) by Rogier van der Weyden (1399/1400–1464), delivered for the city council room, and thus for the court of the city of Brussels, between 1432 and 1445. Its creation was probably ordered by Lionello d'Este somewhere before 1450, and later on it found its way into the collection of Georges de Saluces, bishop of Lausanne. The scenes are represented in contemporary dress, as was fashionable at the court of the dukes of Burgundy (Rapp Buri and Stucky Schürer 2001, p. 41–70).

A rather unexpected example of Trajan's justice is a tapestry from Brussels from around 1510, now in the Museum of Fine Arts in Boston (Fig. 6.6). Here, the meaning is less obvious. It relates to a tale in a Dutch version, printed after 1483, of the *Ludus Scaccorum*, the *Play of Chess*, or *Jeu des Échecs moralisés,* written around 1300 by the Italian author Jacobus de Cessolis (ca. 1250–1322). Here as well, the Emperor Trajan plays the role of the judge. His only son had pushed a boy from a poor family into a river, in which he drowned. According to the Emperor's law, his son should perish in the same way. The Emperor ordered the father of the dead boy to throw the Prince into the river, but then an angel appears and rescues the two children. The tapestry may once have been the property of cardinal Wolsey. Such a piece is cited in his inventory, but its meaning was apparently lost, as it was described as 'two children saved from drowning by an angel' (Delmarcel 1976, 243–253).[4]

6.5 Conclusion

The few examples of the representation of justice in Flemish tapestry, studied in this brief contribution, illustrate the wealth and importance of this medium, so often forgotten by many art historians, for secular iconography. Due to their dimensions, however, they were an expensive means of decorating public halls and princely palaces, places where justice was an important decorative theme, both as a virtue and as an institution.

References

Bennett A (1992) Five centuries of tapestry from the fine arts museums of San Francisco, revised edition. Chronicle Books, San Francisco

Buchanan I (2015) Habsburg tapestries. Studies in western tapestry, vol 4. Brepols, Turnhout

Cavallo AS (1967) Tapestries of Europe and Colonial Peru in the museum of fine arts, Boston. Museum of Fine Arts, Boston

Delmarcel G (1976) De legende van Herkenbald en de gerechtigheid van keizer Trajanus. Een iconografische nota. In: Brusselse wandtapijten van de pre-Renaissance. Tapisseries bruxelloises de la pré-Renaissance (exh. cat.). Musées Royaux d'Art et d'Histoire, Brussels, pp 245–255

Delmarcel G (1979) The triumph of the seven virtues and related Brussels tapestries of the early renaissance. In: Bennett A (ed) Acts of the tapestry symposium, November 1976. The fine arts museums of San Francisco. The Museums, San Francisco, pp 155–170

[4]Cavallo (1967, p. 89–91) labelled it as 'the Miracles of St Claude'.

Delmarcel G (2000) Los Honores, Flemish tapestries for the Emperor Charles V. Pandora, Antwerp
Delmarcel G (2008) David et Bethsabée. Un chef-d' oeuvre de la tapisserie à la Renaissance. Éditions du Patrimoine, Réunion des monuments nationaux, Paris
Franke B (1998) Assuerus und Esther am Burgunderhof. Zur Rezeption des Buches Esther in den Niederlanden (1450 bis 1530). Gebrüder Mann Verlag, Berlin
Heinemann F (1900) Der Richter und Rechtspflege in der deutschen Vergangenheit. Eugen Diederichs, Leipzig
Huygebaert S, Martyn G, Paumen V, Van Poucke T (eds) (2016) The art of law. Three centuries of justice depicted (exh. cat. Bruges). Lannoo, Tielt
Rapp Buri A, Stucky Schürer M (2001) Burgundische Tapisserien. München: Hirmer Verlag
Woldbye V (2006) European tapestries, 15th–20th century. Catalogue of the collection. The Danish Museum of Art & Design, Copenhagen

Guy Delmarcel has a Ph.D degree in Archaeology and History of Art and a MA degree in Romanic Philology. Curator emeritus of Textiles at the Royal Museums of Art and History, Brussels. Emeritus Professor of History of Art, KULeuven. Member of the Royal Flemish Academy of Science of Belgium. Published extensively on the history of ancient Flemish tapestry.

Figures

Fig. 6.1 *Allegory of Justice* Brussels tapestry, 1520–1525, Patrimonio Nacional Madrid, © Patrimonio Nacional Madrid

Fig. 6.2 *Triumph of Justice* Brussels tapestry, ca. 1530, The Fine Arts Museums of San Francisco, © The Fine Arts Museums of San Francisco

Fig. 6.3 *Allegory of Justice* Brussels tapestry, ca. 1545, Kunsthistorisches Museum Vienna, © Kunsthistorisches Museum

Fig. 6.4 *The Court of Honor* Brussels tapestry, 1520–1525, Patrimonio Nacional Madrid, © Patrimonio Nacional Madrid

Fig. 6.5 *Bathseba at the Court of Justice in the Palace of David* Brussels tapestry, ca. 1525, Musée National de la Renaissance, Castle of Écouen, © Réunion des Musées Nationaux

Fig. 6.6 *The Legend of Trajan* Brussels tapestry, ca. 1520, Boston Museum of Fine Arts, Photograph © 2018 Museum of Fine Arts, Boston

Chapter 7
The Judgment of Cambyses: A Rich Iconographical Topic with Multiple Sources and a Long Tradition

Raf Verstegen

Abstract The antique story of the flaying of a corrupt judge, ordered by the Persian King Cambyses, generated an abundance of medieval literature. In the visual arts, the fifteenth century painting *Judgment of Cambyses* (1498; Groeningemuseum, Bruges) by Gerard David was a milestone in how the story was depicted. David represented it in four scenes (a diptych with two scenes on each panel): the bribery, the arrest of the judge, the flaying, and the installation of the son on his father's skin spread over the seat. The better-known Christian iconographical tradition of the flaying of Saint Bartholomew was likely a direct inspiration for David, as well as for some miniaturists. It is my hypothesis that the refined but cruel realism of the painting is the result of a diligent observation of animal flaying—and not of a judicial practice of human flaying. In addition to this, increasingly popular representations of anatomical lessons were also a useful source of inspiration for the elaboration of the diptych. Furthermore, many scholars have interpreted the painting as an early group portrait in disguise of Bruges' aldermen. After David, the depiction of the bribery and the arrest scenes in the Cambyses tale disappeared. Artists started concentrating on the moment of the installation of the young judge on the skin of his father, often with the flaying scene on the background. The Cambyses story, ultimately represented through an emblematic stripped-off skin, was, just as many other exemplary representations of justice, to be replaced by a symbolic iconographic representation of Lady Justice. If flaying was represented at all, it was reserved for other subjects, such as the Marsyas legend, the martyrdom of St Bartholomew and the artistic expression of anatomical structures of the human body.

7.1 Introduction: Literary Tradition

In his *Facta et dicta memorabilia* (VI.3.ext.3), the Roman author Valerius Maximus recounts the story: 'Cambyses' severity was unusual. He flayed the skin from a certain judge and had it stretched over a chair on which he ordered the man's son to

R. Verstegen (✉)
Law Faculty, University of Leuven, Leuven, Belgium
e-mail: Raf.Verstegen@kuleuven.be

S. Huygebaert et al. (eds.), *The Art of Law*, Ius Gentium: Comparative Perspectives on Law and Justice 66, https://doi.org/10.1007/978-3-319-90787-1_7

sit when passing judgment. He was a King and a barbarian, and by the horrible and novel punishment of a judge, he sought to make sure that no judge could be bribed in the future' (Shackleton and David 2000, t. II, p. 43). Numerous medieval writings retell the story, with both minor and major variations (Heckscher 1958, p. 88–89 and 161, n. 162; Ridderbos 2014, p. 287–288; Van der Velden 1995a, p. 7–9 and 11–16). From the fifteenth century onwards, the story found its way into the pictorial arts, epitomised by the famous *exemplum justitiae*, painted by Gerard David (ca. 1450–1523) for the Bruges magistrates in 1498. We do not know which exact version of the story David read and used, but most probably, it was a version that emphasised the aspect of bribery (Ridderbos 2014, p. 287–288; Van der Velden 1995a, p. 11–16 and 22). There is no painted version that appears to have been familiar with Valerius' source Herodotus (V.23), who writes that the judge was first put to death and then flayed, and that his skin was cut in stripes before it was used to cover the seat. If medieval writers had known Herodotus' version of the story, the iconography might have been totally different. Or, if they had known both versions, they most probably would have found the one with the stretched skin more suited to depict. One detail: Herodotus was the only one to mention the name of the corrupt judge (Sisamnes) and his son (Otanes). These names were used in commentaries only since the revival of antique Greek literature in modern times (Ridderbos 2014, p. 280).

According to Herodotus, the judge's son is installed on his father's seat, with the King's admonition to always 'remember what was the judgment-seat whereon he sat'. A story that contained such a striking moral was predestined to become a famous *exemplum justitiae*. However, transposing the story from its literary sources to the visual arts proved a real challenge. Furthermore, current-day research does not offer us much information about the sources of Gerard David's *Judgment of Cambyses* in the Bruges Groeningemuseum (1498), the generally accepted piece of reference for this topic. Hence, the questions I will seek to answer in this paper are the following: What more can we discover about his sources? How important was his work to the later evolution? What were the vicissitudes of the *exemplum* after David?

7.2 Gerard David's *Judgment of Cambyses*

Gerard David distributed the episodes of this story over two panels. The left panel shows the arrest of the corrupt judge Sisamnes, with the bribery scene in the background. The right panel is dominated by the actual flaying, while the background depicts Otanes, seated upon his father's skin, administering justice (Fig. 7.1).

By distributing the subject over two panels with two scenes each, Gerard David was following some famous examples. Van der Weyden initiated this format for the Brussels aldermen chamber with the *exempla* of Trajan and Herkenbald. The Leuven magistrates received a similar showpiece painted by Dieric Bouts, who also distributed the narrative of *Judgment of Otto III* across two panels. David's inclination to artistic competition and emulation, which sometimes led him to copy inventions wholesale, is well-known (Van der Velden 1995a, p. 59–62).[1] However, we may accept that this choice was also a question of collective emulation between the Bruges city magistrates and their colleagues from other leading towns.

Some scholars have raised the question why David represented the episode of the arrest of Sisamnes and the cruel scene of his flaying, in the foreground of the panels, and consigned the installation of the young judge on his father's skin to the background. This is particularly remarkable because the latter scene would go on to become the iconographical anchor of the visualised *exemplum* (Van der Velden 1995a, p. 54). It seems that, once it was decided that the story had to be told in four consecutive, chronological episodes, David had no choice: bribery in the background, arrest and flaying in the foreground, finally the installation of the new judge in the background again (Van der Velden 1995b, p. 59–62). What he was confronted with was the challenge to invent and create a convincing and acceptable iconography for each of the episodes.

In the arrest and flaying scenes, several figures are gathered around the King. It has been generally accepted that David, who emerges here as one of the initiators of group portraiture in painting, did not paint general figures, nor types: the faces are quite individualised, and are very likely to be portraits of the aldermen of the time, despite the fact that it is impossible to identify them. Some faces were replaced in the final stage of painting, probably to bring them into accordance with a recent renewal of the magistrate (Ainsworth 1998, p. 67–72; Borchert 2013, p. 225; Paumen 2016a, p. 89–90; Van der Velden 1995a, p. 52).[2] In this respect, the panels can be read as a manifestation of individual ambition: for the aldermen, it is their legacy to posterity through a group portrait, both in the arrest and in the flaying scene. We may assume, as Van der Velden (1995b, p. 52) observes, that the inclusion of portraits in justice scenes served to emphasise the supposed analogy between the conduct of the just protagonists of the *exempla* and that of the aldermen, in this case a negative analogy *vis-à-vis* the corrupt judge (Ridderbos 2014, p. 287–289).

7.3 David's Iconographical and Other Sources

The choice to depict the story in four episodes probably could not have been taken without a preliminary idea of how each of them could be worked out. The scene of the bribery speaks for itself: a judge accepting a purse. Van der Velden (1995b, p. 55–57) suggested that a miniature of Loyset Liédet served as a source of inspiration to Gerard David. The miniature represented the Judgment of Cambyses

[1]On the influence of Dirk Bouts on David, (see Ainsworth 1998, p. 45 and 148–149).

[2]Van der Velden suggests that the aldermen could have contributed to the costs of the painting. This practice was well-known in the later blooming tradition of guild group portraits. See the contribution by Beatrijs Wolters van der Wey in this volume.

in the manuscript *La Sale,* created in 1461 to edify especially princes, lords and ladies. The resemblance between the position of the executioner on the right side in both representations is too conspicuous to be accidental.[3] The scene of the inauguration of the young judge is also indebted to this miniature (see the suspended skin).[4] Furthermore, Paumen (2016b, p. 94–95) recently pointed out the resemblance between David's arrest scene and another miniature of Liédet, representing the murder of Caesar, in the same book. That three of David's scenes can be linked to two of Liédet's miniatures in the same manuscript shows that he was indeed an important iconographical source. Two questions then arise. What were Liédet's sources for the flaying scene? And did David use any other sources? As I see it, there are, besides the possibility of another illustrated manuscript telling this or another flaying story, three possible traces: medieval judicial practice, the flaying of Saint Bartholomew, and the representation of anatomy lessons.

7.3.1 *Representation of a Medieval Punishment?*

It has been said that David painted the flaying after a common practice in medieval justice (Van Miegroet 1989, p. 155). However, Van der Velden (1995a, p. 40) correctly states that, at least for the Netherlands, 'It was, to be sure, a dangerous age, in which one might be decapitated, buried alive, burned, quartered or even boiled, but there was no tradition of flaying those who offended the law'. Hence, most likely, David never witnessed a criminal being flayed alive. However, there is a lot more to say about this penalty. Shaving the head, up to scalping 'with skin and hair', for sexual abuse is broadly attested in western countries (Maes 1947, p. 418–419 and 422–423; Schowe 1994, p. 143–155). Schowe (1994, p. 154) mentions tearing out strips or parts of the skin on the way to the execution as a supplementary penalty.

Four ancient Assyrian stone reliefs confirm literary sources mentioning captured enemies being flayed alive. In 1571 the Venetian commander, in an attempt to conquer Cyprus on the Ottomans, was captured and publicly flayed alive. It was an event that shocked Western Europe (Wyss 1996, p. 134). And even in Western Europe (although we have to be careful to make any definitive claims here, due to a lack of information), this form of punishment has been applied. In France in 1314,

[3]Van der Velden (1995b, p. 55) also mentions the diagonally positioned table, but see David's early work *Christ nailed to the cross* (London, National Gallery), and precedents in miniatures (Van Miegroet 1989, p. 48). Heckscher (1958, p. 35–36), commenting Rembrandt's *Anatomy of Dr. Nicolaas Tulp*, writes: 'The position diagonal to the picture plane is a common and ages-old device by which a prone body can serve to express the suffering, surrender, and passivity in general of the defenceless, the dying, and the dead'. The diagonal position also functions as a '*repoussoir*', giving depth to the image (Heckscher 1958, p. 18).

[4]For two other miniatures with Otanes sitting on or next to his father's skin, (see Paumen 2016b, p. 94; Van der Velden 1995a, p. 22–24).

two knights who had committed adultery with two daughters-in-law of the French King Philip IV were skinned alive (Favier 1978, 527–529). In England, hanging or flaying were advanced as punishments for high treason (Barron 1978, p. 58). Jean Boutillier, in his *Somme rural* (Northern France, last quarter fourteenth century), sees quartering or flaying as alternative forms of punishment for this crime (Barron 1978, p. 60–61, 1981, p. 192).[5] Flaying is also known in the *Bayerisches Landrecht* of 1346 (Von Simson 1977, p. 349 and 356, fn. 11). The cruelty of the medieval practice of flaying alive was integrated in poetical texts and in medieval animal epics (Barron 1978, 1981). In Savoy, a Jew was flayed alive for having insulted and dishonoured in aggravating circumstances a statue of the Virgin Mary, a crime which was to be punished '*à l'arbitraire du juge*' (Duvillaret 1943, p. 186). In a judicial system where the fundamental principle *nulla poena sine lege* was still unknown, the role of the judge—sometimes the King or the feudal lord—must have been decisive in deciding whether or not, in very exceptional cases, flaying alive was applied. Barron (1981, p. 197) summarises the most recent results of historical research: 'It was apparently always an exceptional penalty, prescribed by ancient usage rather than written code, and reserved for crimes for which society felt a particular abhorrence. But it made an impression on man's mind out of all proportion to its frequency'.[6]

Flaying alive is 'technically' represented in medieval images in a variety of ways. Questions have been raised about the practical feasibility of human flaying (Von Simson 1977, p. 353). After all, the human skin is the strongest tissue of the human body. After assuring a grip on a small strip, it is possible to loosen large flaps of the skin by pulling, a method that can actually be used in today's forensic practice. Preserving the entire skin would need painstaking and patient, meticulous cutting.[7]

7.3.2 The Flaying of Saint Bartholomew Before 1500

According to a popular tradition originating in writings of the church historian Eusebius (fourth century), Saint Bartholomew, one of the twelve Apostles, was flayed alive in Armenia (or India?) (Réau 1958, p. 181–184). From the twelfth century onwards, the legend generated, all over Western Europe, a very rich and diverse iconographical tradition in manuscripts, murals, panel paintings, tapestries

[5]This confirms what Van Miegroet (1989, fn. 59) already suggested: that flaying was a penalty for high treason. Medieval novelists imagined this penalty for the roman emperor Julian the Apostate and for Caïphas, who betrayed Christ, (see Barron 1978, p. 51).

[6]'Paradoxically, because it was only seldom performed and constituted an extremely shocking experience for the public, it incited the medieval imagination and featured frequently in vernacular writings and collective memory', Pinkus (2015, p. 26).

[7]I would like to thank my colleague Wim Van de Voorde from the Department of Forensic Biomedical Sciences at the University of Leuven for this practice-based information.

etc.[8] In a simple version, Saint Bartholomew is depicted holding his attribute, a knife. The flaying can be represented in different positions, with either reservation and competent dedication or brutal and cruel violence on the part of the flayers. In most cases, Bartholomew is being flayed while lying stretched out on a kind of table or rack, or, in exceptional cases, on the ground. We see the saint being flayed at a leg, at both arms and a leg or both legs, at an arm and a knee, at the chest and a leg, at the torso and lower torso, or at a shoulder and a leg. When executed on a standing person, the flaying is particularly bloody and shocking. The flayed Bartholomew can also be represented standing, dressed while holding his skin in his hands or nude with his skin hanging over his shoulder or draped around him.

Loyset Liédet's miniature in *La Sale* is of the brutal type. It is clearly rooted in the rich tradition of depictions of the flaying of Bartholomew. But this iconographical tradition was so widespread that, even without this link, it must have influenced David in the way he conceived his flaying scene.

Besides these, there is another example that deserves our attention. In the *Belles heures du Duc de Berry*, illustrated by the Limburg Brothers between 1405 and 1409 (Metropolitan Museum of Art, Cloisters Collection, Acc. No. 54.1.1) we find a masterfully depicted representation of the martyrdom of Saint Bartholomew (Meiss and Beatson 1975, nr. 79, f. 161). The apostle is tied to a table with ropes over his abdomen and thighs, while three executioners perform the flaying. On the right side, behind the table, the King and four assistants are watching. In the left corner, we see a city (Fig. 7.2). A further comparison with David's flaying scene reveals some interesting facts. The executioner at the centre quietly cuts into an arm, twice. The most active man in the miniature, a knife between his teeth, is on the left side, brutally opening the skin at the chest. David placed the magistrates at this side of the picture, so that it is too crowded there for a detailed rendition of the flaying scene. The artist depicts the executioner as he slices the skin off the chest—as if it were a jacket to be taken off. On the right side of the painting, David, by moving the King and assistants to the other side, created more space for an executioner labouring at stripping off the skin. The latter needs both hands to strip the opened skin of the left leg over the foot. In order to free his hands, he is holding the knife between his teeth. This gesture is similar to Liédet's miniature (Van der Velden 1995a), but is ultimately borrowed from the Bartholomew tradition. Undoubtedly, the Limburg Brothers' miniature was an inspiration for David's central structure of his flaying scene. It most likely offered him a more restrained model, in contrast with the brutality of the Liédet miniature, which was acceptable in the context of a group portrait and reconcilable with the dignity of the Bruges magistrates.[9] The conclusion, fitting David's familiarity with, and even activity in, miniature painting (Ainsworth 1998, p. 44; Graybowski 1985), is that the

[8]Detailed illustration would exceed the limits of this contribution; see for some images Freeman 2008; Stracke 2015).

[9]The Limburg Brothers were not the first to depict concentrated working executioners (Kay 2006, p. 48–53). On the influence of the Limburg Brothers on later miniatures and painting (see Clarck 2005; Dückers 2009).

iconographical tradition in representing the flaying of Saint Bartholomew was both a direct and indirect source of inspiration for David's flaying of Sisamnes.[10]

7.3.3 Anatomical Dissection and Anatomy Lessons

Gerard David was highly skilled in rendering the structures of the human body in an anatomically correct way. Representing the active human body was a real challenge to artists, resulting in a continuous incentive for incisive anatomic exploration, despite the general public's distrust of, and the opposition against, dissection. Opening the body was less general. Dissection of the dead body was practised on demand or with the consent of the family in order to find a medical explanation for death. It was, already in the Late Middle Ages, often ordered by civil authorities in a forensic context of suspicious death. Varying from region to region, with early success in Italy (Bologna), dissection was also organised several times a year in public sessions from the fourteenth century onwards. Apart from sessions such as these, we can see a growing anatomical practice inspired purely by a scientific urge for knowledge. As a result, public sessions became more solemn anatomy lessons (Egmond 2003, p. 108–127; Heckscher 1958, p. 42–51; Park 1994, 2005; Sournia 1991, p. 164–168 and 228–229).

We don't know the specific attitude of civil and religious authorities in Bruges towards anatomy and public dissection, nor whether David had the opportunity to attend public anatomy sessions or not. In any case, his panel does not contain convincing evidence he did. On the flayed leg and foot, veins are visible, but to obtain such a result, the flaying should probably have been done in a more diligent way than is shown in the painting. In fact, the veins in the flayed leg are in accordance with the raised veins in the underarms of Sisamnes and the bluish veins at the surface of a pale skin in the arms of Christ in David's *Deposition*, also painted in the late 1490s. Ainsworth (1998, p. 128) points at the similarity between the body of Sisamnes and the body of Christ in his *Deposition* and in Christ *Nailed to the Cross* (ca. 1480).[11] Perhaps more revealing for the relation to proper anatomy are the details in the careful flaying of the right arm. The thickness and leather structure of the skin, the final bits of muscle fibres: is this really human skin? What David saw with his own eyes, was it human flaying, or rather animal flaying (Decker and John 2015, p. 8; Payne 2015, p. 223)? According to Homann (1995,

---

[10]Therefore, the transposition of David's flaying scene to the painting *Flaying of Bartholomew* (Bruges, Museum Brugse Vrije, sixteenth century, Paumen (2016c, p. 101)) is maybe less a form of plagiarism than it is a logical step in a historical iconographical evolution.

[11]The first representations of anatomical lessons might have been inspired by paintings on the lamentation of Christ (Heckscher 1958, p. 86–87). See also other connections between these early works of David: the motive of the tightening of the cord to immobilise the victim in *The Flaying of Sisamnes* and *Christ nailed to the Cross*, and the shaved brown dog in both, and in a *Crucifixion* of ca. 1475 (Ainsworth 1998, p. 93–98 and 125–128).

col. 1466), in various regions, executioners were assisted by skinners, and skinning dead cattle was often an additional source of income reserved for the executioner by local authorities (see also Borchert 2013, p. 225). The flaying of animals was thus far more common than that of criminals in the Bruges of David's time. Hence, painters would have had a much higher chance of being able to observe the skinning of animals than that of a human being.

7.3.4 Representations of the Upcoming Public Anatomy Lesson

Representations of flaying in medical handbooks are perhaps more probable as an influence on David's the flaying scene than the growing success of public anatomy lessons (Heckscher 1958, p. 86).[12] The fact that, in David's painting, people are placed closely together, directly behind and around the table on which the corrupt judge is positioned, is a perfect stepping stone for the transformation of an anatomy lesson into a group portrait. A miniature in the *Chirurgia* of Guy de Chauliac, a widely known medical handbook from 1363, offers a brilliant example.[13] We see the three traditional actors: the *lector*-professor on a higher seat, the *sector* (surgeon; here two men) behind the table, at work on a corpse with opened abdomen, the *ostensor* pointing with a small stick at features of interest mentioned by the *lector*, and a technical assistant and instruments in the foreground. Next to the *ostensor*, there are five spectators commenting on the spectacle, and on the left, we see three more spectators, two of whom are women. It is a short leap from this visual rendition to David's scene of the flaying of Sisamnes. Another good example is the famous woodcut illustrating Joannes Ketham's editions of Mondino de Luzzi's *Fasciculo de Medicina* (1493–1494).[14]

The influence of these representations of anatomy lessons can also be traced in the iconographical tradition of the martyrdom of Saint Bartholomew. A comparison of Stefan Lochner's *Martyrdom of Saint Bartholomew* (after 1435) with a similar panel by one of his pupils (second half of the fifteenth century), probably part of an altarpiece in Colmar, is telling (Zehnder 1993, p. 359–360 and 468). Lochner gives an original, particularly brutal version of a traditional flaying. His painting emits a feeling of hate and violence, while the atmosphere of the pupil's work is that of an interesting and instructive event. Here two executioners are at work, while, behind the table and bent forward slightly, spectators and a King (or judge) are looking in

[12] A lecture by professor Bob Van Hee, (Antwerp University), 'De anatomische iconografie van Vesalius', held on 16 October 2014 at the occasion of the Vesalius exhibition in Leuven was inspiring.

[13] Montpellier, Musée Anger, Sournia et al. (1980, p. 774).

[14] Heckscher (1958, p. 47). See also *Bartholomaeus Anglicus* (end of the fifteenth century) in Heckscher (1958, p. 84–86); Jost Ammann (1565) with striking isocephalie, *ibidem*, p. 27, 39 and 52.

concentration and talking to each other. The scene is almost a mimicry of an anatomy lesson, with the exception of the executioner closest to the leg (Fig. 7.3).[15] An influence—direct, or through intermediate designs—of the Colmar altar piece on Gerard David is hard to prove. Yet, it is still an attractive hypothesis. The stretched position of the body in both the Colmar and Bruges paintings is in accordance with the model in the anatomy lessons, although the same model is also present in the older Bartholomew tradition.[16] On the right side of the Colmar panel, two men are discussing. We find the same motive at the far left of David's composition, where it perfectly occludes a range of magistrates around the King. The background scene with the young judge forced David to free the right side of his composition, which then again influenced his adaptation of the *Belles Heures* miniature. The emotionless faces here, alternately looking straight ahead and down at the flaying, are revealing by contrast. In depicting a flaying scene, it was impossible for David to maintain the nearly passionate expression of curiosity and interest in the Colmar panel and the representations of anatomy lessons. This much commented and perhaps not yet satisfactory explained lack of emotion could also be seen as a somewhat forced effort to avoid any association with the emotional charge of such a model. Furthermore, compared to the brutality of Lochner's *Martyrdom*, David and Lochner's pupil share the moderation of the Limburg Brothers' miniature which both might have known and used independently. This becomes clear through a comparison of the middle executioner.[17]

Circulating representations of anatomy lessons and perhaps also their transposition to the Colmar Martyrdom of Saint Bartholomew may have reinforced the aldermen in Bruges in their wish to figure personally in their new *exemplum justitiae*. They could also have inspired Gerard David in integrating his commissioners in his painting, in a way that was acceptable for them in a flaying scene converted to a group portrait.

7.3.5 Multiple Sources

Van der Velden's (1995b, p. 57–58) reference to the Loyset Liédet miniature was a first step in the search for the iconographical sources of David's *Judgment of*

[15]The reclining brute in the centre of Lochner's panel returns, seen from the back, in the Colmar representation and evokes the executioner in front of Liédet's miniature, in which David also found inspiration for his man with a knife on the right (Fig. 7.2). The same figure is also present in other Bartholomew miniatures.

[16]This is in contrast with the more dramatically upraised head and shoulders by Lochner, possibly influenced by the Limburg miniature. David also prefers a traditional diagonal setup of the table to the horizontal position in the anatomy lessons and the Colmar panel.

[17]See also Höfler (1987–1988) on the familiarities between later representations of the martyrdom of the apostles and the tradition of French manuscript illustration, and the work of the Limburg Brothers, especially their Bartholomew martyrdom.

Cambyses, especially of the flaying scene. He suggested that Liédet could have doubled his *Judgment of Cambyses* with a *Martyrdom of Saint Bartholomew*, which then could have inspired Gerard David. What he rightly calls 'a pure conjecture' now proves to be an imaginative outlook on what, up until now, was virtually *terra incognita.*[18]

We can find some further connections with David's *Judgment of Cambyses* in an engraving representing the *Death of Regulus*. This picture is often overlooked, and was published by Colard Mansion in Bruges in 1476. In it, Regulus, a Roman commander cruelly executed in Carthage, is lying on a nail bed on a scaffold erected in a cityscape, which includes groups of onlookers (Graybowski 1985, p. 188–189).[19] When we compare the elongated body and the (young) man tightening the cords in both the David panel and the Mansion print, the resemblances are obvious.

We can also compare the engraving *The Flaying of Marsyas*, a woodcut in Sebastian Brant's *Das Narrenschiff* (1495), conceived in pure Bartholomew tradition. A direct influence is hard to prove, but the woodcut is part of a rich iconographical universe surrounding Gerard David, to which his *Flaying of Sisamnes* is indebted in many ways. Borrowing elements from several different sources in inventing panel compositions is one of the most characteristic working methods of Gerard David (Ainsworth 1998; Graybowski 1985, p. 189), which we also recognise in his masterfully constructed *Judgment of Cambyses*.

7.4 From Gerard David to the Eighteenth Century

7.4.1 Half a Century of Diverse Approaches

The literary tradition of the Cambyses story already had an extensive past before it was joined, and in some way marginalised, by the visual arts (Van der Velden 1995a, p. 16). Gerard David was the first panel painter—apart from a lost and otherwise unknown work in Mons (Van der Velden 1995a, p. 22, spec. fn. 79)—to take up the challenge. In the first half of the sixteenth century, there are a few examples of a threefold elaboration of the story. However, the tradition quickly started to reduce it to two or even one scene(s): the installation of the young judge, sometimes with the flaying on the background.

A Touching Bribery Scene. The scenes of the bribery and of Sisamnes' arrest disappear from the iconography very soon after Gerard David's painting. On a side

[18]See also his reference to the booksellers' guild house in Bruges, in a monastery dedicated to Saint Bartholomew, and compare this with the stimulating study of Kay (2006, p. 47–56) on writing on animal skin and some specially well-cared manuscripts holding the story of Saint Bartholomew's flaying.

[19]The engraving is published in a printed edition of Giovanni Boccaccio's *De Casibus Virorum et Feminarum Illustrium;* image in Hollstein (1955, p. 121).

panel of an *exemplum justitiae* in the city hall of Hoorn (Holland, Westfries Museum, after 1522) the bribery, the seated Otanes and the flaying of Sisamnes are shown in the foreground of the composition, rather clumsily structured around the young judge's seat. The enthroned judge reminds us of David's rendition. The flaying scene is awkward, but the bribery scene is original and touching. Sisamnes, sitting on his throne, accepts a coin in an opened hand, in this way confounding his son. The latter is witnessing the scene, and is mildly comforted by the arm gesture of a friend (Fris 1986, p. 634–635).[20] The same three scenes can also be found together, very probably for the last time, in a drawing by Jan Swart van Groningen (ca. 1495–1563). In the centre, the young judge is sitting on a throne with the skin of his father suspended above him. On both sides of the throne, the bribery and the flaying are represented in the background (Huygebaert et al. 2016, p. 145). The way the skin is draped above the young judge's seat, the latter's really young appearance, and the long rod in his hand fit in a tradition that also inspired the designers of two stained-glass windows from the first decades of that century.

Avoiding Explicit Cruelty. From the point of view of the magistrates, it was probably not a very pleasant prospect to be constantly confronted with a bloody flaying spectacle in the courtroom and in their office. After David, the flaying scene, if represented at all, was generally moved to the background of the image. The explicit and shocking cruelty in the flaying scene still survived in a few stained-glass panels or roundels. These were a form of decoration of city halls and courts that was *en vogue* since the second half of the fifteenth century, and was especially popular during the sixteenth and seventeenth centuries. These panels were often part of a decorative ensemble (Paumen 2016c, p. 98–99; Paumen and Desmet 2016, p. 71–77; Van der Velden 1995a, p. 20–21). A glass panel from the Low Countries in a German private collection (ca. 1515–1525) represents a variant of the traditional flaying on a table. In the background, Otanes is seated on a chair above which the skin is suspended (Paumen 2016c, p. 98–99).[21]

In a marvellous piece of creative iconographic mastery, the artist of a stained-glass roundel, presumably created in the city of Leyden and related to the production of Lucas van Leyden (ca. 1525–1530, collection GG, Belgium), evokes the different aspects of the story (Fig. 7.4).[22] At the left side, the standing Sisamnes, an angry, somewhat arrogant expression on his face, is shown with an eye-catching purse at his girdle, and his right hand just above it.[23] The presence of an officer halfway behind him evokes the arrest. In the foreground, the flaying of the corrupt

[20]Van der Velden (1995a, p. 18) omits the bribery and sees 'Otanes being instructed in the impartial dispensation of justice'.

[21]A glass roundel with the same representation is in the Musée Rolin in Autun (1530), Huygebaert et.al. (2016, p. 196, cat. 41).

[22]Both the panel and the roundel were first signalled to me by Joost Caen and Cees Berserik, who are collaborating in the international inventory-project *Corpus Vitrearum*, on which they already published three volumes, Berserik and Caen 2007–2011–2014. I would like to thank them warmly for their generous cooperation and advice.

[23]Compare with the man in front of the judging Otanes by David.

judge on a low rack is depicted in a way that is similar to the one in the glass panel mentioned above. On the right side, we see an absolutely unique, raging King Cambyses, brandishing the sceptre above his head, his anger directed at the arrested judge standing at the other side.[24] In the background between the standing figures, behind a low wall, the young judge, depressed but encouragingly surrounded, is watching his father being flayed alive. The flaying scene is a severe criticism of the corrupt behaviour of judges. It can be seen as a fair admission of occurring guilt in justice administration, and, if it was publicly accessible, as a humbling message to the general public. The outburst of royal rage enhances this humbling tendency of the image. The fact that the admission of guilt, and certainly the open accusation of a judge were moved to the inner parts of the courthouse, or at least reduced to the dimensions of a small stained-glass window, perhaps reveals some reservation towards open self-accusation and self-criticism from the part of the judicial authorities (see Jacob 1994, p. 75–81).

A glass roundel by the Antwerp glass painter Dirck Vellert (Amsterdam, Rijksmuseum, 1542) shows yet another way of depicting the flaying (Paumen 2016c, p. 99). Sisamnes is now lying on his back on the ground in a group of well-formed wrestling Renaissance bodies. This position has its origin in the Marsyas iconography, which was largely developed in Renaissance Italy. The Otanes seated in the background is related to the first above-mentioned stained-glass representations. The clear-cut open skin behind and halfway above the head of the young judge is also present in the mentioned drawing by Jan Swart's, and will remain successful as a motif up until Peter Paul Rubens.

A Group Portrait Saving the Memory of the Arrest Scene. Gerard David is, with his *Judgment of Cambyses*, seen by some scholars as one of the initiators of the group portrait, a genre which knew a clear development in sixteenth-century Bruges (Wolters van der Wey 2015, p. 72–73; Borchert 2013, p. 225). Other than the already mentioned stained glass, the only other known representation of Sisamnes' arrest was painted by Antonius Claeissens (ca. 1576–1600). However, Claeissens painting is hardly an arrest. It should actually be seen more as a group portrait, presumably of magistrates (Paumen 2016c, p. 96–97). David's flaying scene also influenced the tradition of 'anatomy lessons' as a group portrait of the medical guild that was to flourish in later times and which resulted in Rembrandt's famous *Anatomy Lesson of dr. Nicolas Tulp* (Heckscher 1958, p. 89–90). However, since the representation of the arrest and the flaying was omitted in later renditions of the story, the portrait aspect disappeared from the Cambyses tradition. The series of individually portrayed magistrates on the exterior wings of a Judgment of Cambyses in Namur (*cf. infra*) is a group portrait of another type.

[24]In an e-mail (19 April 2017) Caen and Cees Berserik wrote that most roundels are based on drawings and prints (woodcuts and cupper engravings) which surfaced for many roundels, but have not (yet) been found in this case.

7.4.2 Tradition and Innovation in Representations of the Cambyses Story

A Successful Exemplum. The later iconographical development, concentrated on the essence of an admonitory *exemplum*, is continuous with the first attempts of visualising the Cambyses story in two miniatures from around 1425–1440. In these depictions, the entire story was expressed through a single scene: the young judge with the skin of his father on or near his seat (Van der Velden 1995a, p. 22–27). David, on the other hand, depicted the whole story in a pictorial narrative. Nearly the entire iconographical tradition after him concentrated on one image that perfectly expresses the message of the *exemplum*: in the words of Herodotus: the judge should always 'remember what the judgment-seat is upon which he is sitting'. The flaying of Sisamnes was a negative and gruesome example. With the installation of the young judge, the aldermen had, in a sense, a more positive example and a better possibility for identification: they will all be seen as correct judges who take the admonition in the painted *exemplum* to heart.

The installation of the young judge is usually placed in the front, while the flaying scene is rendered in the background, or even completely omitted. Otanes can be depicted while the King is inviting him to sit down, or when he is already sitting down, having followed the King's instructions. In that case, the King can even be absent. The skin is spread over the seat, is folded and is hanging over the back of the seat, or it is suspended at the back of the seat, halfway as a canopy above the judge's throne. The Cambyses motive was very successful in drawings and prints of legal texts during the sixteenth and seventeenth century (Van der Velden 1995a, p. 24–28). The scarcity of larger panels from the sixteenth century is possibly 'ascribable to the disastrous consequences of renovation and modernisation work carried out in prosperous times' (Van der Velden 1995a, p. 34). In the first half of the seventeenth century, new larger paintings are indeed popular in the aldermen's chambers. One such example is Rubens' painting for the Brussels town hall (Van der Velden 1995a, p. 34–39).

The Legend of Apollo Flaying Marsyas. The flaying of Bartholomew (as general Christian iconography, not in the field of *exempla justitiae*) dominated the iconography in the 'flaying field' before David. For more than a century, the flaying of Sisamnes was mainly represented according to a Bartholomew type, in which the subject is lying on a table or rack. Starting in Italy, the reviving classical legend of Apollo flaying Marsyas brought a powerful impulse for a renewal of this iconographical motive.

The flute-playing satyr Marsyas challenged the god Apollo, with the lyre, to a music competition. The victorious Apollo decided to flay Marsyas as punishment for his *hubris* in competing with a god. Italian Renaissance iconography first looked back at antique models (Rawson 1987). There, Marsyas was tied to a tree, with his hands tied together above his head, or with his arms spread, or seated with his arms tied at his back, awaiting his punishment. Marsyas' position evolved constantly and also diverged: only one arm tied, the other free with a greater possibility for vivid activity; Marsyas hung upside down with his feet tied to the tree; or Marsyas lying on the ground as Dick Vellert's stained glass roundel. In the evolution towards the Baroque period, the iconography exploded in terms of movement, passion, cruelty and blood (Wyss 1996). José de Ribera (1591–1652), who incited the contra-reformist ardour in venerating saints and martyrdom, painted the flaying of Saint Bartholomew and of Marsyas with fervour and painful exuberance (Payne 2015).

The iconography of flaying in the depiction of Bartholomew after David has been influenced deeply by the representations of the flaying of Marsyas. The position on a rack was abandoned in favour of a standing or lying figure, or of intermediate positions. However, because the Cambyses iconography avoided an all-too explicit description of the flaying, there were less opportunities to influence this iconography in the same way. David knew the Marsyas story. In his painting, there is a medallion of the seated Marsyas awaiting his punishment that is part of his Renaissance-inspired adaptations for the *Judgment of Cambyses*. His model in Renaissance Italy was an immensely popular reproduction of the scene on an Augustan cameo (Von Simson 1977). There were some drawings and panels in which, the flaying of Sisamnes in the background is exceptionally executed standing up. With respect to the examples known to me, my hypothesis is that the authors passed some time in Italy.[25] Jan Baptist Saive (I) in Namur is a remarkable exception: on the backside of a portrait panel of the aldermen of Namur (1597), he painted a 'full Marsyas' flaying scene of Sisamnes (Fig. 7.5). The victim is standing upright, his right arm tied to a column above his head, his left arm free in a pathetic gesture, while the executioner is flaying his abdomen (Paumen 2016c, p. 99–100).

Vesalius and Masterly Represented Anatomical Structures of the Human Body. In 1543 Andreas Vesalius published his *De humani corporis fabrica libri septem*. The engravings in the book were of outstanding artistic quality. The book was a milestone in the development of anatomical knowledge, and at the same time a breakthrough in the long-lasting search for artistic mastery in displaying the human body in all its beauty and complexity.[26] Renaissance representations of the flaying of Marsyas and of Saint Bartholomew were profoundly influenced by the evolution of anatomical science,[27] but in the Cambyses tradition, the flaying had to make room for the installation of the young judge on, or in front of, the skin of his father. There is little beauty in a poor drooping skin.

---

[25]This is the case for Vellert (glass roundel), Wtewael (*Thronus iustitiae*) and Faber (panel); Boucquet in Nieuwpoort followed Faber in Emden as his model.

[26]Leonardo da Vinci, Raphael and Michelangelo were all dissecting the human body, (see Choulant 1945).

[27]See the statues of Saint Bartholomew as a Vesalian muscle man, like the one in Milan Cathedral.

7.4.3 Emblematical Reduction, Allegorical Personification, Philosophical Reflection and Human Leather

From the seventeenth century onwards, the story of Cambyses appeared repeatedly as an emblematical reduction to an empty skin, for instance as a front page illustration (Paumen 2016c, p. 102–103; Van der Velden 1995a, p. 28–29). In the late seventeenth century, the representation of Lady Justice became increasingly popular, and started to appear in representations of the installation of the young judge on the skin of his father (Nieuwpoort). This was the beginning of the end of the Cambyses story in the visual arts.

In the last decades, historical studies on violence, pain, and destruction of the body are pullulating. They are renewing historical methods by adding anthropological and philosophical analyses to factual research. Particularly with respect to the flaying motive, they join a series of century-old reflections on the skin and its function of protection and identification, on outer and inner, the skin as both the seat of evil and sin and as a source of renewal (e.g. Bohde 2003; Cohen 2003; Decker et al. 2015; Kay 2006; Payne 2015).[28]

In the Cambyses tradition, Sisamnes (just as, in most cases, Bartholomew) is flayed in a way that preserves the entire skin. In another tradition, neat strips of skin are cut off the backs of Crispinus and Crispinianus, patron saints of the shoemakers.[29] Herodotus writes that the judge's seat was covered with what appeared to be leather strips of Sisamnes skin. In medieval literature, it was sometimes said that Sisamnes' skin was nailed to the seat, but in some representations, it rather looks quivering and freshly flayed. From medieval to modern history, the sources reveal traces of, and discussions on, the use of human leather, e.g. for bookbinding.[30]

7.5 Conclusion

Gerard David's *Judgment of Cambyses* was a milestone for the transposition of the Cambyses story to the visual arts. He represented the story in four scenes: the bribery, the arrest of the judge, the flaying and the installation of the son on his father's skin, spread over the seat. The widespread iconographical tradition of the flaying of Saint Bartholomew was a direct inspiration for David and some miniaturists. Most likely, diligent observation of animal flaying—and not a judicial practice of human flaying—resulted in a refined but cruel realism. Upcoming representations of an anatomical lesson very probably offered some useful

[28]See also the contribution by Carolin Behrmann in this volume.

[29]*Martyrdom of Saints Crispinus and Crispinianus*, second half fifteenth century, triptych, Warsaw, (Bücken and Steyaert 2013, p. 247–251; Freedberg 1976, p. 129–131).

[30]See (Bohde 2003, p. 28 (waistcoat); Jung 2007, p. 57) (strips of human skin used by midwifes against cramps); Kay 2006, p. 37 (bookbinding)).

inspiration for the elaboration of an early hidden group portrait of Bruges' aldermen. Following the creation of David's painting for the Bruges aldermen, bribery and arrest quickly disappeared in later renditions of the subject. Artists concentrated on drawing and painting the installation of the young judge on the skin of his father, sometimes with the flaying scene in the background. Hence the iconography of flaying, now dominated by the Marsyas legend and the artistic expression of anatomical structures of the human body, was less important in the Cambyses tradition. The Cambyses story ended with an emblematic empty skin, and was finally supplanted by a symbolic image of Lady Justice.

References

Ainsworth MW (1998) Gerard David. Purity of vision in an age of transition. Ludion, Ghent

Barron WRJ (1978) A propos de quelques cas d'écorchement dans les romans anglais et français du moyen âge. In: Lods J (ed) Mélanges de littérature du moyen âge au XXe siècle. École normale supérieure de jeunes filles, Paris, pp 49–68

Barron WRJ (1981) The penalties for treason in medieval life and literature. J Mediev Hist 7:187–202

Berserik CJ (Kees), Caen JMA (Joost) (eds) (2007–2011–2014) Silver-stained roundels and unipartite panels before the French revolution. Flanders, vol 3. Brepols, Turnhout

Bohde D (2003) Skin and the search for the interior: the representation of flaying in the art and anatomy of the cinquecento. In: Egmond F, Zwijnenberg R, pp 10–47

Borchert T-H (2013) Meesterwerk van Van Eyck tot Rubens in detail, 222–235. Lannoo, Tielt

Bücken V, Steyaert G (2013) De erfenis van Rogier Van der Weyden. De schilderkunst in Brussel 1450–1520. Lannoo, Tielt

Clarck GT (2005) De invloed van de Gebroeders van Limburg in Frankrijk en de Zuidelijke Nederlanden, 1400–1460. In: Dückers et al. 2015, pp 209–235

Choulant L (1945) History and bibliography of anatomic illustration, trans. Mortimer Frank. Hafner Publishing Company, New York

Cohen E (2003) The expression of pain in the later middle ages: deliverance, acceptance and infamy. In: Egmond F, Zwijnenburg R, pp 195–219

Decker JR (2015) Introduction: spectacular unmaking: creative destruction, destructive creativity. In: Decker et al. 2015, pp 1–16

Decker JR, Kirkland-Ives M, Levy A (eds) (2015) Death, torture and the broken body in European Art 1300–1650. Taylor & Francis, Oxford

Dückers R (2009) A close encounter? The Limbourg brothers and illumination in the Netherlands in the first half of the fifteenth century. In: Dückers R, Roelofs P (eds), pp 149–189

Duvillaret H (1943) Essai sur le droit pénal en Savoye (1441–1723). PhD thesis, Université de Grenoble. Plancher, Bonneville

Egmond F (2003) Execution, dissection, pain and infamy. A morphological investigation. In: Egmond F, Zwijnenberg R (eds), pp 92–127

Egmond F, Zwijnenberg R (eds) (2003) Bodily extremities. Preoccupations with the human body in early modern European culture. Ashgate, Farnham

Favier J (1978) Philippe-le-Bel. Fayard, Paris

Freedberg D (1976) The early counter-reformation in antwerp. Burlingt Mag 118:128–138

Fris A (1986) Het Hoornse gerechtigheidsdrieluik ontleed. Antiek. Tijdschrift voor liefhebbers en kenners van oude kunst en kunstnijverheid 20.10:628–639

Freeman J (2008) St. Bartholomew and bookbindings: happy St Bartholomew's day! http://britishlibrary.typepad.co.uk/digitisedmanuscripts/2014/08/st-bartholomew-and-bookbindings-happy-st-bartholomews-day.html. Accessed 4 April 2017

Graybowski SD 1985 (1975) Gerard David and manuscript illumination in the low countries, 1480–1509. PhD Case Western Reserve University, Department of Art. University Microfilm International, Ann Arbor

Heckscher WS (1958) Rembrandt's anatomy of Dr. Nicolaas Tulp. An iconological study. University Press, New York

Höfler J (1987–1988) Zu den Apostelmartyrien vom Weltgerichtsaltar Stephan Lochners. Wallraf-Richartz Jahrbuch. Westdeutsches Jahrbuch für Kunstgeschichte 48–49:65–76

Hollstein FWH (1955) Dutch and Flemish etchings, engravings and woodcuts ca. 1450–1700, vol XII. Hertzberger, Amsterdam

Homann HD (1995) Schinder [Knackers]. In: Lexikon des Mittelalters, vol VII, col. 1466. LexMa Verlag, Munich

Huygebaert S, Martyn G, Paumen V, Van Poucke T (eds) (2016) The art of law. Three centuries of justice depicted (exh. cat. Bruges). Lannoo, Tielt

Jacob R (1994) Images de la justice: essai sur l'iconographie judiciaire du Moyen Âge à l'âge classique. Léopard d'Or, Paris

Jung EG (ed) (2007) Kleine Kulturgeschichte der Haut, mit 120 überwiegend farbigen Abbildungen. Steinkopff, Darmstadt

Kay S (2006) Original skin: flaying, reading, and thinking in the legend of saint bartholomew and other works. J Mediev Early Mod Stud 36(1):35–73

Maes LTh (1947) Vijf eeuwen stedelijk strafrecht. De Sikkel, Antwerpen

Meiss M, Beatson EH (eds) (1975) The belles heures of jean, duke of berry: the cloisters, the metropolitan museum of art. G. Braziller, New York (NY)

Park K (1994) The criminal and the saintly body: autopsy and dissection in renaissance Italy. Renaiss Q 47(1): 1–33

Park K (2005) Anatomy. In: Glick TF, Livesey SJ, Wallis F (eds) Medieval science, technology and medicine: an encyclopaedia. Routledge, New York, pp 32–34

Paumen V (2016a) The skin of the judge: the judgment of Cambyses. In: Huygebaert et al. 2016, pp 81–91

Paumen V (2016b) An illuminated example. In: Huygebaert et al. 2016, pp 93–95

Paumen V (2016c) The popularity of the father's skin: Cambyses after Gerard David. In: Huygebaert et al. 2016, pp 96–103

Paumen V, Desmet M (2016) Translucent exempla. In: Huygebaert et al. 2016, pp. 71–77

Payne E (2015) Bodies suspended in space and time. Execution, suffering and spectatorship in Ribera's martyrdom scenes. In: Decker et al. 2015, pp 213–230

Pinkus A (2015) Guido da Siena and the four modes of violence. In: Decker et al. 2015, pp 19–34

Rawson PB (1987) The myth of Marsyas in the Roman visual arts. An iconographic study. B.A.R, Oxford

Réau L (1958) Iconographie de l'art chrétien. 3. Iconographie des saints. Presses Universitaires de France, Paris

Ridderbos B (2014) Schilderkunst in de Bourgondische Nederlanden. Davidsfonds, Leuven

Schowe U (1994) Mit Haut und Haar. Idiomatisierungsprozesse bei sprichwörtlichen Redensarten aus den Mittelalterlichen Strafrecht. In: Germanistische Arbeiten zu Sprache und Kulturgeschichte, vol XXVII. Peter Lang, Frankfurt am Main

Shackleton B, David R (eds and trans.) (2000) Memorable doings and sayings. Valerius maximus. In: The Loeb classical library, vol 493. Harvard University Press, Cambridge

Sournia J-C (1991) Histoire de la médecine et des médecins. Larousse, Paris

Sournia J-C, Poulet J, Martiny M (eds) (1980). Illustrierte Geschichte der Medizin, vol III. Andreas & Andreas, Salzburg

Stracke R (2015) Saint Bartholomew: the iconography. http://www.christianiconography.info/bartholomew.html. Accessed 23 May 2017

Van der Velden H (1995a) Cambyses for example: the origins and function of an exemplum iustitiae in Netherlandish art of the fifteenth, sixteenth and seventeenth centuries. Simiolus 23(1):5–39

Van der Velden H (1995b) Cambyses reconsidered: Gerard David's exemplum iustitiae for Bruges Town Hall. Simiolus 23(1):40–62
Van Miegroet HJ (1989) Gerard David. Mercatorfonds, Antwerp
Von Simson O (1977) Gerard Davids Gerechtigkeitsbild und der spätmittelalterliche Humanismus. In: Festschrift Wolfgang Braunfels, ed. Friederich Piel and Jörg Traeger. Erst Wasmuth, Tübingen, pp 349–356
Wolters van der Wey B (2015) Corporate splendour. Civic group portraits in Brabant 1585–1800. A social, typological and iconographic approach. In: Pictura nova. Studies in 16th and 17th-century Flemish painting and drawing, vol XVIII. Brepols, Turnhout
Wyss E (1996) The myth of Apollo and Marsyas in the art of the Italian renaissance: an inquiry into the meaning of images. Associated University Presses, London
Zehnder FG (ed) (1993) Stefan Lochner, Meister zu Köln. Herkunft, Werke, Wirkung (exh. cat. Cologne). Wallraf-Richartz-Museum, Cologne

Raf Verstegen studied history (candidate), law and canon law (*iuris utriusque doctor*) at the University of Leuven, where he held the chair of Roman law from 1977 to 2004. He was also teaching, publishing and advising in the field of educational law. After his retirement in 2004 he continued for ten years his activities in the field of law and education. Since several years his main research interests focus on art history and local history.

Figures

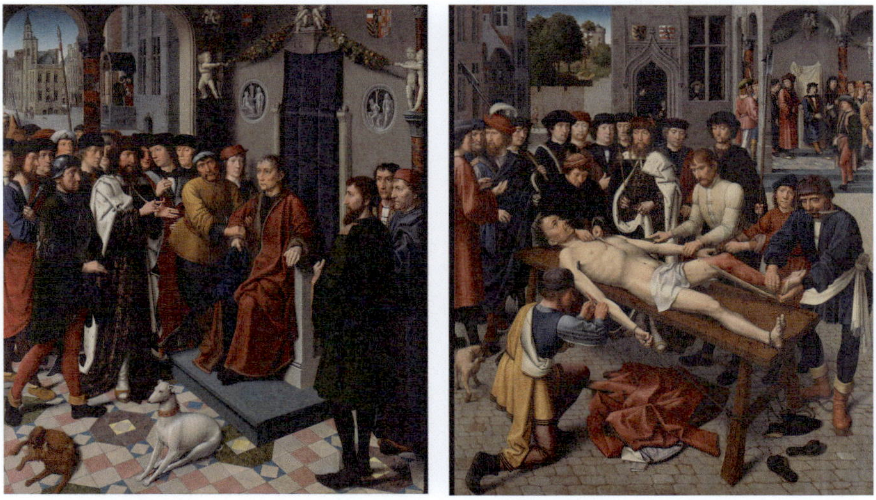

Fig. 7.1 Gerard David, *Judgment of Cambyses*, 1498, oil on panel, 182.3 × 318.6 cm, Bruges, Groeningemuseum, inv. nr. 0000.GRO0040.I-0041.I, © www.lukasweb.be—Art in Flanders vzw, photo Hugo Maertens

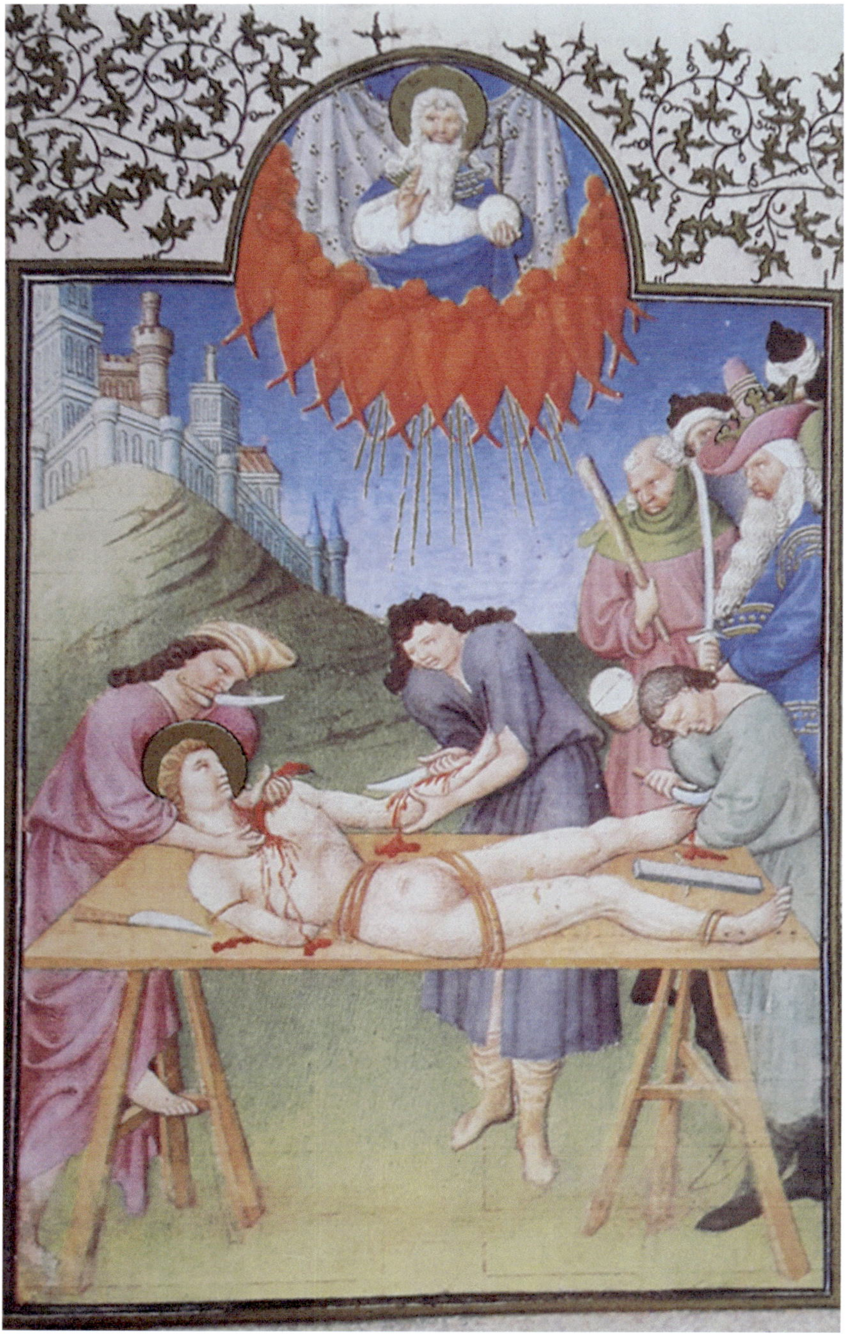

Fig. 7.2 Limburg Brothers, *Martyrdom of Saint Bartholomew*, miniature, 1407–1409, in *Belles heures du duc Jean de Berry*, f. 161, New York, The Cloisters, The Metropolitan Museum of Art, (Meiss and Beatson 1975)

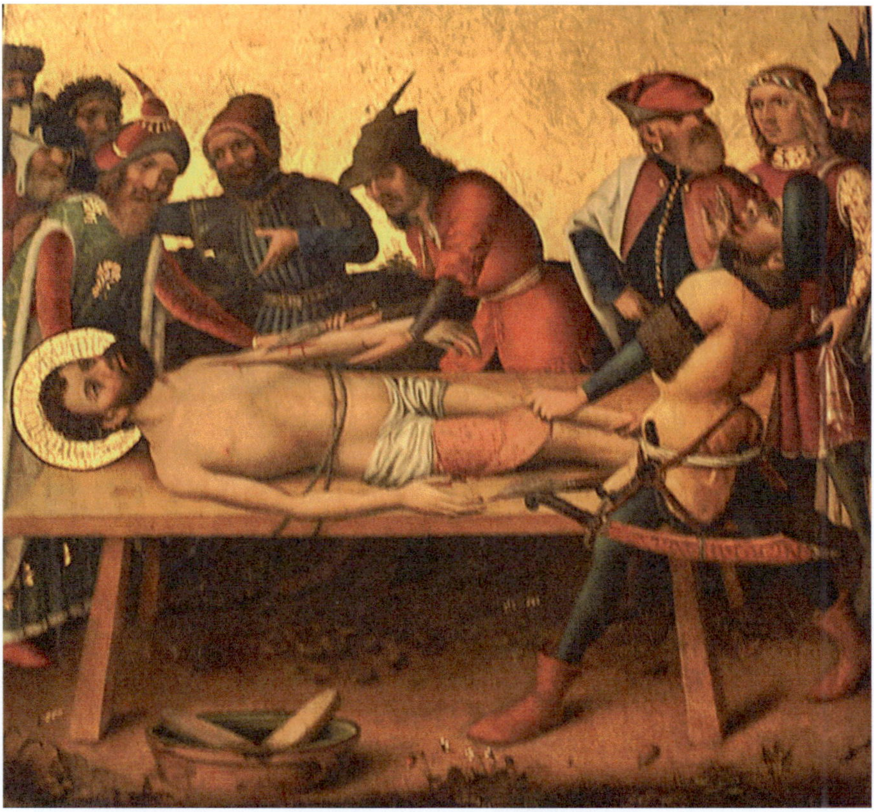

Fig. 7.3 Scholar of Stephan Lochner, *Martyrdom of Saint Bartholomew*, second half fifteenth century, oil on panel, Rome, Pinacotheca Vaticana © http://www.christianiconography.info/bartholomew.html

Fig. 7.4 *Judgment of Cambyses*, glass roundel, ca. 1525–1530, Belgium, private collection GG, © J. Caen and C. Berserik

Fig. 7.5 Jan Baptiste Saive (I), *The Judgment of Cambyses* (left panel), 1597, oil on panel, 117 × 82 cm, Namur, Collections Ville de Namur, © KIK-IRPA, Brussels, photo Jean-Luc Elias

Chapter 8
Multi-layered Functions of Early Modern Courtroom Equipment: Lüneburg for Example

Ann-Kathrin Hubrich

Abstract In early modern Europe, courtrooms were often equipped with a wide range of artworks: paintings, sculpture and furniture as artistic mediums as well as the architecture itself all served to express a certain idea of how justice has been understood or how it was supposed to be communicated to the public. This paper argues that these artistic programmes fulfilled multi-layered functions in their judicial surroundings. The status of images as both material and immaterial objects enables their metaphorical potential, and also allows them to take part as agents in the process of administering justice. The *Niedergericht* ('lower court') in Lüneburg (Lower Saxony, Germany) serves as an exceptional example of the complex meaning of courtroom decorations. The *Niedergericht* itself is decorated with several paintings showing, among other things, stories from the Old and the New Testament. These artworks create an image of justice which, on the one hand, is to be seen as a genealogical derivation of law from heavenly authority, and on the other hand as a meta-comment on the juridical practice of the time. Therefore, courtroom decoration enforces the law and the administering of justice.

For a more detailed analysis, see my dissertation-in-progress, in which I examine the way in which courtrooms in the Early Modern Era were equipped. In my opinion, the interior decoration of courtrooms was highly connected to the legal function of the room itself. As a consequence, the courtroom can be seen as a place where legal practice and visual culture are intertwined. My key questions are based on an interdisciplinary approach: What function did art have in the legal context? Why was there a need to decorate courtrooms in the first place? What kind of iconography do we find in courtrooms? How did members of the court act and interact with their surroundings?

A.-K. Hubrich (✉)
Department of Art History, Graduate School Humanities,
University of Hamburg, Hamburg, Germany
e-mail: Annkathrin.Hubrich@gmail.com

S. Huygebaert et al. (eds.), *The Art of Law*, Ius Gentium: Comparative Perspectives on Law and Justice 66, https://doi.org/10.1007/978-3-319-90787-1_8

8.1 Introduction

'The judge's chambers should be clean and furnished with pictures, and display good, old, wise sayings to be inspired by with wisdom and knowledge; for it is said: seeing provokes reflection; and without a doubt this is true' (Van der Velden 1995, p. 15; see also Martyn 2016, p. 22).

The statement of Jan Matthijsen, a court clerk, in his *Rechtsboek van den Briel* from around 1400 gives us some basic information about how court and deliberation rooms were seen and how paintings were perceived in his time (Martyn 2016, p. 22). As one can deduct from the quote, the choice of interior decoration of early modern courtrooms was not a coincidence. That the chambers 'should be [...] furnished' implies the underlying concept of setting up a courtroom. By asking for good, old, wise sayings, Matthijsen implies that the decoration should embody positive values, and in this way influence the observer. The line 'seeing provokes reflection' refers to the iconic nature of images, of their specific quality as media of communication, which is seen as a potential source of knowledge. In my understanding of this quote, courtrooms are not to be considered as given entities, but as spaces in need of furnishing. As such, they need to be constructed and normatively regulated. The scenography of early modern courtrooms, I argue, played a key role in the process of administering justice. As I will show, the function of the interior design was multi-layered.

In Germany, the fifteenth and sixteenth century were characterised by a profound change in terms of legal concepts (Strauss 1986, p. 65). The reception of Roman law marked a crucial social and cultural development that affected the entire legal system. Not only were trained professionals introduced and employed in the process of administering justice. The requirements in terms of documentation changed as well. Written law was introduced into the modern courtroom and, judicial transcripts for documentation purposes became a necessity (Strauss 1986, p. 77). Revisions in law-enforcement had an impact on the places of jurisdiction as well. Administering justice moved from the open to interior courtrooms (Blümle 2011, p. 28; Klemmer et al. 1993, p. 18). Town halls can be considered as an important pillar of the emerging civic societies (Albrecht 2004). 'The town hall was the focus of civic pride and an expression of the city's wealth, power and prestige and this was emphasised by the building's decorations' (Van der Velden 1995, p. 5). Besides many other functions, town halls served as places for legal practice. These places of jurisdiction were often equipped with a wide range of artwork. Paintings, sculpture and furniture as artistic mediums, as well as the architecture itself, all served to express a certain idea of justice. Hugo van der Velden (1995, p. 5) argues that 'the dispensation of justice was so important as to give rise to an iconography of justice'. The artistic programmes of courtrooms were often inspired by earlier models, such as the interior decorations of churches (Troescher 1939, p. 139–214). Soon a canon of motifs to choose from was established, and the majority of iconographies started following the same tradition. Nevertheless, there were still certain images, stories or combinations of motifs that could vary greatly from town to town.

8.2 The Artistic Programme of Lüneburg's Lower Court

The so called *Niedergericht* ('lower court') which is part of the town hall in Lüneburg (Lower Saxony, Germany) is a great example of early modern courtroom decorations, because of its rich decor and in view of its state of preservation (Fig. 8.1). It is equipped with furniture and decorated with several paintings showing stories from the Old and New Testament: *The Last Judgment*, *The Judgment of Daniel* (Fig. 8.2), *The Judgment of Solomon* (*Fig.* 8.3), a representation of Trinity (Fig. 8.4) and a painting with the coat of arms of Lüneburg. These pictures, as well as the representations of the virtues Pax (peace) (Fig. 8.5) and Justitia (justice), create an 'image' of justice which, on the one hand, can be seen as a construction for judges and members of the court, and on the other hand serves as an ideal for legal practice. The lower court is placed in the north east corner of the façade of the town hall (Fig. 8.1). With its open structure, it gives the public a more or less unobstructed view of what is happening inside. A wooden barrier, and later on an iron gate, separates the public from the inner space, in which only the judicial personnel was allowed (Obert 2014, p. 137). Each member of the court and its personnel was assigned a certain place in the room.[1] When a trial took place, the painting with the coat of arms was folded up, and the representation of the Trinity became visible, as did *The Judgment of Solomon*. In front of the *Judgment of Solomon*—the most prominent spot within the *Niedergericht*—the *Vogt* (representative of the Prince) and the two *Ratsherren* (councillors) were placed. The following remarks will show that the courtroom decoration and its surroundings and the judicial practice were highly intertwined. My main goal is to trace the function of art in this predominantly judicial context.

8.3 Images as Agents Between Heavenly Authority and Mundane Realm of Jurisdiction

When we take a closer look at the architectural setting, it is clear that these paintings are highly connected to their surrounding structure. They fit perfectly into the given frame, by filling in the blank space of the arcade arches. *The Last Judgment*—reading the pictorial programme from the left to the right—is the starting point. With its basic differentiation between good and evil, it can be read as a keynote comment on law and justice. Besides this, it is also a warning to the judges on the

[1]The precise seating arrangement was probably as reconstructed by Katrina Obert. On the left side (that is beneath *The Last Judgment*) the *Vorspraken* (advocates) were seated. Alongside next to them (beneath *The Judgment of Daniel*) probably several more *Vorspraken* were seated as well as a clerk. In front of the judge would be the claimant party as well as the prosecutor. In comparison to the other judicial actors, they were standing, whilst *Vorspraken* and judge were sitting down during the trial (schematic illustration in Obert 2014, p. 137).

one hand, and a legitimation for passing judgment on earth until the Last Day on the other. Christ is shown as the Judge of the World, flanked by angels protruding from the clouds. They carry a sword and a lily, both symbols of jurisdiction, representing the full force of the law and clemency, respectively (Martyn 2016; Merzbacher 1994a, p. 524; 1994b, p. 136–137; Pfister-Burkhalter 1994, p. 101). Mary and John the Baptist appear in their role as intercessors, sitting among a group of saints. Trumpet-playing angels proclaim the inauguration of God's reign. The composition is divided into two parts. While the upper half of the painting is dedicated to the inhabitants of heaven, the bottom half shows people rising from their graves. The saved souls are being sent up to heaven by angels, while the damned are thrown into hell, envisaged as the gaping mouth of a huge dragon-like beast. The painting thus depicts the metaphorical separation of sheep and goats as written in the gospel of Matthew, and as such follows a traditional visualisation of the Last Judgment (Mt. 24). A man in the foreground is looking in the direction of the viewer, as an invitation to get involved in the story. At the same time, however, his gaze is a warning for all those to be judged, which means absolutely everybody. This staring figure forms a bridge between the pictorial space and the real space of the observer. The inner pictorial scene is supposed to be related to the events in the courtroom. As the viewer is directly addressed, he is part of the story, whether he wants to or not.

The presence of the World Judgment motif in a courtroom stems from a long-lasting tradition of church decorations (Troescher 1939, p. 139–214). This parallel between divine and secular jurisdiction can also be found in German law books. Like the general advice given by Matthijsen to install paintings in courtrooms, the *Glosse zum Sächsischen Weichbildrecht* from around 1400 mentions that the motif of the Last Judgment is specifically advisable in order to remind the judges of the fact that they themselves are to be judged for whatever judgment they pass. 'Wherever a judge is passing a judgment, at the same time and at the same place God himself is sitting in his heavenly court above the judge and above the aldermen, and that is why every judge should have the strict and severe tribunal of the Lord painted inside the town hall'.[2]

The cited gloss expresses that, at the very same time when judges administer justice on earth, God metaphorically administers justice above them. *The Last Judgment* puts each trial under divine patronage. The visual representation served as a reminder, both for judges and for those who were to be judged to hold the holy power in high regard (Resnik and Curtis 2011, p. 12).

[2]Quoted after Pleister and Schild (1988, p. 71), see also Haupt (2000, p. 55), Lederle (1937, p. 7–8), trans. A-KH. The original quotation says: '*Wenn wo der richter mit orteiln richtit, in der selbien stat, unde in der selbien stunde, sitzit got in sinem gotlichen gerichte obir den richter, unde obir die schepphen; unde dorum sulde eyn izlichir richter in dem rathuse lazin molen daz gestrenge gerichte unsers herren*' (Daniels and von Gruben 1858, article 16). A similar indication is given in Ulrich Tengler's *Layenspiegel*, first published in 1509, as well as in Justinus Gobler's *Der Rechten Spiegel*, published in 1542.

Looking at the programme in clockwise direction, we come to the second arch, where the painting *The Judgment of Daniel* (Daniel 13) is hung (Fig. 8.2). In the centre of the painting, Daniel is shown as a judge, presiding the trial that leads to the conviction of the elders (Huygebaert et al. 2016, p. 41–43). In the top-left and top-right corner, the attempted assault of Susanna and the stoning of the elders are depicted as the poles of crime and fair conviction, respectively. The focus of the painting is on the trial itself. The earthly jurisprudence is in the limelight, although Daniel's intervention is the result of a divine inspiration. The biblical narrative was transferred into, and modified for, the juridical context. By emphasising the lawsuit, the painting mirrors the events that take place in the lower court itself. The painting is highly connected to its surrounding. As mentioned above, there are some local specificities that need to be taken into account. A couple of aldermen portraits are included in the composition as well. The aldermen are part of the same pictorial space as the biblical figures; they become witnesses of the rightful judgment passed by Daniel. The stoning stands for a fair verdict, and the aldermen—standing in the foreground on the right side of the painting, underneath the stoning of the elders—are therefore to be associated with the fair outcome of the trial. However, despite the fact that they are definitely involved in the historical narrative of the painting, at the same time as being involved in the historical narrative they stand slightly aside. They do not only observe the events in situ, but they also look out of the picture, and to the viewer. The aldermen are intermediary figures, forging a relationship between inner pictorial space and the real space of the lower court. On the one hand, the artistic programme is a general commentary on law and justice, but on the other hand, it is also concretely aimed at the viewer: and thus the judicial personnel as well as the general public and the public sphere in general. The fact that the aldermen attend the trial serves as a proof that they know rightful judgment. They have seen it with their own eyes, and they have heard it with their own ears. They gaze out of the painting, and their determination guarantees that they are willing to enforce the rightful law in Lüneburg. They place themselves in a genealogical tradition with the biblical role model of Daniel.

The next arch is dominated by the canopy construction. The initial state, when the canopy is closed, shows the panel with the Lüneburg coat of arms linking the artistic programme even more with its specific location. As we learn from archival documents, the council of Lüneburg commissioned the paintings for the lower courtroom (Obert 2014, p. 100).[3] They had of course a particular interest in representing themselves as good and wise, and manifesting their reign throughout the artistic programme. The painting with the coat of arms is framed by the virtues of Pax and Justitia, allegories strongly connected to ruling and power: justice serves as a tool for implementing peace (Baer-Henney 1997; Behrisch 2006; Huygebaert et al. 2016, pp 146–147; Kaulbach 2011; Kissel 1984; Kocher 1992). Both female

[3]The documents from 1607 tell us about the payment of the artist Daniel Frese (1540–1611) and about the fact that the motifs of the images were prescribed: '*sowohl auch die Gemelte in die Bögen, darin das Extremun Juridium, auch Juridium Salomonis et Danielis, alle Oliefarbe aufs zirlichste zu fertigen und zu machende*' (Obert 2014, p. 100).

figures are turning their faces towards the canopy construction, and in doing so emphasise the seat that is reserved for the judge.[4]

Before the start of legal proceedings the canopy was opened, and thus a new constellation was established.[5] The panel with the coat of arms disappeared and in its stead, behind the judges, *The Judgment of Solomon* appeared. The composition resembles the one of *The Judgment of Daniel*. The central figure is Solomon, administering justice. Here as well, a crowd of people attends the trial, symbolising the important aspect of free accessibility and publicness of the judicial. And just as in the previous figure, the observing figures in the painting bridge pictorial and real space.

Regarding the specific moment captured by the painting, we notice an important shift. Unlike in *The Judgment of Daniel*, the viewer does not get to see the outcome of the story. The trial is still going on. This fact enables a high level of identification of the inner pictorial story with the trial that takes place in actu. With his place right in front of the painting, the judge of the lower court is equated with the role model of the wise and rightful King Solomon. As a metaphorical climax, the depiction of the Trinity representation roofs over the judge's bench. The Christian concept of justice is epitomised exceedingly well in the arrangement of the canopy. God, His Son and the Holy Ghost are placed literally right above the judge's head, and hence express the permanent presence of the divine power that helps the representatives on earth to administer justice. The influence of religion on the furnishings of courtrooms is undeniable. It clearly affected the design of courtrooms or courtroom architecture in general, as the example of Lüneburg shows. In this case, the decoration programme is in all likelihood based on the structure of the *Biblia Pauperum*-genre. In both cases, typological correspondences between the Old and the New Testament classify the image programme as a Christian-belief-based scheme within a context of salvation history.[6]

In general, the legal tradition of the Early Modern Era was based on religious thought. The Christian concept of justice was founded on the Bible, and all laws were said to ultimately come from God himself. It was He who gave the law to the people. Lay judges are his representatives on earth until the Last Day. The pictorial programme of the lower court represents this idea. The fundamental connection between law and religion is expressed on different levels. These connections become even clearer when we take other visual sources into account.

A woodcut from Ulrich Tengler's *Layenspiegel* shows a courtroom scene.[7] Above the judge's head, Jesus Christ appears in a sea of clouds. His right hand

[4]Ganzert (2014–2015, vol. II, p. 147–245) contextualizes the canopy construction and leads it back to ancient concepts of power and sovereignty.

[5]The canopy construction stands out because of its folding mechanism. The act of opening and closing represents an important ritual. Opening (or closing) the canopy construction indicates a change in the usage of the space and is comparable to the mechanisms of diptychs and triptychs (cf. my upcoming dissertation).

[6]The combination of Solomon and Christ is very popular (Berve 1969; Weckwerth 1957, p. 225–258).

[7]Available on various websites on the worldwide web.

forms the blessing gesture (with three fingers), which can be read as a reminiscence of the Holy Trinity. His left arm is stretched. Next to his head, we see a sword and a lily as symbols of jurisdiction; these two symbols represent mercy and condemnation, respectively (Merzbacher 1994a, p. 524, 1994b, p. 136–137; Pfister-Burkhalter 1994, p. 101). Another woodcut, from the *Bambergensis*, also shows a courtroom scene,[8] probably the taking of an oath. Above the judge, at the top centre of the piece, God's hand reaches out from the clouds and points at a banderol that says: '*Du solst nit falsche zeugknuß geben/Als lieb dir sey das ewig leben*'. The first part refers to the eighth commandment: 'Thou shalt not bear false witness against thy neighbour' (Exodus 20:16). The second part adds: 'if you value and cherish eternal life'. Both woodcuts are part of German law books of the fifteenth and sixteenth century. They represent both the representative function of earthly judges and the legitimisation of mundane jurisdiction through divine power. This close link between law enforcement and religion is present in all mediums, and is transferred in courtrooms, such as that of Lüneburg for example. The reciprocal relationship between the two poles is embodied in the arrangement of the canopy as mentioned (*cf.* supra). The Holy Trinity above the judge's head ensures the permanent presence of divine power, which is supposed to help its representatives on earth to administer justice. The trial stands under the protection, control and care of the Holy Trinity. At the same time, the Holy Trinity serves as a source of wisdom and makes it possible—metaphorically speaking—to pass rightful judgments, and therefore ensures a fair trial.

8.4 Typological Correlations and Influences of the Juridical

The architecture and the pictorial programme of the lower court are strongly intertwined. Firstly, the paintings fill in the blank spaces, whilst the architecture serves both as a frame and as a bridge from one element to another. Secondly, the images themselves interact with each other as well. Jesus Christ as a judge is placed in the middle of the painting, but he is standing slightly to the right. As such, he is, as it were, pointing to the next painting, which again shows Daniel in the centre, but turning to the side, where we find the next section. Solomon, on the other hand, turns to his right, pointing back and thus completing the circle. Furthermore, the three (main) images follow the same formal structure, and can be interpreted semantically by means of a typological approach (Bloch 1969, p. 127–142, 1994, p. 395–404; Ohly 1988, p. 22–63). Daniel as well as Solomon are, from a typological point of view, types of the antitype Jesus Christ. They prefigure His work.

Besides the architecture and the paintings, the personnel also plays a role. There are a couple of connections between the paintings themselves and the spatial sphere

---

[8]Available on various websites on the worldwide web.

of the lower court. As already mentioned, observing figures such as the aldermen in *The Judgment of Daniel* and *The Judgment of Solomon* establishes a relationship between image, content and recipient. In *The Last Judgment*, there is a similar observing figure.

The inscriptions, in Latin on top of the painting and in a German translation underneath it, also connect the images.[9] Here, Matthijsen's instructions find their realisation. As said, he wrote that the judge's chamber should 'display good, old, wise sayings to be inspired by with wisdom and knowledge'. The combination of images and text played an important role in the entire concept of courtrooms' furnishings. The Latin inscriptions are quotes from the Bible, and the German ones are more or less free translations. One example may be sufficient to show how the inscriptions work and how they interact with the paintings. Above *The Judgment of Daniel* the Latin inscription says: '*ivdex debet esse pater pavpervm et cavsam qvam nescit diligentissime investigare. iob 2 9*'. When comparing this with the biblical passage, we find the following text under Job 29:16: 'I was a father to the poor: and the cause which I knew not I searched out'. Obviously, the text—like the iconography—was adjusted to the judicial context. A judge, like Job, must take care of those who cannot help themselves, and has to find the truth. The German translation refers to the judge as well, and adds that 'if he acts diligently, he will gain glory and honour'.[10] The inscription therefore provides the recipients—at least those who were able to read—with a general comment on what quality a judge should especially possess, as well as an emphasis on the very quality of diligence; diligence as the basis of the search for truth. I argue that it is important to underline this very mundane characteristic as an indicator of a changing situation. Despite the fact that the connection between religion and law was still present and important, there were certain changes in law enforcement during the Early Modern Era, such as the inquisitorial procedure, which were also reflected in the changing importance of certain types of iconography. In the judicial system of Lüneburg, these changes made the artistic programme even more important (*cf.* Obert 2014, p. 135–136).

The lower court had a specific status within the judicial system of Lüneburg. It was originally dominated by the sovereign, the Duke of Brunswick-Lüneburg (Haase 1956; Lamschus et al. 1997; Obert 2014; Thurich 1960). His representative was in control of both the blood court (or 'high justice') and lower justice. During the course of the fifteenth century, the city council of Lüneburg gained more and more power. At the latest in the sixteenth century, the city council probably administered justice over blood matters as well as other cases. However, it is important to emphasise that, even though it was de facto the council that made the court decisions, the representative still needed to legitimise the sentences by

[9]The layout of the images reminds of the structure of early modern emblems that consisted of the following parts: *inscriptio*, *pictura* and *subscriptio*. The relationship between emblems, early modern broadsheet production and the Lüneburg images is dealt with in my dissertation.

[10]'*Eyn Richter sey der armen Schutsz, Schaff Gleich undt Recht, nicht egen nütz. Die Wahrheidt auch erforsch mit Fleis, so wirdt ehr haben Rhumb und preis*'.

initialising the court procedure, passing the sentence, and announcing it to the public (Obert 2014, p. 125–126, 135–136).[11] This procedure took place in the lower court. Hence, this court was not only a hinge between inside and outside through its architectural position, but also in terms of its judicial practice (Obert 2014, p. 135–138). If we add this fundamental shift to the fact that (as a result of the reception of Roman law) the proceedings were held indoors, it becomes obvious that there was an urgent need to, at the same time, refer to tradition and visualise those aspects of the legal procedure that were eliminated or made invisible by the new court proceedings.[12] My argument is that the visual programme was able to fill the gap that was created by the withdrawal of visibility within the process. As long as justice was being dispensed in public spaces, with active involvement of the people, there was no urgent need to visualise court procedures. But after the reception of Roman law, and the resulting loss of transparency, images enabled a new way for the public to participate in the realm of jurisdiction.[13]

The Lüneburg lower court is part of the town hall, but it also deeply connected to the neighbouring market places. Its spatial arrangement establishes the *Niedergericht* as public space and refers to what is happening inside the building (Ganzert 2014, p. 7; Obert 2014, p. 136). The painting *The judgment of Daniel* plays a key role in the legal context. The method Daniel used to convict the elders, was a modern one, applied more and more after the reception of Roman law. Despite the fact that the inquisitional method was in practice rarely attended by the public, the image links the act of the newly introduced method with an audience in the present. The image visualises a situation that cannot be observed in practice. The image functions as a substitute, by providing visual accessibility. At the same time, it also reveals itself as meta-commentary on legal procedure. By staging Daniel as judge, Lüneburg, with the image programme, stages itself as a modern city that keeps pace with modern law.

8.5 Constituting Judicial Space

The Lüneburg example provides a complex, pictorial programme inspired by Christian thoughts. Not only does it thematise jurisdiction and a specific idea of justice in each image; all images, as a general programme, establish and affirm a set of values that was supposed to be associated with authority, in this case the council of Lüneburg. Hence, the interior decoration of the lower court of course served to

[11]Obert (2014, p. 135–136) stresses the fact that the decisions derived its legitimacy from the procedure in the lower court.

[12]Certain new habits were introduced into the modern courtroom, like opening the windows and doors while holding a trial, the announcement out in the open as well as law-enforcement in public space (Albrecht 2004, p. 15).

[13]Claudia Blümle (2008, p. 42, 2011 p. 28–29) showed that images contribute significantly 'to the development of this space of juridical visibility'.

express, visualise and make the viewer aware of how justice was seen and executed in Lüneburg. In the function of these artworks lies mainly in their expressive power and versatility to voice the authorities' needs. Additionally, as the description above made clear, the images also fill in the blank spaces of the room. They complete the architectural setting. Furthermore, they play a large part in the constitution of the room as what it is: a courtroom. The decoration constitutes judicial space. The change of status of the canopy—and here again we have a highly dominant parallel with the biblical altarpiece—has its effect on the entire room.

The lower court only manifests itself to us as courtroom when the canopy is opened. The act of unfolding assigns new layers of meaning to the room—physically and metaphorically as well as in a practical sense. The artistic decoration fulfilled the very important function of constituting judicial space. This act of constituting—in German I would call it *Rechtsraumkonstitution*—can happen in a variety of ways, whether it is the opening of a curtain (e.g. in the case of Baegert in Wesel, Zumkley 1988, p. 18) or the installation of the judge's bench (e.g. in the case of Bremen, Albrecht 1993, 2004, p. 110–112).

In addition to this, the judicial practice itself also was attentive of the artistic decor. This can be derived from a large number of visual documents. *The oath taking* by Baegert may serve as an example to underline the assumption that the protagonists in court referred to their surrounding in a physical way. The judge in Derick Baegert's composition resembles Christ's pose when He acts as Judge of the World (Blümle 2011, p. 305–306; Paumen 2016, p. 33). The judge does not only imitate Christ, but also points at the picture-in-picture-depiction of the Last Judgment on his right hand side. With this gesture, he highlights the function of the painting in the courtroom: it served as a metaphorical and at the same as a physical point of reference for both judges and parties. The oath-taking exemplifies both the tradition of including paintings in courtroom furnishings and strengthens the suggestion that images in courtrooms act in a twofold manner: as both material and immaterial objects. In addition to this, the Wesel painting resembles the arrangement of the personnel of the lower court itself: through the similarity of the positions of the judge and the different parties, as well as through the position of *The Last Judgment* at the right hand side of the judge, there is transfer of meaning from the painting to the real space of Lüneburg. As in the picture, one can imagine the judge sitting beneath the canopy and pointing to heavenly judgment, addressing the defendant to keep the Last Day in mind.

With the previous comments on Lüneburg and its furnishings, it becomes clear that courtroom decorations are highly connected with their specific location, and that they have an impact on the space as well as on the protagonists that are part of the judicial act. What was observed in Lüneburg can be seen in other cities as well, as the example of Wesel shows, where a panel depicting the Last Judgment was also included in the overall structure of the chamber.

8.6 Conclusion

The results of our analysis of Lüneburg find their theoretical framing in what Cornelia Vismann (2012) calls *Kulturtechniken des Rechts*. She states that all parts of the furnishings had an influence on how justice was administered. From the seating arrangement to the images, all had an impact on the protagonists as well as their actions. In Lüneburg in particular, one can trace different functions of art in a judicial context. The images display exemplary stories as well as 'good, old, wise sayings', as Jan Matthijsen advised. They fulfil a dual function: they structure the room, and provide a framework for action. They themselves are part of a process of reflection on law and justice, as the example of Daniel shows. The images display a variety of functions: they are a warning and a source of inspiration, they represent, they visualise the authority of legitimisation, they reflect on legal procedure. For this reason, they are an indispensable part of the dramaturgy of administering justice and enforcing the law.

References

Albrecht S (1993) Das Bremer Rathaus im Zeichen städtischer Selbstdarstellung vor dem 30-jährigen Krieg. Wissenschaftliche Buchgesellschaft, Marburg

Albrecht S (2004) Mittelalterliche Rathäuser in Deutschland. Architektur und Funktion. Wissenschaftliche Buchgesellschaft, Darmstadt

Baer-Hennery J (1997) Wie kommt die Jungfrau zur Waage, Schwert und Augenbinde? Zur Darstellung der Justitia. Juristische Arbeitsblätter. Zeitschrift für Studenten und Referendare 29:610–613

Behrisch S (2006) Die Justitia. Eine Annäherung an die Allegorie der Gerechtigkeit. Verlag und Datenbank für Geisteswissenschaften, Weimar

Berve M (1969) Die Armenbibel. Herkunft. Gestalt. Typologie. Beuroner Kunstverlag, Beuron

Bloch P (1969) Typologische Kunst. In: Lex et Sacramentum im Mittelalter, vol 6, pp 127–142

Bloch P (1994) Typologie. In: Kirschbaum E (ed) Lexikon der Christlichen Ikonographie, vol IV. Herder, Rome, pp 395–404

Blümle C (2008) The omnipresent eye of the judge: juridical evidence in Albrecht Dürer and Lucas Cranach the elder. In: Vismann C (ed) Image and Law. A Troubled Relationship. Parallax. A journal of metadiscursive theory and cultural practices 14(4): 42–54

Blümle C (2011) Der Zeuge im Bild. Dieric Bouts und die Konstitution des modernen Rechtsraumes. Fink, Munich

Daniels A, von Gruben F (eds) (1858) Das Sächsische Weichbildrecht. Jus municipale saxonicum. Mylius, Berlin

Ganzert J (ed) (2014–2015) Das Lüneburger Rathaus. Ergebnisse der Untersuchung 2008 bis 2011 (Beiträge zur Architektur- und Kulturgeschichte, Leibniz Universität Hannover, Abteilung Bau-/Stadtgeschichte, Fakultät für Architektur und Landschaft, vol X.1) Imhof, Petersberg

Haase C (1956) Das Lüneburger Stadtrecht. In: Wendland U (ed) Aus Lüneburgs tausendjähriger Vergangenheit. Heliand-Verlag, Lüneburg, pp 67–86

Haupt MG (2000) Die Große Ratsstube im Lüneburger Rathaus (1564–1584). Selbstdarstellung einer protestantischen Obrigkeit. Jonas-Verlag, Marburg

Huygebaert S, Martyn G, Paumen V, Van Poucke T (ed) (2016) The art of law: three centuries of justice depicted (exh. cat. Bruges). Lannoo, Tielt

Kaulbach H-M (2011) Friede. In: Fleckner U, Warnke M, Ziegler H (eds) Handbuch der Politischen Ikonographie, vol I. Beck, Munich, pp 381–387

Kissel OR (1984) Die Justitia. Reflexionen über ein Symbol und seine Darstellung in der bildenden Kunst. Beck, Munich
Klemmer K, Wassermann R, Wessel TM (1993) Deutsche Gerichtsgebäude. Von der Dorflinde über den Justizpalast zum Haus des Rechts. Beck, Munichn
Kocher G (1992) Zeichen und Symbole des Rechts. Eine historische Ikonographie. Beck, Munich
Lamschus C, Lamschus H, Reinhardt U (1997) Alles was Recht ist. 750 Jahre Stadtrecht in Lüneburg. Stern'sche Druckerei, Lüneburg
Lederle U (1937) Gerechtigkeitsdarstellungen in deutschen und niederländischen Rathäusern. Kruse, Philippsburg
Martyn G (2016) Divine judgement, worldly judges. In: Huygebaert et al. pp 14–27
Merzbacher F (1994a) Reich. In: Kirschbaum E (ed) Lexikon der Christlichen Ikonographie, vol III. Herder, Rome, p 524
Merzbacher F (1994b) Schwert. In: Kirschbaum E (ed) Lexikon der Christlichen Ikonographie, vol IV. Herder, Rome, pp 136–137
Obert K (2014) Architektonische Manifestationen von Gerichtsbarkeit. Die Befunde am Lüneburger Rathaus. In: Ganzert 2014–2015, vol II, pp 7-156
Ohly F (1988) Typologie als Denkform der Geschichtsbetrachtung. In: Bohn V (ed) Typologie. Internationale Beiträge zur Poetik. Suhrkamp, Frankfurt am Main, pp 22–63
Paumen V (2016) Judging by example of the divine judge. In: Huygebaert et al. pp 32–34
Pfister-Burkhalter M (1994) Lilie. In: Kirschbaum E (ed) Lexikon der Christlichen Ikonographie, vol III. Herder, Rome, p 101
Pleister W, Schild W (eds) (1988) Recht und Gerechtigkeit im Spiegel der europäischen Kunst. DuMont, Cologne
Resnik J, Curtis D (2011) Representing justice: invention, controversy and rights in city-states and democratic courtrooms. Yale University Press, New Haven
Strauss G (1986) Law, resistance, and the state: the opposition to Roman Law in reformation Germany. Princeton University Press, Princeton
Thurich E (1960) Die Geschichte des Lüneburger Stadtrechts im Mittelalter. Museumsverein für das Fürstentum Lüneburg, Lüneburg
Troescher G (1939) Weltgerichtsbilder in Rathäusern und Gerichtsstätten. Westdeutsches Jahrbuch für Kunstgeschichte. Wallraff-Richartz-Jahrbuch 11:139–214
Van der Velden H (1995) Cambyses for example: the origins and function of an *exemplum iustitiae* in Netherlandish art of the fifteenth, sixteenth and seventeenth centuries. Simiolus 23(1): 5–39
Vismann C (2012) In judicio stare. Kulturtechniken des Rechts. In: Gephart W (ed) Rechtsanalyse als Kulturforschung. Vittorio Klostermann, Frankfurt am Main, pp 323–334
Weckwerth A (1957) Die Zweckbestimmung der Armenbibel und die Bedeutung ihres Namens. Zeitschrift für Kirchengeschichte 68:225–258
Zumkley B (1988) Das Weseler Gerichtsbild *Die Eidesleistung* von Derick Baegert: Quellengeschichtliche und technologische Studie zu einem Gemälde des 15. Jahrhunderts, Rheinland-Verl., Cologne

Ann-Kathrin Hubrich studied Art History, Italian Literature and Political Science at the University of Hamburg and Genoa. She received her Master of Arts with a thesis on *Das Bildprogramm des Lüneburger Niedergerichts. Zu Funktionen von Gerechtigkeitsdarstellungen im Rechtskontext*. The dissertation is on the scenography of courtrooms in the early modern period and analyzes the multilayered correlations between art and jurisdiction. Since the fall of 2014 she has been a scholar of the Graduate School Humanities at the University of Hamburg. Since 2015 she is part of the committee of Ulmer Verein. Since 2018 she works at Hamburger Kunsthalle.

Figures

Fig. 8.1 Town hall of Lüneburg, © Fred Dott, Hamburg

Fig. 8.2 Daniel Frese, *The Judgment of Daniel*, 1603–1607, oil on panel, 275 × 140 cm, Lüneburg, Town Hall, *Niedergericht*, © Fred Dott, Hamburg

Fig. 8.3 Daniel Frese, *The Judgment of Solomon*, 1603–1607, oil on panel, 165 × 125 cm, Lüneburg, Town Hall, *Niedergericht*, © Fred Dott, Hamburg

Fig. 8.4 Daniel Frese, *Holy Trinity*, 1603–1607, oil on panel, 167 × 125 cm, Lüneburg, Town Hall, *Niedergericht*, © Fred Dott, Hamburg

Fig. 8.5 Daniel Frese, *Pax*, 1603–1607, oil on panel, 49 × 186 cm, Lüneburg, Town Hall, *Niedergericht*, © Fred Dott, Hamburg

Part III
Lawyers and Justices: Their Books, Their Work, Their Symbols

Chapter 9
Civic Bodies and their Identification with Justice and Law in Early Modern Flemish Portraiture

Beatrijs Wolters van der Wey

Abstract This paper relies on object-based—i.e. starting from the concrete preserved works of art—research in art history. Its starting point is formed by a number of specific, too often overlooked, paintings of a particular subgenre of Flemish portraiture from before 1800. It focuses on artworks in which the commissioners had themselves portrayed in a setting of historical and allegorical motifs, or scenes that were appropriate to the group's judicial authority or legal privileges. This contribution's principal aim is to bring some of these paintings, together with their interpretive challenges, back into the limelight, and present a multifaceted understanding of their functions and their commissioners' intentions.

9.1 Introduction

In the Southern Netherlands during the Ancien Régime, there was a long-standing tradition of adorning places where judgments were handed down with scenes of justice.[1] Since among others Juliaan de Ridders reference work *Gerechtigheidstaferelen* (1989), these scenes and the role they played as *exempla justitiae* have become widely known. Less known is the fact that portraits of the people who had commissioned the artworks were often integrated into the paintings.[2] These include judicial authorities

[1]The term 'Early Modern Flemish portraiture' refers to portraits painted in the Southern Netherlands or in the corresponding part of the Low Countries which, around 1585, was under Spanish Habsburg rule, was then passed in 1715 to Austrian Habsburg control, which lasted until annexation by the French just before 1800. It consisted of a number of principalities, of which the Duchy of Brabant, the Lordship of Malines and the Counties of Flanders, Namur and Hainaut were the principal producers of civic group portraits. In literature, from art history especially, 'Flemish' is used as *pars pro toto* for 'Southern-Netherlandish'.
[2]See the in-depth and integrated study of Flemish civic group portraiture before 1800: Wolters van der Wey (2015a).

B. Wolters van der Wey (✉)
Royal Institute for Cultural Heritage (KIK-IRPA), Brussels, Belgium
e-mail: Beatrijs.Woltersvanderwey@kikirpa.be

S. Huygebaert et al. (eds.), *The Art of Law*, Ius Gentium: Comparative Perspectives on Law and Justice 66, https://doi.org/10.1007/978-3-319-90787-1_9

such as a town's bench of aldermen, or even the entire town council. As a result, these scenes of justice should then be interpreted in a broader sense, as an allusion to the members' responsibility of good governance.

Proportionally, compared to other bodies (groups, institutions, confraternities, guilds etc.) who had themselves portrayed during the Early Modern Era (militia and craft guilds, charitable institutions and religious confraternities) civic authorities are thin on the ground.[3] Before 1800, in the Duchy of Brabant, only eight or perhaps nine out of a total of one hundred and twelve traceable group portraits were ordered by a town council, a bench of aldermen or by other administrative bodies. In the County of Namur, two group portraits of burgomasters and aldermen were painted, at the end of the sixteenth and the beginning of the seventeenth century. In Ghent (County of Flanders) another one was created in the second half of the seventeenth century.

It may be noted that, in the Dutch Republic between the sixteenth and eighteenth century, the proportion of town councils' portraits was equally low, with only one known example from Amsterdam (Holland), one from Deventer (Overijssel) and six from The Hague (Holland), out of an estimated total of 335 surviving Dutch group portraits.[4] In Paris, on the other hand, for almost two hundred years—from the second half of the sixteenth century to the second half of the eighteenth—successive officers of the municipal administration or *Bureau de la Ville* had themselves painted in corporate portraits, which must have resulted in a good one hundred paintings (of which only about ten have been preserved). They were hung in a chamber in the Paris town hall (Wolters van der Wey 2015a, p. 23). In Venice too, there was, during the sixteenth and seventeenth century, a tradition of painting official group portraits of city magistrates, assembled in one of the city councils (Wolters van der Wey 2015a, p. 23).

In the Southern Netherlands, we have six examples of judicial or civic authorities who had themselves portrayed in combination with a scene or motif of justice. The oldest surviving portrait, a highly allegorical work, is from Antwerp, of the council of the Brabant Mint, painted by Maarten de Vos (1532–1603) in 1594 (Fig. 9.1, Wolters van der Wey 2015a, p. 198–199, no A8). In Brussels, there is a portrait of what is assumed to be the bench of aldermen in the company of Lady Justice, painted for the town hall by Anthony van Dyck (1599–1641) in 1634–1635. It is well-known thanks to its extant *modello*. The final artwork must have been an impressive painting with life-sized figures, which unfortunately was destroyed during the French bombardment of Brussels in 1695 (Wolters van der Wey 2015a,

[3]See in particular in Wolters van der Wey (2015a), p. 408–415 (Tables 1a–b) for the Duchy of Brabant before 1585, p. 422–423 (Table 4) for Brabant 1585–1800, p. 434–445 (Table 10) for civic group portraits with a Southern Netherlandish origin outside Brabant. In order to compile the corpus and obtain the broadest possible sample of the subgenre of Flemish civic group portraiture, systematic use was made of different photo libraries, of the contemporary collection catalogues of as many domestic and major foreign museums as possible, and of a number of eighteenth- and nineteenth-century (published and unpublished) topographical descriptions. A number of portraits also came to light by chance in sales catalogues and archival documents. For the resources used, see Wolters van der Wey (2015a, p. 20, 127–128, note 29).

[4]The majority of which being, of course, the well-known militia, surgeon and regent portraits (Wolters van der Wey 2015a, p. 23, 131, endnote 69).

p. 230–232, no B19). Two older group portraits from the 1560–1570s, of the Brussels town council members gathered around a *Judgment of Solomon*, have not been preserved either (Wolters van der Wey 2015a, p. 410–411, Table 1a, no 18a–b, and p. 412–413, Table 1b, no 6a–b). In Namur, the burgomaster and aldermen had themselves painted with a *Last Judgment*—the central panel is now lost—by Jan Baptist (I) Saive (1540–1624) in 1597 (Wolters van der Wey 2015a, p. 444–445, Table 10 g, no 1; Huygebaert et al. 2016, p. 99–100, Fig. 45, cat. 46). Finally, there is a painting from 1686 by Gillis Le Plat (1656–1724) in Ghent, representing the aldermen of the Ghedeele in combination, again, with Lady Justice (Wolters van der Wey 2015a, p. 442–443, Table 10e, no 3).

None of these paintings are still in situ: some have been moved, some were destroyed or have disappeared and are known only from archival sources. Thus, if we want to interpret these paintings correctly, it is vitally important to reconstruct their history, in the hope of getting as close as possible to the circumstances of their production and original destination. Unfortunately, for these six paintings from the Southern Netherlands, explicit indications as to why, at that specific moment, the commissioning bodies elected to order a group portrait for their room, are rather scarce. However, we can infer from our contextual study that they had different motivations and thus, also, a varying degree of personal involvement with the themes of justice and law in combination with which they were depicted. I will illustrate this with a few examples.

9.2 Maarten de Vos' Commission for the Brabant Mint

In 1594, the executive of the Brabant Mint commissioned a painting from Maarten de Vos (Fig. 9.1) for its Antwerp office, which was situated on the corner of *Kloosterstraat* and *Oever* square.[5] The minters worked within a closed corporation, as membership was hereditary, serving the financial institution of the Mint, where they enjoyed extensive fiscal, military and judicial privileges. The Mint even had had its own tribunal, the *Vierschaer*: an independent judiciary that could uphold the law to its members and their families. The minters' executive council, consisting of two provosts and seven sworn members of the guild, was responsible for both civil and criminal matters relating to the minters.

The work painted by Maarten de Vos in 1594 is one of the earliest examples in Antwerp of a secular group portrait on an autonomous support, which means that it has not been integrated into a larger triptych and combined with a religious theme (Wolters van der Wey 2015a). It is a highly allegorical work: a scene of justice, meant to be hang in their courtroom or *rechtcamer*, and encourage the virtue it

[5]Oil on panel, 142.5 × 187.5 cm sight size (with frame 157 × 215 cm), Antwerp, Museum Rockoxhuis (KBC Bank), inv. 77.4. For the full text of the extensive catalogue entry about the painting, with archival and bibliographic references, see the online publication Wolters van der Wey (2015b), http://balat.kikirpa.be/object/43827.

depicts. As a result, the exemplary part of the image is the most conspicuous, with a stately Lady Justice in the centre, and four historical paragons of law and justice in the foreground. From left to right we recognise Moses, the Byzantine emperor Justinian, Numa Pompilius (the second King of Rome) and Pliny (author of *Historia Naturalis*). Juliaan de Ridder considered Maarten de Vos' composition not simply as an allegory of justice, but as one of the 'justice scenes'. It was indeed intended to encourage just action, since it was hung in the courtroom itself.[6] The composition is rigidly symmetrical: the sitting figures are split into two groups and arrayed on either side of the painting. The portrait group stands behind the allegorical figures, and the sitters are shown only in half length. However, from the addition of an inscription that gives us their names, we can infer that the portrait element was regarded as important.[7] Over the years, the Antwerp minters commissioned at least three group portraits for their courtroom.[8] It is worth noting that payment for the paintings came (at the very least in 1594 for Maarten de Vos' piece), not out of their own funds, but *ex pecunia publica*. In other words, the paintings were acquired with public money or tax revenue (Wolters van der Wey 2015a, p. 136, fn. 134).[9] We have no idea whether the two other paintings, which have not been preserved, also combined portraits with a judicial theme.

A description of the Antwerp minters' courtroom, which was installed and decorated as early as 1566, suggests that great play was made with the theme of

[6]In this way, he expanded the concept of 'justice scene' somewhat, compared to the definition he himself had given earlier: a scene that 'always represents something specific: a true or believed story, a real or legendary event or act, and even a real or unreal character. Lady Justice, on the other hand, is simply an attempt at the sensory representation of the abstract idea of justice. In any case, the proper justice scenes are derived from very disparate sources', both secular and religious (De Ridder 1989, p. 119 and 11 resp., trans. BWvdW).

[7]Just when this inscription was added, and whether it was on a separate plaque or (less likely) painted on the support itself, is not known with certainty. The content of the inscription, now lost, is known to us thanks to a transcription by the Antwerp chronicler Jan Baptist Van der Straelen, from before 1847: '*Iustitiae S[acrum]/Petrus Borremans, christophorus Brabants,/Prepositi.,/ Michael van Bolenbeke, joannes van der/Heijden, gualterus van Craesbeeck, Joannes/Hoons, georgius Pannis, Petrus van/papevelt, Franciscus van Bijlant jurati.–/theodorus Everwijn, viator./ Ex pec. pub. colleg. monetar. Duc./Brab. P. C. CIƆ. IƆ. XCIIII [Ex pecunia publica collegium monetarium Ducatus Brabantiae poni curavit 1594]*'. See Wolters van der Wey (2015b), http://balat.kikirpa.be/object/43827, fn. 31.

[8]There is archival evidence that the Antwerp minters ordered at least two more group portraits in 1638 and 1663 (Wolters van der Wey 2015a, p. 202, no A15, and p. 209, no A21 respectively; full text of the catalogue entries in Wolters van der Wey 2015b).

[9]I thank Professor Erik Aerts (KU Leuven, History Research Unit, Early Modern History) for confirming that the *pecunia publica* alluded to in the inscription probably refers to public money or tax revenue rather than to the funds of the Brabant Mint itself, given that it was not an ordinary public institution and thus the use of the adjective *publicus* would have been less fitting.

justice in this room's decoration, which indicates that the minters regarded it as important. In addition to Maarten de Vos' painting from 1594, and perhaps the two other group portraits that hung on the panelled walls, a boss above the fireplace was decorated with figures representing the *Judgment of Solomon* and a plaque inscribed with a verse from the Psalms: '*Zalig is den rechter die den oprechten recht*' ('Blessed are those who observe justice, who do righteousness at all times')[10] (Wolters van der Wey 2015b).[11] Moreover, one of the stained-glass windows in the courtroom bore the inscription '*pace et iustitia*', which was also inscribed on coins minted from 1576 onwards.[12] More broadly speaking, this was an allusion to the then very relevant desire for political peace and justice in this era of the Dutch Revolt.

For the governing body of the minters, the anniversary of an important privilege around 1594 may have been the reason for ordering a group portrait. Indeed, three hundred years earlier, in 1291, they had received judicial independence as a privilege from John I, Duke of Brabant (Jennes 1978, p. 45). In this case, it is obvious that the minters' intention when ordering the new painting was more than to present a paradigm or example of justice, and evoke an inducement to just judgments. By including their likenesses, the sitters also fully identified with the virtue depicted in their company. They represented, at the same time, as living personifications, as it were, the centuries-old tradition of fair justice of their institution, which they were keen to reaffirm.

9.3 Group Portraits Painted for the Brussels and Malines Town Hall

Another example, from Brussels and some twenty years older, reveals that the sitters did not necessarily attach much importance to the complementary theme in the painting, but instead focused mainly on the portraits or, in other words, on their personal representation. Nevertheless, we must still consider the case in its historical context.

In January 1566, the Brussels town council commissioned two wing panels with portraits from the Brussels artist Lucas van Nevele (1509–1566), which were to be attached to an already existing centre panel with a *Judgment of Solomon* (Wolters

[10]The text is a free rendering of Psalms 106:3.

[11]See in particular document 3, with transcriptions from the manuscript by Frédéric Verachter: *Histoire monétaire de la ville d'Anvers, ancien Chef-lieu Du marquisât du St. Empire, prouvée par les monuments* (1855), Antwerp, City Archives (Felixarchief), PK 2957.

[12]*Ibidem*, ch. VII (*Le Serment, le Tribunal, le Greffe et la Prison de la Monnaie*), f. 4v.

van der Wey 2015c, p. 294–295). Undoubtedly, this theme was also chosen for the biblical King's legendary wisdom, a quality that the council members ought to be showing too. Because of Van Nevele's premature death, another (anonymous) painter finished the work in 1571. It is not clear from the sources whether the portraits were on the inside or the outside of the wings, but since they were meant to be combined with a *Judgment of Solomon* in the *raetcamer* (council chamber) of the Brussels town hall, it is likely that they were on the inside, so that the justice scene and the portraits were visible at the same time. The decision to commission the portraits was taken by the two burgomasters, three of the seven aldermen, four of the then serving receivers, and three or four of the six council members, which suggests that the entire town council was to be portrayed. As a result, a large number of figures, up to twenty-three, had to be depicted on the wings.[13] Only six years later, in 1577, the Brussels town council passed a resolution to have the portraits on the pair of wings replaced with the likenesses of the then serving council: '*in den jaere 1577 (...) geresolveert de contrefeijtsels staende op de schilderijen van Salamon [sic] ende van het oordeel hangende in de raetcamer uyt te doen ende daer op te doen schilderen de wethouders ende rentmeesters als dan dienende. d. lib. fol. 314 verso*'.[14]

Edmond Roobaert (2005, p. 153–204) provides a detailed explanation of the painting from 1577 (which did not survive either) and in my view rightly suggests that the town council's decision to have the portraits of their predecessors replaced by those of the new administration was not the result of the 'neutral' annual change of council, but of the political situation around 1577, given that the administration was Calvinist at that time. Apparently, the portraits of individuals who had fallen from grace were removed.[15] Meanwhile, the *Judgment of Solomon* continued to serve as the centre panel of the town council's triptych. After all, it was equally applicable to the functions with which the new sitters were entrusted, and to the room, the council chamber, where the painting was permanently placed. However, the relation between the sitters and the central scene of justice may not have been that strong after all. The portraits could be changed more easily because of the formal characteristics of the painting's support and composition—a triptych, in which the sitters were depicted on the wings. As such, the portraits seemed to function more autonomously, as paintings in their own right.

---

[13]See about the composition of the Brussels town council, Henne and Wauters (1845, vol. II, p. 508*ff*). The still extant triptych with portrait wings of the Confraternity of Our Lady of the Dry Tree of Bruges, painted a few decades later (1607–1611) by Pieter II Claeissens (after 1542–1623) (Bruges, St Walburga's Church) (Fig. 9.2), gives an idea of what the Brussels town council's triptych must have looked like.

[14]Brussels, City Archives, Historical Archive, no 1230 (*Index der Resolutien raeckende de stadt Brussel*, ca.1660), f. 82v.

[15]There is a similar case in Haarlem in 1615–1619, in which the portraits of four members of a civic guard company, who had refused to swear a loyalty oath to the Remonstrant town council, were painted out of a group portrait, only to be painted in again a few years later when the political situation was reversed (Levy-van Halm 1988, p. 112).

Furthermore, civic authorities did not necessarily have themselves depicted in combination with an iconography that specifically referred to the content of their duties. When the Malines town council ordered a painting from Michiel Coxcie (1499–1592) in September 1585, to be hung in the *Schepene-kamer* (the aldermen's chamber), they opted for a single support without wings, with the members' portraits arrayed on either side of a central Crucifixion.[16] Of course, they felt equally supported in the performance of their duties by this Christ on the cross, who was depicted as protecting them.[17]

9.4 Antwerp Militia Portraits and the Guilds' Historical Legitimation

Starting from the first half of the seventeenth century, another type of painting appeared. They were ordered by various guilds in Antwerp, and their context was different than that of the paintings in Malines and Brussel. The commissioners did not have themselves placed in a judicial context, but in a historical-allegorical scene appropriate to the group's legal privileges. Here, the patrons were clearly concerned first and foremost with their portraits, and the complementary scene was specifically chosen in relation to the commissioning company, in order to affirm their identity as a group. The paintings were subsequently hung in the guild's own meeting room.

In two group portraits of the Antwerp *Kolveniers* (arquebusiers), painted by Cornelis de Vos (1584/1585–1651) (Fig. 9.3) and Peter Thys (1624–1677) (Fig. 9.4) in 1644 and 1677 respectively, the guildsmen are anachronistically represented in the company of the Holy Roman Emperor Charles V, who in 1524 had granted the guild an exclusive privilege (Wolters van der Wey 2015a, p. 205–207, no A18, and p. 212–213, no A26).[18] Both paintings show how the inclusion of a much earlier ruler was intended to provide historical legitimation for the rights of the portrayed group. This is probably also true in the case of another composition by Peter Thys, painted in 1664, which depicts the deans of several Antwerp guilds in the presence of John II,

[16]Resolution passed by the city magistrates on 16 September 1585, Malines, City Archives, Old Archive, *Stadsbestuur, C. Magistraat (Resolutiën)*, series I, no 1 (1585–1615), f. 7v–8; partially published in *Provincie, Stad ende District van Mechelen* (1770, p. 219).

[17]In the context of the time, such a combination of civic portraits, in which the sitters are shown in prayer before a saint or a sacred scene and a secular environment such as a room in a town hall, probably seemed less strange than it does now (De Munck 2009, p. 27). See Wolters van der Wey (2015a, p. 428–430), Table 7, which lists Brabant's civic group portraits according to their accompanying iconography. It shows not only that Christological and Marian motifs were particularly popular, but also that they were used in a variety of ways. Pairing a group portrait with a Crucifixion was the most common combination.

[18]For the full text of the extensive catalogue entry about the paintings, with archival and bibliographic references, see the online publication (Wolters van der Wey 2015b); http://balat.kikirpa.be/object/11007212 and http://balat.kikirpa.be/object/55093.

Duke of Brabant (1275–1312) (Fig. 9.5), but whose exact meaning is still elusive (Wolters van der Wey 2015a, p. 209–210, no A22, and 2015b).[19]

The three Antwerp paintings give visual expression to the practice of calling on one's own past, in the form of potent texts, such as statutes and privileges, to legitimise oneself as a group. As historian Marc Jacobs has shown (1997), this was common practice among Southern-Netherlandish craft guilds in the eighteenth century. Furthermore, Cornelis de Vos' *Kolveniers* portrait and Thys' 1664 painting both feature an enthroned ruler in a 'charter-granting scene'—a fairly standard, well-established iconographic and formal component.[20] For the Antwerp *Kolveniers*, this charter-granting model was indeed perfectly in keeping with what the guild wished to commemorate. Perhaps their hope was that, in doing so, they would partially recover not only the form, but also the underlying significance of this older pictorial model; it gave expression to the dominion and power of the ruler, and specifically to his legal authority.[21] For the *Kolveniers*, this was a pleasant reminder: it was a powerful reaffirmation of the privilege they were granted a century earlier. Thus, despite the fact that, at the moment of the painting's commission, the portrayal of the guild's council was the prime motive, it was the historical component that ultimately determined the form of the composition.

9.5 Conclusion

When commissioners had themselves portrayed in combination with a scene or motif of justice or a privilege-granting scene, they had a variety of motivations, depending on who they were and what the painting's intended destination was.[22] Generally speaking, one of the most important motives for commissioning a portrait

---

[19]http://balat.kikirpa.be/object/161619. The image was probably related to the socio-political troubles in 1659 in Antwerp, when craft and militia guilds rebelled against their own town council, because it was in their opinion too indulgent towards the central and royal authorities, to the detriment of the town's privileges (Wolters van der Wey 2012, 2013).

[20]I borrow this term (*overhandigingspatroon*) from Cyriel Stroo, who in connection with the 'presentation model' in fifteenth-century presentation miniatures has made a particularly insightful analysis of the related 'charter-granting'—formula, see Stroo (2002, p. 26–33, 42–47) (of inter alia French and Burgundian miniatures, last quarter of the tenth century to 1460).

[21]Cyriel Stroo (2002, p. 44–47) noted that the *overhandigingspatroon* or 'charter-granting model' is found almost exclusively in miniatures illustrating a legal text or, more occasionally, a charter and saw in that an expression of the legal content of this compositional formula—i.e. the ruler shown in a legal action.

[22]In the matter of public access, in the sixteenth and seventeenth centuries, the courtroom of the Antwerp minters and the town hall formed a separate category, as they were certainly accessible to a wider audience than the semi-public guild rooms; see on this particular topic: Wolters van der Wey (2015a, p. 51–56). Given the function of those spaces and the higher turnover in the composition of the municipal administration, the different council chambers in the town hall probably saw also a greater variety of people.

seems to have been the desire to document and commemorate the depicted group and its composing members or a particular event related to the group's history. The latter was clearly the case for the Antwerp *Kolveniers* and also the Brussels town council in 1577.

The representation of exemplary behaviour played a significant part in images of justice, where the portraits gave more weight to the message expressed in them. They were intended to evoke an empathic response from the viewer. This could be a more determined motivation to bring about true justice, but also an increase in trust from the general public. The sitters themselves could identify with this message to a greater or lesser degree. In the case of the Antwerp minters, the composition suggests that they had themselves painted as embodying the same virtues of justice and respect for the law as the figures in the foreground, which was also a means of affirming the identity of their institution.

The latter aspect, presenting a picture of group identity, and the historical legitimating that underpinned that identity, seem to have played the most important part in portraits in a privilege-granting scene.

References

De Munck, B (2009) Van religieuze devotie naar zakelijk streven? Enkele kanttekeningen bij de religieuze materiële cultuur van Antwerpse ambachten in de zestiende eeuw. In: Aerts W, Van Hout N (eds) Reünie. Van Quinten Metsijs tot Peter Paul Rubens. Meesterwerken uit het Koninklijk Museum terug in de kathedraal (exh. cat. Antwerp). Exhibitions International, Antwerp, pp 21–31

De Ridder JHA (1989) Gerechtigheidstaferelen voor schepenhuizen in de Zuidelijke Nederlanden in de 14de, 15de en 16de eeuw. Koninklijke Vlaamse Academie voor Wetenschappen, Letteren en Schone Kunsten van België, Brussels

Henne A, Wauters A (1845) Histoire de la ville de Bruxelles. Perichon, Brussels

Huygebaert S, Martyn G, Paumen V, Van Poucke T (eds) (2016) The art of law: three centuries of justice depicted (exh. cat. Bruges). Lannoo, Tielt

Jacobs M (1997) Zonder twijfel dat waarschijnlijk… Ambachtelijke geschiedenissen in de Zuidelijke Nederlanden aan het einde van het 'oude regime'. In: Lis C, Soly H (eds) Werelden van verschil: ambachtsgilden in de Lage Landen. VUBPress, Brussels, pp 243–292

Jennes M (1978) Een schilderij van Maarten de Vos voor de rechtbank van de Brabantse Munters. Jaarboek Koninklijk Museum voor Schone Kunsten Antwerpen 1978:41–50

Levy-van Halm J (1988) De Haarlemse schuttersstukken. In: Carasso-Kok M, Levy-van Halm J (eds) Schutters in Holland, Kracht en zenuwen van de stad (exh. cat. Haarlem). Waanders, Zwolle, pp 104–123

Provincie, Stad ende District van Mechelen opgeheldert in haere Kercken, Kloosters, Kapellen, Gods-huysen, Gilden, publieke Plaetsen, etc. 2 (1770). J.B. Jorez, Brussels

Roobaert E (2005) Het 'Oordeel van Salomo': archivalische toelichting bij het leven en werk van Michiel van Coxcie (1499–1592) te Brussel. Handelingen Koninklijke Kring voor Oudheidkunde, Letteren en Kunst van Mechelen 109(1):153–204

Stroo, C (2002) De celebratie van de macht. Presentatieminiaturen en aanverwante voorstellingen in handschriften van Filips de Goede (1419–1467) en Karel de Stoute (1467–1477). Koninklijke Vlaamse Academie van België voor Wetenschappen en Kunsten, Brussels

Wolters van der Wey B (2012) 350 jaar Antwerpse Academie (1663–2013): geen reden tot feestvieren voor het schilderij 'Stichting der Academie' (1664) van Peter Thys. Antwerpsche Tydinghen 33(4):115–122

Wolters van der Wey B (2013).'Stichting der Academie' van Peter Thys: kanttekeningen bij een iconisch beeld. In: Pas J, Dockx N, De Bruyn E (eds) Contradicties. Koninklijke Academie voor Schone Kunsten Antwerpen 2013–1663. MER Paper Kunsthalle, Ghent, pp 261–267

Wolters van der Wey B (2015a) Corporate splendour: civic group portraits in Brabant 1585–1800: a social, typological and iconographic approach. In: Van der Stighelen K, Vlieghe H (eds) Pictura nova, vol XVIII. Brepols, Turnhout

Wolters van der Wey B (2015b) Groepsvertoon. Catalogus van publieke groepsportretten in Brabant 1585–1800. http://balat.kikirpa.be/groepsvertoon/index.html. Accessed 12 Jul 2017

Wolters van der Wey B (2015c) Brusselaars in beeld. Een nieuwe kijk op portretten van Brusselse groepen vóór 1800. Cahiers Bruxellois 47(1):289–329

Beatrijs Wolters van der Wey studied Classical Philology and History of Art at the Universities of Antwerp and Leuven, where in 2012 she successfully defended her dissertation on civic group portraits painted in Brabant 1585–1800. She is currently working in a project about the confiscation of works of art during the French occupation (1794–1815) at the Royal Institute for Cultural Heritage (KIK-IRPA, Brussels) and is guest lecturer at the University of Leuven. Her main interests are Flemish painting and cultural history from the sixteenth to eighteenth centuries with a focus on the authentic sources and an interdisciplinary approach to the artworks.

Figures

Fig. 9.1 Maarten de Vos, *The Executive Council of the Brabant Mint at Antwerp with Lady Justice*, 1594, oil on panel, 142.5 × 187.5 cm, Antwerp, Museum Rockoxhuis (KBC Bank), inv. 77.4, © KBC Antwerpen, Snijder and Rockoxhuis

Fig. 9.2 Pieter II Claeissens, *Triptych with portrait wings of the Confraternity of Our Lady of the Dry Tree of Bruges*, 1607–1611, oil on panel, 115 × 150 cm centre panel, 120 × 67, 5 cm each wing, Bruges, St Walburga's Church, © Brussels, KIK-IRPA

Fig. 9.3 Cornelis de Vos, Modello *The Council of the Antwerp Arquebusiers' Guild Receives its Privilege from Emperor Charles V*, 1644, oil on panel, 53.5 × 124.5 cm, Collection of Lady Elizabeth Ashcombe, Sudeley Castle, Winchcombe, Gloucestershire, © Rubenianum, Antwerp, photo Clovis Whitfield, Whitfield Fine Art Ltd., London

Fig. 9.4 Peter Thys, Modello *The Council of the Antwerp Arquebusiers' Guild with Emperor Charles V, their President Hendrick van Halmale and the Abbot of Saint Michael's Abbey*, 1677, oil on canvas, 57.5 × 98 cm, Averbode Abbey, © Brussels, KIK-IRPA

Fig. 9.5 Peter Thys, *The Deans of the Antwerp Guilds Receive a Charter from John II, Duke of Brabant*, 1664, oil on canvas, 246 × 529 cm, Antwerp, Royal Academy of Fine Arts, AP Hogeschool, © Brussels, KIK-IRPA

Chapter 10
Lawyers and Litigants: The Corrupting Appeal and Effects of Civil Litigation in Hendrick Goltzius' *Litis abusus*

Alain Wijffels

Abstract The series *Litis abusus* by Hendrick Goltzius (later recast in different versions by Philips and Theodoor Galle) entails a strong moral criticism of civil litigation. Although the artist highlights conventional targets of attacks on litigation, in particular the duration and costs of civil proceedings, the litigant himself, rather than legal professionals, is the central character whose greed and acrimony are the driving forces behind his procedural obstinacy, which ultimately leads to the exhaustion of his patrimonial, physical, mental and spiritual resources. The representation of civil litigation as a monstrous predator also suggests that the system of civil procedure is per se flawed. The sequence of eight prints offers a mostly secular view of the artist's moral censure of greed and querulous abuse of the system of justice. The addition of several Biblical quotes, at the bottom of each print, gives religious force to the general moral message of the series.

10.1 Civil Litigation as a Minor Topos in Art History

Civil litigation, unlike criminal justice, has rarely been prominently represented in the early modern Western iconographic tradition, at least in pictorial representations. The scales of Lady Justice may arguably be more closely associated with the adversarial system of proceedings which has prevailed in civil litigation since the

A. Wijffels (✉)
Faculteit Rechtsgeleerdheid, Universiteit Leiden, Leiden, The Netherlands
e-mail: Alain.Wijffels@law.kuleuven.be

A. Wijffels
Faculteit Rechtsgeleerdheid, KU Leuven, Leuven, Belgium

A. Wijffels
Faculté de Droit, Université catholique de Louvain, Louvain-la-Neuve, Belgium

A. Wijffels
CNRS, Centre d'histoire judiciaire, Université de Lille 2, Lille, France

S. Huygebaert et al. (eds.), *The Art of Law*, Ius Gentium: Comparative Perspectives on Law and Justice 66, https://doi.org/10.1007/978-3-319-90787-1_10

Second Middle Ages than with the inquisitorial principle of criminal prosecutions (at least on the European continent), yet as a symbol it remains, however powerful, a comparatively abstract image of the administration of justice between private litigants. Although in the Western tradition, the volume of civil litigation has traditionally far outweighed that of criminal cases, the latter have usually attracted the most attention from public opinion and non-legal writers, and that is still true in modern coverage of legal proceedings in the press and other media. Similarly, artists appear to have been more readily inspired to represent scenes of criminal justice.

A few exceptions stand out. In the Low Countries, the illustrations in Joos de Damhouder's printed work on civil proceedings have contributed to reach a wider readership beyond legal professionals and to formalise to some degree the representation of particular stages and actors of the administration of civil justice (Monballyu 2016).

A more committed genre of artistic representations deals with moral and social criticism of civil litigation: recurrent topics in that genre are corruption through bribery, and, more specifically associated with civil litigation, undue delays and costs of litigation. Bribery appears very explicitly linked to the adversarial model of (civil) procedure in Hans Vredeman de Vries' (1527–1607) allegory of human justice in the series on public governance painted around 1595 for the town hall of Danzig (Wijffels 2011). Costs and delays are hinted in various parts of Marinus van Reymerswale's (1490/1495–1546/1556) detailed representation of a lawyer's office (ca. 1542–1545, Monballieu 1972, 1973). In those examples, professional lawyers or legal officials (counsel, judge) appear to be the main instruments and beneficiaries of the flaws in the administration of justice, although dishonest or inordinately ingenuous litigants share part of the blame.

In sixteenth-century critical pictorial representations of civil litigation, the series *Litis abusus* holds a special place. While it primarily censures the moral flaws of litigants who unreasonably pursue theirs claims before the courts, and less unequivocally the lawyers' part in the detrimental effects of litigation, it also conveys the idea that civil litigation is per se pernicious. The series offers no positive alternative to the corrupting nature of civil proceedings.

10.2 *Litis abusus*: Three Closely Related Versions

Following *The New Hollstein*, three main versions of the series comprising a sequence of eight numbered plates were produced in the Netherlands (Leesberg 2012 [NHD], vol. II, n° 186–193; Strauss 1977). The original series is said to have been 'designed and executed' by Hendrick Goltzius (1558–1617) himself, after a concept from his then teacher Dirck Volckertsz. Coornhert (1522–1590), who is credited with the first (and unsigned) edition in Haarlem around 1576 (Leesberg 2012 [NHD], vol. I, p. xlv.).[1]

A second edition with Goltzius' signature added on all plates appeared in Haarlem (Marten Spiegel for his father Hendrick Laurensz. Spiegel) in 1597, and a third edition at The Hague (by Hendrick Hondius) around 1604. Copies, including several variations with regard to size, orientations and captions in different languages, are reported in Italy (*partim* s.l.n.d.), in Germany (Frankfurt 1614) and France (s.l.n.d.).

Possibly before the second edition of the Goltzius version, an adapted version featuring the same sequence of eight plates was published in Antwerp by Philips Galle (1537–1612), who is also credited with the new design of the engravings around 1590.[2] That version, signed by Philips Galle's eldest son Theodoor (Sellink and Leesberg 2001 [NHD], vol. I, p. lxii), may have been published again by the latter (in Antwerp) before 1636 and certainly by Joannes Galle (also in Antwerp) some time before 1677.

Finally, a third version published in the Netherlands—if, as in the present contribution, Goltzius' version may be regarded as the first version, and Philips Galle's version as the second—was also published in Antwerp by Theodoor Galle before 1636: the eight scenes are here incorporated in one larger plate (37.0 × 45.5 cm).[3] In the three versions published in the Netherlands, the sequence

[1]Around the same time, Coornhert published a series which, as in *Litis abusus*, combined, sometimes in the same plate, realistic and allegorical figures (Puhlmann 2007, p. 159–60; the book in which the plates are included, published by Plantijn in Antwerp in 1575, is available on-line on *Gallica*). On the collaboration between Coornhert and Goltzius, see Veldman (1990), p. 23–26 (emphasising *inter alia* how Coornhert's experience as a notary may have influenced some elements in plates 2 and 3). Greed and avarice were a main theme in Coornhert's work, *ibidem*, p. 56–57.

[2]That version by Philips and Theodoor Galle is discussed more in detail by Martyn (2016) (including reproductions of the copies exhibited, from the collection of the Royal Library in Brussels, the same copies I have consulted for the preparation of my paper).

[3]I shall not discuss hereafter in my contribution that third version, limiting a few elements of comparison to the versions by Goltzius and Philips Galle. The smaller plates in the all-in-one version are very close to Philips Galle's adaptation of Goltzius. In the copies I have seen, plates 1 and 8 in the last version are arranged as mirror images of the Galle engravings, but the other plates follow the same arrangement as Galle. The main difference in the texts below is that, for each plate, the Dutch verses are preceded by an equivalent set of verses, first in Latin, then in French. The Biblical references which follow (see Appendix) are the same as in Philips Galle's version. The Dutch texts in the all-in-one version are almost identical to those in Philips Galle's version, but for the odd misprint and a few more or less consistent spelling variations. Occasionally, the text has been slightly adapted: for example in plate 7, where in the one-in-all version the last verse reads '*Voor Goey rechters ist goet, voor Quaden ist mommescansen*' (perhaps the change has been inspired by the need, in that version, to identify the figures on the picture with a reference number, which is not the case in Philips Galle's version: the all-in-one version identifies the good judges with a n° 2, the bad judges with a n° 3). The Latin verses in the all-in-one version are original and replace the Latin verses published in Philips Galle's version. The general title on top of the engraving in the all-in-one version is trilingual, in capital letters: *Litis abusus. Abus du proces. Misbruyck van't process*. Bottom right of the plate: 'Theodorus Galle excudit Antverpiae cum privilegiis. Utiliter evulgabitur P. Coens C.A.'. I have consulted (on-line) the copy of Rijksmuseum Amsterdam, inv. RP-P-OB-80.477.

of eight plates is the same, in the sense that each plate in the different versions illustrates the same scene, although the setting and the arrangement of the characters may differ significantly. However, the versions by Goltzius and Galle also share many crucial original features. The graphic styles of both artists are nonetheless strikingly different.[4]

10.3 The Sequence of the Scenes

The plates in Goltzius' and Galle's versions are numbered. The captions under the pictures give a brief description of the scene in verse form and a number of quotes from the Bible (discussed *infra* and listed in the Appendix). The captions which can be regarded as the subtitles describing the individual scenes are in Goltzius' series as follows (original Dutch and modern English translation (AW)):

1. '*LITIS ABUSUS. Mijnn en dijn verdriven door onmatich begeren/die zoete Liefde, Eendracht, Vreed. en Vrees des heeren*' (THE ABUSE OF LITIGATION. Mine and Thine chase away through immoderate greed/the sweet Love, Concord, Peace and the Fear of the Lord, Fig. 10.1).

Each of these characters mentioned in the caption is depicted and identified in the picture in Latin and Dutch.[5] The fleeing characters are preceded by a barking dog looking back.

2. '*Door t'scalke bedroch, door valscheit argelistich/ooc door scryvers zot werdt de coopman meest twistich*' (Through devious fraud, through deceitful falsehood/and also through foolish scribes has the merchant become most litigious).

Against the backdrop of a harbour and quayside with ships, two men, at least one of them a merchant, are striking a deal: they shake hands, encouraged by Falsitas (a woman), holding a bent measuring rod. Another woman, Fraus (with a small trap on

---

[4]As I am not an art historian, I cannot venture any attribution based on stylistic features. From what I have seen of other engravings attributed to Philips Galle, many share several features of style and concept with the series of *Litis abusus* attributed to Goltzius, while the same series attributed to Philips Galle seems stylistically rather different from other, comparable, pictures attributed to the same artist. The connection between Philips Galle and Hendrick Goltzius should not be underestimated, especially during the 1570s, when both Galle and Goltzius, encouraged by Coornhert, strongly developed their production of prints on moralising topics (Sellink and Leesberg 2001 [NHD], vol. I, p. xlix and lxii). To my untrained eye, the Goltzius *Litis abusus* series often presents more similarities with the style of some of Cornelis Cort's works, although the latter's backgrounds are often more sophisticated than the somewhat raw background setting in Goltzius' present early series (Sellink 2000 [NHD]).

[5]*Tuum/Dijn*; *Meum/Mijn* (both men); *Concordia/Eendracht* (woman); *Charitas/Liefde* (woman, with boy and young child); *Pax/Vrede* (woman); *Timor Dei/Vrese Goods* (man).

her head),[6] holds up the right arm of one merchant, as if to gesture an oath, and pulls the other merchant's right hand to shake the first merchant's left hand. Behind them, sitting among the barrels and bales (some adorned with merchants' signs) a blindfolded man (identified as '*Notarius imperitus*') is sitting and writing up a document.[7]

3. '*Waenr[ec]ht hartneckich, duister testament, myn en dyn/met begeerte blint, halen t'Proces, eendrachts venyn*' (An obstinate delusion of one's right, an obscure will, Mine and Thine/together with blind desire, fetch Litigation, the venom of concord).

Walking out of a cave, with a city in the distance, a procession led by a Cupido whose upper part of the head, including his eyes, is covered by (possibly) a handbag turned upside down,[8] a woman whose head has turned into a skull ('*Testamenta*'),[9] holding with her right hand the left arm of Litigation ('*Lis*', dressed as a gentleman, *cf. infra* for his description), whose right arm is held by another woman ('*Opinio*', whose hair is held by several reading-glasses),[10] and followed by Mine ('*Meum*') and Thine ('*Tuum*'), both engaged in a discussion.

4. '*Hi behoeft drie sacken die met process is gequelt,/Een vol onscamelheit, een vol gedult, een vol gelt*' (He who is affected by litigation needs three bags:/One full of shamelessness, one full of patience, one full of money, Fig. 10.2).

A male litigant ('*Litigator*') walks up the steps towards a building (which can be understood to be the courthouse) carrying in each hand a labelled case bag. He is followed by three women, all carrying a large and full bag over their shoulder: on the bags, the inscriptions, respectively, '*Impudentia*', '*Patientia*', '*Pecunia*'. On top of the steps, a pair of gentlemen engaged in conversation, two others leaning casually against the railing, one looking down at the figures walking up.

5. '*Huis en hof verslint het Proces onversadelijck/Met gesindts, tyds en der zielen versuym scadelijck*' (Litigation insatiably devours house and yard,/detrimental because of the neglect of one's home, one's time and one's soul).

---

[6]In Galle's representation, also a fishing-rod with a fish hanging from the hook, as in his general representation of *Fraus*, Sellink and Leesberg 2001 [NHD], vol. III, p. 28, n° 353.

[7]For a brief analysis (and a good quality reproduction), see the entry by Eva Fußwinkel in Eichler et al. (2010), p. 142–143.

[8]For more conventional representations of a blinded Cupid in Goltzius' *œuvre*, see Leesberg 2012 [NHD], vol. I, p. 154, n° 79.

[9]Similar depictions of a skull to which locks of hair are still clinging in the Goltzian corpus: Leesberg 2012 [NHD], vol. III, p. 223–225.

[10]*Opinio*, very much represented in the same way, plays a central part in the series *The world ruined by wrong opinion* (Leesberg 2012 [NHD], vol. III, p. 207–209). Spectacles were also associated with *Temerarium iudicium*, e.g. *ibidem*, vol. I, p. 153, n° 76; see also *ibidem*, vol. IV, p. 156, on the vain effect of the use of spectacles on a fool's mind.

Inside a hall, the male litigant (‘*Litigator*’) serves to the mouth of the monster Litigation, sitting on a raised bench, a house surrounded by land (Fig. 10.3). From the trunk of the monster, two small monsters sprout (caption in the picture: ‘*Lis lites generans*’). Behind the litigant, three women: one holding a wrecked building (‘*Negligentia domus*’), one an hourglass (‘*Negligentia temporis*’), while the third one (‘*Negligentia animæ*’) hangs a lifeless corpse (‘*Anima litigatoris*’) over a horizontal pole along the wall (Seelman 1988, p. 207, Fig. 341).

6. ‘*Onrust des herten craeyt wacker den pleyter verstijft/Door ancxstige sorge, die den zoeten slaep verdrijft*’ (Crowing unrest in his heart keeps awake the litigant who has become stiff/because of his anxious worries, which chase away sweet sleep).

In a bedroom: in his four-poster bed, the litigant (‘*Litigator*’, with nightcap) is busy writing, while a lady at his bedside (‘*Inquietatio cordis*’), holds a candle and (possibly) a clapper.[11] Next to her, a rooster, wide awake. In the same room: a woman with a whip (to which bats are attached), ‘*Anxia cordis*’, is chasing away another woman, ‘*Somnus dulcis*’ (with closed eyes).

7. ‘*Goede saec moet dic na zeech door den spietsen danssen./Voor goey rechters ist goet, anders ist mommescanssen*’ (A sound case often has to struggle its way to victory through the stakes./It is all right when one deals with good judges, otherwise, it is a hazardous game, Fig. 10.4).

On a town square, a woman (‘*Bona causa*’) is running towards Lady Victory (‘*Victoria*’). On both sides of her way men are standing holding huge quills as if they were spears: on the left hand side of her flight, eight men with captions ‘*Testes veraces*’, ‘*Procuratores fideles*’, ‘*Advocati periti*’, ‘*Judices justi*’; on the right, nine men with the captions ‘*Judices iniusti*’, ‘*Advocati imperiti*’, ‘*Procuratores negligentes*’, ‘*Testes falsi*’.

8. ‘*Wat wint donwijse pleiter met syn moeilick draven? Dat hem quaey conscientie en armoey begraven*’ (What does the unwise litigant achieve with all his heavy toil? That Bad Conscience and Poverty will bury him).

On a town square, two women are digging a hole from which flames flare up. One is identified as ‘*Conscientia mala*’, the other, very dishevelled, as ‘*Paupertas*’. Behind the first woman, the litigant (‘*Litigator*’), lifeless, lies on a straw bedding laid out on the square. A smaller version of the litigation monster, but winged as a devil, is fluttering above him and pulling a small human figure (viz. the litigant’s soul) escaping from the litigant’s mouth.

The general sequence of the plates conveys a clear message: civil litigation can be a descent into hell—literally. The first two plates show attitudes and the moral

---

[11]See the attributes of Inquietudo (viz. a weasel or squirrel, and, as in *Litis abusus*, a *crotalum* and a *horarum machina*, a wheel mechanism drilling into a heart) in Sellink and Leesberg 2001 [NHD], vol. III, p. 24, n° 346.

perversion of actions which lead to litigation. In plates 3 and 4, litigation and the litigant are on their way to the court. Plates 4 and 5 show how, as the proceedings drag on, the litigant is wasting, respectively, his patrimonial, physical and mental resources. Plate 6 warns that even a case which deserves to win on its merits will face numerous procedural hurdles. Finally, plate 8 ends with the by now destitute litigant's death, losing his soul to the devil whose shape replicates that of the litigation monster.

10.4 Graphic Mise En Scène: Some Main Differences Between Goltzius' and Galle's Representations

The series of Goltzius and Galle follow the same sequence, representing in each plate the same characters involved in the same action, more or less in the same display 'on stage' in both series. In most plates, the general setting is the same, i.e. outdoors, indoors, or city centre. The only major difference occurs in the last plate, which Goltzius has set on a city square, whereas Galle shows a cavern.

In a few plates, Galle has opted for a 'mirror image' in the arrangement of the characters: in plate 1, the chase runs from the left of the picture to the right in Goltzius' representation (Fig. 10.1), whereas Galle makes the same figures run in the opposite direction; a similar mirror-image arrangement occurs in plate 2.

Only in plate 5 has Galle rearranged the position of the characters on stage, so as to place the litigation monster at the centre, reinforcing the similarity with the traditional representation of a judge overlooking a courtroom.

Both series are closely related, except for the style, and share many original features and details, but at the same time, Galle has departed from the presumed original version in his specific representations of the settings and characters. Some of these changes which appear relevant for understanding the central theme of the series will be discussed further on.

10.5 The Recurrent Actors of Litis abusus

A few characters appear in different plates. Firstly, the pair Mine and Thine, in plates 1 (Fig. 10.1) and 3. Their recurrent appearance emphasises their role both as a deeper cause of litigation and the initiation of legal proceedings.

The litigant, a central character in the theme of the series, appears in four plates (4, 5, 6 and 8). We see him at the outset of the court proceedings and at the very end of the tale, when he expires, exhausted by the litigation. The two middle plates depict how that ending is reached, through the consumption of property, body and soul. In the first three of those plates, he appears as an active agent of his own downfall.

The last of the recurrent actors is the litigation monster (plates 3 and 5 (Fig. 10.3), and, transformed as a devil, in Table 8). A well-dressed male figure in Goltzius' series, his head is that of a predatory animal (usually referred to as a wolf, though he may also suggest a rodent),[12] he has treble hooks for hands and large wooden screws (similar to those of a wine press, linen press or printing press) for legs. His trunk opens as a monstrously faced blazing furnace, spewing out (in plate 5) litigation cubs drawn after his own image, illustrating the caption '*Lis lites generans*' (Fig. 10.3). In one single picture, Goltzius thus refers to the criticism of both the costs and the duration of civil litigation.[13]

All other (allegorical) figures appear only once. Galle's version includes the same (identified) figures as Goltzius, sometimes under a slightly different name.[14]

10.6 The Props

10.6.1 Writing Utensils

Some of the 'props' displayed by the various allegorical figures are the iconological symbols conventionally associated with the figures represented, like Peace's palm leaf and The Fear of God's clarion (both in plate 1) (Fig. 10.1).

---

[12]Galle's version may also suggest a bear, comp. with Sellink and Leesberg (2001) [NHD], vol. III, p. 261, n° 524/1 (bear hunt) and p. 265, n° 528/1 (wolf hunt; also on p. 266). For a bear's representation in the Goltzian tradition, see Leesberg (2012) [NHD], vol. III, p. 252, n° 560/1.

[13]Goltzius' allegorical representation of litigation appears to have been recycled in 1641 in England, not for referring to legal proceedings, but for criticising the system of patents. The wolf's head, the (quadruple) hooks instead of hands, and the legs in the shape of pressing screws are the features which show how the monster is a 'wolfe like devourer of the Common Wealth' (Leesberg 2012 [NHD], vol. II, p. 4 and 12, n° 188e).

[14]Goltzius has inserted the names of the characters in the plate, in Dutch and Latin, Galle only in Latin. Apart from an occasional spelling variation, the different designations are: in Plate 2 Galle has replaced '*Falsitas*' by '*Fallacia*', '*Notarius imperitus*' by '*Scriba imperitus*', and has added the designation '*Mercator*'; in Plate 3, '*Opinio*' became '*Opinio mala*', '*Testamenta*' simply '*Testamentum*', while Goltzius' '*Cupido cęcus*' became '*Cupido caeca*' (a grammatical transgender change not warranted by the character's physical attributes); in Plate 4, '*Litigator*' became, perhaps more negatively, '*Litigiosus*', a change Galle has also made in the other plates, where the same character appears (5, 6 and 8), and '*Pecunia*' became '*Pecuniae*'; in Plate 5, '*Anima Litigatoris*' is changed into '*Anima Litigiosi*', and the same applies for that character himself in the same picture, while '*Lis lites generans*' is changed into '*Lis lites procreans*'; in Plate 6, '*Inquietatio cordis*' is changed into '*Inquies cordis*', '*Somnus dulcis*' into '*Sopor*'; in Plate 7, all the names are identical in both versions; in the last plate, apart from the litigant's name, '*Paupertas*' became '*Pauperies*'. In the all-in-one version, the names follow those in Galle's version (the only striking difference being a change in the sequence of forensic actors in Plate 7). The names appear in the picture (in Latin), with a reference number, which is mentioned in the French and Dutch versions of the verses under each picture, suggesting that the French or Dutch reader may not have been assumed to understand the Latin captions – although the Latin Bible quotations remain untranslated.

Some of the items included by Goltzius are directly linked with the imagery associated with lawyers and litigation. The writing utensils and (legal) documents have thus been included in several plates:[15] the small whips brandished by Mine and Thine in plate 1 (Fig. 10.1) consist of quill-cases to which inkpots are attached with a string; in plate 2, the blindfolded notary is writing up a document, presumably the spurious contract being concluded next to him; in plate 3, the woman's skull (identified as '*Testamenta*') is capped by a deed to which five seals are attached; in plate 4 (Fig. 10.2), the litigant's case-bags are already full and have been labelled ('evangelised', according to sixteenth-century practitioners' jargon); in plate 6, the litigant is busy writing yet another document in the middle of the night (and in Galle's corresponding plate, more documents and case bags can be seen in the room next door); finally, the most spectacular and original reference to the legal professionals' inclination for producing and exchanging written documents is highlighted in plate 7 (Fig. 10.4), where the judges, advocates, proctors and witnesses on both sides are wielding oversized quills as spears, alluding to the need, in all civil proceedings influenced by the Roman-canonical model, for written documents which were ubiquitous at every stage of the adversarial procedure, a practice reflected in the saying *Quod non est in actis, non est in mundo.*

10.6.2 The Courthouse

Goltzius (in contrast to Galle) also gave the outer courthouse a prominent place,[16] thus strengthening the importance of litigation in the whole sequence. In plate 1 (Fig. 10.1), there is no indication that the nearest building immediately behind the chase by Mine and Thine is a courthouse, but its characteristic features (especially the railing and the bench on the top stair) reappear in plate 4 (Fig. 10.2), where the litigant and his lady companions are about to climb the stairs to the building where it is suggested the proceedings will take place. The background view of a square and an avenue bordered by buildings is (almost) the same as in the first plate, the most striking difference being that the fountain on the square in plate 1 has vanished in plate 4—giving the latter a more desolate outlook.[17]

The same building, which may now be identified as the courthouse, is also seen in the far background in plate 7 (Fig. 10.4), behind the almost inaccessible figure of

[15]The representation of such items in a different context has been discussed by Gustav Kalm in his contribution to the present volume.

[16]The insistence on the courthouse in Goltzius' series may also link the moralistic central theme of the series to that of the individual's duties in the civic space, see Resnik and Curtis (2011), p. 18–37.

[17]It would probably be stretching too far the interpretation of the disappearance of the fountain as a symbol of the 'fountain of justice' having dried up.

Victory, and as the immediate backdrop of the last scene (plate 8) where the dead litigant is lying on the city square, and Poverty and Bad Conscience are digging a grave in hell.

No such persistent theme of the courthouse appears in Galle's series, though in both versions, one may assume that the scene of plate 5 takes place in the courtroom.

10.7 Secular Iconography and the Religious Subtext

In critical or satirical representations of justice, the flaws of legal professionals tend to be a central topic. In the *Litis abusus* series, the lawyers do not appear the prime targets of Goltzius' charges. Two of the four figures on the doorstep of the courthouse in plate 4 (Fig. 10.2), presumably proctors or advocates, may look somewhat haughty, but the essential criticism of the scene is directed towards the litigant. Perhaps surprisingly, the only courtroom scene (plate 5) does not include any professional lawyers: again, the litigant's foolish squandering of his estate, time and soul are the main theme of the scene.

The only picture where professional lawyers take centre stage is plate 7 (Fig. 10.4), but the representation is not unambiguously disparaging for the legal profession. The picture does not make it clear whether the 'good case' will eventually attain victory, but it conveys the message that there are just judges, experienced advocates, and trustworthy proctors (as there are also truthful witnesses). The caption under the picture suggests that when a case is sound and in the hands of fair judges, the litigant may rely on an appropriate outcome. However, even the travails of the good legal professionals with their quills and endless paperwork may be seen to impede a straightforward progress to the final judgment. Moreover, one notes that the corrupt legal professionals and witnesses outnumber (by nine to eight in Goltzius' series, eight to seven in Galle's) their honourable counterparts. The inference must be that the artist's aim was not to present the whole legal professional as a corrupt lot—the picture implies that a substantial number (though a minority) are honest and competent—, but the giant awe-inspiring quills on both sides of the case's forensic trajectory point out that the very structure of civil proceedings is the principal impediment preventing that a just case may count on a straightforward administration of justice.

The litigant and the litigation monster appear as the two main characters of the series. The role of the legal professionals in the litigant's downfall is ancillary. The litigant's own moral flaws are the principal cause which bring him to initiate and, against all reasons, to pursue interminably the legal proceedings. The monstrous appearance of civil litigation seems to imply that civil litigation does not have any redeeming features, but on the contrary that it is harmful per se. It is, as suggested in the last plate, an instrument of the devil, which can bring no good to mankind. In other words, the implication of *Litis abusus* is that civil litigation is inevitably corrupting. Whereas most critical depictions of the administration of justice tend to show how the court's system can be corrupted by various actors of the system, here the system only needs to be triggered into action as the result of greed or fraud, and it will inescapably grind down the litigant. In that sense, *Litis abusus* does not fit in the tradition of positive or negative representations of justice, who as an allegorical figure remains conspicuously absent from the whole sequence. This is essentially different from the representations of justice *v.* injustice, or good justice *v.* corrupt (ed) justice, or even of the standard representations of justice in the broader sense of just policies underlying good public governance, as for example in the traditional imagery coupling justice and peace. Those traditions assume that public governance is also exercised through a fair administration of justice which contributes to maintain the social peace. That political and social dimension of the administration of justice is not a primary concern of *Litis abusus.* The social and public virtues only appear prominently in the first plate (Fig. 10.1), where they are from the outset driven away. The series' concern consists almost entirely in documenting the individual downfall of the litigant.

That downfall is largely represented in secular terms. The illustrations contain very few, and rather oblique, religious references: '*Timor Dei*' in Plate 1, and the evocation of hell and the devil in the last plate—the latter discreetly anticipated in Plate 5 where the litigant is seen to neglect his soul. None of these references is specifically Christian. By contrast, the textual additions under the plates bring the whole storyline back into a Christian and Biblical orbit. Admittedly, a closer look at those Biblical quotations[18] does not reveal many specifically religious references (e.g. to God, heaven, or spirituality), as most of them express moral exhortations or condemnations which could also apply in a pagan or secular society. Nevertheless, the explicitly stated provenance of those quotes as Biblical texts underlines that these are moral statements which have a divine foundation. Moreover, the last plate's sting is that after losing all his physical, material and spiritual assets, the litigant is finally doomed and will face eternal damnation in his afterlife.

Bearing in mind the religious character of the quotes which underpin each plate, one may speculate whether, or to what extent, the artists' purpose has been to give a figurative expression to the quotes, or whether the quotes have been added afterwards in order to strengthen the plates' message. Any speculation on that relationship is blurred by the presence of the verses, which match much more closely and literally the various elements of the pictures, and here, too, one may wonder whether the artist made his drawings directed by those verses, or whether the latter were composed afterwards. An intermediate possibility is that the drafts and the

[18]In Goltzius' series, the Biblical quotations are given in Latin and German (Galle only gives the Latin text). The German Bible translations follow closely the Zürich Bible (I have collated the excerpts with the corresponding verses in the 1570 Froschauer edition on-line).

verses were the product of a combined effort.[19] In any case, it seems more likely that the Biblical references were sought to back up (and perhaps, here and there, to adjust) the phrasing of the verses, and that, in some cases, a verse of the Bible may have directly influenced an element of the imagery.

An example could be the insistence on the litigant's insomnia in Plate 6, both in the Biblical passages and in the whole depiction of the scene. In Plate 8, the reference to Prov. 11:7 expresses the essential message of the picture. On the other hand, it is plausible that several of the Biblical references were simply selected because they included some key phrase or term reflecting an essential theme of the picture, for example 'fraud' in Plate 2, or 'cupidity' and 'concupiscence' in Plate 3 (which, in turn, may have inspired its representation by the somewhat incongruous figure of a blind Cupid).

Other Biblical quotations have obviously been selected because they included an explicit reference to litigation, or at least a phrase associated with litigation (e.g. '*iudicium*' in Plates 1 (Fig. 10.1) and 7 (Fig. 10.4); '*lis*', borrowed from closely related verses in Ecclesiasticus 8:1-2 in Plates 4 (Fig. 10.2) and 5; '*lites*' again in Plate 4; arguably, '*consilium*' in Plate 7 (Fig. 10.4), and in the same plate, '*testimonium*'; similarly, '*adversarius*' in Plate 8, where '*solicitorum expectatio*' may have been meant ironically: some of the latter examples show that general terms in their original Biblical context may have been given here, because of the context of a criticism on litigation, a more specific legal connotation, well established in legal jargon).

10.8 Conclusion

Hendrick Goltzius' *Litis abusus* is a warning against greed and unethical behaviour leading to civil litigation and the ruin of the litigant's property, of his physical and mental welfare, and, ultimately, of his soul. The series considers mainly the moral flaws of the individual driven to litigation. Contrary to most other representations

[19]These speculations about the relationship between verses, Biblical quotations and images refer of course to the presumed inspiration and influence of Dirck Volkertsz. Coornhert on the young Goltzius, at a time when the series *Litis abusus* may have originated. A few other moralistic series have also been linked to some form of collaboration between Coornhert and Goltzius: for example, the series *How mistaken belief brings the world to its downfall* has the central *Opinio* (as mistaken belief) which is represented with spectacles covering her hair, as in *Litis abusus* Plate 3, Rijksmuseum Amsterdam, inv. RP-P-BI-6597 (*Mistaken belief carries the world to hell*, with a winged Justice in the background, whose sword and scales lay on the ground, http://hdl.handle.net/10934/RM0001.collect.295403). In the same series, the plate showing Foolish World attacking Truth with a sword while *Opinio* (here also recognisable by the spectacles on her hair) is reading a book and, in the background, Justice throws herself (without wings!) from a rock, inv. RP-P-BI-6594, http://hdl.handle.net/10934/RM0001.collect.98193. The *Opinio*-plates just referred to also display Biblical quotations (in Latin) and a moralistic explanatory verse (in Dutch) under the picture. On the association between Goltzius and Coornhert in several series: Leeflang et al. (2003), p. 36–37

criticising the administration of justice, legal professionals are not depicted as the main agents of the individual's corruption. However, the series conveys the idea that corruption is inherent to litigation as a process. Legal proceedings are an obstacle to the achievement of justice, the latter a figure and theme which do not appear in the series. The core message seems therefore to resist falling prey to immoral and unreasonable passions which urge the individual to venture into litigation, presented as systemically evil. Civil litigation is ultimately seen as an instrument of the devil, with no redeeming features. The moral message is thus supported by a religious reference, enhanced through the Biblical quotations accompanying each plate.

Appendix: Synopsis of Biblical References

	Goltzius (1597)	Ph. Galle (ca. 1590)	Th. Galle (all-in-one)
Plate 1	1 Cor. 10:24[a]	1 Cor. 10:24	1 Cor. 10:24
	Phil. 2:21[b]	Phil. 2:21	Phil. 2:21
	Mt. 24:12[c]	Mt. 24:12	Mt. 24:12
	Isaiah 59:8[d]		
	Ecclesiasticus 1:28[e]		
Plate 2	1 Cor. 6:8[f]		
	Marc 10:19 [g]		
	Prov. 20:23 [h]	Prov. 20:23	Prov. 20:23
	Prov. 20:14[i]		
	Mt. 7:12[j]	Mt. 7:12	Mt. 7:12
Plate 3	1 Tim. 6:10 [k]		
	Jac. 4:1 [l]	Jac. 4:1	Jac. 4:1
	Prov. 15:18 [m]		
	1 Tim. 6:9[n]	1 Tim. 6:9	1 Tim. 6:9
Plate 4	Ecclesiasticus 8:2[o]	Ecclesiasticus 8:2	Ecclesiasticus 8:2
	Prov. 12:26[p]		
	Ecclesiastes 10:15[q]		
	Prov. 20:3[r]	Prov. 20:3	Prov. 20:3
	Isaiah 58:4 [s]		
Plate 5	Ecclesiasticus 8:1[t]	Ecclesiasticus 8:1	Ecclesiasticus 8:1
	Prov. 30:15[w]		
	Isaiah 9:19-20[x]		
	Gal. 5:15[y]	Gal. 5:15	Gal. 5:15
Plate 6	Ecclesiastes 2:26[z]		
	Prov. 4:16[aa]		
	Ecclesiastes 8:16[ab]	Ecclesiastes 8:16	Ecclesiastes 8:16
	Ecclesiastes 2:23[ac]	Ecclesiastes 2:23	Ecclesiastes 2:23

(continued)

(continued)

	Goltzius (1597)	Ph. Galle (ca. 1590)	Th. Galle (all-in-one)
Plate 7	Prov. 18:5[ad]	Prov. 18:5	Prov. 18:5
	Prov. 12:5[ae]		
	Psalms 13:6[af]		
	Prov. 10:26[ag]		
	Prov. 25:18[ah]	Prov. 25:18	Prov. 25:18
Plate 8	Prov. 11:7[ai]	Prov. 11:7	Prov. 11:7
	Isaiah 66:24[aj]	Isaiah 66:24	Isaiah 66:24
	Prov. 11:24[ak]		
	Mt. 5:25[al]		
	Ecclesiasticus 13:30[am]		

[a]'*Nemo quod suum est quaerat, sed quod alterius* 1. Cor.10. *Niemants suche seinen eignen Nutz, sunder den nutz des anderen.* 1. Co[r]int. 10.'

[b]'*Omnes quae sua sunt quaerunt.* Phil. 2.' [no translation included: '*dann sie suchen all das ir [nit das Jesu Christi] ist.*'

[c]'*Et quoniam abundavit iniquitas: refrigescet charitas multorum.* Matthei. 24. *Und dieweyl die ungerechtigkeit wirdt uberhand nemmen wirdt die lieb in vilen erkalten.*'

[d]'*Viam pacis nescierunt, et non est iudicium in gressibus eorum.* Esai. 59. *Den waeg des fridens kennend sy nit: in iren gengen ist kein billigkeit.* Esai. 59.'

[e]'*Qui sine timore est, non poterit iustificari, iracundia enim animositatis illius, subversio illius est.* Ecli. 1. *Das ungerecht gemut mag nit gerechtlich hanlen, dan das wanken seines gemuts macht in fallen.* Ecli. 1.'

[f]'*Sed vos iniuriam facitis et fraudatis: et hoc fratribus.* 1 Cor. 6. *Sunder ir thund unrecht, und verforteilen, und soelichs an den bruederen.* 1 Corint. 6.'

[g]'*Ne fraudem feceris.* Mar. 10' [no translation included]

[h]'*Abominatio est apud Dominum pondus et pondus, statera dolosa non est bona.* Pro. 20. *Dem Herren ists ein greuwel zweierley gewicht, und ein falsce wag ist ein boesz ding.*'

[i]'*Malum est, malum est, dicit omnis emptor: et cum recesserit, tunc gloriabitur.* Pro. 20. *Est ist boesz, es ist boesz, spricht der, der etwas kauft: so es aber im wirt so lobt ers.* Prov. 20.'

[j]'*Omnia ergo quecunque vultis ut faciant vobis homines: et vos facite illis.* Matth. 7. *Alles nun das ir woellend d[a]z euch die leut thun sollend, dasz thund auch ir inen.* Math. 7.'

[k]'*Radix enim omnium malorum est cupiditas: quam quidam appetentes erraverunt a fide.* 1. Tim. 6. *Dann geyt ist ein wurtzel alles ubels: welcher hat etliche gelustet und sind etcet.*' [The spelling '*geyt'* also occurs in the 1570 edition of the Froschauer Bible I have consulted; other editions appear to have the spelling '*geyz*'.]

[l] '*Unde bella et lites in vobis? nonne hinc: ex concupiscentiis vestris quae militant in membris vestris.* Jac. 4. *Wohaer ist streit und krieg under euch? ist nit dahaer ausz euweren wollusten, die etcet.'*

[m]'*Vir iracundus provocat rixas: qui patiens est mitigat suscitatas.* Proverb. 15. *Der zormuetig richtet zanck an: der dultmuetig aber stillet den zanck und hader.*'

[n]'*Desideria multa, intilia et nociva que mergunt homines in interitum et perditionem.* 1. Tim. 6. *Vil torecht[ig]e und scaedli[c]he lust, welche versenckend die menschen ins verde<r>ben.*'

[o]'*Non contendas cum viro locuplete, ne forte contra te constituat litem tibi.* Eccli. 8. *Zouck nit mi einem reichen, das er nit wider dich einen schwaren handel anrichte.*'

[p]'*Iter impiorum decipiet eos.* Prov. 12. *Den gottlosen verfurend seine waeg.* Pro. 12.'

[q]'*Labor stultorum affliget eos.* Eccs. 10. *Das bemuyet und bekumberet die thooren etcet.*'

[r]'*Honor est homini qui separat se a contentionibus: omnes autem stulti miscentur contumeliis.* Pro. [...]. *Der mensch der sich von zanck und hader huetet wirt eerlich: ein yeder aber der sich etcet.*'

[s]'*Ecce ad lites et contentiones ieiunatis, et percutitis pugno impie*. Esaias. 58. *Sich ir fastend zu zancken und haderen, und das ir den zugesprochenen mit der etcet.*'
[t]'*Non litigas cum homine potente, ne forte incidas in manus illius*. Ecclesiasti. 8. *Stryt nit mit dem gewaltigen, das du im nit in seine hend fallist.*'
[w]'*Sanguisugae duae sunt filiae, dicentes, Affer, Affer*. Proverbior. 30. *Die aeglen hat zwo toechteren*: *(die eine heiszt) Traghaer (die ander) Bringha[e]r.*'
[x]'*Vir fratri suo non parcet.—Unusquisque carnem brachii sui vorabit*. Esai. 9. *Es wirt yeder das fleisch seines arms essen.*'
[y]'*Quod si invicem mordetis et commeditis: videte ne ab invicem consummamini*. Gal. 5. *So ir euch aber under einander byssend und fraessend, so sehend zu das ir nit under einander verzeert werdind.*'
[z]'*Peccatori autem dedit afflictionem et curam superfluam*. Ecclesiastes. 2. *Dem s[ue]nder aber gibt es mouy und kumber.*'
[aa]'*Non [... et] rapitur somnus ab eis nisi supplantaverit*. Proverb. 4. *Kein slaaf ficht sy an, sy habend dann vor einen unfal angerichtet.*'
[ab]'*Est homo qui diebus ac noctibus somnum non capit oculis*. Ecclesiastes. 8. *Es ist ein mensch der weder tag noch nacht seinen augen keinen schlaaff günnet.*'
[ac]'*Cuncti dies eius doloribus et aerumnis pleni sunt, nec per noctem mente requiescit*. Eccl [esiastes] 2. *Das er alle seine tag mit traurigkeit, mit leid und iamer vertreibt, das auch sein hertz bei nacht kein ruh hat.*'
[ad]'*Accipere personam impii in iudicio, non est bonum, ut declines a veritate iudicii*. Pro. 18. *Vast boesz ists so man am gericht den unsculdigen [a]usz ansehen des gotlosen verurteilt.*'
[ae]'*Consilia impiorum fraudulenta*. Pro. 12. *Die ratsleg der gotlosen sind falsch.*'
[af]'*Consilium inopis confutistis*. Psalm. 13. *Ir habend den raat des armen verspottet.*'
[ag]'*Sicut acetum dentibus, et fumus oculis, sic piger his qui miserunt eum*. Proverb. 10. *Wie der essig den zaenen ist, und der rauch den augen, also ist der faul denen die in auszendend.*'
[ah]'*Jaculum, et gladius, et sagitta acuta, homo qui loquitur contra proximum suum falsum testimonium*. pro. 25. *De wider seinen naec < h>sten falsche zeugnusz gibt, ist wie ein bickel, ein schwaert un<d>* scarpffe pfeyl'
[ai]'*Mortuo homine impio nulla erit ultra spes, et solicitorum expectatio peribit*. Pro. 11. *So der gotlos stirbt, so ist sein hofnung usz: dan das hoffen der frae[f]leren ist verderbnusz.*'
[aj]'*Vermis eorum non morietur, et ignis eorum non extinguetur: et erunt usque ad satietatem*. Esa. < 66 > . *Ire wurm werdend nit sterben, noch ir fheur erloscen*. Esai. 66.'
[ak]'*Alii rapiunt non sua et semper in egestate sunt*. Proverbi 11.'
[al]'*Esto consentiens adversario tuo cito dum es in* via *cum eo, ne forte tradat te adversarius iudici*. Mat. 5. *Bisz wilfertig deinen widersacher bald, dieweil du noch mit im auf dem waeg bist.*'
[am] '*Bosz ist die Armut in dem mund des gottlosen*. Ecclesiasti. 13.' No Latin text included; in the Vulgate, the verse Ecclesiasticus 13:30 is '*et nequissima paupertas in ore impii*'.

References

Biblia, das ist, Alle Bücher Alts unnd Neüws Testaments (1570). Froschauer, Zürich. http://dx.doi.org/10.3931/e-rara-9023

Eichler A, Fußwinkel E, Löffler N (eds) (2010) Spott und Respekt. Die Justiz in der Kritik. Michael Imhof Verlag, Petersberg

Leeflang H, Luijten G, Engelsman WJ, Nichols LW (2003) Hendrick Goltzius (1558–1617). Tekeningen, prenten en schilderijen (exh. cat. Amsterdam). Waanders, Zwolle

Leesberg M (2012) Hendrick Goltzius. In: Leeflang H (ed) The New Hollstein. Dutch & Flemish Etchings, Engravings and Woodcuts (1450–1700), vol. I-IV. Sound & Vision Publishers, Ouderkerk aan den IJssel

Martyn G (2016) Greedy lawyers and courtroom monsters. In: Huygebaert S, Martyn G, Paumen V, Van Poucke T (eds) The Art of Law. Three Centuries of Justice Depicted (exh. cat. Bruges). Lannoo, Tielt, pp 132–135

Monballieu A (1972) The Lawyer's Office by Marinus van Reymerswael in the New Orleans Museum of Art. Jaarboek van het Koninklijk Museum van Schone Kunsten Antwerpen 1972:109–144

Monballieu A (1973) Een 'advokatenkabinet' (1545) van Marinus van Reymerswael en een proces voor de Grote Raad van Mechelen. Handelingen van de Koninklijke Kring voor Oudheidkunde, Letteren en Kunst te Mechelen 27(2):69–112

Monballyu J (2016) Joos de Damhouder, an internationally influencial jurist from Bruges. In: Huygebaert S, Martyn G, Paumen V, Van Poucke T (eds) The art of law. Three centuries of justice depicted (exh. cat. Bruges). Lannoo, Tielt, pp 107–119

Puhlmann H (2007) Ethik in Wort und Bild. Dirck Volckertszoon Coornhert und das moralisierende Emblembuch De rerum usu et abusu (Antwerpen 1575). Scaneg Verlag, Munich

Resnik J, Curtis D (2011) Representing Justice. Invention, Controversy, and Rights in City-States and Democratic Courtrooms. Yale University Press, New Haven

Seelman K (1988) Relativierung von Recht und Gerechtigkeit. In: Pleister W, Schild W (eds) Recht und Gerechtigkeit im Spiegel der europäischen Kunst. DuMont Buchverlag, Cologne, pp 195–213

Sellink M (2000) Cornelis Cort. In: The New Hollstein. Dutch & Flemish Etchings, Engravings and Woodcuts, 1450–1700, vol. I-III, ed. Huigen Leeflang. Sound & Vision Publishers, Rotterdam

Sellink M, Leesberg M (2001) Philips Galle. In The New Hollstein. Dutch & Flemish Etchings, Engravings and Woodcuts, 1450–1700, vol. I-IV, ed. Manfred Sellink. Sound & Vision Publishers, Rotterdam

Strauss WL (ed) (1977) Hendrik Goltzius: The Complete Engravings and Woodcuts. Abaris Books, New York

Veldman IM (1990) De Wereld tussen Goed en Kwaad. Late prenten van Coornhert. The Hague, SDU

Wijffels A (2011) Justitie en behoorlijk bestuur. Hans Vredeman de Vries' schilderijen in het stadhuis van Danzig (Gdańsk). Pro Memorie 13.1:103–116

Alain Wijffels (Dr. jur. [Amst.], Ph.D [Cantab.], DLitt [Cantab.]) is professor of legal history and comparative law at the universities of Leiden, Leuven and Louvain-la-Neuve. He is also senior research fellow of the French CNRS. His work specialises on comparative legal history in Western Europe, from the late Middle Ages until Modern Times.

Figures

Fig. 10.1 Hendrick Goltzius, *Litis abusus* (Plate 1), 1597, Rijksmuseum Amsterdam, inv. RP-P-1886-A-10435, http://hdl.handle.net/10934/RM0001.COLLECT.381062

Fig. 10.2 Hendrick Goltzius, *Litis abusus* (Plate 4), 1597, Rijksmuseum Amsterdam, inv. RP-P-1886-A-10438, http://hdl.handle.net/10934/RM0001.COLLECT.381066

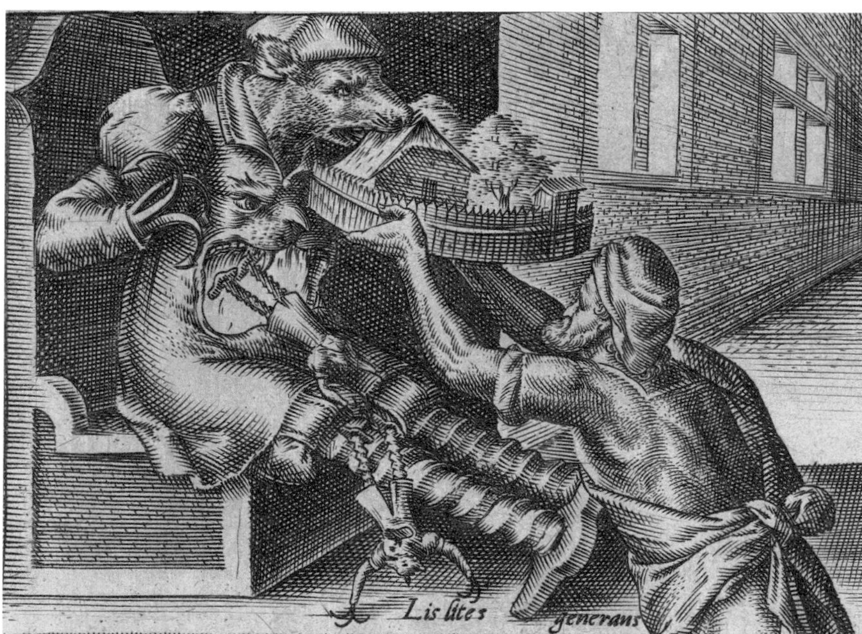

Fig. 10.3 Hendrick Goltzius, *Litis abusus* (Plate 5, detail: the litigation monster), 1597, Rijksmuseum Amsterdam, inv. RP-P-1886-A-10439, http://hdl.handle.net/10934/RM0001.COLLECT.381066

Fig. 10.4 Hendrick Goltzius, *Litis abusus* (Plate 7), 1597, Rijksmuseum Amsterdam, inv. RP-P-1886-A-10441, http://hdl.handle.net/10934/RM0001.COLLECT.381068

Chapter 11
The Paradoxes of Lady Justice's Blindfold

Valérie Hayaert

Abstract Of all the issues involved in the representation of Lady Justice, that of her blindfold is undoubtedly the most disputed one. Sightlessness is problematic: is it a sign of disability, or a token of impartiality? One way of contributing to this issue is to show how the blindfold itself is polysemic. Its nature is ambivalent: Justitia must see, she is *oculatissima*. According to the Renaissance thinker Cælius Rhodiginus, the eye is the symbol of justice, *iustitiæ servator* (Lady Justice's servant) and Chrysippus (279-206 BC), quoted by Aulus Gellius, emphasised the glance of her eyes. At the end of the fifteenth century, Lady Justice's blindfold was used as a negative attribute. The earliest known representation of a blindfolded Lady Justice is a satirical woodcut for Sebastian Brant's *Das Narrenschiff* (*The Ship of Fools*, 1494), in which the author criticised the abuse of trials and the foolishness of court quarellings. However, Lady Justice's blindfold is not necessarily meant as a negative attribute. The act of blindfolding Justitia is a paradoxical gesture, and as such it deserves a detailed analysis. The paradoxical nature of the blindfold is very productive: Is it a sign of blindness? A necessary avoidance of lucidity? A momentaneous disregard of the evidence put before the eyes? A mark of ecstasy? A shameful stigma? A trick? A game? A mark of derision? The list of questions shows the many ways of reading this sign, dependent on its viewers, contexts, and intentions.

This article/book benefitted from a fellowship at the Paris Institute for Advanced Studies (France), with the financial support of the French State, programme "Investissements d'avenir" managed by the Agence Nationale de la Recherche (ANR-11-LABX-0027-01 Labex RFIEA+).

V. Hayaert (✉)
Käte Hamburger Kolleg "Recht als Kultur", Internationales Kolleg für Geisteswissenschaftliche Forschung / Center for Advanced Study in the Humanities "Law as Culture", Bonn, Germany
e-mail: Valerie.Hayaert@eui.eu

S. Huygebaert et al. (eds.), *The Art of Law*, Ius Gentium: Comparative Perspectives on Law and Justice 66, https://doi.org/10.1007/978-3-319-90787-1_11

11.1 Introduction

Of all the issues involved in the representation of Lady Justice, that of her blindfold is undoubtedly the most disputed one (Von Moeller 1905; Zdekauer 1909; Perelman 1966; Rawls 1971; Kissel 1984; Jacob 1994; Ferreira da Cunha 1996; Robert 1993 and 1998; Schild 1995; Sbriccoli 2005; Resnik and Curtis 2011; Goodrich 2014; Huygebaert et al. 2016). Since its invention in the second half of the fifteenth century, Lady Justice's most controversial attribute has generated a constantly growing body of glosses and interpretations, taken up as a topic today by a scholarly debate of considerable size.

Sightlessness is problematic: is it a sign of disability or a symbol of impartiality? One way of contributing to this issue is to show how the blindfold itself is polysemic: as a word as well as a representation, it remains ambivalent.

An investigation into several interpretations of Lady Justice's attributes, made by lawyers, orators and legal Humanists, shows that, as a *res,* the object has different uses, meanings and functions. The noun itself, *velum, -i* (a veil, a curtain, but also the stage curtain of a theatre) is less frequently used than the verbs associated to the process of blindfolding: *oculis velatis, oculis tectis, oculis obductis*. If the gesture of blindfolding Justice cannot be reduced to a stable meaning, the process of veiling her body is not fixed either:, her composite body is at the heart of various blindfolding processes. Justitia can exist without head, or without ears, her head can be covered by bandages, impairing her sight but also modifying her perception of the world around her. Moreover, there is a large variety of possible translations in Latin of the Renaissance French vernacular '*bandeau*' and, as we will observe, the idea of the blindfolding process is conveyed, by texts and images alike, in a great variety of ways.

The focus of this contribution is multi-layered: first, it intends to offer new modes of defining the power of the visual allegory of justice. Far from seeing the allegory as nothing more than a vehicle for abstract and transcendent meaning, underpinning stable conventions designed to articulate fully-formed ideas, this chapter makes use of a phenomenological approach to the uses and functions of an incarnate form within the legal sphere. Lady Justice is a sensual and spiritual body. In methodological terms, allegory is open to an analysis that tries to find a balance between a semiotic trend, articulated in the Early Modern Era by iconological coding, and a more phenomenological point of view (Baskins and Rosenthal 2007), focussed on cognition and frames of perception, pertaining to all individuals as part of a *civitas*. The examples analysed here aim at revealing the essentially dynamic function of a civic allegory: its invention and composition, derived from iconological treatises and emblematic sources, its role in the dissemination of meaning and the ways in which the image is perceived by different audiences. More generally, my aim is to investigate to which extent this device fulfilled didactic, persuasive, mnemonic, evidential or deontological functions.

11.2 The Velum of Gaspard Heuvick's Allegory

Lady's Justice blindfold can be seen as a *velum* covering her eyes, but it can also relate to what Ovid (*Metamorphoses* 5, 110) calls a *velatus tempora vitta*, i.e. 'a head covered with bandages', which may be a verbal translation of Gaspard Heuvick's (ca. 1550–1590/1611) painting from 1589 (Fig. 11.1; Huygebaert et al. 2016, p. 152–153 and ill. 85). In it, the Flemish painter depicts an allegory of justice as an adornment of the courtroom of the town hall of Oudenaarde. Justice is blindfolded and seated on a throne. Behind her head, at her right hand side, one can read '*praemium et poena*' (reward and punishment). She holds a bare sword in one hand and the scales in the other hand. The phrase *suum cuique tribuo* ('I give to each what is his due'), situated on her left hand side, is a truncated version of the opening words of the first title of the first book of Justinian's *Institutes* '*De justitia et jure* '('On justice and law'). Each legal student or trained lawyer looking at this painting might be tempted to think of the full doctrinal definition of justice: '*Justitia est constans et perpetua voluntas jus suum cuique tribuens*' ('Justice is a constant and perpetual will, rendering everyone his right'). This is one way of observing and reading the inscription. Another way is to refer to Cicero's (106-43 BC) earlier observation '*Suum cuique tribuere, ea demum summa justitia est*' (to render to each person his due, that indeed is the ultimate justice). The Ciceronian reading of the motto allows for broader perception, including Humanists or a more general literate readership. Finally, citizens unable to read any of these Latin allusions could be assisted by means of an interpreter. The plasticity of allegory, as a crossroad of interpretations, collides with the interpretative plurality of how the motto might be developed.

Visually, Heuvick's creation contains letters inscribed into the surface of the represented space, and the written golden letters between the two pans of the scales attract the spectator's attention. One side bears the initial capital M, for *meum* ('mine', and the other bears the initial capital T for *tuum* ('thine'). Lady Justice's will (*voluntas*) is represented as a double gesture, perfectly firm and balanced: the sword (incumbent *poena*) is held upwards, whereas the tips of the scales are somehow magically balanced by a force that exceeds human vision. The allegorical body of Lady Justice sits on a throne under a shroud or curtain (one of the senses of the Latin *velum*) high up before humans. Lady Justice's body is designed to remain composite and multivalent.

Aby Warburg's (1866–1929) bushman might wonder how a 'natural' human body is able to hold up an even-balanced scale alongside an upward sword in one perfect and steady gesture, if its eyes are covered. The allegorical impulse does not happen within the natural order of beings; it comes from a monstrous body, a composite assemblage of several gestures, much in the same way a chimera is structured: by borrowing each piece from a different species. Only because the body of Justitia stands as a composite structure is it able to play its role of mediator between two orders of reality: ideal justice and human deeds.

The figures of the letters (M and T) celebrate, as the architect Leon Battista Alberti (1404–1472) would put it, the pictographic language of hieroglyphs as an esoteric language of eternity. Allegories only gesture towards meaning. In doing so, they trigger a diversity of interpretative responses to the image. The absurdity of Justice's gesture immediately indicates to the spectator that a literal exegesis is irrelevant. Ancient grammarians explain that the word 'allegory' implies *alla* ('other') and *agoreuein* ('say'): the trope that says one thing, but signifies another. Allegory says one thing, but provides a notion of something else by means of similarity. As a rhetorical trope and a method of commentary, the process is crucial to understand the articulation between textual interpretation applied to a reference text and the interpretative plurality required by images. Renaissance Humanists often stress the importance of Heraclitus (sometimes called 'the Allegorist', Russell and Konstan 2005) who lived perhaps toward the end of the first or the beginning of the second century AD. He introduced the term *sêmainein*, referring to the interpretation of oracles, which he asserted, neither speak openly nor conceal their meaning, but rather 'indicate' it. When allegorised, the oracles of divine law may thus be interpreted by a style of explication that has little to do with deciphering codes. The earliest purpose to which allegorical criticism might have been used, was to the interpretation of the oracles of divine laws in Homer and Hesiod. But above all, the allegorical impulse is an appeal: the spectator is first brought to a state of astonishment, indicating that the seat of intelligence might be located in the heart. The oddity of the gesture is a way to signal something that is hidden beyond nature.

Today, scholars frequently treat allegory, as opposed to metonymy, as the systematic application of transferred or hidden meanings of terms in an extended passage or argument. Allegorical images of justice tell a quite different story. Allegorical readings of Heuvick's painting may be harnessed in particular, but in order to come to a coherent interpretation, we must first map the network of meanings and references present in the painting. Lady Justice serves as a paradigm for virtuous behaviour: as a heroin of exceptional integrity, she becomes an exemplar of wisdom and endurance in service of divine law. Visually speaking, Heuvick substitutes writing for representation, spelled out in the central fragment '*Suum cuique tribuere*'. The observer may then gain access to the intended meaning of the allegory by an act of reading, from the enigmatic letter of the law to its enshrouding within the open books of the codes and the *jura propria* of customary law. The reading of the letter of the law may then serve as a frame of reference for understanding the whole composition. Pictorial composition is interpreted through the cardinal texts of the *Digest*, but as an icon, it hints towards premodern classical rhetoric. Heuvick's Lady Justice encapsulates a fourfold method of *compositio*: the letter (M & T), the adage (ancient wisdom here conveyed by an elliptic motto), the attributes (visual conventions are perfectly respected) and finally, the personification (Lady Justice as the embodiment of a figurative body). Once the *compositio* is understood as an overall structure, the allegorical interpretation becomes possible. However, this does not imply that the eyes of the observer will stick to the 'authorised' interpretation of the allegorical content displayed in the picture. Anyone prepared to delve deeper into the routes indicated by Justitia will recognise that an allegorical reading is an initiation endowed with deep wisdom. The allegorical body of Justitia is plausible rather than true. Its *raison d'être* is to give an ethical interpretation of the inevitable conflict between human and divine laws.

On her right hand side, there is an allegory of piety, with a stork holding a chalice and an enormous wooden cross, which might become more salient to an observer who would articulate a lenient interpretation of the principle of equity. On her left hand side, prudence, with her traditional attributes (a snake, recalling the biblical '*estote prudentes sicut serpentes*' ('be wise like serpents', Mt. 10:16) and a convex mirror with a handle) might resonate differently to the observer who notices the shadowy bodies reflected into the convex surface of the mirror facing Prudentia. Under her feet, envy is crawling, trying to grasp the fallen amount of heavenly riches (scepter, golden coins).

The appearance of the blindfold itself is unusual: normally, using a double knot in the back of one's head is enough to keep the blindfold from slipping. In this case, however, Heuvick designed a peculiar blindfold with two different prominent knots on each side of Justitia's face, rather than at the back. The blindfold seems more salient than in other representations. As a sophisticated ornament, it is all the more solid as the scarf used is longer than usual and its two edges fall on her shoulders. The blindfold is placed firmly over the ears and the two knots add a symmetrical dimension to this tight-fitting blindfold, this symmetry echoes the even tipped pans of the scales.

11.3 A Phenomenological Approach of the Allegory of Justice

The ubiquitous nature of the allegorical imagery in the physical spaces of early modern Europe should not obscure the fact that these images, when located in courts, serve as a visual memorandum of judicial duties.

Much in the same way as the visual allegory is always in tension, the word *allegoria* itself has, ever since it first appearance, pertained to different configurations and rhetorical traditions. Any attempt at a definition of the visual allegory of justice shows that this device is always a struggle between figure and conceit, image and idea, or compositional coherence and perceived multivalence. I will argue here that the visual allegory of justice, as a civic theophany, excludes all forms of contact between the figure (the embodiment) and the idea (divine justice). The blindfold is more than a semi-latent attribute, it is an *index animi*. It indicates that Lady Justice's body is meant to be perceived as a theophany. As Walter Benjamin (1892–1940) recalls Charles Baudelaire's (1821–1867) reflection upon this notion: allegory is a relic, re-enacted by memory. The cardinal force of the virtue (in both senses of *virtus*—an impulse or an ethical stand) is to be found in its struggle with the ambivalent essence of the blindfold.

Why is the allegory of Justice still readily identified today? How can we explain the constant revival of its paradoxical gaze? One way of answering these questions is to look at the ways in which the allegory of Lady Justice has been used as a vehicle or medium within the legal sphere. Law is an art (*ars boni et æqui*), an art of interpretation and an art of measurement. As Carolin Berhmann investigates in *The Nomos of Images. Manifestations and Iconology of Law*,[1] visual allegories must not be separated from their *nomos*, which connotes 'both the written and the unwritten law' and includes customs, rituals, manners and habits. The crosscurrent dialogue operating between art and law dates back from an ancient tradition, traced by Ernst Kantorowicz in one of his last articles, written in honour of Erwin Panofsky (Kantorowicz 1961). The main driving force of the '*démon de l'analogie*' (Mallarmé 1897) is an art of *æquiparatio*, (literally, a comparison made by similar pairing) which used to rely on very practical techniques of reasoning *a simili*. One of the achievements of Kantorowicz's article is the development of a set of analogical tools common to art and law. Trained *in utroque jure*, the architect Alberti became an innovative thinker of *compositio*. From the technical terms of grammar to the technical practicalities of legal analogies, Kantorowicz showed the ubiquity of *æquiparatio* as a rhetorical tool aimed at persuasion. Paintings, in the eyes of humanist lawyers, can thus be analysed as a specific, visual language. The principle of a comparison such as *æquiparatio* is to equate a *res* with a *res* and not to reduce a thing to a word. In other words, lawyers are very much aware that the meaning of the blindfold can never satisfactorily expressed by means of language, as it is impossible to compare things to words adequately. The method of allegory is very well applicable, to the art of law as both languages communicate truths that are not expressed in ordinary language.

11.4 Representation

A 'representation' includes abstract renditions of justice as well as 'images', understood as signs that bear a resemblance to the object represented. An image always reproduces the relevant features of an object, no matter what level of mimesis is achieved. But in order to understand how the allegorical process works, the image of justice has to be located in its spatial context. The allegorical process constitutes a time and space which is different from the time and space experienced during a court session, or recorded into the writing of *consilia*. Courthouse designs, civic spaces as well as mental spaces are to be scrutinised if one wants to discover where the power (Freedberg 1991) of an image of justice lies. Images are able to express more vividly an order or a normative message, because they act as substitutes for real people (judges). The anthropology of images may serve to question whether representations of justice are in any sense performative *imagines agentes*: is there a causal connection between the efficacy of an image and subsequent actions? Efficiency and action are not necessarily linked. Moreover, if the people represented can have an effect on us through their images, than the reverse is also

[1]Dr. Carolin Berhmann is head of the Minerva Research Group 'The Nomos of Images. Manifestations and Iconology of Law' at the Kunsthistorisches Institut in Florence.

true. We produce images to honour or dishonour people. Wolfgang Brückner (1986) and David Freedberg (1991) have underlined the distinct role of effigies in legal practice and mob violence.

The very notion of representation has a double face. On the one hand, a representation is a projection of the mind. On the other hand, something is represented inside it. Too often, this Janus-faced nature of representation is quickly rephrased as follows: a representation possesses a content. Thus, we are naturally tempted to think that the signified *res* is expressed by a signifying 'form'. We need to be aware, however, that the very essence of a representation is dynamic. The way we experience symbolic forms is different from the mental processes we project onto them. As Jean-Pierre Changeux (2016) and other neuroscientists have been able to show, the human brain proceeds in exactly the opposite way of the entry/exit functioning mode long postulated by cybernetics. The human brain projects, on a permanent basis, 'mental representations' onto the world, in a spontaneous and endogenous way. In doing so, it attempts to interpret an exterior reality which is intrinsically meaningless. This projective activity, generating mental forms, constitutes an essential predisposition of the human brain towards creation.

We can use these insights to interpret early modern judicial images of justice, by using the projective mental images of the human brain as models to approach the complex problem of mimesis. The relationship between the body of a figure and the idea it reveals is not static. A symbolic picture is and remains an inchoative process. From the mental image ('the bare emblem') to its internalisation and from the engraving to its potential applications (as a hat badge, a piece of mosaic, an ornament in the margins of a fresco, a heraldic device worn on a shield), there is an infinite number of symbolic uses of these iconotexts. In his famous commentary on the title of the *Digest* '*De verborum significatione*' ('On the meaning of words'), the humanist lawyer Andrea Alciato (1492–1550) had inserted a comment on the symbolic form of the emblem he had just invented. He asserts that 'words signify' (*verba significant*) and 'things are signified' (*res significantur*), but 'things can also sometimes signify, such as the *Hieroglyphica* by Horapollo and Chæremon' ('*tametsi et res quandoque significant ut hieroglyphica apud Horum et Chæremonem*') for example, and he adds that he has invented an ingenious little book of epigrams wherein he first describes an object, and subsequently attaches an ingenious meaning to it. Since their creation during the first half of the sixteenth century, emblems are active tools for construing legal lessons for the mind.

11.5 Justitia's Blindfold

11.5.1 Did It Start with an Error?

The enigma of Justitia's blindfold is probably one of the best examples of the inchoative nature of the emblematic process. As an official token of impartiality, it aims to disseminate the idea that justice is no respecter of persons. Nevertheless, as is well known, it started out as a negative attribute in a satirical woodcut for the lawyer Sebastian Brant's (1458–1521) *Das Narrenschiff* (1494) (Huygebaert et al. 2016, p. 179–180, Fig. 103 and cat. 126). Several lawyers show that its symbolism contains both positive and negative valences, which has resulted in a series of lively comments and philological inquiries. Moreover, the reception of the image of Justitia's blindfold is not always carefully controlled: in its profound ambiguity, it bears a fear of misleading interpretations. The blindfolding process is paradoxical at several levels. Has Lady Justice been blindfolded by painters, by the King, by God, or is it a self-imposed hindrance? Is the blindfold a way to deprive sight, to enhance an inward-glance, or to render Justice's sight more acute? Is it a way of indicating that Justice cannot see or cannot be seen? Lawyers stress that the blindfold is not simply an enigma; it is the depiction of the blindfold itself that remains paradoxical.

In an attempt to reconstruct the power of allegory within the legal sphere and the legal profession, we should also examine the judicial *act*. Traditional uses of visual allegories may well interact with functions more acquainted to legal practice, such as its evidential and deontological nature. The image of Lady Justice often appears to freeze social categories into a totalising scheme, yet the very selectivity and seriality of these images undermine any attempt at a unifying reading. The plurality of viewers (legal scholars, lawyers, litigants, citizens) ascertains that these images resonate differently and can lead to opposite perceptions. In contrast to an erudite jurist who proposes an iconological reading, harnessing meaning to a particular, telling detail (Morellian method[2]), a litigant might experience the allegory's more provisional and fugitive effects. Judicial allegories are to be scrutinised on the premise that several specific interpretative communities react differently to allegorical imagery, and that the issue goes well beyond the notion of a literal visual interpretation.

The blindfolding process is often referred to as an error, a crime against ancient wisdom and ancient texts. According to the Renaissance thinker Cælius Rhodiginus (1469–1525), the eye is the symbol of justice is the eye, and therefore Justitia must see, she is *oculatissima*. Her eye is '*justitiae servator*', justice's servant, and Chrysippus, in his treatise about the nature of beauty and pleasure (*Aulus Gellius* 14:4), insisted upon her sight and the keen gaze of her eyes.

[2]The Morellian method has its nearest roots in Giovani Morelli's (1816-1891) own discipline of medicine, with a particular way of identifying disease through several symptoms, each of which may seem, at first, totally trivial. This technique has been used by art historians, namely by Carlo Ginzburg in the manner of a detective method. It serves to identify from clues unnoticed by others, the author of a painting, in much the same way as the author of a crime is revealed by a particularly telling detail. The identity of the artist is expressed most reliably in the details that are least attended to.

11.5.2 *Jacob de Gheyn's Justitia*

In a roundel engraved by Jacob (II) de Gheyn of circa 1593 (Fig. 11.2, Huygebaert et al. 2016, Fig. 83, cat. 103), there is a striking example of a paradoxical blindfold: the bandage covers only half of her sight, as well as her revolving eyes and half-open mouth. Along with her hardened nipples, it makes her look as if she is in a state of ecstasy. Crowned with laurels, her ecstatic mind expands her interior sight and spiritual awareness: she stands as the exact opposite of strict justice, the kind that seeks to provide adequate compensation. This ecstatic justice goes beyond the mere norms of human justice: her excess shows the enthusiasm of pure love as she embodies the superior sight of divine justice. Lady Justice, represented into the convex and circular shape of a shield, acts as the visual depiction of the Latin legal proverb '*In gremio legis*' (in the bosom of the law), which is an interpretation of the idea 'under the protection of the law'. But here, the depiction of an erotic body with a technical virtuosity stages a freestanding act of statuary, echoed by the six other virtues of the series.

Instead of painting, like Heuvick, a more or less inscrutable hieroglyph, de Gheyn celebrates justice as ecstasy, more than a century before Bernini (1598–1680) used the same ambiguous method of representation to carve out his famous Saint Theresa of Avila in a quite different context. The ecstatic Lady Justice presents a dual appeal, to the learned and the unlearned. Without any accompanying text except from the fragmented wording '*IUSTI/TIA*', Lady Justice carries her sword in a very negligent way, as a warrior would do, and she seems to be holding the scales at the balancing point, making the observer wonder why they are off-balance. Ecstatic justice is precisely the opposite of firmness, as a visual representation of order.

11.5.3 *De Iusticia Pingenda*

The question raised by the dialogue *De Iusticia pingenda* ('On the Painting of Justice'), already discussed by several scholars (Resnik and Curtis 2011), is still productive today. The piece is a fictitious and ironic dialogue between Momus and the painter Andrea Mantegna (1430/1431–1506), set sometime around 1488–1490. Momus, the ironic face of knowledge, addresses the same question as the one puzzled observers ask themselves today:

> Momus: 'How can you represent Justice both with one eye and many eyes; and how can you depict her with one hand only, and yet measuring, and at the same time weighing, and simultaneously brandishing a sword? Unless of course they are all raving mad. Flatly, the thing cannot be done…'
>
> Mantegna: 'Justice [the Carmelite said] is the will of God…'

Both disputants seek a consensus around the depiction of human justice, which is said to be imprinted on the human mind. From the outset, justice is embedded in the core of our nature, as an instinct of self-protection, to such an extent that Mantegna says justice and life should be sisters. This allegorical dialogue ends with the affirmation that, only when a decree of divine justice will decide to put all men equal under her guard, only then death will reveal us all and attain some sort of consensus about real justice. Allegory only reaches a form of stability when all men are revealed equally in the trial of the Last Judgment. Momus hints at the very essence of the allegorical process. Death only can fulfil a narrative of allegoresis, since when we die, we automatically give up our interpretative plasticity. Death ironically reaches some sort of coherence: the univocity of a tomb.

11.5.4 The Paradox of Blindfolding

The act of blindfolding is a paradoxical gesture and as such, it deserves a detailed analysis. Justice's blindness is the result of an emblematic process: the inherent polysemy of the blindfold shows that any blindfolded allegory taken alone can accommodate several textual interpretations that can, effectively turn into a different emblem, depending on the preferences of an active viewer.

When the erring meanings of the blindfold are framed into an attribute, the sign still remains ambiguous: the official language tends to interpret it in a positive way, but many people today still see it as a sign of derision: Lady Justice's blindfold is often understood as proof of her helplessness. Nevertheless, it is always possible that the blindfold escapes the intention of its observers; this is why there is no end to the conflicts about what is considered as a 'right' attribute for justice. Judges will not necessarily argue for a sign of virtuous celebration, as they are well aware that it is a potentially derisive mark. Again, the question arises when a representation of justice as an institution needs to be displayed publicly. The same is true for the citizen: depending on his view about justice as an institution, he will opt or not for an irreverent disfiguration of Justitia.

Because the blindfold is essentially ambivalent, it has generated a wide array of glosses or alleged misinterpretations: the blunt opposition between a clear-sighted justice and a blindfolded one is unable to capture the complexity of this articulation. Justice's sight is paradoxical, and it is too simplistic to state that sight is valuable; and the failure to see derided. In the Early Modern Era, the blindfold is a *symbolon*, it bears multiple meanings; conflation is essential. As a token of mutual identification, the *symbolon* is essentially tensive. Moreover, images are able to more express an order or some other normative message more vividly than texts, since they act as substitutes for real people (judges). Justice wears a blindfold, which is an enigma, an index of mystery and not a straightforward signifier. The only method that seems relevant for apprehending the variegated nature of Lady Justice's blindfolds is looking at the spatial frames of reference that her images institutes.

To consolidate this stand, the collection of contemporary accounts of how these blindfolds were viewed and translated into texts will help sharpen the focus of the study. Renaissance lawyers were very much aware of the paradoxical nature of this symbolism. Justice's blindfold revives the paradoxical games of legal aphorisms. '*Audi* (or *audite*) *et alteram partem*' (Hear—singular or plural—the other side) is built on a dialogical principle. Justice needs a powerful form of symbolism to articulate the fact that legal words both compliment and contradict each other. Judicial discourse is itself constituted by a vast network of interrelated texts. Perhaps only a paradoxical emblem can do justice to the very essence of adjudication.

11.6 Clear-Sighted Justice in Greek and Roman Antiquity

According to classical authors, the goddess of Justice was clear-sighted. Athenaeus of Naucratis (2nd-3th c.) (*The Deipnosophists*, 12:65) recalls that several people made an effigy of justice bearing a golden face with golden eyes. This was meant to signify that all citizens were equal in the eyes of justice. Plato says that Justice 'looks abroad' ('*foras spectat*') and that she is the 'trustworthy observer' (*fida speculatrix*) of others (Pl. 2.7.229). According to Cælius Rhodiginus (*Lectiones Antiquarum*, liber 29), justice's symbol is an eye, and her gaze is penetrating. Aulus Gellius, the second-century jurist and rhetor, reproduced an ecphrasis of Justitia from Stoic sources in Greek in his *Attic Nights*. The description was taken from Chrysippus, according to whom Justice is 'an awe-inspiring virgin with penetrating eyes ('*luminibus oculorum acribus*') and with some venerable grief in her dignity'. The purpose of this appearance was that 'she might inspire fear in the wicked and courage in the good: to the latter, as her friends, she presents a friendly aspect, to the former a stern face'.

Another intention was to set an example for the good judge, who 'ought to be dignified, holy, austere, incorruptible, not susceptible to flattery and inexorable towards the wicked and the guilty, vigorous, lofty and powerful, terrible by reason of the force and majesty of equity and truth'. This famous passage is regularly quoted by humanist lawyers and orators alike. Diodore of Sicily refers to a part of Egypt, where the doors of truth stand, and mentions a statue of justice which bears no head. In his *Hieroglyphica*, namely in the hieroglyph dedicated to Cælio Curione devoted to the theme of justice (ed. Siena 1626, p. 797), the poet and Humanist Pierio Valeriano gives an interpretation of the theme of an headless Justice. It is because her head needs to be inside the clouds, as a sign of divinity, that she bears no head. He adds that Athenians, when sitting on the Aeropagus, had their head covered by a veil, in order to avoid the gaze of spectators (Fig. 11.3).

11.7 The Blindfolding of Justitia

Except for this last case (Lady Justice without head), Justitia was known in Antiquity for her clear-sightedness. The idea of placing a blindfold around her eyes arose only in 1494, in Germany, when in the first edition of *The Ship of Fools* by the lawyer Sebastian Brant, a woodcut showed a jester tying the eyes of Justitia with a blindfold. The blindfold was intended to imply an absence of judgment, and was originally meant to mock justice and criticise the ignorance and dishonesty of the courts. In this derisive context, the blindfold is not to be considered an attribute on equal footing with the sword or the scales: instead it is momentaneous; it has to be removed as it is an obstacle created by human folly. Brant expects his readers to remove Lady Justice's blindfold and restore her penetrating gaze.

Justice is not only an institution or an academic discipline. It is, for most people, a formalised ritual susceptible to mockery. The blindfolding process is and remains an intriguing gesture. As an attribute for Lady Justice, it has never been a fully formed idea. It is, at best, a semi-attribute; its value as a tool for allegorical identification is not fully efficient. This is the reason why many commentators have underlined the absurdity of such a symbolic choice for the representation of Justice.

The official explanation of the blindfold is that Lady Justice without eyes or hands cannot be corrupted. Blindfolds make it harder for her to solicit or receive bribes. Her eyes are covered so that the rich and poor appear the same, as we can read in an inscription written in the antechamber of the old Tübingen town hall, where Justice is painted as blindfolded on a mural. In Ripa's *Iconologia*, one of the many models for justice is depicted as blindfolded. The device aims to clarify knowledge: 'Justice's eyes are bandaged and thus she cannot see anything that might cause her to judge in a manner that is against reason' (ed. Padua 1611, p. 203).

Is the blindfolding process read by humanist lawyers as a token of Justitia's ability to clarify the reason of the Law? The Angevin criminal law scholar Pierre Ayrault (1536–1601) wrote an influent treatise called *L'ordre, la formalité et instruction judiciaire*, a discourse on judicial procedure first published in 1576. In it, he argues that every suspect must receive a formal judicial proceeding with cross-examination of witnesses in order for the justice system to work properly. He has an original statement about the blindfold of Justice: 'We say that, even if Justice is blindfolded, she is not blind. As when she's seeking truth (which is the task of the investigation procedure) she rightfully opens up her eyes. It is only when truth has been obtained that she blindfolds her eyes in order to judge.' The blindfolding process is thought of as a momentaneous time span and it happens only when truth has been settled down.

The figure of a blindfolded Justice is often used in public spaces, so as to appear under public purview. Christian-Nils Robert showed that it was not by chance that, in Northern Europe, many statues and fountains of blindfolded Justitia were placed in town squares next to newly erected buildings, in which a nascent public sphere was gradually emerging. One particularly telling example is a wooden sculpture of a judge kneeling in front of a blindfolded Justice, currently exhibited at the Musée municipal de Cambrai. It was originally placed on the front façade of the courthouse of Cambrai, in memory of a judicial error committed by a judge. The French *bailli* of Marcoing, Jean de Bove, who had sentenced an innocent person to jail, had, in 1552, the sculptor Guillaume Dannolle create a statue in which he kneeled in front of an effigy of a blindfolded Lady Justice. The Museum of Cambrai still holds a wooden model of this statue (*Jehan de Bove, bailli de Marcoing, demande grâce à la Justice*). It is the bronze version of it that was placed above the entrance of the courthouse of Cambrai to perpetuate the memory of his punishment. Lady Justice wears a kind of peplum tied at her waist; she is blindfolded, holds scales in her left hand and lean on a no longer existing sword. Jean de Bove is kneeling, bareheaded, hands in prayer. Imploringly, he looks up at Justice. In his unequal eye-dialogue with the goddess, the penitent judge pays homage to Lady Justice in return her blindfold makes her look implacable and merciless. This scene is above all an effigy of public humiliation.[3] Being unable to meet the eyes of the sculpture is part of his penance Here, the blindfold shows clearly and painfully the limits of law officials and their earthly incapacities.

11.8 Seventeenth-Century Apologetics of the Blindfold

11.8.1 Jacob de Cater

In an engraving by Jacob de Cater (1593–1657) from 1645,[4] the blindfold has become a powerful attribute for impartiality, and the upright sword and aligned scales reinforce the clarity of what was at first a disconcerting attribute. Justitia is seated on her throne, and the Latin text in a cartouche below the image underlines her incorruptibility. This image is extracted from a book of emblems, the Latin text displayed behind the image dwells on the significance of the blindfold:

> Iconism of Justice
>
> True Justice is blind and deaf, but this blindness is not due to the fact that the object of her desires is gold, and her deafness is not due either to the fact that she is often exposed to rich promises. She sees too much, if she sees gold; she hears too much, if she listens to flattery. And nonetheless she's able to see, but at the same time she is blind. And she's able to listen and nonetheless she is deaf. She uses her faculty of sight to investigate the motives of the crimes she punishes and to evaluate the merits that she greets with rewards; however, she is blind, so as to be no respecter of persons.

[3]See the contribution by Paul De Win in this volume on works of art as part of the execution of criminal sentences in the Early Modern Era.

[4]De Cater, Jacob. 1645. *Virtutes Cardinales Ethico Emblemata Expressae*. Antwerp: Balthazar Moretus, vol. II, p. 10-11, trans. VH.

As a didactic interpretation of the paradoxical attribute of the blindfold, the text first isolates its possible misunderstandings. The exemplar shows that conflict about whether the blindfold ought to be seen in a positive light had generated a number of possible misinterpretations. Whether this explanation of justice's even-handedness actually convinced his readers is not known, but the message is conveyed through a dialogical poem, not by means of a doctrinal discourse.

One oft-used rationale argues that the blindfolding device, as a way of robbing the judges of their direct sight, urges them to focus on their hearing of the cause instead. The blindfold encourages a higher reliance on the sense of hearing. Many painters, Ole Worm says,[5] have put a blindfold on Lady Justice's face to prevent her from looking at litigating persons, in order to better focus on listening to the trial instead, and hence give to everyone their due. In Roman law, the testimony of eyewitnesses is not trustworthy enough: one eyewitness account alone is not sufficient to prove that someone is guilty. Whenever possible, lawyers sought to convert hearsay or single-witness testimony into a record established by multiple eye-witnesses. The blindfold's function here is clear: it is meant to avoid the limitations of eyewitness testimony in order to focus on the legal principle of *Audi alteram partem* instead

Lady Justice's body is used as an 'animative' (Taylor 2016) to make the observer imagine having the very limited perception that is the result if a blindfold. It acts as an animated form and serves as a virtual model to experience a shift in perception. If one defines the body as a coordinate structure of gestures, the allegorical body can articulate virtual gestures that are different from our usual ones. Justice's body, as perceived in the brain of the observer, may be seen as a conflation of three human bodies: the litigant, the judge and the executioner. Under the bosom of divine justice, the eye of the observer is caught by the mirrored gestures of Lady Justice. As a composite structure of various gestures, Justitia's body may be perceived and made intelligible by the gradual understanding of her gestures as elements of symbolic acts. Taken together, sculptural virtuosity and Latin mottos almost never point in the same direction. An observer, instead of being caught by the moralisation of the allegory, might applaud the pleasure of the senses first. Conversely, it can be argued that aesthetic pleasure can drive one's imagination to contemplate Justice as an ideal. In the judicial sphere of legal *actio*, the allegorical body of Lady Justice might distract jurists from their focus on the text of the law.

11.8.2 Jacques Gouthière

Other contemporary testimonials show that Justice's blindfold is a constant object of paradoxical interpretation. In 1618,, Jacques Gouthière (d. 1638), an early

[5]Worm, Ole. 1643. Danicorum onumentorum libri sex, e spissis antiquitatum tenebris et in Dania ac Norvegia extantibus ruderibus. Copenhagen: Joachim Moltke.

seventeenth-century French Humanist and lawyer, wrote a paradoxical eulogy of blindness,[6] in which he comments extensively on Justitia's blindfold. His piece is entitled *Tiresias or a praise of blindness* (*Tiresias, seu caecitatis encomium*):

> At first, Lady Justice was clearsighted, as we know from Aulus Gellius quoting Chrysippus and from other ancient testimonies (…) So why do we apply a blindfold on *Justitia*? Does it signify that Lady Justice serves the blind circumstances of the time? Or is it because she seems to find in an iniquitous situation an example for meditation? A thing she would not be able to do if she did not show some blindness of the mind. Or does she wear a blindfold because her piercing eyes dazzle with the lightnings she throws, while her eyes look up at the ultimate summit of law, the extreme right (*summus ius*), which often produces extreme wrong (*summa iniuria*)? Or does she wear a blindfold to signify that justice defines itself as a constant and perpetual will to grant every person his due? It is this last hypothesis that seems the most relevant to me because justice's will serves reason. Justice's will is similar to a blind person who is driven by reason only.

This explanation is close to the one we find in Cesare Ripa's *Iconologia*. The Paduan edition of 1611 (p. 203) mentions, as noted before, that the blindfold aims to clarify knowledge. It prevents the use false judgment and keeps justice's reason free of bad influences: it indicates that justice is a matter of inner conscience. Wearing the blindfold enables one to see the true dimension of equity and reason. As a sign of metaphorical blindness, the blindfold may also be a sign for an inward-directed gaze. This volitional blindfolding is not an imposed hindrance; rather, it is a sign that she relies upon an inner source of wisdom as a source of equitable judgment.

11.8.3 Nicolas Reusner

The lawyer Nicolas Reusner (1545–1602) heavily criticised the use of a blindfold as a proper attribute for justice. In one of the three speeches[7] he devotes to the theme of the Theban Judges, written in 1581, he warns against the use of this controversial attribute.

> The allegory of justice is a goddess, virgin, eyes closed or blindfolded so as men's faces will not disturb or move her when she pronounces her judgment. Indeed, instead of using her eyes, she should focus on her hearing when pronouncing her judgment. From this point, she must reach the truth and the value of the trial. But these two things, as far as I can judge, seem ridiculous to me. Because of this attribute, the allegory may also signify the following: either it means that the magistrate might sometimes turn a blind eye to vices and crimes, or it might also signify that the knowledge and perception of all that occurs are not always relevant to investigate cases, because, as it often happens, the magistrate ignores or

---

[6]Gouthière, Jacques. 1618. *Tiresias, seu de Caecitatis and Sapientiae cognatione*. Paris: Héritiers Nicolas Buon, p. 25–26, trans. VH.

[7]Reusner, Nicolas. 1581. De officiis Magistratus et Subditorum in Republica tam civili quam literaria oratio. In *De Statuis principum et judicum Thebanorum Orationes Tres*. Lauingen: Leonard Reinmichel, Oratio prima-, f. B5v, trans. VH.

> dissimulates what has happened, if he wants the others to continue to rule in peace and serenity. (…) As far as I'm concerned, I'm fully against this opinion, as I am highly convinced that the good Prince, or the magistrate, not only should not be blind, but also should never turn a blind eye to the case.

Reusner underlines that the application of the blindfold can be understood as an attempt to limit, rather than focus, Justitia's knowledge of a given case. The blindfold prevents her from seeing and knowing all there is to see and all there is to know when issuing judgment. As a well-trained lawyer, Reusner gives a cynical explanation of the symbol of the blindfold. For him, the blindfold can only be deceptive, derisive and equivocal: it should be banned from the allegory of Justice.

11.8.4 Blindfold or Diadem? André de Nesmond's Remonstrance

One final example deserves an in-depth analysis. It is a remonstrance entitled *Le bandeau ou le diadème de Justice* by the magistrate André de Nesmond (1553–1616) at the opening session of the *Parlement de Bordeaux* in 1613. The text is quite long (42 pages),[8] so the following account will only stress the main points of the argument. De Nesmond's discourse is remarkable for its erudite wealth and complex symbolic thinking. His first concern is to state that ancient painters should be blamed for having forgotten to put a blindfold on Lady Justice. The magistrate criticizes what he understands as a *lèse-majesté*. He wishes to rectify the fault by honouring Lady Justice with a blindfold or a diadem. His goal is fixed from the very beginning: the new attribute is intended to make justice more venerable. The author gathers all the positive valences of the blindfold he can find and invent. All his interpretations are supported by long and thorough quotes in Latin or Greek from ancient authorities.

The first reason he gives is that Astraea, when abandoning the earth during the Iron Age, fleeing from the new wickedness of humanity, blindfolded herself and became the constellation of Virgo. In her quality of goddess, Astræa wears a blindfold. He then underlines that justice, as a most sacred institution, is rightly covered with a blindfold. The next argument praises Lady Justice's virginity. As a symbol of modesty and chastity, the principal rationale for the blindfolding of Justitia is the protection of her integrity. The orator then makes a more original statement when he says that the blindfold is a sign of mourning: Lady Justice regrets and mourns her more unpleasant functions, especially when she has to ordain criminal judgments. The blindfold is also understood as a *flammeum*, a bridal veil, which was a kind of cloak Roman women used to cover themselves on their

[8]Nesmond, André de. 1617. *Neufiesme Remonstrance faicte en Parlement à l'ouverture de la Sainct Martin, l'an 1613: le bandeau ou le diadème de Justice*. Poitiers: A.Mesnier, http://gallica.bnf.fr/ark:/12148/bpt6k94691k. Accessed 4 July 2017.

wedding day. As the Roman bride wore the *flammeum* as a good omen for a lasting marriage, a symbol of constancy and lifelong fidelity, Lady Justice's blindfold demonstrates her respectability. Even if these interpretations are given as hypotheses, they nevertheless enrich his reflexion and show how the symbol of the blindfold could resonate at the time.

De Nesmond then comes to his core argument: the significance of the 'emblem' and the 'declaration of the symbol'. Unsurprisingly, he states that justice is no respecter of persons and that it should not give preferential treatment to anyone based on quality or rank. De Nesmond adds that 'favour' is represented by the hieroglyph of the eye. He points out that Lady Justice doesn't need to become blind. She ought to remain clear-sighted when she investigates the case, but she must put her blindfold back on when the time has come to pronounce judgments. This reading has been proposed by Pierre Ayrault, as noted above.

The final part of the speech is probably the most adventurous. De Nesmond refers to the *splenium* (a bandage) used by Roman lawyers to cover their eyes, as Pliny says about Regulus (*Epistles* 6:2). De Nesmond interprets the *splenium* as a sort of mask (*persona*) or blindfold, and adds that it was meant to signify that lawyers should not be concerned with people, but only with equity and the generality of the case. This is probably an extrapolation. Nevertheless, the orator dwells on the lawyer's veil which is understood as a mask to unmask passions and reveal true Justice.

The last part of the speech is devoted to the transformation of the blindfold into a diadem. This might be related to a wordplay on *fascia, -ae* (a headband or blindfold) and *fasces* (a bundle of rods, symbol of coercion). Here, the blindfold becomes a sign of justice's power and authority: it is a royal bandage or diadem, suitable for a queen. The orator imagines a peculiar diadem which is to cover her eyes, adorned with precious gems symbolising each of justice's virtues. Lady Justice's blindfold is wiped out from any negative connotation to appear as a luminous diadem. In itself, this transformation is remarkable. André de Nesmond transforms a potentially derisive mark into a unquestionable mark of honour. From the blindfold to the diadem, this is a strong plea to maintain the blindfold as an appropriate attribute for Justice.

11.9 Conclusion

The list of the multiple significations of Lady Justice's blindfold shows that this attribute is a constant matter of interpretation, or, at times, a bone of contention. The blindfolding process is ambiguous at several levels; it solicits a true art of interpretation, masterfully adopted by erudite lawyers. Is Lady Justice blindfolded by painters, by the King, by God, or is it a self-imposed hindrance? Is the blindfold a way to deprive sight, to enhance an inward gaze, or to render her sight more acute? Is the blindfold a way of indicating that justice cannot see or cannot be seen?

Lawyers stress that the blindfold is not simply an enigma; it is the depiction of the blindfold itself that remains paradoxical.

Lady Justice's blindfold is a telling case study if one thinks of Renaissance traditions of arguing for opposite points of view. The apparent absurdity of blindfolding Lady Justice is soon taken over as a serious matter for a true art of interpretation. At the very beginning, Folly was the first to dare blindfold Lady Justice. The act of blindfolding the virtue of justice is not to be put on equal footing with the trivial games of blindfolded Cupids. Dame Fortune is blindfolded, Cupid may well be blindfolded too, but Lady Justice needs some sort of dignity. A virtue, and even an institution, such as Justice might be vilified by the Humanists' rhetorical paradoxes of *joco-seria*, but when allegorical imagery is displayed onto the façades of courthouses, some sort of allegorical dignity needs to be retained. This difficult task is discussed extensively by architects, lawyers and citizens in contemporary courthouse building. The enigma of the blindfold, which led to a plethora of sophisticated arguments, might seem to be irrelevant today, if we think of the necessity to revive a powerful symbolism for contemporary justice. However, the increasing opacity of interpretation, moving in a sense from a headband to a blindfold, to a mask, and finally to a veil, shows that this attribute will always generate tensions and attempts to justify its paradoxical gesture.

John Rawls, in *A Theory of Justice* (1971), famously built on this positive meaning to define the essence of justice and its 'veil of ignorance'. Despite the assumption that allegory is dead, Justitia's blindfold is still a source of widely shared fascination.

References

Baskins CL, Rosenthal L (eds) (2007) Early modern visual alleghory: embodying meaning. Ashgate, Aldershot

Berhmann C (2017) The nomos of images. Manifestations and Iconology of Law, Kunsthistorisches Institut in Florenz. http://www.khi.fi.it/en/Nomos. Accessed 8 Aug 2017

Brückner W (1966) Bildnis und brauch. Studien zur Bildfunktion der Effigies. Schmidt Erich Verlag, Berlin

Changeux J-P (2016) La Beauté dans le cerveau. Odile Jacob, Paris

Ferreira da Cunha P (1996) Arqueologias Jurídicas. Ensaios Juridico-Humanísticos e Jurídico-Políticos. Lello, Porto

Freedberg D (1991) The power of images. Studies in the History and Theory of Response. University of Chicago Press, Chicago

Goodrich P (2014) Legal emblems and the art of law: obiter Depicta as the vision of governance. Cambridge University Press, Cambridge

Huygebaert S, Martyn G, Paumen V, Van Poucke, T (ed) (2016) The art of law. Three Centuries of Justice Depicted (exh. cat. Bruges). Lannoo, Tielt

Jacob R (1994) Images de la justice. Essai sur l'iconographie judiciaire du Moyen Âge à l'âge classique. Le Léopard d'Or, Paris

Kantorowicz, Ernst Hartwig. 1961. The Sovereignty of the Artist: A Note on Legal Maxims and Renaissance Theory of Art. In *De artibus opuscula XL. Essays in Honor of Erwin Panofsky*, 267–279. New York: Millard Meiss

Kissel OR (1984) Die Justitia. Reflexionen über ein Symbol und seine Darstellung in der bildenden Kunst. Beck, Munich

Mallarmé S (1897) Le démon de l'analogie. In Divagations. Paris: E. Fasquelle

Panofsky E (1939) Studies in iconology: humanistic themes in the art of the renaissance. Harper Torchbook, New York

Perelman C (1966) Études de logique juridique. Bruylant, Brussels

Rawls J (1971) A theory of justice. Harvard University Press, Cambridge (MA)

Resnik J, Curtis D (2011) Representing justice. Invention, Controversy, and Rights in City-States and Democratic Courtrooms. Yale University Press, New Haven (CT)

Robert C-N (1993) Une allégorie parfaite. La Justice: vertu, courtisane et bourreau. Georg Éditeur, Genève

Robert C-N (1998) Naissance d'une image: la balance de l'équité. Histoire de la Justice 11:85–97

Russell DA, Konstan D (ed. and trans.) (2005) Heraclitus: homeric problems. Society of Biblical Literature, Atlanta

Sbriccoli M 2005 (2003). La triade, le bandeau, le genou. Droit et procès pénal dans les allégories de la justice du Moyen Âge à l'âge moderne. *Histoire, crime & société* 11.1:1–42

Schild W (1995) Bilder von Recht und Gerechtigkeit. DuMont, Cologne

Taylor D (2016) ¡Presente! The Politics of Presence. Ediciones Universidad Alberto Hurtado, Santiago de Chile

Von Moeller E (1905) Die Augenbinde der Justitia. Zeitschrift für christliche Kunst 17:107–122 and 141–152

Zdekauer L (1909) L'idea della giustizia e la sua imagine nelle arti figurative. Bianchini, Macerata

Valérie Hayaert is a classicist, historian, linguist and humanist researcher on the early modern European tradition. Her particular interest lies in the mens emblematica, the humanist lawyers' invention of woodcut depictions of legal and theological themes, in the tradition of serio-ludere or playful seriousness. Her 2008 book Mens emblematica et humanisme juridique studied the genesis of the emblem tradition. Her subsequent work has added works on the key figures and works of the legal humanists and has also looked at the aesthetics of justice. Valérie Hayaert has taught in Cyprus, Tunisia, England, France and is now an associate researcher at the Institut des Hautes Études sur la Justice in Paris.

Figures

Fig. 11.1 Gaspard Heuvick (or Gaspar Hovic), *Justitia*, 1589, oil painting on panel, 150 × 125 cm, Oudenaarde, MOU Museum Oudenaarde en de Vlaamse Ardennen, © www.lukasweb.be—Art in Flanders vzw, photo Dominique Provost

Fig. 11.2 Workshop of Jacob (II) de Gheyn, *Justitia*, ca 1591–1595, engraving, diam. 145 mm, Antwerp, Museum Plantin-Moretus, © www.lukasweb.be—Art in Flanders vzw

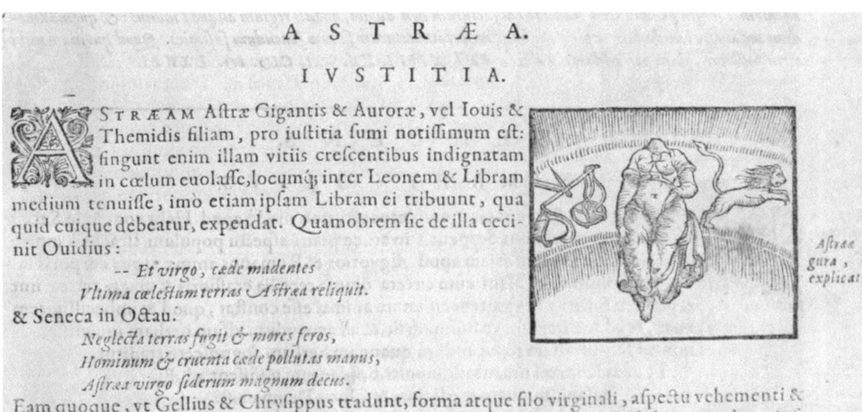

A S T R Æ A.

I V S T I T I A.

ASTRÆAM Aſtræ Gigantis & Auroræ, vel Iouis & Themidis filiam, pro iuſtitia ſumi notiſſimum eſt: fingunt enim illam vitiis creſcentibus indignatam in cœlum euolaſſe, locumq; inter Leonem & Libram medium tenuiſſe, imò etiam ipſam Libram ei tribuunt, qua quid cuique debeatur, expendat. Quamobrem ſic de illa cecinit Ouidius:

-- Et virgo, cæde madentes
Vltima cæleſtum terras Aſtræa reliquit.

& Seneca in Octau.

Neglecta terras fugit & mores feros,
Hominum & cruenta cæde pollutas manus,
Aſtræa virgo ſiderum magnum decus.

Eam quoque, vt Gellius & Chryſippus tradunt, forma atque filo virginali, aſpectu vehementi & formidabili, luminibus oculorum acribus, neque humilem, neque atrocem, ſed reuerendæ cuiuſdam triſtitiæ dignitate pingi ſolitam, omnes ferè norunt: cui noſtri pictores modò lancem, modò

b 2

Aſtræa fi- gura, c- explicati-

Fig. 11.3 Pierio Valeriano, *Astrœea/Justitia*, figure of an acephal Justitia, 1556, wooden engraving in *Hieroglyphica, sive, De Sacris Ægyptiorum literis commentarii*, p. 599. Basel: Michael Isengrin, © Collection Getty (archive.org resource)

Chapter 12
Framing the Law: Joos de Damhouder and the Legal Iconology of the Grotesque

Felix Jäger

Abstract This paper considers legal aspects of grotesque imagery in Northern Mannerism by examining the illustrations in Joos de Damhouder's *Praxis Rerum Criminalium* from 1554. The Bruges jurist advocated for the disciplinary control of the community through the exercise of criminal law, which would deter the public from future deviance. The intended fear of punishment is not so much demonstrated but enforced through the accompanying images, which show scenes of crime and criminal procedure framed by haunting grotesque settings. Popularised in Italy, the grotesque in the Low Countries developed distinctly individual forms and connotations. Rather than embodying creativity or aesthetic refinement, ornamental prints reveal intensely phobic qualities. I argue that the ambivalent characteristics of *furore* and *terribilità*, attributed to grotesques by art theory, appeal to a general sense of crisis that also permeated political discourse. Seeking to contain the upheavals of the time, theorists envisioned fear as the emotional basis and primary tool of power. Wrapped in grotesque armour, the Sovereign issued law by playing on the same politics of affect. Such images, both printed and on armour, acted on specific aesthetic sensibilities and political strategies laid out by contemporary thought. They transcend the pure logics of legal reasoning and pinpoint the irrational infrastructure of law. The grotesque does not elicit rational judgment, but, on the contrary, imposes on the beholder physically. Framing the law, the iconology of the grotesque thus sheds a different light on the visual culture of law and the constitution of normativity in the sixteenth century.

F. Jäger (✉)
Minerva Research Group 'The Nomos of Images: Manifestation and Iconology of Law', Kunsthistorisches Institut in Florenz, Max-Planck-Institut, Florence, Italy
e-mail: Felix.Jaeger@khi.fi.it

S. Huygebaert et al. (eds.), *The Art of Law*, Ius Gentium: Comparative Perspectives on Law and Justice 66, https://doi.org/10.1007/978-3-319-90787-1_12

12.1 Introduction

The woodcuts in the legal manual *Praxis Rerum Criminalium*, published by the Bruges jurist Joos de Damhouder (1507–1581) in 1554, depict various crimes and scenes from criminal procedure, intriguingly framed by ornate architectural settings, anthropomorphic supports and mascarons. The original fifty-six illustrations were created by an unknown artist, whose designs Damhouder considered vital to the setup of the book as his editorial epilogue to the first French edition underscores (De Damhouder 1555, p. 293).[1] Largely plagiarising a manuscript by Filips Wielant (1441/1442–1520), who sought to propagate the criminal law practices of the Council of Flanders (*Raad van Vlaanderen*) and the Great Council of Malines (*Grote Raad van Mechelen*), Damhouder added contextual commentaries and an unusual set of images in his version. Its visual allure and usability seem to have been essential to the lasting success of the book, which was translated into various languages, numerously reissued and widely used in legal practice (Bauer 2000; Dufrasne 2014, pp. 5–11; Feenstra 1995; Maihold 2016; Monballyu 2016; Prinz 2006, pp. 131–133; Strubbe 1970).

Unlike previous law books, such as the *Laienspiegel* (1509) by Ulrich Tengler (1447–1511) or the *Praxis Criminis Persequendi* (1541) by Jean Milles de Souvigny (1490–1563), Damhouder's illustrated handbook reveals a much more conflicted relationship between text and image, as well as a general shift in the meaning and use of legal imagery. This shift, I argue, is especially evident in the framing of the illustrations. Usually attributed to a Mannerist sense of *decorum*, these accessories are fashioned with extreme artistic care and demand as much attention as the scenes they enclose. Appealing directly to the viewer, the deformed bodies and staring heads in particular evoke a visual history of the grotesque, which is not confined to aesthetic taste, but, in fact, fundamental to the enforcement of law and the constitution of normativity in the sixteenth century.[2]

12.2 Envisioning Crime: Damhouder's Woodcuts

In contrast to its predecessors, the *Praxis Rerum Criminalium* is much less concerned with the depiction of the proceedings than with the manifestations of crime, such as manslaughter, sexual offences, extortion, theft and fraud, which account for

[1]For a review of attempts at identifying the artists involved as well as a discussion of Damhouder's personal role, see Dufrasne 2014, pp. 28–29.

[2]The hermeneutic sterilisation of the frame echoes the larger dismissal of legal imagery as illustration or decoration of a set text (Prinz 2006, pp. 63–67; Röhl 2005, pp. 335–340); for a typology, see Fehr 1923, pp. 20–26; Von Amira and Schwerin 1943, pp. 117–119. Generally, the devaluing of such visual accessories derives from the modernist discourse on ornament (Irmscher 1984, pp. 286–291).

the vast majority of images.[3] This conspicuous imbalance suggests a displacement of emphasis from the enactment of law to the criminal act that echoes the rationale attributed to prosecution by Damhouder in the preface. Punishment, then, does not so much serve to 'correct' past damages but to prevent future misdeeds. 'Crimes', Damhouder asserts, 'have to be punished so that the punishment of one can be the fear of many.'[4] This fear of punishment would provide a compelling 'medicine' for public discipline and benefit the wellbeing of the community.[5]

Among the most severe offences is 'parricide' (Fig. 12.1), visualised by a young man in front of a brick building, stabbing his father with a dagger and beating his mother to death (De Damhouder 1554, pp. 304–308, cap. 87). The scene is framed on both sides by two towering caryatids, half tree trunk, half man, facing outwards as if shielding off the scene. Their long beards and prominent noses uncannily recall the physiognomy of the murdered father, who thus appears to be multiplied, but in different representational states. In the lower strip two symmetrically arranged cranes peck at heaps of fruits and vegetables, turned inwards towards a central *bucranium*. The upper strip is fashioned as an entablature with two leonine mascarons in the corners and, at the centre, a gaping, double-mouthed head mounted on a curved base with overhanging volutes. The lions seem to allude to the punishment of *damnatio ad bestias* that Damhouder mentions as alternative to the more specific *poena cullei* of Roman law. Torn apart by wild beasts, the anguish of the perpetrator, which is somewhat hinted at by the gorgonic head in the middle, is said to serve as deterrent.[6] The intensely menacing rendering of the framing figures and heads, thrown into sharp relief by deep shadows, mirrors the act of violence pictured in the central scene. The horror of the crime, in other words, reappears displaced from the narrative setting and recast into expressive formulas of the grotesque, so as to act all the more directly on the viewer.[7] Stylistically, the simple

---

[3]Dufrasne (2014, pp. 41–45), Follain (2015, pp. 233–234 and 249–261) and Monballyu (2016, pp. 113–117) provide a detailed overview of their contents and classification.

[4]Trans. FJ, Damhouder (1554), p. 2: '*Punie[n]da ergo sunt maleficia, ut unius poena, metus possit esse multoru[m]*'.

[5]*Ibidem*, pp. 1–2: '*Publicae disciplinae favore[m] dictare ac suadere, ut maleficia puniantur. (…) Dare poenas maximi mali evitatio est: facit enim alibi prudentiores et iustiores, et medicina quaeda[m] iniquitatis, ipsum est iudicium. (…) Castigare noxam oportet, no[n] ob pr[a]eteritum delictu[m], cum id corrigi nequeat, sed ne iteru[m] peccet: tu[m] ne ipsius exe[m]plo caeteri quoqu[ue] pecce[n]t. (…) Et quos ad vitae decora domesticae laudis exe[m]pla no[n] provoca[n]t, correctionis salte[m] medicina co[m]pellat*'.

[6]*Ibidem*, pp. 306–307 (cap. 87): '*Alioquin huiusmodi parricidae obiiciuntur discerpendi atq[ue] devora[n]di leonibus, ursis, lupis, canibus, aut his similib[us] feris anima[n]tibus. […] Porro si res aut ratio ita postulet, ut his poenis aliquid propter enormitatem adiiciendum foret, hoc totum in Iudicis arbitrio situm est, cui dictis poenis semper aliquid adiicere permittitur, ut his poenis et exemplis alii exterriti, a similibus co[n]mittendis abstineant*'.

[7]Erasmus of Rotterdam (1466/1469–1536) adopted the figure of Terminus as personal emblem and interpreted it as a symbol of inevitable death (Wind 1937). Apart from signalling a claim to antiquity, both *bucrania* and Gorgon-like heads or masks were considered to incorporate talismanic powers that deflect the 'evil eye' (Elliott 2016, pp. 212 and 244–248).

but evocative modelling indicates the work of a single artist, who seems to have devised narrative and frame as a compositional whole, even to the degree of replicating iconographic types.[8]

In another illustration visualising 'sins against nature' (Fig. 12.2), such as homosexuality and bestiality, the content of the text is not represented literally, but by re-telling a biblical story (De Damhouder 1554, pp. 351–361, cap. 97). The woodcut shows the burning cities of Sodom and Gomorrah in the background with Lot and his daughters, escorted by two angels, passing into wilderness in the foreground. The scene is split by a central herm that seems to allude to Lot's wife, who froze to a pillar of salt when disobeying the angels' warnings and looking back at the cities. Curiously rendered into a terminal figure, she marks the confines of the civilised but degenerate world, condemned by God's judgment. The architectural frame, overhung by a heavy architrave with mascarons, again, redoubles the narrative by picturing two brooding herms, one male and one female, glancing sideways, exactly in the same direction Lot and his companions are heading. Set behind the frame in the upper part but trespassing outwards in the lower part, the herms seek to involve the reader who, in facing that same boundary, is allocated to the realm of earthly laws himself. Should he not succeed in curtailing the moral decay of society, as the illustration suggests, he also will be judged by God. Anthropomorphic supports such as these were a common feature of judicial and administrative spaces at the time. They rendered sensible captivity and pending punishment through the visual play of tectonic forces (Sölch 2014, pp. 84–90). Similar to 'parricide', accordingly, these herms prefigure punitive measures that were meant not only to kill the perpetrator, but also to terrify the public.[9]

As these examples demonstrate, the images and the texts they illustrate are often only loosely associated, as are the grotesque frames and the narrative scenes they enclose. Even if a frame shows compositional and stylistic overlaps with a specific scene, it could also be reused with another one from a different context. The design for 'parricide', for instance, is duplicated in 'pledging surety', while the one for 'sins against nature' reappears with slight modifications in 'theft from burning houses', in this way also generating new connotations (De Damhouder 1554, pp. 365–371, cap. 98, and pp. 424–427, cap. 114). Still more puzzlingly, in some editions, the narrative scenes were relocated to other chapters, apparently without compromising the integrity of the book.[10] The elaborate grotesque frames, however, feature exclusively in the first four Latin, French and Flemish editions from 1554 to 1555 (Dufrasne 2014, pp. 31–37). They are subsequently

[8]For a detailed analysis of technical, compositional and stylistic features as well as their intended effects, see Follain and Papillard (2015), pp. 243–247.

[9]De Damhouder (1554), p. 358 (cap. 97): '*Cu[m] enim hoc peccatu[m] sit omniu[m] maximu[m] et execra[n]du[m], no[n] simplici et levi morte punie[n]du[m] est, sed maximis suppliciis, et execrandis modis, ad terrore[m] alioru[m] mulctandu[m] est*'. For the polemical address of the reader and strong moral claims of this chapter, see Puff (2003), pp. 247–249.

[10]For the reuse of woodcuts in law books, see Prinz (2006), pp. 81–85 and 171–173; on the broader context of print culture, see Kunze (1993), pp. 108–109.

replaced by purely graphic, ornamental borders or omitted altogether, while the illustrations themselves gradually vanish from later editions, first the crimes, then the procedural scenes. The disavowal of the grotesques soon after the first editions thus seems to anticipate the reversal of aesthetic sensibilities taking hold in the seventeenth century. The spectacle of crimes and violence, staged by Damhouder to avert criminalisation, ironically then was considered to have a detrimental effect on the morals of young practitioners of law, for which reason they were banned from reprints by the Dutch authorities in 1656 (De Damhouder 1656, pp. [iii–iv]). In the same line of reasoning, some of the procedural images were eligible for reproduction in Damhouder's treatise on civil procedure, *Praxis Rerum Civilium* (1567), though without their grotesque frames and unaccompanied by any of the images of crimes (Bauer 2000; Monballyu and Dauwe 1999, pp. 14–23; Follain and Papillard 2015, pp. 237–238). The grotesques appear to have eluded the sphere of civil jurisdiction in that they do not resonate with dispute resolution and redress, but with incarceration, physical punishment and deterrence.[11]

The seemingly haphazard recombination of text, narrative and frame does not indicate a purely decorative meaning, but rather suggests the effect these illustrations were expected to exert on the viewer. In contrast to previous law books, which were equipped with far fewer images, they do not so much seek to visualise offences to be identified, nor legal actions to be performed during trial. They do not serve to instruct the reader. Similar to emblems, which were enormously popular at that same time, they are based on legal precepts, complicate a visual reading and provoke engagement. In this regard, the grotesque frames may be considered to elucidate the scenes they encase in the same way that in emblems *inscriptio* and *subscriptio* reflect on the *pictura* so as to elevate its literal sense to a universal norm. The Italian jurist Andrea Alciato (1492–1550), who had invented the emblematic genre, compared his method of philological criticism with grotesque painting, which, as he argued, upsets the rules of pure reasoning (Behrmann 2015, pp. 41–52, Hayaert 2008, pp. 156–158). Damhouder's images of crimes, however, do not conceal humanist learning and moral concepts, but diffuse contexts and references, which, in turn, underpins their blunt visual appeal. Ushered in by the adoption of Roman and canon law, the ambivalent status of these images thus signals a shift in legal culture, which moved away from ritual, gestural and symbolic actions, as in customary law, towards codification, which confined the administration of justice to the interpretation of a set of legal propositions.[12] Although stripping them of their didactic quality, Damhouder still does not discard

[11]On the interdependence of image practice, criminal law and corporal punishment, see Röhl (2005), pp. 330 and 344. In general, for the preventive and deterrent use of legal imagery, see Dufrasne (2014), pp. 68–69; Fehr (1923), p. 25; Prinz (2006), pp. 151–152.

[12]On the reconciliation of customary or decree-based law, Roman and canon law, see, among many others, Dezza (2017), pp. 83–84; Monballyu (2014), pp. 17–19.

images from his treatise, as will be the case in later law books. On the contrary, images proliferate.[13] These illustrations no longer explicate the texts they accompany, but endow them with visual force. Rather than specifying meaning, they generalise legal power. They do not mirror legal practices, but transcend them. This generalised legal effect, then, lies less in the represented stories than in the emotional pull of the images themselves, which emerges most plainly in their grotesque framing.[14]

12.3 Figures of Fear: The Northern Grotesque

Around the same time that Damhouder devised his law book, grotesque imagery, named for the purported 'grottos' of Nero's rediscovered palace in Rome, migrated from Italy to the Netherlands as a popular feature of Mannerism. Originally adopted from antique models in the Renaissance, the Northern grotesque developed distinctly individual forms and connotations. Rather than embodying creativity, playfulness or delectation, ornamental prints, produced copiously from the 1550s onwards, reveal intensely phobic qualities and often refer to motifs of *vanitas*. Contrary to its accessory use, in these prints the grotesque is elevated to a subject in its own right, imbued with a self-referential, iconic or atmospheric charge rather than narrative meaning.[15]

Hans Vredeman de Vries (1527–1607), who had extensively studied Italian art practice and theory, is particularly known for his creation of various sets of prints with grotesque imagery. These sets were intended for collection, embellishment of houses or use as artistic models. After having assisted in devising the ceremonial decorations for the sumptuous entry of Charles V (1500–1558) and Philip II (1527–1598) in Antwerp in 1549, he not only produced designs for the growing print market but also garnered commissions from the most powerful princes of the time (Borggrefe 2002; Heuer 2009, pp. 99–109; Veldman 2002). One set of twelve engravings, manufactured around 1555, pictures admonitory quotes from classical authors, framed by strikingly elaborate cartouches of strapwork. A phrase by

[13]For the prehistory of 'iconophobia' in law, see Röhl (2005), pp. 284–287 and 341–346. For the upsurge of legal image production in the sixteenth century, see *ibidem*, pp. 311–315.

[14]For the tension between literal illustration and conceptual generalisation, see Hayduk (2011), pp. 201–205.

[15]On the adoption and transformation of the Renaissance grotesque in Northern Europe, see Connelly (2012), pp. 34–35; Hedicke (1913), pp. 294–307; Heuer (2009), pp. 109–123; Irmscher (1984), pp. 207–222; Schéle (1965); in particular on the coalescence of the ornamental grotesque *all'antica* and the medieval *drôlerie*, see Chastel (1997), pp. 63–72; Warncke (1979), pp. 71–74. For the phobic subtext, see Hocke (1957), pp. 72–74; for a psychopathological characterisation of the period, see *ibidem*, pp. 9–11 and 55–57.

Aristotle, for example, is mounted on a massive base with plastically modelled volutes, a horned and bespectacled mask at the bottom as well as a small lion head on bat-like straps at the top (Fig. 12.3). More than merely decorative, the overwhelmingly rich frame is rendered with such visual weight that the quote seems to yield to the impact of its surroundings, reducing the lesson to be learned to a diffuse sense of transience. The same moral impetus also pervades another series of four engravings, most probably created by Vredeman de Vries and Jan van der Straet (1523–1605), who worked most of his life in Florence. Similar to the images in Damhouder's law book, these prints illustrate a story with a legal background, that is, the parable of the ungrateful servant, enclosed by a broad ornamental frame. The terms of this parable on guilt and pardon evoke concepts of absolute rule and legal violence that find close analogies in the political thought of the time (Mt. 18:21–35; Jeremias 1984, pp. 138–141). In this scene, the servant, who had been released from his debt by the King, attacks a fellow servant, who, in his turn, owes him money (Fig. 12.4). The strapwork, as in the other print, looms menacingly over the narrative, with birds, salamanders, lion and goat heads as well as garlands of fruits and vegetables filling the plate with teeming life. Although symmetrically arranged, the sprawling shapes testify to a horror of devouring forces, rather than drawing attention to the content of the story. Instead of guiding the viewer towards the narrative, they unsettle the gaze, which moves restlessly from one detail to the other.

Pushing the affective appeal of this imagery to its most extreme, the Flemish, artist and architect Cornelis Floris (II) de Vriendt (1514–1575), who in his early years had travelled to Rome, created enigmatic ornamental compositions that undermine any such simple notions as taste or visual delight (Hedicke 1913, pp. 9–23; Huysmans et al. 1996, pp. 9–16 and 37–70; Schéle 1965, pp. 39–59). In a particularly sinister set of etchings published in 1556, Floris pictured a nightmarish, tree-like chimaera, engineered of architectural elements, auricular ornament, plants and ghostly human figures entrapped in their surroundings (Fig. 12.5). Rather than eliciting consideration or aesthetic apprehension, this monstrous brutality evokes a nameless terror that suspends rational judgment and imposes on the imagination of the beholder. Seen against this backdrop, Damhouder's illustrations seem to act on psychological sensibilities implied by the visual culture of the time. Their grotesque frames impart a subtle horror and admonitory undertone that relay the preventive effects of legal practice as stipulated by Damhouder. This affective impact, in fact, is not only implicit in the formal rendering of these figures, but also conceptualised explicitly by Mannerist art theory.

The Italian painter and writer Gian Paolo Lomazzo (1538–1592), for instance, in his highly influential *Trattato dell'Arte della Pittura, Scoltura et Architettura* from 1584, recapitulated the controversy on the grotesque, underlining its double-edged character. On the one hand such imagery is seen to liberate artistic fantasy from the restraints of representation and *decorum*; yet, on the other, it is believed to retain a sense of order and convey cryptic messages. Just as in emblems, Lomazzo (1977, p. 2694) points out, in these images 'concepts acquire an external form' (trans. FJ), although at the same time confusing the viewer.[16] The *furore* and *terribilità* of the artist thus instils them with ambivalent meaning, neither legible as natural or conventional signs, nor simply capricious, that is, devoid of significance, as previous approaches had argued.[17]

Exploring its sway over the morals of the viewer rather than semiotic properties, the Cardinal and Archbishop of Bologna Gabriele Paleotti (1522–1597) set out to review the grotesque within the framework of the Counter-Reformation. Damhouder, who held public offices under the Spanish Habsburgs and participated actively in the legal reforms of the notorious Duke of Alba, Fernando Álvarez de Toledo (1507–1582), seems to have shared the same confessional agenda and visual concerns that later were cast into theological terms by Paleotti.[18] In his *Discorso intorno alle Imagini Sacre et Profane*, published in 1582, the Italian Cardinal traced grotesque imagery to pagan cults of infernal gods, worshipped in subterranean chambers, where, as he argues, there 'existed other bodies and other forms very unlike the ones visible on the face of the earth',[19] that had to be accommodated by the surrounding decoration. What is more, these cavernous images not only defy Christian worship, but also animate political revolt. They were encrypted in such a way that 'individuals could speak secretly and more freely against sovereigns or great persons who were feared' (Paleotti 2012, p. 268 (lib. 2, cap. 38)).[20] For these reasons, they should be considered harmful to the wellbeing of society.

[16]For their emblematic meaning, see Lomazzo (1977), p. 2694: '*Venivano fatte non altrimente che enimmi o cifere, o figure egizzie, dimandate ieroglifici, per significare alcun concetto o pensiero sotto altre figure, come noi usiamo negli emblemi e nelle imprese*' ['Like riddles or ciphers or Egyptian figures, called hieroglyphs, they were made to represent a certain concept or idea through other figures, in the same way we use emblems and devices', trans. FJ]. On the equilibrium of fantasy and formal order, see *ibidem*, pp. 2695–2697.

[17]*Ibidem*, p. 2695: '*Nell'invenzioni delle grottesche più che in ogn'altra vi corre un certo furore et una natural bizarria. (...) Perché in ciò l'una e l'altra hanno da concorrere insieme giuntamente, furia naturale et arte*' ['In the invention of grotesques more than anywhere else you need a certain frenzy [*furore*] and natural folly [*bizarria*]. (...) For in this the one and the other have to act closely together, natural fervor [*furia*] and art', trans. FJ]. The emphasis on *furor* points to the irrational sources and visual efficacy of the grotesque. The term comprises connotations of ingenuity as much as of madness and violence (Plackinger 2016, pp. 119–128). For a comprehensive account of Lomazzo's concept of the grotesque, see Scholl (2004), pp. 453–578; on his semiotic thought, see Morel (1997), pp. 44–47 and 88–91.

[18]Under the impression of growing unrest against Spanish Habsburg rule, Damhouder (1571, pp. [xi–xxii]) even dedicated his late theological treatise *Paraeneses Christianae* to the Duke. For his legal activities in that period, see Dezza (2017), p. 83.

[19]Paleotti (2012), pp. 269–271 (lib. 2, cap. 39): 'Just as the temples of other gods were always decorated and painted with things befitting their cult (...) it is highly likely that those dedicated to the underworld gods were adorned with images and forms appropriate to their condition. Our inference is that the pagans (...) believed (...) that (...) these cavernous places, deprived of light and filled with horror, abounded in phantasms, monsters, and counterfeit things—indeed that the infernal gods themselves sometimes took the shape of wild beasts, serpents, and other monsters. (...) The painters, then, (...) strove to accommodate their art to these fabulous creatures'.

[20]For Paleotti's account of the origins of grotesques and the art theoretical context, see Morel (1997), pp. 119–122; Scholl (2004), pp. 181–194.

Inspiring insurgence by evading the control of the ruler, however, they may also be used in the service of power. Disproportionate or deformed bodies, accordingly, are recommended for representing acts of justice against malefactors so as to cause 'extreme horror'.[21] Their particularly disrupting power is said to lie in their compelling appeal. Grotesques, he points out, 'capture the immediate attention of those who view them for the first time and do not reflect on them at all' (Paleotti 2012, p. 273 (lib. 2, cap. 39)).[22] Usually understood as symptomatic of a general sense of crisis encapsulated in Mannerist art, the horror of the grotesque proves to be functional to both political power and the administration of justice. The ambivalent characteristics of *furore* and *terribilità*, attributed to the artist by Italian art theory, however, in Northern Mannerism reappear as impersonal sensations exuding from the artwork itself. They subdue rather than liberate the fantasy of the viewer. Highlighted by the use of grotesques in legal imagery, this shift of emphasis from artistic freedom to political coercion and from imagination to horror mirrors a reversal in political theory that installed fear as medium of power.

12.4 The Grotesque Body of the Law: Bandinelli's Portrait

Upsetting the ethics of rule, Niccolò Machiavelli (1469–1527) in his *Il Principe* (1513–1515) advised princes to make strategic use of their reputation, especially stressing the merits of cruelty and fear as tools to maintain authority. The restraints of law may be bypassed by force if benefitting tactical play (Machiavelli 2005, p. 60 (cap. 18)). Governing prudently according to necessity, the Sovereign thus should embrace the infamy of being inhumanly violent to keep his subjects united (Machiavelli 2005, pp. 57–59 (cap. 17)). Given the deceitful nature of men he is required to keep them in awe, emanating a mystic *tremendum* that is both venerable and terrifying. Similar to the artist's creative *furore*, although not by divine vocation but by political reasoning, the ruler claims the mystic majesty of God (Machiavelli 1971, p. 94 (lib. 1, cap. 11)).[23] Not by free obligation of his citizens,

[21]Paleotti (2012), p. 258 (lib. 2, cap. 35): 'Such a subject embraces exaltation of the justice administered by the judges, reproof of the iniquity abhorred by the holy laws, and the divine anger against wicked deeds'. This particular visual strategy suspends the didactic or edificatory backdrop of violent imagery. Dismissing a possible re-orientation of the viewer towards virtuousness, these images evoke nothing but fear (Steinemann 2006, pp. 447–449).

[22]On the place of grotesques in Paleotti's theology of images, see Hecht (2012), pp. 356–359; Steinemann (2006), pp. 51–59; in particular on the legal and normative dimension of his theory of signs, see Behrmann (2015), pp. 78–91.

[23]For the homology of Sovereign and artist, see Kantorowicz (1961). Machiavelli's pessimistic anthropology serves as prerequisite for a repressive notion of rule, see Machiavelli (2005), p. 82 (cap. 23): 'Men always turn out bad for you, unless some necessity makes them act well'; *ibidem*, p. 58 (cap. 17) and 61 (cap. 18); for a comprehensive analysis, see Münkler (2007), pp. 263–280.

therefore, but through the threat of force, which is sustained, above all, 'by a dread of punishment' (Machiavelli 2005, p. 58 (cap. 17)), the Prince exercises control.[24]

Although he rejected Machiavellian thought as condoning tyranny, the French jurist and political philosopher Jean Bodin (1530–1596) in his *Les Six Livres de la République* from 1576 nevertheless upheld the political appraisal of fear. Bodin closely observed the Dutch Revolt and later allegedly took part in the negotiations between the States General and the French Prince François d'Alençon (1555–1584), who contended for the role of 'protector' of the Low Countries against Spain. The latter's spectacular failure to assert his authority prompted Bodin to highlight the necessity of force to substantiate legal claims. His conceptual terms seem to have served as a common frame of reference in the political discourse of the time as various popular pamphlets suggest (Machielsen 2013). Remoulding Machiavelli's tactical instructions into a legal framework, Bodin in his *République* outlined a concept of government based on the absolute power of a sovereign legislator.[25] Ruling a commonwealth 'originally founded on violence',[26] the Sovereign, exempt from positive law himself, rules by the force of law, which does not depend on rational deliberation but his own free will alone.[27] Just as Damhouder had argued, laws are not as much understood to passively secure the wellbeing of the State by sanctioning delinquency, but rather to actively shape the subjects by exerting a generalised prohibitive threat.[28] Accordingly, they do not imply permissions or assignments but solely 'prohibitions and sanctions',[29] which entail a threat of punishment. Without this threat, Bodin concludes, 'no law is

[24]For Machiavelli's break with the legal tradition of the *ius commune*, see Pennington (1993), pp. 269–272.

[25]On the legislative transformation of rule in Bodin, see Skinner (2004), pp. 284–301, here 289.

[26]Trans. FJ, Bodin (1993), pp. 92–93 (lib. 1, cap. 6): '*La raison et lumière naturelle nous conduit à cela, de croire que la force et violence a donné source et origine aux Républiques. Et quand la raison n'y serait point, il sera montré (...) par le témoignage indubitable des plus véritables historiens (...) que les premiers hommes n'avaient point d'honneur et de vertu plus grande que de tuer, massacrer, voler, ou asservir les hommes*'; for the violent origins of the State, see *ibidem*, pp. 317–319 and 323–324 (lib. 4, cap. 1).

[27]Bodin (1992), p. 13 (lib. 1, cap. 8): 'The laws of a sovereign prince, even if founded on good and strong reasons, depend solely on his own free will'. For the concept of sovereignty, see *ibidem*, pp. 1–45 (lib. 1, cap. 8). However, while 'absolute' by definition, the power of the Sovereign is confined by natural law, divine commandments, the 'constitutional' laws of the State (*loix du Royaume*) and the *ius gentium*.

[28]Essentially, on the notion of 'general deterrence' (*Generalprävention*), see Feuerbach (1847), pp. 38–39. Based on the assumption that crimes originate in sensual desires (*Sinnlichkeit*), Feuerbach argues for a psychological counterforce encapsulated by a legal threat. This threat is to be implanted in the imagination of all and targets the public at large. For a contemporary discussion, see Meier (2015), pp. 22–24.

[29]Trans. FJ, Bodin (1993), pp. 293–294 (lib. 3, cap. 5): '*La loi n'a rien que la prohibition et les menaces à faute d'obéir, attendu que celui qui commande défend de contrevenir à son commandement. Et, quant à la permission, ce n'est pas loi, car la permission lève les défenses, et ne porte ni peine ni menace, sans lesquelles la loi ne peut être, vu que loi ne signifie autre chose que le commandement du souverain*'.

conceivable, which is nothing else than the command of the Sovereign'.[30] Much like Machiavelli, Bodin advises the ruler to enact his power by avoiding direct contact with his subjects and cloud himself in ambiguity. He should emulate God's arcane presence and communicate by 'visions and dreams and through a small number of chosen ones'.[31] Seen in this context, the specific emotional pull of grotesques as used in legal imagery seems to meet strategical demands elaborated by contemporary political discourse. Drawing on the fear of punishment rather than insight or common agreement, they impart law with a visual force directed as much at the practitioners of law that handled the book as at the general public. In this sense, they seem intended to inspire a specific legal habitus and theatricality of prosecution expected to transpire through to the community at large. Transcending the pure logics of legal reasoning, they pinpoint the fictional, irrational and violent basis of law. Hence, they do not simply illustrate legal practices, but secure their enforcement.

Given the monopolisation and personalisation of power in the sixteenth century, underpinned by the notion of sovereignty, the same political economy of affect seems to be at work in representations of rulers. Notably, so-called grotesque armour suggests a framing of authority that at the same time displaces the legislator beyond the law and imposes a generalised threat of force. A portrait of Cosimo I de' Medici (1519–1574) (Fig. 12.6), for instance, engraved after a drawing by Baccio Bandinelli (1493–1560) in 1544, shows the Grand Duke of Tuscany standing in three-quarter profile, absorbed by his overwhelmingly sumptuous suit. Flanked by a shield, a plumed helmet as well as a banner and fasces behind him, he demonstrates physical strength and military prowess (Hegener 2008, pp. 332–334; Heikamp and Paolozzi Strozzi 2014, p. 308, cat. 19). The design of his garniture reproduces models actually crafted at the time, in particular a richly embossed and engraved breastplate by the Milan workshop of Giovan Paolo Negroli (1513–1569) from around 1545 (Fig. 12.7).[32] Similar to the engraving, Negroli's haunting creation shows a menacingly sprawling siren at the top as well as two horned chimaeras with satyr-like physiognomies facing each other at the bottom. Outstanding for its artistic quality and visual intensity, this piece exemplifies a large group of grotesque armours manufactured by the Negroli for the aristocratic elite of the time and marketed from a network of business outlets, such as in Antwerp, Brussels and Paris. However, these suits were not so much intended for military purposes, but to

[30]*Ibidem* and in the same vein Bodin (1992), p. 11 (lib. 1, cap. 8). Like Machiavelli, Bodin (1993, 216–219 (lib. 2, cap. 4) and pp. 328–331 (lib. 4, cap. 1)), in this context, values prudence over the reputation of cruelty.

[31]Bodin (1993), p. 384 (lib. 4, cap. 6): '*[Il] semble que ce grand Dieu, souverain, Prince du monde, a montré aux Princes humains, qui sont ses vraies images, comment il se faut communiquer aux sujets, car il ne se communique aux hommes que par visions et songes, et seulement à bien petit nombre des élus, et plus parfaits*'. In these enigmatic remarks Bodin evokes a liturgical notion of kingship that echoes medieval political theory (Giesey 1973).

[32]The piece was originally part of a horseman's armour (Pyhrr and Godoy 1998, pp. 226–229, cat. 43; Williams 1999, pp. 113–114).

serve the representation of their owners, who wore them at ceremonial occasions or showed them off in princely collections. Grotesque armour does not distinguish the wearer by means of heraldic or allegorical attributes. On the contrary, such objects diffuse iconographic meaning, while intensifying the visual impact. His gaze turned absently away, Cosimo is portrayed in strangely schematic terms that undermine the notion of lifelikeness, eschew physiognomic characterisation and complicate identification. Instead, he dissolves into the ornamental design of his suit, which is rendered with such exuberance, sharp contrast and clear-cut detail that it captivates the full attention of the viewer. Rather than addressing his subjects, the Grand Duke avoids their inquiry, as Bodin recommends.[33] His representation, accordingly, does not so much impose authority by evoking personal virtues to be deliberated by self-empowered citizens, but by dissimulating the portrayed, which is then disseminated in prints. In other words, in as much as he acts as source of law, he withdraws from view. Camouflaged as grotesque, Cosimo veils himself in mystery, therefore not communicating with the viewer by being represented, but enforcing his rule on him through the affective forces of his visual modelling.[34] Far from showcasing refined aesthetic taste, his self-fashioning caters to the same sense of fear conceptualised by contemporary art theory. Just as in Damhouder's illustrations grotesque imagery seeks to impose a legal threat, so, in turn, Cosimo, framed by grotesques himself, figures as sovereign legislator. Dispelling the critical gaze of his subjects and relieving himself of legal obligations, he paradoxically seeks to evoke impersonal powers that act directly on the awed beholder.

12.5 Legal Violence

In his essay *Critique of Violence*, published in 1921, Walter Benjamin explored the place of violence in law and justice, contrasting natural law, defined by just ends, with positive law, measured by the legality of its means. Fluctuating between manifestations of making and preserving legal order through power, law is said to be structurally compromised by violence. At the moment of legislative enactment, as Benjamin argues, violence 'establishes as law not an end unalloyed by violence, but one necessarily and intimately bound to it, under the title of power' (Benjamin 1986, p. 295). Punishment is understood to serve the preservation of law by transposing violence into a threat of force, which does not imply deterrence but a generalised fear of fate.[35] What is more, with the institutionalisation of the State,

[33]On the stylistic characteristics of this type of portrait and its implications for the visual strategies of Cosimo, see Springer (2010), pp. 132–142; for a broad contextualisation, see Forster (1971). On the allegorical and art theoretical meaning of portrayed armour, see Bodart (2012).

[34]For the 'mystic' dimension of law envisaged by Montaigne and Pascal, see Derrida (1992), pp. 11–14.

[35]On the notion of 'legal threat' (*Rechtsdrohung*): 'For law-preserving violence is a threatening violence. And its threat is not intended as the deterrent that uninformed liberal theorists interpret it

this legal threat tends to set ends by itself so as to spare 'law-preserving violence more taxing manifestations' (Benjamin 1986, p. 290). Shifting its focus from retribution through punishment towards the act of crime, as Damhouder's illustrations imply, law increasingly enforces itself as prohibitive and preventive restraint, in that sense, exerting symbolic rather than physical force. Just as much as violence is morally ambiguous, law takes shape mythically, not as legal means to a just end but as materialisation of a higher will.[36] Driven by the fear of fate that pervaded early baroque culture, as Benjamin expounded in his later study on the *Origin of German Tragic Drama* (1925/1928), rulers at the time did not act on timeless ethical norms, but operated by sovereign violence, seeking to preserve order in face of imminent catastrophe (Benjamin 2003, pp. 65–68 and 131–132). This historical constellation of power thus particularly highlights the working of 'legal violence'.

12.6 Conclusion

In this context, the grotesque imagery used in law books and representations of rulers feeds into the irrational infrastructure of legal order. Given their specific connotations, pinpointed by Lomazzo and Paleotti, these images not only evoke mythic powers but also visual violence, thus fostering a pervading sense of fear. They do not appeal to rational deliberation or an abstract notion of justice, but impose on the viewer physically, enforcing his compliance. In other words, they do not work iconographically but iconically. Considering the erosion of political power at the time, in fact, grotesque imagery may be said to unearth sources of physical force, usually hidden underneath the self-sufficient functionality of legality. They reveal the self-assertion of political power through law. Emerging on the verge of absolutism, grotesques signal a shift towards a preventive, institutional, that is, juridical formation of power, prefigured by Bodin (Foucault 2007, pp. 154–156). In as much as this new order of legal means and just ends rises, however, the violence of law again recedes behind the veil of representation, while the grotesque haunts the caricatures of the Sovereign.[37]

---

to be. A deterrent in the exact sense would require a certainty that contradicts the nature of a threat and is not attained by any law, since there is always hope of eluding its arm. This makes it all the more threatening, like fate' (Benjamin 1986, p. 285).

[36]On the mythic dimension of lawmaking, see *ibidem*, pp. 294–297. For a discussion, see Derrida (1992), pp. 29–63.

[37]For the philosophical discourse on power and representation in the age of absolutism, see Marin (1988), pp. 3–15.

References

Bauer A (2000) Joos de Damhouder und seine 'Practica Gerichtlicher Handlungen in Bürgerlichen Sachen'. In: Hausmann J, Krause T (eds) Zur Erhaltung Guter Ordnung: Beiträge zur Geschichte von Recht und Justiz. Böhlau, Cologne, pp 269–318
Behrmann C (2015) Tyrann und Märtyrer: Bild und Ideengeschichte des Rechts um 1600. De Gruyter, Berlin
Benjamin W (1986) 1921 Critique of violence. In: Demetz P (ed) Reflections: essays, aphorisms, autobiographical writings, trans: Jephcott E. Schocken Books, New York, pp 277–300
Benjamin W (2003) 1928 The origin of German tragic drama, trans: Osborne J. Verso, London
Bodart D (2012) Le Prince Miroir: Métaphores optiques du corps politique. In: Morel P (ed) Le mirroir et l'espace du prince dans l'art italien de la Renaissance. Presses Universitaires François Rabelais, Tours, pp 123–142
Bodin J (1992) 1576 On sovereignty: four chapters from the six books of the commonwealth, ed and trans: Franklin JH. Cambridge University Press, Cambridge
Bodin J (1993) 1583 Les six livres de la République: Un abrégé du texte de l'édition de Paris de 1583. In: Mairet G (ed). Librairie Générale Française, Paris
Borggrefe H (2002) Hans Vredeman de Vries (1526–1609). In: Borggrefe H et al (eds) Hans Vredeman de Vries und die Renaissance im Norden (exh. cat. Lemgo-Antwerp). Hirmer, Munich, pp 15–40
Chastel A (1997) Die Groteske: Streifzug durch eine Zügellose Malerei, trans: Günther H. Wagenbach, Berlin
Connelly FS (2012) The grotesque in western art and culture: the image at play. Cambridge University Press, Cambridge
De Damhouder J (1554) Praxis rerum criminalium. Johannes Bellerus, Antwerp
De Damhouder J (1555) La practique et enchiridion des causes criminelles. Stephanus Gualtherus & Joannes Bathenius, Leuven
De Damhouder J (1571) Paraeneses christianae. Johannes Bellerus, Antwerp
De Damhouder J (1656) De practijke of gebruyk zoo van civile als criminele zaken. Joannes Naeranus, Rotterdam
Derrida J (1992) Force of law: the 'mystical foundation of authority'. In: Cornell D et al (eds) Deconstruction and the possibility of justice. Routledge, New York, pp 3–67
Dezza E (2017) Geschichte des Strafprozessrechts in der Frühen Neuzeit: Eine Einführung. In: Vormbaum T (ed). Springer, Cham
Dufrasne J (2014) Les gravures de la Praxis rerum criminalium de Jos de Damhouder: La représentation de la justice pénale du XVIe siècle à partir du programme iconographique de l'œuvre (1554–1618). Unpubl. MA thesis Université catholique de Louvain
Elliott JH (2016) Beware the evil eye: the evil eye in the bible and the ancient world, vol. II (Greece and Rome). Cascade Books, Eugene
Feenstra R (1995) Damhouder, Joos de. In: Stolleis M (ed) Juristen: Ein Biographisches Lexikon von der Antike bis zum 20. Jahrhundert. Beck, Munich, pp 158–159
Fehr H (1923) Das Recht im Bilde. Eugen Rentsch, Munich
Feuerbach PJA (1847) Lehrbuch des gemeinen in Deutschland gültigen Peinlichen Rechts. Georg Friedrich Heyer, Gießen
Follain A, Papillard C-A (2015) Figures du crime et de la violence au XVIe siècle: Les singulières gravures insérées dans la 'Praxis Rerum Criminalium' de Damhoudère. In: Follain A (ed) Brutes ou braves gens? La violence et sa mesure (XVIe–XVIIIe siècle). Presses Universitaires de Strasbourg, Strasbourg, pp 227–275
Forster K (1971) Metaphors of rule: political ideology and history in the portraits of Cosimo I de' Medici. Mitt des Kunsthist Inst Florenz 15:65–104
Foucault M (2007) The meshes of power. In: Jeremy WC, Elden S (eds) Space, knowledge and power: Foucault and geography, trans: Moore G. Ashgate, Aldershot, pp 153–162

Giesey RE (1973) Medieval jurisprudence in Bodin's concept of sovereignty. In: Denzer H (ed) Jean Bodin: Verhandlungen der internationalen Bodin-Tagung in München. Beck, Munich, pp 167–186
Hayaert V (2008) 'Mens emblematica et humanisme juridique: le Cas du 'Pegma cum Narrationibus Philosophicis' de Pierre Coustau (1555). Droz, Geneva
Hayduk HS (2011) Rechtsidee und Bild: Zur Funktion und Ikonografie der Bilder in Rechtsbüchern vom 9. bis zum 16. Jahrhundert. Reichert, Wiesbaden
Hecht C (2012) Katholische Bildertheologie der Frühen Neuzeit: Studien zu Traktaten von Johannes Molanus, Gabriele Paleotti und anderen Autoren. Gebrüder Mann, Berlin
Hedicke R (1913) Cornelis Floris und die Florisdekoration: Studien zur Niederländischen und Deutschen Kunst im XVI. Jahrhundert. Julius Bard, Berlin
Hegener N (2008) Divi Iacobi Eques: Selbstdarstellung im Werk des Florentiner Bildhauers Baccio Bandinelli. Deutscher Kunstverlag, Munich
Heikamp D, Paolozzi Strozzi B (eds) (2014) Baccio Bandinelli: scultore e maestro (1493–1560) (exh. cat. Florence). Giunti, Florence
Heuer CP (2009) The city rehearsed: object, architecture, and print in the worlds of Hans Vredeman de Vries. Routledge, London
Hocke GR (1957) Die Welt als Labyrinth: Manier und Manie in der Europäischen Kunst. Von 1520 bis 1650 und in der Gegenwart. Rowohlt, Hamburg
Huysmans A, Van Damme J, Van de Velde C, Devisscher H (eds) (1996) Cornelis Floris (1514–1575): beeldhouwer, architect, ontwerper. Gemeentekrediet, Brussels
Irmscher G (1984) Kleine Kunstgeschichte des Europäischen Ornaments seit der Frühen Neuzeit (1400–1900). Wissenschaftliche Buchgesellschaft, Darmstadt
Jeremias J (1984) Die Gleichnisse Jesu. Vandenhoeck & Ruprecht, Göttingen
Kantorowicz EH (1961) The sovereignty of the artist: a note on legal maxims and renaissance theories of art. In: Meiss M (ed) De artibus opuscula XL: essays in honor of Erwin Panofsky. University Press, New York, pp 267–279
Kunze H (1993) Geschichte der Buchillustration in Deutschland, vol. IV (Das 16. und 17. Jahrhundert). Insel-Verlag, Leipzig
Lomazzo GP (1977) 1584 Composizione de le grottesche. In: Barocchi P (ed) Scritti d'Arte del Cinquecento, vol. III. Riccardo Ricciardi, Milan, pp 2692–2697
Machiavelli N (1971) 1531 Discorsi sopra la prima deca di Tito Livio. In: Martelli M (ed) Tutte le Opere. Sansoni, Florence, pp 72–254
Machiavelli N (2005) 1532 The prince, trans: Bondanella P. Oxford University Press, Oxford
Maihold H (2016) Praxis rerum criminalium. In: Dauchy S, Martyn G, Musson A, Pihlajamäki H, Wijffels A (eds) The formation and transmission of western legal culture: 150 books that made the law in the age of printing. Springer, Cham, pp 99–102
Marin L (1988) Portrait of the king, trans: Martha MH. Palgrave Macmillan, Basingstoke
Machielsen J (2013) Bodin in the Netherlands. In: Howell AL (ed) The reception of bodin. Brill, Leiden, pp 157–192
Meier B-D (2015) Strafrechtliche Sanktionen. Springer, Cham
Monballyu J (2014) Six centuries of criminal law: history of criminal law in the Southern Netherlands and Belgium (1400–2000). Brill, Leiden
Monballyu J (2016) Joos de Damhouder, an internationally influential jurist from Bruges. In: Huygebaert S et al (eds) The art of law: three centuries of justice depicted (exh. cat. Bruges). Lannoo, Tielt, pp 107–117
Monballyu J, Dauwe J (eds) (1999) Joos de Damhouder en zijn 'Practycke in Civile Saecken'. In: Joos de Damhouder: Practycke in civile saecken. Tijdschrift voor Privaatrecht, Ghent, pp 1–23
Morel P (1997) Les grotesques: les figures de l'imaginaire dans la peinture italienne de la fin de la Renaissance. Flammarion, Paris
Münkler H (2007) Machiavelli: die Begründung des politischen Denkens der Neuzeit aus der Krise der Republik Florenz. Fischer, Frankfurt am Main
Paleotti G (2012) 1582 Discourse on sacred and profane images, trans: McCuaig W. Getty Publications, Los Angeles

Pennington K (1993) The prince and the law, 1200–1600: sovereignty and rights in the western legal tradition. University of California Press, Berkeley (CA)
Plackinger A (2016) Violenza: Gewalt als Denkfigur im michelangelesken Kunstdiskurs. De Gruyter, Berlin
Prinz F (2006) Der Bildgebrauch in Gedruckten Rechtsbüchern des 15. bis zum Ausgang des 18. Jahrhunderts. Lit, Münster
Puff H (2003) Nature on trial: acts 'against nature' in the law courts of early modern Germany and Switzerland. In: Daston L, Vidal F (eds) The moral authority of nature. University of Chicago Press, Chicago (IL), pp 232–253
Pyhrr SW, Godoy J-A (eds) (1998) Heroic armor of the Italian Renaissance: Filippo Negroli and his contemporaries (exh. cat. New York). Abrams, New York
Röhl KF (2005) Bilder in gedruckten Rechtsbüchern. In: Lerch KD (ed) Recht vermitteln. De Gruyter, Berlin, pp 267–348
Schéle S (1965) Cornelis Bos: a study of the origins of the Netherland grotesque. Almquist & Wiksell, Stockholm
Scholl D (2004) Von den 'Grottesken' zum Grotesken: Die Konstituierung einer Poetik des Grotesken in der Italienischen Renaissance. Lit, Münster
Skinner Q (2004) The foundations of modern political thought, vol. II (The Age of Reformation). Cambridge University Press, Cambridge
Sölch B (2014) Architektur bewegt: Pugets Rathausportal in Toulon oder Schwellenräume als 'Sympathetische' Interaktionsräume. Mitt des Kunsthist Inst Florenz 56:71–93
Springer C (2010) Armour and masculinity in the Italian Renaissance. University of Toronto Press, Toronto
Steinemann H (2006) Eine Bildtheorie zwischen Repräsentation und Wirkung: Kardinal Gabriele Paleottis 'Discorso intorno alle imagini sacre e profane' (1582). Olms, Hildesheim
Strubbe EI (1970) Joos de Damhouder als criminalist. Tijdschrift voor Rechtsgeschiedenis 38:1–65
Veldman I (2002) Hans Vredeman de Vries und das Ornament als Vorlage und Modell. In: Borggrefe H et al (eds) Hans Vredeman de Vries und die Renaissance im Norden (exh. cat. Lemgo-Antwerp). Hirmer, Munich, pp 61–70
Von Amira K, von Schwerin C (1943) Rechtsarchäologie: Gegenstände, Formen und Symbole des Germanischen Rechts. Ahnenerbe-Stiftung-Verlag, Berlin
Warncke C-P (1979) Die ornamentale Groteske in Deutschland 1500–1650. Volker Spiess, Berlin
Williams AR (1999) The steel of the Negroli. Metropolitan Museum Journal 34:101–124
Wind E (1937) Ænigma Termini. J Warbg Inst 1:66–69

Felix Jäger is a Ph.D. candidate in History of Art at Humboldt University of Berlin. His dissertation surveys the political and legal dimensions of Mannerist art, and is supervised by Prof. Dr. Horst Bredekamp. He studied Medieval History, Art History and Philosophy at Humboldt University of Berlin and University College London, and worked as freelance curatorial assistant for the exhibitions *Von mehr als einer Welt: Die Künste der Aufklärung* at the Berlin State Museums, 2011–2012, and *Signes des Temps: OEuvres Visionnaires d'avant 1914* at the Beaux-Arts, Mons, 2013–2014. Since May 2014 he has been a pre-doctoral fellow in the Minerva Research Group 'The Nomos of Images: Manifestation and Iconology of Law' at the Kunsthistorisches Institut in Florenz—Max-Planck-Institut.

Figures

305 RERVM CRIMINALIVM

2 Iure ciuili ſcripto.
3 Parricidarum pœna ex { Conſuetudine, varia.
10 12 Iure canonico, biſaria.
Latronum ac parricidarum pœnis, Iudici aliquid adijcere permittitur. 4
Filius

Fig. 12.1 *De Parricidio*, woodcut, in: Joos de Damhouder. 1554. *Enchiridion Rerum Criminalium*, Cap. 87, p. 305. Leuven: Stephanus Gualtherus and Joannes Bathenius, © Rare Book Collection, Lillian Goldman Law Library, Yale Law School

Fig. 12.2 *De Peccato contra Naturam*, woodcut, in: Joos de Damhouder. 1554. *Enchiridion Rerum Criminalium*, Cap. 97, p. 352. Leuven: Stephanus Gualtherus and Joannes Bathenius, © Rare Book Collection, Lillian Goldman Law Library, Yale Law School

Fig. 12.3 Frans Huys after Hans Vredeman de Vries, *Cartouche with Quote by Aristotle*, etching on paper, in: Hans Vredeman de Vries. 1555. *Variarum Protractionum*. Antwerp: Gerard de Jode, © Creative Commons CC0 1.0

Fig. 12.4 After Hans Vredeman de Vries and Jan van der Straet (?), *Parable of the Ungrateful Servant*, engraving on paper, Antwerp, 1568–1577 (?), pl. 2, © Creative Commons CC0 1.0

Fig. 12.5 Joannes or Lucas van Doetecum after Cornelis Floris (II) de Vriendt, *Auricular Cartouche with Figures*, etching on laid paper, in: Cornelis Floris de Vriendt. 1556. *Veelderleij Veranderinghe van Grotissen ende Compertimenten*, pl. F. Antwerp: Hieronymus Cock, © Creative Commons CC0 1.0

Fig. 12.6 Niccolò della Casa after Baccio Bandinelli, *Portrait of Cosimo I de' Medici*, engraving on paper, 1544, © Creative Commons CC0 1.0

Fig. 12.7 Giovan Paolo Negroli, *Breastplate*, steel and gold, Milan, ca. 1540–1545, New York, Metropolitan Museum of Art, acc.no. 14.25.1855, © The Metropolitan Museum of Art, URL: www.metmuseum.org

Chapter 13
The Mechanical Art of Rhetoric in an Ordinary Sixteenth Century German Formulary

Gustav Kalm

Abstract The title pages of multiple editions of the most popular German language notarial treatise from the sixteenth century, *Rhetoric und Teutsch Formular*, feature woodcuts depicting an array of writing utensils, sometimes complemented with a writing notary and some further tools. Those pictures bare striking similarity to the imagery used to illustrate the booming genre of practical guidebooks for artisans of various sorts. As such they bring to the fore a peculiarly materialist understanding of legal work and offer thus a welcome counterpoint to most jurisprudence. In some title pages, the composition of writing utensils is supplemented with emblematic tools of both mechanical and liberal arts thus pointing to notarial art as carrying elements of both and standing between the two. Those illustrations also match the vision of the book which in its theoretical section defines the notarial art as consisting in saving transactions and agreements from the feebleness of human memory and oblivion by giving them endurance by way of diligent writing. Overall, the book and its title page illustrations thus emphasise what is becoming the central contribution of the craft of law to the development of capitalist modernity: fixing agreements in potent writing. Understanding notarial art as the artisanship of document fabrication, those images also show the transformative power of writing.

13.1 Introduction

Open any treatise in jurisprudence, a legal review or attend an introductory law class at a university and one thing becomes clear: legal theory considers its object to be the various texts of legislation and adjudication and the commentary of both of them. It barely, rarely, or, rather, almost never considers the mundane practical (paper)work that goes into the upkeep of those texts and the legal machinery at large. Indeed, all discussion of the practical materialities of the trade is seen as

G. Kalm (✉)
Department of Anthropology, Columbia University, New York, USA
e-mail: gustav.kalm@columbia.edu

S. Huygebaert et al. (eds.), *The Art of Law*, Ius Gentium: Comparative Perspectives on Law and Justice 66, https://doi.org/10.1007/978-3-319-90787-1_13

somewhat dirty or at least not worthy of being discussed in public, or taught. Two of the most famous recent scholars to have tried to make inroads into a more materialist approach to legal work and its tools have also both deplored this situation.

> Bruno Latour, in his ethnography of the French administrative supreme court Conseil d'État, observes that 'jurists always speak of texts, but rarely of their materiality' (2010, 71). Even more critically Vismann (2008, 11), in her grand history of law and administration through filing systems, claims that 'legal studies lack any reflection on their tools' and goes on to dismiss this state of affairs as a failure of the contemporary discipline.

Perhaps instead of focusing on high level theorisation, a closer view of what law is about can be gained by studying how it is theorised by its very practitioners. One way to gain a practical emic vision of legal work is to look at the various professional guidebooks and trade manuals. Unfortunately, legal scholarship, both historical and contemporary, has generally ignored this precious material. Although these books can also be a valuable source for writing social, cultural or political history—see for example the call by Schuler (1984)—, their primary and little exploited merit is to provide critical insight into law as it is practiced by providing indications on how the practitioners who make law work see their labour.[1]

A notarial practice guide and formulary published by the Strassburger-Frankfurter printer-publisher Christian Egenolph (1502–1555) in 1530, under the title *Rhetoric vñ Teutsch Formular* belongs to this genre.[2] One of the most striking features of this book is the woodcut print on its title page (Fig. 13.1). Illustrating legal books is certainly not uncommon in sixteenth-century German publishing (Röhl 2005; Prinz 2006), but what is perhaps surprising is the peculiar choice of imagery for the title page of this book. The two most prominent features on the page are the haphazardly levitating writing tools and the capital R of the first word of the title of the book. The main title *Rhetoric vñ Teutsch Formular/ In allen Gerichts Haͤndlen* (Rhetoric and German Formulary/ In all Legal Documents[3]) and the following titles *Kunst und Regel der Notarien und Schreiber* (Art and Rules of Notaries and Scribes) and *Titel unnd cantzlei Buͤchlin* (Manual of Chancellery and Titles) tell us that the book is about rhetoric and German model documents, intended for all sorts of legal proceedings that is possibly conducted by notaries and scribes. But what has this book to do with rhetoric and what are the writing tools doing on its title page?

---

[1]As such this proposal has some bearing with Riles' (2005) and Vismann's (2011) calls to study law through the mundane technicalities of quotidian legal work.

[2]The spelling of all the words in the title varies slightly between different editions with *Rhetoric und Teutsch Formular* being most prevalent.

[3]Gerichts Haͤndlen could be translated in several different ways, either as judicial proceedings understood broadly as legal proceedings or simply as lawsuits. However, especially in the sixteenth century, it can also be taken to mean legal documents and writing related to judicial proceedings. The latter meaning sits best with the content of the book that specifically provides instruction in legal writing, although for documents that are not only related to litigation. See the entry for 'Gerichts'handel' in *Deutsches Rechtswörterbuch (Wörterbuch der älteren deutschen Rechtssprache)*, vol. IV, 1951.

It is my contention that the title page is telling us to look at the art of the notary and scribe through its tools, the writing implements and the manual and mechanical activity of writing. As such it could be portraying the notarial art and rhetoric, and by extension law more broadly, as mechanical arts, or at least celebrating law as a practical art ingrained in doing rather than in haughty bookish learning. A cursory look at the genre and the history of the concrete book and its title page illustrations are necessary (2), before exploring how the first two generations of title page images see the notarial art as uniquely grained in the material activity of crafting documents (3) and how this depiction resonates with modern public and private administration that is taking shape in the sixteenth century (4).

13.2 The Book

This book is part of the broader history of adoption and dissemination of the learned legal literature in Germany during late medieval and early modern times. The particular genre of notarial art, '*ars notaria*', and its manuals by the same title had their beginnings in thirteenth century, when the letter-writing focused medieval version of rhetoric, the dictaminal art ('*ars dictaminis*' or '*ars dictandi*') met with Roman law renaissance in Northern Italy.[4] Both dictaminal and notarial art were always closely related to the formulary tradition as the dictaminal art itself had developed in the preceding centuries from a combination of formularies and Ciceronian rhetoric (Murphy 1974). As the institution of the notary developed in Germany, so the Italian *ars notaria* manuals were translated and disseminated through print.[5] All in all, from thirteenth to fifteenth century, the Italian *ars notariae* were either partially incorporated or at least mentioned in various law books written in Germany. Smaller formularies were either translated or composed, and since the end of fifteenth century widely disseminated thanks to print. Overall, the notarial guidebooks and formularies were a key genre of rhetoric books in German-speaking Europe and constituted a much bigger section of the total rhetoric book production than elsewhere in Europe.[6] According to one overview, out of the 164 editions and

---

[4]For the emergence of *ars notariae* in Bologna in the thirteenth century, see Orlandelli (1965). There is some disagreement whether *ars notaria* and *ars dictaminis* were rivalrous, as claims Murphy (1974), or complementary, as argues Ronald Witt (2015). On *ars dictaminis*, see Murphy (1974) and Camargo (1991), and on its downfall, see Camargo (2001) and the other contributions in the same issue of *Rhetorica*. Gero Dolezalek (2002) gives bibliographic indications to the German reception of the Italian *artes*.

[5]The importance of the *ars notaria* manuals for the development of the notary in Germany is somewhat disputed. Wilhelm Schmidt-Thomé (1961) claims the manuals to have played a crucial role for the development of *Notariat*, yet several contributions in *Rolandino e l'ars notaria da Bologna all'Europa* (2002) point out how the role of the Italian *ars notariae* in the conception of the notarial profession north of the Alps has been exaggerated in most historiography.

[6]See Mack (2011, 282–306) for a comparison of rhetoric book developments in the early Renaissance period across Latin, German, French, Italian and English.

twenty titles on rhetoric published in German between 1476 and 1620, 125 editions and eleven titles were notarial formularies and letter-books.[7]

The book in question *Rhetoric und Teutsch Formular* was the most widely published German language rhetoric book in sixteenth century (Mack 2011, 283). It was printed in over thirty editions by different printers-publishers.[8] The first edition was released by Christian Egenolph in 1530 and the last print was again issued by Egenolph's heirs in 1602. Besides the first and last editions by the Egenolphs in Straßburg and Frankcfort am Mayn, the book was also published at least in Wittemberg, Leipzig, Nuremberg, Augsburg, Ingolstadt and Dillingen.

The book itself consists of three parts: a formulary, a short treatise of notarial art and instructions on how to address various dignitaries. Although the author in most library catalogues is identified as Ludwig Fruck, it appears that Egenolph also had a considerable hand in composing the book. Indeed, the tripartite composition is probably of Egenolph's making. The formulary part was first published in Vienna in 1522 under the title *Teutsch Formulari* with Ludovicus Fruck as its author. Egenolph republished the book in 1529 under the title *Teütsch Formular*, combining it with a short *Cantzlei Büchlin* listing various titles and addresses without, however, modifying the original formulary itself. For the first 1530 edition under the title *Rhetoric uñ Teutsch Formular*, Egenolph slightly modified the earlier formulary[9] and combined it with the short treatise on notarial art and added the curious title page illustration. In the second 1530 edition *Rhetoric uñ Teütsch Formular*, Egenolph also expands the last section by adding instructions on how to write to various dignitaries. This publishing history sits with the broader prodigious business strategy of Egenolph's that consisted in copying and recombining already published books (Jäcker 2002).

The first and longest part is a formulary providing models for a wide range of documents. The collection is very diverse, indicating that the book must have been catered to a broad audience of writers. The formulary contains samples for various forms of witness statements and affidavits, letters, rent agreements, quittances of different sorts, letters for describing goods, stipulations, donations, cessions, promissory notes, contracts, birth certificates and various forms of testaments and codicils. Some pertain more to private everyday life, others to diplomacy, whereas yet others more to the realm of business. Some samples are only a couple lines long, whereas others occupy several pages.

---

[7]Mack (2011, 283) gives those numbers, but in this book, like in Green and Murphy (2006), the boundaries of rhetoric books and notarial manuals are not very clear and the list excludes some of those practice books whilst including others, especially when they contain the word 'rhetoric' in their title.

[8]Green and Murphy (2006, 209–210) provide a list, which however, does not include all the editions I came across.

[9]He also explains this in the preface. Oddly enough, all the later editions of the book by other publishers also reprint word-to-word Egenolph's preface, even including the first person singular initially referring to Egenolph.

The second and shortest part, comprising only seven pages and titled *Notariat und Schreiber Kunst*, furnishes some theoretical definitions, introduces some key legal concepts deriving from Roman law, and provides a code of conduct for the notary. This section is actually a slightly modified version of a book that Egenolph had already published in 1528 under the same title and which had already featured a title page image with a smaller compilation of writing tools. This very short book (six folios or twelve pages) in 24 chapters seems itself to have been an abbreviated and reworked version of a popular short treatise *Ars notariatus* that had appeared in many manuscript and print editions in at least Italy, Germany, France and the Netherlands.[10] Even the 1512 *Reichsnotariatsordnung* was based on *Ars Notariatus* as its model (Schmoeckel 2012, p. 42–45). Given its brevity, this short treatise seems to have been meant to be combined with other books.[11] The edition published by Egenolph is quite peculiar. It is a fair bit shorter than the first German translation *Kunst desz Notariat und wie sich der Notarius in seinem Ampt halten und regieren soll*, printed in Nürnberg in 1502, and its content has been considerably modified, with some chapters removed and others added, and the order of chapters considerably reworked (Feenstra 1998, p. 158). Confirming Furtenbach's (1979) thesis on the canonical origin of *Ars Notariatus*, one of the two modifications that Egenolph brings to *Notariat und Schreiber Kunst* when incorporating it in *Rhetoric und Teutsch Formular*, is to change the manual from being addressed to notaries in canonical practice to notaries in civil practice by renaming the other order to which the same definition of notary applies, without, however, otherwise modifying the work.

Finally, the third section, titled *Kurtz Titel oder Cantzlei Bu^e^chlin*, provides instructions in addressing various secular and ecclesiastical dignitaries as well as basic guidance in diplomacy, even including advice as precise as what is the proper way for a city to wish luck to a *Fürst* (Prince) fighting in a regiment whilst also trying to obtain a favour from him. This part is likely an abbreviated compilation of different addresses assembled from the various *Cantzlei büchlein* and *Büchlein der Titel* published by different printers in the preceding decades.

The title *Rhetoric und Teutsch Formular* matches, or more likely mimics, the earlier German language books *Formulare und deutsch Rhetorica*.[12] Although the title of Egenolph's compiled volume contains both 'Rhetoric' and 'Formulary' simply with the epithet German attached to the other noun,[13] its content differs considerably from these earlier books that were far less legalistic and contract-driven, concentrating instead on generic letter writing in the dictaminal

[10]On the genealogy of *Ars Notariatus*, see Furtenbach (1979) and Feenstra (1998). Feenstra mentions also the combined edition by Egenolph. However, neither article addresses the title page illustrations in the printed books or possible illuminations in the preceding manuscripts.

[11]For example, also the *Kölner Sammelwerk* described by Roderich Stintzing (1867, 482–484) contains it as one of its eight constituent parts.

[12]For a comparative pedigree of those books, see Joachimsohn (1893).

[13]Also in the later editions of *Rhetoric und Teutsch Formular*, by accident or design, the two components of the title switch places, and thus the book becomes *Teutsch Formular und Rhetoric*.

tradition. Overall the different notarial and letter writing manuals appear in multiple editions bearing confusingly similar titles, thus creating a proper bibliographic maze. For example, Egenolph also publishes other notarial guidebooks with very similar titles like *Notariat und Teutsche Rhetoric* (1538), *Rhetoric und Teutsch Notariat* (1551). Although they all vary slightly in their content, some of them also featuring more elaborate treatments of rhetoric and many of them in bigger formats and illustrated with more woodcuts, a number of them also include either the short German version of *Notariat und Schreiber Kunst* or elements from Fruck's formulary.

That the title of the book begins simply with *Rhetoric* makes sense if we consider the book to the backdrop of the adaption and dissemination of dictaminal and notarial art treatises in Germany. According to a thesis initially put forth by Kristeller (1945) and further developed by Witt (1982, 2012) *ars dictaminis* merges into Renaissance Humanism with many humanists earning their living working as *dictatores*. As these authors argue, rhetoric became synonymous with *ars dictaminis* in Italy and France in the twelfth century. Likewise, in the fifteenth and sixteenth century German vernacular adaption of *ars dictaminis* and *ars notaria*, it seems that both these traditions and a book stemming from either could simply be dubbed 'rhetoric/k(a)'. For example when Friedrich Riedrer publishes in 1493 the first German language rhetorical treatise *Spiegel der wahren Rhetorik* that combines *ars notaria* and *ars dictandi* with an exegesis on classical rhetoric, he adds the epithet *wahre* (true) to distinguish his treatise from a generic understanding of 'Rhetoric/k(a)' as a book providing instructions and models on letter and document composition, like for example in the title of Heinrich Geßler's formulary *New practicirt rethoric* from the same year (Knape 2000, p. 207–210). Similarly, Egenolph names his book *Rhetoric und Teutsch Formular* when he adds the vernacular treatise *Notariat und Schreiber Kunst* to Fruck's formulary, thus seemingly simply calling the German readapted notarial art manual by the title *Rhetoric*.

Although the at least twelve publishers who took to printing the book stuck to the text of Egenolph's *Sammelwerk* even reprinting verbatim his preface written in first person singular, they did, however, vary the title page illustrations, either copying or building from earlier editions or by introducing new themes in line with broader trends in the illustration of legal and other practice manuals. Among the editions I was able to access, I could broadly distinguish four tendencies or generations. The first editions by Christian Egenolph from 1530 (Fig. 13.1) and 1531 present a central image with a multitude of writing devices, which in at least two editions are accompanied by various animals on the side. A number of other publishers, starting with Hans Weiss in Wittemberg (Fig. 13.4), keep the writing tools from Egenolph's initial edition, but drop the animals and add instead a number of elements of which most notably a writing notary or scribe and some further tools. A couple editions also appear portraying only notaries at work without the floating tools. Since the 1530s Egenolph and after him some other editors used rather generic legal illustrations with a lawgiver king sitting on a throne with often a more humble looking man presenting a sealed document to him. The latest editions all come without a title page illustration, however they do expose a more exquisite typography.

The first 1530 edition of *Rhetoric und Teutsch Formular* published by Christian Egenolph in Straßburg (Fig. 13.1) comes with a frontispiece illustration featuring a plethora of writing devices: a straightedge, quills, quill knife, pounce or sand pot, comb possibly used for obtaining parallel lines, penner and ink horn wearable over belt, string, scissors, a seal matrix, probably wax for seals next to it, a letter or document and an envelope, a small sharp object, three piles of what are possibly abacus disks[14] and an amorphous object that could be a piece of bread or sponge or some other device for cleaning and erasing.[15] The two succeeding editions keep the same composition with the tools. On the second 1530 edition, four birds are added, two on each side, all with their pecks turned towards the writing implements. In an edition published a year later, the birds are replaced with a springing rabbit on the right and a bird watching out of its nest on the left. These small animals on the side were part of a wider repertoire of woodcuts that Egenolph had at his disposal and that he also used to illustrate many other books around that time.

Röttinger (1933, p. 5) attributes the panoply of tools to artist Hans Weiditz (II), who has sometimes also been identified as the *Petrarcameister* or the author of the illustrations to the 1530s German translation of Petrarch's *De remediis utriusque fortunae*. The relationship between Egenolph and Weiditz is somewhat curious. Another editor Johannes Schott had sued Egenolph in one of the first publishing copyright cases for copying a number of illustrations Schott had commissioned from Weiditz for a herbal by Otto Brunfels (Parshall 1993, p. 567–569). Although the outcome of the case is not known, apparently after the lawsuit Egenolph stopped using the woodcuts in his cheaper smaller herbals and commissioned new ones instead. This curious instance of early copyright litigation seems however not have barred the two from having a productive business relationship otherwise as Weiditz conceived illustrations for a wide range of Egenolph's books (Röttinger 1904).

Only a couple years later, in 1533, the Wittemberger printer Hans Weiss publishes a copy that builds on the themes from the first Egenolph editions (Fig. 13.4). Most prominently, an image of a notary clad in fancier garb sitting on an ornate bench behind a desk, writing onto a multipage document or cahier, is added. Also behind the notary stands a disproportionately large candle. New utensils are also added to the cloud of floating tools. A pair of candlewick scissors appears next to the candle and a double-edge comb appears below the straightedge to the left of the larger scissors. On the bottom of the image a knife and what looks like a scraper

[14]These small round disks are often featured on the desks of notaries, just like on the desks of accountants or calculation masters pictured in contemporaneous arithmetic books (*Rechenbücher*).

[15]Gumbert (1998) has also identified some of the tools from the illustration claiming the woodcut to be from a 1545 Egenolph title *Instruction Wie gegen trefflichen personen*, although the version he reproduces looks precisely like the lower section of the title page of the 1530 Frankfurt edition *Rhetoric uñ Teütsch Formular*. Otherwise, Rosenfeld (2002) provides a good list of writing implements and their depiction in writing and iconography, although concentrating on a slightly earlier period.

stand crossed. Next to them stands a tool with a roughed working surface and a wooden handle. It could likely be the woodwork tool surform, given especially how it stands next to two other construction tools. On the right-hand side of the image appear a winged flute and a viol with a bow. Next to them stand a pair of glasses and a richly bound book.

A similar assembly also appears on some further editions. First, a 1537 Leipzig edition from Valentin Schumm uses the precise same image as the earlier Wittemberger edition, probably Schumm having acquired the block. A further 1537 Augsburg edition by Valentin Othmar takes up the same composition as in the original Wittemberger edition but drops some elements. There are only two (and not three) piles of abacus disks and the small sharp object or knife, seal matrix and what was possibly wax are all gone. Instead of the winged flute now a wing or a brush stands on its own, without the flute. Also the single candle is replaced with a roughly sketched candelabrum. The writer who also takes up a larger proportion of the image sits behind a more prominent desk and is not writing into a book, but composing on a sheet of paper. Also a further 1539 Augsburger edition (Fig. 13.5), printed by Alexander Weyssenhorn, depicts all the same tools as the 1533 edition from Wittemberg, albeit slightly shuffling the positions and proportions. The image is generally more clear and robust than the two other versions with the various elements being depicted in a broader line and less detail.

Amongst the editions I was able to browse, two other editions—a 1537 Dillingen edition printed by Sebaldum Mayer and a 1559 Wittemberger edition printed by Veit Creutzer—depict notaries or scribes at work, in one case in a small workshop and in the other individually tilting over a desk. In these images, however, the earlier panoply of tools is gone. From the 1540s onward the images with notaries become replaced with scenes featuring an enthroned lawgiver king that had been an habitual generic motive both in illuminated legal manuscripts (L'Engle and Gibbs 2001, chap. 5) and continued be so in printed law books (Röhl 2005; Prinz 2006). A recurring theme in those woodcuts, which are also often used in other notarial and legal manuals, is a more moderately dressed man humbly presenting a sealed document to an enthroned king. Finally after this trend, the last editions of the book come without title page illustrations.

What remains particularly arresting about those title pages is the unique focus on writing implements in the first and second generation illustrations. Instead of portraying the work of notaries broadly, they ignore several aspects such as consulting clients or even dealing with imperative law. Perhaps most importantly, unlike most legal book illustration, they do not directly extol a certain virtue like justice or prudence. Instead they associate the notarial art specifically to the manual activity of writing and its products. This choice seems even more odd given that the book title begins with the word 'rhetoric'. Indeed, what has rhetoric to do with this almost fetishistic interest in writing and its tools? Could it be that this book and specifically its title page illustrations portray the liberal art of rhetoric, the honourable member of *trivium* through the manual activity of writing, thus possibly portraying it as a mechanical art? After all, as Murphy (1974, p. 264) summarizes the work of the Italian predecessors, '[b]asically the *ars notaria* concerned itself with the physical forms of documents'.

13.3 Rhetoric as a Mechanical Art

The association of 'rhetoric' and writing tools indeed strikes as odd. Even if we understand rhetoric as referring to a manual of *ars dictaminis* or *ars notaria* as was common at the time, the panoply of writing implements still seems by no means an obvious iconographic choice for the title page illustration. Displaying writing and its tools does give a particularly materialist portrayal of legal work and rhetoric. But how so precisely? And what are the implications of this choice? Or more precisely, would this portrayal mount to depicting notarial art and therefore rhetoric as mechanical arts? Of course, all mental and conceptual activity that goes through writing is also manual activity inasmuch as writing itself does demand leaving traces on a surface by moving the hand. In this regard written rhetoric, grammar, logic, philosophy and other arts of thinking are all manual to the extent that they depend on writing. Yet this does not make them mechanical arts. However, rarely are also writing implements chosen to depict those arts. Perhaps the comparison with mechanical arts becomes better understood in comparison with the depiction of those arts.

The focus on writing and its tools in our notarial manual bears great similarity to the illustrations in various practical artisanal how-to guidebooks of mechanical arts that were printed in great numbers during this time (Long 2001; Smith 2012). Starting in late scribal period and culminating in early print age, a great number of books providing technical guidance sometimes in combination with theoretical elaboration were written for a diverse set of domains including alchemy, metallurgy, mining, artillery, machine-building, fortification, architecture, martial arts, painting, pottery, printing, dentistry, surgery, book-keeping, practical arithmetic, cocking and even gondola steering. The reasons for the technical guide book publishing boom were multiple, going from valuing the knowledge acquired through the artisanal experience of the world (Smith 2004), to promoting a particular art and sharing its knowledge (Long 2001) or quite simply advancing the career of the author (Smith 2012). Many of those books were also richly illustrated and in the case of architecture, machine building or botany the success of the books was directly linked to the quality of the illustrations (Smith 2006). *Rhetoric und Teutsch Formular* likewise provides practical instructions to professionals exercising a trade and could thus be seen as belonging to this group of technical literature.

Although the book contains no technical drawings, the focus on the tools of the trade and attention to the actual working process of the notary in many of the title page illustrations further accentuate the affinity with the technical and artisanal guidebooks. According to Röttinger (1933, p. 1–5), many of the early woodcuts that Hans Weiditz designed for Christian Egenolph were for various professional practice books. In the illustrations for these technical books, Weiditz apparently sought to appeal to the chefs, gardeners, distillers and others buying those books by giving a detailed depiction of their work. The first-generation title page illustrations with the panoply of writing implements indeed greatly resemble the title page illustrations of at least two other technical guidebooks also depicting the tools of the trade in question. The Hans Weiditz title page illustration to Ioannis Charetani's surgical manual *Wundartznei: Zu allen Gebrechen des gantzen Leibs* (Fig. 13.2) features syringe, scissors, knives, clyster pump, tool case, bandage etc. A further 1535 *Kunstbüchlin* (Little Book of Skills) (Fig. 13.3) on alchemy, metal work, colour fabrication, gilding and working with precious stones conceived by another artist following Weiditz's manner (Röttinger 1933, p. 18) proudly presents crucible with fire and bellows, forger's tongs, saws, metal cutters, a plane, mallets, chisels and gouges, a hammer, a file, a burin, and callipers etc.[16] That Egenolph and Weiditz saw fit to illustrate the title page of a notarial *rhetoric* in the same manner as a guidebook for surgeons and a popular booklet of practical alchemy shows that for these actors of the publishing world these three books belonged to the same genre or type of publications. These images identify the work of surgeons, notaries and all sorts of users of practical alchemy by the tools that are necessary for mechanically exercising the activity in question.[17] It is also noteworthy that all the three fields were practical applied counterparts to some discipline of theoretical learning: medicine for wound doctoring, law for notarial art and physics and alchemy for practical alchemy. The display of tools could thus also have served to distinguish the applied technical art from a theoretical form of learning.

The pre-eminence of writing implements on the title page illustration of *Rhetoric und Teutsch Formular* also matches the definition of notarial art offered in the short theoretical section *Notariat und Schreiber Kunst*. The very first sentence of this theoretical elaboration defines the notary precisely by the activity of writing: '*Was Notariat Kunst [?] Ist ein beschreibung dadurch die gescheft menschlicher bloedigkeyt behalten/unnd in glaubliche gedaechtnuss kommen*', roughly translated into English: 'What is notarial Art? Is a description/writing, by which affairs/ transactions are saved from human weakness and preserved in credible memory'. The definition in *Notariat und Schreiber Kunst* that Egenolph had published in 1529 as a separate volume differs slightly in seeing agreements as not saved but strengthened (*gesterckt*) by the notarial art and saved in a memory that is not only credible but also lengthy or prolonged (*langwirig*). Both these versions as well as the different Latin versions of *Ars notariatus* (Furtenbach 1979) and the initial longer German translation show the notarial art as that which casts agreements into credible and sometimes perennial, or at least long lasting, memory, thus saving them from the frail human forgetfulness.

[16]I follow the identification of tools by David Landau and Peter Parshall (1994, 27). William Eamon's website (2017) provides a nice little history of the book.

[17]Writing utensils also feature as tools and even weapons of lawyers in Goltzius' *litis abusus* series discussed by Alain Wijffels in this volume.

Although the *Ars notariatus* is a mix of sources from different Italian medieval predecessors, the definition and the whole first chapter are copied from the original Italian master Rainerius Perusinus (Furtenbach 1979, p. 17). This formulation also resonates with a motive appearing already in tenth and eleventh century Italian *arrenghe*, referring to the memory of human events living only in writing, in contrast to the oblivion inexorably induced by the passing of time (Petrucci 1995). Although in the Italian *artes* this formulation is replaced with an emphasis on *publica fides* of the new notarial acts also called notarial instruments (Petrucci 1995, p. 240–243), the definition that finds its way to the sixteenth-century German manual derives from this earlier medieval obsession with the perduration of memory in writing. Notwithstanding the later developments in documentary modes of veridiction, this formulation continues to praise the notarial art for its ability to save agreements thanks to writing. In all those cases it is promoting the external object—document—that is supposed to better record and remember an agreement than the mere fleeting human memory could.

This promotion of the superiority of documents that outlast human forgetting, and can thus save agreements, is also possibly what the austere choice of writing implements is evoking. According to Röttinger (1933, p. 4–5), the title page panoplies of tools, in notarial just like in surgical treatises, focus on the utensils rather than production processes, because the tools themselves outlast the temporary moments of production. The display of implements instead of processes therefore also denotes the perdurance of the produced object. This focus on the lasting object in the title page illustration matches the self-congratulatory definition of the power of the notary to make agreements gain credible and long-lasting memory through being saved in writing. Inasmuch as the title page illustration can be understood as an advertisement that at the same time festively aims to attract a potential buyer whilst also providing a peak or some insight into the content of the book, it both matches the definition offered in the book and furthermore aims to flatter the notary and his ability to save agreements, and give them lasting existence through his labour.

Although the addition of the writing notary in the 1533 Wittemberg edition (Fig. 13.4) interrupts the trend of sole focus on the writing utensils, it keeps the focus on writing as an activity. It also sets the work more in line with other depictions of notaries in contemporaneous legal book illustration whilst still remaining within the standard tropes of technical practice book illustration. Although depictions of scribes had been relatively rare in medieval manuscripts (Gullick 2006, p. ix), portraying (legal) writers became a far more common theme in the early printed books on notaries and continued to be so well into the nineteenth and twentieth centuries.[18] Several other books intended for notarial practice, a number of which were also printed by Egenolph, included woodcuts portraying notaries at work: either writing solitarily or collectively in a workshop, consulting

[18]See the collections of notarial iconography in Salerno and Brandizzi (1958), Schatborn and Szénássy (1971), Van der Marck and Eisma (2013).

clients, noting down a bed sick dying man's last will, or taking the minutes of some proceedings.

One particularly widely used woodcut portrays several notaries or scribes in a workshop with three notaries or scribes engaged in writing work, a fourth one possibly consulting a client jotting down some first notes, various readymade documents hanging from the wall and a dog sitting in the centre of the floor, looking out of the picture sideways (Fig. 13.6). This image was initially conceived for the German translation of the Petrarch's *De remediis utriusque fortunae* that had been prepared for years and was finally published in 1532. Whether the same artist Hans Weiditz, author of famous herbals and the title page illustrations with tools, was also the Petrarcameister, author of the woodcuts in the German translation of Petrarch, remains unclear. Notwithstanding the precise attribution of authorship, that particular image had a long history in legal book illustration. Along with a couple other woodcuts from the same ensemble it had already been used in a 1531 German translation of Cicero's *De Officiis* before the publication of Petrarch's translation.[19] After Egenolph had acquired the woodblocks in 1546 following the bankruptcy of Heinrich Steiner who had already used them for the German translations of Cicero and Petrarch and some rhetoric books, Egenolph and his heirs used this and a couple other woodcuts from that ensemble in many notarial and legal treatises.[20] This popular image seems to have had given a lasting impact on the depiction of notaries. For example even the title page illustration of the 1537 Dillingen Sebaldum Mayer edition *Rhetorica unnd Teutsch Formular* appears to be a simplified copy of this notarial workshop scene.

What is most important for present purposes, is that the way Petrarcameister depicts the notaries' workshop is quite similar to the depictions of workshops of painters, sculptors, boilersmiths, builders and alchemists in the same luxurious richly illustrated book. The similar portrayal and their positioning within the book indicates that Petrarcameister and possibly Sebastian Brant who instructed the translation and illustration of Petrarch's work sought to depict the work of notaries and scribes as manual work similar to that of the various technical arts. That both printers Steiner and Egenolph used the images so widely in other practical and theoretical law books also shows that this portrayal of notaries' work as the labour of writing sat well with sixteenth century readers of legal treatises.

The proper classification of the notarial art gets addressed explicitly in the second-generation title page illustrations where the initial set of writing utensils is complemented with a writing notary and additional tools. The introduction of the notary writing tilted over a desk is itself not a distant motif from the original panoply of writing utensils. However, several of the newly added tools bare little connection to the trade of the notary. Rather all the supplementary tools not directly related to the activity of writing, could be related to and seen as standing for either

[19] On the word-image assemblies in that book and its publishing history, see Enenkel (2013).

[20] To name just a few *Rhetoric vnnd Teutsch Notariat*, 1556; *Notariat vnd Teutsche Rhetoric*, 1561; *Formular Allerlei Schrifften Brieffe und Instrumenten*, 1561.

mechanical or liberal arts. Some of them, like the woodwork tools, possibly evoke material fabrication and the mechanical arts, whereas others like the musical instruments, book and spectacles all probably allude to theoretical learning. A *lira da braccio* or more simply viol was used in woodcuts of the period to symbolise a return to Antiquity or simply poetry and philosophy (Winternitz 1967, p. 86–98). The book and spectacles possibly stand quite straightforwardly for theoretical book knowledge acquired through reading the written word. Unfortunately, I was unable to find any literature on the striking object that is the winged flute, but quite likely it belongs to the same group with the string instrument and book and glasses evoking theoretical learning. On the other hand, the small scissors, knife and surform are all construction tools not unlike those depicted in the mechanical arts trade books such as *Kunstbüchlin* (Fig. 13.3). Coupled now with a broader array of tools that are not only used for writing but that refer to either liberal or mechanical arts, the illustration is possibly aiming to show how the notarial art stands between the two, having elements of both.

That the initial choice of the Hans Weiss 1533 Wittemberg edition was also copied by the Augsburg printers Valentin Othmar and Alexander Weißenhorn, and that the initial 1533 woodcut was reused in 1537 by Valentin Schumann in Leipzig, and that Othmar deemed it appropriate also to use the same woodcut for another notarial formulary, Moritz Breunle's *Ain Kurtz formular und Canzley büchlin*, all show that this composition resonated with an accepted understanding of the work of the notary.

In similar terms, French notarial theorist Claude Berguère in his *ars notaria* from a century later asks '*si le Notariat est Science ou art méchanique*' (Poisson 1990). Although by the seventeenth century the point of reference had become the new concept of science and the artisanal knowledge was no longer held in such high esteem as it had been earlier—Berguère's treatise continues by calling mechanical arts vile and abject –, it is nonetheless significant that the question be posed in those terms. In his discussion, this seventeenth century French notarial theorist reasons that since the work of the notary is writing work and thus manual activity, and since it is often quite routine, it ought to be considered a mechanical art. Acknowledging this much, but trying to show otherwise, Berguère claims the question to be a difficult one. He finally concludes with a workaround by distinguishing perfect and imperfect notaries. When practised by perfect notaries, the notarial art is a science, because the careful reduction of the parties' agreement into contractual clauses also demands the contemplation of laws, knowledge of doctrine and understanding of the parties' psyche. Yet, as he admits in regret, few notaries correspond to such a high standard.

Treatises from other technical arts were likewise discussing the proper classification of their art. Several authors from diverse arts were specifically trying to show how their arts as liberal rather than mechanical (Smith 2012). Yet several architecture treatises from the time explicitly emphasised the importance of combining theoretical humanistic learning and practical technical experience (Long 2001, p. 222–234). For example the multitalented painter, architect and military engineer

Cesare Cesariano (1475–1543) argued that all arts are made up of fabrication and reasoning which each depend on the other (Long 2001, p. 224).

However, the replacement of the writing utensils and writing notaries with more generic legal iconography on the title pages of later editions of *Rhetoric und Teutsch Formular* casts some doubts, if not over my interpretation of the title page illustrations portraying notarial art as akin to mechanical arts, than at least over the popularity of such imagery. Looked to the backdrop of the evolution of chancellery literature more broadly, the slow phasing out of the iconography with the writing tools from the 1540 s onwards could be related to the progressive emergence of writing master manuals (*Schreibmeisterbücher*), starting with Johann Neudörfer's *Fundament ... seinen schülern zu einer unterweysung gemacht*, published in 1519. Those books gave practical calligraphic instructions for bureaucratic penmanship by showing, with the help of woodcut and copperplate illustrations, how to produce particular hands. Although the emergence of the printing press had somewhat depressed the status of the copyist of manuscripts, it did, however, provide a tool for the furtherance of the art of the writing master, just like it had helped popularise the various mechanical trades (Osley and Wolpe 1980, p. 18). Notarial and dictaminal art manuals and formularies had quite an overlap with the new writing manuals that sometimes also gave general advice on letter writing and occasionally even provided model documents. For example, Urban Wyß' *Canzlÿ und Formular Buch mit vÿl hupschen Copien* from 1553, produced in elaborate prints of calligraphy, provides simultaneously samples of letters and hands as well as schemes on the proper way to handle quills. Since the emergence of writing master books, a depiction of writing tools could become associated with this new genre of books focusing specifically on writing as a manual activity, rather than referring to chancellery books more broadly.

From the twenty-first century perspective the belief in the ability of writing to precisely safeguard the initial agreement of course looks somewhat naive. We know that writing gains its own agency and goes far beyond merely replicating what was said. In writing it is no longer the past agreement but a new deed that speaks. Writing is difficult to master or control and it often ceases to be the policeman of the initial agreement, instead halting and wrecking the various efforts of control (Kafka 2012). Most famously, Jacques Derrida (centrally 1967, but also 1972) has shown how writing instead of being the record of the spoken word, comes to take primacy. What the Derridan unique focus on writing, however, misses, and that Latour (1986) has aptly pointed out, is that writing *per se* never achieves the broad scale social changes often attributed to it. Most importantly in order for writing to be able to change society, the users of writing must also trust the truth claims made by means of writing. The radical social changes brought by the printing press also demanded considerable trust-building and convincing labour on behalf of book printers and sellers as Johns (1998) has shown in his extensive critique of Eisenstein's (1979) classical thesis. Likewise, it is not enough that notaries produce written agreements, they also need to promote those agreements and their ability to be trusted as independent points of reference, a process that had been slow in the coming over the preceding centuries (Arlinghaus 2008). To procure that trust to documents, the notaries also needed to promote themselves as capable "brokers of public trust" as Nussdorfer (2009) dubs the contemporaneous Roman practicioners.

To show that notaries and their products are worthy of trust, the title page illustrations proclaim the perdurance of notarial acts and proudly portray the art of notaries as the craft of transforming agreements into trustworthy acts requiring both artisanal skill and theoretical wordsmithery. Although the text and illustrations of notarial treatises might not have fully appreciated how much writing transforms the meaning of a preceding oral agreement, they specifically celebrate the ability of writing to enhance the effect of agreements and thus alter future courses of action. This understanding of the art of the notary is perhaps then not too different from that of artisans more generally (Smith 2006). Both seek first to imitate something already existing, agreements or nature, to then make the product of that imitation act upon the world whence it came from.

What the prints from the sixteenth century notarial treatises aim to do is to instil trust in the work of notaries and their writing. In the middle of the notarial office in Petrarcameister's woodcut sits a dog showing the centrality of trust in notaries work. The title pages, the self-laudatory definitions of legal writing and even adages from the time speak of earnest promotion of writing as technique to manage agreements. As writing gains importance in the following decades and centuries, the depictions of bureaucratic work increasingly also turn to derision. For example Pieter Brueghel the Younger's (1564–1638) *The Village Lawyer*, sometimes also called *The Notary's Office*, and its various renderings specifically mock the excessive paperwork and the haughty lawyers manipulating their tortuous mounds of documentation (Martyn 2013). Yet, during the sixteenth century notarial guidebook publishing boom, the emphasis remains on the ability of writ to found trust.

13.4 Contractualisation

The concentration on writing and its tools also resonates with radical changes in pragmatic writing in Germany and Europe during this period. For documentation in public administration the shift from governing through *Urkunden* (translated as documents, charters or acts) to governing through *Akten* (translated either as files or acts) incites a general increase in paperwork in the various administrative offices (Vismann 2008, chap. 3). Simultaneously the growing long-distance trade and the general complexification of business increasingly require and depend on written documentation.

With the shift from *Urkunden* to *Akten* emerge the first administrations to correspond to the key element in Max Weber's (1978, p. 957) definition of the modern office management that is the storage of drafts. In the German realm, the administration of Maximilian I (1486–1519) was the first to do so. Indeed, as Vismann observes, it is broadly during the sixteenth century that the modern filing based administration arises. As a result of this change the amount of written matter and the demand for the scribal staff and space for storing the new filing systems increase exponentially.

Perhaps somewhat characteristically of the general preoccupation in legal history and theory with public rather than private matters, there is considerably less literature dedicated to the evolutions in private documentation during this period which, saw a no less important increase in bureaucratisation.[21] On the one hand, with the *Reichskammergerichtsordnung* from 1495 and other smaller reforms judicial proceedings become increasingly written, also profoundly modifying the composition of legal professions (Strauss 1986). It is also a period of increasing trade, trade networks, creation of bills of exchange etc. (Braudel 1979), which all require concomitant private paper supports. Expanding business ventures demand expanding bureaucracies. Again somewhat characteristically for legal scholarship, both sixteenth century and contemporary, the vast changes in local laws that ease this commercial expansion have been far less discussed than doctrinal and theoretical works on *ius commune* (Berman 2003, p. 158–160).

The precise role of the notaries in this growth of pragmatic writing remains open. No comprehensive study of notarial documentation in Germany in the sixteenth to eighteenth centuries has been written (Schubert 2012, p. 650). On the one hand the abundant practical notarial literature leaves an impression of a thriving profession. The many editions and prints of *Rhetoric und Teutsch Formular* between 1530 and 1602 show that it clearly had a market meaning that in all likelihood the provided models were also handy for contemporaneous practitioners. On the other hand, by the seventeenth and eighteenth centuries the notarial profession was in a general decline compared to their peak in late Middle Ages (Schubert 2012, p. 650). The strength of the notarial institution also varied considerably across regions. In Silesia for example, the number of notarially certified documents started declining already in the fifteenth century (Luschek 1940). It seems quite likely that the notarial manual publishing boom concurred with a declining institution and thus did not only address notaries in particular, but was catering to a broader audience of business scribes.

One of the most important changes in private documentation during the sixteenth century, and the one that also dealt a serious blow to notaries and their certified documents or public instruments, is the importation of the principle *pacta sunt servanda* from canon law to German civil law.[22] As Harold Berman (2003, p. 157) writes, '[i]n sharp contrast both to Germanic customary law and to the rediscovered Roman law, the twelfth-century canonists asserted that the legally binding force of various types of agreements depended ultimately neither on their solemnity nor on their form, nor on part performance by one of the parties, but rather on the intention of the parties. It was the consent of the parties to enter into a contract that made it a

[21]See for example Martyn (2000), 60–65.

[22]On the theological elaboration of this principle, see Decock (2013), which albeit offering an interesting intellectual history fails to consider the singular impact of writing in the social import of contracting.

contract'. Although the principle had meant to serve much narrower ends in canon law, the civil law jurists who adopted it in the sixteenth century gave the new principle of contractual faith (*Vertragstreue*) a central place in contracts (Berman 2003, p. 158). This principle in turn entered positive law either by becoming codified as statutory law under the new legislative prerogatives of princes and urban communes or through reference to *ius commune* as subsidiary law to various local statutes and customs (Berman 2003, p. 157–166).

The notarially certified act with its protocol might have been crucial when paper is not yet so abundantly available, literacy not so widespread and *Vertragstreue* not yet accepted. Yet in the sixteenth century the new contractual freedom is combined with the growth of pragmatic literacy expanding in Germany through public literacy drives (Gawthrop 1987), new business models and abundance of writing surfaces. Indeed, if contracts become relieved of formal requirements, and if writing surfaces become more abundant and contracting parties more literate, the registered notarial act or instrument loses its specific market and generic contract writing can burgeon.

However, those contracts still need writers. Indeed, the services of notaries were also mostly used for such private deeds. Notaries during this period mostly produced sale-purchase agreements, donations, lease agreements and testaments which are not all forcibly notarial instruments (Schubert 2012, p. 650). As such, the business documentation from the time seems to have been more fluid. For example, although notarially certified acts ought to refer to a notary's protocol or registry from which copies can be released to parties, it is not certain to what degree the German notaries in the sixteenth century actually kept those registries, even if they were mandated to do so by the *Reichnotariatsordnung* of 1512 (Schubert 2012, p. 649–650). Also the boundaries between notaries in private exercise, various city writers, and all sorts of semi-professional scriveners were quite fluid (Mostert and Adamska 2014). *Rhetoric und Teutsch formular* could have served a practical scrivener engaged in some of those affairs somewhere between private praxis, notarial or not, and fulfilment of public duties. The model documents offered in the formulary cover a wide range of situations: official letters, litigation documents, various contracts, loan management, different types of testaments, copying of documents etc. Some of these are better suited for the administrative chancellery whilst others for the conduct of private business, and yet others for judicature.

The prominent position given to contract formation in the formulary and theoretical section of *Rhetoric und Teutsch Formular* is in line with a broader evolution towards a society where an increasing share of social relations are mediated through contracts. This rise of contractual relations has found oddly little take-up in contemporary legal scholarship, albeit having been seen as a central feature of modern law by some of the principal legal theorists of the last turn of century. Henry Sumner Maine, Karl Marx, Friedrich Engels, Emile Durkheim and Max Weber all saw the contractualisation of social relations as a key feature of capitalist modernity. Weber (1978, p. 669) deemed that the pre-eminence of contractual relations, which itself was a reflex of the 'market orientation of our society', had become so characteristic 'that one can *a potiori* designate the contemporary type of society, to the extent that private law obtains, as a “contractual” one’.[23] Reaching farthest, Sumner Maine (1908, p. 274–275) argued that for social contract theory to make contract the very origin and organising principle of all legislation was made imaginable because of the wide scale contractualisation of human relations that had preceded its elaboration:

> [Social contract theory] is a theory which, though nursed into importance by political passions, derived all its sap from the speculations of lawyers. True it certainly is that the famous Englishmen, for whom it had first had attraction, valued it chiefly for its political serviceableness, but, as I shall presently attempt to explain, they would never have arrived at it, if politicians had not long conducted their controversies in legal phraseology. (…) They had observed the fact, already striking in their day, that of the positive rules obeyed by men, the greater part were created by Contract, the lesser by Imperative Law.

Although Maine’s observation is fabulous, he and the other mentioned authors do not actually establish how the greater part of rules would have come to stem from contracts in the time preceding the elaboration of the social contract theory. More importantly still, Maine but also Weber and the others miss something that the authors of our notarial tractate and its title page illustrations point out: the social power of the contract lies with it being written, and I should add, that writing being trusted.

The specificity of this new contractual legal development is vast: a new form of human relations can emerge. Suddenly, the agreement of the parties can come to be considered creating a mutually binding obligation that, if not fulfilled, can be enforced through the State judiciary. The increasing contractualisation of interpersonal relations reshapes not only the judiciary, which will henceforth increasingly be dealing with judging the correspondence of action and the written word of private agreements, but also modifies social relations more broadly. The title page illustrations of *Rhetoric und Teutsch Formular* remind us of the importance of writing in making the contractualisation of social relations a reality.

13.5 Conclusion

From the perspective of grand conceptual history of legal theory, *Rhetoric und Teutsch Formular* probably appears as insignificant. It does not re-theorise contracting like did the famous Jesuit theologians. Although transmitting Roman legal notions, it does not specifically elaborate on their adoption in German local laws like did *Laienspiegel* or *Klagspiegel*. It is but a compilation of odd pieces and translations by a non-specialised publisher-printer. It is certainly not an original work of a legal genius. Even further from the traditional legal historical and

[23] Wim Decock (2013), however, argues that although contractual freedom might have been crucial for the development of capitalism, its origins are rather in theological reasoning than economic necessity.

jurisprudential canon than the text of the book are its title page illustrations. Although it is not certain how the themes were chosen, the artists who created them were certainly no experts of legal theory either. Despite all this the book and its illustrations offer valuable insights into understanding the role of law in society. *Rhetoric und Teutsch Formular* was a legal bestseller and reached a great number of professionals. It offers an insight into how the role of law would have been seen from the perspective of quotidian legal practice.

In continuance to the medieval Italian *artes* the theoretical section of the book sees the art of the notary consisting in giving trustworthiness and endurance to agreements through diligent writing. The title page illustrations with writing tools endorse this idea and advertise the perdurance of writing. Although these images are also likely reflections on the contemporaneous bureaucratisation of public and private administration, they do portray the work of notaries as either akin to the work of various artisans or as containing elements of both mechanical and liberal arts. Indeed those title page illustrations go a step further from the text of the book that also predates them by a couple centuries and offer a more critical or reflexive understanding of legal writing. The austere display of writing tools akin to artisan book illustration does show notaries as artisans but through the display of mere implements also evokes the perdurance of the produced written agreements and thereby the agreements themselves. Yet the later careful retraction to a display of notarial art as both mechanical and liberal assumes the transformative force of writing. The artefact of artisanal imitation is neither the same as the original that it is imitating neither is it a pure new creation like positive legislation.

Writing and its increased distribution thanks to print is thoroughly transforming European societies at the time. One form of practical writing that is particularly influential is the formation of written contracts. Many social theorists have considered contractualisation as a key condition for capitalist modernity in early modern Europe. Yet it is not the mere expansion of contractual freedom in law that allows contracting to reshape European societies so profoundly. Contracting can ground the broad social changes, because the independent written object of contract can come to serve as a point of reference that can direct and mediate relations between humans and things over time. This is where we can admire the theoretical savvy of the folk jurisprudence that are the title page illustrations of *Rhetoric und Teutsch Formular*. Those images depict legal writing as an artisanal activity in which a new artefact is fabricated in the imitation of the preceding agreement understanding that this new object will come to outlast its original ground and thus have its own agency. Crafting those objects is the everyday art of law.

Acknowledgments I thank Mike Widener from Yale Law Library for showing me to this gem and Brinkley Messick, Adam Kosto, Pamela Smith, Nomos fellows, conference participants and the editors for their questions and advice.

References

Arlinghaus F-J (2008) Point of reference: trust and the function of written agreements in a late medieval town. In: Schulte P, Mostert M, van Renswoude I (eds) Strategies of writing. Utrecht Studies in Medieval Literacy 13. Brepols Publishers, Turnhout, pp 277–299

Berman H (2003) Law and revolution, II: the impact of the protestant reformations on the western legal tradition. Belknap Press, Cambridge

Braudel F (1979) Les Jeux de l'échange. Vol. II. Civilisation matérielle, économie et capitalisme, XVe-XVIIIe siècle. Armand Colin, Paris

Camargo M (1991) Ars dictaminis, ars dictandi. Typologie des sources du Moyen Age occidental 60. Brepols, Turnhout

Camargo M (2001) The Waning of Medieval Ars Dictaminis. Rhetorica: J Hist Rhetoric 19:135–140

Decock W (2013) Theologians and contract law : the moral transformation of the ius commune (ca. 1500–1650). Martinus Nijhoff Publishers, Leiden

Derrida J (1967) De la grammatologie. Minuit, Paris

Derrida J (1972) Signature, événement, contexte. In Marges de la philosophie. Paris, Minuit

Dolezalek G (2002) La diffusione delle opere di Rolandino in Germania e nelle zone contigue. In Rolandino e l'ars notaria da Bologna a Europa. Atti del Convegno nazionale di studi storici sulla figura e l'opera di Rolandino, ed. Giorgio Tamba. Giuffrè, Milano, pp 739–757

Eamon W (2017) Practical Alchemy in the Renaissance. The Official Website of Author William Eamon. http://williameamon.com/?p=640. Accessed May 24

Eisenstein EL (1979) The printing press as an agent of change. Cambridge University Press, New York

Enenkel KAE (2013) Illustrations as Commentary and Readers' Guidance. The Transformation of Cicero's De Officiis into a German Emblem Book by Johann von Schwarzenberg, Heinrich Steiner, and Christian Egenolff (1517–1520; 1530/1531; 1550). In: Karl AEE (ed) Transformation of the Classics via Early Modern Commentaries. Brill, Leiden, pp 167–259

Feenstra R (1998) Deux traités notariaux du XVe siècle: l'Ars notariatus anonyme et le Doctrinale florum artis notarie d'Etienne Marcillet. Une orientation bibliographique. In: Jacobs B, Coppens EC (eds) Een rijk gerecht: Opstellen aangeboden aan prof. mr. P. L. Nève 149–175. Rechtshistorische Reeks van het Gerard Noodt Instituut XLI. Gerard Noodt Instituut, Nijmegen

Furtenbach S (1979) Ars Notariatus. Ein kurialer Notariatstraktat des 15. Jahrhunderts. Österreichisches Archiv für Kirchenrecht 30:3–22 & 299–327

Gawthrop RL (1987) Literacy drives in preindustrial germany. In: Arnove RF, Graff HJ (eds) National literacy campaigns. Springer, Boston, pp 29–48

Green LD, Murphy JJ (2006) Renaissance rhetoric short-title catalogue 1460-1700. Ashgate, Aldershot

Gullick M (2006) Pen in hand: medieval scribal portraits, colophons and tools. Red Gull Press, Walkern

Gumbert JP (1998) Les outils du copiste. Gazette du livre médiéval 32:1–7

Jäcker C (2002) Christian Egenolff 1502-1555: Ein Frankfurter Meister des frühen Buchdrucks aus Hadamar. Glaukos Verlag, Limburg

Joachimsohn P (1893) Aus der vorgeschichte des "Formulare und deutsch rhetorica". Zeitschrift für deutsches Altertum und deutsche Literatur 37:24–121

Johns A (1998) The nature of the book: print and knowledge in the making. University of Chicago Press, Chicago

Kafka B (2012) The demon of writing: powers and failures of paperwork. Zone Books, New York

Knape J (2000) Allgemeine Rhetorik: Stationen der Theoriegeschichte. Reclam, Stuttgart

Kristeller PO (1945) Humanism and Scholasticism in the Italian Renaissance. Byzantion 17:346–374

Landau D, Parshall P (1994) The Renaissance Print: 1470–1550. Yale University Press, New Haven

Latour B (1986) Visualization and cognition. Knowl Soc 6:1–40
Latour B (2010)/(2002) The Making of Law: An Ethnography of the Conseil d'Etat. Polity Press, Cambridge
L'Engle S, Gibbs R (eds) (2001) Illuminating the law: legal manuscripts in Cambridge collections. Harvey Miller Publishers, London
Long PO (2001) Openness, secrecy, authorship: technical arts and the culture of knowledge from antiquity to the renaissance. Johns Hopkins University Press, Baltimore
Luschek F (1940) Notariatsurkunde und Notariat in Schlesien von den Anfängen (1282) bis zum Ende des 16. Jahrhunderts. Hermann Böhlaus Nachfolger, Weimar
Mack P (2011) A history of renaissance rhetoric 1380–1620. Oxford University Press
Martyn G (2000) Het Eeuwig Edict van 12 juli 1611: zijn genese en zijn rol in de verschriftelijking van het privaatrecht. Algemeen Rijksarchief, Brussels
Martyn G (2013) Naar het museum met een jurist als gids. Recht in de kunst in Gent (2). De dorpsadvocaat van Pieter Brueghel de Jonge. Strop & Toga 4:12–17
Mostert M, Adamska A (2014) Studying medieval urban literacy: a provisional state of affairs. In: Mostert M, Adamska A (eds) Uses of the written word in medieval towns. Brepols, Turnhout
Murphy JJ (1974) Rhetoric in the middle ages: a history of rhetorical theory from Saint Augustine to the renaissance. University of California Press, Berkeley
Nussdorfer L (2009) Brokers of public trust: notaries in early modern rome. Johns Hopkins University Press, Baltimore
Orlandelli G (1965) Genesi dell'"ars notariae" nel secolo XIII. Studi Medievali 6:329–366
Osley AS, Wolpe B (eds) (1980) Scribes and sources: handbook of the chancery hand in the sixteenth century: texts from the writing-masters. D. R. Godine, Boston
Parshall P (1993) Imago contrafacta: images and facts in the Northern Renaissance. Art History 16:554
Petrucci A (1995) The illusion of authentic history: documentary evidence. In: Writers and Readers in Medieval Italy: Studies in the History of Written Culture, tran. Charles M. Radding. Yale University Press, New Haven, pp 236–250
Poisson J-P (1990) L'apport des formulaires notariaux à la connaissance de la vision des notaires sur eux-mêmes et sur la société aux XVIe et XVIIe siècles. Premières données. In Notaires et société: Travaux d'histoire et de sociologie notariales. Economica, Paris, pp 21–53
Prinz F (2006) Der Bildgebrauch in gedruckten Rechtsbüchern des 15. bis zum Ausgang des 18. Jahrhunderts. LIT Verlag, Münster
Riles A (2005) A new agenda for the cultural study of law: taking on the technicalities. Buffalo Law Review 53:973–1033
Röhl KF (2005) Bilder in gedruckten Rechtsbüchern. In Recht vermitteln: Strukturen, Formen und Medien des Kommunikation im Recht, ed. Kent D. Lerch, 3:267–347. Die Sprache des Rechts. Walter de Gruyter, Berlin
Rosenfeld RA (2002) Tools for producing books and documents in roman antiquity and the middle ages: a summary list of classes. Scriptorium 56:156–176
Röttinger H (1904) Hans Weiditz: der Petrarkameister. J.H. Ed. Heitz, Strassburg
Röttinger H (1933) Der frankfurter Buchholzschnitt 1530–1550. J.H. Ed. Heitz, Strassburg
Schmidt-Thomé W (1961) Das Notariat. In: Kaspers H (ed) Vom Sachsenspiegel zum Code Napoléon: Kleine Rechtsgeschichte im Spiegel alter Rechtsbücher. Wienand-Verlag, Cologne, pp 153–176
Schmoeckel M (2012) Die Reichnotariatsordnung von 1512. Entstehung und Würdigung. In Handbuch zur Geschichte des deutschen Notariats seit der Reichsnotariatsordnung von 1512, ed. Werner Schubert and Mathias Schmoeckel. Nomos, Baden-Baden, pp 29–74
Schubert W (2012) Die Geschichte des Beurkundungsrechts und der notariellen Beurkundszuständigkeiten bis zu deren Vereinheitlichung durch das Beurkundungsgesetz vom 28. August 1969. In: Schubert W, Schmoeckel M (eds) Handbuch zur Geschichte des

deutschen Notariats seit der Reichsnotariatsordnung von 1512. Nomos, Baden-Baden, pp 645–682
Schuler P-J (1984) Formelbuch und Ars dictandi. Kaum genutzte Quellen zur politischen und sozialen Geschichte. In: Jäger H (ed) Civitatum communitas: Studien zum europäischen Städtewesen. Festschrift Heinz Stoob zum 65. Geburtstag. Böhlau, Cologne, pp 374–389
Smith PH (2004) The body of the artisan: art and experience in the scientific revolution. University of Chicago Press, Chicago
Smith PH (2012) Making things: techniques and books in early modern Europe. In: Findlen P (ed) Early modern things. Routledge, New York, pp 173–203
Smith PH (2006) Art, science, and visual culture in early modern Europe. Isis 97:83–100.
Stintzing R (1867) Geschichte der populären Literatur des römisch-kanonischen Rechts in Deutschland am Ende des fünfzehnten und im Anfang des sechszehnten Jahrhunderts. S. Hirzel, Leipzig
Strauss G (1986) Law, resistance, and the state: the opposition to roman law in reformation Germany. Princeton University Press, Princeton
Sumner Maine H (1908) Ancient law. Cheap edition. John Murray, London
Tamba G (ed) (2002) Rolandino e l'ars notaria da Bologna all'Europa. Atti del Convegno internazionale di studi storici sulla figura e l'opera di Rolandino. Giuffrè, Milano
van der Marck L, Eisma M (eds) (2013) De notaris in woord en beeld. De cultuurhistorische collectie van de Stichting tot Bevordering der Notariële Wetenschap. Waanders Uitgevers, Zwolle
Vismann C (2008)/(2001) Files: law and media technology. Translated by Geoffrey Winthrop-Young. Stanford University Press, Stanford
Vismann C (2011) In judicio stare. Law and Literature 23:309–323
Weber M (1978)/(1922) Economy and society: an outline of interpretive sociology. University of California Press, Berkeley
Winternitz E (1967) Musical instruments and their symbolism in Western Art. W. W. Norton, New York
Witt R (1982) Medieval "Ars Dictaminis" and the beginnings of humanism: a new construction of the problem. Renaissance Quarterly 35:1–35
Witt R (2012) The two Latin cultures and the foundation of Renaissance humanism in medieval Italy. Cambridge University Press, New York

Gustav Kalm completed a masters in law in Paris at Sciences Po with a master thesis on the aesthetics of legal paperwork at international business law firms. This inquiry into visual in contemporary business law firms was based on fieldwork at law firms in London, Paris and Tallinn and analyzed the role of visuality in legal veridiction. He is now pursuing a doctorate in anthropology at Columbia University focusing on bureaucratic management of complex areas of global regulation and the differences in the construction of political and technical. He was also previously a pre-doctoral fellow with the Minerva Research Group at the Kunsthis-torisches Institut in Florence.

Figures

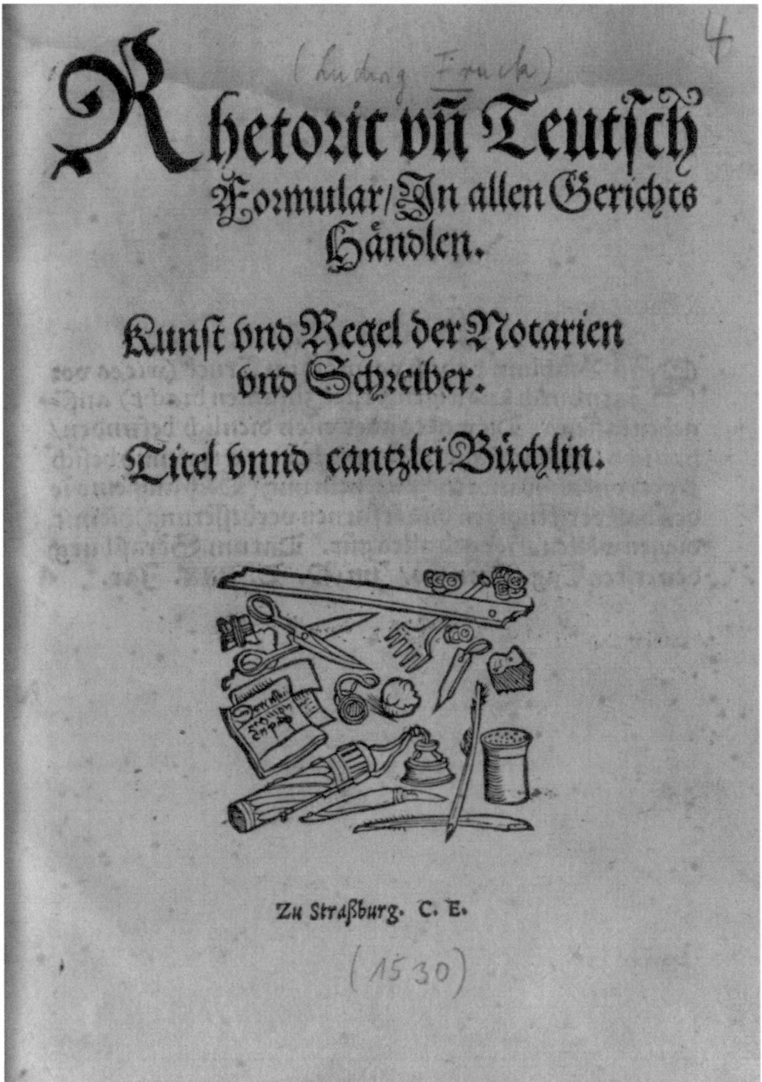

Fig. 13.1 Title page of *Rhetoric uñ Teutsch Formular*, 1530, Straßburg, Christian Egenolph, © Bayerische Staatsbibliothek München, inv. Res/4 J.pract. 85

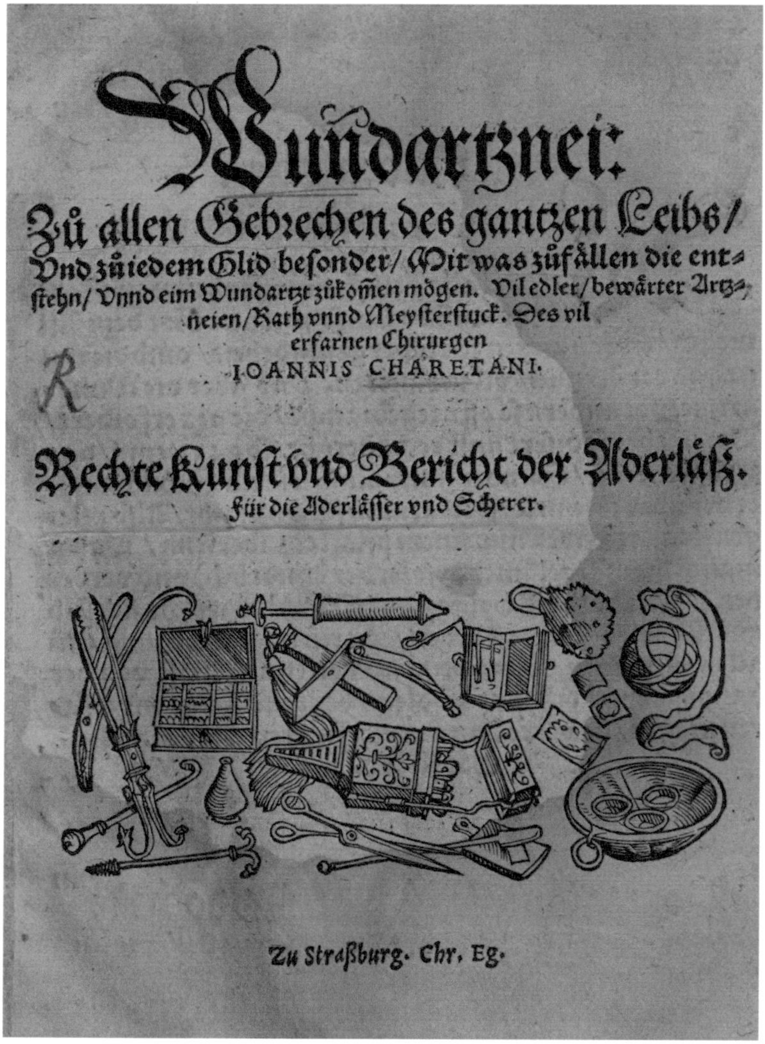

Wundartznei:
Zů allen Gebrechen des gantzen Leibs/ Vnd zů iedem Glid besonder/ Mit was zůfällen die entstehn/ Vnnd eim Wundartzt zůkom̃en mögen. Vil edler/bewärter Artzneien/Rath vnnd Meysterstuck. Des vil erfarnen Chirurgen
IOANNIS CHARETANI.

Rechte Kunst vnd Bericht der Aderläß.
Für die Aderlässer vnd Scherer.

Zu Straßburg. Chr. Eg.

Fig. 13.2 Title page of Ioannis Charetani, *Wuñdartznei*, 1530, Straßburg, Christian Egenolph, Illustration possibly by Hans Weiditz, © Bayerische Staatsbibliothek München, inv. Res/4 Chir. 110,1

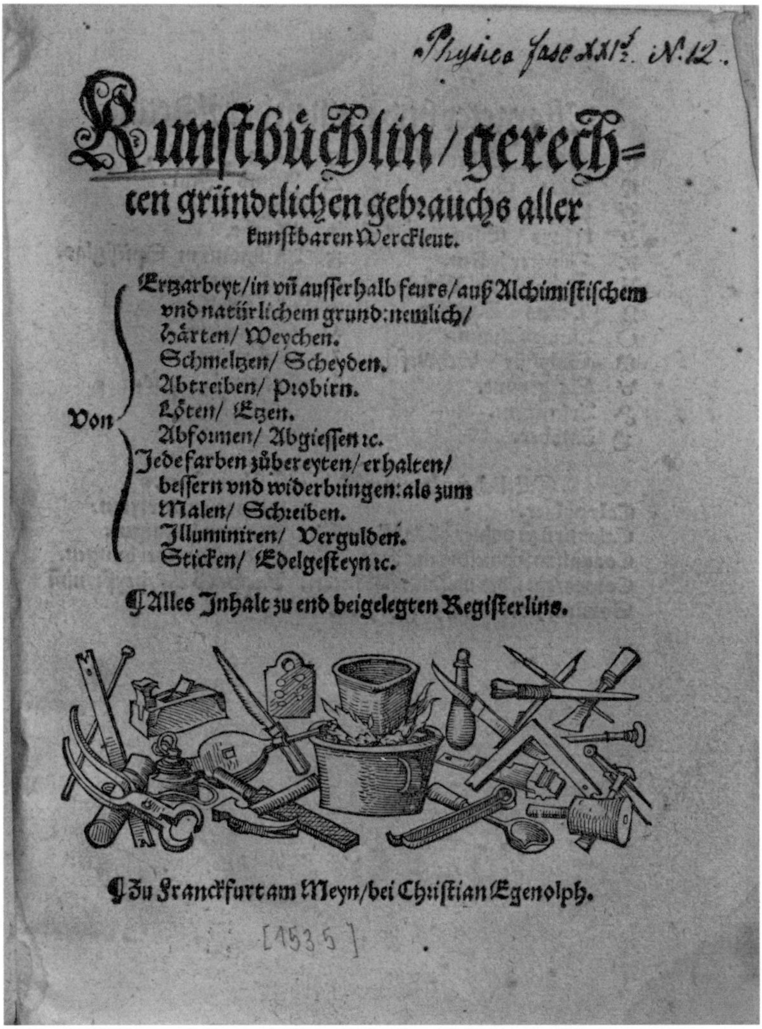

Physica Fasc XXI½. N:12.

Kunstbüchlin/gerechten gründtlichen gebrauchs aller kunstbaren Werckleut.

Von

Etzarbeyt/in vñ ausserhalb feurs/auß Alchimistischem vnd natürlichem grund: nemlich/
Härten/ Weychen.
Schmeltzen/ Scheyden.
Abtreiben/ Probirn.
Löten/ Etzen.
Abformen/ Abgiessen ꝛc.
Jede farben zůbereyten/erhalten/ bessern vnd widerbringen: als zum
Malen/ Schreiben.
Illuminiren/ Verguldẽn.
Sticken/ Edelgesteyn ꝛc.

¶ Alles Inhalt zu end beigelegten Registerlins.

¶ Zu Franckfurt am Meyn/bei Christian Egenolph.

[1535]

Fig. 13.3 Title page of *Kunstbuͤchlin*, 1535, Franckfurt am Meyn, Christian Egenolph, © Augsburg, Staats- und Stadtbibliothek, inv. 037/4 Techn 193

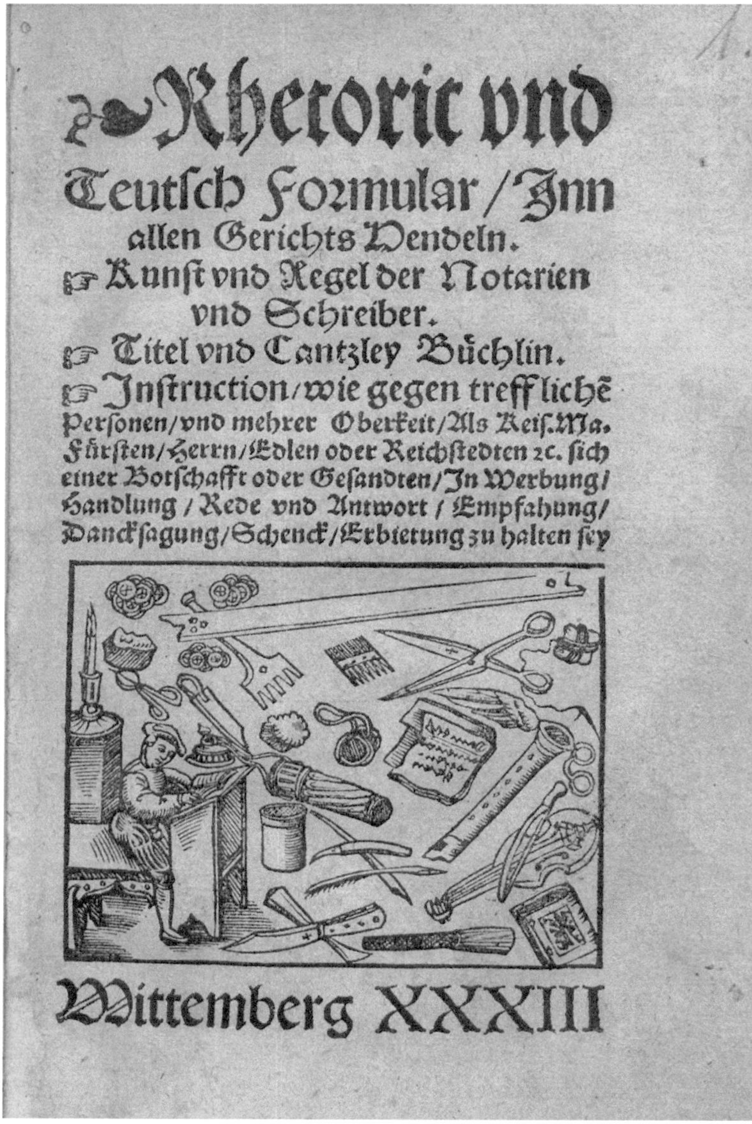

Rhetoric vnd
Teutſch Formular / Inn
allen Gerichts Hendeln.
☞ Kunſt vnd Regel der Notarien
vnd Schreiber.
☞ Titel vnd Cantzley Büchlin.
☞ Inſtruction / wie gegen trefflichē
Perſonen / vnd mehrer Oberkeit / Als Keiſ. Ma.
Fürſten / Herrn / Edlen oder Reichſtedten ꝛc. ſich
einer Botſchafft oder Geſandten / In Werbung /
Handlung / Rede vnd Antwort / Empfahung /
Danckſagung / Schenck / Erbietung zu halten ſey

Wittemberg XXXIII

Fig. 13.4 Title page of *Rhetoric und Teutsch Formular*, 1533, Wittemberg, Hans Weiss, © Universitätsbibliothek Leipzig, inv. 8-B.S.T.221/1

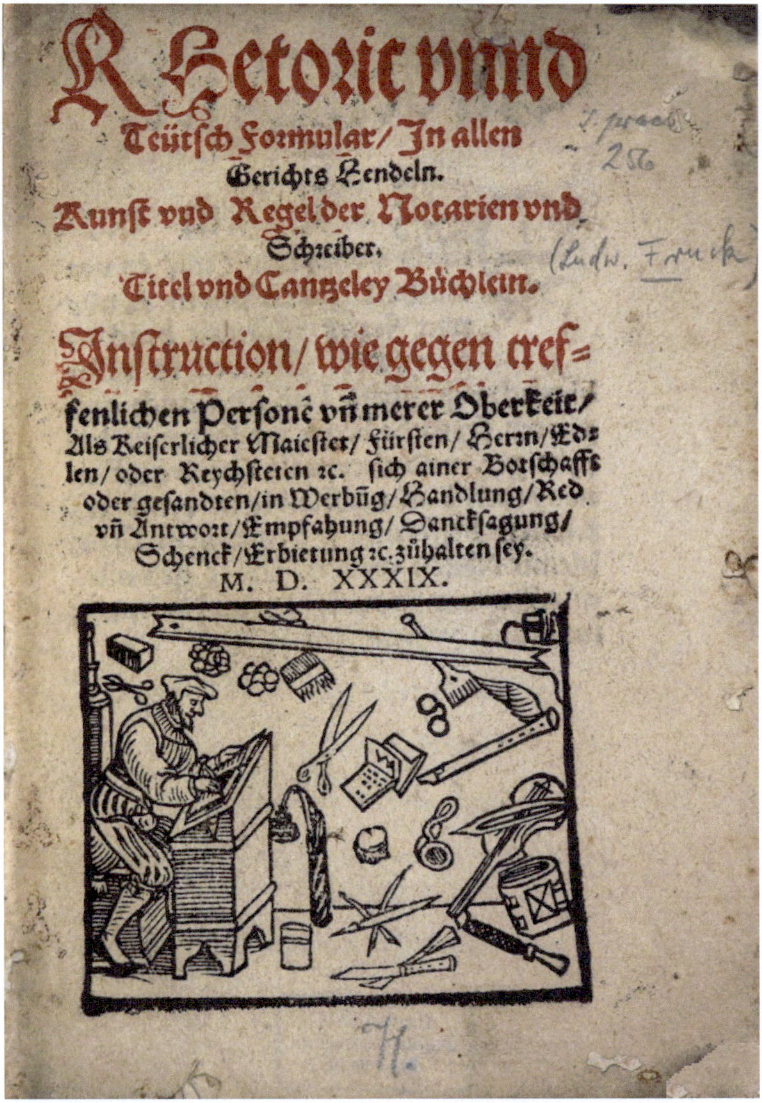
Rhetoric vnnd
Teütsch Formular / In allen
Gerichts Hendeln.
Kunst vnd Regel der Notarien vnd
Schreiber.
Titel vnd Canzeley Büchlein.
Instruction / wie gegen tref=
fenlichen Personē vñ merer Oberkeit /
Als Keiserlicher Maiestet / Fürsten / Herrn / Ed=
len / oder Reychsteten ꝛc. sich ainer Botschafft
oder gesandten / in Werbūg / Handlung / Red
vñ Antwort / Empfahung / Danckſagung /
Schenck / Erbietung ꝛc. zůhalten sey.
M. D. XXXIX.

Fig. 13.5 Title page of *Rhetoric vnnd Teütsch formular*, 1539, Augspurg, Alexander Weyssenhorn, © Bayerische Staatsbibliothek München, inv. J.pract. 256

Fig. 13.6 Petrarcameister, *Notaries' workshop*, engraving, here from *Von der Artzney bayder Glück*, but also used in numerous notarial and legal treatises: Francesco Petrarca, *Von der Artzney bayder* Glück, 1532, Augspurg, Heynrich Steyner, p. LVIIIv, © Bayerische Staatsbibliothek München, inv. Rar. 2266

Chapter 14
Liberté, égalité, fraternité ou la mort. The Iconography of Injustice in the Work of Pierre Goetsbloets

Brecht Deseure

Abstract Liberty and justice were central to the political iconography developed in the course of the French Revolution. Revolutionary iconography was introduced in the Southern Netherlands as a result of their annexation to France in the 1790s. The reception of this visual language has hitherto scarcely been investigated, despite offering valuable indications about the degree of popular acceptance of the new legal order. This chapter focuses on a rare example of a visual source that explicitly engages with the revolutionary iconography. The *Tydsgebeurtenissen* chronicle by the Antwerp nobleman Pierre-Antoine-Joseph Goetsbloets contains a unique collection of watercolour drawings made under the French regime. Despite his repudiation of the revolution and its principles, Goetsbloets was well acquainted with the revolutionary symbolism. Not only did he carefully copy revolutionary ceremonial into his chronicle, he also appropriated the new iconography in a subversive way. The elaborate satires he drew contained ironic reversals of the revolutionary representations of liberty and justice. By systematically undermining the revolutionary symbolism in the privacy of his chronicle, Goetsbloets created a powerful yet little-known visual counter-narrative to the French occupation of his hometown.

14.1 Introduction

In his classical article on the revolutionary calendar, Bronislaw Baczko observed that it is virtually impossible to separate the French Revolution from its representation (Baczko 1984, p. 40). Few changes of regime have witnessed a more

B. Deseure (✉)
Institute of Philosophy, University of Leuven, Leuven, Belgium
e-mail: Brecht.deseure@kuleuven.be

S. Huygebaert et al. (eds.), *The Art of Law*, Ius Gentium: Comparative Perspectives on Law and Justice 66, https://doi.org/10.1007/978-3-319-90787-1_14

profound iconographical transformation, while few political iconographies have had a stronger impact on the course of history. The close relationship between the Revolution and its representation partly results from the fact that the destruction of the old regime and its replacement by a new order was so fundamental that it required a completely new symbolic language. However, it is as much due to the deliberate use of the new iconography as a tool for education and administration by the authorities, especially under the Directory (Agulhon 1979, p. 23; Baczko 1996, p. 20; Hunt 1984, p. 60; Jainchill 2008, p. 75; Martin 2007, p. 19; Ozouf 1976, p. 280; Vovelle 1988).

Not only the calendar was reinvented, also a cycle of republican festivals aimed at instilling patriotism and republican values was put in place. Carefully designed iconographical programs and republican rituals accompanied these festivals. Equally important were the various attempts at establishing a secular State religion to channel the religious feelings of the people in a more useful direction than the 'obscure' and 'fanatic' learnings of Roman Catholicism (Aulard 1892; Mathiez 1904, p. 102; Soboul 1957, p. 197). Temples were raised to the Supreme Being, the goddess of Reason and the goddess of Law respectively. In order to convey the revolutionary message, a distinctive iconography was developed. Central to the revolutionary imagery was the figure of Liberty. Liberty and justice were indeed the fundamental concepts of the legal order instated by the Revolution.

The history of the symbolic representation of the revolutionary order and the accompanying iconographical transformations is well known, but its reception is not. Especially in territories annexed to France, like the former Southern Netherlands—more or less present-day Belgium—research into the circulation and acceptance of revolutionary symbolism is very limited. Nevertheless, official iconography was an important arena for the expression of political allegiance. Research has shown that the introduction of political iconography never worked one way: it entailed adaptation to the local context and negotiations over meaning and interpretation (Hebel and Wagner 2011). Traditional, national historiographies on the revolutionary period have generally looked down upon the iconographic aspect of French rule, considering it ridiculous at best, cynical at worst. Also, sources for the study of its reception are notoriously scarce. Press censorship was harsh during most of the period, hampering the free circulation of texts and images.

This chapter will shed light on the reception of revolutionary iconography of liberty and justice by using a rare visual source: the *Tydsgebeurtenissen* manuscript, owned by the Royal Library of Belgium.[1] The manuscript's author is the relatively obscure Pierre-Antoine-Joseph Goetsbloets, a wealthy aristocrat from Antwerp.[2] The title can be translated as 'events of the time', revealing the nature of the

[1]Brussels, Royal Library of Belgium, Manuscripts, inv. II 1492.

[2]Goetsbloets easily switched between Dutch and French in his writings. In this text, the French version of his first name is used because he consistently signed with 'Pierre (A.J.) Goetsbloets', both in official and private documents.

manuscript: it is a day-by-day eyewitness account of noteworthy events in Antwerp under French rule. Keeping chronicles was a widespread practice among city dwellers in the early modern period, especially in times of crisis and turmoil (Deseure 2014a; Pollmann 2016). The exceptional circumstances incited their authors—mostly literate men from the middle and upper strata of society—at recording public events as historical evidence for the future.

What makes the *Tydsgebeurtenissen* stand out among similar chronicles of the time is Goetsbloets' taste for the visual: the manuscript is interspersed with around two hundred full-folio water colour drawings. They stand in close relationship to the text, usually illustrating or commenting upon the events described. Despite their naïve style and their lack of artistic pretentions, these drawings betray a skilled hand and a sharp sense of observation. They offer unique visual evidence of life in Antwerp under French revolutionary rule. Many scenes resulted from Goetsbloets' own observation and constitute the single known visual trace of the depicted events. As such, Goetsbloets' drawings have been used extensively to illustrate publications on the revolutionary period in Belgium. Remarkably though, the manuscript and its images have never been thoroughly analysed in their own right.[3] This chapter aims at making a start with such an analysis by focusing on Goetsbloets' reception of revolutionary iconography, especially relating to the subject of law and justice (and its counterparts).

14.2 Revolutionary Iconography and Public Opinion

The importance of the study of political iconography for French revolutionary scholarship hardly needs introduction. Ever since the cultural turn and the rise of the revisionist school, the role of images in political communication has been at the centre of attention (Brunel 2003; Germani and Swales 1998; Reichardt 2003). Following the ground-breaking work done by Maurice Agulhon, Lynn Hunt, James Leith, Mona Ozouf and Michel Vovelle, among others, political representation has been promoted from the category of historical effects to the one of historical causes. The creation and circulation of imagery—both in the literal and the figurative sense—are now recognised as essential components of the revolutionary dynamic and as historical impact factors in their own right (Clark 2004; Hunt 1989).

The French Revolution brought about a moment of acceleration in the history of political iconography. The quick succession of radical political, cultural and social changes engendered an explosion of images and symbols. Innovative visual forms

[3]The best informed sources on the manuscript are Donnet (1910) and Welten (2015). Basic facts can be found in D'Hainaut-Zveny (2005) and Van den Gheyn (1907, pp. 649–658). Extensive use of the manuscript is made in Deseure (2014b).

were created to express and to perform the destruction of the old regime and its replacement by the revolutionary order. Soon these spontaneous visual innovations were institutionalised and used as an instrument of policy making (Baczko 1996, p. 20; Jainchill 2008, p. 75; Jourdan 1997; Ozouf 1976, p. 125). The revolutionary ideologists were strongly convinced of the importance of sensorial experiences for the communication of ideas; hence the central importance of political imagery in revolutionary political culture (Hunt 1983, p. 98; Jourdan 1997, p. 11; Leith 1960, p. 31; Ozouf 1976, pp. 241–244).

Political iconography has provided an ideal test-case for another historiographical turnabout of recent decades: the rise of transnational and entangled history. Leaving the national a priori's of comparative history behind, researchers have shifted their focus to communicative processes of interaction and exchange (Espagne and Werner 1988; Lüsebrink and Reichardt 1997; Owzar 2008; Reichardt 1990; Schönpflug 2004; Te Velde 2005). As these processes are being driven by the needs of both senders and receivers, it is understood that cultural and political goods are constantly being appropriated, reinterpreted and creatively adapted (Jourdan 2009). This is a fortiori the case with images and symbols, especially in a political context. Images of power are never static, but reflect changing political realities. The French occupation of the Southern Netherlands is exactly the kind of case where the meaning of political images was dependent on their circulation and reception in a trans-cultural context.

It is well known that the revolutionary symbols were a source of controversy in the occupied Southern Netherlands. Public opinion was for the most part conservative and in favour of a restoration of the Austrian regime. The first one and a half years of French occupation were not of a nature to engender popular support: it was a harsh military regime accompanied by state-organised plunder. Famine, banditry and large-scale social and economic disruption were the results (Devleeshouwer 1967; Hasquin 1993, p. 61; Rapport 2002, p. 61). Only from 1 October 1795 did the Belgian departments become properly integrated into the French state system. Nevertheless, the anti-religious policies, the high levels of taxation and the military conscription kept a majority of the population from sympathising with their new rulers.

Open rebellion against the regime was scarce, but its symbols became a target of popular discontent. The tree of liberty was one of the most prominent symbols of the new order. The planting of liberty trees by the victorious French armies was often accompanied by the destruction of symbols of the old regime, such as coats of arms and portraits of former kings and emperors (Deseure 2010, pp. 221–251; Prims 1935, pp. 231–238). The revolutionary symbolism drew on this antagonism between, on the one hand, the corrupt, delegitimised order of the old regime and, on the other hand, the new order based on the true principles of natural law and universal justice (Idzerda 1954; Poulot 1996, p. 165; Thamer 2005, p. 101). Numerous examples are known of liberty trees which were cut down by angry villagers under the cover of darkness. Another typical victim was the French flag flying above the doors of former town halls, now the seats of the republican municipalities.[4]

Indignation with the French revolutionary regime was exactly what prompted Pierre Goetsbloets to perform the truly Herculean task of creating the *Tydsgebeurtenissen.* The collecting of materials, the writing and drawing must have consumed most of his waking hours: in less than two and a half years' time he produced ten large in folio volumes, totalling around 5,000 handwritten pages. Each volume has a luxurious leather binding stamped with the gilded Goetsbloets coat of arms.[5] The penmanship is extraordinary: each volume opens with several lavishly decorated frontispieces, while the neatly aligned pages of handwriting are enlivened by fine pen drawings. Apart from his own eyewitness accounts, Goetsbloets inserted or copied in handwriting a flurry of other documents, including newspapers articles, official proclamations, tax documents, French paper money, popular songs and official speeches. He also integrated a rich collection of prints, including town maps, government propaganda, caricatures and portraits. Above all, each volume contains around twenty extraordinary watercolours.[6]

Not much is known about the background and personal life of Pierre Goetsbloets, who was born in 1765.[7] A passport included in the chronicle provides an impression of his physical appearance at thirty-three: 'five foot and two thumbs high, blond hair and eyebrows, blue eyes, medium nose, mouth idem, round chin, round forehead, full face'.[8] Goetsbloets scarcely mentions any personal events in his chronicle, except when they serve to illustrate the disasters brought about by French occupation. Such is the case with one of the rare drawings in which he depicts himself: a candlelit scene set in the hallway of his spacious residence on the *Sint-Jacobsmarkt* (Saint James Market).[9] Domestic peace is brutally violated by two French gendarmes who enter the house by force in order to arrest an alleged deserter hiding under Goetsbloets' roof.[10] Also present in the scene is Goetsbloets'

[4]For a more positive reception of revolutionary iconography in the work of local artists, see Deseure (2017).

[5]The first of the ten volumes is lost. Photographs of the drawings and a few pages of text it contained have been preserved. A description of the volume's content is included in the manuscripts catalogue (Van den Gheyn 1907, pp. 649–651).

[6]Goetsbloets probably took lessons at Antwerp's reputed art academy, as was customary for young urban aristocrats (Welten 2015, p. 348).

[7]Antwerp, City Archives, Parochial registers, Saint-James parish, baptism register 1751–1771: 5 May 1765. His parents were Petrus Arnoldus Josephus Goetsbloets (1733–1775), hereditary director of the Royal Mint of Antwerp, and Joanna Francisca Josepha Wellens (1732–1808) (Goethals 1857, p. 442).

[8]Brussels, Royal Library of Belgium, Manuscripts, inv. II 1492, vol. V, f. 213.

[9]Brussels, Royal Library of Belgium, Manuscripts, inv. II 1492, vol. VI, f. 176. Another self-depiction occurred at the occasion of an attempted robbery at his home (vol. X, f. 106).

[10]This information turned out to be false: the soldier in question was billeted on Goetsbloets' address. Goetsbloets was nevertheless prosecuted for offending the French gendarmes conducting the search, but he was acquitted.

wife, Henriette de Wael (born 1759), whom he married in 1785.[11] They had five children together but divorced in 1799 due to conflicting characters.[12] Both descended from affluent families that belonged to the urban patriciate since several generations (Goethals 1849, p. 248). The couple's family relations, as well as occasional glimpses of their social life in the chronicle, indicate that they frequented the highest social circles of the old regime urban establishment.[13]

Work on the chronicle probably started in the last months of 1794 or early in 1795, not long after the second French invasion of Antwerp. Goetsbloets grew more obsessive with his chronicle along the way, progressively devoting more and more space to the events described. In February 1797, the chronicle suddenly stops. Untimely, as it seems: additional pages had been lay-outed and waited to be filled. The manuscript provides no indication for the reason of that sudden halt, although it seems plausible that the daily rhythm of completing it became untenable.[14] Goetsbloets lived at least until 1838 but did not leave any further personal records.[15]

The contents of the chronicle are diverse. The watercolour drawings can roughly be divided in four topical categories: celebrations and ceremonies, local back pages (crimes, natural disasters, disturbances, executions),[16] foreign news (often concerning the French armies or French state officials) and allegories. The first and the last category will concern us here. These are the drawings in which Goetsbloets engages with revolutionary iconography. We will show his familiarity with this iconography and his own creative adaption of it, via three categories of analysis: accuracy, irony and parody.

---

[11]Antwerp, City Archives, Parochial registers, Saint-George parish, baptism register 1742–1760: 22 July 1759; marriage register 1747–1796: 1 February 1785.

[12]Antwerp, City Archives, Parochial registers, Saint-James parish, baptism register 1779–1793: Petrus Josephus Hyacinthus, 18 July 1788; Maria Josepha Henrica, 24 May 1789; Joannes Maria Petrus Josephus, 5 June 1790; Teresia Henrica Josepha, 26 November 1791; Joannes Baptista Josephus, 5 June 1793. The divorce was registered not in Antwerp but in Brussels (Eeckhoudt 2010, p. 148).

[13]E.g. an evening for cards described in vol. IX, f. 16. See also the list of émigrés from the Deux Nèthes department published on 19 fructidor year IV (5 September 1796) and copied in the chronicle. Goetsbloets mentions being related to 14 out of 93 of the listed individuals, including several former mayors and aldermen, a canon and the former bishop Corneille François de Nelis (vol. VIII, f. 433).

[14]Donnet (1910, p. 189) argues that Goetsbloets was assisted in his work by an anonymous helper.

[15]The address book for 1838 indicates *Steenhouwersvest* as his residence (1838. *Guide commercial ou livre d'adresses de la ville d'Anvers édité par les frères Ratinckx pour l'année 1838*, p. 87. Antwerp: Ratinckx).

[16]For Goetsbloets' many depictions of public punishment and executions, see the contribution by Jérôme de Brouwer and Xavier Rousseaux in this volume.

14.3 Accuracy

As a staunch supporter of the time-honoured order of the old regime, and as a devout Catholic, Goetsbloets considered the Revolution a disastrous event.[17] The experience led him to faithfully copy what he saw. Like his fellow chroniclers, Goetsbloets was strongly aware of the future historical value of his recordings. His desire for historical accuracy is reflected in the many details of costume, decoration, inscription and architecture. Added to this was a clear fascination for revolutionary festivals and iconography. Despite his aversion for the revolutionary order, he missed out on few of the public events staged by the new rulers. This is noteworthy in itself: other chroniclers insisted on avoiding these ceremonies, where no 'good citizen' would want to be seen. They even complained of city spaces becoming virtually inaccessible to them, as they were too closely associated with the new regime (Deseure 2013b). Goetsbloets was less easily deterred. Along with the more famous Jean-Baptiste Lesueur (1749–1826) series from Paris, the *Tydsgebeurtenissen* are among the most accurate and elaborate visual sources depicting the festivals of the French Revolution (De Carbonnières 2005).

The drawings and their captions show that Goetsbloets was familiar with the rituals and iconography as well as with their meaning. Often these were explained in a legend underneath the image. The destruction of the symbols of the old regime is a recurring theme: one example shows the removal of the royal coats of arms from a city gate at the orders of the town administration.[18] Another one depicts the public burning of a chariot laden with the symbols of royalty and religion and the instruments of torture.[19] The liberty tree on Antwerp's Great Market Square figures dozens of times in the *Tydsgebeurtenissen*, surrounded by ever-changing revolutionary festivities and processions.

A noteworthy series is devoted to the Festival of Liberty in 1796, staged in memory of the storming of the Bastille and the foundation of the Republic. The drawings prove that the local organizers carefully followed the instructions for the ritual and the decoration imposed by the central government. The end of royalty was represented by a group of armed young citizens who storm and trash a throne laden with symbols of monarchy. After that, fire was set to the throne and to a copy of the monarchical Constitution of 1791. Finally, the statue of the goddess of liberty, surrounded by French flags, was carried in procession by the authorities and installed on a podium replacing the destroyed throne (Fig. 14.1).[20] Liberty returns many times in the drawings, as her statue was often used in ceremonies. She was depicted in a neoclassical fashion, dressed in white garments with a red sash. In her

[17]Welten's characterisation of Goetsbloets' political position as 'relatively indifferent' seems hard to defend given the anti-French and anti-revolutionary tone pervading the entire manuscript (Donnet 1910, p. 17; Welten 2015, p. 79).

[18]Brussels, Royal Library of Belgium, Manuscripts, inv. II 1492, vol. VII, f. 206v.

[19]*Ibidem*, vol. I, f. 144.

[20]*Ibidem*, vol. VIII, f. 36–40.

left hand she held the revolutionary pike, crowned with a red Phrygian or Jacobin cap. Her right hand sometimes rested on the fasces, representing justice and authority.

Other festivals involved more exotic symbolism, such as the Festival of Agriculture with its ceremonial cultivation of a plot of land by use of a tricolour plough.[21] On other occasions, the symbols were explicitly political. One drawing shows the celebration of the *Fête de la Réunion* in Brussels on 12 October 1795, celebrating the annexation of the Southern Netherlands to France. First came the public burning of a cardboard pyramid topped with the coats of arms of the Austrian imperial House and the Duchy of Brabant.[22] The next drawing depicts the allegory of union displayed in the Temple of Law: two Roman soldiers are shown shaking hands over the altar of the fatherland, which is adorned with the constitution and the pike of liberty.[23] The left soldier's helmet carries a Gaulish rooster, while the right one's is adorned with a 'Belgian' lion. Apart from the revolutionary symbolism, Goetsbloets had a clear predilection for official costumes. He rendered them with much precision, up to the point of hand-copying prints depicting the new official robes for the various administrators under the Directory (Welten 2015, p. 82).

All in all, his detailed renderings of symbols, decorations and inscriptions show a great familiarity with the signs and meanings of the visual language introduced by the revolutionary authorities. Written sources, such as organisational files relating to the festivals and eyewitness accounts, corroborate Goetsbloets' depictions (Donnet 1910, p. 173). Evidently, he relied on existing visual codes and pictorial traditions when composing his drawings. Also, he reduced the scenes to what he considered important; often leaving out elements like the background setting or indications as to the number of spectators. Nevertheless, his representations of the revolutionary ceremonial show a clear intention of historical accuracy.

14.4 Irony

His desire for accuracy did not prevent Goetsbloets from satirising the revolutionary iconography. He did so by adding captions to the scenes and by integrating ironic twists in the images. One of his first depictions of a ceremony under the tree of liberty, set in 1795, is a case in point.[24] It shows a gathering of soldiers and civilians attending a speech given by a member of the military authorities. He and a

[21]*Ibidem*, vol. VII, f. 149–152.

[22]*Ibidem*, vol. III, f. 142.

[23]*Ibidem*, vol. III, f. 207.

[24]*Ibidem*, vol. I, f. 157r.

municipal officer are shown standing on a platform adorned with a statue of the goddess of liberty on a pedestal. She is equipped with her usual attributes, but her face is covered in dirty spots, giving the statue a pockmarked or worm-eaten look. In the foreground a crouching dog is ostensibly shown in the act of defecating and urinating. The association of the image with disease and scatological elements conveys an unmistakable message of disapproval to the viewer.

More defecation is going on in an image from a series depicting the procession for the opening of the Temple of Reason in 1794.[25] A marching cavalry brigade is shown, commanded by its sabre-brandishing captain. A small bird flies above and sends its droppings down on the captain's head. To prevent the detail from going unnoticed, a legend has been added reading: '*malum signum in urina*'. Whether the incident really happened or not is of secondary importance; Goetsbloets' explicit depiction of it is all the more meaningful. In the same procession, the goddess of Reason was personified by a woman of flesh and blood, as was customary. The image shows her sitting majestically enthroned on a rock with a French flag flying above (Fig. 14.2).[26] Goetsbloets again uses the captions to prevent the viewer from taking the revolutionary message seriously. He explains that the lady personifying the goddess was in reality the daughter of a wigmaker, while the horses pulling the godly chariot had been requisitioned by force. That way, the elevated register of Reason's cult was contrasted with the dismal reality of military occupation by a penniless regime.

Another symbolic animal is present in the image showing an oath-taking ceremony in front of the town hall. The tree of liberty in the foreground had obviously died, as written sources confirm. On top of the protective wooden casing sits a small, fully dressed monkey, looking the viewer directly in the eye (Fig. 14.3).[27] The presence of such an animal in reality is highly improbable. Goetsbloets much more likely used it as symbol of human folly, as known from the painting genre of the *singeries*.

Textual additions to the images, too, functioned as counterpoints to the display of revolutionary symbolism. One example shows a ceremony in the Temple of Law, installed in a former church. On the platform is the French representative of the people Lefebvre de Nantes, who reads out the new French Constitution of the year III to an audience of soldiers. One soldier expresses his boredom in a line escaping from his mouth: '*Il nous embête avec sa sacré* [sic] *Constitution*' (he bores us with his blasted Constitution).[28] The services in the temple were indeed known

[25] *Ibidem*, vol. I, f. 138.

[26] *Ibidem*, vol. I, f. 137.

[27] *Ibidem*, vol. IV, f. 168.

[28] *Ibidem*, vol. III, f. 18.

to be exceedingly dull, up to the point that even French officials stopped attending them (Deseure 2014b).

Often, pen-drawn human or animal figures appear at the bottom of a page, from whose mouths similar comments escape. The mastery of Goetsbloets' penmanship does not fail to impress, as most of these drawings are done with one single, uninterrupted line. Often, a rooster and a lion are shown in conversation, as the symbols of France and Belgium respectively. One drawing stages the pair in a dialogue at the occasion of the abolishment of the transit duties imposed on the River Scheldt by the Dutch Republic. French intervention removed this fiscal barrier, which had harmed Antwerp's position as a commercial centre for almost two centuries.[29] The rooster proudly announces the 'liberation' of the river, clearly expecting an expression of gratitude from the *sinjoren* (nickname for the inhabitants of Antwerp). The lion's sarcastic answer reads: 'Yes, yes, Uncle Rooster, you brave republican, as a reward we offer you all the fish this river contains, including its mussels, shrimps, snail shells and periwinkles'.[30] In this and other scenes, mild sarcasm was used as means to comment on events that were otherwise truthfully represented.

14.5 Parody

The case is different in those images where Goetsbloets targeted the revolutionary iconography itself. From time to time he integrated full-blown allegories satirising the exalted revolutionary representations of liberty and justice. In these images, the tone was much grimmer. The underlying message was that the revolutionary order was illegal and would lead to the total destruction of 'Belgium' and its inhabitants. The revolutionary abuses Goetsbloets cried out against were many: the ousting of the legitimate sovereign the Austrian emperor, the annexation to France, the burden of taxation, the disastrous introduction of paper money, the plundering of Church property, the famine…

The use of allegory allowed Goetsbloets to emphasise the contrast between the idealistic revolutionary rhetoric and the experienced reality of brutal occupation. It is no coincidence that the allegories often preceded, or followed directly after, a series of images depicting revolutionary festivals. Goetsbloets used them to react to the imposition of revolutionary imagery in a more direct way than the ironic twists discussed above. It seems almost as if crude parody provided him with compensation for the painstaking accuracy he applied in depicting the symbols of a regime he despised.

[29]On the recuperation of the Scheldt theme by the French administration: Deseure (2013a) and (2016).

[30]Brussels, Royal Library of Belgium, Manuscripts, inv. II 1492, vol. II, f. 21v.

His allegory on the union of Belgium and France probably echoes the iconographical program of the *Fête de la Réunion* celebrated in Antwerp on 8 October 1795. The design of that program has not been preserved, but presumably resembled the one of the Brussels edition of the *Fête*. Under the title 'Forced reunion', Goetsbloets depicted a rooster and a lion sitting beneath the altar of the fatherland and holding a fasces bundle together as a sign of unity. A hybrid allegory of liberty (pike) and justice (scales) towers over the altar.[31] As the caption explains, the rooster represents the country formerly known as France, which is now called 'the land of Carmagnoles' (nickname for French revolutionaries derived from the *sansculotte* song *La Carmagnole*). The rooster is being supported by a richly dressed lady wearing a plumed headdress, who represents 'puffed-up Pride'. The lion, by contrast, is accompanied by a savage-looking figure brandishing iron chains. As the author explains, 'the fierce and furious lion would rather dispatch the pluck bird for lunch', but the tortures inflicted on him by Hate and Envy force him into the reunion. Tellingly, the allegorical figure above the altar suspends the scales of Justice above the lion, whereas she extends the 'bloody cap of Liberty' in the direction of the rooster.

In this case, an existing allegory used in a festival was being parodied. But most allegories drawn by Goetsbloets were of his own invention. They did not refer to a given example and concerned subjects that preoccupied him. A typical example is an allegory on the 'emprunt forcé' or forced loan (Fig. 14.4).[32] These 'loans' were heavy financial obligations imposed on the propertied classes in the annexed territories in order to relieve the financial needs of the French Republic.[33] Being a member of the elite and liable to the second highest taxation rate, Goetsbloets worried a lot about financial matters.[34] He regularly copied tax bills into the chronicle and complained about taxes more than about anything else.

The allegory not only criticizes the forced loan, but attacks the new legal order itself. The law is depicted as a worn-out scrap of paper bearing the words: 'Liberty. Lex. Requisition. Forced loan. Contribution'. It is held by a hideous lady wearing the cap of Liberty, whom Goetsbloets identifies as Cruelty. She menacingly brandishes her sword while speaking the words: 'Your purse or your life, fraternity

[31]No blindfold is present. Brussels, Royal Library of Belgium, Manuscripts, inv. II 1492, vol. III, f. 131. Typical allegories of Justice with blindfold, sword and scales can be found in vol. III, f. 17 and vol. VI, f. 20. In the latter case, an Assumption-like scene shows Justice rising to Heaven after being chased from the earth by Falseness, Violence and Deceit.

[32]*Ibidem*, vol. IV, f. 213.

[33]Donnet (1910) asserts, without reference, that Goetsbloets was taken hostage in August 1794 in order to compel him to pay his part of 4,000 *livres* in the contribution imposed on the propertied classes after the capture of Antwerp.

[34]Goetsbloets belonged to the financial sub-top of the city. He was among Antwerp's two hundred richest inhabitants (Welten 2015, p. 86).

or death'. The centre of the image shows the robberies and outrages committed on an innocent people under the cover of this false and crooked law. The Belgian coffer is being plundered by 'the Carmagnoles' regime', depicted as a ragged lady bearing the French standard. Meanwhile, a soldier in Roman dress strangles an innocent inhabitant whom he calls an 'aristo-fanatic', right under the liberty tree. The languishing Belgian maiden looks on impotently, her wrists bound with iron bracelets symbolising 'the miserable century of iron she is living in'. A kneeling, half-naked boy is shown holding up a heart and weeping for the King.[35] He stands for the 'poverty of the good inhabitants of France who for lack of bread eat up their own hearts, being truly deprived of pants (sans culottes)'. Goetsbloets sardonically captioned the image with a classic *sansculotte* slogan: 'Freedom, Equality, Brotherhood or Death. War on the castles, peace to the huts'.

Goetsbloets took existing symbols from revolutionary iconography and used them in a way that reversed their intended significance. In his view, turning the symbols around revealed their true meaning. He regularly expressed the idea that the revolutionary symbols were only a cover: a hypocrite ideological cloaking of a much more cynical truth. The tree of liberty was among his preferred targets, being one of the most visible symbols of the revolutionary regime. He qualified it as 'the so-called tree of liberty' or as 'the tree of misery and distress'. For him, the tree grew on the ruins of the legal order and was therefore a symbol of slavery. In one of his allegories, the tree of liberty is chained to a pole with iron shackles. From the tree flows an inscription reading: 'I am truly very free now'.[36] Goetsbloets abundantly associated the republican and revolutionary imagery with the symbols of death, violence, misery and oppression. In another allegory he presents the French regime as a skull crowned with thorns, surrounded by shackles, a French flag and a pike of liberty. The caption reads: 'Misery, distress, slavery, despotism, shackles, chains and death or famine'.[37] Elsewhere, the goddess of liberty is herself chained up or put under the joke.[38]

Goetsbloets' attempts at exposing the dire truth behind the revolutionary iconography culminated in his literal unmasking of the goddess of liberty. The caption of one particularly impressive allegory reads: 'Hypocrisy, under the guise of liberty, sitting on the spoliations and holy vessels of the Netherlands, raises its mask. Over the course of time it leaves the Netherlands nothing but bad hope, evil government and death or the bed of poverty' (Fig. 14.5). The image shows the goddess of Liberty enthroned under an obelisk adorned with French flags. Her attributes point both to Liberty (pike, Phrygian cap) and to France (helmet with Gaulish rooster), but she has claws for feet, placed on confiscated gold coins and

---

[35]The heart was also used as an emblem by the anti-revolutionary resistance in the Vendée region.

[36]Brussels, Royal Library of Belgium, Manuscripts, inv. II 1492, vol. I, f. 66. The distinctive style of this drawing suggests that it may have been made after a cartoon.

[37]*Ibidem*, vol. II, f. 11.

[38]*Ibidem*, vol. III, f. 2; VI, f. 46.

sacred vessels. With her left hand she lifts her charming mask, revealing the frightening features of Medusa that lurk behind it. To her left sits worried-faced Time, with his hour-glass, scythe and wings. To her right lies the half-naked Belgian maiden, recognizable by her city crown. Her hands chained, she languishes dispiritedly between the symbols of death and destitution. Hope, recognizable by her anchor, vainly tries to relieve her.[39]

In a similar example, set in barren and rocky surroundings, the enchained Belgian maiden seeks protection against a tomb (Fig. 14.6). She tries to ward off an enraged goddess of liberty on the verge of stabbing her to death with her pike. On the horizon appears the frightful figure of Revenge, hurling down a thunderbolt to stop this act of tyranny. In the caption, Goetsbloets points out that the terrifying goddess is only 'pretended liberty'.[40] Both images are powerful examples of Goetsbloets' reversal of the liberty symbolism. Liberty, whose graceful statue he so often drew when used in revolutionary festivals, was now reduced to her true character: a merciless, blood-thirsty fury who led the French in the unlawful subjugation and extortion of an innocent people. It is no coincidence that Goetsbloets' Liberty carried armour and displayed the colours and symbols of the French Republic. In her hands, the pike of liberty became an offensive weapon aimed not at liberation but at submission.

14.6 Conclusion

There is room for much more research on the historic and artistic aspects of the drawings in the *Tydsgebeurtenissen* chronicle. Many questions remain on Pierre Goetsbloets' use of visual sources and the relationship of his drawings to contemporary visual culture. Looking at the drawings from the point of view of revolutionary iconography reveals that, for a convinced supporter of the old regime, Goetsbloets showed a remarkable interest in the symbols of the French Revolution. The images in his chronicle show that he engaged with this iconography on various levels and with various goals. As a chronicler, he was interested in preserving his experiences of French occupation as accurately as possible.

But Goetsbloets did more than accurately record what he saw. The private space of the chronicle allowed him to appropriate and comment upon the new iconography. This makes the *Tydsgebeurtenissen* manuscript a rare but very illuminating example of iconographical reception in the territories occupied in the wake of the French Revolution. It shows the creative transformation of the dominant political

[39] *Ibidem*, vol. VII, f. 14.

[40] *Ibidem*, vol. VII, f. 262.

and visual narrative by a supporter of the old regime. This narrative was deeply bound up with notions of law and justice: the ever-present goddess of liberty suggested the advent of a new and right order of things, in which true justice might finally triumph. In his striking parodies of the revolutionary iconography, Goetsbloets created a visual counter-narrative to that message. By satirising the revolutionary festivals and iconography, he delegitimised the revolutionary claims to truth and lawfulness. Instead, he pointed at the illegality of the new regime and the fundamental injustices he associated with it.

Such a degree of creative transformation was only possible due to Goetsbloets' familiarity with French revolutionary iconography. He gained this knowledge not only through the festivals he witnessed in Antwerp, but also through the printed media he collected and included into the manuscript. His captions and comments prove that he was well aware of the intended meaning of these symbols. In his allegories, he reused them in a more hybrid context, changing the codes of revolutionary iconography and adding figures from local tradition (e.g. the Belgian maiden) and of his own invention. Doing so allowed him to reveal what he considered to be the true meaning of the revolutionary iconography. Previous research has shown that the French administrators adapted the symbolism they used to the local context. The *Tydsgebeurtenissen* manuscript proves that the process went both ways: the inhabitants themselves actively engaged with the new iconography. Pierre Goetsbloets turned this engagement into an art, by producing one of the most captivating and inventive visual testimonies of the revolutionary experience.

References

Agulhon M (1979) Marianne au combat: l'imagerie et la symbolique républicaines de 1789 à 1880. Flammarion, Paris

Aulard F-A (1892) Le culte de la raison et le culte de l'Etre suprême (1793–1794). Essai historique. Alcan, Paris

Baczko B (1984) Le calendrier républicain. Décréter l'éternité. In: Nora P (ed) Les lieux de mémoire, vol I. La République, Gallimard, Paris, pp 37–83

Baczko B (1996) Le tournant culturel de l'an III. In: Dupuy R, Morabito M (eds) 1795: Pour une République sans Révolution. Presses Universitaires de Rennes, Rennes, pp 17–38

Brunel F (2003) L'histoire politique de la Révolution française. Quelques réflexions sur l'historiographie récente. In: Lapied M, Peyrard C (eds) La Révolution française au carrefour des recherches. Publications de l'Université de Provence, Aix-en-Provence, pp 115–137

Clark EA (2004) History, theory, text. historians and the linguistic turn. Harvard University Press, Cambridge

D'Hainaut-Zveny B (2005) Pierre-Antoine-Joseph Goetsbloets, Tydsgebeurtenissen. In: Delsaerdt P, Duvosquel J-M, Simons L, Sorgeloos C (eds) Honderd schatten uit de Koninklijke Bibliotheek van België. Mercatorfonds, Brussels, pp 179–180

De Carbonnières P (2005) Lesueur: gouaches révolutionnaires. Collections du musée Carnavalet. Paris-Musées, Paris
Deseure B (2010) Boom van Vrijheid/Boom van Slavernij. De Antwerpse vrijheidsbomen tussen oud en nieuw. Belgisch Tijdschrift voor Filologie en Geschiedenis 88:221–251
Deseure B (2013a) 'Rappelez-leur, pour mieux les persuader'. French political legitimation and historical discourse in Belgium (1792–1799). In: Andress D (ed) Experiencing the French revolution. Voltaire Foundation, Oxford, pp 221–244
Deseure B (2013b) 'Al ongehoorde nieuwigheden'. Beleving van de Antwerpse stedelijke ruimte in revolutietijd. In: Bertels I, Furnée JH, Sintobin T et al (eds) Tussen beleving en verbeelding. De stad in de negentiende-eeuwse literatuur. Universitaire Pers Leuven, Leuven, pp 221–244
Deseure B (2014a) 'Den ouden luijster is verdwenen'. Geschiedenis, herinnering en verlies bij Jan Baptist Van der Straelen (1792–1817). Belgisch Tijdschrift voor Nieuwste Geschiedenis 10:517–555
Deseure B (2014b) Onhoudbaar verleden. Geschiedenis als politiek instrument tijdens de Franse periode in België. Leuven University Press, Leuven
Deseure B (2016) La représentation du pouvoir français en Belgique (1792–1799): entre révolution et tradition. Annales historiques de la Révolution française 384:109–130
Deseure B (2017) Een wemeling van zinnebeelden. Kunst en politiek in de Franse tijd door de ogen van de Antwerpse schilders Nicolas en Jean Delin. Jaarboek De Achttiende Eeuw 1:53–64
Devleeshouwer R (1967) Occupants et occupés. La répression en Belgique en l'an III. Annales historiques de la Révolution française 215:199–220
Donnet F (1910). La vie intime anversoise sous le régime républicain. Bulletin de l'Académie Royale d'Archéologie de Belgique 171–198
Eeckhoudt L (2010) Comparatieve studie van de huwelijksdissoluties in de stad en het platteland tussen 1796 en 1830. Unpublished master's thesis Ghent University
Espagne M, Werner M (eds) (1988) Transferts: les relations interculturelles dans l'espace franco-allemand. Recherches sur les Civilisations, Paris
Germani I, Swales R (eds) (1998) Symbols, myths and images of the french revolution. essays in honour of James A. Leith. Canadian Plains Research Centre, Regina
Goethals F-V (1849) Dictionnaire généalogique et héraldique des familles nobles du Royaume de Belgique, vol II. Polack-Duvivier, Brussels
Goethals F-V (1857) Miroir des notabilités nobiliaires de Belgique, des Pays-Bas et du Nord de la France, vol I. Polack-Duvivier, Brussels
Hasquin H (1993) Van Fleurus tot de annexatie: een gekneusd land. In: Hasquin Hervé (ed) België onder het Frans bewind (1792–1815). Gemeentekrediet van België, Brussels, pp 41–72
Hebel U, Wagner C (2011) Introduction. In: Hebel U, Wagner C (eds) Pictorial cultures and political iconographies: approaches, perspectives, case studies from Europe and America. De Gruyter, Berlin, pp 7–12
Hunt L (1983) Hercules and the radical image in the French revolution. Representations 2:95–117
Hunt L (1984) Politics, culture and class in the French revolution. University of California Press, Berkeley
Hunt L (1989) Introduction: history, culture and text. In: Hunt L (ed) The new cultural history. University of California Press, Berkeley, pp 1–22
Idzerda SJ (1954) Iconoclasm during the French revolution. Am Hist Rev 60(3):13–26
Jainchill A (2008) Reimagining politics after the terror. The republican origins of French liberalism. Cornell University Press, New York
Jourdan A (1997) Les monuments de la Révolution, 1770–1804. Une histoire de représentation. Champion, Paris
Jourdan A (2009) Politieke en culturele transfers in een tijd van revolutie. Bijdragen en Mededelingen tot de Geschiedenis der Nederlanden 124:559–577

Leith JA (1960) The idea of art as propaganda during the French revolution. Rep Annu Meet Can Hist Assoc 38:30–43
Lüsebrink H, Reichardt R (1997) Kulturtransfer im Epochenumbruch. Frankreich-Deutschland 1770–1815. Leipziger Universitätsverlag, Leipzig
Martin J-C (2007). Introduction. In: Scholz N, Schröer C (eds) Représentation et pouvoir. La politique symbolique en France (1789–1830), Presses universitaires de Rennes, Rennes, pp 1–19
Mathiez A (1904) Les origines des cultes révolutionnaires (1789–1792). Société nouvelle de librairie et d'édition, Paris
Ozouf M (1976) La fête révolutionnaire, 1789–1799. Gallimard, Paris
Owzar A (2008) Vom Topos der Fremdherrschaft zum Modernisierungsparadigma. Zur Einführung. In: Dethlefs G, Owzar A, Weiß G (eds) Modell und Wirklichkeit. Politik, Kultur und Gesellschaft im Großherzogtum Berg und im Königreich Westphalen. Schöningh, Paderborn, pp 1–14
Pollmann J (2016) Archiving the present and chronicling for the future in early modern Europe. Past Present 230:231–252
Poulot D (1996) Surveiller et s'instruire: la Révolution française et l'intelligence de l'héritage historique. Voltaire Foundation, Oxford
Prims F (1935) De Fransche Vrijheidsbomen. In: Prims F (ed) Antwerpiensia, vol VIII. De Vlijt, Antwerp, pp 231–238
Rapport M (2002) Belgium under French occupation: between collaboration and resistance, July 1794–October 1795. Fr Hist 16:53–82
Reichardt R (1990) Die Französische Revolution und Deutschland. Thesen für einen komparatistischen, kulturhistorischen Neuansatz. In: Freiherr von Aretin KO, Härter K (eds) Revolution und konservatives Beharren. Das alte Reich und die Fransösiche Revolution. Von Zabern, Mainz
Reichardt R (2003) Histoire de la culture et des opinions. In: Lapied M, Peyrard C (eds) La Révolution française au carrefour des recherches. Publications de l'Université de Provence, Aix-en-Provence, pp 115–137
Schönpflug D (2004) So far, and yet so near: comparison, transfer and memory in recent German books on the age of the French revolution and napoleon. Fr Hist 18:446–462
Soboul A (1957) Sentiment religieux et cultes populaires pendant la Révolution: saintes patriotes et martyrs de la liberté. Annales historiques de la Révolution française 29:193–213
Te Velde H (2005). Political transfer: an introduction. Eur Rev Hist 12:205–211
Thamer H-U (2005) Die Aneignung der Tradition. Destruktion und Konstruktion im Umgang der Französischen Revolution mit Monumenten des Ancien Régime. In: Reichardt R, Schmidt R, Thamer H-U (eds) Symbolische Politik und politische Zeichensysteme im Zeitalter der Französischen Revolution (1789–1848). Rhema, Münster, pp 101–111
Van den Gheyn J (1907) Catalogue des manuscrits de la Bibliothèque royale de Belgique, vol VII. Lamertin, Brussels
Vovelle M (1988) Les images de la Révolution française. Publications de la Sorbonne, Paris
Welten J (2015). Een monument van papier. Het levenswerk van Petrus Goetsbloets. In: Welten J (ed) Antihelden. Bijzondere levens van gewone mensen uit de tijd van Napoleon. Davidsfonds, Leuven, pp 75–94

Brecht Deseure is a historian specialising in the political history of the revolutionary era. The focus of his research is on the political culture of the succeeding regimes in Belgium between the end of the eighteenth and the middle of the nineteenth century. In his dissertation he has investigated the politics of history pursued by the French revolutionary and Napoleonic governments in the annexed territories. His current research as a postdoctoral fellow at the University of Leuven focuses on the genesis of the Belgian Constitution of 1831.

Figures

Fig. 14.1 A statue of the goddess of liberty is carried in procession at the occasion of the Festival of Liberty in Antwerp on 27 July 1796, © Royal Library of Belgium, Brussels

Fig. 14.2 The goddess of reason in the procession for the inauguration of the temple in Antwerp on 30 November 1794, © Royal Library of Belgium, Brussels

Fig. 14.3 Celebration for the anniversary of the execution of Louis XVI on Antwerp's Great Market Square on 21 January 1796, © Royal Library of Belgium, Brussels

Fig. 14.4 Allegory on the '*emprunt forcé*' or forced loan (1796), © Royal Library of Belgium, Brussels

Fig. 14.5 Hypocrisy, under the guise of liberty, sitting on the spoliations and holy vessels of the Netherlands, raises its mask (1796), © Royal Library of Belgium, Brussels

Fig. 14.6 Armed liberty persecuting the Belgian maiden (1796), © Royal Library of Belgium, Brussels

Part IV
Criminal Justice: Art, Object and Locus

Chapter 15
Works of Art as a Form of Criminal Punishment in the Low Countries (14th–17th C.)

Paul De Win

Abstract From the fourteenth to the sixteenth century, and even in the seventeenth century, it was not uncommon for judicial sentences to require the convicted person to acquire, or finance, a work of art, or to have to provide specific objects. One can distinguish two types of artistic objects: those that were only intended as decorations, and those that bore an explanatory text mentioning the crime and the name of the condemned. The objects that were only used for embellishment are, strictly speaking, works of art. They can be found inside churches or public buildings (often the courtroom) in the form of a painting, a stained-glass window or a statue, but also as ornaments on the façade of a church or a town hall. Objects bearing explanatory notes, such as a description of the crime, the date of conviction and the name of the convicted person, are better referred as 'shaming penalty pieces': pieces imposed as punishment intending to shame offenders for their wrongdoing. The purpose of these pieces is not too primarily to decorate the room or façade, but rather to damage the reputation of the convict and serve as examples and warnings to those who read them. In these cases, the aesthetic quality of the work is subordinated to the message. These pieces in the form of metal fists and heads with explaining plaques, paintings and stained-glass windows were often exhibited in or near the courtroom. The theme was usually chosen in accordance with the misdeeds. In matters of high treason or *lèse-majesté*, columns of infamy were sometimes erected as an exceptional measure.

P. De Win (✉)
Formerly Legal History Institute, Ghent University, Ghent, Belgium
e-mail: pauldewin1@gmail.com

P. De Win
Federal Public Service of Foreign Affairs, Brussels, Belgium

S. Huygebaert et al. (eds.), *The Art of Law*, Ius Gentium: Comparative Perspectives on Law and Justice 66, https://doi.org/10.1007/978-3-319-90787-1_15

15.1 Introduction: Two Types of Art Objects

From the fourteenth to the seventeenth century, it was not uncommon for a convicted person to be sentenced to the acquisition of a work of art or to have to provide specific objects. This was particularly the case in the context of an *amende honorable* or 'honorable fine' (*eerlijke betering* in old Dutch), which in fact was a kind of public penance (De Win 2003). The penalty involved public reparation, firstly by begging forgiveness to God, the magistrates, the victim, its family and the community. The person undergoing this penance had to kneel, barefooted and bare-headed, and usually wore nothing but undergarments. Most often, a pecuniary fine was added to the penance as well. Within this 'profitable' part (*amende proufitable*, *profijtelijke betering*), the judges could impose the destination of (parts of) the sum(s) to be paid. For example, they could force the condemned to finance the distribution of alms, to share in the costs of public buildings under construction (such as the ramparts of the city or the tower of the church), but also to the acquisition of works of art. In some cases, the condemnation could even consist of the obligation to commission specific objects.

Aside from criminal sentences imposed by the courts, these obligations were also often agreed upon in the context of a 'peace' (i.e. an agreement between parties, particularly between the victim's family and the perpetrator), in the context of a 'composition' (i.e. a settlement with the authorities) or in a case of judicial reconciliation (which is imposed by the court). A peace-agreement (*pax*, *paix*, *zoen*) is a convention, usually on a voluntary basis, but sometimes carried out under the pressure of the authorities, between the victim (and its family) on the one hand and the perpetrator of a homicide or an act of violence on the other.[1] In the vast majority of cases, the convention included an *amende honorable* vis-à-vis the injured party, but it sometimes also stipulated the erection of a commemorative cross or the founding of a chapel in honour of the victim (De Win 2003, pp. 132–133 and 211–213). In some rare cases, there could be an obligation to (contribute to) finance stained-glass windows. However, in this paper, I will focus specifically on public criminal convictions imposing an investment in works of art.

One can distinguish two types of artistic objects: those that were only intended to decorate (par. 2), and those that bore an explanatory text mentioning the crime and the name of the condemned (par. 3).

15.2 An Imposed Investment in Works of Art

Objects used only for decoration are, strictly speaking, works of art. They can be found inside churches, in the form of a statue of a saint, the work of a goldsmith or stained-glass windows, or in a public building, often the courtroom, in the form of a

[1]For a nineteenth-century invented depiction of such a peace agreement or *mondzoen*, see the contribution by Stefan Huygebaert in this volume.

painting, a stained-glass window or a statue. But they could also be ornaments on the façade of a church or a town hall. Churches and monasteries especially have benefited from these measures.

15.2.1 Paintings, Statues, Jewelry…

According to the accounts of towns and judicial officers, payments were often made to goldsmiths to make gold or silver objects, such as crucifixes, chalices, ampoules, censers and candlesticks, the creation of which was imposed by a court sentence.[2] These records are a rich source of information for art historians who want to know the names of the artists working during this period. Besides gold and silver objects, there was a large diversity in the kind of investments that were imposed:

- In 1367, the inhabitants of Diksmuide (county of Flanders) were condemned to put pinnacles above some statues outside the church of Saint Donatian in Bruges (Gilliodts-Van Severen 1874, pp. 422–425, no 46, with publication of the judgment).
- In 1375, the aldermen of the town of Sluis assaulted the dean of the goldsmiths' corporation, and were condemned by the magistrate of Bruges to deliver ten polychrome statues for the façade of the city hall of Bruges (Gilliodts-Van Severen 1892, pp. 533–536, no 11, with publication of the judgment). In 1483, a couple belonging to the nobility was condemned to, among other things, finance nine statues representing the Counts of Flanders to decorate the façade of the same building (Gaillard 1847, p. 22).
- In 1378, Jan Blancquaert, who had behaved badly at the Ghent city hall, was condemned by the aldermen of the *Gedele* bench to have a statue of the Blessed Virgin made, destined to adorn the *Gedele* courtroom in the city hall (Cannaert 1835, p. 188).
- In Ypres, at the end of the fourteenth century, someone was condemned to an *amende honorable*, and had to pay twelve *livres parisis* '*à faire une nouvelle clocque en l'église de Saint-Martin*' ('to create a new bell for the church of Saint Martin') and the same sum '*à la nouvelle ouvraige de la tour de la dicte église*' ('for the new work of the tower of this church') (De Pelsmaeker 1914, p. 302, no 380).
- A representation of the *Last Judgment*, painted by the Ghent artist Lievin van den Clite (d. 1422) in 1413 for the courtroom of the Council of Flanders in Ghent, was largely paid for by the fine imposed by the Council in 1411 on the bailiff of Axel and Hulst, who was convicted for disobedience and abuse of power (Pinchart 1854, p. 189).[3]

---

[2]Some examples between 1460 and 1473 are cited in De Keyser (1984), p. 170.

[3]De Ridder (1989, pp. 19–38, no 2 and Fig. 10; 1989–91, pp. 91–123) identifies this painting with the *The Last Judgment*, formerly preserved in the Museum of Diest and currently in the Royal Museums of Fine Arts in Brussels.

- In 1475, Jean de Corioulle was convicted for abuse of power by the Council of Namur, the supreme court of the county, and had to pay a fine of 200 *écus* to the sovereign and commission a painting at his own expense that represented the *Last Judgment*. The painting should be worth 40 florins of the Rhine, and was to be placed in the courtroom (Pinchart 1860–81, vol. II, pp. 159–162; not mentioned by De Ridder 1989).[4]
- In 1510, Daniël van Eggherswaerde was condemned for having seriously injured Cornelis Heym, and had to pay the Paschal candle and a stained-glass window representing the patron saint of the wounded person, as well as the costs for the decoration of the statue of Saint Godelieve in the church of Wenduine in the county of Flanders (Weale 1868–69).
- In 1515 in Middelburg (county of Zeeland), Cornelis Symons was among others condemned to donate a statue in order to embellish the façade of the town hall of the city (De Wind 1827, p. 55).
- In 1516 in Kortrijk (county of Flanders), the draper Joos Adin was condemned to pay, among other sums, 24 *livres parisis* for the making of a jewel for the altar of Saint John the Baptist in the church of Saint Martin in Kortrijk.[5]
- The fresco of the *Last Judgment* (Fig. 15.1) painted by Frans Sanders in 1526 for the courtroom of the Great Council in Malines (today *Oud Schepenhuis*, i.e. Old Aldermen's Hall), was paid for from the fine of 100 Carolus florins imposed by the Council in 1523 on Gregoire Lommelin, a Genoese merchant. It was explicitly stated that this fine should be used for the repair and decoration of the palace of the Council (‘*pour ester convertiz et employez à la reparation et decoration du palais [du Conseil]*’).[6] Although the painting is known to historians and art historians (De Ridder 1989, pp. 79–82 no 10 and Pl. 27–28; Maes 1949, Pl. V–VI), the fact that it was paid for with money from a fine was, up until now, unknown.
- Steven Du Gardin was condemned by the aldermen of the Keure of Ghent in 1592 to pay 50 Carolus florins to have a stained-glass window made for the Ghent church of Saint Nicholas, of which he was a parishioner (Cannaert 1835, pp. 175–177).[7]
- In 1602, the court of Ekeren in the duchy of Brabant condemned a man to an *amende honorable*, a fine of 100 florins for the poor and 8 florins for the restoration of the altar of Saint George in the parish church for insulting the Corporation of Saint George (Bresseleers and Kanora 1963, pp. 83–84).

Only a few of the works belonging to this category have survived to the present day. An interesting example in this context is the case of a Lutheran who was condemned to produce the statue of a saint for the church of Saint Walburga in Oudenaarde (county of Flanders). A few years later, in 1539, some of his sympathizers removed the statue from the church during a revolt and destroyed it (Van Lerberghe and Ronsse 1845, p. 57). This illustrates the fate suffered by many of

---

[4]Brussels, State Archives, Chamber of Accounts, no 10948, f. 27 and 43.

[5]Kortrijk, State Archives, Old City Archives of Kortrijk, no 2052, f. 150 (August 8th, 1516).

[6]Brussels, State Archives, Chamber of Accounts, no 21469, f. 45r (fine) and 46v–47r (painting).

[7]Ghent, City Archives, Series 214 (*Boec van den Crime*), no 13 (1591–1594), f. 10v–11r.

these objects during the Iconoclastic Fury in the sixteenth century. Although the work itself probably did not carry a defamatory inscription, the context of its making remained alive and engraved in the collective memory.

In the Southern Netherlands, one of the few objects still in existence (as far as I know) is the statue of Saint Bartholomew (Fig. 15.2), made in 1572 for the collegiate church of Saint Waltrude in Mons (capital of the county of Hainaut) by the sculptor Jacques Dubroeucq (ca. 1505–1584) as a condemnation (on the order of the Council of Troubles) for having sympathised with the heretics at the capture of the city of Mons by the troops of the Prince of Orange (*Jacques Du Broeucq* 1985, pp. 29, 90, 91 and 93; Pinchart 1854, p. 197–198; Wellens 1962, pp. 29–30).

Recently, I discovered that another work of art, the fresco of the *Last Judgment* by Frans Sanders (Fig. 15.1), mentioned above, was also paid for by a fine.

There might be other works of art of this kind in our churches, museums and collections, which we cannot qualify as such for lack of proof. The reason for their creation has been lost over time and has not been recovered yet. If the painting formerly preserved at Diest could be identified as the already mentioned painting of the *Last Judgment* painted by Lievin van den Clite in 1413 for the courtroom of the Council of Flanders, this would constitute another example.

15.2.2 Stained-Glass Windows

The example of a stained-glass window in the Old Church (*Oude Kerk*) in Amsterdam, which still exists, but has been almost completely renewed in 1761–1763, shows how easy it is to camouflage the initial reason for its making by misleading historians and art historians. In 1550, a bourgeois from Amsterdam, Jan Claesz. van Hoppen (who afterwards went on to become alderman and mayor of the city) was accused of heresy and forced to go on a pilgrimage to Rome, and place a large stained-glass window in the Old Church on his return (Commelin 1693, pp. 425–426; Le Long 1729, pp. 491–492; Pinchart 1854, p. 197). The stained glass represents the Annunciation and Visitation, and was created by Digman Meynaert (active 1525–1574) of Antwerp, based on the cartoons of Lambert van Noort (ca. 1520–1571), who also executed the superb stained-glass windows of the church of Gouda. It was placed in the choir of the chapel of the Holy Virgin (*Mariakapel*) of the church in 1555. What is particularly striking about this example is that the convict was represented on the stained-glass window with his family and his coat of arms, suggesting that the window was offered as an act of patronage rather than as a result of a repressive judgment (Noordegraaf 2009, pp. 345, 362 and 365).

As already stated above, the obligation to finance stained-glass windows or to contribute to their execution in a context of a peace-agreement was rather rare. In 1597, in the Saint Lawrence church of Betekom in Brabant, two stained-glass windows were paid for by the perpetrator of a homicide in the context of a peace-agreement, one containing the image of Our Lady of Sorrows and the other depicting the crucifixion (Scheys and Willems 1981, p. 29). In these cases, it was less a voluntary agreement between parties than a semi-imposed composition or reconciliation. In Antwerp the father of a man guilty of homicide of a German merchant had to pay a stained-glass window for the church of Our Lady in Antwerp representing four German Electors, at the behest of the German merchant's guild, not because of the homicide, but because he had insulted German merchants. The window itself is not present anymore, but we still have a partial drawing of the work (Papebrochius 1845, pp. 368bis and 357–361; Prims 1938).

As already mentioned in the Amsterdam case of Van Hoppen financing stained-glass windows was sometimes imposed on people of a certain position. The noble lady Johanna van der Leck, lady of Heeswijk and Dinther (duchy of Brabant), was severely punished by Duke Philip the Good for abuse of power. Claiming to have been robbed by a Brussels citizen, she ordered her officers to prosecute the suspect, who was arrested in ducal territory and brought to the castle of Heeswijk. He was then tortured and hanged. The Duke subsequently confiscated the domains of the lady. Furthermore, the magistrate of Brussels seized the property of her sheriff (*schout*, *écoutète*), whom he banished in perpetuity. Finally, in 1436, the authorities moderated the imposed sentences by way of composition. To settle, Johanna had to do an *amende honorable* and pay 100 *ridders* for the creation of a large stained-glass window for the collegiate church of Saint Gudula in Brussels (Henne and Wauters 1845, pp. 242–243).

At the beginning of the fifteenth century, the sheriff and aldermen of Turnhout were condemned by the magistrate of Antwerp for abuse of power against an Antwerp bourgeois, and had to pay 12 crowns as a contribution to the creation of a stained-glass window for the church of Our Lady in Antwerp.[8]

In the sources, there is even a trace of a payment of stained-glass windows as a collective punishment. In 1429, the Brabant town of Lier was condemned by the main towns of the Duchy (Leuven, Brussels and Antwerp) to pay for the delivery of 600 feet of stained-glass windows, equally shared between the churches of Saint Peter in Leuven, Saint Gudula in Brussels and Our Lady in Antwerp (Henne and Wauters 1845, pp. 230–231).

Another example is the case of Nicolaes van Ruyven, sheriff of Haarlem in Holland, who was killed during a riot. In 1492, the cities of Haarlem and Alkmaar were condemned to pay 200 florins each for the creation of stained-glass windows for the church of Saint Bavo in Haarlem and the Saint Lawrence church in Alkmaar, representing the murdered sheriff, kneeling in prayer, with his escutcheon and an explanatory text (Groenveld 2012, p. 145; Noordegraaf 2009, pp. 330–331). These stained-glass windows have now disappeared, but a drawing made in 1616 of the Alkmaar window can still be found in the archives of Haarlem.[9] These 'penalty pieces' were to serve as means of commemoration, and were not really meant to damage the reputation of the convict.

[8]Brussels, State Archives, Chamber of Accounts, no 12902, f. 64v–65r (accounts of Jean de Grimberghe, 1408–1412).

[9]The drawing has been published in De Bye Dolleman (1966), p. 160bis.

15.3 The Obligation to Create Objects with Defamatory Connotations

In the case of objects bearing explanatory notes, such as the recall of the crime, the date of conviction and the name of the convicted person, one could speak of 'shaming penalty pieces': pieces imposed as punishment intending to shame offenders for wrongdoing. The purpose of these pieces is not to embellish, but to damage the reputation of the convict—and indirectly his family—and serve as examples and warnings to those who read them. In these cases, the aesthetic of the piece is subordinated to the message. These pieces were often exhibited in or near the courtroom. This should not come as a surprise, since the creation of these objects was generally imposed by the judges in the context of an attack on their prestige or on their rights and privileges. They are, therefore, visible and permanent witnesses to the reparation of their injured honour, and a warning to those who read them. The theme was usually chosen in accordance with the misdeeds.

15.3.1 Metal Fists and Heads with Explaining Plaques

Metal fists and heads with their accompanying plaques are at once the most striking and the least aesthetic expression of this punishment. A closed metal fist refers to someone who physically assaulted or threatened a judicial official, sometimes using a knife, a dagger or a small axe. A metal head, its lips sealed by a ring, refers to someone who had insulted the court, a judge or an agent in office. These pieces did not replace a beheading or an amputation of the hand, as some think, but were part of the array of punitive measures at the magistrate's disposal.

The metal fists, heads and plaques now preserved in the town hall of Veurne (county of Flanders) have already been the subject of several studies (De Win 1989, vol. II-B; De Win 1991b; Huygebaert and Van Audenaeren 2016; Schimmer 1974, pp. 297–299; Strubbe 1938, 1940; Van Molle 1974, pp. 141–148). In the museum of Bruges, one can also admire a silver fist and a silver bust. Although the accompanying plaques are not available anymore, archival research has revealed the judgment, the name of the condemned and the name of the goldsmith that belong to the bust (De Win 1989, vol. II-B; Huygebaert and Van Audenaeren 2016, pp. 127–131; Martens 1990, pp. 235–242; Van Molle 1974, p. 154). In this context, the copper plaque preserved in the museum of Oudenaarde is interesting as well. In 1533, François Alaert was condemned to have an iron fist made, with the metal plaque. Today, only the plaque has been preserved (Van Molle 1974, pp. 155 and 157, Fig. 16).

Flanders was not the only region in which penalties of this kind were imposed. In 1546, François Aerts, mayor of Heverlee in the duchy of Brabant, was condemned by the aldermen of the city of Leuven to do an *amende honorable*, pay a 'profitable' fine to the city and the Prince, and have an iron fist made together with a metal plaque '*ter eewigher memorie[n]*' ('in eternal memory'). He had captured a citizen of Leuven on the territory of the city and imprisoned him in Heverlee, thereby violating the privileges of the city and its citizens. Only the plaque has been preserved, and can still be seen in the town hall of Leuven (De Win 1989, vol. II-B; De Win 2003, p. 209, with illustrations; Van Even 1853; Van Even 1895, pp. 275–276; Van Molle 1974). In 1547, Nicolas Waubert, attorney at the court of the city of Tournai, was condemned to have an iron fist made, accompanied by an explanatory plaque, for having given two slaps to a city functionary. The iron fist, still attached to its explanatory plaque, is preserved in the museum of Tournai (Bozière 1864, pp. 300–301; De Win 1989, vol. II-B; Van Molle 1974, pp. 158–159, Fig. 20–21). These examples also prove that this sentence could be imposed on persons of rank.

In the Netherlands as well, there are some of these metal fists that have been preserved: the iron fist, quite primitive, accompanied by its explanatory plaque at the town hall of Sluis (Zeeland),[10] three metal fists in museum *De Vierschaar* of Veere (Zeeland), among which the Bremboes fist with axe, and the sandstone fist with an explanatory plaque in stone in the *Fries Museum* of Leeuwarden (Friesland) (Moelands and de Smidt 1999, pp. 118–119, no 64 and 65;[11] Schimmer 1974, pp. 295–297, Fig. 2–7 with the three metal fists preserved in Veere; Van Molle 1974, p. 159-161 and 163, Fig. 22–26 with the Veere fists). A very unknown case is the broken copper plaque excavated around 1957 in Hulst (Zeeland), which is kept in the local city archives (Fig. 15.3). According to its text, a certain Cornelis was convicted in 1525 to have a fist made because he had physically assaulted judicial officials.[12]

All the fists, heads and plaques mentioned here escaped destruction after the end of the Ancien Régime. There is no doubt that a thorough and systematic archival research could reveal many more examples of this kind of punishment (De Win 1989, vol. II-B; De Win De Win 1991a, pp. 215–221). Furthermore, for historians and especially for art historians, these archives are an important source of knowledge for the names of artists, painters, sculptors, goldsmiths, blacksmiths etc. active in the decorative arts.

The well-documented case of Willem vander Schage can serve as an example. He was banished from the county of Flanders by the aldermen of the Keure of Ghent, but returned to Bruges without permission shortly afterwards. In 1481, for having infringed the rights and privileges of the city of Ghent, he was condemned to make '*een mottalen hooft van der grootte van eenen manshoofde*' ('a metal head the size of a man's head'), with an explanatory plaque to be displayed on the façade of the alderman's house of the Keure. Engraved on the plaque was the following: '*Dit es eene van de amende die Willelme vander Schage gheordonneert syn te*

[10]Penalty piece of the condemnation (1548) of the merchant Jan Pauwels Cornelissen for striking a judicial officer in office (Schimmer 1974, pp. 296–297, Fig. 6–7; Van Molle 1974, pp. 156–157, Fig. 17–19).

[11]No 64 is the Bremboes fist with axe, 1550. Bremboes had thrown an axe at a city messenger's head. No 65 is the fist of Oosterwolde, with explanatory plaque in stone, 1574, preserved in the *Fries Museum* of Leeuwarden; Oosterwolde hit, injured and knocked down a magistrate in the execution of his duty.

[12]Hulst, City Archives, Series *Bijzondere Stukken*, no 106.

doene omme dat hy ballinc synde van deser stede hem vervoordert heeft up zeker inland by hem vercreghen te comen binnen Brugghe sonder consent van scepen[en] van der Keure. Aldus hier ghestelt den XV July MCCCCLXXXI' ('This is one of the fines to which Willem vander Schage was condemned, because, being banished from this city, he returned to the county in Bruges without permission from the aldermen of the Keure. Thus put here on July 15th 1481'). A second head with a more general message threatening observers to refrain from such offenses was exposed to the *Collatiezolder*, the courtroom of the aldermen. On the basis of the accounts that have been kept, we are well informed about the artists who participated in the realisation of these heads: the local sculptor Pieter Bulteel, who built the small roof over the head against the façade, the female artist Agnes van den Bossche (ca. 1435–1504), who painted the *tabernacle*, Willem de Jaghere, a founder of tin pots, and the blacksmith Jan van Belle, who delivered lead and iron for more than 14 lb, and Lieven vanden Bossche (active 1459–1500), who decorated the head of the *Collatiezolder* (Cannaert 1835, pp. 127–129; Van Tyghem 1978, vol. I, pp. 59–60 and vol. II, p. 105).

15.3.2 Paintings and Stained-Glass Windows with Defamatory Inscriptions

Besides fists and heads, the court would sometimes also order the creation of a painting, often symbolic, or of a stained-glass window. Some of these paintings are still preserved. However, none of the stained-glass windows survived wars, fires or voluntary destruction (e.g. by iconoclasts during the Iconoclastic Fury in the sixteenth century, or by the French revolutionaries at the end of the eighteenth century).[13]

Paintings. Several sources inform us about the financing of paintings, of which some are still preserved. A rather unknown example is a painting representing the *Judgment of Solomon*,[14] which is currently exhibited at the municipal museum of Huy (Fig. 15.4). It was financed in 1570 by an official who offended the court of the *Douze Hommes*, and it bears the mention of the name of the convict, Gérard de Baillonville, and the reason for, and date of, his condemnation. The picture once decorated the courtroom at the *Grand Hôpital* of Huy. In 1687, a family member of the forced donor tried to replace the defamatory inscription with a neutral text, but eventually failed to do so (Jopken 1906–07; Van Der Made 1960, pp. 31–33).[15]

[13]On the destruction of Ancien Régime symbols in the French period, see the contribution by Brecht Deseure in this volume.

[14]On the importance of Solomon's judgment as *exemplum iustitae*, see the contributions by Ann-Kathrin Hubrich and Beatrijs Wolters-van der Wey in this volume, as well as the *The Art of Law* exhibition catalogue, Huygebaert et al. (2016), pp. 39–41, 58, 61, 66 and 183–184 and cat. 9, 21–23, 108 and 118.

[15]Jopken and Van Der Made also mention two other comparable paintings, which sadly have not been preserved (De Win 1989, vol. II-B).

At the Nieuwpoort town hall, there is still a very large painting, representing the biblical story of Esther and Ahasverus. It was painted in 1578, following the condemnation of Cornelis Coeman and Claijs Ondercouter for having attempted to take the life of Pieter Adriaens. The inscription at the bottom of the painting recalls the names of the perpetrators and their crime, and issues a general warning (De Ridder 1981, p. 458; De Ridder 1989, pp. 107–109, no 19 and Fig. 42; De Win 1989, vol. II-B).

A less symbolic example is a painting representing a crucifixion, now preserved in the church of Saint Nicolas in Veurne. The defamatory inscription on the original frame was found during the restoration of the painting in the 1970s. It informs us that Willem de Wale was condemned in 1517 by the aldermen of Veurne to have this painting created for having insulted an official of the city and having rebelled against the bailiff and the mayor at the time of his arrest. Hence, it is a defamatory painting, which was probably originally intended to decorate the courtroom of the city's aldermen (De Ridder 1981, p. 457; De Win 1989, vol. II-B; De Win 1991c, with colour illustration; Van Molle 1974, p. 151).

In this context, we need to mention a painting with an explanatory text, situated on the Burg Square in Bruges. At first sight, this painting could be seen as a defamatory piece. Nevertheless, although its aim was certainly to serve as a warning, it is not a defamatory piece in the strict sense since the name of the condemned person is not explicitly cited in the text, and the creation of the painting was not a direct consequence of a court order (De Win 1991d, with colour illustration; Vermeersch 2016, with colour illustration).[16]

Stained-glass windows. The financing of stained-glass windows is—at least in the Low Countries—only known to us by written sources. In Middelburg (Zeeland) in 1512, for instance, J. van Domburg was condemned to pay for a '*cruys glas*' (glass with a cross) representing the Prince's coat of arms, his own name and the crime he had committed (Hermesdorf 1955, p. 276).

In 1533, the Kortrijk aldermen condemned draper Jan Wille to an *amende honorable*, a high 'profitable' fine, and the payment of a stained-glass window of 100 *livres parisis* for the church of Saint Martin of Kortrijk, representing the shield of the city, as well as his name and the reason for his condemnation, in large letters (Pinchart 1854, pp. 193–194).

In 1538, Jehan Ruyschzone was condemned by the Privy Council in Brussels for having injured Claes Geryt Matheeuszone, mayor of Amsterdam, to an *amende honorable* in the Privy Council in Brussels, in the High Court of Holland and in the *vierschaar* (courtroom) of the city of Amsterdam, and to have placed, at his expense, a stained-glass window of 100 Carolus florins in the New Church (*Nieuwe Kerk*) of Amsterdam, bearing the following text: '*Ceste verrière a fait faire Jehan Ruyschzone pour réparation des injures par luy proférées all'encontre de Claes Geryt Matheeuszone, burgmestre de ceste ville d'Amsterdam, en l'an XVc XXXVIII*' ('this stained-glass window was commissioned by Jehan Ruyschzone as reparation

[16]Bruges, State Archives, Registers Brugse Vrije, no 17028 (*Crim-Boeken*, 1766–70), f. 24r–36v.

for the insults uttered by him against Claes Geryt Matheeuszone, mayor of this city of Amsterdam in the year 1538') (Pinchart 1854, pp. 194–196).[17]

In 1545, some inhabitants of Jodoigne were condemned by the Council of Brabant for having rebelled against the authority of the lieutenant-bailiff of Walloon Brabant. The court imposed on them, among other things, the obligation to do an *amende honorable* in the church of Saint Medardus of Jodoigne, and to have placed, at their own expense, a stained-glass window worth 48 florins. They themselves were to be depicted in the window while carrying out the honourable fine. The entire scene was to be accompanied by an inscription recalling their misdeed (Tarlier and Wauters 1865–73, p. 15).

In 1568, the aldermen of the town of La Roche-en-Ardenne condemned the butcher Remacle de Marche to an *amende honorable* and the payment of a commemorative window for the church of the city, with mention of his name and the misdeeds committed. He had refused to take his turn of duty, as every citizen was ought to do, had insulted the provost, and had even threatened to set fire to a city gate (Marquet 1977, pp. 92–94).

Gerrit van Raephorst, a nobleman of Holland, was condemned by the High Court of Holland in 1515 for the abduction of a thirteen-year-old noble girl with the intention of marrying her. His condemnation consisted of an honourable fine and the payment of a stained-glass window for the church of Wassenaar, with the representation of the coat of arms of the Prince and the mention of his name and his crime. During the Iconoclastic Fury of 1566, the stained-glass window was destroyed by a group of iconoclasts led by Herbert van Raephorst, a descendant of the convict (Van Nierop 1984, p. 103).

15.3.3 Erection of a Column of Infamy in Case of High Treason and Lèse-Majesté

A special case is the sixteenth century column of Culembourg, erected in Brussels, on the exact place of the *Hotel de Culembourg* (De Win 1989, vol. II-B; De Win 2016, pp. 494–496; Schuermans 1870). In 1566, the famous *Banquet des Gueux* took place in the palace after the signing of the request to King Philip II, known as the Compromise of Nobles. The King rejected all of the signatories' demands and sent the Duke of Alba as Governor-General to the Netherlands, endowed with unlimited powers to quell the Iconoclastic Fury and to put order in a general. In 1567, the Duke set up an exceptional tribunal, the Council of Troubles. The signatories and sympathizers of the Compromise of Nobles were regarded as traitors and prosecuted for high treason and *lèse-majesté*. Several were sentenced to death and executed, including the counts of Egmont and Hornes. By judgment of the Council of Troubles, pronounced on May 28th, 1568, the count of Culembourg was

[17]With transcription of the judgment of February 21th, 1539 (n.s.).

banished in perpetuity and declared an enemy to the King. His property was confiscated, and his hotel in Brussels, a meeting place for the 'conspirators', was demolished from top to bottom. The ground was levelled and salt spread on the now cursed ground, on which building was prohibited in perpetuity. Moreover, the following year, on this very site, an expiatory or defamatory column was erected in order to damn the memory of the events that had taken place in this palace. The blue stone column, about five meters high, commissioned to a master-tailor of Arquennes in January 1569 and erected at the end of May of the same year, bore a *dictum* in four languages on the four sides of a cubic architrave.[18] This measure was not ordered in the judgment itself, but happened on the orders of the Duke of Alba. However, the column did not survive the departure of the latter. Article 13 of the Pacification of Ghent (1576) stipulated the destruction of all the monuments and inscriptions erected by the Duke of Alba '*en déshonneur et blasme*' ('in dishonour and blame'). After the publication of the text in Brussels on the same day, the inhabitants of Brussels destroyed the infamous column. The count of Culembourg obtained the payment of an annuity of 5,000 florins from the States of Brabant in compensation for the demolition of his hotel in Brussels.

As far as I know, this is the only example of an erection of a column of infamy in case of high treason in modern times in the Low Countries.[19]

15.4 Conclusion

Condemnations containing an obligation to fund a work of art were especially common from the fourteenth to the sixteenth century. This is not really surprising. Typical for the criminal law in this period was the arbitrary nature of punishments, which left much to the judges' discretion. For the Low Countries, this was a period of splendour and wealth, an epoch characterised artistically and architecturally by exuberant taste. It was also a period of construction and embellishment of town halls, palaces, churches and monasteries. Beautiful but expensive. 'Why not make the perpetrators contribute to these enterprises?', might have been the ulterior motive of the judges of the time. But it was also a period in which the 'public justice' of the state was expanded through the creation of new central institutions

[18]With regard to the monument itself, we are well informed by archival documents, particularly the overview of the expenses for the execution of the work and a drawing; for the expenses: Lille, Archives Départementales du Nord, Archives Civiles, Series B, Chamber of Accounts of Lille, B. 3619, 1569 (account of Martin Vandenberghe); Finot, Jules. 1895. *Inventaire sommaire des Archives départementales antérieur à 1790*, vol. VIII, p. 343. Lille: Archives Départementales du Nord; for the drawing: Brussels, State Archives, Maps and Plans, no 2810; Piot, Charles. 1879. *Inventaires divers. Troisième supplément à l'Inventaire des Cartes et Plans*, p. 90. Brussels: State Archives); see also Schuermans (1870), pp. 18–28, with the reproduction of the drawing on p. 18bis; Henne and Wauters (1845), p. 416 (augmented and illustrated edition, 1969, vol. III, p. 339–341).

[19]Other examples outside the Low Countries are cited in De Win (2016).

and courts. Through architecture and decoration, the court buildings and courtrooms were transformed into 'theatres of justice' with the aim not only of impressing the law-seeking and the perpetrator but, above all, to legitimise the power and authority of the court and the judges.

The primary purpose of works of art without connotation was to decorate. They can be regarded as a payment in kind rather than in cash. Objects bearing explanatory information, such as the record of the crime and the name of the convict, are defamatory pieces or 'shaming penalty pieces'. Their aim is not primarily to adorn, but to serve a public and permanent shame to the convict and his family, and as an example and warning to others. However, the convict was not the only one suffering from this public shame. As is demonstrated by the Van Raephorst case and the case of the Huy painting, the victim's family was affected as well. In these two cases, relatives of the victim actively tried to destroy the work (Van Raephorst) or at least change the inscription (Huy). But even for a work of art that did not bear a defamatory inscription, the context of its making remained alive and engraved in the collective memory. This is illustrated by the case of a Lutheran, who had been condemned to produce the statue of a saint for the church of Saint Walburga in Oudenaarde; only a couple of years later, sympathizers removed the statue of the church during a revolt and destroyed it.

Sentences that contained the obligation to pay for a work of art were ordered by local, provincial and central courts. Generally speaking, these penalties were usually imposed to people who had sufficient financial means (merchants, tradesmen), but sometimes also to persons of rank (officers and civil servants, patricians and persons belonging to the nobility), or even to communities (the officials of a town, the board of a merchant or craft guild).

This kind of punishment was especially imposed for offense and rebellion against authority, in its various expressions. The most common offences were abuse of power, and thus infringements of the rights and privileges of magistrates and serving officials on the one hand, and insults, acts of resistance, disobedience or even violence against the authorities on the other hand.

References

Bozière A-F (1864) Tournai ancien et moderne. Adolphe Delmée, Tournai

Bresseleers F, Kanora H (1963) Op de drempel van de polder: Ekeren, ontstaan en groei. Davidsfonds, Leuven

Cannaert JB (1835) Bydragen tot de kennis van het oude strafrecht in Vlaenderen. Gyselynck, Ghent

Commelin C (1693) Beschryvinge van Amsterdam. Wolfgang, Waasberge, Boom, van Someren en Gorthals, Amsterdam

De Bye Dolleman T (1966) Genealogie van Ruyven. Jaarboek van het Centraal Bureau voor Genealogie 20:149–173

De Keyser B (1984) Goud- en zilversmeden uit het graafschap Vlaanderen. Ons Heem 38:170–172
De Pelsmaeker P (ed) (1914) Coutumes du Pays et Comté de Flandre. Quartier d'Ypres, vol VI. Registres aux sentences des échevins d'Ypres, vol VI. Goemaere, Brussels
De Ridder J (1981) Vonnis-, boete- of strafstukken. Spiegel Historiael 16:456–458
De Ridder J (1989) Gerechtigheidstaferelen voor schepenhuizen in de Zuidelijke Nederlanden in de 14de, 15de en 16de eeuw (Verhandelingen van de Koninklijke Academie voor Wetenschappen, Letteren in Schone Kunsten van België, Klasse der Schone Kunsten, vol XLV). Koninklijke Academie, Brussels
De Ridder J (1989–91) Vlaamse primitief op de dool: 'Het Laatste Oordeel' van Lieven van den Clite. Bulletin des Musées royaux de Beaux-Arts de Belgique 1–3: 91–123
De Win P (1989) De schandstraffen in België van de Middeleeuwen tot de 19e eeuw. Een rechtshistorische en rechtsarcheologische studie. Unpubl. PhD thesis, University of Ghent, Law Faculty
De Win P (1991a) De schandstraffen in het wereldlijk strafrecht in de Zuidelijke Nederlanden van de Middeleeuwen tot de Franse Tijd bestudeerd in Europees perspectief (Verhandelingen van de Koninklijke Academie voor Wetenschappen, Letteren en Schone Kunsten van België, Klasse der Letteren, vol CXXXIX). Koninklijke Academie voor Wetenschappen, Letteren en Schone Kunsten van België, Brussels
De Win P (1991b) Vier koperen schandstrafstukken. In: Van der Stock J (ed) Stad in Vlaanderen. Cultuur en maatschappij, 1477–1787 (exh. cat. Brussels). Gemeentekrediet van België, Brussels, pp 339–340
De Win P (1991c) Schandstrafschilderij. In: Van der Stock J (ed) Stad in Vlaanderen. Cultuur en maatschappij, 1477–1787 (exh. cat. Brussels). Gemeentekrediet van België, Brussels, pp 341–342
De Win P (1991d) Terechtstelling. In: Van der Stock J (ed) Stad in Vlaanderen. Cultuur en maatschappij, 1477–1787 (exh. cat. Brussels). Gemeentekrediet van België, Brussels, pp 342–344
De Win P (2003) Analyse van een merkwaardige straf: de openbare bede om vergiffenis, 'eerlijke betering' of *amende honorable*. Handelingen van de Koninklijke Kring voor Oudheidkunde, Letteren in Kunst van Mechelen 107:117–232
De Win, P (2016) La maison rasée. Regard historique sur les mesures et sanctions envers la demeure des contrevenants et malfaiteurs du moyen âge à nos jours. In: Bousmar É, Desmette P, Simon N (eds) Légiférer, gouverner et juger. Mélanges d'histoire du droit et des institutions (IXe–XXe siècle) offerts à Jean-Marie Cauchies à l'occasion de ses 65 ans. Presses de l'Université Saint-Louis, Brussels, pp 494–501
De Wind S (1827) Bijzonderheden uit de geschiedenis van het strafregt in de Nederlanden. Gebroeders Abrahams, Middelburg
Gaillard J (1847) Ephémérides brugeoises. Gaillard, Bruges
Gilliodts-Van Severen L (ed) (1874) Coutumes des Pays et Comté de Flandre. Quartier de Bruges, vol I. Goemaere, Brussels
Gilliodts-Van Severen L (ed) (1892) Coutumes des Pays et Comté de Flandre. Quartier de Bruges, vol IV. Goemaere, Brussels
Groenveld S (2012) Schenkingen van gebrandschilderde glazen in de zestiende en zeventiende eeuw. Ontwikkelingen in argumenten en methoden. Bulletin van de Koninklijke Nederlandse Oudheidkundige Bond 111:142–157
Henne A, Wauters A (1845) Histoire de la ville de Bruxelles, vol I. Perichon, Brussels
Hermesdorf BHD (1955) Recht en Taal te hoofde. Opstellen over de ontmoeting tussen middelnederlandse letteren en oudvaderlands recht. Tjeenk Willink, Zwolle
Huygebaert S, Martyn G, Paumen V, Van Poucke T (eds) (2016) The art of law. Three centuries of justice depicted (exh. cat. Bruges). Lannoo, Tielt

Huygebaert S, Van Audenaeren K (2016) Making a good fist of early modern Criminal Law. In: Huygebaert S et al (eds) 2016. Lannoo, Tielt, pp 127–131
Jacques Du Broeucq, sculpteur et architecte de la Renaissance (exh. cat. Mons) (1985). Crédit Communal, Brussels
Jopken E (1906–07) Note sur trois tableaux provenant du Grand Hôpital de Huy. Annales du Cercle hutois des Sciences et Beaux-Arts 15:198–200
Le Long I (1729) Historische Beschryvinge van de Reformatie der Stadt Amsterdam. Johannes van Septeren, Amsterdam
Maes LT (1949) The Parliament and the Great Council at Malines. Wellens-Godenne, Malines
Marquet L (1977) Témoignages sur la justice d'autrefois au comté de La Roche-en-Ardenne. Bulletin trimestriel de l'Institut archéologique du Luxembourg-Arlon 53:71–103
Martens M (1990) Een gerechtigheidsbuste in het Gruuthusemuseum aan een Brugs zilversmid van de 15de eeuw toegeschreven. Jaarboek Stad Brugge, Stedelijke Musea 1989–90:235–242
Moelands M, de Smidt JT (1999) Weegschaal & Zwaard. De Verbeelding van Recht en Gerechtigheid in Nederland (exh.cat. The Hague). Jongbloed, The Hague
Noordegraaf L (2009) Van vlas naar gras. Aspecten van de sociale en economische geschiedenis van Nederland. Verloren, Hilversum
Papebrochius D (1845) Annales Antverpienes. Mertens FH, Buschmann E (eds), vol I. Buschmann, Antwerp
Pinchart A (1854) Notice sur Liévin Van den Clite, peintre gantois du XVe siècle. Bulletins de l'Académie royale des Sciences, des Lettres et des Beaux-Arts de Belgique 21:186–200
Pinchart A (1860–81). Archives des Arts, Sciences et Lettres. Documents inédits. Hebbelynck, Ghent
Prims F (1938) Het glasraam van de vier keurvorsten (1433). Antwerpiensia 1937:53–58
Scheys F, Willems A (1981) De Kronijk door Adrien Carpentier en Charles Millet van 1597 over Baal, Betekom en Gelrode in het Hertogdom Brabant (Bijdragen tot de Geschiedenis van het Land van Aarschot, vol V). Lannoo, Tielt
Schimmer J (1974) Een merkwaardig rechtsgebruik: Middeleeuwse gerechtshanden. Spiegel Historiael 9:294–299
Schuermans H (1870) La Colonne de Culembourg à Bruxelles. Bulletin des Commissions royales d'Art et d'Archéologie 9:17–107
Strubbe E (1938) De opstand van Jan Reingoot. Het masker en de plaat te Veurne. Biekorf 64:169–178
Strubbe E (1940) Een opstandige schuldenaar te Westvleteren. De plaat en de vuist te Veurne 1551. Biekorf 66:1–7
Tarlier J, Wauters A (1865–73) Géographie et histoire des communes belges. Arrondissement de Nivelles, canton de Jodoigne. Decq, Brussels
Van Der Made R (1960) Le Grand Hôpital de Huy. Organisation et fonctionnement (1263–1795) (Anciens Pays et Assemblées d'États, vol XX). UGA, Heule
Van Even E (1853) Une amende honorable en 1546. Messager des Sciences historiques 1853:385–393
Van Even E (1895) Louvain dans le passé et dans le présent. Fonteyn, Leuven
Van Lerberghe L, Ronsse J (1845) Audenaerdsche Mengelingen, vol I. Van Peteghem-Ronsse, Oudenaarde
Van Molle F (1974) Koperen koppen en vuisten in het oude Vlaamse strafrecht. Antiek 9:141–166 (also published 1976. De Gidsenkring 14.3:2–28)
Van Nierop H (1984) Van ridders tot regenten. De Hollandse adel in de zestiende en de eerste helft van de zeventiende eeuw (Hollandse Historische Reeks, vol I). Bataafsche Leeuw, The Hague
Van Tyghem F (1978) Het Stadhuis van Gent (Verhandelingen van de Koninklijke Academie voor Wetenschappen, Letteren en Schone Kunsten van België, Klasse der Schone Kunsten, vol XXXI). Koninklijke Academie voor Wetenschappen, Letteren en Schone Kunsten van België, Brussels
Vermeersch M (2016) Execution on Burg Square. In: Huygebaert S et al (eds) 2016. Lannoo, Tielt, pp 127–131. Lannoo, Tielt, pp 124–126

Weale J (1868–69) Droit pénal au XVe siècle. Sentence arbitraire au sujet de coups et blessures. La Flandre, New Series 2, pp 117–120
Wellens R (1962) Jacques Du Broeucq. Sculpteur et architecte de la Renaissance (1505–1584). Renaissance du Livre, Brussels

Paul De Win has a Ph.D. in Law and Master in History (Ghent University), was scientific collaborator in Ghent University (Law Faculty), and is honorary advisor for Foreign Affairs of the Belgian Federal Government. He is honorary secretary of the *Conseil de Noblesse* (College of Arms of Belgium).

Figures

Fig. 15.1 Frans Sanders, *The Last Judgment*, 1526, fresco, Malines, *Oud Schepenhuis* (former palace of the Great Council), from Maes 1949, Pl. V

Fig. 15.2 Jacques Du Broeucq, *Saint Bartholomew*, 1572, Mons, Collegiate church of Saint Waltrude, © KIK-IRPA

Fig. 15.3 Explanatory plaque of Hulst (Zeeland), 1525, copper, Hulst, City Archives, © Paul De Win

Fig. 15.4 Anonymous, *Judgment of Solomon* (with infamous inscription), 1570, Huy, Municipal Museum, © KIK-IRPA

Chapter 16
"*ut experiri et scire posset*": Pictorial Evidence and Judicial Inquiry in Hans Fries' *Kleiner Johannes Altar*

Tamara Golan

Abstract Featuring scenes of John the Evangelist's trial on Ephesus and his later visions of the Apocalypse on Patmos, the *Kleiner Johannes Altar* by Hans Fries is his most intensely juridical work. The altar reveals his particular attunement to the investigative mode of truth-seeking refined by the judicial *inquisitio*, or inquiry, which further established the standards of evidence required to prove the miraculous and visionary. Fries conforms his representation of visionary experience to new concepts of the sacred redefined in the judicial sphere; his innovative pictorial and material strategies strongly elicit a judicial investigation of the image itself, thus allowing him to make distinctive claims about the visual certitude of his work. Fries' own participation as an expert witness in an inquisitional trial, tasked with investigating a purported miracle, suggests that the altar's claims of certitude were based not only on the increasing acknowledgement in this period of the epistemic value of the artisan's craft, but also on the shared rhetoric between artisanal and judicial modes of inquiry.

16.1 Introduction

In the early hours of the morning on June 24th, 1507, Hans Jetzer, a young novice at the Dominican church in Bern, found himself compelled by a strange force to visit the church's Marian chapel. As he approached, he heard the voices of a female and male conversing, as well as distressed sobbing. When he entered the chapel, he discovered the source of these voices: a large *Pietà* sculpture sitting upon the altar, with bloody tears streaming down the Virgin's face. The weeping statue quickly attracted attention and on June 25th hundreds of people gathered in the chapel to witness the miracle. Some in the crowd, however, remained sceptical. Anton Noll, a glass painter and member of the Bernese Grand Council, reported that when he visited the church that day a priest named Johannes Teschenmacher climbed upon

T. Golan (✉)
History of Art Department, Johns Hopkins University, Baltimore, MD, USA
e-mail: tgolan1@jhu.edu

S. Huygebaert et al. (eds.), *The Art of Law*, Ius Gentium: Comparative Perspectives on Law and Justice 66, https://doi.org/10.1007/978-3-319-90787-1_16

the altar, touched the cheek of Mary, and cried out to the crowd: '*Ei, glowends nit! es sind nit plutstrahen, es ist nur farb*' (Would you believe it? It is not blood, only paint).[1]

Teschenmacher's disdainful proclamation instigated what would soon be known as the *Jetzerhandel*, or Jetzer affair, a criminal investigation conducted jointly by civic and ecclesiastical authorities into the veracity of a series of apparitions and miracles at the Dominican monastery.[2] The judicial authorities were keenly aware of the possibility that the bloody tears were a product of deceit; and in the summer of 1507, the Fribourg artist Hans Fries (ca. 1465–1520) was summoned to Bern because, according to a trial document dated August 9th, 1508, he was best suited 'to test and know, whether or not the red appearance of the tears was brought about by human industry or art'.[3]

Fries' participation in the *Jetzerhandel* corresponds with the introduction of a new type of legal participant in criminal and civil courts towards the end of the fifteenth century: the expert witness.[4] In 1215, the Fourth Lateran Council issued a proscription against the *judicium Dei*, or trial by ordeal, and in its place introduced the *inquisitio* as the judicial standard for obtaining proof in ecclesiastical trials (Bartlett 1986; Fraher 1992; Vauchez 1997). But as the trial by ordeal, with its certainty guaranteed by divine intervention, was replaced by a careful examination of human testimony, there was increasing pressure to ensure this testimony was exhaustive and accurate. During the development of the inquisitional method in the thirteenth century, the corresponding statements of two eyewitnesses became one of the primary means by which 'full proof' (*plena probation*) was established (Brundage 1996; Franklin 2001; Lepsius 2003). However, increasing understanding of the fallibility of sight meant that eyewitnesses were gradually required to possess a particular skill or knowledge to verify what they had seen (Lepsius 2003). By the end of the fifteenth century, the expert witness took precedence over all other witnesses; expert testimony was frequently provided by professionals from both medical and artisanal fields.

Thus Fries participated not as an eyewitness, someone who saw the miracle itself, but as an expert witness, someone with the requisite knowledge to determine its authenticity. In his lecture 'Truth and Juridical Forms', Foucault (2002, p. 52) traces the transition from the trial by ordeal to the *inquisitio* in the medieval period, arguing that while the test 'was a legal device, not a truth device', the *inquisitio* was 'a way of authenticating truth, of acquiring and transmitting things that would be

[1]From *Zeugenverhör Anton Noll* (12 August 1508), reprinted in Villiger et al. (2001), p. 280, fn. 217.

[2]The bibliography on the *Jetzerhandel* is too lengthy to provide an exhaustive list. The most prominent scholar on the *Jetzerhandel* is Kathrin Utz Tremp, who has written on numerous aspects of the affair in many different publications. My summary of the events draws heavily on her history of the affair (Utz Tremp 1988 and 1993).

[3]Question 136 *Artikelverhör des Priors* (9 August 1508), reprinted in Villiger et al. (2001), p. 280: '*ut experiri et scire posset, si humana industria vel arte lachrime rubentes apparebant vel non*'.

[4]On the development of expert witness, see Lepsius (2003), p. 99–107.

regarded as true'. As Foucault and legal historians have argued, the *inquisitio* was not just a method of procuring and authenticating truth, but a form of truth in and of itself. Moreover, Elliott (2004) has traced the dissemination of an 'inquisitional culture' outside of the judicial sphere, convincingly demonstrating that, by the fourteenth century, the inquisitional procedure was a mode of inquiry that informed methods of truth-seeking in multiple contexts, such as medical, theological, and academic.

Fries' investigatory role in the *Jetzerhandel* raises questions about the ways in which artists responded to the ascendency of the judicial inquiry as the surest means for establishing truth. How did the material and manual expertise called upon by inquisitors extend to the sorts of claims that Fries could make for his art? Could the image itself function as a category of proof, one that met the standards established by judicial *inquisitio*? In order to address these questions, I will explore the intersections of judicial and artisanal modes of knowledge highlighted by Fries' role in the *Jetzerhandel* and their thematisation in his *Kleiner Johannes Altar* (Figs. 16.1 and 16.2).

The altar addressed the growing desire to verify the sacred through observation and examination of the material world, compellingly demanding a judicial investigation of the work itself. With a representation of the trial of John the Evangelist on the exterior, the interior of the altar features a scene of his apocalyptic visions of the Last Judgment, in which the earthly realm of Patmos rendered in exquisite naturalistic detail abruptly transitions to the flat, metallic gold ground that constitutes the visionary arena of the altar. His representation of visionary experience met the standards of proof required by the judicial *inquisitio*, thereby allowing him to make distinctive claims about the visual certitude of his work.

After first overviewing the altarpiece (par. 2) and the events of the *Jetzerhandel* (par. 3), this paper will consider the sort of specialised knowledge possessed by Fries that made him particularly suited to authenticate a miracle. While many of his altarpieces indicate his suitability for the task, it is the *Kleiner Johannes Altar*'s thematic constellation of miracle, judgment, and artistic conceit that most strongly resonates with the issues at stake in the *Jetzerhandel*. This is not to suggest a direct correlation between the altarpiece and the affair. Instead, a reading of the two together demonstrates the ways in which artists adapted to the concepts of miraculous and visionary redefined in the judicial sphere and, in turn, reveals the juridical potential of images to test or prove the sacred as it appeared to the senses. The second half of this paper examines the pictorial strategies of this altarpiece (par. 4 and 5), and argues that Fries used both the iconography and materiality of the altarpiece to impart a new kind of epistemic value to his work, thus assigning it an evidentiary status that met the new standards of proof established by the judicial inquiry.

16.2 The Kleiner Johannes Altar

The *Kleiner Johannes Altar* is a striking altarpiece with an unusual iconographic program (Villiger et al. 2001, p. 159–168). The exterior wings portray the miracle of the poisoned cup, an apocryphal account from Jacobus da Varagine's *Golden Legend*.[5] In front of a crowd of spectators, separated by a wall, John, standing barefoot and adorned in voluminous white, green, and red drapery, raises the poisoned chalice to his lips. On the right sits Aristodemus, the high priest of Ephesus, accompanied by another high official. Aristodemus raises his gloved hands in what appears to be a gesture of incitement or anticipation, his left hand jabbing toward John with a rod. His companion extends his right hand across the frames' divide towards John, while simultaneously pointing to the two dead figures occupying the foreground, their corpses divided by the split in the frame. They already appear to be in a state of decomposition, evidenced by their grossly distended abdomens, their eerie half-open eyes, the slight greenish tinge of their flesh, and the fly that has alighted next to their bodies.

The miracle narrative is rather rare in the standard iconography of John the Evangelist. One finds the scene most frequently in thirteenth-century English Apocalypse cycles or occasionally in small vignettes in French books of hours.[6] The scene is always accompanied by depictions of John's other miracles in Ephesus, such as the raising of Drusiana or his destruction of the temple of Artemis, and almost always continues to show either or both the resurrection of the two prisoners or the baptism of Aristodemus. The miracle scene in the *Kleiner Johannes Altar*, however, is unique as it neither accompanies other accounts from John's *Vita* nor represents the resurrection of the prisoners or the conversion of Aristodemus.

Instead, the altarpiece opens to reveal dazzling scenes from John's visionary experience on Patmos. The left panel depicts John on Patmos with a vision of the Virgin and Child as the Apocalyptic Woman. An inscription in Latin runs below the vision, inscribed on the gold ground: '*Non erit ultra tempus gracie sed justitie*' (It will no longer be a time of grace, but of justice). John holds his pen in mid-air as if he were about to write. The ground is tilted downwards providing a view of the torrential waters surrounding the island. The next panel portrays John floating above the island and moving toward the vision of the Son of Man and the seven candlesticks. John's mediatory role is cleverly emphasised as he hovers between the two spheres, his drapery billowing behind him.[7] He approaches the vision with his hands clasped as the Son of Man holds his palm outward, holding a book in his other hand that is opened to the first lines of the Gospel of John, written in German.

---

[5]Consulted in the English translation edited by William Granger, p. 50–55. Princeton (NJ): Princeton University Press.

[6]See for example a Parisian book of hours from ca. 1480 at the Morgan Library (M 815, f. 14r) or the Westminster Apocalypse Group from 1260 at the British Library (Add. 35166, f. 32r-33v).

[7]For the significance of depicting John as an intermediary in medieval Apocalypse cycles, see Ganz (2008), particularly p. 20–21.

The line 'He was not that Light, but was sent to bear witness of that Light' (John 1:8), referring to John the Baptist, nevertheless seems particularly suitable here as he approaches the golden material of the upper sphere. The opening lines of the Gospel also appear in the open book on Patmos.

Neither panel depicts John directly gazing upon the subject of his vision. This is not unusual in representations of the Apocalypse (Klein 1998). However, from each panel he appears to look at the visions in the opposite panels, complicating a clear or sequential reading of the narrative. John's gaze might have been directed at something in the centre of the altarpiece. Unfortunately, nothing is known about the lost middle section, which would have most likely contained a sculptural shrine (Villiger et al. 2001, p. 159). Identifying the subject of the sculptural group from the altar is difficult due to its unusual iconography.[8] To the best of my knowledge, there are no contemporary or parallel examples of altarpieces featuring an apocryphal scene of John's *Vita* on the exterior and a selection of scenes from Revelation on the interior.[9]

The altarpiece has received very little attention in part due to the ambiguity of its date, which has been put forth as early as 1505 and as late as 1509, as well as the lack of any documents confirming its original location, function, or patron. Claudia Blümle (2005, p. 77–78) argues that the altar evidences the impact of the *Jetzerhandel* on Fries, as he would have been particularly attuned to juridical modes of investigation due to his involvement in the affair. The suggestion is rather compelling. However, Blümle (2005, p. 75) does not draw any meaningful connections between the artist's involvement and his work, except for a rather cursory observation that the exterior of his *Kleiner Johannes Altar* represents a trial by ordeal. The altar's sophisticated thematisation of judicial inquiry suggests that Fries already possessed a certain skill-set that made him particularly suited for authenticating (or discrediting) a miracle. As further examination of the trial and his role in it demonstrates, it was his own material experimentation as an artist that gave him the requisite knowledge for participating in a juridical investigation.

[8]For the *Kleiner Johannes Altar*'s central sculptural group, a scene of the Last Judgment or the Ascension would seem most suitable; however, such suggestions must ultimately rest in the realm of speculation.

[9]The only known monumental works solely dedicated to the Apocalypse are the mid-fourteenth century Neapolitan panels at the Stuttgart *Staatsgallerie* and Master Bertram's 1400 Apocalypse Altarpiece at the Victoria and Albert Museum. Most altarpieces feature only one panel dedicated to the Book of Revelation, such as the right interior wing from Hans Memling's 1479 *Mystic Marriage of Saint Catherine* altarpiece.

16.3 The Jetzerhandel (1506–1509) and the Investigation of Miracles

The *Jetzerhandel* was one of the most notorious clerical scandals to take place in Europe in the early sixteenth century. From November 1506 until September 1507, Hans Jetzer experienced numerous visions of the Virgin Mary and several other saints, each one more sensational than the last. Most of the visions consisted of conversations between the saints; however, the Virgin Mary sometimes left behind physical traces of her miraculous presence, such as a linen cloth with drops of blood on it (Steck 1904, p. 214). On several occasions, Jetzer was physically altered or marked by some and capof these visions: in one particularly creepy encounter with the Virgin Mary, he received the wounds of the Stigmata, and every day at noon following this event, he would fall into a trance and re-enact the stages of the Passion before collapsing in a dramatic faint (Steck 1904, p. 192). Jetzer's visionary experiences reached a climax on the evening of June 24th, 1507, when the *Pietà* sculpture in the Dominican convent's Marian chapel began to weep blood.

These visions contained a thinly veiled polemic against the Franciscan concept of the Immaculate Conception, which had been a recent focus of debates for the past decade, advertising the Dominican position that even the Virgin Mary was afflicted with original sin (Utz Tremp 1988, p. 221–249). During the miracle of the *Pietà* sculpture, for instance, Jetzer reportedly overheard a conversation between the figures of the Virgin and Christ. According to Jetzer's statement from August 2nd, 1508, 'The son asked "Mother, why are you crying?" The Madonna answered: "Son, I cry, because they have taken an honour away from you and given it to me". The son responded: "Cry not, mother, this honour will not be withheld from me long, soon the discussion on the conception will come to an end and I will receive my award again"' (Steck 1904, p. 112).[10] As Kathrin Utz Tremp (2001, p. 24) has pointed out, the 'honour' stolen from Christ and bestowed upon his mother is that of his virgin birth.

At the end of 1507, the Bishop of Lausanne opened an inquiry into Jetzer and four friars at the Dominican convent: the prior Johannes Vatter, the subprior Franz Ueltschi, the lector Stephan Bolzhurst, and the steward Heinrich Steinegger.[11] After two years of trial and investigation, the visions and miracles were revealed to be a complete fraud. Jetzer confessed under torture that the visions were a hoax played on him by four of his superiors. After discovering that it was, in fact, his fellow

[10]Utz Tremp (1993), p. 326: '"Mater, quid ploras?" Respondit filius: "Mater, ego ploro, quod honor tuus tibi aufertur et mihi attribuitur". Et dixit filius: "Non plores, pia mater, quia non diu auferetur honor meus a me, sed illico terminabitur materia conceptionis et restituetur mibi honor meus".'.

[11]There were three trials in total: an examination before the episcopal court of Lausanne (8 October 1507 to 15 December 1507), the main inquisition into the allegations of heresy (26 July to 7 September 1508) and finally the revision process (2 to 30 May 1509) carried out by judicial authorities in the city of Bern.

friars who were dressing up as female saints and visiting him in the night, he was forced to continue to play along. Towards the end of the inquisitors' interrogation, it was eventually revealed that the monastery's manuscript illuminator, Lazarus von Adlau, had painted the Virgin's bloody tears (Steck 1904, p. 237).

At the final trial in Bern in 1509, Jetzer was exiled and the four other friars involved in the hoax were sentenced to death. They were burned at the stake on May 31st, 1509. The *Jetzerhandel* caused irreparable damage to the reputation of the Bernese Dominicans and sowed a pervasive distrust of clerical authority in the city. The political and religious uproar it caused has led scholars to regard the scandal as a watershed moment leading to the Swiss Reformation (Gordon 2002, p. 32–33). The *Jetzerhandel* gained widespread notoriety through the writings of critics of the Catholic Church, such as Erasmus (1466–1536), and through the dissemination of broadsheets illustrating the affair, such as Urs Graf's (1485–1529) woodcut series, originally produced for Thomas Murner's (1475–1537) *Von den vier ketzeren* (1509), a satirical poem lampooning the Dominican friars involved in the scandal (Günthart 2009).

When the priest Teschenmacher climbed upon the altar and publicly denounced the miraculous tears as red paint, it would have conceivably stirred up a debate over the nature of the sculpture's tears that necessitated the authority of an expert to settle the issue. The notion that a miracle, even a dubious one, must be proven through an inquiry was established by Innocent III's mandate in 1215 that canonisations follow the format of inquisitional procedures, ensuring that all individual's supernatural powers, visions, and miracles were now subject to an intensive, judicial interrogation (Vauchez 1997, p. 33–58). The crucial formative years of the canonisation proceedings occurred in the thirteenth century, at the same time as scholastic theologians were working out the ontological distinction between natural and supernatural, redefining the miracle as a genuine suspension of the laws of nature.[12]

Canonisation proceedings began to integrate this new concept of the miraculous. Both the sponsors of the saint and the canonists tasked with investigating his or her sanctity had to prove that there were no natural causes behind the potential saint's miracles (Kleinberg 1989; Smoller 1997). However, as scholars such as Elliott (2004) and Fogleman (2009) have shown, there was soon little that distinguished between canonisation proceedings and heretical trials. In other words, the sacred could no longer be taken for granted, it had to be tested and proven. In contrast to the trials by ordeal where miracles served as evidence, in the medieval judicial inquiry, the miracle itself was now subject to investigation.

The type of investigation now entailed by these new standards of proof can be seen in the painting *Verification of the Stigmata* attributed to Giotto di Bondone (1266–1337) from the Upper Church of Assisi. With Francis' body laid out upon the funeral bier, a local townsman, Girolamo, probes the deceased saint's wounds to determine their authenticity. In Bonaventure's biography of Francis, Girolamo is

[12]On the shifting concepts of the miraculous and its evidentiary potential, see Daston (1999).

described as a local laymen and knight. However, in the fresco, Giotto identifies the investigator as a medical doctor. He is dressed as a doctor, in a long robe with a fur collar and cap, and the titles beneath the mural describe him as a 'doctor and renowned man of learning' (Rubin 2007, p. 120). Thus, Giotto's fresco represents Francis' wounds as meeting the highest standard of proof demanded by the *inquisitio*; they are authenticated through the expertise of a doctor.

The town physician Valerius Anshelm also participated in the trial as an expert witness, assigned to investigate Jetzer's stigmatic wounds. However, he was not asked to examine the bloody tears, suggesting that Fries possessed a specialised knowledge that made him uniquely suited to the task at hand. But what sort of specialised knowledge were they calling on when they summoned him? And, would any artist have sufficed, or was Fries uniquely suited to the task at hand? Both the doctor and the artist possessed a practical knowledge of the respective materials of their trade, blood and paint, that would have allowed them to make an informed ruling on the controversial red substance. Yet, Fries was an expert in more than the scientific properties of various pigments. Through his profession, he was also skilled in the use of paint to imitate nature.

Bialostocki (1963) has discussed the two conceptions of nature, as established in Antiquity, that were frequently discussed throughout the medieval and early modern period: *natura naturata* (the products of nature) and *natura naturans* (the generative forces of nature). Although an artist's imitation of nature could be understood as producing an accurate representation of created nature, over the course of the fifteenth and sixteenth century, artists frequently made bold claims for their ability to imitate the powers of creation itself. Koerner (2016, p. 227) has pointed out the inherent risks of such assertions, stating 'through their novel products, artists implied that God's creation was mutable and incomplete, and that human *poiesis* could generate entirely new species…Whether consciously or not, artists vied dangerously with the Creator'. The deceptive use of red paint to create the illusion of miraculous tears in the *Jetzerhandel* was one example of the potential perils associated with the artist's imitation of *natura naturans*.

Yet it was precisely this familiarity with the creative forces of nature that provided Fries with the skill-set to undertake an investigation of the evidence. Indeed, the trial document suggests that the material experimentation that defined his profession was a form of knowledge in its own right. The document uses the word *experiri* (to test or prove). The word is also used in juridical texts, where it means to try by law or submit to a trial. In a judicial context, the use of the word *experiri*, placed before *scire*, connotes Fries placing the tears on trial and then deriving knowledge from the result.[13] The artist possessed not only the necessary expertise to understand the nature of the evidence, but also the expertise to discover the truth by subjecting it to rigorous inquiry. The revelation of the truth would have required

[13]I am grateful to Dr. Christopher Geekie for helping with the translation and pointing out the full range of possible connotations for *expirere* in the Middle Ages and Early Modern Era.

an intensely sensorial examination, in which Fries observed, touched, smelled, and perhaps even tasted the red material.

The trial document reveals the latent judicial dimensions of what Pamela Smith (2004, p. 6) has called an 'artisanal epistemology', that is, the idea that 'certainty is located in matter and nature and that knowledge can be gained by observing and experiencing—often by bodily struggle—the particularity of nature'. Smith convincingly argues that fifteenth- and sixteenth-century Northern artists increasingly asserted their specialised knowledge of nature that was yielded to them by the manual labour and experimentation that defined their craft. The document's recognition of Fries' facility for putting materials 'on trial' in order to obtain knowledge, however, suggests that the efficacy of these claims was also based on the shared rhetoric between artisanal and juridical modes of inquiry. Fries thematises in his *Kleiner Johannes Altar* a mode of inquiry that approximates both methods. Further examination of the panels reveals that Fries was attuned to the evidence sought after when claims for what was shown were couched in the rhetoric of visionary experience, and that he was aware of the power of the material of the work to generate this proof.

16.4 The Exterior Panels: Judge, Witness, and the Locus of Justice

The *Miracle of the Poisoned Cup* represents the moment when Aristodemus challenges John to prove his God by drinking poison, envisioned in the panel as a trial by ordeal, in which the truth will be revealed by the performance of a miracle thus signifying divine intervention. While Aristodemus sits in the position of judge, he is merely a mediator for the true judge, God. Medieval courtrooms were often decorated with images that both expressed and legitimated the judge's ruling as an extension of divine justice (Huygebaert et al. Chap. 1 and 2). The iconography of the *Miracle of the Poisoned Cup* narrative derives from Netherlandish *exempla* of justice, such as Dieric Bouts' (ca. 1420/1420–1475) *Justice of Otto III* (1473–75), Derick Baegert's (d. ca. 1525) *Oath-taking in Courtroom* (1493–94) (Huygebaert et al. p. 31–35, Fig. 9 and cat. 5), and Gerard David's (ca. 1460–1523) *Judgment of Cambyses* (1498) (Huygebaert et al. Chap. 3, Fig. 37–38 and cat. 28), which were particularly prevalent in the mid- to late-fifteenth century.[14] The most characteristic element is a depiction of the seated judge with his legs crossed in the act of dispensing justice, often holding or pointing a rod. The observation and participation of witnesses, usually surrounding the scene in a semi-circle, was another important feature.

---

[14]For general studies of this particular iconography, see Huygebaert et al. ch. 2; Martyn (2006), Pleister and Schild (1988), Schild (1980) Sutter (2008); Van der Velden (1995).

In addition, the composition of the *Miracle of the Poisoned Cup* scene would have recalled settings of justice in contemporary Switzerland, as can be seen, for example, in a trial scene (f. 110a) from Gerold Edlibach's illustrated *Zürcher Chronik* (1486–1530), in which the trial proceedings take place in an arena-like setting, enclosed on all sides by short walls, upon which a group of spectators rest their arms and observe the trial. Fries' panel bears even more striking similarities to Diebold Schilling the Younger's *Degradation of the Monks* (f. 319b) from his 1513 *Luzerner Chronik* (Zemp 1897, p. 97 and 118). Like the *Miracle of the Poisoned Cup* panels, the scene takes place on an open, raised platform, which appears to be located in Bern's *Kramgasse*, and features a dense crowd of spectators pressing against the front balustrade. And although the bishop does not sit under an elaborate baldachin, the seats in both scenes are squat and bench-like, with ornately carved sides.

The crowd of spectators in the *Kleiner Johannes Altar*, pressing against each other and craning their necks, dynamically reinforces the act of looking. The barrier in front of the crowd serves to emphasise their role as observers, not participants, while simultaneously evoking the setting of a theatre. The dramatic scene unfolds on a stage, where the spectacle is not only visually accessible, but in fact demands the attention of the viewer. The contemplative manner of the prominent figure in red in the background, who watches the trial with his head resting on his hand, directs our gaze back to the proceedings.

According to Rothstein (2008, p. 24), in the late Middle Ages 'seeing is (…) a prelude to knowing'. Rothstein (*ibidem*) is concerned with fifteenth-century Netherlandish justice exempla, which stimulate an active looking on the part of the viewer so that they may 'draw intellectual or spiritual sustenance' from the image. Yet Fries' panel also sets up the viewer of the painting in order to lead them to a type of knowledge. By relying on recognizable iconographies and contemporary settings of justice, Fries stimulates the viewer's judicial gaze. And in the late Middle Ages, it was the 'judicial gaze [which had become] the decisive factor for the judicial establishment of the truth' (Blümle 2008, p. 48). Fries thus encourages the viewer's active, visual engagement and casts them in the role of an eyewitness.

Fries' panel is unusual, however, in that the viewer is not shown the miraculous results of this 'trial by ordeal'. In earlier depictions of the *Miracle of the Poisoned Cup*, the artist depicts either or both the conversion of Aristodemus or the resurrection of the dead prisoners.[15] Instead, Fries portrays John with his eyes closed as he slowly and emphatically drinks from the poisoned cup. He stresses the deadness of the prisoners through his meticulously realistic depiction of their tinged, rotting flesh. The scene is a moment of anticipation, without any revelation of the justice administered by divine will.

Because the exterior portrays a moment of suspense without resolving it, the juridical gaze does not dissipate when the altarpiece is opened to reveal the interior. The Latin inscription underneath the Maria in Sole, 'It will no longer be a time of

[15]The lack of the miracle would also be unusual in contemporary depictions of trials by ordeal.

grace, but of justice', points to the thematic continuity between the exterior and interior.[16] Such a transition is further emphasised by the visual parallel between the unbelieving pagan sitting on a throne in judgment to the heavenly enthroned Son of Man on the interior. When the altarpiece is opened, the viewer is plucked from the cramped and dramatically tense judicial stage at Ephesus where he witnesses the trial of John to the spectacular, dazzling realm of Patmos, where now it is John who witnesses the ultimate trial of mankind.

16.5 The Interior Panels: Evidence, Inquiry, and the Visionary

John's particular role as witness to the Judgment Day is emphasised not only through his physical gaze, but also the twofold presence of the opening lines of John's Gospel. The purpose of John's ability to 'see' and 'testify' is to lead his readers to believe (Koester 1989). In the numerous Apocalypse manuscripts produced between the tenth and fifteenth centuries John was depicted, according to Emmerson (2010, p. 152), as 'first, a visionary witness; second, an active participant within his visions; and, third, a human intermediary between his otherworldly revelatory experience and the earthly reception of that experience by the medieval viewer/reader'. Artists experimented with different pictorial devices to explicate the physical and metaphysical mechanics of John's sight and to present a model of viewing to the reader (Camille 1992; Emmerson 2010; Klein 2010; Lewis 1991). In order to emphasise John's role as a witness to a higher truth, his spiritual sight was shown as distinct from the viewer's own earthly, corporeal sight. This can be seen, for example, in the prevalence of the window device in the thirteenth-century Westminster Apocalypse cycles, in which John peers through openings in the frames of the illumination in order to suggest that his view of the vision is different from the reader's (Klein 2010, p. 179–184).

In the *Kleiner Johannes Altar*, Fries certainly emphasizes the distinctiveness of John's sight and his role as a medium between the spiritual and earthly. John's sight is not spatio-temporally bound; he gazes at each vision from a different narrative point in the frame. Moreover, his depiction of the Son of Man departs from the standard iconography, which usually shows John kneeling on an indeterminate ground in front of the vision, as can be seen, for example, in Albrecht Dürer's (1471–1528) depiction of the Son of Man from his Apocalypse woodcut cycle (1498). Instead, John is represented as transcending the earthly sphere into the heavenly, hovering precisely in between the two. Thus, one could argue that the

[16]I have not been able to identify a source for this particular inscription. It is possible that it refers to the *tempus gratiae*, or grace period, at the beginning of an inquisitional process. First established in 1235, the grace period lasted for several days and confessions made during this window would receive lighter judicial punishment. I am grateful to Prof. Dr. Georges Martyn for the suggestion.

altarpiece merely follows earlier, traditional artistic depictions of John, which emphasise his role as visionary intermediary (Ganz 2008, p. 20–21). However, there are elements in this altarpiece that suggest Fries emphasised John's role as witness, not in order to relay a spiritual truth to a passive audience, but instead to facilitate the viewer's own inquiry into the material truth of the vision.

At first glance, the interior of the altarpiece seems to set up a categorical distinction between the earthly and spiritual realms, between which only John is able to navigate. Fries paints the bottom register with such crystalline naturalism that each flower and insect can be precisely identified: a lily of the valley, strawberries, thistle, woodruff, bluebells with a white butterfly, and a housefly (Villiger et al. 2001, p. 160). The recognizable reality of the natural world starkly contrasts with the hyper-materiality of the gold ground in the upper register. The density and flatness of the material seems incongruous with the meticulously rendered world below. Moreover, the upper register does not conceal its own artifice; the stars, the moon, the mandorla, and rays are clearly incisions made by the artist. The upper portion is of a different material reality than that of the earthly realm below. This division is highlighted by the erosion of John's halo as he moves from the exterior to the interior panels. On the exterior, in Ephesus, John's halo is a solid, gold disk that becomes more ethereal and transparent in the mystical liminal space of Patmos, finally disintegrating into nothing once he enters the visionary realm on the right panel.

Despite the perceived separation of the two realms, closer investigation of the image reveals a subtle blurring of the two realities. The murky grey of the sky in the middle of both images neutralizes the abrupt break between the earthly and spiritual. Furthermore, John is not the only traveller between the two realms. The feathery leaves on top of the slender tree in the left panel delicately brush the bottom portion of the gold material. The dense, rocky outgrowth on the right breaches the upper portion as well. The most striking evidence of the porosity between the two realms, however, can be found in the depiction of the Son of Man on the right panel.

The Book of Revelation describes John's vision of the Son of Man as follows: 'And I turned to see the voice that spake with me. And being turned, I saw seven golden candlesticks; And in the midst of the seven candlesticks one like unto the Son of man' (Revelation 1:12–13). To the casual eye, the seated figure with a sword and stars, surrounded by candlesticks, seems a standard representation of the apocalyptic Son of Man. Yet, curiously, the Son of Man in Fries' altarpiece is surrounded not by seven candlesticks, but by six. And to the best of my knowledge, there is no iconographic precedent for this; the Son of Man is always depicted amidst seven candlesticks.

Such a minor variation might seem insignificant, merely an unintentional omission by the artist. Closer inspection of the panel, however, reveals a calculated displacement of the candlestick by Fries. On the bottom left corner, peculiarly affixed to the rocky outgrowth, resides the missing seventh candle. The candle is no longer contained by a golden candelabrum, but it is almost identical to the slender, tawny coloured candles surrounding the Son of Man albeit slightly taller and thinner. Removed from the visionary arena above, the candle is now subject to the laws governing the earthly realm. A wisp of smoke trails upwards from its now extinguished flame. Illuminated by an indeterminable light source, it casts a faint shadow against the rock behind it.

Given the themes of trial and judgment emphasised throughout the whole altarpiece, the seventh candle functions as a visionary deposit, available to the viewer's inquisition. Fries brings a remnant from the visionary realm, something miraculous, and plants it in the natural world so that it is tangible and obtainable for the viewer.[17] The viewer might not have the special sight given to John that allows access to the higher level of spiritual reality; however, with John as a corroborating witness, the manifestation of the miraculous in a pointedly earthly, natural realm becomes a piece of evidence that can be investigated by the viewer with their physical faculties. The altarpiece, therefore, corresponds to the growing impetus to test the sacred through empirical investigation as brought about by the judicial inquiry. Fries constructed the altar as a metaphorical judicial stage, wherein it is the veracity of both the depicted visionary experience, as well as the artwork itself, which the viewer is asked to investigate.

16.6 Conclusion

At the turn of the sixteenth century, the growing criticism of images, as seen in the writings of Jean Gerson, Johann Geiler von Kayersberg, and Erasmus, accompanied by the fermenting distrust in the certitude of vision led to what Wimböck (2007, p. 426) has described as an 'epistemological transition in the valuation of sight'. The period from the mid- fifteenth century to the late seventeenth century was marked by an intense visual crisis, in which an increasing awareness of the disconnect between appearance and reality severely undermined the primacy of sight in the Aristotelian hierarchy of the senses. Clark (2007, p. 2) has charted the developing distrust of sight in this period, arguing that 'in one context after another, vision came to be characterised by uncertainty and unreliability, such that access to visual reality could no longer be normally guaranteed'. Yet as Cacciola (2003), Elliott (2004) and Anderson (2011) have convincingly argued, the judicial *inquisitio* was a method for procuring the truth and re-establishing certainty. The preciseness and rationality of its methodology was an effective corrective to the unstable epistemological value of sight, and it was understood to be 'the most obvious and up-to-date safeguard against deception' (Elliott 2004, p. 71).

Considering that the *Kleiner Johannes Altar* was created on the eve of the Reformation, when scepticism of the miraculous and visionary took on increasingly

[17]Of course, there is a distinction to be made between a miracle and a visionary experience. However, as evidenced in the *Jetzerhandel* itself, in which the visionary Virgin Mary left behind 'miraculous' deposits during the vision, the same rules still apply to the investigation of a visionary experience as a miraculous event.

litigious dimensions, the activation of a judicial mode of inquiry can be understood as the surest way of guaranteeing the certitude of the viewer's investigation. The certitude, however, would have been guaranteed not only by the mode of inquiry, but by the altarpiece itself. Fries' artisanal profession gave him a familiarity with the processes of nature, or *natura naturans*, that would have made him particularly adept at discerning any potential natural causes behind seemingly supernatural effects. For if artists were experts on the processes of nature, then they were also experts on its limitations. It was this kind of specialised knowledge sought after when Fries was summoned to Bern to authenticate the bloody tears. As an artist, he also had experience in the use of red paint to simulate blood. The judicial officials summoned Fries because his profession granted him the ability not only to distinguish paint from blood, but illusion from reality.

Thus, the *Kleiner Johannes Altar* not only speaks to Fries' awareness of the new concepts of the miraculous and visionary redefined by the judicial inquisition, but also expresses the epistemic claims he strove to make for the products of his profession that were based on his knowledge of nature. For it is precisely Fries' own craft that both generated and constituted the evidence that met the standards of proof demanded by the judicial inquiry. The truth, therefore, resided in matter itself; its certainty guaranteed by the labour of its creation.

References

Anderson WL (2011) The discernment of spirits: assessing visions and visionaries in the late middle ages. Mohr Siebeck, Tübingen

Bartlett R (1986) Trial by fire and water: the medieval judicial ordeal. Clarendon Press, Oxford

Bialostocki J (1963) The renaissance concept of nature and antiquity. In: The Renaissance and Mannerism. Princeton University Press, Princeton (NJ), pp 19–30

Blümle C (2005) Dünne rote Linie. Verhandlung zwischen Substanz und Täuschung. In: Lauper A (ed) Transfusionen: Blutbilder und Biopolitik in der Neuzeit. Diaphanes, Zürich, pp 71–83

Blümle C (2008) The omnipresent eye of the judge: juridical evidence in Albrecht Dürer and Lucas Cranach the Elder. Parallax 14:42–54

Brundage J (1996) Proof in canonical criminal law. Contin Change 11:329–339

Caciola N (2003) Discerning spirits: divine and demonic possession in the middle ages. Cornell University Press, Ithaca (NY)

Camille M (1992) Visionary perception and images of the apocalypse in the later middle ages. In: Emmerson RK, McGinn B (eds) The apocalypse in the middle ages. Cornell University Press, Ithaca (NY), pp 276–292

Clark S (2007) Vanities of the eye: vision in early modern european culture. Oxford University Press, Oxford

Daston L (1999) Marvelous facts and miraculous evidence in early modern europe. In: Platt PG (ed) Wonders, marvels, and monsters in early modern culture. University of Delaware Press, Newark (NJ), pp 76–104

Elliott D (2004) Proving woman: female spirituality and inquisitional culture in the later middle ages. Princeton University Press, Princeton (NJ)

Emmerson RK (2010) Visualizing the visionary: John in his apocalypse. In: Hourihane C (ed) Looking beyond. Visions, dreams, and insights in medieval art and history. Princeton University Press, Princeton (NJ), pp 148–176

Fogleman A (2009) Finding a middle way: late medieval naturalism and visionary experience. Vis Res 25:7–28

Foucault M (2002) Truth and juridical forms. In: Grabinow P (ed) Power, the essential works. Penguin, London, pp 1–89

Fraher R (1992) IV Lateran's revolution in criminal procedure: the birth of *Inquisitio*, the end of ordeals, and Innocent III's vision of ecclesiastical politics. In: Castillo Lara RJ (ed) Studia in honorem eminentissimi cardinalis Alphonsi M. Stickler. LAS, Rome, pp 97–111

Franklin J (2001) The science of conjecture: evidence and probability before pascal. Johns Hopkins University Press, Baltimore (MD)

Ganz D (2008) Medien der Offenbarung: Visionsdarstellungen im Mittelalter. Reimer, Berlin

Gordon B (2002) The swiss reformation. Manchester University Press, Manchester

Günthart R (2009) Von den vier Ketzern: 'ein erdocht falsch history etlicher Prediger münch' und 'Die war History von den vier ketzer prediger ordens'. Edition und Kommentar. Zürich, Chronos

Huygebaert S, Martyn G, Paumen V, Van Poucke T (eds) (2016) The art of law. Three centuries of justice depicted (exh. cat. Bruges). Lannoo, Tielt

Klein P (1998) From the heavenly to the trivial: vision and visual perception in early and high medieval apocalypse illustration. In: Kessler H, Wolf G (eds) The holy face and the paradox of representation. Nuova Alfa Editoriale, Bologna, pp 247–278

Klein P (2010) Visionary experience and corporeal seeing in thirteenth-century english apocalypses: John as external witness and the rise of gothic marginal images. In: Hourihane C (ed) Looking Beyond. Visions, dreams, and insights in medieval art and history. Princeton University Press, Princeton (NJ), pp 177–202

Kleinberg AM (1989) Proving sanctity: selection and authentication of saints in the later middle ages. Viator 20:183–205

Koerner J (2016) Bosch and Bruegel: from enemy painting to everyday life. Princeton University Press, Princeton (NJ)

Koester C (1989) Hearing, seeing, and believing in the gospel of John. Biblica 70:327–348

Lepsius S (2003) Von Zweifeln zur Überzeugung: der Zeugenbeweis im gelehrten Recht ausgehend von der Abhandlung des Bartolus von Sassoferrato. Vittorio Klostermann, Frankfurt am Main

Lewis S (1991) English Gothic Illuminated Apocalypse, Lectio Divina and the Art of Memory. Word and Image 7:1–32

Martyn G (2006) Painted exempla iustitiae in the Southern Netherlands. In: Schulze R (ed) Symbolische Kommunikation vor Gericht in der Frühen Neuzeit. Duncker & Humblot, Berlin, pp 335–356

Pleister W, Schild W (1988) Recht und Gerechtigkeit im Spiegel der europäischen Kunst. DuMont, Cologne

Rothstein B (2008) Looking the part: ruminative viewing and the imagination of community in the early modern low Countries. Art History 31:1–32

Rubin PL (2007) Images and identity in fifteenth-century florence. Yale University Press, New Haven (CT)

Schild W (1980) Alte Gerichtsbarkeit: Vom Gottesurteil bis zum Beginn der modernen Rechtsprechnung. Callwey, Munich

Smith PH (2004) The body of the artisan: art and experience in the scientific revolution. University of Chicago Press, Chicago (IL)

Smoller L (1997) Defining the boundaries of the natural in fifteenth-century Brittany: the inquest into the miracles of saint Vincent Ferrer. Viator 28:333–359

Steck R (1904) Die Akten des Jetzerprozesses nebst dem Defensorium. Verlag der Basler Buch- und Antiquariatshandlung, Basel

Sutter C (2008) Flämische Gerechtigkeitsbilder des 15. Jahrhunderts: die Visualisierung spätmittelalterlicher Auffassungen von Recht und Moral. VDM, Saarbrücken

Utz Tremp K (1988) Welche Sprache spricht die Jungfrau Maria? Sprachgrenzen und Sprachkenntnisse im bernischen Jetzerhandel (1507–1509). Schweizerische Zeitschrift für Geschichte 38:221–249
Utz Tremp K (1993) Eine Werbekampagne für die befleckte Empfängnis: der Jetzerhandel in Bern (1507–1509). In: Opitz C (ed) Maria in der Welt: Marienverehrung im Kontext der Sozialgeschichte 10.-18. Jahrhundert. Chronos, Zürich, pp 323–337
Utz Tremp K (2001) Die Zeit des Malers Hans Fries. In: Villiger V, Schmid AA, Cavizel N (eds) Hans Fries: ein Maler an der Zeitenwende. München: Hirmer, pp 21–29
Van der Velden H (1995) Cambyses for example: the origins and function of an *exemplum iustitiae* in Netherlandish art of the fifteenth, sixteenth, and seventeenth centuries. Simiolus 23:5–62
Vauchez A (1997) Sainthood in the later middle ages. Cambridge University Press, Cambridge
Villiger V, Schmid AA, Caviezel N (eds) (2001) Hans Fries: ein Maler an der Zeitenwende. Hirmer, München
Wimböck G (2007) 'Durch die Augen in das menschliche Gemüth kommen': Sehen und Glauben —Grenzen und Reservate. In: Wimböck G, Leonhard K, Friedrich M (eds) Evidentia. Reichweiten visueller Wahrnehmung in der Frühen Neuzeit LIT-Verlag, Münster, pp 425–450
Zemp J (1897) Die schweizerischen Bildchroniken und ihre Architektur-Darstellungen. Schultheiss, Zurich

Tamara Golan is a Ph.D candidate at Johns Hopkins University working on a dissertation project titled: Hans Fries and Niklaus Manuel: Evidence, Inquiry, and Artistic Knowledge in Swiss Painting, 1430–1530. Her research focuses on the growing distrust of visions and miracles on the eve of the Reformation. Since August 2016, she has been a Samuel H. Kress pre-doctoral fellow at the Zentralinstitut für Kunstgeschichte in Munich. Previously she was a pre-doctoral fellow with the Minerva Research Group The Nomos of Images: The Manifestation and Iconology of Law' at the Kunsthistorisches Institut in Florence.

Figures

Fig. 16.1 Hans Fries, *Miracle of the Poisoned Cup of John the Evangelist*, exterior panels of the *Kleiner Johannes Altar*, ca. 1505. Zürich, Swiss National Museum, LM-1893a, © Schweizerisches Landesmuseum, Zürich

Fig. 16.2 Hans Fries, *John on Patmos*, interior panels of the *Kleiner Johannes Altar*, ca. 1505. Zürich, Swiss National Museum, LM-1893a, © Schweizerisches Landesmuseum, Zürich

Chapter 17
A Ghostly Corpse in the City? Spatial Configurations and Iconographic Representations of Capital Punishment in the 'Belgian' Space (16th–20th C.)

Jérôme de Brouwer and Xavier Rousseaux

Abstract This contribution addresses the complex relation between 'sovereign' power, legitimate State violence, and public space in the 'Belgian' territories. By linking the spatiality of the execution and its iconographic representation to changing socio-political power configurations, it studies the role of the Belgian 'culture of capital executions' in its specific path of State formation. The trend of removing the death penalty from the communal agora is a general issue in the West. From the Middle Ages, capital executions were characterised by specific appropriations of space by central authorities, local elites and ordinary citizens. During the eighteenth century, local powers faced attempts of the central governments to control the public execution, and more specifically the death penalty. Data from the 1770s to the 1850s, during several quickly succeeding political regimes, supports the hypothesis of a decline of publicly exposed death penalties. In nineteenth century Belgium, the gradual disappearance of the public execution as a spectacular expression of the State runs parallel with the (all but) inexistence of an iconography' of public executions. The guillotine appears as the expression of a change in criminal justice and it also influences the representation of capital execution. It focuses now on the cutted head, the seat of the mental faculties. During the same period, cell confinement is considered by the State as a mean of control the criminal's mind.

J. de Brouwer (✉)
Centre for Legal History and Legal Anthropology, Free University of Brussels (ULB), Brussels, Belgium
e-mail: Jerome.de.Brouwer@ulb.ac.be

X. Rousseaux
Fonds National de la Recherche Scientifique, Centre for Law and Justice History, Université catholique de Louvain, Louvain-La-Neuve, Belgium
e-mail: Xavier.Rousseaux@uclouvain.be

S. Huygebaert et al. (eds.), *The Art of Law*, Ius Gentium: Comparative Perspectives on Law and Justice 66, https://doi.org/10.1007/978-3-319-90787-1_17

17.1 Introduction

By opening up law and justice to the study of perception, experience and emotion, (as developed by the social sciences during the last few decades), it becomes possible to highlight the 'spatial' and 'iconic' aspects of legal and socio-political history (Mitchell 1994, 1999 and 2015). In this context, the public expression of punishment is a particularly interesting 'event' for an approach that combines image and space, since visual representation and space are at the very heart of the ritual (and its memory) (Wilf 1993; Merback 2001; Mills 2005).

In this contribution we want to develop a historical reflection on public executions in the area we today call Belgium. The aim is to shed light on the complex relations between 'sovereign' powers, legitimate State violence and the public space. Historians have pointed out the gradual disappearance of public execution as a highly visible expression of the State's claim to the monopoly of the legitimate use of violence (Weber 2015). The Belgian case is interesting because: (i) the monopolisation by the 'State' of executions dates back to the end of the eighteenth century and the annexation by revolutionary France, (ii) the 'national' State only exists officially since 1830, and (iii) there is no national iconography on public executions within the 'Belgian space' (contrary to, for example, the tradition around the beheading of Charles I in England, or that of Louis XVI in France, or the *auto da fé* in Mediterranean Inquisitions) (Arasse 1987; Bethencourt 1992).

Our hypothesis is that the iconographic representation of public execution was regarded as taboo by the new liberal-Catholic elites governing young 'Belgium'. The Belgian case invites us to go beyond 'national' historiographies in order to understand how various political authorities engaged in a discussion with their ordinary subjects on the meaning of capital punishment. Although the power configurations, and the participating elites changed profoundly between the fifteenth and the twentieth century, the urban traditions provided consistency within the recently created national State.

The development of the display of public execution in the community space, followed by the trend to expel capital punishment—and by extension its common representation—from this common space, is a general theme in the West. As a social fact, the specific nature of the death penalty has been analysed as a key element of a long process of civilisation (Bastien 2006; Blok 1989; Evans 1996; Friedland 2012; Gatrell 1994; Martschukat 2000; Spierenburg 1984; Van Dülmen 1990; Ward 2015). In an archaeology of long-term power, recent research has focused on the relation between the death penalty and local authorities. Punitive rituals in England have been studied extensively (Gatrell 1994; Ward 2015), but similar trends can be found in a variety of continental European cities—Amsterdam, Hamburg, Paris, Toulouse and Rome—as well.

17.2 The Scaffold in the City: The Construction of Public Execution in the Long Term

Since the Middle Ages, public executions have been characterised by specific appropriations of the public space by central authorities, churches, local elites, and ordinary citizens (Goffman 1963; Blok 1989; Cohen 1989; Terpstra 2008). Research on legal executions and the people ordering them in the Low Countries between the fourteenth and sixteenth centuries stresses the multiple roles and the ambiguities of the representations of the executioners. Between 1450 and 1550, public torture and executions became increasingly prevalent in the cities of the Low Countries (Demaret 2016; Klemettilä 2006). The practice of submitting the condemned to public suffering developed from an occasional performance into a routine public spectacle (Handelman 1998). From the sixteenth century onwards, the wooden scaffold, mounted and reassembled for each separate execution, made way for a more permanent infrastructure in more durable materials (brick or stone). Specific instruments—cages, pillories, chains and the like—were added to extend the spectrum of public punishments to also include lesser crimes (Rousseaux 1997, 2012).

The role of the executioner broadened as well. As an officer of the Prince, the executioner was frequently paid by the urban authorities, for example in Valenciennes, Mons, Brussels, Leuven, Antwerp, or ‘s Hertogenbosch. Power relations were part of the landscape. In more rural regions, for example in the small city of Nivelles at the fringes of Walloon Brabant, the competition between a princely officer and a seigneurial power (in this case the abbess of the powerful monastery of Nivelles) was played out in the only urban space of the region. The city had no executioner of its own, and used the services of the executioner of the officer of the Duke of Brabant: the bailiff of the Roman Pays. Spatial competence was strictly organised: executions ordered by the urban court took place on the market place, in front of the town hall, and the bodies were exhibited on the abbey gallows, the *Happart* or *Hapeau.* Those executed by the princely justice were hanged on the edges of the city, at the crossing of two main roads: a place called *Trois Tilleuls* (Three Lime trees) (Van der Sanden and Luning 2010; Rousseaux 2012).

As shown for many medieval and early modern cities, this public display of punishment underlines a double spatial polarisation. On the one hand, public executions of judicial sentences took place in the main spaces of urban community life: in front of the church or town hall, or on the market square (Rebecchini 2013; Stuart 2000; Terpstra 2008). On the other hand, the fact that there was a permanent punishment infrastructure, not only on the centre, but also on the boundaries of the jurisdiction illustrates the power to expel the deviant body from the ‘civilised’ space of the city (Spierenburg 2013; Van der Sanden and Luning 2010).

The popularity of public executions in medieval towns was concomitant with the phenomenon of commissioned representations, by and of the urban elite, for the adornment of courtrooms (Edgerton 1985; Jacob 1994; Schild 1980). In the cities of Northern Italy, the Low Countries, the Rhineland or the Helvetic region (Boomgaard 1992; Gyger 1998), the majority of these representations were linked to urban sovereignty, symbolised by the image of the 'good judge' (Jacob 1994; Robert 1996; Schild 1980). In contrast to other European political entities (such as the English or French monarchies), the medieval principalities which constituted the Burgundian and Habsburg Low Countries, hardly produced an iconographic programme focused on public executions at all (Klemetillä 2006). While many works described civic propaganda and public demonstrations of power in the cities (Arnade 1996; Brown 2007; Lecuppre-Desjardins 2004), the image of criminal justice, inspired by biblical or antique models, remained confined to courtrooms (Harbison 1975; Lederle 1937). Parallel to this efflorescence of 'justice paintings', archival research confirms that the 'punishment theatre', which found its way into the urban spaces of the fifteenth to the seventeenth centuries, was based on both practical experience and visual representation (Boes 2013; Demaret 2016; Musin 2017; Silverman 2001; Van Dülmen 1990).

17.3 The Printing Revolution, Political Unrest and Criminalisation of Justice

Under the first Habsburgs, the 'printing revolution' transformed representations and the dissemination thereof. This was a time when jurists were attempting to structure civil and criminal justice on the basis of Roman law. This process also included the publishing of (often illustrated) manuals. In the 1550s, Bruges jurist Joos de Damhouder enjoyed European success with his *Praxis rerum criminalium* and his programme of illustrations of 'legal practices' (Dauwe and Monballyu 1981, Monballyu 2016). These images represent the various types and places of punishment. On the one hand, there was the urban prison, which was linked to the exercise of the secret so-called 'extraordinary procedure', including the use of torture. On the other hand, there was the scaffold, at the heart of the market. The great symbols of capital punishment (the stake, hanging and beheading), are found in the illustrations of criminalists (Fig. 17.1) (Dufrasne 2014, 2015; Follain and Papillard 2015), but also in, for instance, the decorated initial letters in Vesalius' best-seller *De humani corporis fabrica* (Lambert 1952).[1]

Pieter Bruegel's (1525–1569) drawing *Justitia* crystallizes all representations of this kind of justice (Fig. 17.2). Outwardly allegorical, in a series devoted to the virtues, the design draws on the actual practice of the criminal courts of Antwerp or Brussels (Vancauwenberghe 2003). The action is taking place at the heart of the city, while in the background the landscape, including the gallows, unfolds. However, this does not mean that the rural world is absent in representations of capital punishment. In 1568, Pieter Bruegel painted a vast landscape in which

[1]See the contributions of Behrmann and Verstegen, on the representation of skinning, in this volume, as well as the contribution by Jäger in this volume and the *The Art of Law* exhibition catalogue (Huygebaert et al. 2016, *passim*) for more information, and illustrations, on Damhouder.

peasants dance not far from a twisted gallows on which a magpie is perched. It is generally thought that in *The Magpie and the Gallows*, Bruegel is criticising the political and religious repression by Philip II of Spain, who was, via the Council of Troubles, responsible for over 150 executions in 1568 alone (Goosens 1997–1998; Verheyden 1961).

The same year, the execution of counts Egmont and Hornes on the *Grand'Place* in Brussels gave rise to the first representation of a real execution, in the form of a double engraving by Frans Hogenberg (ca. 1538/1540–1590) (Figs. 17.3 and 17.4; Van der Kooij 2012; Voges 2016). The better-known of the two (Fig. 17.3) shows the moment when the executioner is about to kill Hornes, with Egmont's body covered by the sheet of the scaffold. The second (Fig. 17.4) presents the same scaffold transformed into a catafalque, with the two heads exhibited before an audience of judges and citizens of both sexes. The two engravings present a stylised urban décor, vaguely evoking the *Grand'Place*. These engravings were one of the most popular representations of an execution, in a place of symbolic importance for royal power. After 1830, the event would go on to be reinterpreted as a key moment in the crystallisation of the young Belgian nation (*cf. infra*). More than the execution itself, the concealed corpses and executed heads form the determining element of the political liturgy of execution at the centre of Spanish power in the Low Countries.

17.4 The Softening of Practices, the Enlightenment, and Debates on Public Execution

At the beginning of the seventeenth century, representations of public execution change. Archdukes Albert and Isabella censored the iconographic programme of legal textbooks (Dufrasne 2015).[2] As a result, we find very few representations of actual executions. At the Saint Martin's Church in Halle, a small town close to Brussels, 21 paintings represent miracles attributed to Our Lady of Halle, at least three of which depict a hanging. These scenes from daily life, probably painted in David Teniers' (1582–1649) Brussels workshop in the early seventeenth century, are ex-votos offered by pilgrims. Places of devotion such as Our Lady of Halle were privileged destinations for pilgrims, and hence were often visited by individuals condemned by the courts to go on a pilgrimage, as a physical and religious exercise. In the context of Catholicisation, the Archdukes, members of the Fraternity of Our Lady of Halle, supported pilgrimages to the Counter-Reformation sanctuaries of Scherpenheuvel, Dinant, Walcourt and elsewhere.

Two paintings–inspired by religious representations—depict hangings on the outskirts of Halle. A group of spectators is gathered around the gallows, where the

[2]J. de Damhouder (1656) *De practijke of gebruyk zoo van civile als criminele zaken*, foreword, referring to an Archdukes Albert & Isabella Statute of 3 July 1623.

condemned man is to be hanged. In the upper left, a ray of sunlight, accompanied in one case by an image of the Virgin and in the other by a bird, lights up the gallows and the head of the condemned man.[3]

Another of these miracle paintings, recently restored, shows a pilgrim kneeling at the feet of Our Lady (Fig. 17.5). Depicted in the background are various scenes of the vagaries of life: sickness, a vehicle accident, drowning and, on the other side of the river, an execution under the gaze of two assisting religious officers. Hence, being hanged is presented as one of the risks of daily life for people of the seventeenth century.

Do these rare representations confirm what archive-based criminal justice studies teach us: that the death penalty in Western Europe gradually became less prevalent from the mid-seventeenth century onwards.? During the eighteenth century the local authorities in the Southern Low Countries (at that time under Austrian rule) found themselves (as the depositories of the right to condemn individuals to death) confronted with attempts from the central government to control public executions. After 1750, capital punishment was under the control of provincial courts and lawyers through judicial recourses, and under that of the government through the system of royal pardons. As early as 1765, the Low Countries, the debate initiated by Cesare Beccaria and Voltaire reached the Low Countries (Rousseaux 1997). The government sought to persuade provincial elites to invest in prisons and abolish torture and banishment. Local authorities had mixed reactions. While there was indeed a general decline of the number of executions, some studies show a surge of death sentences in some specific regions, Bruges for example. Public banishment from cities, accompanied by stigmatising punishments (whipping, branding), was gradually replaced by long-term imprisonment in the new 'houses of enforcement' created in Ghent (Flanders) and Vilvoorde (Brabant) (Spierenburg 1991).

The mapping of the territory is another source testifying the transformations of criminal punishment in the landscape. The first complete map of the territory of the Austrian-ruled Southern Low Countries, produced by Count Joseph de Ferraris between 1770 and 1778,[4] reflects the desire of the Austrian government to encapsulate these very fragmented Low Countries in a permanent representation (De Coene et al. 2012). The map's defects are well-known. Its objectives were primarily military and political. As a result, rural areas and borders are described better than urban centres. Looking at the rural areas, we notice that the legends mention 'gibbets' or 'gallows'; 111 of the 275 plates indicate places of justice. On most of these places gibbets and gallows predominate (146 occurrences), but there

---

[3]The second case is the staging of a legend, recounted in the *Guldenboek*, the book of the fraternity, of the falconer condemned to death for losing his master's falcon, and saved *in extremis* by the bird's return (*Dit siin die privilegien van der kerke, die miraclen ende die teekene die broeders ende zusters onser vouwen van Halle, 1341–1789. Integrale tekst van het Guldenboek, met toelichtingen*. 1989. Halle: VVV-Halle).

[4]Ferraris, Joseph. 1770–1778. *Carte de cabinet des Pays Bas autrichiens, levée à l'initiative du comte de Ferraris*, accompanied by *Mémoires historiques, chronologiques et économiques, sur les feuilles du numéro de la carte de cabinet pour son Altesse royale le duc Charles*. XII vols.

are also nine fields, eight trees, one hill and one fountain of justice. We can also see two prisons, the octagonal prison in Ghent and the Vilvoorde 'house of correction' (Montignie and De la Croix 2015).

In contrast to the rural areas, the written comments accompanying the map highlight the new buildings of the 'criminal revolution': courts of justice and provincial councils are referred to as *loci justitiae*, and houses of correction as *loci poenae*. The new prison in Ghent is a telling example. 'The house of enforcement being built there recently, is considered the largest in the country. Its shape is octagonal. It contains eight lateral courtyards and one in the centre'.[5] Of the royal castle of Vilvoorde, we learn that 'this was demolished in 1775 for the materials to be used in building a house of enforcement, which the States of Brabant had resolved to establish at a short distance from this old castle'.[6]

The Ferraris map reflects a slow transformation of mentality. While reflecting an unchanged image of a rural world dotted with gibbets and gallows—witnesses of the disparity of local seigneurial powers—the comments insist on the urban and peri-urban centralisation of the mechanisms of justice and punishment. In the same vein, since the sixteenth century, depictions of urban executions are rare in the Southern Netherlands. Only one representation exists, from the end of the *Ancien Regime*, painted by J.A. Garemijn.

This painting depicts the hanging of Josef Mesuere (Fig. 17.6), condemned for perjury and forgery, as we can read on the sign carried by the body of the hanged man, and in subscription (Everaert 2005; Gyselen 1958; Vermeersch 2014 and 2016). Probably commissioned by the Magistrate of the Liberty of Bruges (a rural judicial district), the painting was destined for its courtroom. In other words, it was intended as a tool of communication with the public, aimed at deterring its viewers from the crime of forgery. The painting itself is divided into two parts: above is the image, below a text describing the crime. Even so, the individual is anonymised ('N …. A certain inhabitant', trans. JDB and XR). The space taken up by the text in the painting reflects both the expansion of writing in an increasingly bourgeois society and a crime—forgery—perceived as threatening, doubled by perjury, and calling for an unusually severe sentence in the last third of the eighteenth century. The physical representation of the execution matches with our knowledge of how criminal justice operated in Bruges (De Win 1991 and 1992a; Vermeersch 2014 and 2016). The gallows was erected on Burgh Square, on the corner of the Liberty of Bruges hall and the former 'Civil Registry'. The emphasis in the paiting is on the finished hanging, represented as a genre scene (Hofman 2017). The hierarchy of Ancien Régime society is illustrated by the opposition between the lower plane, representing ordinary Bruges society, and the upper plane, where the judges are seated behind the windows. The priest provides the link between these separate worlds: the body of the condemned, the persons wielding justice, and the general population. Another contrast is between the majesty of the stone building of justice

[5]Ferraris, *Mémoires*, vol. IV, p. 86 (ref. map G.2), trans. JDB and XR.

[6]Ferraris, *Mémoires*, vol. I, pp. 127–138 (ref. map K.1), trans. JDB and XR.

and the make-shift character of the wooden gallows. It is also notable that the painter has opted to show the hanging from the back, away from the judges, but with the hanged man's body, and the notice board indicating his crime turned towards the spectators.

17.5 Public Execution and the Use of the Guillotine, from the Penal Revolution to the Bourgeois Order

Our analysis of Garemijn's painting needs to be extended by that of a work of another artist from the beginning of the penal regime introduced with the French annexation of the Low Countries: Antwerp chronicler P.A.J. Goetsbloets' (Fig. 17.7) representation of the execution, three decades later, of Henri Demeliez.[7] His *Tijdsgebeurtenissen* (1793–1797) is illustrated with numerous watercolours depicting persons being pilloried and capital executions in Antwerp and Brussels (Deseure 2014; D'Hainaut-Zvény 2005).[8] While capital executions are widely represented in France itself during the revolutionary period (the execution of King Louis XVI providing the archetype), there are few depictions of executions in the conquered *départements*, neither during the revolutionary nor during the imperial period.[9] For this reason, these watercolours form an iconographic ensemble of exceptional value. One example of these representations is the illustration of the execution of Henri Demeliez. Condemned by the Criminal Court of the *Département* of the Dyle, he was the first person sentenced to death to be executed on the guillotine in Brussels, on 16 July 1796. Between the execution of Mesuere and that of Demeliez, 29 years had passed. Each of the two representations expresses a view on capital execution at the end of the eighteenth century. Nevertheless, while Garemijn's painting was intended to be seen by that part of the general public that had access to its location, this is not the case for Goetsbloets' work, which remained unpublished.

Both paintings represent the public and the instrument of execution (gallows or guillotine), but they do so from a different vantage point. While Garemijn presents the scene from the ground, at the level of the spectators, Goetsbloets seems to hover above as if he himself was positioned slightly above it.[10] The guillotine alone,

[7]See the contribution by Deseure in this volume.

[8]Goetsbloets, PAJ, [1793-1797], Tydsgebeurtenissen, 10 vol. Royal Library Ms. II 1492. Goetsbloets presents other representations of capital executions from a different angle, see De Win (1992b), pp. 141–143, Figs. 1–54.

[9]One of the few artists who represented French justice in the new United Departments is the Liège painter Léonard Defrance (1735–1805). His scene of the Criminal Court could very well represent a real court session, but the place is not specified. Defrance did not leave any painting of a judicial execution.

[10]It is possible that Goetsbloets was present at the execution, which is mentioned in the first regular periodical of the *département*, *Le Républicain du Nord*, which fills in some of the details: 'Brussels, 26th Messidor. Yesterday, at 3 o'clock in the afternoon, the man named Deméliez,

exposed on a high scaffold, takes in half of the painting. The depiction also makes a fairly marked distinction between the population and the soldiers surrounding the scaffold. This division is much less marked in Garemijn's work, where the forces of order share a space with the general population, and do not appear to be there specifically to protect the gallows. The separation of these groups in Goetsbloets' work reflects the tension inherent in an event organised by the new regime, which could turn into confrontation. Finally, Goetsbloets, unlike Garemijn, is focused on the scaffold and makes no reference to the urban environment.

Hence, there are indeed significant differences between these two representations of capital punishment, 29 years apart.[11] But there is another consequence, not visible in Goetsbloets' work, of the appearance of the guillotine during the Revolution, and of the systematic use of decapitation as a mode of execution. The guillotine is the most appropriate means of responding to the demand for a transformation of the death penalty, from the perspective of the authors of the 1791 Penal Code, into 'the simple deprivation of life'.[12] Decapitation by the guillotine makes capital punishment at once mechanical and instantaneous. Unlike previous forms of execution, the deprivation of life now only takes a very short time. With the extreme swiftness of execution making it difficult for the spectators to take in the 'passage from life to death', the severed head now became an object of questioning, repulsion and fascination. Of course, these were elements which also concerned the artist whose job it was to represent the execution, and who is faced with the difficulty of representing an event which seems irreducible to representation (Arasse 1987; Bethencourt 1992).

Execution by guillotine remained fairly common in the years following the French annexation. It was performed on Belgian territory, in a public place—as prescribed by article 5 of the 1791 Penal Code and article 26 of the 1810 Penal Code—over 500 times during the two decades of the French regime. However, the number of executions decreased significantly with the Dutch regime, a trend which continued after the Belgian Independence (De Brouwer 2005b). Capital execution and the public spectacle that surrounds it gradually became less common in the public space during the course of the nineteenth century.

---

condemned to death for the crime of premeditated murder, suffered his punishment, dressed in a red shirt. He was taken to the Communal Square and decapitated by the instrument called the guillotine, after its inventor. An immense crowd of inhabitants of this city wanted to enjoy a spectacle that is always hideous, but imprints a salutary terror in the souls of the wicked, while reassuring the good citizens, who cannot be unaware that, under the reign of the Constitution and the law, and by means of the benevolent institution of jurors, it is morally impossible that the sword of justice, which sometimes spares the guilty, could strike an innocent man' (trans. JDB and XR).

[11]A link does exist, however, between the two executions, even if one takes place in Bruges and the other in Brussels: the person of the executioner. Mesuere was hanged by Pieter-Jan Boutquin, the executioner of Bruges and of the Liberty of Bruges, Demeliez by Frans-Jan Boutquin, the executioner of the *département* of the Dyle, nephew of the aforementioned (De Brouwer 2005a; Gerlache 1914).

[12]Art. 2 Penal Code 1791.

From the 1830s onwards, the public nature of capital punishment was increasingly questioned or criticised in the press. The press did not speak out against the appropriateness of carrying out the death penalty in public, but rather expressed embarrassment or discomfort: about the prolonged public exposure of the guillotine before or after the execution, about the presence of women and children at the place of execution, about the manifestations of drunkenness, contentment, or merely good humour. This sentiment started to appear on the pages of the daily press as early as the 1830s, at the day after the execution of Dominique Nys, which marked the return of capital execution in Belgium (De Brouwer 2009). This embarrassment would grow and become expressed more precisely in the years to come. The late 1830s saw the emergence of a series of negative stereotypes about the execution process that were common to all press accounts: the over-representation of women and children among the spectators, the eager curiosity of the crowd, and the signs of joy or drunkenness.

The manner in which capital execution took place during this period, and more particularly its installation in the heart of the city, was rejected by a part of the population. The representation of urban order spreading among the elite, is ill at ease with the behaviour of the lower classes which executions engender. The bourgeois population denounces the manifestations of indecency that accompany executions. It is not so much the principle of the public nature of the execution which is questioned, but rather the way in which it is carried out. There is little doubt that these citizens would be perfectly happy to see these executions taking place elsewhere. The bourgeoisie's major concern was to their district rid of an event that hurts its sensitivity (Bergman 2001; De Brouwer 2009).

However, whatever their disadvantages, the modalities of capital punishment remained set in law. Pending a revision of the 1810 Penal Code, article 26 remained applicable. The execution therefore had to take place 'at one of the public places of the town to be indicated in the sentence' (trans. JDB and XR). Hence, the most important challenge was to handle the requirement for the public nature of the execution in a way which, as far as possible, reconciled local complaints with compliance with article 26. In 1847, the Minister of Justice addressed the prosecutors-general, asking them to assess whether the sentence would be any less effective for being applied less publicly.[13] Following the example of other countries, the letter was meant to encourage the organisation of capital executions outside city centres, while still maintaining its public nature (Bergman 1996; Evans 1996; Foucault 1975; Franke 1985; Gatrell 1994; Martschukat 2000 and 2002). This displacement happened in Brussels a few months later. In February 1848, sentenced criminals Rosseel and Vandenplas were executed in front of the *Porte de Hal*,[14] at the outskirts of the city, and not on the *Grand Place*. However, the initiative of the Brussels authorities remained an isolated case. The Minister of

[13]Circulaire du ministre de la Justice adressée aux procureurs généraux près les cours d'appel (26 November 1847). *Recueil des circulaires, instructions et autres actes émanés du ministère de la Justice (...)*, series III, vol. I (1847–1849), p. 188. Brussels: Weissenbruch.

[14]See the contribution by Feyaerts in this volume.

Justice was obliged to address a new circular—more directive this time—to the prosecutors-general.[15]

The relocation of capital execution to a less frequented place, is one of the most tangible manifestations of the desire to ascertain a certain degree of 'de-publicisation' of the event. It was also complemented by other initiatives. In Brussels, from the 1840s onwards, various measures were taken to make executions 'more discrete': the press observed that the scaffold was transported to its destination and mounted during night-time, and also that the guillotine was removed immediately after the execution.

This process of reducing the public element also affected the convict's journey to the place of execution. The displacement of the place of execution had not necessarily decreased the duration of the journey. Some observers, including members of the Penal Code Review Commission, considered this to be an extra, moral form of suffering inflicted on the convicted person, whereas the sole punishment to be imposed was death. In their view, the journey elicited an unhealthy curiosity on the part of the population, and could even lead to manifestations of indecency. The solution the Commission proposed was simply to organise the execution in the prison yard in front of a selected audience. However, this solution was seen as an excessive reduction in publicity, and the Parliament preferred a less radical alternative: they chose to organising executions in one of the public places of the locality stated in the sentence, but rid the journey of its public nature by transporting the convicted person in a closed rather than an open vehicle (De Brouwer 2011 and 2014).

The increasing rarity of capital executions, their marginalisation in the urban space and the other measures meant to reduce their public nature turned execution into a less visible event. Moreover, the moment of putting to death was extremely brief. Consequently, the iconographic representation of the execution, and of the executed criminal, changed noticeably.

Up until the know, the research that has been carried out on this topic has produced only very meagre results. It has proven to be impossible to collect more than a very small number of iconographic representations of execution by guillotine, or of the executed persons. However, even this tiny sample allows us to formulate certain hypotheses. Representations can be divided into two categories: those that were essentially intended to communicate and inform, and those that reflected a more artistic approach. A first observation relates to the extreme brevity of the actual putting to death. This peculiarity forms an obstacle for the artist to represent this very precise moment. In this respect, the execution of Demeliez, as represented by Goetsbloets in 1796, is an exception (Fig. 17.7). Nevertheless, this exceptional case can be explained by a contextual peculiarity: the artist depicts the executioner beheading the condemned man with the aid of a sharp instrument, following a technical failure of the guillotine. The manual intervention of the

[15]Circulaire du ministre de la Justice adressée aux procureurs généraux près les cours d'appel (10 June 1848), *Recueil*, pp.188–189.

executioner, called in as a substitute for the defective machine, is an exceptional circumstance. This intervention of the executioner has an important consequence: the execution is exceptionally shown as a process that takes longer than it was normally supposed to since the use of the guillotine. It is precisely this feature that allows it to be represented. This particular case is the only one of its kind. None of the engravings or paintings collected from the following period, in whatever category, represents the putting to death itself, i.e. the separation of the convict's head from his body.

The first category of representations consists, in principle, of ad hoc printed material, generally referred to as broadsheets, published on the occasion of executions. Their publication is mentioned several times in the press reports, but research has brought to light only a very limited number of them. Intended for a broad audience, they generally consisted of a single sheet containing the main elements of the case—both the criminal facts and elements from the criminal court trials—in most cases in both French and Dutch and they are generally illustrated by a single image.

The first two images (Figs. 17.8 and 17.9) represent the execution of François Rosseel and Guillaume Vandenplas, which took place in front of the *Porte de Hal*, in February 1848. The third image (Fig. 17.10), simpler still and clumsily drawn, represents the execution of Jean-Baptiste Boucher and Auguste Leclercq (the two leaders of the *Entre-Sambre-et-Meuse* gang), which took place in March 1862 in Charleroi, on the *Place de la Ville-Haute* (Didier 2013).

As can be seen from these three illustrations, the execution is depicted in an extremely simplified form, with little or no background. The elements represented are the scaffold and the guillotine, as well as the figures deemed to be the most important: the condemned man (Fig. 17.10) or men (Figs. 17.8 and 17.9), one (Fig. 17.10) or more priests (Figs. 17.8 and 17.9), one (Fig. 17.10) or two (Fig. 17.8) *gendarmes* on horseback, and the executioner, accompanied by one of his assistants (Figs. 17.8, 17.9 and 17.10). The two illustrations depicting the execution of Rosseel and Vandenplas are distinguished from the third through the representation of other elements: the *char-a-bancs* in which the second condemned man is waiting, and (in Fig. 17.9) the silhouette of buildings surrounding the scaffold. It should be noted that the two engravings depicting the execution of Rosseel and Vandenplas accurately represent the two condemned men. However, this is not the case in the engraving representing the execution of Boucher and Leclercq, which depicts only one condemned man. In some cases, the engravings were probably prepared before the execution, to illustrate a broadsheet to appear on the morning of, or immediately after, the event. In the case of a trial ending in multiple death sentences, the public is unaware until the day of execution itself of exactly how many sentenced men will actually be executed. At the end of the *Entre-Sambre-et-Meuse* gang's trial, nine defendants were sentenced to death. Only two of them—Boucher and Leclercq—saw their petitions for commutation dismissed (Didier 2013). While the scaffold had been mounted during the night, the number of convicts to be executed would have been unknown until the morning itself. It is possible that, in the case of the execution of Boucher and Leclercq, the engraving was done before the news was known. It should be noted that certain representations had already been disseminated even before the petition for commutation could have been presented, i.e. several days or weeks before the execution the press actually reported on this phenomenon with regard to the execution of the *Entre-Sambre-et-Meuse* gang members.[16]

The simplicity of the illustrations we have just examined is in stark contrast with the representations of the heads of the guillotined men. While the scene of execution is very sketchily depicted, the guillotined head is represented with detail. This is the case for Pierre-François Breck, executed in Brussels in October 1847,[17] as well as—and above all—for Rosseel and Vandenplas (Fig. 17.12). This observation suggests that, given the impossibility of depicting the precise moment of the killing, the representation of the severed head, after death, forms the most meaningful representation of the execution. 'By referring to this here-and-now of the event, the portrait of the guillotined head has the incomparable merit of fixing the ultimate expression while permitting one to see close-up what one could scarcely make out from a distance' (Arasse 1987, trans. JDB and XR).

Moreover, the importance of the representation of the severed head was reflected in the public's interest in the face of the criminal. This was relayed in the press, even in those publications least suspected of 'sensationalism'. Thus we find full-page portraits of Rosseel and Vandenplas during their trial in *La Belgique judiciaire*, normally an unillustrated legal periodical (Fig. 17.11).

The medical and scientific spheres showed particular interest in the guillotined head and the facial features of the accused or condemned man. In Brussels, the heads of decapitated men were transported to one of the two city hospitals or to the university. The heads of the two Janssens brothers, and those of Rosseel and Vandenplas, underwent an experiment of 'galvanism', which was a procedure commonly applied to the heads of guillotined persons Europe from the early nineteenth century onwards.[18] Interest in the guillotined head was demonstrated in the Belgian territory as early as the 1820s, as shown by the preservation of the heads of Magonette and Gena, executed in Liège in 1821 (Vandevoir 1935).

---

[16]*La Meuse* (22 January 1862), two months before the execution of Boucher and Leclercq, signals the dissemination of an 'abominable paper' representing the execution. This also happened with the execution of the brothers Pierre-Joseph and Corneille Janssens (Brussels, 9 February 1847). *Le Précurseur* observes that 'yesterday morning, [the] public criers were selling outside the *Porte de Namur* printed placards announcing the execution of the Janssens and Rouffé brothers, as taking place in the morning. A crowd of peasants have purchased these posters and will take them and announce in the villages the death of these unfortunates, while the execution was not decided' (trans. JDB and XR).

[17]*Tête du fratricide P.-F. Breck*, [1851], Brussels, Royal Library, *Brochures relatives à la Belgique*, vol. XXXV.

[18]There is mention of the transportation of the heads of convicts Pierre-Joseph and Corneille Janssens, executed in Brussels on 9 February 1847, to the Université Libre de Bruxelles, where they were exhibited in the amphitheatre and subjected to an experiment with galvanic current (*Le Précurseur*, 10 February 1847). There is also a mention of the removal of the bodies of François Rosseel and Guillaume Vandenplas to the Université Libre de Bruxelles, and of their heads to the Saint-Jean hospital, where they would be subjected to experimentation with galvanic current.

The emergence of phrenology in the 1830s, which connected each mental function to a particular zone of the brain and studying the shapes of skulls, made the human head an object of systematic examination (Carol 2012; Renneville 2000). Beyond the advancement of science, phrenology was clearly quite popular with the general public. In one of the pamphlets published in the Evenepoel case, an observer, carefully examined the reliefs of the heads of Rosseel and Vandenplas (deposited at University after execution). Of the first head, he noticed the size of the 'destructiveness bumps'. With regard to the second one, he mentions 'the defect of the bumps to which phrenology relates the disposition to crime' (Fig. 17.12).[19] The heads of all persons guillotined in Brussels would have been examined at the university (Dubreucq 1996, p. 26).

The iconographic representation of executions by guillotine and of the executed were also a theme in the work of certain artists. The depiction of guillotined heads in nineteenth-century painting– especially by French artists—has been the subject of several studies (Boariu 2012 and 2015; Clair 2010; Hanselaar 2017). We can also find similar representations by Belgian artists (Boariu 2012 and 2015). Among them, Louis Gallait (1810–1887) and Antoine Wiertz (1806–1865), each treating the guillotined heads from a very different perspective, are of particular interest to us.

The work by Louis Gallait is a preparatory study. The guillotined man's head is represented not for its own sake, nor with reference to a contemporary event, but to be included potentially, with as much realism as possible, in one of the historical canvases on which Gallait built his reputation: the execution of the counts of Egmont and Hornes. Gallait did not want to paint the moment of the execution nor the relation between the condemned, the public and the authorities, but rather a more private moment that took place after the two men had been decapitated (Figs. 17.13 and 17.14).

In order to do so, the painter took steps to obtain the head of Rémy Bomal, sentenced to death by the Brabant *cour d'assises* on 27 February 1851. This was not easy, since the heads of men executed in Brussels were sent to university. The press mentions that the family, exceptionally, requested to obtain the condemned man's head.[20] It is very probable that Gallait contacted Bomal's family. Rather than competing with the university by asking for the judicial authorities' direct authorisation, this was undoubtedly the most obvious way for the painter to obtain the head he wished to sketch.

Gallait made an oil painting, with (in upper part) the inscription 'Rémy Bomal. 15 April 1851. Half an hour after the execution' (Le Bailly de Tilleghem 1987, trans. JDB and XR) (Fig. 17.13).[21] It would function as a preparatory study for one of his most important historical works, *The Last Honours given to Counts Egmont*

---

[19]*Assassinat de la place Saint-Géry. Procès, condamnation et exécution des nommés F. Rosseel et G. Vandenplas, condamnés par la Cour d'assises du Brabant, le 13 février 1848, à la peine de mort, convaincus d'avoir commis cet horrible assassinat*. s.d. Brussels: Imprimerie de Josse Sacré, Brussels, Royal Library, *Brochures relatives à la Belgique*, vol. IX.

[20]*La Gazette de Mons*, 17 April 1851.

[21]'*Rémy Bomal/ 15 avril 1851/ Une demi-heure après l'exécution*'.

and Hornes, also referred to as *Severed Heads* (Le Bailly de Tilleghem 1987) (Fig. 17.14).

Far removed from Gallait's point of view, Antoine Wiertz painted the guillotined head as a part of a contemporary event and as a way to take part in the contemporary debate about capital punishment. This perspective is obvious in his triptych *Thoughts and Visions of a Severed Head* (Fig. 17.15). Here, Wiertz is very clearly involved in the questioning of the death penalty since the appearance of the guillotine, by painting a 'composition that follows as closely as possible the clinical debate on the pain of decapitation and the faculty of perceiving it' (Boariu 2012, p. 191, trans. JDB and XR). Apparently, he wanted to show the suffering endured by the guillotined person during his execution. It is even said that Wiertz was not afraid of lying under the scaffold himself. (Potvin 1912; Watteau 1865).The first panel of the triptych, entitled *First Minute: On the Scaffold*, depicts the already severed man on the tilting board. The second panel, entitled *Second Minute: Under the Scaffold*, represents the body precipitated to the foot of the scaffold. The third panel finally, entitled *Third Minute: In Eternity*, represents the outcome of the condemned man's path: death. One of Wiertz's commentators points out that the idea of his painting supposedly came to the painter during the trial of Rosseel and Vandenplas (Watteau 1865).

Another painting by Wiertz, *A Severed Head* (1855), depicts a guillotined head placed on straw and being observed by three persons (Fig. 17.16). According to a commentator, it was painted 'from nature' (De Laveleye 1870).

Finally, Wiertz delivered a second *Severed Head* (Fig. 17.17), undoubtedly intended as a preparatory study. In it, he attempts to render, in an apparently rigorous manner, the expulsion of the blood as a result of the decapitation, as well as the flesh on the inside of the severed head

Wiertz' works are the result of an engaged point of view. By emphasising the suffering endured by the guillotined person after the moment of the separation of the head and the body, Wiertz seeks to make a contribution to the abolitionist debate. As he writes to one of his friends: 'Perhaps one day my painting will serve as an argument against the death penalty. I hope so' (Potvin 1912, trans. JDB and XR). The painter's intention is obvious in *Thoughts and Visions of a Severed Head*. The triptych appears here as the most appropriate means of expressing a sequence. This is underlined by the different title given to each panel. In this way, the painter makes the viewer see an execution as an event with a certain duration. Wiertz endeavours to contest, by painting, the instantaneousness of death by means of the guillotine. He overcomes the obstacle of the iconographic representation of an event of extreme brevity by the artifice of the sequence in a triptych. And in this way, he opposes the representation of the guillotine, cultivated by those defending its use in the name of humanity, as an instrument that makes it possible to ensure that the death penalty consists, as prescribed by the 1791 Penal Code, of nothing more than the deprivation of life.

17.6 Conclusion

The long-term analysis of representations of executions, regardless of who governed the country at the time, highlights their role as a collective ritual in the urban communities of the Ancien Régime, as well as their progressive withdrawal from the urban and cultural space of city dwellers during the nineteenth century.

Between 1450 and 1600, the growing number of executions in what is now Belgium, modelled by urban civilisation, leads to two phenomena. Firstly, a civic ritual of public executions comes into being. This ritual was polarised between the place of execution, which was at the heart of the urban space, and that of the exhibition of the corpses, at the limits of the jurisdiction. Between the two, two processions were organised: first the procession of the condemned individuals, and thereafter that of their dead bodies. This penal geography develops a spatial symbolism of the city as a place of social pacification, largely nurtured by an anthropological religious ritual (Terpstra 2008). At the same time, this ritual is supported by the development of representations of justice (judgment paintings). These depictions intended to 'dramatize' the place of justice and, with the rise of the printing press, mediate a highly schematic typology of executions centred on the stake, decapitation and hanging.

From 1600 onwards, the decline in the number of executions and their gradual replacement by penal confinement did not result in the end of such representations. These depictions show two types of executions used for particular crimes, although decapitation decreased in favour of hanging in a religious or urban setting. Transformed into scenes of miraculous relief in the seventeenth century, and even into genre scenes in the eighteenth, the representation of the treatment of the condemned persons, the authorities and the public became less harsh. The blood disappeared, the role of religious officers became more important, and the civil authorities as spectators seemed to share a consensus on the legitimacy and inevitability of the execution.

The annexation of the Low Countries and the Principality of Liège to France in 1795 brought about three major changes: the monopolization of public executions by the central authorities, the introduction of the guillotine as the standard, mechanical method of putting to death, and the concentration of public criminal rituals in the capital cities of the new *départements*. However, there was another element that was soon add to these changes: the execution ad an event became less visible in the public space. Not only were there fewer death sentences (due to the increasing number of royal pardons) but the public nature of the execution, prescribed by the Penal Code, was questioned, and executions gradually moved out of the public space. However, when the question of public execution within the city was submitted to Parliament, it was reaffirmed as a legitimisation of the death penalty, and more generally of the exercise of justice. The displacement of the execution to the inside of the prison compound was postponed. Thus, while the execution becomes *less* public, it still has to take place *in* public.

Whatever the evolution of the public nature of executions during the nineteenth century, since the French conquest, its representations focused on two material elements: the guillotine as an execution machine, and the heads of the executed persons. The iconographic representation of the executions was increasingly limited, at least when the entire scene is represented. The representations disseminated by the press and by broadsheets are archetypal, and contain four categories of actors: the condemned person, the priest, the executioner and the gendarme. The spectators are invisible and the urban environment is all but absent. The only thing that is presented in detail is the head of the guillotined man. Interest in the guillotined head is quite characteristic of the nineteenth century. Particularly noticeable after 1830, it finds its expression in experiments with galvanism and in phrenology, but also in the work of painters. However, this phenomenon is not entirely new.

The importance of the severed head as a representation of the punishing omnipotence was already evident in the paintings of Dierick Bouts (Judgment of Otto III, ca 1473–1475 (ca. 1410/1420–1475) or Hans Memling (Saint John Altar, ca 1479). In this respect, the representations of the heads of Egmont and Hornes and those of the nineteenth century executed criminals provide a certain continuity. Through its mechanical functioning, the guillotine does nothing more than systematise, in another form, an archaic mode of the representation of penal power.

While providing a continuity of representation, the guillotine also appears as the expression of a change in criminal justice in the nineteenth century. The punishment and its representation are directed towards the head, the seat of the mental faculties. During the same period, cell confinement became, alongside the guillotine, the ultimate punishment. Hence, it is in the brain that the seeds of crime lie, and it is in prison that surgery must take place to remove its evil.

From the public place to the prison yard, the moving execution away from the public sphere also resulted in a limiting of its depiction by images, etching, photography, or even cinematography. This was clearly the case in France. The reduction of the process of execution to the guillotine, and of the corpse to the severed head, corresponds to the transformation of a collective ritual into a mechanised and disembodied symbol.

References

Arasse D (1987) La guillotine et l'imaginaire de la Terreur. Flammarion, Paris

Arnade P (1996) Realms of ritual. Burgundian ceremony and civic life in late medieval Ghent Cornell University Press, Ithaca

Bastien P (2006) L'exécution publique à Paris au XVIIIe siècle. Une histoire des rituels judiciaires. Champ Vallon, Seyssel

Bergman M (1996) Dödstraffet, kyrkan och staten i Sverige från 1700-tal till 1900-tal. Nerenius & Santérus, Stockholm

Bergman M (2001) The penalty of death and executions: the tensions between national government, local authorities and population. In: Ågren M, Åsa K, Rousseaux X (eds) Guises

of power. Integration of society and legitimation of power in Sweden and the Southern Low Countries, ca. 1500–1900. University of Uppsala, Department of History, Uppsala, pp 91–108
Bethencourt F (1992) The auto da fé: ritual and imagery. J Warbg Court Inst 55:155–168
Blok A (1989) The symbolic vocabulary of public executions. In: Starr J, Collier JF (eds) History and power in the study of law: new directions in legal anthropology. Cornell University Press, Ithaca (NY), pp 31–54
Boariu D-A (2012) L'arrière-douleur. Peinture et décapitation au XIXe siècle. In: Baudoin S, Bricault C, Hadeh M (eds) Représentations littéraires et picturales de la douleur du XIXe au XXIe siècle. Actes du colloque coordonné par Makki Rebai. Presses Universitaires Blaise Pascal, Clermont-Ferrand, pp 181–197
Boariu, D-A (2015) La tête coupée. Clinique et peinture de la décapitation au XIXe siècle, unpubl. PhD thesis, University of Fribourg
Boes MR (2013) Crime and punishment in early modern Germany: courts and adjudicatory practices in Frankfurt am main, 1562–1696. Ashgate, Farnham
Boomgaard J (1992) Misdaad en straf in Amsterdam. Een onderzoek naar de strafrechtspleging van de Amsterdamse schepenbank 1490–1552. Waanders, Zwolle
Brown A (2007) Court and civic society in the Burgundian Low Countries, c.1420–1530. Manchester University Press, Manchester
Carol A (2012) Physiologie de la veuve. Une histoire médicale de la guillotine. Champ Vallon, Seyssel
Clair J (ed) (2010) Crime et châtiment. Musée d'Orsay & Gallimard, Paris
Cohen E (1989) Symbols of culpability and the universal language of justice: the ritual of public executions in late medieval Europe. Hist Eur Ideas 11:407–416
Dauwe J, Monballyu J (eds) (1981) Joos de Damhouder, Practycke ende handbouck in criminele zaeken, verchiert met zommeghe schoone figuren ende beilden ter materie dienende, Anastatische herdruk naar de editie Leuven 1555. Den Wijngaert, Roeselare
De Brouwer J (2005a) En marge de la cité, en marge de la justice: le bourreau dans la province de Brabant (1810–1867). In: Dolan C (ed) Entre justice et justiciables: les auxiliaires de la justice du Moyen Âge au XXe siècle. Presses de l'Université Laval, Québec, pp 261–276
De Brouwer J (2005b) Statistique et peine de mort en Belgique (1795–1875): grandeur et servitude du chiffre. In: Vesentini F (ed) Les chiffres du crime en débat. Regards croisés sur la statistique pénale en Belgique (1830–2005). Academia-Bruylant, Louvain-la-Neuve, pp 253–277
De Brouwer J (2009) « Un peuple civilisé n'use du dernier supplice qu'avec répugnance… ». La peine de mort en Belgique au 19e siècle, unpubl. PhD thesis, Université catholique de Louvain
De Brouwer J (2011) Répondre aux exigences de l'ordre et de la moralité publique? La dépublicisation de l'exécution capitale (Belgique, 19e siècle). Annales de droit de Louvain 71 (2):97–111
De Brouwer J (2014) La résistance au processus de dépublicisation de la peine capitale en Belgique au XIXe siècle. In: Bastien P, Fyson D, Garneau J-P, Nootens T (eds) Justice et espaces publics en Occident, du Moyen Âge à nos jours. Presses Universitaires du Québec, Montréal, pp 99–122
De Coene K, Ongena T, Stragier F, Vervust S, Bracke W, De Maeyer P (2012) Ferraris, the legend. Cartogr J 49(1):30–42
De Laveleye E (1870) Catalogue du Musée Wiertz. Parent et fils, Brussels
Demaret N (2016) Le bourreau: icône de la haute justice. Le maître des hautes œuvres, la torture et les exécutions criminelles dans deux principautés en mutation: Hainaut et Brabant (ca. 1350-ca. 1570), unpubl. PhD thesis, Université catholique de Louvain
Deseure B (2014) Onhoudbaar verleden. Geschiedenis als politiek instrument tijdens de Franse periode in België. Leuven University Press, Leuven
De Win P (1991) Terechtstelling. In: Van der Stock J (ed) Stad in Vlaanderen: cultuur en maatschappij, 1477–1787. Gemeentekrediet, Brussels, p 344
De Win P (1992a) Rechtsarcheologie en rechtsiconografie in België. Ter illustratie: De rechtsarcheologische en rechtsiconografische rijkdom van de stad Brugge. In: De Win P

(ed) Rechtsarcheologie en rechtsiconografie: een kennismaking. Koninklijke Vlaamse Academie van België, Brussels, pp 101–136
De Win P (1992b) De kaakstraf in België van de Franse Tijd tot 1867. Koninklijke Vlaamse Academie van België, Brussels
D'Hainaut-Zvény B (2005) Tijdsgebeurtenissen, le manuscrit de Pierre-Antoine-Joseph Goetsbloets (1793–1797), (10 vol.). Notice sur ce manuscrit inédit. In: Cent Trésors de la Bibliothèque royale de Belgique. Mercator Fund, Antwerp, pp 75–76
Didier L (2013) La Bande noire (1855–1862), Le banditisme dans l'Entre-Sambre-et-Meuse et ses liens avec l'affaire Coucke et Goethals. Presses Universitaires de Louvain, Louvain-la-Neuve
Dubreucq J (1996) Bruxelles 1000, une histoire capitale. Vol. 1: Section des Sablons, s.n, Brussels
Dufrasne J (2014) Les gravures de la Praxis rerum criminalium de Jos de Damhouder: la représentation de la justice pénale du XVIe siècle à partir du programme iconographique de l'oeuvre (1554–1618), unpubl. MA thesis (History), Université catholique de Louvain
Dufrasne J (2015) Les gravures dans l'oeuvre du juriste Jos de Damhouder (1554–1618). Représentation de la violence dans un manuel juridique illustré, Louvain-la-Neuve, 2015. Unpublished MA in Art History. Université catholique de Louvain
Edgerton S (1985) Pictures and punishment. Art and criminal prosecution during the florentine Renaissance. Cornell University Press, Ithaca (NY)
Evans RJ (1996) Rituals of retribution: capital punishment in Germany, 1600–1987. Oxford University Press, Oxford
Everaert D (2005) Het verhaal achter het gerechtsschilderijtje van Jan Garemijn. Brugs Ommeland 2005(3):174–180
Follain A, Papillard CA (2015) Figures du crime et de la violence au XVIe siècle: les singulières gravures insérées dans la Praxis rerum criminalium de Damhoudère. In: Follain A (ed) Brutes ou braves gens? La violence et sa mesure (XVIe–XVIIIe siècle). Strasbourg, Presses Universitaires de Strasbourg, pp 37–41
Foucault M (1975) Surveiller et punir. Naissance de la prison. Gallimard, Paris
Franke H (1985) De dood in het leven van alledag. Rouwadvertenties en openbare strafvoltrekkingen in Nederland. Nijgh & Van Ditmar, The Hague
Friedland P (2012) Seeing justice done: the age of spectacular capital punishment in France. Oxford University Press, Oxford
Gatrell VAC (1994) The hanging tree: execution and the english people, 1770–1868. Oxford University Press, Oxford
Gerlache J (1914) Le bourreau de Bruxelles. Émile Kumps, Brussels
Goffman E (1963) Behavior in Public Places. Notes on the Social Organization of Gatherings. Free Press of Glencoe, New York
Goosens A (1997–1998) Les Inquisitions modernes dans les Pays-Bas méridionaux (1520–1633). Université de Bruxelles, Brussels
Gyger P (1998) L'épée et la corde: Criminalité et justice à Fribourg (1475–1505). Université de Lausanne, Lausanne
Gyselen G (1958) Schilderijen in het Gerechtshof te Brugge. Handelingen van het Genootschap voor Geschiedenis 95:25–58
Handelman D (1998) Models and mirrors: towards an anthropology of public events. Berghahn Books, New York
Hanselaar S (2017) Edification et peinture d'histoire: des limites à la représentation du criminel et du fait divers dans le premier 19e siècle. Tétrade. Revue du Centre de recherche en arts et esthétique 4:45–53
Harbison C (1975) The Last Judgment in sixteenth century Northern Europe, a study in the relation between art and the Reformation. Garland, New York
Hofman E (2017) The tears of a killer. Criminal trials and sentimentalism in the Austrian Netherlands. Low Ctries Hist Rev 132(2):3–26
Huygebaert S, Martyn G, Paumen V, Van Poucke T (eds) (2016) The art of law. Three centuries of justice depicted (exh. cat. Bruges). Lannoo, Tielt

Jacob R (1994) Images de justice. Essai sur l'iconographie judiciaire du Moyen Âge à l'âge classique. Le Léopard d'Or, Paris

Klemettilä H (2006) Epitome of evil. Representations of executioners in Northern France and the Low Countries in the Late Middle Ages. Brepols, Turnhout

Lambert SW (1952) The initial letters of the anatomical treatise *De humani corporis fabrica* of Vesalius. In: Three Vesalian essays to accompany the Icones Anatomicae of 1934. Macmillan, New York, pp 3–24

Le Bailly de Tilleghem S (1987). Louis Gallait, 1810–1887. La gloire d'un romantique. Crédit communal, Brussels

Lecuppre-Desjardins E (2004) Vade mecum. La ville des cérémonies. Essai sur la communication politique dans les anciens Pays-Bas bourguignons. Brepols, Turnhout

Lederle U (1937) Gerechtigkeitsdarstellungen in deutschen und niederländischen Rathäusern. Kruse, Philippsburg

Martschukat J (2000) Inzseniertes Töten. Eine Geschichte der Todesstrafe vom 17. bis zum 19. Jahrhundert. Bölhau, Cologne

Martschukat J (2002) Die Geschichte der Todesstrafe in Nordamerika. Von der Kolonialzeit bis zur Gegenwart. Beck, Munich

Merback MB (2001) The thief, the cross and the wheel: pain and the spectacle of punishment in medieval and renaissance Europe. Reaktion Books, London

Mills R (2005) Suspended animation. Pain, pleasure and punishment in medieval culture. Reaktion Books, London

Mitchell WJT (1994) Picture theory: essays on verbal and visual representation. University of Chicago Press, Chicago

Mitchell WJT (1999) Iconology. Image, text, ideology. University of Chicago Press, Chicago

Mitchell WJT (2015) Image science: iconology, visual culture and media aesthetics. University of Chicago Press, Chicago

Monballyu J (2016) Joos de Damhouder, an internationally influential jurist from Bruges. In: Huygebaert et al (eds), pp 107–117

Montignie N, De la Croix M (2015) La carte de Ferraris: étude des lieux de justice sur la carte de cabinet et dans les mémoires, unpubl. paper Université catholique de Louvain

Musin A (2017) Sociabilité urbaine et criminalisation étatique. La justice namuroise face à la violence de 1360 à 1555. Brepols, Turnhout

Potvin J (1912) Antoine Wiertz, l'époque, l'homme, l'œuvre. F. De Nobele, Brussels

Rebecchini G (2013) Rituals of justice and the construction of space in sixteenth-century Rome. I Tatti Stud Ital Renaiss 16(1–2):153–179

Renneville M (2000) Le langage des crânes. Une histoire de la phrénologie. Institut d'édition Sanofi-Interlabo, Paris

Robert C-N (1996) La justice dans ses décors (XVe-XVIe siècles). Droz, Genève

Rousseaux X (1997) Doctrines criminelles, pratiques pénales, projets politiques : le cas des possessions habsbourgeoises (1750–1790). In: Michel P (ed) Cesare Beccaria (1738–1794) et la culture juridique des Lumières. Actes du colloque européen de Genève, 25–26 November 1994. Droz, Genève, pp 223–252

Rousseaux X (2012) De la « bonne justiche » à la « honteuse execution » à Nivelles. Réflexions sur la matérialité de l'exécution publique des sanctions (1350–1550). In: Porret M, Fontana V, Maugué L (eds) Bois, fers et papiers de justice. Histoire matérielle du droit de punir. Georg, Genève, pp 167–188

Schild W (1980) Alte Gerichtsbarkeit. Vom Gottesurteil bis zum Beginn der modernen Rechtsprechung. Callwey, Munich

Silverman L (2001) Tortured subjects: pain, truth, and the body in early modern France. University of Chicago Press, Chicago

Spierenburg P (1984) The spectacle of suffering: executions and the evolution of repression from a preindustrial metropolis to the European experience. Cambridge University Press, Cambridge

Spierenburg P (1991) The prison experience: disciplinary institutions and their inmates in early modern Europe. Rutgers, New Brunswick

Spierenburg P (2013) Violence and punishment: civilizing the body through time. Cambridge University Press, Cambridge
Stuart K (2000) Defiled outcasts. Honor and ritual pollution in early modern Germany. Cambridge University Press, Cambridge
Terpstra N (2008) The art of executing well. Rituals of execution in renaissance Italy. Truman State University Press, Kirksville (MO)
Vancauwenberghe A (2003) Le dessin Justicia de Pierre Bruegel l'Ancien (1559) Revue des Archéologues, historiens d'art et musicologues de l'UCL 1:31–45
Van der Kooij J (2012) In het theater van sententie. Pieter Spierenburgs 'mentaliteitsverandering' in executiegrafiek, unpubl. paper University of Amsterdam
Van der Sanden W, Luning H (eds) (2010) Over galg en rad. Executieplaatsen in Drenthe. Waanders, Zwolle
Vandevoir W (1935) Magonette et Gena: les brigands ardennais, d'après les documents officiels et les légendes locales. Steinmetz et fils, Remouchamps
Van Dülmen R (1990) Theatre of horror: crime and punishment in early modern Germany. Polity Press, Cambridge
Verheyden ALE (1961) Le Conseil des Troubles. Liste des condamnés (1567–1573). Académie Royale de Belgique (Commission Royale d'Histoire), Brussels
Vermeersch M (2014) Terechstellingtafereel voor het Landhuis van het Brugse Vrije. Pro Memorie 16:66–75
Vermeersch M (2016) Execution on Burg Square. In: Huygebaert et al (eds) 2016, pp 124–126
Voges R (2016) Power, faith, and pictures. Frans Hogenberg's account of the Beeldenstorm. Low Ctries Hist Rev 131:121–140
Ward R (2015) A global history of execution and the criminal corpse. Palgrave, Basingstoke
Watteau L (1865) Catalogue raisonné du Musée Wiertz précédé d'une biographie du peintre. Louis Watteau, Brussels
Weber M (2015) Rationalism and modern society (Waters T, Waters D, trans). Palgrave, London
Wilf S (1993) Imagining justice: aesthetics and public executions in late eighteenth-century England. Yale J Law Humanit 5(1):51–78

Jérôme de Brouwer is lawyer (1997) and historian (1999), Université catholique de Louvain. He has defended his Ph.D. dissertation on the history of death penalty in Belgium in nineteenth century. He is currently assistant professor at the Law Faculty, Free University of Brussels (ULB) and director of the Center for Legal history and Legal anthropology. His research activities on the history of law and justice are focused on nineteenth and twentieth century in Belgium and are organised along three main axes: the evolution of penal codifications, the publicity of justice execution, the representations of judiciary activities and the development of legal education.

Xavier Rousseaux is research director (FRS-FNRS), and professor at the Université catholique de Louvain, Centre d'histoire du droit et de la justice. Working extensively on the history of crime and justice, he is coordinating the IAP Justice and Populations. The Belgian experience in international Perspective, 1795–1950. He co-edited with M. De Koster and D. Heirbaut *Tweehonderd Jaar Justitie. Historische Encyclopedie van de Belgische Justitie, Deux siècles de justice belge. Encyclopédie historique de la justice belge* (Bruges, La Charte-Die Keure, 2015) and with A. Hondeghem and F. Schoenaers *Modernisation of the Criminal Justice Chain and the Judicial System. New Insights on Trust, Cooperation and Human Capital* (Springer, 2015).

Figures

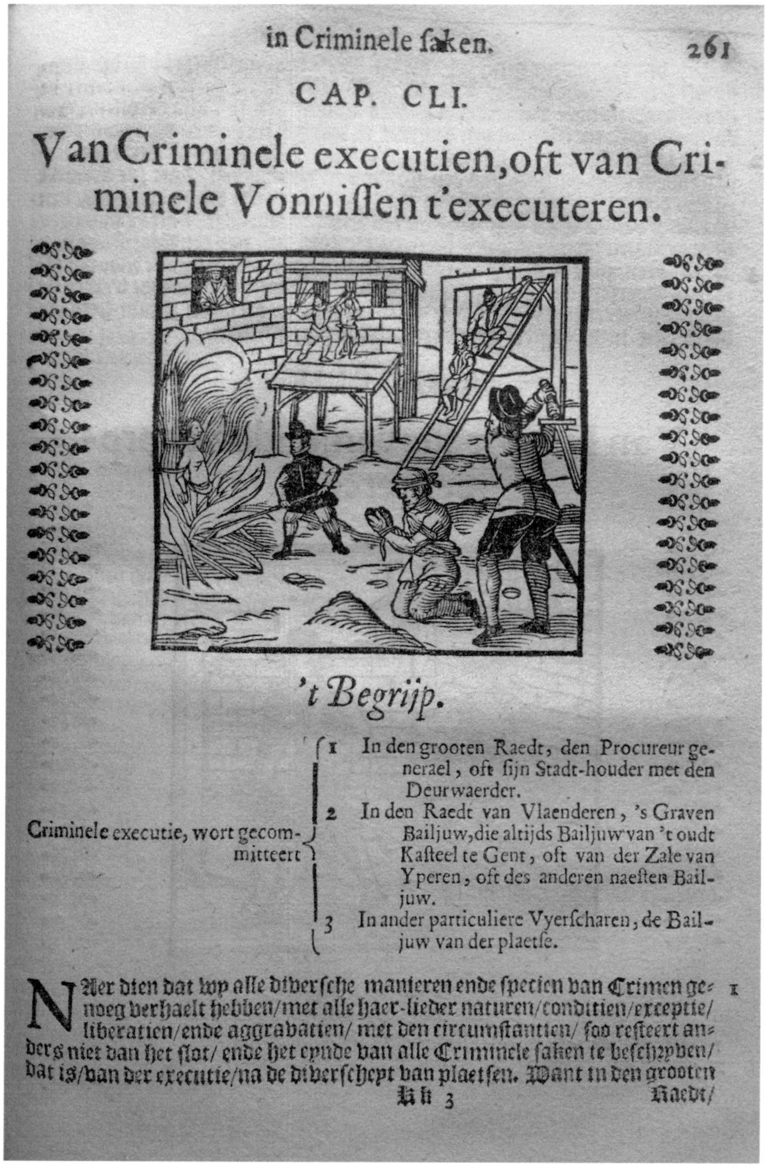
in Criminele ſaken. 261

CAP. CLI.

Van Criminele executien, oft van Criminele Vonniſſen t'executeren.

't Begrijp.

Criminele executie, wort gecommitteert

1 In den grooten Raedt, den Procureur generael, oft ſijn Stadt-houder met den Deurwaerder.

2 In den Raedt van Vlaenderen, 's Graven Bailjuw, die altijds Bailjuw van 't oudt Kaſteel te Gent, oft van der Zale van Yperen, oft des anderen naeſten Bailjuw.

3 In ander particuliere Vyerſcharen, de Bailjuw van der plaetſe.

Naer dien dat wy alle diverſche manieren ende ſpecien van Crimen genoeg verhaelt hebben/met alle haer-lieder naturen/conditien/exceptie/ 1
liberatien/ende aggravatien/ met den circumſtantien/ ſoo reſteert anders niet dan het ſlot/ ende het eynde van alle Criminele ſaken te beſchryven/ dat is/van der executie/na de diverſcheyt van plaetſen. Want in den grooten

Kk 3 Raedt/

Fig. 17.1 First page of chapter 151 on executions in De Damhouder, Joost. 1660. *Practycke in criminele saken*. Rotterdam: Pieter van Waesberge, © Private collection GM, Belgium

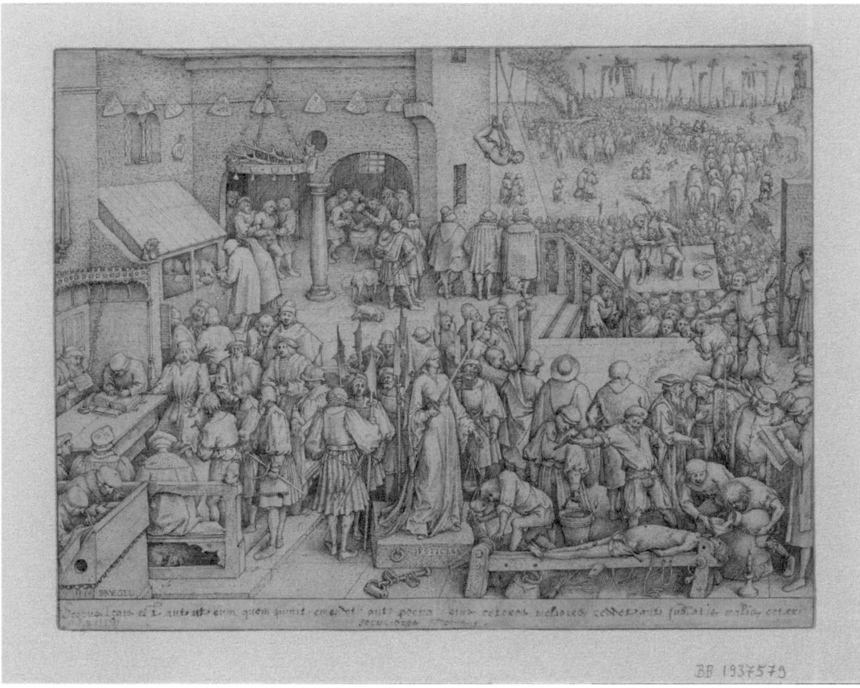

Fig. 17.2 Pieter Bruegel the Elder, *Justitia*, from the series *The Seven Virtues*, ca. 1559, drawing, pen and brown ink, 22.5 × 29.5 cm, © Brussels, Royal Library

Fig. 17.3 Frans Hogenberg, *The Executions of Counts Egmont and Hornes* (in *Frederik Muller Historieplaten*), © Rijksmuseum, Amsterdam

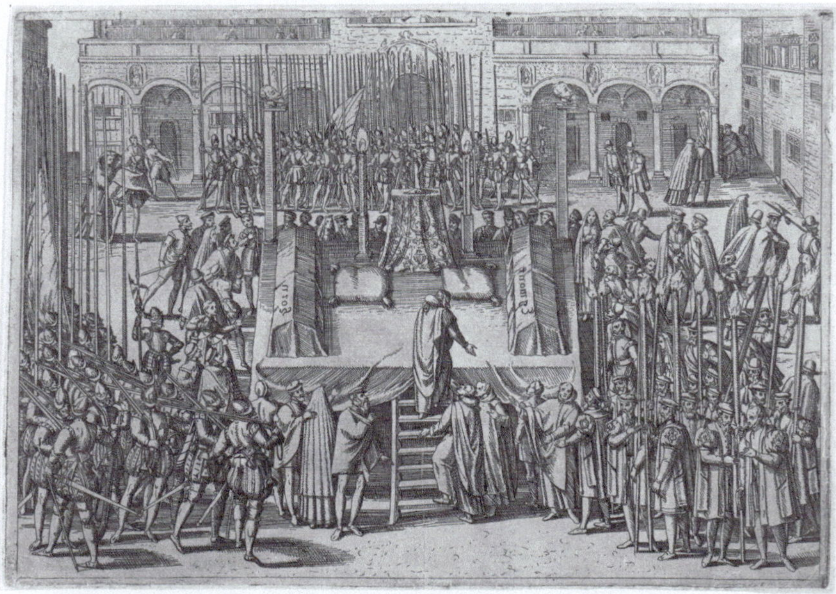

Fig. 17.4 Frans Hogenberg, *The Executions of Counts Egmont and Hornes*, 1568, *Frederik Muller Historieplaten*, © Rijksmuseum, Amsterdam

Fig. 17.5 Anonymous, *Our Lady of Halle Saving a Hanged Man*, ca. 1600–1650, 108.5 × 83 cm, Halle, Saint Martin's Church © Sint Martinus Kerk, Halle (Belgium)

Fig. 17.6 Jan Anton Garemijn (attributed to), *The Execution of Joseph Mesure in front of the Manor of the Brugse Vrije*, 1767, oil on canvas, 120 × 85 cm, Bruges Museum Brugse Vrije, © www.lukasweb.be—Art in Flanders vzw, photo Dominique Provost

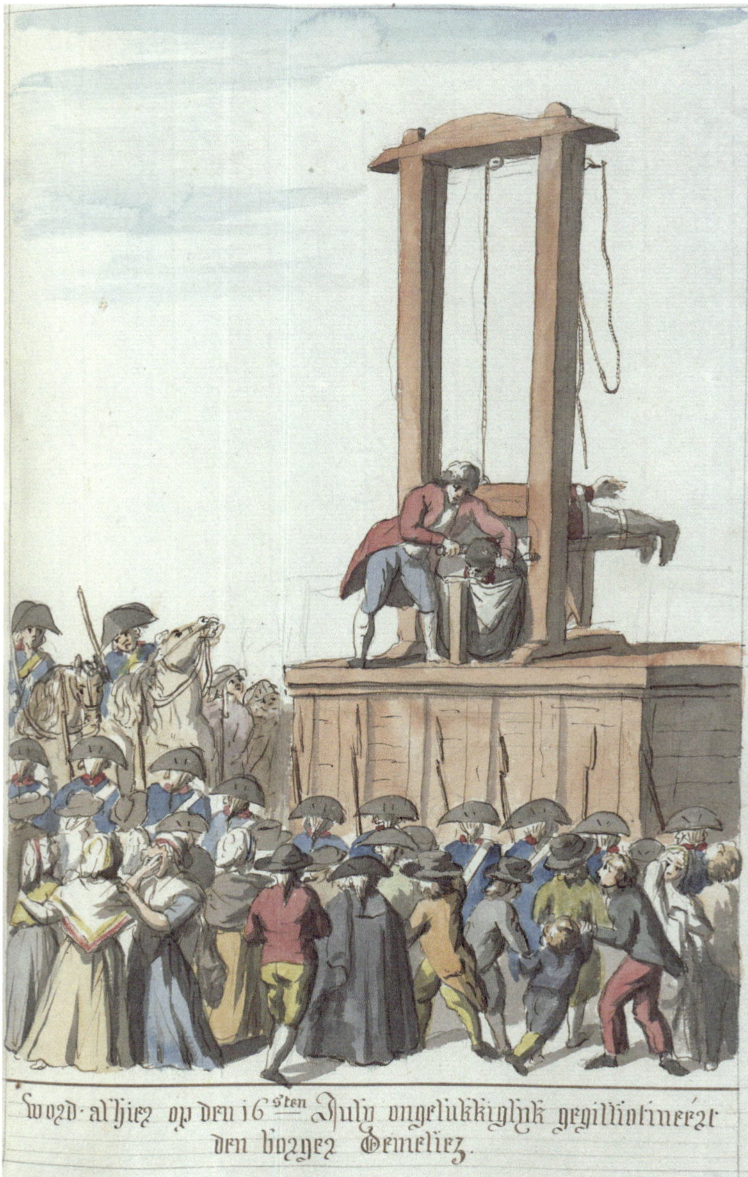

Fig. 17.7 P.A.J. Goetsbloets *The execution of Henri Demeslier, in: Tijdsgebeurtenissen*, 1796, Brussels, Royal Library © Royal Library, Brussels

Fig. 17.8 Execution of Rosseel and Vandenplas (broadsheet detail), in-folio, Imprimerie Gambin, Brussels, Royal Library, *Brochures relatives à la Belgique*, vol. XXXIX. © Royal Library, Brussels

Fig. 17.9 *Assassinat de la Place Saint-Géry. Procès, condamnation et exécution des nommés F. Rosseel et G. Vandenplas* (broadsheet detail), in- 8°, Brussels, Royal Library, Brochures relatives à la Belgique, vol. XL. © Royal Library, Brussels

Fig. 17.10 Execution of Boucher and Leclercq (broadsheet detail), 42 × 17 cm, Imprimerie d'Alphonse Deghistelle, Musée de Cerfontaine, Cerfontaine © Musée de Cerfontaine, Cerfontaine

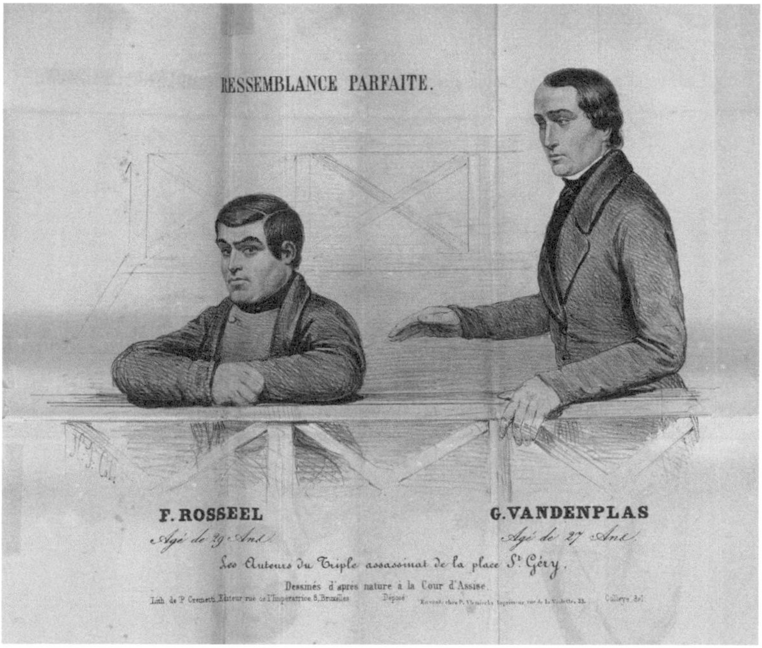

Fig. 17.11 Portraits of Rosseel and Vandenplas, *La Belgique judiciaire*, 1848 © Centre d'histoire du droit et d'anthropologie juridique (ULB), Brussels

Fig. 17.12 Heads of Rosseel & Vandenplas, in: *Assassinat de la place Saint-Géry. Procès, condamnation et exécution des nommés F. Rosseel et G. Vandenplas, condamnés par la Cour d'assises du Brabant, le 13 février 1848, à la peine de mort, convaincus d'avoir commis cet horrible assassinat*. s.d. Brussels: Imprimerie de Josse Sacré, Brussels, Royal Library, Brochures relatives à la Belgique, vol. XL. © Royal Library, Brussels

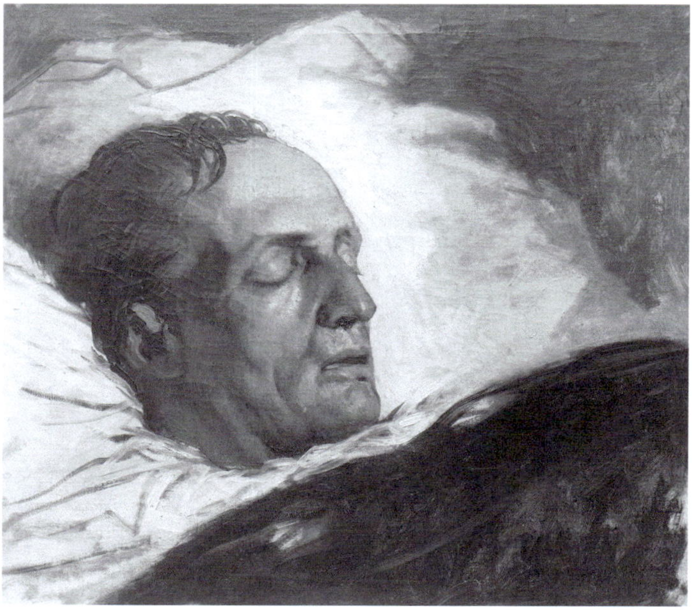

Fig. 17.13 Louis Gallait, *Study of a head for 'The Last Honours given to Counts Egmont and Hornes'*, 1851, oil on canvas, 55.5 × 64.5 cm, Brussels, Royal Museums of Fine Arts of Belgium. ©KIK-IRPA, Bruxelles

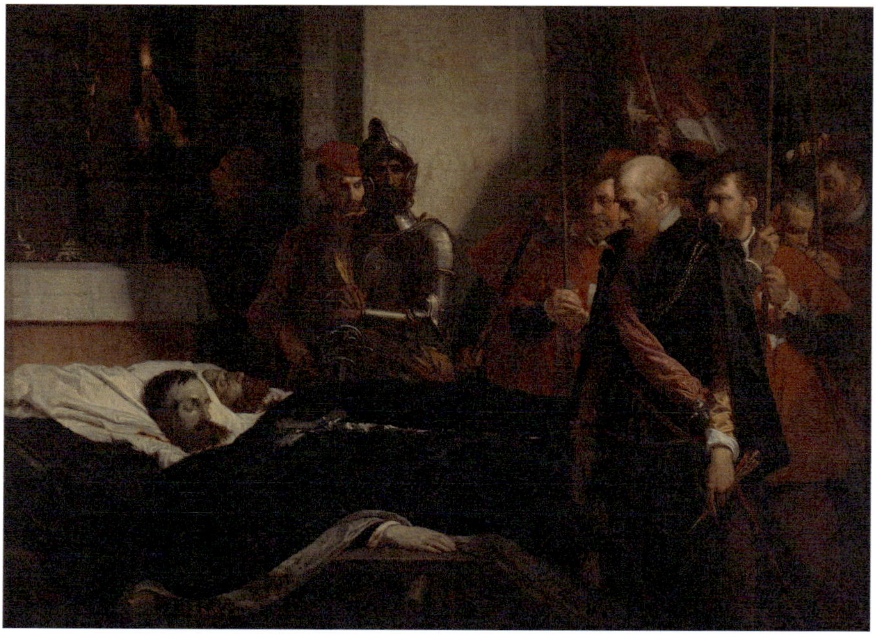

Fig. 17.14 Louis Gallait, *The Last Honours given to Counts Egmont and Hornes*, 1851, oil on wood, 35.5 × 50.5 cm, Brussels, Royal Museums of Fine Arts of Belgium © Royal Museums of Fine Arts of Belgium, Brussels/photo: J. Geleyns—Art Photography

Fig. 17.15 Antoine Wiertz, *Thoughts and Visions of a Severed Head, oil on canvas*, 70 × 265 cm, 1853, Brussels, Royal Museums of Fine Arts of Belgium (Wiertz Museum). © Royal Museums of Fine Arts of Belgium, Brussels/photo: J. Geleyns—Art Photography

Fig. 17.16 Antoine Wiertz, *Severed Head*, oil on paper, 43 × 55 cm, 1855, Brussels, Royal Museums of Fine Arts of Belgium (Wiertz Museum). © Royal Museums of Fine Arts of Belgium, Brussels/photo: J. Geleyns—Art Photography

Fig. 17.17 Antoine Wiertz, *Severed Head*, oil on paper, 23.5 × 33 cm, s.d., Brussels, Royal Museums of Fine Arts of Belgium (Wiertz Museum). © Royal Museums of Fine Arts of Belgium, Brussels/photo: J. Geleyns—Art Photography

Part V
Justice Architecture and Decorations in the Long Nineteenth Century

Chapter 18
Joseph-Jonas Dumont's Prison Gatehouses: *Architecture Parlante* in Neo-Tudor Style

Jozefien Feyaerts

Abstract Between 1850 and 1919, nearly thirty new cellular prisons were built in Belgium to facilitate the strictly cellular regime. Joseph-Jonas Dumont (1811–1859), Belgium's most important prison architect in the first decade(s) of the cellular building campaign, introduced the English neo-Tudor style in his prison designs. This paper explores the underlying motives and meanings of his stylistic choice.

18.1 The 'Ducpétiaux Prison': More than Ducpétiaux

Between 1850 and 1919, nearly thirty new cellular prisons were built in Belgium to facilitate the strictly cellular regime. Édouard Ducpétiaux (1804–1868), appointed General Inspector of prisons after the Belgian independence, had advocated the implementation of this new regime in the wake of an international prison reform movement (Maes 2009).

With the aim of moral improvement, prisoners were incarcerated night and day in a single cell. Radically countering the hitherto prevalent community regime, the specific spatial requirements of the cellular regime demanded a thorough makeover of the outdated infrastructure. Anno 1850 most Belgian prisons in use were not originally designed to accommodate detainees, as they were often established in confiscated monasteries and obsolete city gates. An initially gradual adaptation of some institutions ultimately led to a large-scale construction campaign for radial

This paper is part of my doctoral research *Design and construction of the cellular prison in Belgium (1830-WWI)*, Ghent University.

J. Feyaerts (✉)
Department of Art History, Ghent University, Ghent, Belgium
e-mail: Jozefien.Feyaerts@UGent.be

S. Huygebaert et al. (eds.), *The Art of Law*, Ius Gentium: Comparative Perspectives on Law and Justice 66, https://doi.org/10.1007/978-3-319-90787-1_18

cellular prisons to the Anglo-Saxon model.[1] Both because of the rigorous implementation of the cellular regime and because of the deployment of a completely new prison infrastructure throughout its territory in just a few decades, Belgium attained a solid penitentiary reputation abroad (Maes 2009, p. 203).

Prison historiography traditionally ascribes a leading role to Ducpétiaux in the success of the star-shaped penitentiary in Belgium.[2] The common use of his name as an epithet when referring to this typology, affirms this narrative even more. Leuven Central Prison (1860), for instance, is considered Belgium's most prototypical 'Ducpétiaux-prison' (Fig. 18.1). The radial and cellular concept indeed was quintessential for prison reformers, as it was the tangible expression of the solitary regime. Nonetheless, the penal concept alone does not determine the design of the prison. Other fundamental components are: building techniques (heating, lighting, ventilation and sanitation), necessitated by an increased concern for health (Nys et al. 2002); the technical and architectural concretisation of all program requirements; and the stylistic design. Hence, the realisation of the 'Ducpétiaux prison' involved various contributors—not the least the prison architect—that have been undervalued in the (thus far fairly limited) historiography of the Belgian prison system.

18.2 Neo-Tudor: A Historical Style for a New Prison Type

More than half of Belgium's nineteenth-century cellular patrimony is the work of only two architects. Joseph-Jonas Dumont (1811–1859) was considered the pre-eminent prison architect in the 1840s and 1850s. After his death in 1859, his collaborator François Derre (1826–1888)[3] finished the on-going projects and made a name for himself as a prison expert in the following decade.

[1]The prison of Tongeren was the first one in Belgium to be adapted to the cellular regime, through a renovation in 1844. In 1850, a new cell quarter for women was opened in the Brussels *Prison des Petits Carmes* (Fig. 18.4). In the same year, a cellular prison in Liège (Fig. 18.2) and a small one in Marche-en-Famenne were built. In the Bruges new cell quarter adjacent to the Bruges prison *'t Pandreitje* (1851), the cell wings were arranged in a radial plan for the first time. Except for Verviers (1853), the radial type would further develop and spread throughout Belgium: Dinant (1853), Charleroi (1854), Kortrijk (1856), Antwerp (1857), Hasselt (1859), Leuven Central Prison (1860, Figs. 18.1 and 18.6), Ghent (1862), Dendermonde (1863), Mons (1867), Leuven Auxiliary Prison (1869), Arlon (1870), Tournai (1871), Huy (1872), Malines (1874), Neufchâteau (1875), Veurne (1876), Ieper (1876), Namur (1876), Saint-Gilles (1885, Fig. 18.3), Verviers (1891), Nivelles (1903), Turnhout (1908), Forest (1910) and Oudenaarde (1919) (Maes 2009, pp. 200–201, verified and corrected, based on research in a.o. the State Archives in Brussels).

[2]This is however considered problematic by Vanhulle (2010, p. 180–182), who claims that this unilateral focus is the result of an image created and cultivated by Ducpétiaux himself. It moreover improperly reduces Belgian prison history to a handful of protagonists.

[3]The primary sources and literature do not provide conclusive information on the correct spelling (Derre/Derré) and date of birth and death. I base myself on Thieme et al. (1999, vol. IX, p. 100) and Van Loo et al. (2003, p. 290).

The rigid spatial and hygiene requirements of the new prison system drew the architect to indulge his creativity on the stylistic, rather than on the programmatic plane. In particular the prison gatehouse was well-suited to showcase architectural craftsmanship. It is not surprising then that Dumont, who had established not only a reputation of prison-architect expert but also of pioneer of the gothic revival style in Belgian architecture (e.g. the Ixelles Saint Boniface church, *cf.* infra), adopted the neo-Tudor style to adorn the radical new typology of the cellular prison. Or is it?

Identifying a style as 'neo-' or 'revival' implies the re-use of features of a historic style. Especially in the nineteenth century this was a widespread architectural practice (Haslinghuis and Janse 2005, p. 337). Neo-Tudor or Tudor revival, as part of the broader gothic revival movement, refers to the re-use of elements from the English domestic architecture of the early sixteenth century. In particular in the context of this paper, neo-Tudor refers to the idiom of Henry VIII's building works, including Hampton Court. This Tudor idiom is characterised by the use of brick and military elements such as battlements, and grafts Italian detailing on a largely gothic structure (Clark and Clark 2001; Stratton 1946, pp. 5–11).

The neo-Tudor style of Belgian prison gatehouses has been abundantly explained by architectural historians as a reference to the intimidating and impregnable medieval castle (De Keyser et al. 1997; Van Cleven 1996; Vandenbreeden et al. 1994; Vandendaele et al. 1980). This paper wants to present a more extensive and nuanced reading of Dumont's stylistic choices (Figs. 18.2 and 18.3).

The scientific approach of art history granted the concept of 'style' a different meaning in nineteenth-century architecture historical discourse. No longer would it refer to the personal signature of the artist, as it did in the eighteenth century. Instead, it related to a chronological and formal classification of art and architecture, raising the question in what style to build (Schoonjans 2007, pp. 159–162). Architectural historian Yves Schoonjans states that this nineteenth-century science not only defined a multitude of styles based on a shared iconography, but, moreover, linked this iconography to an iconology: 'The nineteenth-century concept of style was more than a method to classify the historical plurality and diversity; it could also detect societal significance in artistic design' (Schoonjans 2007, pp. 162–164, trans. JF). Schoonjans refers to the 'national character' some styles are attributed, but also to the ability of style to make architecture 'readable' and to evoke associations. He considers style the language that grants architecture a narrative character (Schoonjans 2007, pp. 164–166), and emphasizes the function of architecture as a medium of communication: 'The nineteenth-century architect's interest in architectural history lies mainly in the connection of form and sentiment. The history of architecture is regarded as a reservoir of different recognizable styles, hence characters that can be incorporated in his own designs. (…) Style is not a matter of personal architectural preference, but of societal encodings' (Schoonjans 2007, pp. 194–196, trans. JF).

18.3 American and English Precursors and Models

Stylistic choices are therefore far from arbitrary. Yet, Dumont's primary reason for favouring neo-Tudor probably was an inspiring visit to England's newest cellular prisons. In 1846, the Belgian Ministry of Justice sent out a delegation of prison officials, including Ducpétiaux and prison architect Dumont, to study the prison infrastructure of Pentonville, Reading and Aylesbury.[4]

Pentonville was Europe's first fully developed radial penitentiary, influencing prison design in the rest of continental Europe in the second half of the nineteenth century. It was built in 1840–42 based on the 'separate system'; a regime developed in the United States in the 1820s, where prisoners were isolated in order to avoid moral contamination and thus 'demanding a purpose-built prison to enforce the complete separation of prisoners' (Brodie et al. 2002, p. 85). Pentonville and all subsequent adaptations of this kind of prison system are formally derived from the Eastern State Penitentiary in Cherry Hill, Philadelphia. Built in 1823–29 by architect John Haviland (1792–1852) (Johnston 1960, pp. 91–112), it is considered the prototype of the radial cellular prison. Haviland was the first architect to bring together in Cherry Hill the characteristic elements of this typology: a radial plan, a central observatory and cell galleries (Johnston et al. 1994, pp. 31–32; Brodie et al. 2002, p. 86).

According to the nineteenth-century concept of style as a messenger of meaning, Haviland opted for the heavy and gloomy gothic to intimidate the (potential) criminal, both psychologically and physically (Johnston et al. 1994, p. 36). John Haviland was born in England, and completed his architectural education under the London architect James Elmes (1782–1862). Elmes was a prison architect and a committed penal reformer himself,[5] apparently passing on this interest to his pupil who later emigrated to the United States. Haviland moreover received his education at the height of the gothic revival, flourishing in English literature and architecture under the influence of the broader cultural movement of Romanticism. For the façade of the Eastern State Penitentiary, he adopted a sober neo-gothic style with which he must have been well-acquainted (Johnston et al. 1994, pp. 33–36 and 109). He further developed his radial concept in the New Jersey State Penitentiary at Trenton, which he designed in an equally heavy and gloomy 'Egyptoid' style to convey the same message (Johnston 1960, pp. 106–107).

Haviland actually applied the upcoming historical styles of the nineteenth century to an idea that had already been formulated by eighteenth-century French architect

[4]Brussels, State Archives, T022, no 258, dossier 13 (*Délégation de divers fonctionnaires, Roget, Ducpétiaux, Vleminckx, Dumont, Rousseau, pour visiter la prison de Pentonville*, 1832–1866); *Le Progrès. Journal d'Ypres et de l'arrondissement,* January 14, 1847; Vandendaele et al. (1980), p. 148.

[5]In 1817, Elmes published a pamphlet on prison planning: *Hints for the Improvement of Prisons, and for a more Economical Management of Prisoners, partly founded on the Principles of John Howard* (Johnston et al. 1994, p. 33).

Jacques François Blondel (1705–1774). In his *Cours d'architecture* (1771–77), Blondel prescribed an *architecture terrible* for the exterior of prisons. To evoke the power and authority of detention as well as the gloomy life inside the prison walls, he proposed an expressive and massive interpretation of the classical idiom (Blondel 2002 (1771), p. 426; Bergdoll 2000, p. 91). This growing relevance of the appearance of the prison is, according to architectural historian Barry Bergdoll, a result of the success of the 'invisible' custodial sentence in the nineteenth century, superseding the former corporal and scandal punishments in the public space.

This idea of *architecture terrible*, be it directly or indirectly inspired by Blondel, is put into practice (among others) in Newgate Prison in London, built by George Dance the Younger (1741–1825) in 1768–75. Heavily rusticated and with enforced walls, barely interrupted by window openings, it evokes a dark and deterring impression, even more articulated by overt symbolism such as carved chains over the entrances (Bergdoll 2000, p. 91). It is the same idea of how the prison exterior should have an impact on the beholder that was translated into the nineteenth-century neo-gothic style in Havilland's Eastern State Penitentiary.[6]

Although modelled to resemble the Eastern State Penitentiary's plan, a neo-classical rather than a neo-gothic idiom was found to fit Pentonville's purpose best. As the radial prison concept gained success in England though, more architects embraced the gothic neo-Tudor style.[7] Reading Gaol (1842–1844),[8] Armley Gaol (1843–1847), Birmingham Borough Gaol (1847) and Holloway House of Correction (1848–1852) were constructed in the same picturesque neo-Tudor style. The contrast with Haviland's rather sober gothic composition is striking. According to architectural historian Robin Evans (1982, p. 377), the reason architects preferred a detailed and elaborated style is that the main concept and technical aspects of prison design had already been so rigorously established in England, that architects especially seized the stylistic adornment of the prison as an opportunity to showcase their talent.

Considering, moreover, the functional similarities between nineteenth-century prison gatehouses and gatehouses of sixteenth-century Tudor manors, the suitability of this style seems evident. Just like the cellular prison building, the Tudor manor

---

[6]Haviland must have been familiar with Newgate prison given his education in London with Elmes, who praised the style and exterior of Newgate prison in his pamphlet *Hints for the Improvement of Prisons* (Johnston et al. 1994, p. 36). According to Johnston et al. (1994, p. 36), some English prisons had been constructed in neo-gothic style already before Haviland's departure to the United States. However, the question whether Haviland was the first to design a neo-gothic prison, is irrelevant. Crucial is the fact that the neo-gothic Eastern State Penitentiary, combining cell wings directly and radially connected to a central observatory, eventually had a major impact on the dissemination of the radial prison typology.

[7]See also Johnston's reference to neo-gothic English prisons (*cf. supra*), or other 'early' examples such as Leicester Prison (1825–1828). These however are not radial types. Leicester for instance, features a 'detached radial plan', in which the radially arranged cell wings are not connected directly to the central observatory (Brodie et al. 2002, p. 63).

[8]J.J. Dumont visited Reading Gaol during the Belgian study mission (Vandendaele et al. 1980, p. 148, referring to Brussels, State Archives, T022, no 258, dossier 13, file 52 (report from the Minister of Justice to the King, 1848).

was hidden from view and only accessible by a gatehouse, controlling inbound and outbound traffic. Based on the design of medieval castle gatehouses and city gates, with military features such as battlements, machicolations, embrasures and turrets, the Tudor gatehouse no longer served a military function since the invention of artillery warfare in the fourteenth century. 'Yet, these gatehouses were still formidable deterrents to less well-equipped intruders. (…) By virtue of its situation and size, the early Tudor gatehouse was often also a showpiece, a symbol of power and status, that dominated the entrance' (Henderson 2005, pp. 35–39). In particular, these former military elements were used more for their symbolic and decorative associations. As such, sixteenth-century Tudor gatehouses proved to be an excellent model for nineteenth-century prison gateways, serving the same practical purposes (controlling traffic), and evoking the same symbolic associations (intimidation and military or authoritarian power).

18.4 Neo-Tudor Style in Belgium

In England, Dumont not only became acquainted with the new typology of the cellular prison, but also with the (neo-)Tudor style which he applied right away in his first prison design (Fig. 18.4). Around that time, the Belgian government had commissioned him to design a new cellular quarter for women in the Brussels *Prison des Petits Carmes*.[9] Dumont's design, although not radial (for it was not until 1851 that the first radial cellular prison in Belgium was taken into use in Bruges), drew the attention of the *Journal de l'Architecture et des Arts relatifs à la Construction en Belgique*. An article in the very first issue in 1848, praised Dumont not only for introducing the neo-Tudor style in Belgium, but also for the meticulous and appropriate application to the prison typology.[10]

The introduction of neo-Tudor in Belgium was part of a broader gothic revival movement (Vandenbreeden et al. 1994, p. 65). The cultural connection with the strong and continuous gothic tradition in England through a colony of English artists in Bruges gave impulse to the revival of gothic architecture in Belgium from the mid-nineteenth century. With his Saint Boniface church in Ixelles (1847–1849), a milestone in the development of gothic revival architecture in Belgium, Dumont is considered to be one of the pioneers (*Brussel* 1979, p. 171). The neo-gothic style became the pre-eminent idiom to express national identity, and it was affiliated with the Catholic movement for a long time. Although the style soon became fashionable in private and public religious architecture, it would only become common in secular public building in the last quarter of the nineteenth century (Van Loo et al. 2003, p. 25). That Dumont already in 1848 preferred an eminently foreign late gothic style like neo-Tudor in secular public architecture, is therefore noteworthy.

[9]T.L. 1848. Prison cellulaire en construction à Bruxelles, *Journal de l'Architecture et des Arts relatifs à la Construction* 1: 4–6.

[10]*Ibidem.*

There is yet another secular public typology that often adopted the same idiom: military architecture. Barracks *Caserne du Petit-Château* and *Caserne Rolin* in Brussels, *Fort 4* in Mortsel and the Antwerp *Stedelijke Schietbaan* (city shooting range) were, however, all built after Dumont's first prison. Significant is the construction of the *Caserne du Petit-Château* between 1848 and 1852. Originally designed in Byzantine revival style, it was redesigned to neo-Tudor shortly after the publication of Dumont's neo-Tudor prison façade in the *Journal de l'Architecture* (Van Aerschot-Van Haeverbeeck 1993, p. 465). For this typology, the military symbolism of the neo-Tudor style is overt. For the prison typology on the other hand, the same military associations appear to be read more indirect. According to the common architecture-historical interpretation (*cf.* supra), the (military) power and authority of the neo-Tudor prison gatehouse ought to bring a feeling of security for society, and at the same time act as a psychological deterrent for potential criminals.

18.5 The Analogy Between City Gate and Prison Gate

The formal and functional analogy between the neo-Tudor prison gatehouse and the medieval city gate[11] also underlines this function of 'deterrent' through the association of the new penitentiary with the old, dehumanising prison system. As medieval city gates often contained prison cells (Johnston 2000, p. 12) and several of them perpetuated this function of confinement through the eighteenth and even until the middle of the nineteenth century,[12] medieval defensive architecture thus was already associated with the prison function. The Tudor style, as a late-gothic aesthetic redefinition of this medieval utilitarian idiom, was well-fit to link this function with the nineteenth-century penchant for picturesque architecture. The gatehouse of Leuven central prison appears to refer almost literally to the city's medieval gates that had maintained their prison function through the first half of the nineteenth century—be it in a more picturesque, elaborated way (Figs. 18.5 and 18.6).

18.6 Conclusion

Between 1850 and 1870, the English late-gothic Tudor style was a favoured inspiration for the architecture of the new cellular prison typology. Joseph-Jonas Dumont is considered to be the pioneer of neo-Tudor in Belgium. In the 1840s, the

---

[11]After all, the sixteenth-century Tudor gatehouses were based on the architecture of the medieval castle gatehouses and city gates as they were designed to control traffic and evoke power (Henderson 2005, pp. 35–39).

[12]Belgian examples include the Brussels *Porte de Hal* (Van Haegendoren 1988, p. 4), the *Porte Saint Léonard* in Liège (Brussels, State Archives, T063, no 30) and the *Biestpoort* and *Diestsepoort* in Leuven (Debonne 2017; Van Even 1860, pp. 30–31 and 59).

Ministry of Justice assigned him to study the prison infrastructure in England, where several penitentiaries were designed in neo-Tudor style under the influence of the gothic revival movement. Conforming the dominant discourse on the role of 'style' in architecture, the iconology of neo-Tudor was fit to make prison architecture 'legible'. Through historical and typological associations with the military architecture of medieval city gates and Tudor gatehouses, the neo-Tudor style granted the prison gatehouse societal significance as a guardian of public safety. Moreover, the picturesque style could showcase the architect's craftsmanship.

Yet, the enthusiasm for Dumont's stylistic choice was not at all unanimous. Where the *Journal de l'Architecture* praised the 'harmony that exists between the form of the building and its function'[13] in Dumont's design for the Brussels cellular quarter, a reviewer of the Brussels salon interpreted the same design as an anachronism: 'Today, the prison no longer tortures, but amends and corrects. It is a place of zeal and labour, a cloister of repentance that does not need machicolations, nor bastions or battlements. That is the serious mistake that Dumont has made' (Van Roy and Decamps 1848, p. 181, trans. JF).

This paper explored the architectural choice for the neo-Tudor style as well as its societal meanings. The divergent appreciation for Dumont's neo-Tudor façade in 1848 raises questions about the general appreciation for historicising prison architecture in the nineteenth century. Further research options include the contemporary reception of prison architecture in the written press, and an analysis of the government's role in the choice of style within the prison building campaign.

References

Bergdoll B (2000) European architecture, 1750–1890. Oxford University Press, New York

Blondel JF (2002) 1771 Cours d'architecture. Monum, Paris

Brodie A, Croom J, Davies JO (2002) English prisons. An architectural history. English Heritage, Swindon

Brussel, breken, bouwen. Architectuur en stadsverfraaiing, 1780–1914 (1979) Gemeentekrediet van België, Brussel

Clark M, Clark D (2001) Tudor. In: The concise oxford dictionary of art terms. http://www.oxfordartonline.com. Accessed 29 June 2017

De Keyser B, Verpoest J, De Maeyer L (1997) De ingenieuze neogotiek. Techniek en kunst, 1852–1925. Davidsfonds, Leuven

Debonne V (2017) Hulpgevangenis/arresthuis, agentschap onroerend erfgoed. https://id.erfgoed.net/erfgoedobjecten/72854. Accessed 29 June 2017

Evans R (1982) The fabrication of virtue: English prison architecture 1750–1840. Cambridge University Press, Cambridge

Haslinghuis EJ, Janse H (2005) Bouwkundige termen. Verklarend woordenboek van de westerse architectuur- en bouwhistorie. Primavera Pers, Leiden

[13]T.L. 1848. Prison cellulaire en construction à Bruxelles, *Journal de l'Architecture et des Arts relatifs à la Construction* 1:5 (trans. JF).

Henderson P (2005) The Tudor house and garden: architecture and landscape in the sixteenth and early seventeenth centuries. Yale University Press, New Haven (Conn.)
Johnston NB (1960) John Haviland, 1792–1852. In: Mannheim H (ed) Pioneers in criminology. Stevens, London, pp 91–112
Johnston NB (2000) Forms of constraint. A history of prison architecture. University of Illinois Press, Champaign (Il)
Johnston NB, Finkel K, Cohen JA (1994) Eastern state penitentiary: crucible of good intentions. Philadelphia Museum of Art, Philadelphia (PA)
Maes E (2009) Van gevangenisstraf naar vrijheidsstraf. 200 jaar Belgisch gevangeniswezen. Maklu, Antwerpen
Nys L, De Smaele H, Tollebeek J, Wils K (2002) De zieke natie. Historische Uitgeverij, Groningen
Schoonjans Y (2007) Architectuur en vooruitgang. De cultuur van het eclecticisme in de 19de eeuw. A&S Books, Gent
Stratton A (1946) Introductory handbook to the styles of English architecture, vol. II. Tudor & Renaissance, Batsford, London
Thieme U, Becker F, Vollmer H (1999) Allgemeines Lexikon der Bildenden Künstler von der Antike bis zur Gegenwart. Seemann, Leipzig
Van Aerschot-Van Haeverbeeck S (1993) Bouwen door de eeuwen heen in Brussel: inventaris van het cultuurbezit in België: architectuur. Deel Brussel 1B: Stad Brussel, Binnenstad H-O. Mardaga, Liège
Van Cleven J (1996) Dumont, Joseph Jonas (1811–1859), architect. In: Grove art online. http://www.oxfordartonline.com. Accessed 29 June 2017
Van Even E (1860) Louvain monumental ou description historique et artistique de tous les édifices civils et religieux de ladite ville. Fonteyn, Leuven
Van Haegendoren M (1988) Prisons de Bruxelles. Registres d'écrou 1692–1847. Archives générales du royaume, Brussels
Van Loo A, Dubois M, Strauven F, Poulain N (2003) Repertorium van de architectuur in België van 1830 tot heden. Mercatorfonds, Antwerpen
Van Roy L, Decamps T (1848) Exposition nationale des beaux-arts 1848. Revue du Salon de Bruxelles. D. Raes, Brussels
Vandenbreeden J, Evrard J, Bastin C, Dierkens-Aubry F (1994) De 19de Eeuw in België: Architectuur en interieurs. Lannoo, Tielt
Vandendaele R, Gosse A, Geerinck A-M, De Smedt-Massant E (1980) Poelaert en zijn tijd. Gemeentekrediet van België, Brussels
Vanhulle B (2010) Geschiedenis achter slot en grendel? Bedenkingen over de Belgische en internationale gevangenishistoriografie. In: De Koster M, Rousseaux X, Velle K (eds) Bronnen en perspectieven voor de sociaal-politieke geschiedenis van justitie in België (1795–2005). Algemeen Rijksarchief, Brussels, pp 171–190

Jozefien Feyaerts obtained a master's degree in Art History (2012) at Ghent University, with a specialisation in Architecture, Interior and Heritage Conservation. She wrote her master's thesis on Philippe Van Boxmeer's function as municipal architect in the Flemish town of Malines in the late nineteenth century. As an assistant to the Ghent University Department of Art History since 2013, she is preparing a PhD dissertation on the design and construction of the cellular prison in Belgium (1830-World War I).

Figures

Fig. 18.1 Model of Leuven central prison, designed by J.J. Dumont and opened in 1860, © Universiteitsbibliotheek Gent (Ghent University Library), BRKZ.TOPO.1165.O.09

Fig. 18.2 Prison Saint-Léonard in Liège, designed by J.J. Dumont and opened in 1850, © Universiteitsbibliotheek Gent (Ghent University Library), BRKZ.TOPO.1165.N.01

Fig. 18.3 Prison of Saint-Gilles, designed by J.J. Dumont and opened in 1885, © Universiteitsbibliotheek Gent (Ghent University Library), BRKZ.TOPO.1166.E.14

Fig. 18.4 Façade of the cellular quarter of the *Prison des Petits Carmes* (Brussels) designed by J. J. Dumont, as published in the *Journal de l'Architecture* (1848), © Universiteitsbibliotheek Gent (Ghent University Library), BIB.ARCH.0257.0001

Fig. 18.5 Biestpoort, in use as prison between 1778 and 1819, from: Van Even (1860), p. 22

Fig. 18.6 Prison gatehouse of Leuven central prison (1860), © Universiteitsbibliotheek Gent (Ghent University Library), BRKZ.TOPO.1165.O.04

Chapter 19
Experiencing Justice in the *Cour d'assises* of Brabant (1893–1913): A Place of Education and Entertainment

Gaëlle Dubois and Amandine De Burchgraeve

Abstract On the one hand, the spectator sees the judicial space as a theatre where he attends a specific play: the judicial ritual. Hence, the courtroom of the *cour d'assises* is a place of entertainment. On the other hand, the spectator also undergoes an experience of education and warning: by being present, he is confronted with the norms according to which society assesses behaviours, determines the limits of the tolerable, and punishes those who transgress them. He leaves trial with a message, as the initiatory architecture of the courthouse, the layout of the courtroom and the ritualised performance contribute to the expression and the transmission of a discourse on justice and, more broadly, on society. He then spreads the word, willingly or unwillingly, and as such participates in legitimising it. The public thus plays an active role in the strategy of the well-oiled machine that is the justice system.

19.1 Introduction

Since the beginning of the nineteenth century, the *cour d'assises* gathers a few times a year inside the Brussels Courthouse (Fig. 19.1) to judge and punish the most severe offences.[1] During trial, actors with different status come together to discuss and judge these cases. The scientific experts join the judicial world of lawyers and magistrates, as do the jury, the accused, the witnesses, the public and the press, all of whom come from different social and geographical horizons. Inside an area, delimited in time and space, they actively participate in placing the accused

[1]Crimes against persons, the state and property but also press offenses could all be considered severe offenses These were tried by the cour d'assises, which was authorised to hand out the most severe sentences, the '*peines afflictives et infamantes*', of which the death penalty was the gravest.

G. Dubois (✉) · A. De Burchgraeve
FRS-FNRS (Université catholique de Louvain, IUAP 9/22 Justice and Populations), Louvain, Belgium
e-mail: Gaelle.Dubois@uclouvain.be

A. De Burchgraeve
e-mail: Amandine.DeBurchgraeve@uclouvain.be

S. Huygebaert et al. (eds.), *The Art of Law*, Ius Gentium: Comparative Perspectives on Law and Justice 66, https://doi.org/10.1007/978-3-319-90787-1_19

and his crime within the limits of tolerance that are defined according to the societal norms of transgressions (Kalifa 2005, p. 10). Whatever their role and status, they thus experience justice that is at once singular, through its uniqueness, and conventional, since it is guided by a well-regulated ritual.

This paper scrutinies the way in which the public of the *cour d'assises* lived this judicial experience in Belgium at the end of the nineteenth and the beginning of the twentieth century.[2] What is the spectator's impression when he visits the temple of Themis? Is he more surprised by the strange spectacle that unfolds before him than by the legal discussion? What are the various means used to influence his experience? Finally, what is the impact of visual (architecture, scenography, decorum), discursive (discourses of magistrates, lawyers, experts, witnesses and accused) and sensorial experiences (noises, smells, emotions, atmosphere) on their interpretation of justice? The hypotheses presented in this paper are the result of a collaboration between two researchers whose expertise and research subjects differ, but are highly complementary. Both study the representations of justice: Gaëlle Dubois through the architecture of Belgian courthouses and Amandine De Burchgraeve via the debates of the *cour d'assises* of Brabant (Brussels).

The notion of 'justice' refers to both an ideal and a system. First, it is a moral high ground society tries to achieve. In order to do so, it relies on a system composed of institutions that manage the application of law. This system also acts as the creator and transmitter of a top-down message. Justice has always spread discourses on norms, values and the workings of society by using a series of tools, such as buildings and judicial or punishment rituals. It teaches moral imperatives, determines limits and cautions us about the consequences of missteps.

The trials of the *cour d'assises* often attracted a large crowd. Spectators played an important part in the judicial ritual, and a special place was reserved for them inside the courtroom. Indeed, there can be no discourse without a recipient, and no performance without audience (Marrani 2011, p. 72). For Antoine Garapon (2001, p. 110–114), the audience represents society as a whole within the judicial area. It is an image of its divisions, its composite character. At the court session, it represents the public opinion, taken as a collective witness of respect for the forms, the impartiality of the judges, the conduct of the debates— and therefore the regularity of the ritual. It is there to 'control the application of law' according to the general principle of Publicity.

The judicial ritual takes place in a courtroom that is included in a courthouse, vector of visual and spatial representations. On the eve of the First World War, there were twenty-six courthouses in Belgium.[3] The majority was established in

[2]On the decoration of another Belgian *cour d'assises*, in Antwerp, see the contribution by Stefan Huygebaert in this volume.

[3]What we call a 'courthouse' in Belgium, is a building that houses various courts and is located within a judicial district ('*arrondissement*'). Between 1839 and 1988, there were 26 judicial districts. Courthouses do not include justices of the peace ('*justices de paix*'), of which there are one or more per canton (subdivision of the judicial districts) and more than 200 in total.

new buildings constructed between 1830 and 1914, but around a third was placed in already existing buildings. An example of the latter is the courthouse of Liège, which was installed in the former *Palais des Princes-Évêques* (Palace of the Prince-Bischops, Fig. 19.2), whose various parts were erected between the sixteenth and eighteenth centuries. From 1850 until the beginning of the twentieth century, it was continuously renovated and enlarged in a variety of styles (for example neo-Gothic in the *cour d'assises*) (Godinas 2008, Fig. 19.3). The largest courthouse of Belgium—and Europe—was constructed in Brussels from 1850 to 1883, in an eclectic style by architect Joseph Poelaert (*Poelaert et son temps* 1980; Loze 1983). The *cour d'assises* had its seat in one of its most prestigious rooms (Fig. 19.4).

The trials often attracted Belgian newspaper journalists. As a result, an abundance of information on judicial representations—visual and discursive—can be found in press reports. On a critical note, one should be aware that the journalist's point of view is not a certified reality. He tends to embellish most of his accounts in order to sensationnalise, impress and provoke emotions. He also often reconstructs and rearranges the words expressed during the audiences for his own purposes, mostly in order to get a specific (political) message across. Yet, most of the narratives possess a grain of truth, which can often be verified by comparing multiple accounts of the same trial in various newspapers.[4]

From the viewpoint of the staging of justice and its consequences, the *cour d'assises* of Brabant is an interesting case. Hence, this will be the focus of our study. Nevertheless, we will also compare this case with the courthouse of Liège in order to analyse whether the means of expression used to influence the viewer are similar in a building that was not originally intended as a courthouse.

This contribution covers the period between 1883 and 1913. The year 1883 marks the inauguration date of the Brussels Courthouse. In Liège, the renovation of the *cour d'assises* had just been completed a year earlier. Due to the sudden growth of the press, the number of articles written on trials of the *cour d'assises* multiplied during this period. In order to anchor our analysis in a homogeneous context, we choose the last year before the First World War, when the world would change forever, as our *terminus ad quem*.

The anthropological and sociological study of the judicial ritual, through sensorial experiences, the construction of discourse or visual rhetoric, is a developing research area. Antoine Garapon, Frédéric Chauvaud and David Marrani are among the leading figures. Robert Jacob, Katherine Fischer Taylor and Judith Resnik and Dennis E. Curtis, in their turn, are more interested in the imagery and the architectural and spatial representations of justice. Belgium, however, is all but absent from this body of historiography. There are some studies on the courthouses of Brussels and Liège, but none have taken interest in the representations developed through its visual aspect, especially its architecture. Similarly, the *cour d'assises* of

[4]For more information on this subject, see the doctoral thesis of Amandine De Burchgraeve (Université catholique de Louvain).

Brabant has not yet been studied, neither its functioning nor its judicial ideology which it helped to construct. The purpose of this paper is to fill part of this gap.

Our analysis relies mainly on a corpus of press articles and photographs, dating from the chosen period. The articles are from two liberal Brussels newspapers,[5] *L'Indépendance belge* (in French) and *Het Laatste Nieuws* (in Dutch). The photographs were incorporated into postcards that now belong to collectors. Plans and sketches, as well as archival documents from the *Fonds du Ministère des Travaux publics* (Ministry of Public Works) were also used.[6]

The structure of this chapter follows the path of the visitor, from the moment when he is about to penetrate the universe of the courthouse, over when he goes into its heart, the *cour d'assises,* until he leaves the building at the end of the trial. His trajectory takes place in three distinct phases, which 'link and connect the ritual with the psychoanalytic experience' (Marrani 2011, p. 68). We study his experience throughout this three phased voyage and conclude with a brief reflection on how and what this experience may—or may not—have brought forth when the spectator walked out of the judicial world.

19.2 The Initiatory Journey in the Courthouse

19.2.1 Approaching the Judicial Space

When the citizen sees, from the street, the majestic façade of the courthouse, his experience of justice begins. At this point, he is equal to all other protagonists of the trial. Once he enters the compound of the courthouse, he acquires the specific status of a spectator. At this stage of the journey, the viewer is neither quite inside nor outside the judicial space. Antoine Garapon calls this phase the 'preliminary rite of separation' by Antoine Garapon (1985, p. 34–35). It is a transitional phase between the exterior and the interior of the building that is prior to the creation of the judicial event, which occurs as soon as the viewer has passed the front door (Marrani 2011, p. 68–69).

[5]If only two (liberal) journals are used in the context of this paper, this is because of all the studied press, they are the most verbal about the "life" that takes place around the trials. While the catholic and socialist newspapers speak about the sidelines of the debates in some cases, they are much more austere and less detailed in their accounts.

[6]For Brussels: Brussels, State Archives, *Fonds du Ministère des Travaux publics. Administration des Bâtiments. Cartes et plans du Palais de Justice*, 1862–1950, n° 887. For Liège: Liège, State Archives, *Ministère des Travaux publics. Administration des Ponts et chaussées. Direction de Liège*, n° 4216 and 4257; Brussels, State Archives, *Administration des Ponts et chaussées. Bâtiments civils*, n° 274 (*Devis et cahier des charges relatif à l'entreprise des travaux pour la construction, en bois de chêne, de la voûte, portes, lambris,* etc., *de la salle d'audience de la Cour d'assises, plafond et lambris de l'antichambre de ladite Cour et appropriation et restauration des plafonds et lambris sculptés des salles Louis XV, servant aux délibérations du Jury et de la Cour*, 1881).

At the Brussels Courthouse, this first stage is marked by the ascent of a monumental eighty-two metres[7] wide staircase that leads to a central entrance portico as high as a six-story building. A thirty metres long peristyle with a double colonnade of Doric pillars flanks this imposing portico (Loits and Vandenbreeden 2001, p. 35).[8] In Liège, despite the fact that the building was not originally intended to be a courthouse, the citizen makes the same transition from the outside to the inside of the judicial world by going through the palace's first external courtyard, which is framed by an Italian-styled portico (Godinas 2008, p. 109).

The architecture of the Brussels Courthouse evokes a sacred place, the temple, suggesting a link between justice and the divine. Yet, it also creates a panoramic space that extends on a horizontal plane. Given that divine values tend be expressed by verticality,[9] this can be seen as an evocation of the more humanistic and materially inclined nineteenth-century bourgeoisie (Dubois 2014, p. 95; Loze 1983, p. 129–130). The Courthouse of Liège, on the other hand, combines elements of classical architecture, reminiscent of the temple, with neo-Gothic style components that remind us if medieval gothic churches. However, as in Brussels, the space is organised around rigorous horizontality. Hence, one could say that the potential for a symbolism similar to that of Brussels is definitely there, despite the fact that the basic structure of the building dates from well before the nineteenth century. The courthouse is a secular building, built by men for themselves.

The spectator, on the lookout for stories, scandals, mysteries and extraordinary confessions, is seemingly unaware of this separation. Before big trials, the atmosphere on the threshold of the courthouse resembles that of a theatre. A crowd of people arrives *en masse*, climbing the stairs to the palace while the Brussels police are stationed on the steps in order to maintain a minimum of order. In the eyes of the public, in search of juicy details about the case, the courthouse briefly becomes an 'attraction', in which lawyers and the accused are the stars of the day (Chauvaud 2010, p. 24). It is superfluous to point out that there are many people streaming out of all streets adjacent to court. In the Wijnand Street, where the public entrance is to be found, the police rallies to keep order. The carriage with the prisoners, used every day to transport them, arrived at 8 o'clock in the morning in order to avoid the public demonstrations at the Marolles. Everyone who can walk hurries to the court, through the smallest alleys. The district of the Marolles is abuzz![10]

---

[7]Measurable on an authentic plan of the courthouse, abstracted from *Le Nouveau Palais de Justice par J. Poelaert, architecte*. Undated. Collection of plates. Brussels, Paris.

[8]Note that the public enters through the doors located on the main façade, but also by means of two others entrances, rue aux Laines/Wolstraat and rue de Wynants/Wynantsstraat.

[9]In architecture, especially Gothic, verticality suggested the elevation to God (Watkin 2001, p. 87).

[10]'*Het zal wel overbodig zijn hier aan te stippen dat er veel volk toestroomt door al de aanpalende straten van het gerechtshof. In de Wijnandsstraat waar de toegang is voor het publiek moet de politie de orde handhaven. Het rijtuig van het gevang, waarmee de betichten alle dagen vervoerd moet worden, is heden morgen om acht ure al toegekomen om zooveel mogelijk de betoogingen der Marollen te voorkomen—want tot uit de kleinste steegjes en gangskens daagt alles op wat beenen heeft. 't Marollenkwartier staat in rep en roer*' (*Het Laatste Nieuws*, March 13, 1897).

19.2.2 The Labyrinth of the Courthouse: From Its Entrance into the Courtroom

The entrance. The second stage consists of entering the building through the front entryway, followed by the crossing of the *salle des pas perdus*. In Brussels, the double entrance door seems rather small, given the size of the building. It leads to a gigantesque *salle des pas perdus* with a Piranesian appearance.

The salle des pas perdus. This area consists of several volumes within a panoramic space, creating a play of lights and a monumentality pushed to the extreme (Loze 1983, p. 92, 104–105). The *salle des pas perdus,* witness to an everlasting back and forth, is a space of transition between the outside world and the judicial space. According to Antoine Garapon (1985, p. 35), 'its uniformity, its obscurity and the freedom enjoyed within it, makes it the most profane place in the judicial area, allowing it to be related, after the separation phase, to the phase of undifferentiation, imprisonment and death'. For David Marrani (2011, p. 70–71), the latter is not only experienced physically, but also constitutes a place and time for reflection, a time to understand, a moment when the observer begins to perceive the singular setting in which he is placed.

The Courthouse of Liège, for its part, does not possess a *salle des pas perdus*, firstly because it is mainly a creation of the nineteenth century, but also because it is a structure that was only used for public and administrative buildings—which the *Palais des Princes-Évêques* originally was not. The main entrance to the courthouse merges with entrances of various courts, and gives direct access to the multiple corridors of the building. The *grande galerie* precedes the *cour d'assises* on its own floor, and is decorated in a Louis XIV style. The hall is adorned with portraits and busts of great men who have marked the history of Liège (Godinas 2008, p. 157–159). As a combination of a *salle des pas perdus* and a portrait gallery, the *grande galerie* marks the transition space, isolates the viewer and allows him to pursue the judicial experience. Incidentally, this court is the only one served by this gallery. It may not be a coincidence that this specific site was chosen when the courts were installed in the former *Palais des Princes-Évêques*, as it was very much frequented by the general public.

The staircases. The spectator becomes part of the judicial world as soon as he crosses the front entrance. But in order to access the heart of justice, he has to go through a preparation that goes beyond the passage of this door, and the crossing of the *salle des pas perdus* (Garapon 1985, p. 35). In order to access the *cour d'assises,* usually situated on the first floor or *bel stage*, the spectator must climb some stairs, a nameless monumental staircase in Brussels, and the *escalier royal* in Liège (Godinas 2008, p. 151). In the capital, the staircase presents itself as soon as the *salle des pas perdus* has been crossed. Its appearance reflects an idea of progression, an evolution and an elevation, which is also evident in the passage from one space to another during this second phase (entrance, *salle des pas perdus*, stairs) (Garapon 1985, p. 35). The spectator's ultimate progression lies in this final ascension, after which he is ready to enter the courtroom, having triumphed over the judicial labyrinth. In Liège, however, the staircase leads to the *grande galerie* mentioned above, as such slightly disturbing the preconceived arrangement. However, this disruption is not absolute, since the isolation, the evolution and the elevation that the building's architecture is trying to achieve is accomplished once the doors of the *cour d'assises* are reached.

It is with excitement that the people step through the entrance door and wait for the 'play' that is about to start in the *cour d'assises.* In Brussels and Liège, the *cour d'assises* is one of the most accessible rooms, practically located at the end of the stairs, preventing the spectator to get lost in the labyrinth of corridors. When entering, the visitor goes through the aggregation phase, meaning he fully enters the universe as an active agent.[11]

19.3 Experiencing Justice: A Trial of the *Cour d'assises*

19.3.1 Open Sesame

The courtroom of the *cour d'assises* has several doors, which are intended for the various actors of the trial. The public enters through the main entrance, which gives access to the space outside the trial area. This two-door entrance of the *cour d'assises* of Brabant is framed by two columns surmounted by an entablature and a pediment, which gives it a monumental character—a style which is in accordance with the rest of the building. In Liège, the double doors are made of oak and decorated with cordonnets, clusters, ribbons, rosettes and various geometric motifs (Godinas 2008, p. 163). While its neo-Gothic style is different from that of the *cour d'assises* of Brabant, it is not less solemn.

The crowd gathers impatiently in front of this door, knowing that once it opens, they will be able to satisfy their curiosity about the accused and the victim, obtain scandalous details about the case and finally hear the verdict. Only a select group of people who obtained 'privilege cards' distributed by the president of the *cour d'assises,* can afford to wait calmly, knowing that they have a reserved seat inside. Once the doors open, men and women rush inside and sit down on the benches at the back of the room, often with a packed lunch. By doing so, they avoid the risk of losing their place at lunch hour.

19.3.2 A Judicial Theatre

'In the public space, there is an invasion. A few screams, accompanied by the rattling of the gendarmes' arms. The curious stay silent and at once become very

[11]Only in the antropological sense, not in the judicial one.

calm. The prestige of the *cour d'assises*, left in a dim light due to curtains hanging over the windows, strikes them'.[12] The audience, exalted and eager, settles in order to experience the great spectacle of justice. In truth, as we will see later on, they are confronted with a double experience that goes beyond simple entertainment. Decor, scenography, costumes, gestural and verbal rituals, and even the actors themselves, are organised according to a controlled theatricality that aims to convey a message of caution as well as an education on shared values and the path to follow.

This sensation-seeking public finds its way into an artificial, ceremonious, grandiloquent space, the organisation of which is an inheritance of the past centuries. During the nineteenth century, the courtroom has indeed retained several elements of the original judicial assembly, which took place under a tree planted on the top of a hill. The relationship with nature seems preserved through the stone-wood duo manifested in the separation between the judicial space (*parc*) and the outer space (*carreau*) (Jacob and Marchal-Jacob 1992, p. 27–28, 40–41). Inside the *parc* a second barrier isolates the heart of the judicial space where the trial takes place. Antoine Garapon (2001, p. 34–35) refers to this area the *cancel*, delimited by what he calls the *cancella*. In Brussels, a wooden barrier delimits the *parc* and the *cancel*, while the *cour d'assises* of Liège was provided with wrought-iron fences decorated with volutes. Archival research on the restoration of the Palace of the Prince-Bischop indicates that a wooden balustrade was constructed in 1835.[13] An iron fence might have replaced the balustrade during the restoration of the *cour d'assises* room in 1881.[14] These boundaries are reminiscent of the vegetal enclosure, which once surrounded the space where the judicial ritual took place. The high (er) emplacement of the court session, in turn, evokes the hill on which the plaids were held, and invites the viewer to look up (Jacob and Marchal-Jacob 1992, p. 41).

'The world of judicial debate remains deeply human and terrestrial' (Jacob and Marchal-Jacob 1992, p. 41). Communication with the sky is, moreover, limited by the architecture of the room. The rather high ceilings are often flat or box-like, and not curved, which would refer to the celestial order. The Brussels *cour d'assises* is a very good example of this. In Liège, on the other hand, the neo-Gothic styled courtroom has a vault ceiling supported by double arches.

Within the *cancel*, a relationship with the divine can be found in the layout of the room, even if this specific feature is limited to the person of the presiding judge.

---

[12]'*Dans l'enceinte publique. C'est un envahissement. Quelques cris accompagnés du cliquetis des armes des gendarmes. Mais les curieux se taisent, aussitôt devenus très calmes. Le prestige de la salle des assises, que de larges rideaux tombés sur les fenêtres laissent dans la pénombre, les frappe*' (*L'Indépendance belge*, 4 June 1902).

[13]Liège, State Archives, *Administration des Ponts et chaussées. Direction de Liège*, 1835, n° 4216 (*Devis de divers ouvrages neufs ou de reconstruction*, p. 2, art. 8).

[14]Brussels, State Archives, *Administration des Ponts et chaussées. Bâtiments civils*, n° 274 (*Devis et cahier des charges relatif à l'entreprise des travaux pour la construction, en bois de chêne, de la voûte, portes, lambris*, etc., *de la salle d'audience de la Cour d'assises, plafond et lambris de l'antichambre de ladite Cour et appropriation et restauration des plafonds et lambris sculptés des salles Louis XV, servant aux délibérations du Jury et de la Cour*, 1881).

The judge faces the courtroom and the public from behind a desk, which is situated in the middle of the width of the room. His two assessors flank him, on each side. The judge's position, emphasised by the presence of a central aisle, creates a horizontal axis of symmetry, which separates good from evil. This axis is fundamental for the structuration of the space, as it constitutes the ritual benchmark of the actors' play and it gives direction to the staging of the ritual (Jacob and Marchal-Jacob 1992, p. 41–42). The courtroom is also crossed by a vertical axis, which distinguishes the ordinary citizens from the magistrates, by hierarchically separating the people who sit on the top of the platform from those who sit down (Fischer Taylor 2013, p. 458). The judges' desk is the culmination point of these vertical and horizontal axes; it is closest to the divine (Garapon 2001, p. 38–39).

Nevertheless, the president's place is not the judicial space's centre of gravity. For Antoine Garapon (1985, p. 34; 1997, p. 38), it is organised around an empty space (between the president and the bar or the chair where the witnesses are interrogated) that might symbolise the place of the Law, 'inaccessible to all citizens, and around which social exchanges are organised'.

In the court session, each actor is assigned a specific place, embedded in a codified relationship with the other seating arrangements. As Linda Mulcahy (2011, p. 38) points out, this rigorous layout determines which actors are allowed to take part in the ritual, and the kind of respect that has to be accorded to them. The public prosecutor is usually seated on the platform at the right side of the president,[15] at a separate table or at the same one. He is placed next to the judges. The clerk sits at the other side of the president, as do his assessors. Sometimes, the clerk is looking in the same direction as the judges, but much more often, he directly faces the public prosecutor, as can be seen in the Waddington trial in Brussels (Fig. 19.5). On the ground, the jury sits on the right of the judges' desk, facing the accused and his lawyer who are on the other side. Most of the time, the jurors and defence are aligned with the judges, as is the public prosecutor. In Liège however, they are placed, side by side, in front of the judge's desk (Fig. 19.5). The civil party, the witnesses[16] and a part of the public sit outside the *cancel*, in what Antoine Garapon calls the '*petit parc*' (Garapon 2001, p. 27). The public is behind them, sitting on the benches or standing on the '*carreau*'.

This traditional arrangement could, however, undergo some adjustments depending on the case and the needs. In Liège the accused is placed on the right of the president, in order to prevent him from escaping through the windows situated

[15]'Originally conceived for the civil trial and then transposed to the criminal trial', the arrangement of the judicial area 'always conveys the idea of a superiority of the personage placed to the right'. It thus 'reflects a preference in principle for the plaintiff, most likely because he is a victim and demands the fulfillment of his sacred duty of justice from the State despite the principle of the presumption of innocence, which is favourable to the accused' (Jacob 1994, p. 131–133).

[16]Except during the hearing of the witnesses. After the call of witnesses, the latter retreat from the courtroom. Separate rooms are reserved for the prosecution and for the defense witnesses. Doing so, they could not influence each other (v° 'Cour d'assises'. In Picard et al. 1888, col. 275, art. 1085–1086).

on the left side of the room. A fence made out of wrought iron surrounds the benches reserved for him and his defence. It should be noted that, in the *cour d'assises* of Liège and Brabant, there was no fence before 1910; the witnesses sat on an elevated chair placed in front of the judge.

Right in the middle of this theatrical setting, there is the table of exhibits, which makes the decor even more fascinating and impressive to the viewer. Bloody objects, heads or hands put into jars, the washbasin the assassin used to clean his hands, or the armchair in which the accused was shot; all are placed in the space reserved for trial. These objects play the role of figurative material that participates in the creation of a 'theatrical scene'. 'On the exhibit table, in front of the judges, a cluster of clothes and shapeless packages and boxes are placed. Among these items are—a gruesome list—the clothes of Vandevelde and Anne Pallenholz, a part of the victim's larynx and part of Vandevelde's lips, debris from the safe, etc'.[17]

Seated in the *parc* or standing in the *carreau*, the spectators watch the scene, the actors and the setting. The crowd consist of occasional viewers as well as of 'regulars'—usually ladies who come to amuse themselves, looking for lively emotions that they cannot find anywhere else. 'Once again, the same mass of people as the previous days. Ladies and girls largely occupy the reserved seats, and as a result, the assembly is a spectacle showcasing a variety of looks and dresses. Behind the public fence, one can also notice some women, and many men and young people from the working class'.[18]

19.3.3 Living the Trial: Entertainment and Education

The audience experiences the courtroom as a 'place of spectacle' with the same kind of people and exchanges as in theatres and churches: a stage, actors, gestures and an oratory. The story and the actors provoke laughter, exclamations, tears and applause. The *cour d'assises* incarnates the spectacle: it is a place where the public can come to observe the machine that creates figures of monsters, mad and abnormal people, poisoners and degenerates. It is a territory that speaks to people's imagination. At the same time, it is a theatre of reality, which deals with questions of the couple, conjugality, relationships between parents and children, jealousy, envy, etc. (Chauvaud 2010, p. 25.) In short, those who do not follow the moral

[17]'*Sur la table des pièces à conviction, devant les juges, un amas de vêtements et de paquets informes et de boîtes est placé. Parmi ces pièces à conviction se trouvent – liste macabre – les vêtements de Vandevelde et d'Anne Pallenholz, une partie du larynx des victimes et une partie des lèvres de Vandevelde, des débris du coffre fort, etc.*' (*L'Indépendance belge*, 4 April 1901).

[18]'*Weer dezelfde volkstoeloop als de vorige dagen. De voorbehouden plaatsen zijn grootendeels ingenomen door damen en juffertjes, zoodat het geheel een bonte verscheidenheid uitmaakt van toiletten. In de publieke omheining bemerkt men ook eenige vrouwen en verder talrijke mannen, jongelingen en knapen uit den werkman stand*' (Het *Laatste Nieuws*, 1 July 1907).

blueprint of the time fascinate the spectators. One comes to the courthouse, to the trial, to be entertained.

Yet, in the nineteenth century, the architecture of the courtroom was more akin to the architecture of a church[19] than to that of a theatre. Furthermore, it was from the vocabulary of religious architecture that Antoine Garapon (1985, p. 30–31) borrowed the words *cancel* and *cancella.*[20] The courtroom was designed as a rectangle and arranged in the same direction as the nave of the church, whereas the traditional theatre is organised in a circular arch. The courtroom of the *cour d'assises* in Liège depicts the idea of sacred architecture very well. The neo-Gothic style used by Liège architect Lambert Noppius (1827–1889) for its renovation in the 1880s is undoubtedly well chosen. Elisabeth Fischer Taylor divides the church in three zones: the nave, which welcomes the faithful, the choir, which corresponds to the clergy as mediators, and the sanctuary, with a main altar (at the far end beyond the choir), which represents sacred authority. The courtroom is, for its part, only divided in two parts. According to Taylor, this contrast originates from the different relationship the clergy has with the public: the priest is an intermediary between God and the faithful, while the judge is a final authority, subject only to the authority of another judge at a higher level (Fischer Taylor 2013, p. 461).

In the courtroom, the part of the audience that was sitting in the back did not enjoy much comfort. In Brussels and in Liège the room was flanked on each side by high windows. However, the room wasn't very bright, and hence spectators could easily miss some of the visual details. The public faced the court and was able to see the faces of the seating magistrates, but not those of the other actors, who were placed in profile or with their back to them. They often struggled to hear the speakers—who were too far, did not speak in their direction, and whose words were covered by a permanent hubbub. Camille Roussel, appointed judicial columnist at the *Indépendance belge*, often mentioned the bad acoustics of the room: 'The interrogations have taken place in the unpleasant acoustics of the courtroom, which is very beautiful, but horribly tiring for those who have to perceive what is being said'.[21] The public regularly had to stand up, and didn't possess the comfort given to the protagonists of the trial. The jury and the parties sat on wooden benches, while the magistrates were entitled to individual chairs. The president's chair, richly decorated and luxurious, marked his pre-eminence within the trial.

In Liège and Brussels, the *cour d'assises* was not very different from that of the other courtrooms. Nevertheless, the general public much less visited the latter. One might conclude that, although the theatre of justice was open to the public, the

[19]On the origins of this arrangement and its comparison with that of the church: Fischer Taylor (2013, p. 459–461).

[20]In the architecture of christian churches and cathedrals, the *cancella* was the barrier, wall of hek that separated the liturgical choir, in other words the *cancel*, from the other parts of the buidling (Pérouse de Montclos 2009, p. 409).

[21]'*Les interrogatoires se sont effectuées dans la fâcheuse acoustique de cette salle d'audience des assises qui est très belle, mais terriblement fatigante pour ceux qui doivent percevoir ce qui s'y dit*' (*L'Indépendance belge*, 12 December 1913).

architecture of the premises may not have been organised in function of it, but rather according to the nature of the ritual. Nonetheless, through the solemn architecture of the courthouse, the layout of the courtroom and the rigorously staged ritual, the spectacle of justice exerted a strong impression on the viewer coming to be entertained.[22] In truth, the public does not simply see the *cour d'assises* as a place of entertainment; it also becomes aware of it as a place of education and warning.

The changing attitude of the spectator when entering the room is the first signal that he is receptive to the messages transmitted to him through the various judicial rituals. Once having passed the oak doors, the noisy theatrical atmosphere makes way for a calmer, more subdued attitude. It is as if the spectator is aware that he is confronted with the functioning of justice. In contrast, the people left in the hall, in the corridors and in the stairs leading to the entrance of the courtroom, maintain a noisy atmosphere. 'In the great staircase which leads from the peristyle of the courtroom to the correctional courtrooms in the basement, there is a crowd of human bodies (…). Their groans are perfectly heard in the courtroom, notwithstanding the care with which the padded doors are kept closed'.[23]

Once having entered the room, the viewer adopts several roles at once. He is the spectator who comes to entertain himself, but he is also a figure who, like the jury, the assessors, the press, the witnesses and the experts, becomes an integral member of the play. He is not a mere observer, but a participant. Beyond his role as a witness of the ritual, he also serves to breathe new life into the debates: his murmurs and gestures are an expression of changes in opinion that are likely to have an impact on the jury and the verdict that follows. As Denis Salas (2010, p. 100) says: 'it is he (the public) who constructs our representations of criminality, it is his degree of indignation that determines the limits of tolerance'. Through his murmurings, he shares his thoughts and his approvals, and therefore some standards of society (Kalifa and Flynn 2005, p. 36).

During trial, social barriers and norms are constructed by the appreciation of accepted and unacceptable behaviours. 'Just as in a melodrama, the court's narrative provides ethical clarification: we simplify human behaviour, strip it of all ambiguity and complexity in order to better underline the moral imperatives' (Shapiro 1990, p. 67). Denis Salas (1992, p. 325) explains: 'In a world without reference other than human law, all representations of the world are valid, none are

---

[22]Originally, the symbolism of the place and of the ritual was less intended for the public than it was for legal professionnals. However, in the seventeenth century, this judicial symbolism became secular. Justice became a virtue, independent of religion and the supernatural, equiped with a symbolism of its own. Henceforth, the discourse of justice was no longer addressed to the judges, but to the public (Garapon 2001, p. 28–29).

[23]'*Dans le grand escalier qui mène du péristyle de la salle des assises aux bas fonds de la correctionnelle, il y a là un grouillement de foule, un entassement de corps humain (…). Cette multitude turbulente et agitée de constants remous, des poussées formidables (…). Des gémissements (…) s'entendent parfaitement dans la salle d'audience, malgré le soin avec lequel on maintient fermées les portes matelassées*' (*L'Indépendance belge*, 16 March 1897).

absolutely true or false, all are equivalent, those of the State and the various other that germinate in society. Every human community must, at the risk of disappearing, impose a legal representation of the world on everyone in order to regulate what it considers necessary for its perpetuation. Only rites of discussion such as the trial are likely to foster a consensus on inappropriate values because they are recognised by everyone as a common good'.

In its educational role, through its staging, the judicial ritual aims to install these rules into public, but also to warn them these regulations must be respected. It is in this sense that the participation of the viewer corresponds to the aggregation phase. He undergoes a transformation during trial, a renaissance towards the moral and judicial values that are reaffirmed. It is a 'time of light', in contrast to the darkness of the *salle des pas perdus* and the corridors of the courthouse. It does not mean that the spectator understands all of this, but at the end of the trial, he is able to act in a free and responsible manner within society (Garapon 1985, p. 36; Marrani 2011, p. 71–73). As David Marrani (2011, p. 71–73) puts it: the ritual overwhelms the individual and brings back order.

The public is receptive to the different types of messages that the judicial ritual suggests. A prosecutor once noted the importance of the visual messages brought to the public. An acquittal allows the accused to exit through the big oak door and through the central entrance, while a condemnation forces him to go through the small door behind the bench of the accused. As is clear from the requisitory of a public prosecutor, this type of visual ritual, and the symbolic message it carries, seems to matter greatly: 'If he's acquitted, he'll leave the room through the big door! Is this possible? No!'[24]

In addition, the public also acquires a role of transmitter, as it is often called out to share the messages that were dispensed during the audience. Indeed, the same prosecutor noted to the jury that 'in the crowd, at the back of the room, there are friends and acquaintances of the accused, people waiting for the verdict, and they will take note. They must not say that murder is allowed in Belgium'.[25]

19.4 Leaving the Judicial Space: Impression, Reception, Diffusion

While the spectator may attend trials of the *cour d'assises* in order to be entertained, once the door closes behind him at the end of the hearing, the feeling that sticks with him is one of being warned rather than of being entertained. When going back

[24]'*S'il était acquitté, il quitterait la salle par la grande porte! Est-ce possible? Non!*' (*L'Indépendance belge*, 11 July 1900).

[25]'*M. Janssens termine en faisant remarquer au jury que dans la foule qui garnit le fond de la salle, se trouvent des amis et des connaissances des accusés, des gens qui attendent le verdict et ils en feront leur profit. Il faut qu'ils ne puissent pas dire qu'on peut assassiner en Belgique*' (*L'Indépendance belge*, 11 July 1900).

to the vestibule, through the *salle des pas perdus,* many spectators have the feeling that someone took them aside and spoke to them. 'It may as well be as if the State is the invisible and confidential speaker, expressing itself in general, but addressing itself to the particular. The trial spectator is asked that the game ceases to appear to him as a game, that the 'fiction' of the trial integrates with reality' (Garapon 2001, p. 113).

Journalistic chronicles sense the contrast and observe how people leave the theatrics behind in order to discuss the moral that was shared through the judicial rituals. As David Marrani (2011, p. 71) said, the vestibule is a transition phase between two spaces as much when one goes in as when one goes out. It is a place of reflection, a zone between the inside and the outside. While one may feel entertained, one is also left behind with questions and impressions about the judicial ritual itself. The already quoted Camille Roussel wrote: 'As soon as we find ourselves under the dome of the *salle des pas perdus*, between the colonnades of giant stones, reason blows on tears and dries them'.[26] In another case, the same journalist noted that 'the attitude of the crowd in the corridors, in the hall, on the stairs, is, moreover, perfectly decent (…) They gather in groups to discuss the indictment, the arguments, the reply of Mr. Janson, which made a great impression'.[27]

Once they leave, the people disperse the words and impressions they have collected inside the courtroom and the courthouse. Moreover, once they leave the space that keeps moral indignation and public fury at bay (Garapon 2001, p. 19), at the bottom of the courthouse steps, they often seem to want to enforce the judicial message. They create their own 'externationalisation' mechanism, their own judgment of the case through a particular ritual. The mass of people does not stay quiet once the verdict is rendered. In cases of acquittal for example, the spectators of the trial and the people that were stationed outside of the courtroom and courthouse during the debates show the desire to reintegrate the free man or the woman in the bosom of society, as much by his chosen discourse as by his gestures, as the following newspaper excerpts illustrate:

- A compact crowd who uttered cheers, followed the acquitted, through the hall of the Pas-Perdus, towards the Poelaert Place to the astonishment of foreigners who are now visiting the Themis palace…[28];

[26]'*Ces émotions ne passent pas, pour le public, la porte de chêne de la cour d'assises. Dès que l'on se retrouve sous le dôme de la salle des Pas-Perdus, entre les colonnades de pierres géantes, la raison souffle sur les larmes et les sèche*' (*L'Indépendance belge*, 11 July 1900).

[27]'*L'attitude de la foule, dans les couloirs, au prétoire, dans les escaliers, est d'ailleurs d'une parfaite décence. […] Dans les groupes on commente l'acte d'accusation, le réquisitoire, les plaidoiries, la réplique de M. Janson, qui a fait grande impression*' (*L'Indépendance belge*, 29 March 1897).

[28]'*Une foule compacte, qui a poussé des acclamations, a suivi l'acquitté, à travers la salle des Pas-Perdus, vers la place Poelaert—au grand étonnement des étrangers qui visitent actuellement le palais Thémis*' (*L'Indépendance belge*, 16 September 1909).

- Meanwhile, some people, believing that they recognised the heroine of the drama that had just ended, accompanied her, clapping their hands;[29]
- Meanwhile, in the corridor of the detainees, Mme De Bruyn is surrounded by members of her family (…) arriving in the *Rue des Laines*, the crowd, warned, no one knows how, arrives and gives her ovations[30].

Interestingly, condemnations elicit inverse reactions. Once the accused has left the courtroom and the courthouse through the small doors, there is often a crowd waiting for him when he enters the carriage that brings him to prison. Many react with intense sentiments: howls, boos, etc.; messages that are meant to marginalise him further from society: 'The crowd growls, there are rumours of bad anger (…) one whistles, one cries, "Assassin!" It is a sad spectacle. As in a movement of commiseration and revolt, we [journalists] say around us, "No, no, let go, justice is done, have mercy now!" Whatever! This crowd avenged is wild and barbarous! Now the cellular carriage sets off at a gallop, still followed by the screaming crowd'.[31]

19.5 Conclusion

Between 1883 and 1913, attending a trial at the *cour d'assises* represented a double experience of justice for the audience. On the one hand, it sees the judicial space as a theatre in which social events take place and where sordid and shocking stories are shared. In the eyes of the spectator, the *cour d'assises* is more than an arena where he can obtain a form of revenge and where he can observe how order reigns over chaos. He comes here looking for entertainment, trying to get a glimpse of the heroes and villains everyone is talking about.

Yet, he leaves trial with a message, as the initiatory architecture of the courthouse, the layout of the courtroom and the ritualised performance contribute to the expression and the transmission of a discourse on justice and, more broadly, on society. Through the court session, whose scenes cause cries, laughter and tears, the

---

[29]'*Pendant ce temps place Poelaert, quelques individus croyant reconnaître dans une passante l'héroïne du drame qui venait de se terminer, se mirent à l'accompagner, claquant des mains et d'autres personnes, commettant la même erreur se joignirent à eux*' (*L'Indépendance belge*, 19 December 1902).

[30]'*Quand on la fait sortir par des couloirs détournés du palais, arrivée rue aux Laines, la foule prévenue on ne sait comment, arrive et lui fait des ovations*' (*L'Indépendance belge*, 18 February 1902).

[31]'*La foule pousse de sourdes rumeurs de colère mauvaise (…) on siffle, on crie: "Assassin!" C'est un spectacle navrant. Comme dans un mouvement de commisération et de révolte, nous [journalistes] disons autour de nous "Non, non, laissez passer, justice est faite, ayez pitié maintenant!" N'importe! Cette foule qui est vengée est d'aspect sauvage et barbare! Maintenant la voiture cellulaire s'est mise en course au galop, toujours suivie par la cohue hurlante*' (*L'Indépendance belge*, 27 March 1897).

spectator is confronted with the norms according to which society assesses behaviours, determines the limits of the tolerable, and punishes those who transgress them.

Besides entertainment, the spectator also faces an experience of education and warning. This implies a communication from top (Justice) to bottom (Society). Through an initiatory journey within the courthouse, from its exteriors to the courtroom, architecture elevates and opens the mind of the citizen to the message of justice. The layout of the *cour d'assises* room for its part supports the conduct of the judicial ritual. Its roots lie in a distant past, where it was born together with the judicial ritual. The two are inseparable, as the arrangement is part of the ritual.

Even if the comfort of the courtroom is not great and seems to have been organised to serve the ritual itself above all else, the audience fully takes part in it, if not in a literally legal sense, then at least anthropologically. The spectator is more than a mere observer. His presence both guarantees the proper conduct of the ritual and validates the act of reparation that takes place. Moreover, he has an influence on the members of the court and the jury through his behaviour and reactions during the procedure.

Therefore, when he leaves this 'ritualised comedy' (Fillon 2010, p. 114) behind, the spectator does so with these representations in mind. He then spreads them, willingly or unwillingly, and as such participates in legitimising. He thus plays an active role in the strategy of the well-oiled machine that is the justice system. As this paper suggests, entertainment, education and warnings are not incompatible. On the contrary, it is their conjunction that allows the system to function. For Shapiro (1990, p. 67), 'the public trial fulfils the same function as a melodrama in the theatre of the nineteenth century. That is to say, it tells a dramatic story, nourished by an emotional hyperbole aimed at making the universe readable'. Consequently, even if one goes in search of amusement, the temple of Themis and the trials of the *cour d'assises* always bring forth a judicial lesson at the exit. Justice subtly draws advantage from the theatricality of its ritual, placed in a sacred space, and from the entertainment that this procedure engenders to mark the minds. The architecture, the decor, the disposition and the gestures of the actors, the role allotted to the public, etc. are all elements that actively participate in the development of this ritual which, under the cover of a spectacle, ensures the balance of society.

References

Chauvaud F (2010) La chair du prétoire. Histoire du sensible de la *cour d'assises* (1881–1932). Presses universitaires de Rennes, Rennes

Dubois, G (2014) La symbolique architecturale du palais de justice de Bruxelles. In: Van Eeckhoutte W, Maes B (eds) Genius, Grandeur & Gêne. La Fin de Siècle autour du Palais de Justice de Bruxelles et la figure controversée d'Edmond Picard. Het Fin de Siècle rond het Justitiepaleis te Brussel en de controversiële figuur van Edmond Picard. Knops, Herentals, pp 83–113

Fillon C (2010) Faites entrer le témoin. Léon Werth, chroniqueur judiciaire. Histoire de la justice 20(1): 107–118

Fischer Taylor K (2013) Geometries of power: royal, revolutionary, and postrevolutionary French courtrooms. J Soc Archit Hist 72(4):434–474

Garapon A (1985) L'Âne portant des reliques. Essai sur le rituel judiciaire. Le Centurion, Paris
Garapon A (2001) Bien juger. Essai sur le rituel judiciaire. Odile Jacob, Paris
Godinas J (2008) Le palais de Liège: cœur de la Cité ardente. Institut du patrimoine wallon, Namur
Jacob R (1994) Images de la justice. Essai sur l'iconographie judiciaire du Moyen Âge à l'âge classique. Le Léopard d'Or, Paris
Jacob R, Marchal-Jacob N (1992) Jalons pour une histoire de l'architecture judiciaire. In: Association française pour l'histoire de la Justice (ed) La justice en ses temples. Regards sur l'architecture judiciaire en France. Errance, Paris, pp 23–68
Kalifa D (2005) Crime et culture au XIXe siècle. Perrin, Paris
Kalifa D, Flynn MJ (2005) Criminal investigators at the Fin-de-siècle. Yale French Studies 108:36–47
Kalifa D, Flynn MJ (2005) Criminal investigators at the Fin-de-siècle. Yale French Studies108:36–47
Le Nouveau Palais de Justice par J. Poelaert, architecte. Undated, Collection of plates, Brussels, Paris
Loits A, Vandenbreeden J (2001) Le Palais de Justice. Ministère de la Région Bruxelles-Capitale, Direction des Monuments et Sites, Brussels
Loze P (1983) Le palais de justice de Bruxelles. Monument XIXe. Atelier Vokaer, Brussels
Marrani D (2011) Rituel(s) de justice. Essai Anthropologique sur la Relation du Temps et de l'Espace dans le Procès. EME, Brussels
Mulcahy L (2011) Legal architecture: justice, due process and the place of law. Routledge, New York
Pérouse de Montclos J-M (2009) Architecture. Méthode et vocabulaire. Éditions du patrimoine, Centre des monuments nationaux, Paris
Picard E et al (1888) Pandectes belges. Encyclopédie de législation, de doctrine et de jurisprudence belges, vol XXVII. Ferdinand Larcier, Brussels
Poelaert et son temps (1980) Catalogue de l'exposition (Bruxelles, Palais de Justice, 29 novembre–27 décembre 1980). Crédit communal de Belgique, Brussels
Salas D (1992) Du procès pénal. Presses universitaires de France, Paris
Salas D (2010) Opinion publique et justice pénale. Une rencontre impossible? Le temps des médias 15:99–110
Shapiro A-L (1990) L'amour aux assises: la femme criminelle et le discours judiciaire à la fin du 19e siècle. Romantisme 68:61–74
Watkin D (2001) Histoire de l'architecture occidentale. Könneman, Cologne

Gaëlle Dubois is a FRS-FNRS Research Fellow and an associated member of IAP Justice & Populations. In this framework, she is writing a Ph.D thesis about justice representations studied towards courthouses architecture in Belgium from 1914 to 1830 at the Centre d'histoire du droit et de la justice (Université catholique de Louvain). In 2010, she graduated in history (2010) and, in 2012, in archaeology and history of art (Université catholique de Louvain). Her research interests concern legal architecture, nineteenth century history, law and justice history, history of architecture, history of representations and cultural history.

Amandine De Burchgraeve is a FRS-FNRS Research Fellow, currently completing a Ph.D on *The Social Construction of Crime. The actors of the Assize Court of Brabant and their discourses on murder, murderers and victimes* (*1893–1913*) at the Centre d'Histoire du Droit et de la Justice in Louvain-la-Neuve. She graduated in History at Université catholique de Louvain in 2011 and in Social and Cultural Anthropology at the University College of London in 2012. She's a member of IAP Justice & Populations. Her research interests include history of crime, criminal anthropology, judicial history, *histoire du sensible* and contemporary history.

Figures

Fig. 19.1 The Brussels palace of justice, ca. 1910, postcard (private collection GD)

Fig. 19.2 The courthouse of Liège, ca. 1910, postcard (private collection GD)

Fig. 19.3 Courtroom of the *cour d'assises* in the courthouse of Liège, ca. 1910, postcard (private collection GD)

Fig. 19.4 Courtroom of the *cour d'assises* of Brabant (Brussels), ca. 1910, postcard (private collection GD)

Fig. 19.5 Positions of the actors of the judicial ritual, Waddington trial, *cour d'assises* of Brabant (Brussels), 1907, postcard (private collection GD)

Chapter 20
The Judge, the Artist and the (Legal) Historian: Théophile Smekens, Pieter Van der Ouderaa, Pieter Génard and the Antwerp *cour d'assises*

Stefan Huygebaert

Abstract This paper presents an iconological interpretation of the courtroom decorations in the Antwerp *cour d'assises*. These decorations were created between 1886 and 1893 by three traditionalist artists and a legal historian, and commissioned by a conservative Catholic judge, Théophile Smekens. In the 1880s, under the influence of the international criminology movement, Belgian criminal law started to gravitate towards the so-called 'social defence' theory. However, not all members of the legal and political elite agreed with the changes propagated by Adolphe Prins, and installed by Minister of Justice Jules Le Jeune. Several conservative Catholics in particular held on to a moralising view on crime and criminality. This paper argues that, in the decoration commission, Smekens demonstrated his combined artistic and legal conservatism and his opposition to recent legal changes in his choice of collaborators and iconography. This is particularly clear in town archivist Pieter Génard's coloured reading of Antwerp criminal history and artist Pieter Van der Ouderaa's characteristic mode of depicting this subject matter.

20.1 Introduction

In October 1890, the Antwerp *Palais de Justice* received a group of international visitors. The criminologists, legal scholars and practitioners were not there to visit the *cour d'assises*,[1] despite the fact that three artists were busy decorating the room with five large historical scenes. The visitors were there to conclude a five-day international

[1]The Belgian *cour d'assises*, modelled after its French predecessor, is the competent court for capital crimes and press and political offences, see also the contribution by Dubois and De Burchgraeve in this volume and Monballyu (2014).

S. Huygebaert (✉)
Department of Art History, Musicology and Theatre Studies, Ghent Legal History Institute, Ghent University and Research Foundation Flanders (FWO), Ghent, Belgium
e-mail: Stefan.Huygebaert@UGent.be

S. Huygebaert et al. (eds.), *The Art of Law*, Ius Gentium: Comparative Perspectives on Law and Justice 66, https://doi.org/10.1007/978-3-319-90787-1_20

conference on patronage of released convicts and the protection of abandoned children, organised by Belgium's progressive Catholic Minister of Justice Jules Le Jeune (1828–1911). In 1887, Le Jeune had started modernising the criminal legal system in order to improve reintegration and individualise punishment. In doing so, he was inspired by Adolphe Prins (1845–1919), a progressive liberal professor at the university of Brussels and Belgium's quintessential representative of the international criminology movement, which was started by Cesare Lombroso. Prins believed in the freedom of choice and personal responsibility of criminals, and he was convinced that their behaviour was determined by their social background. An opponent of solitary confinement, Prins' *défense sociale* (social defence) theory was aimed at both rehabilitating convicts by means of patronage and defending society from inveterate malefactors. Le Jeune's bill on probation (1888) was the first of a series of laws inspired by scientific input (e.g. 1891 statute on vagabondage, 1912 statute on child protection) that were signed by subsequent Ministers of Justice. (Christiaensen 2004; De Ruyver 1998; Fijnaut 2014, pp. 469–496).

Together with other conservative Catholics such as Charles Woeste (1837–1922), who often clashed with Le Jeune over criminal legal reforms in parliament (Weber 1996, p. 15, 57, 81, 92–93, 121–122 and 130), Théophile Smekens (1823–1921), president of the Antwerp first instance court, appears to have had a very different view on criminal law. The proceedings of the above-mentioned 1890 conference (*Congrès International* 1891) give us a rare look into his legal thinking. During his interventions, Smekens referred to his eighteen years of experience as a judge. Although he agreed with the patronage system, he vividly defended paternal correctional power and authority, which could be overruled only by the higher power of the magistrate. Likewise, his idea of a correctional regime for delinquent youths was harsher than what was suggested by other conference participants. More generally, he adhered to a penal legal doctrine summarised by Donald Weber under the banner of 'objectivism'. Objectivism focussed on the committed crime, which men such as Woeste and Smekens interpreted as a moral fact, as sin. Several of Smekens' fellow conservative Catholics, such as Woeste, defended capital punishment, and at the same time opposed Prins and Le Jeune's rigorous incarceration plans for inveterate malefactors, whom Woeste thought could still be saved by means of education and religious moralising (Weber 1996, p. 15, 57, 81 and 92–93).

We can gain a deeper insight into Smekens' thoughts on contemporary changes of the country's criminal legal system by analysing the paintings he commissioned for the *cour d'assises* between 1886 and 1893. In her work on Belgian monumental painting, Ogonovszky-Steffens (1999, p. 13 and 404) refers to this medium as one of the 'heads of the official hydra', or 'the official art par excellence'.[2] Much like public sculpture, monumental painting as a medium is a form of top-down communication. This is an expression of a legal (sub-)culture, an interpretation of what the law should be according to the commissioners. In what follows, I argue that the commissioner (Smekens) instrumentalised the legal historian (Pieter Génard) and artist's (Van der Ouderaa) specific way of reading and depicting criminal legal

---

[2]All citations are my (SH) translation from the original French, unless stated otherwise.

history. Hence, an analysis of courtroom decorations can give us insight into hidden aspects of a legal (sub-)culture. Moreover, the courtroom in question and its monumental paintings are currently undergoing major restorations, which makes a focus study all the more relevant.[3]

Up to this point, scholars have largely ignored the decoration history of the Antwerp *cour d'assises*. The most important study appeared in a book from 1953 by Charles Laenens, clerk of the court, followed by an exhibition catalogue from 1977, lacking footnotes (Laenens 1953, pp. 615–618; Laenens 1977, p. 205). Both works were mostly based on town archivist Pieter Génard's (1891, pp. 106–123) own account and the relevant fund in the Antwerp provincial archives. As a result, they did not fully consider the role of Théophile Smekens, let alone his views on law and art, as well as the preceding oeuvre of the artists involved. The timing of the commission, on the eve of crucial changes in Belgian criminal law, urges us to interpret the decorations iconologically and scrutinise them as symptoms of a legal culture, or rather, as I will argue, a legal subculture, opposed to the mainstream movement of Belgian criminal law.

The purpose of my investigation is to gain insight into what Théophile Smekens was aiming at with these decorations, and how the latter could achieve this. Unmistakably, Smekens was the leading force. To achieve his objective, he first chose a team of five protagonists: himself, Génard as archivist, and Pieter Van der Ouderaa (1841–1915), Karel Ooms (1845–1900) and Juliaan De Vriendt (1842–1935) as artists (originally, Juliaan's brother Albrecht (1843–1900) stood on Smekens' wish list as well). I will show how these men shared a mostly conservative Catholic, traditionalist and pro-Flemish view. These five men chose the subject matter, and with this also the main message of the five paintings. A focus on the previous work of Van der Ouderaa and Pieter Génard (the main artist and the archivist-gone-legal historian), and the oeuvre of Van der Ouderaa resulting from their collaborations, helps us understand the specific rationale behind the decorations. Firstly, it is important to emphasise the close collaboration between Pieter Génard and Pieter Van der Ouderaa and the resulting written and artistic oeuvre. In doing so, I will both elaborate on, and provide solid ground for, Laenens' claim that the men were 'intimate friends' (Laenens 1953, p. 616). Secondly, because of the importance of legal history within this collaboration, I aim to demonstrate how, for Smekens, Van der Ouderaa's legal historical artistic oeuvre was a vehicle for the communication of his view of the law. In particular, the notion of emotion in Van der Ouderaa's works—and the presumed lack thereof—is quintessential for an understanding of how Smekens could instrumentalise his work in a *cour d'assises* as a comment on contemporary criminal law.

---

[3]Origin Architecture and Engineering, *Palais de Justice d'Anvers*, http://www.origin.eu/project.cfm?pro=114, accessed 4 July 2017.

20.2 Selecting the Team: The Protagonists

The five protagonists of this story had several traits in common: firstly their role as leaders in the Antwerp art scene, of which they shared the traditional view; and secondly their (conservative) Catholic and Flemish conviction.[4]

20.2.1 (Conservative) Catholic and Flemish

At his ninetieth birthday in 1893, several speeches described Théophile Smekens as having three passions: law, art and charity.[5] The last word referred to his Catholic charitable work as a devote Christian. Some referred to his first name—Théophile, 'friend of God'—to emphasise his Catholic spirit. It seems that the judge was not shy of putting his convictions into practice outside the church.[6] For example, during a trial in 1882, a witness brought up that Smekens was known to be opposed to divorce.[7] Smekens himself would remain a bachelor throughout his 98 years long life. Some liberals reproached him for being 'very clerical', and for favouring the *Meetingpartij*, a political party in Antwerp closely connected to the Catholic party and the Flemish struggle, during several elections. As president of the court, Smekens officially organised the elections in Antwerp.[8] Probably the most visible reminder of Smekens' conservative Catholicism is the enormous crucifix conspicuously placed in the centre of the monumental perjury painting by Van der Ouderaa the main painting in the *cour d'assises* (Fig. 20.1). According to a persistent rumour, Smekens demanded a painted crucifix that would be impossible to remove from his courtroom, whatever political wind might blow through it. The only source I have been able to find that substantiates this rumour is a crossed-out phrase in a note from the Royal Commission for Monuments (RCM), which describes the painted crucifix as a substitute for the traditional specimen.[9] However, judging by

---

[4]The following journals and newspapers were used for this contribution: *L'Art Moderne* (Brussels, progressive), *Le Bien Public* (Ghent, conservative Catholic), *La Chronique des Arts de la Curiosité. Supplément à la Gazette des Beaux-Arts* (Paris, conservative), *L'Echo du Parlement* (Brussels, liberal), *Fédération Artistique* (Antwerp, conservative), *Het Handelsblad* (Antwerp, Catholic), *L'Indépendance Belge* (Brussels, liberal), *Journal de Bruxelles* (Brussels, Catholic), *De Koophandel* (Antwerp, liberal), *Het Laatste Nieuws* (Brussels, liberal), *Le Matin* (Antwerp, Catholic), *L'Opinion* (Antwerp, liberal), *Rotterdamsch Nieuwsblad* (Rotterdam, centre) and *De Tijd* (Amsterdam, Catholic).

[5]*Journal de Bruxelles*, 5 December 1913.

[6]*Journal de Bruxelles*, 4 December 1882.

[7]*L'Echo du Parlement*, 9 December 1882.

[8]*L'Indépendance Belge*, 8 June 1878; *De Koophandel*, 5 June 1880; *Het Handelsblad*, 26 May 1881; *De Koophandel*, 10 June 1882.

[9]Antwerp, Archives of the Royal Commission for Monuments (RCM), KCML A/0804, Letter from the Royal Commission to Van der Ouderaa, 10 February 1887.

Smekens' vigour in the decoration program, there is little doubt that he had a hand in the specific iconographic choice.

The four artists Smekens put on his first wish list for the governor (Van der Ouderaa, Ooms and the two De Vriendt brothers) mostly shared his (conservative) Catholic convictions. Eventually, Smekens was forced to omit Albrecht De Vriendt, due to the latter's overlapping assignment from the government to decorate the gothic room inside the Bruges town hall, which would start in 1892 (VandenBorre et al. 1999, pp. 14–15, Demeyer 2008). Albrecht's brother, Juliaan, would base his courtroom paintings on his brother's sketches.[10] Van der Ouderaa and Juliaan De Vriendt both ran for office for the Catholic *Meetingpartij*. De Vriendt eventually became a Member of Parliament for the national Catholic party in 1894.

Religious paintings form a large part of these artists' oeuvre. Juliaan De Vriendt's most praised work is his *Chant de noël* (*Christmas carol*) from 1894. Despite his success in religious painting, and despite the fact that he had travelled to the Middle East in 1894 with his friend Van der Ouderaa, Ooms (contrary to Van der Ouderaa) did not start to paint many biblical or religious scenes in the last part of his life. (De Taeye 1894, p. 615; Van Huerck 1919). Although of the three courtroom decorators, Ooms was the least engaged Catholic, he was a devout believer and allegedly intended to paint religious scenes at a later part in his relatively short life (Dumon 1987, pp. 17–19).

In 1863, Pieter Génard (1830–1899) became Antwerp's town archivist, thanks to the support from the same Catholic *Meetingpartij* (Van den Nieuwenhuizen 2002). His contemporaries saw him as a (moderate) Catholic (Van Doorslaer 1984, p. 80, 92). His work as a town archivist included moving over 20,000 procedural bags, from which he would draw material for a number of legal historical writings, and a chapter on Antwerp's legal history in his *magnum opus*, *Anvers à travers les ages* (*Antwerp through the ages*, 1888). Additionally, Génard was involved with the restauration of the *Steen* (the *Burgh)*. Originally built as a fortress, this ancient building was eventually used as a prison during the Middle Ages and Early Modern Era. From 1862, it housed the Antwerp Museum of Antiquities, for which Génard, together with Smekens, founded the commission. These elements suffice to label Génard as a legal historian, although with a clear focus on early modern criminal law in Antwerp.

Furthermore, the words used to describe Génard in an obituary were 'religion, language and art, and fatherland' (Caeymaex 1899, p. 14). The language aspect had to do with another characteristic of the protagonists. Except Smekens and Ooms, all protagonists were clearly involved in the Flemish movement, which at the end of the nineteenth century strived for the equal treatment of the Flemish language, as compared to French, within the Belgian society and State. The literary, political or other figures involved in the struggle were called *flamingants*. One of the most important milestones in their struggle, the 1898 *Gelijkheidswet* (*Equality Act*), was a proposal from Juliaan De Vriendt, together with a fellow Member of Parliament. Like Van der Ouderaa, Juliaan De Vriendt stood for office on the list of candidates

[10]Beveren, State Archives, PAA656-112, Letter from Smekens to the Governor, 4 October 1886.

of the *Meetingpartij*, which was part of the Flemish movement (Goovaerts and Vandeweyer 1998). The De Vriendt brothers published several articles in which they voiced their view on art, nationalism and the Flemish movement, which for them consisted most of all of blocking foreign influences (De Bruyn 1872, pp. 40–58). Génard was a founder of *De Vlaamsche School* (*The Flemish School*), a leading conservative artistic journal advocating the Flemish movement. The archivist frequently wrote contributions and was considered an important member of the movement (Snieders 1893). Smekens is harder to pinpoint as *flamingant*, apart from the occasions on which he gave speeches in Flemish despite the fact that he did not seem to have mastered the language well enough (*Het Laatste Nieuws*, 3 December 1913). Again, Ooms seems to be the odd man out, since no proof exists that he was in anyway involved in the Flemish movement. Likely, together with his more indistinct Catholicism, this might explain why he was originally commissioned to paint only one of the five paintings.[11] Eventually, an explanation in Dutch was added to all the paintings, whilst the struggle for the use of Flemish in court was still ongoing. The use of Flemish in criminal cases in the Flemish part of the country only became obligatory from 1873 onwards (Van Goethem 1985, p. 32). However, what is clear, is that Smekens, Génard, Van der Ouderaa, De Vriendt and Ooms' collaboration in 1886–1893 was far from surprising, given their shared political views. Furthermore, they also had a common artistic taste, and an authoritative voice to spread it.

20.2.2 Leaders Within the Antwerp Art Scene

The symbiosis of art and law in the Brussels art scene is a known fact in the scholarship on *fin de siècle* Belgian culture (Block 1997; Huygebaert and Vandenbogaerde 2014; De Smet and Verleysen 2016). Men such as Edmond Picard, Octave Maus and Emile Verhaeren combined legal careers or training with intensive writing and organising within the avant-garde art scene, through legal circles such as the *Jeune Barreau* and art societies such as *Les Vingt* (1883–1893) and *La Libre Esthétique* (1893–1914). Smekens' activities seem to indicate that the same is true for at least part of the Antwerp art scene. However, there is one crucial difference. Picard and his fellow art-minded lawyers were organising *salons* that challenged the official institutes, but Smekens was part of Antwerp's artistic establishment (Persoons et al. 1976, p. 44). From 1853 onwards, he was a member of the *Société d'encouragement des beaux-arts* (Society for the Encouragement of Fine Arts) and of its commission, which organised the triennial Antwerp art exhibition or *salon* (alternating with Brussels and Ghent). He eventually presided the *Société* from 1889 onwards, and thus became the organiser of the 1894 Antwerp World Fair art exhibition. Together with artist Henri Leys (1815–1869) and Génard,

[11]In 1889–1890, Ooms received the commission for the sixth painting, on the balcony wall.

Smekens was a founding member of *Artibus Patriae* (1864), which brought together Antwerp art fanatics and purchased works for the local Royal Museum of Fine Arts (Artibus 1865). Later, Van der Ouderaa would become a member as well (*Het Handelsblad*, 25 January 1909). Smekens was a member of the museum's administrative commission since 1889, and of many other organisations, such as the RCM (*Journal de Bruxelles*, 5 December 1913). Also together with Génard, Smekens founded the commission of the Museum of Antiquities inside the *Steen*. Van der Ouderaa joined this commission, together with Albrecht De Vriendt (Génard 1881). Smekens' legal career as a judge started in 1862, and he became president of the first instance court in 1872 (*Le Matin*, 2 December 1913).

In his view on art, Smekens embodied the late-nineteenth-century Antwerp art scene, characterised by art historian Jean Buyck as provincial, traditional and epigonic. The epigonic nature came from the fact that it closely imitated Antwerp's leading, innovative artist from the mid-nineteenth century, Henri Leys (Buyck 1980). His historical scenes set in late-medieval and sixteenth-century Antwerp would dominate the extended historicism of Van der Ouderaa, Ooms and the De Vriendt brothers. In the early 1870s, Smekens combined an influential voice with a conservative view. For example, under the guise of the pseudonym 'T.', the judge wrote a scathing review of the stained glass windows by the French artist Édouard Didron (1836–1902) in the Holy Sacrament chapel of the Antwerp cathedral. Smekens, who in the midst of a paper war was forced to drop his pseudonym, denounced both Didron's iconographic and stylistic anachronisms and his Parisian fashion fads. The reason was that they were incompatible with the judge's view on national character (Smekens 1873; *Het Handelsblad*, 26 June 1873). Smekens was also held responsible for the fact that the 1876 Antwerp *salon* would only feature two paintings that contained nudes, much to the dislike of the liberal and Brussels press (*L'Opinion*, 8, 10–11 and 14 August 1876). Other liberals reproached him for wanting to turn the Academy into a prudish institution in line with his Catholic convictions (*De Koophandel*, 11 and 30 December 1885). As a magistrate and court president, Smekens remained a respected figure, despite some incidental conflicts with the local bar. The latter's disciplinary board resigned collectively in 1891 as an act of protest against the judge.[12]

The artists involved were part of a similar generation and style, and each of them would succeed in securing a teaching job in the Antwerp art scene. At the actual start of the decoration works in 1886, Van der Ouderaa and Albrecht De Vriendt led both painting studios of the Antwerp academy (*Journal de Bruxelles*, 2 October 1886). In 1891, Smekens welcomed—with a speech in Flemish—Albrecht De Vriendt as the new president of the Antwerp Academy (*Journal de Bruxelles*, 9 February 1891). By 1898, Smekens, Van der Ouderaa, Ooms and Albrecht De Vriendt were all members of the steering committee of the earlier mentioned

[12]Apparently, Smekens had insulted members of the bar when they made too much noise in the *Palais* during one of his trials (*L'Indépendance Belge*, 29 March 1891; *Journal de Bruxelles*, 31 March 1891).

Societé (Persoons et al. 1976). By Smekens' ninetieth birthday celebration in 1913, Juliaan De Vriendt was the president of the Class of Fine Arts of the Belgian Academy of Arts and Sciences (*Journal de Bruxelles*, 5 December 1913).[13] Génard, too, occupied a central position in the Antwerp cultural scene, due to his contacts with historians, writers and artists (Somers and van Roey 1998). As such, he was asked to provide Henri Leys with historical background for his monumental paintings inside the Antwerp town hall in 1864–69, creating a precedent for the *cour d'assises* (Baetens 2012).

The outspoken nationalist and traditionalist view on art seems to be the most important link between Smekens and the De Vriendt brothers. The De Vriendts' traditionalism was intrinsically linked with their flamingantism. Inveighing against classicism, pseudo-Rubensian romanticism (which, in their eyes, was French) and realism, the artists renounced modernism in favour of a national, Flemish art inspired by Flemish artists, and free of foreign influences (De Vriendt 1871 and 1874; Todts 1998). As for Smekens, the way poet and art critic Émile Verhaeren (1855–1916) described the president of the *Société* and organiser of the Antwerp 1891 *salon* is telling with respect to both the judge's influence and his vision. Fulminating from the Brussels avant-garde perspective, and very much opposed to the Antwerp school of Ooms and Van der Ouderaa, Verhaeren wrote: 'President of the court, he also wants to preside art. He is an austere kind of person. He has outdated opinions. Certainly, he takes up his role—unfortunately. He incarnates tradition, the typical kind of painting, the banal "chef d'oeuvre". He is one of those men who appear in public only to be stately. Always provincially dressed up in their Sunday suit' (*La Nation*, 29 July 1891; see Aron 1997, p. 462).

20.2.3 Commission History

Smekens' position as a leading member of the official Antwerp art scene and his preferences and views on art converged in his organisation of the courtroom decorations. He took it upon himself to contact the governor of the province of Antwerp. He did so after having spoken with the Catholic Prime Minister Auguste Beernaert, who was also Minister of Finance, and with the Minister of Public Works, Alphonse de Moreau, responsible for the fine arts, at the occasion of a history conference inside the *cour d'assises* on 27 September 1885.[14] 'Taking up the reigns' would be an understatement to describe how Smekens obtained what he wanted. He immediately proposed a financial plan and he himself selected the team of artists, namely Albrecht and Juliaan De Vriendt, Karel Ooms and Pieter Van der

---

[13]However, around the turn of the century, a part of the Antwerp Catholic press turned against Juliaan De Vriendt in favour of Pieter Van der Ouderaa as director of the Academy (*Het Handelsblad*, 24 March 1901).

[14]Beveren, State Archives, PAA656-112, Letter from Smekens to the Governor, 16 December 1885.

Ouderaa, accompanied by Pieter Génard. Smekens also took it upon himself to serve as a liaison between these men and help distribute the different subjects.[15] However, the absence of an open competition for the *cour d'assises* decorations led to reproaches of favouritism in *La Fédération Artistique*—despite the fact that this was a conservative art journal which had originated in Antwerp (Verbruggen 2009, p. 238). In their eyes, if all Belgians were equal before the law or before repressive justice, should this not be the case for distributive justice too? (*Fédération Artistique*, 22 January 1887, p. 111; *Fédération Artistique*, 12 February 1887, p. 138) The liberal Antwerp Newspaper *L'Opinion* (4 January 1887) added: 'We can tell by these names [Ooms, De Vriendt and Van der Ouderaa] that official art is not separated from politics. There are still pleasant days ahead for historico-religious imagery'. The article thus linked the commission to the homogeneous Belgian Catholic government.

According to Smekens, the artists would work well together, and would ensure a harmonious style, since they were, as the judge described them, 'equally faithful to the traditions of Flemish art'.[16] By the time of the decorations, Smekens' favourite artists were mostly grouped together in reviews of the *salons*. In 1880 already, the liberal newspaper *L'Indépendance Belge* (4 September 1880) specifically mentioned the names of Van der Ouderaa, Ooms and De Vriendt as the quintessential painters of medieval and early modern patriotic history. Hence, they shared the same negative critical appreciation. Several critics described the art of Ooms, Van der Ouderaa and the De Vriendt brothers as outdated, cold and emotionless, and the artists themselves as mere epigones of Henri Leys (*Chronique des Arts et de la Curiosité*, 29 November 1890).

A painter called Karel Pont also got involved in the *cour d'assises* decorations. He was commissioned to paint imitation oak on the ceiling, imitations of marble on the pilasters, tapestry imitations above and underneath the paintings and the gilding of several lines.[17] Analogous to Smekens' suggestions, the entire project was under double supervision of the palace's architect, Jan-Lodewijk (Louis) Baeckelmans (1835–1871), and the RCM.[18] The latter was supposed to give her approval for a small sketch/cartoon, a ca. 1/3 sketch on canvas, and the definitive creation of each of the five paintings. The archives show few remarks from the RCM, apart from some details about colour and the number of figures.[19] The RCM's inspection committee for the *cour d'assises* included RCM president François-Joseph Wellens (1812–1897), who had built the Brussels *Palais de Justice*, together with Joseph Poelaert, and Jan-Baptiste Rousseau (1829–1891), the national director of fine arts. As I have shown in earlier papers, the RCM and these same men had insisted on

---

[15]*Ibidem*.

[16]*Ibidem*.

[17]Beveren, State Archives, PAA656-112, Letter from Baeckelmans to the Governor, 10 February 1886.

[18]Beveren, State Archives, PAA656-112, Letter from Smekens to the Governor, 4 October 1886.

[19]Antwerp, RCM Archives, KCML A/0804.

portraits of historical jurists for the *Cour de Cassation* decorations in Brussels (Huygebaert 2014 and 2017). For the Antwerp case, the historicist paintings were already to their liking. Moreover, Smekens had good contacts with the RCM, since he himself as well as Van der Ouderaa and Génard were corresponding members by 1887.[20]

20.3 Selecting the Theme: The Decorations' Subject Matter

In consultation with the artists and Génard, Smekens decided that the *cour d'assises* would best feature subjects that (1) related to the kind of cases that were discussed in this courtroom, (2) were taken from local history and (3) were taken from a period of which the corresponding costumes would create a harmonious ensemble.[21] This de facto meant that the paintings would consist of legal historical scenes taken from the late fifteenth and sixteenth centuries, Antwerp's golden age. Smekens attached a clearly educational objective to the paintings' subjects, much like the tradition of monumental paintings (Ogonovszky-Steffens 1999, p. 301 and 310). The message was in line with his own artistic and legal views, his preference for national art, his local Antwerp city pride, and his disgust for French modernism. He explicitly opposed general and often repeated subjects, which according to him would inevitably result in banality. It is safe to assume that Smekens was referring to the *Palais de Justice* in Brussels, where four large statues of antique (i.e. pagan) jurists and legislators were a thorn in the Catholic flesh (Huygebaert 2016, p. 182).

Documents in Génard's personal archive show the evolution of the shortlist of specific scenes and subject matters. Some were referred to by means of legal historical terminology or anecdotes ('*purge criminelle*' (*cf. infra*), 'free slave'), others by more general legal principles ('No-one can be deprived of his competent judge').[22] In his letter to the governor, Smekens had headed each painting with a title based on legal texts, followed by a short summary of the story. Génard repeated this in his 1891 publication on the decorations. In the actual room, a legal principle, cited from old legal texts, would eventually be written above each painting. The story itself would then be summarised in a single phrase underneath (Fig. 20.2).

[20]In 1880, Frans Vinck (1827–1903), a historicist late romantic painter (like Van der Ouderaa, Ooms and the De Vriendts) but at the same time also a liberal (like his tutor Henri Leys) allegedly had contacts with the liberal Minister of the Interior, Gustaaf Rolin-Jaequemyns, about the decoration of the Antwerp *cour d'assises* (Ogonovszky-Steffens 1999, p. 386). *La Fédération Artistique* of 17 April 1880 mentions one of his designs, which was intended for the rear wall (which Ooms would eventually decorate). It featured Charlemagne discussing the *capitularia*. However, during the discussions of the 1886–1893 decorations, no one made a single reference to this project.

[21]Beveren, State Archives, PAA656-112, Letter from Smekens to the Governor, 3 March 1886.

[22]Antwerp, City Archives (Felixarchief), PK # 3101, scrap paper [wedding invitation 31 August 1885].

The first scene (A1-A2), painted by Juliaan De Vriendt, was an expression of the principle 'All are free and there are no slaves'.[23] It showed the story of a black man named Jean-Marie who was freed by his master, the dean of an Antwerp chamber of rhetoric. The next scene (B) showed that 'No-one can be deprived of his competent judge'. This was done by means of a story from 1425, painted by Pieter Van der Ouderaa, in which 2,000 armed men from Antwerp went to Bergen-op-Zoom to destroy the gallows of Jean de Glimes. This lord of Bergen-op-Zoom was about to hang a forger despite the fact that the Antwerp magistrate was the only one who had the juridical authority to do so. The third and most visible, central scene (C), also by Van der Ouderaa, showed that in capital crimes, false testimony was punishable by death. The painting featured a convict (a German man-at-arms) on his way from the *Steen* prison to his execution. Next to the perjury scene, Juliaan De Vriendt showed how the law is equal to all (D). This principle was illustrated by a scene depicting a story about two noblemen convicted for insults toward the mayor, whose families had unsuccessfully tried to persuade archduke Matthias to grant them mercy. The fifth and final scene (E1-E2), the only one of the originally intended works that was painted by Karel Ooms, showed a so-called *purge criminelle* procedure: a nobleman was accused of forgery and was freed of guilt in 1564 (Génard 1891; on this kind of procedure: Van Caenegem 1956, p. 154 and 199).

According to Smekens (in 1886), these five chosen subjects would show the citizen's rights and duties, and more specifically that: '[A] The citizen is naturally free; [B] He can only be tried by his or her competent judge; [C] to whom [judge] he [citizen] owes the truth; [D] When the citizen is guilty, there is no privilege that allows him to avoid punishment; [E] When the citizen is innocent, no-one can do him harm'.[24]

After publication of the subject matters and chosen painters, some of the artistic and mainstream press interpreted the message as if the five paintings showed principles from legal history that were still typical for the current criminal legislation (*Het Handelsblad*, 12 December 1886; *Journal des Beaux-Arts*, 31 December 1886). However, extrapolating these individual cases to the entire legal system in sixteenth-century Antwerp was actually quite a bold thing to do. Pieter Génard even went one step further in his published article on the decorations. His words are very close to those used in Smekens' letter to the governor, when he writes that, based on ancient Antwerp law (customary law, usages and statutes) 'at all times the lives and rights of our citizens were protected by the law' (Génard 1891, p. 108). Furthermore, the *Vierschaerboeken* containing the judgments of the Antwerp aldermen demonstrated the 'eternal principles of the law'. The personal and suggestive reading of Antwerp legal history on the walls of the *cour d'assises* was written down even more explicitly in Génard's *Anvers à travers les ages*. In this

[23]For four of the five scenes, Génard referred to the 1582 Antwerp customary law codification, both to the original pages and to the 1871 edition (de Longé 1871). For Van der Ouderaa's central scene, Génard referred to Joos de Damhouder's *Praxis Rerum Criminalium*.

[24]Beveren, State Archives, PAA656-112, Letter from Smekens to the Governor, 3 March 1886.

two-volume history of Antwerp, Génard opened his chapter on legal history, in which he hopped from one anecdotic case to another as stepping stones through (mostly criminal) legal history, with an equally bold statement: In Antwerp, a sixteenth-century citizen had the same rights and duties that characterised the contemporary, late-nineteenth-century *Rechtstaat*. 'The *keuren* (town charters) or *coutumes* (codified costumary law) show that, in matters of civil rights, our ancestors enjoyed more or less the rights which are enshrined by the French code' (Génard 1888, vol. II, p. 295). In other words, Génard largely ignored the importance of the French Revolution in establishing and guaranteeing civil rights.

Apart from this, Génard also wrote that he had searched for exemplary episodes that would inspire love for the fatherland and respect for the law in the contemporary citizen (Génard 1891, p. 108). According to Ogonovszky-Steffens, this combination of an educational with a moral objective is often found in nineteenth-century monumental painting programs. Equally characteristic is the local nature of the subject matter, despite the fact that the city of Antwerp was not one of the funding parties (Ogonovszky-Steffens 1999, p. 299 and 407–408). In general, Génard's coloured reading of Antwerp's legal history might be more inspired by his unlimited local city pride than by a critique of the law—old or new. Smekens, however, had a different agenda, as he aimed to comment on contemporary criminal law.

Despite the fact that the RCM was only expected to judge the composition and the pictorial aspect of the paintings, and was not supposed to say anything about their content and subject matter, its members did voice their opinion about the chosen iconography.[25] In a letter to Van der Ouderaa, the RCM asked whether the chosen subjects were really in line with what happened inside a *cour d'assises*. After all, the five scenes were pre-eminently about the execution of the punishment of convicts, while in a *cour d'assises* magistrates presided over a procedure in which a jury judged an accused, who could just as well be acquitted. As a result, the RCM suggested to show deliberating magistrates, rather than the executing '*force publique*'.[26] Seen in this light, the five scenes show (next to (A) a judgment regarding the freedom of a citizen) (B) the prevention of an execution, (C) a dramatic moment during an execution, (D) the refusal of mercy (and the preparation of an execution), and (E) the acquittal of a wrongfully convicted subject. The contemporary reality was completely different since, by means of a royal pardon, Belgian Ministers of Justice had, from 1863 onwards, consistently made sure that capital punishment was never executed.[27] The fact that no one paid attention to the RCM's comment is proof of Smekens' determination and influence, as well as the Commission's limited authority in this particular case, as opposed to the earlier

[25]Commission Royale des Monuments: Résumé des Proces-Verbaux: Peinture et sculpture. 1887. *Bulletin des Commissions Royales d'Art et d'Archeologie* 1887: 100–101.

[26]Antwerp, RCM Archives, KCML A/0804, letter from the RCM to Van der Ouderaa, 2 February 1887.

[27]See the contribution by De Brouwer and Rousseaux in this volume.

mentioned Brussels *Cour de Cassation* case, where the RCM succeeded in forcing through its plans for the subject matter.

20.4 Van der Ouderaa's Preceding Oeuvre

'Mister Van der Ouderaa has ingeniously illustrated the Antwerp archives' (*Journal de Bruxelles*, 19 September 1891). These words were written by a critic after having seen Van der Ouderaa's *La veille de l'exécution* (1891), one of his many paintings set inside the *Steen* prison (Génard's museum, which had just been renovated). The critic also complained about the lack of a 'perfume of the past' and 'intimate penetration'.

The next section in this paper aims to show the close collaboration between Pieter Génard and Pieter Van der Ouderaa, as well as how the latter's legal historical artistic oeuvre and the lack of emotion therein enabled Smekens to communicate his view on the law.

20.4.1 The Artist and the Legal Historian: Collaborations

A first documented cooperation between Génard and Van der Ouderaa took place in 1875, when baron Henri Marie van de Werve de Schilde had his hotel (demolished in 1957) in the Antwerp *Kipdorp* street decorated. For the monumental paintings, the baron hired the well-established painter Godfried Guffens (1823–1901), but the design of the stained glass windows containing 38 medallions was given to Van der Ouderaa. Both artists were able to rely on Génard for guidance in the subject matter, the history of the family. Génard issued a publication with this research, a modus operandi he would also use for his other assignments (Génard 1879). Twelve of Van der Ouderaa's medallions, made by renowned stained-glass artists Auguste Stalins (1839–1906) and Alfons Janssens (1836–1915), show the gruesome story of the assassin Simon Turchi. As told by Hendrik Conscience in his novel *Simon Turchi*, the Van de Werve family played an important part in this historical story, since both Turchi, the assassin, and his victim, Jeronimo Deodati, courted Marie van de Werve (Conscience 1859; Génard 1879; Van Langendonck 2002, pp. 218–219; *Het Handelsblad*, 30 December 1875). The last windows showed the execution scene, when Turchi was burned in the armchair in which he had killed his victim. One of the stained-glass window designs provides us with an image of the artist, explaining his work, and the legal historian, holding the documents (Fig. 20.3). These designs form Van der Ouderaa's oldest work on legal history, and Génard was there to guide him.

In 1876, the archivist published an article in his *De Vlaamsche School*, in which he stipulated how magistrates were dressed in the sixteenth century because several artists had asked him what they looked like (Génard 1876). Van der Ouderaa was undoubtedly among them, since at the Antwerp *salon* of that year, he showed his painting of the widow of count Egmont being introduced to the Antwerp magistrates. In 1877, *De Vlaamse School* published an account of a judicial reconciliation in Turnhout in 1577—a piece that was probably written by Génard (1877). Two years later, Van der Ouderaa presented *La reconciliation judiciaire* (*The Kiss of Peace*, Royal Museum of Fine Arts, Antwerp, 1879, Fig. 20.4), which puts this legal procedure inside one of the chapels of the Antwerp cathedral. However, it features a fictional female protagonist, kissed on the lips by her father's murderer.[28] The chronology, however, leaves little doubt about Van der Ouderaa's inspiration.

The team that collaborated for the Hotel De Werve de Schilde—Génard as a historian and iconographer, Van der Ouderaa as the designer, and Stalins and Janssens as the glass painters—was responsible for several of the stained glass windows in the Antwerp cathedral. Following Smekens' harsh criticism of Didron's windows in 1872–1873, Génard's help would keep Van der Ouderaa safe.[29] Factual, antiquarian exactitude was Van der Ouderaa's trademark—similar to the De Vriendts and, to a lesser degree, Ooms. The collaboration between the artist and the legal historian continued the following decade, and by the time Génard published his two-volume *Anvers à travers les ages* in 1886–1887, he could benefit from their collaboration. Génard was able to use no less than six paintings painted by Van der Ouderaa between 1876 and 1882 as double page illustrations. They all had to do with legal history, or at the very least featured the Antwerp magistrates.[30]

Several of Van der Ouderaa's paintings are set in, or in the vicinity of, the *Steen*. In the catalogue of the Antwerp *salon* of 1882, Van der Ouderaa referred to Génard's museum catalogue to explain his painting *Une réparation judiciaire à Anvers en 1593* (*Exposition nationale* 1882, pp. 181–182). Génard, in his turn, lectured and published a note on the criminal case Van der Ouderaa had put into painting as *En route pour le supplice* (*The Road to the Execution*, or *The Last Appeal* as it was also called, *cf. infra*, Fig. 20.5), in 1880–1881, and ended his account with an entire page devoted to an explanation and eulogy of the painting (which he called *La dernière prière*).[31]

---

[28]For the procedure, see Petkov (2003), which uses Van der Ouderaa's invention as a cover illustration. Historically, women were unlikely to be kissed on the lips in such a procedure.

[29]Eventually, Smekens, Génard and Van der Ouderaa would each be a member of the stained-glass window commission (G.S. 1896). In 1887, Stalins and Janssens also designed and executed the stained-glass windows for the Smekens family in the Saint John Berchman chapel inside the Antwerp cathedral (including a window for Saint Theophilus), whilst Van der Ouderaa painted the chapel's altarpiece, a historicist triptych placed right in front of the Smekens windows (Grieten et al. 1996, pp. 152–153; Evens 2002, pp. 77–81).

[30]These paintings include *La veuve d'Egmont présenté au magistrat d'Anvers* (1876), *L'archiduc inauguré au serment de la grande arbalète en 1515* (1876), *Ouverture de la Foire* (a.k.a. *La distribution des roses*) (1878), *Le baiser de justice* or *La réconciliation judiciaire* (*The Kiss of Peace*) (1879), *Marguerite Harstein* or *En route pour le supplice* (1880), and *Une réparation judiciaire à Anvers en 1593* (1882).

[31]Génard (1880, p. 9) had read the note in the *Académie d'Archéologie de Belgique* on 6 June 1880.

20.4.2 Emotional Deficit

Unlike Génard, a large number of critics did not care much for Van der Ouderaa's art. To them, it lacked emotion—a criticism Ooms and the De Vriendt brothers were also subjected to. Critics from the local, Catholic newspaper *Het Handelsblad* always spoke highly of Van der Ouderaa's work (unsurprisingly, since the artist was one of their journalists: Van Maanen 2017, p. 163), but most other critics were less favourable, and deemed his historical scenes to be cold and emotionless.[32]

Within the scope of this paper, it is useful to focus on Van der Ouderaa's *En route pour le supplice (Anvers le 12 février 1555)*. On the one hand, the setting and composition of the work, painted in 1880–1881, are conspicuously close to Van der Ouderaa's largest work, the central, monumental painting *La punition du parjure* in the Antwerp *cour d'assises*. On the other hand, the criticism the painting was subjected to, is exemplary for Van der Ouderaa's legal historical scenes. As I argue, this lack of emotion can help us understand what Smekens had in mind for the *cour d'assises* paintings.

As mentioned above, the story depicted in the painting was read and subsequently published by Génard in 1880, probably when Van der Ouderaa had just finished the artwork, which he would only show for the first time at the Brussels *salon* in 1881. The large painting (three metres across) showed a Viennese woman Marguerite (probably Margareta, 'Margriete' in the Dutch source published by Génard) Hartstein, kneeling in front of a Calvary during a procession which led her from the *Steen* prison to her execution. Hartstein had been sentenced to the stake after having killed her aggressor, a Spanish doctor called Hieronymus Abanzo, in February 1555. Van der Ouderaa placed the gaunt looking woman on the left of his composition, flanked by a monk and her executioner. Behind her is the executioner's helper, kneeled next to the faggots which remind us of her imminent punishment. In the centre, we can find the magistrates in their costumes as described in Génard's helpful article from 1876, and the audience. The gate of the *Steen* can be seen in the back. The scene is set on the historical *Palingbrug* just outside the *Steen*, a bridge that was destroyed a few years after Van der Ouderaa created the painting. In his days, the spot where he painted a Calvary (a crucified Christ flanked by Our Lady and John the Baptist) was occupied by a large, single crucified Christ, as can be seen on a postcard of the time (Fig. 20.6). The actual crucifix was too high to fit into the composition, but the location was known as the last place where convicted criminals prayed before their execution. Hence, Van der Ouderaa did not need to do anything more than place his costumed actors in the existing setting.

When in 1887–1888 Van der Ouderaa painted his *La punition du parjure* for the *cour d'assises*, he simply reused his composition from *En route pour le supplice* (compare Figs. 20.1 and 20.5). However, he turned the perspective 45°, so that the viewer is placed opposite the Calvary. The kneeling helper of the executioner

---

[32]On the lack of emotion in *The Kiss of Peace* (1880), see *L'Art Moderne*, 10 September 1882; *Le Bien Public*, 21 June 1885; *Rotterdamsch Nieuwsblad*, 24 June 1879; Coppieters (1883), p. 20.

became the convicted perjurer,[33] the observing, standing man and kneeling woman were moved from the right to the left. There, together with the large crowd and the chart which would transport the convict, they provide balance to the composition. The Calvary was turned into the single crucifix again, and as such also functioned as a traditional courtroom crucifix. Contemporary critics also noted the resemblance between the two artworks. (*De Tijd*, 4 October 1889; *L'Indépendance Belge*, 23 September 1890).

Like most of Van der Ouderaa's history paintings, *En route pour le supplice* drew the attention of critics at the many exhibitions (Brussels and Paris in 1881, Amsterdam in 1883, London in 1885, Melbourne in 1888 and Philadelphia in 1894) in which it appeared, and where it would eventually receive *The last appeal* as its international title (*Catalogue of over Seven Hundred Paintings* 1894; *P. Van Ouderaa's Great Picture* 1888). The bystanders on the painting were especially problematic, because of their indifference. In the long catalogue note, Van der Ouderaa himself wrote that the audience was in silent contemplation, repeating the monk's prayer (*Exposition générale* 1881, p. 108). The critic of *L'Indépendence Belge* interpreted this as a weakness, a lack of indignation, and the progressive art journal *L'Art Moderne* concurred.[34] It was this weakness and lack of indignation, and Marguerite Hartstein suffering, that formed the essence of Van der Ouderaa's message. His catalogue note started with an explicit reminder of the 'excessive severity' of sixteenth-century criminal law (*Exposition générale* 1881, p. 108, no 799). He then gave some examples of excessive 'mirror punishments', in which criminals (e.g. forgers) were given a punishment (e.g. being boiled alive) that reflected the crime (forgery) (Monballyu 2006). Van der Ouderaa opposed all this to his main point: however harsh their punishment, convicts always received spiritual consolation, and the audience silently agreed (at least according to Van der Ouderaa). First and foremost, the artist wanted to demonstrate the religious respect for the law that was present in sixteenth-century Antwerp, ignoring, among others, the Calvinist regime (1577–1585). By emphasising how spiritual consolation was an inherent part of sixteenth-century punishment, and by presenting this ancient punishment as morally superior, Van der Ouderaa's paintings provided the objectivist criminal legal doctrine with historical arguments.

The conservative Catholic press welcomed this message. The Dutch newspaper *De Tijd* (7 July 1883), whose former editor in chief was Jan Willem Brouwers (1831–1893), a Catholic priest and correspondent of Génard, was wildly enthusiastic after seeing the painting at the 1883 Amsterdam *salon*:

> [Van der Ouderaa's] painting is no "fashionable" work, no work created for political, clerical or anticlerical purposes; it just wants to render an episode from the life of the Middle Ages, seen through the eyes of the artist. Whether that woman, brought to the

---

[33] Van der Ouderaa often included such kneeled figures, turned with their back to the beholder, as also noted for his stained glass window designs by Leen Evens (2002, p. 80).

[34] For the lack of emotion in *En route pour le supplice*, see *L'Indépendance Belge*, 29 August 1881; *L'Art Moderne*, 2 October 1881, p. 243.

> scaffold, is guilty or not guilty; whether medieval justice should be rated inferior compared to modern justice, or whether the "superstition" and "lust for power" of the clergy can be held accountable for the cruelty of justice, from all these questions, the artist has wisely kept away, and, as an artist, he is not to interfere with them. Only this did he want to express in his painting: all these people, even the simple observer and the assistant executioner, all feel, right there in front of the crucifix (…), the lofty gravity of the moment. Neither the magistrates, nor the audience, nor the soldiers are the kind of nervous and oversensitive people from the nineteenth century; they are, at least in that moment, serious medieval Christians, who see, rightfully or wrongly, the judgment's execution, which will be implemented, as an utterly just—and even, in a certain way, religious—deed. They might be wrong, but their good faith is undeniable.[35]

In this light, Van der Ouderaa's work could easily be used to advocate a more severe criminal law and punishment—as opposed to what 'oversensitive' contemporary legislators thought. His emotionless rendering of the subjects facilitated such interpretations. Jules Bosmans (1853–1928) a priest and archivist known for his less-than-factual historical publications, saw divine and human justice at work in the painting, which he discussed in his 1881 *salon* review. With Hartstein's imminent punishment in mind, Bosmans trenchantly referred to an ongoing Belgian murder case in which the French Communard and murder suspect Edmond-Auguste Baraquin (b 1845) wanted to be tried in Belgium in order to escape the possibility of a French death penalty (Bosmans 1881; De Ghellinck Vaernewyck 1961; Le Maitron 2007–2017).

In 1887, the critic of *Het Handelsblad* also gave his interpretation of modern criminal law after seeing Van der Ouderaa's *La punition du parjure* (Fig. 20.1), the retrial of *En route pour le supplice*. The perjurer deserved the highest penalty, according to the critic (*Het Handelsblad*, 9 November 1887): 'Our ancestors were not so benevolent and forgiving as our contemporary legislators, and although we do not wish those past days to come back, it is good to illustrate the punishment for perjurers back then'. Again, *L'Indépendance Belge*'s (23 September 1890) critic was not convinced of the emotional qualities of the painting. Due to its antiquarian exactness, the sketch for the *cour d'assises* supposedly lacked character and life. And concerning the latter, 'one would learn more about the sixteenth-century judicial mores from the naive images accompanying Damhouder's *Praxis rerum criminalium* than from paintings such as those of Van der Ouderaa'.[36]

In his account of the story of Marguerite Hartstein, Génard added that, whatever opinion nineteenth-century readers might have about the harshness of early modern criminal law and the barbarism of its punishment, at least the trial followed the rules (Génard 1880, p. 8). However, as we have seen, Génard later wrote that, in matters of civil rights, these rules were no different from those of the nineteenth century. A painting form 1882 called *Une réparation judiciaire à Anvers en 1593* showed the Antwerp magistrates apologising to a wealthy tradesman after days of wrongful torture. Again, the focus is not at all on the actual torture or abuse of the law. We only see an old nobleman who needs to be supported after his days of agony, which

[35] *De Tijd*, 7 July 1883 (trans. SH).

[36] On Damhouder, see Jäger in this volume, and Monballyu (2016).

are thus only implicitly present. The focus is on the grandness of the magistrates and the mutual respect between the (wrongfully) accused and the judiciary. As written in the catalogue note (a quote from Génard's museum catalogue for the *Steen*), the tradesman was asked what kind of indemnity he wanted. Because he had enough money, the man asked for the torturing device that was used on him to be exhibited in his former cell, were it hung until French Revolutionaries burned it in the 1790s (Deseure 2014, pp. 195–197; Génard 1888, pp. 268–269).

The message behind these artworks was such that they painted a coloured, rosy picture of the criminal legal past. As an epigone, the painter monumentalised Leys' sixteenth-century scenes. Furthermore, to paraphrase art historian Herwig Todts, he not only turned them into 'pictorial inventories of picturesque old Antwerp' (Todts 1985), but also into costumed expressions of conservative Catholic standards. Because it presented the (legal) past as morally superior (Van Cleven 1994 p. 127), it was not difficult for Smekens to instrumentalise Van der Ouderaa's oeuvre for the *cour d'assises*.

20.5 Conclusion

Firstly, this paper showed how Théophile Smekens, a conservative Catholic judge and traditionalist leading figure in the Antwerp art scene, gathered a number of like-minded members of said scene to decorate 'his' *cour d'assises*.

Secondly, the chosen subject matter was such that it fitted into a broader frame that was the result of the close professional relationship between Pieter Van der Ouderaa and Pieter Génard, which scholars have neglected up until now. Specifically with respect to Antwerp criminal legal history, there was a kind of bilateral inspiration: a two-way traffic between the artist and the legal historian, the former as illustrator of the work of the latter, and the latter as scholar and explainer of the oeuvre of the former.

Thirdly, both Génard's historiography and Van der Ouderaa's depictions of history allowed Smekens to make his point about Prins and Le Jeune's contemporary modernisation of criminal law. On the one hand, Génard's Antwerp city pride equated local late-medieval with post-revolutionary civil rights in criminal matters. On the other hand, both the emotional deficit and the absence of actual torture, punishment or execution in Van der Ouderaa's paintings implied a moral superiority of the legal past. In the decoration programme for the Antwerp *cour d'assises*, Smekens instrumentalised these presentations of history in order to subtly express his disagreement with the social defence doctrine which he deemed less repressive and therefore inferior. As a response, the judge generalised the repressive regime and moral guidance, which the social defence doctrine installed for inveterate malefactors. For Smekens, negating the importance of the French Revolution and modernity was one and the same thing as keeping foreign and modern influences away from Belgian or Flemish art, in line with the writings of the De Vriendt brothers. Hence, his artistic conservatism proved to be in symbiosis with his view on criminal law.

Acknowledgment I would like to thank Dirk Heirbaut, Georges Martyn, Marjan Sterckx and Bruno De Wever for their comments, as well as Jan Caudron, Brecht Deseure, Rita S'Jegers, Jeroen Van Steenkiste, my fellow editors and all conference participants.

References

Aron P (1997) Emile Verhaeren: Écrits sur l'art (1881–1916). Labor, Brussels

Artibus P (1865) Journal des Beaux-Arts et de la Litérature 1865:164

Baetens JD (2012) Voor vorst en vaderland. Een nieuwe lezing van de muurschilderingen van Henri Leys in het Antwerpse stadhuis. Belgisch Tijdschrift voor Filologie en Geschiedenis/ Revue belge de philologie et d'histoire 90(2):513–539

Block J (1997) The art of law: le jeune barreau: patron of arts and letters. In: Block J (ed) Belgium. The golden decades. Peter Lang, New York

Bosmans J (1881) Le Salon de 1881 (Bruxelles, Palais des Beaux-Arts, 14 août-16 octobre 1881): Catalogue explicatif. Imprimerie Adolphe Mertens, Brussels

De Bruyn H (1872) Exposition triennale des Beaux-Arts de Bruxelles 1872 (15 août-15 octobre 1872): compte rendu du salon. C. Muquardt, Brussels

Buyck J (1980) Antwerp, Als Ik Kan, and the Problem of Provincialism. In: Botvinnik MM, Robert-Jones P, Block J (eds) Belgian art, 1880–1914. Brooklyn Museum, New York, pp 71–80

Caeymaex C (1899) P. Génard (repr. from Dietsche Warande). A. Siffer, Ghent

(1894) Catalogue of over Seven Hundred Paintings forming the Present Valuable Stock of the Haseltine Galleries. Davis & Harvey, Philadelphia

Christiaensen S (2004) Tussen klassieke en moderne criminele politiek. Leven en beleid van Jules Lejeune. Samenleving, Criminaliteit & Strafrechtspleging, vol XXVIII. Universitaire Pers Leuven, Leuven

(1891) Congrès International pour l'Etude des questions relatives au patronage des détenus et à la protection des enfants moralement abandonnés Anvers 1890. Compte rendu sténographique. Guyot, Brussels

Conscience H (1859) Simon Turchi of de Italianen te Antwerpen (1550): historische tafereelen uit de XVIe eeuw. J.P. Van Dieren en C°, Antwerp

Coppieters EL (1883) Critique du Salon Triennal de Gand, 1883. Volksdrukkerij, Ghent

De Ghellinck Vaernewyck X (1961) Bosmans, Jules. In: Biographie nationale. vol XXXI. Bruylant, Brussels, pp 103–106

De Longé G (ed) (1871) Coutumes du Pays et Duché du Brabant, Quartier d'Anvers, vol II (Coutume de la Ville d'Anvers). Gobbaerts, Brussels

Demeyer F (2008) De muurschilderingen van de gebroeders De Vriendt in de gotische zaal van het Brugse stadhuis (1886–1905), panorama en pantheon van de Brugse geschiedenis. De rol van Louis Delacenserie, Albrecht en Juliaan De Vriendt, François Van den Abeele, Louis Gilliodts-Van Severen, Julius Sabbe en Georges Rodenbach, Master thesis, University of Leuven

De Ruyver B (1998) De transformatie van het Belgisch strafrecht tegen de achtergrond van de politieke en sociaal-economische ontwikkelingen in het laatste kwart van de negentiende eeuw. In: Heirbaut D, Lambrecht D (ed) Van oud en nieuw recht. Kluwer Rechtswetenschappen, Antwerp, pp 191–218

Deseure B (2014) Onhoudbaar verleden. Geschiedenis als politiek instrument tijdens de Franse periode in België. Universitaire Pers, Leuven

De Smet J, Verleysen C (ed) (2016) Emile Verhaeren, de schrijver-criticus en de kunst van zijn tijd, 1881–1916. Snoeck, Gent

De Taeye E-L (1894) Les artistes belges contemporains: Leur vie, leurs oeuvres, leur place dans l'art. Alfred Castaigne, Brussels

De Vriendt J (1871) Over de noodzakelijkheid van een Vlaamse kunstbeweging. De Zweep 3:17, 18, 19, 21, 22 and 26

De Vriendt J (1874) Over Nationalisme en Kosmopolitisme in de Beeldende Kunst. De Vlaamse Kunstbode 4:1

Dumon M (1987) De Antwerpse schilder Karel Ooms (1845–1900): een studie van zijn leven en werk. Master thesis, University of Leuven

Evens L (2002) Stalins en Janssens: Een Antwerps glazeniersatelier uit de late negentiende en vroege twintigste eeuw. Een historische en stilitische studie, Master thesis, University of Leuven

(1881) Exposition générale des Beaux-Arts 1881 (Bruxelles, Palais des Beaux-Arts, 14 août-16 octobre 1881): Catalogue explicatif. Imprimerie Adolphe Mertens, Brussels

(1882) Exposition nationale: catalogue des ouvrages de peinture, sculpture, architecture, gravure et dessin, exécutés par des artistes vivants, et exposés au Salon d'Anvers, ouvert par la Société Royale d'Encouragement des Beaux-Arts le 13 août (-1er octobre 1882). J.P. van Dieren & Co, Antwerp

Fijnaut C (2014) Criminologie en strafrechtsbedeling: een historische en transatlantische inleiding. Intersentia, Antwerpen

G.S (1896) P. Génard en de glasschildering. De Dietsche Warande. Nieuwe reeks 9:89

Génard P (1876) De oude kledij van het magistraat te Antwerpen. De Vlaamsche School 1876:30–31

Génard P (1877) Een doodslag te Turnhout in 1577. De Vlaamsche School 1877:146–147

Génard P (1879) Les Peintures Monumentales de l'Hôtel et du Château de Schilde. Van Os-De Wolf, Antwerp

Génard P (1880) Une exécution au XVIe siècle. Imprimerie G. van Merlen, Antwerp

Génard P (1881) Catalogue du Musée d'Antiquités. Buschmann, Antwerp

Génard P (1888) Anvers à travers les âges. Bruylant, Brussels

Génard P (1891) Les Peintures Murales du Palais de Justice d'Anvers. Province d'Anvers, Bulletin du Comité des Membres Correspondants de la Commission Royale des Monuments et de la Commission du Musée d'Antiquités, etc. d'Anvers 3:107–123

Goovaerts A, Vandeweyer L (1998) Meetingpartij. In: De Wever B, De Schrijver R (eds) Nieuwe encyclopedie van de vlaamse beweging. Lannoo, Tielt, pp 2026–2028

Grieten S, Mees M, Van Damme J, Van Langendonck L (1996) Een venster op de hemel: de glasramen van de Onze-Lieve-Vrouwekathedraal van Antwerpen. Provinciebestuur, Antwerp

Huygebaert S, Vandenbogaerde S (2014) Êtes-vous Justice, Minerve ou Thémis? Een tijdschriftlogo als *numen mixtum* en symptoom van de versmelting van kunst en recht in het Belgische *fin de siècle*. Pro Memorie. Bijdragen tot de rechtsgeschiedenis der Nederlanden 16 (2):244–258

Huygebaert S (2014) "Le décor au milieu duquel ils vivront": Beeldhouwkunst en decoratie in het Justitiepaleis. In: Van Eeckhoutte W, Maes B (eds) Genius, grandeur en gêne. Het Fin de Siècle rond het Justitiepaleis te Brussel en de controversiële figuur van Edmond Picard. Cassatio, vol. I. Knops, Gent, pp 117–183

Huygebaert S (2016) Het ‘Justitiepaleis der schone kunsten’ als symbiose van kunst en recht in het *fin-de-siècle*. In: Debaenst B (ed) De Belle Époque van het Belgisch recht (1870–1914). Die Keure, Bruges, pp 155–184

Huygebaert S (2018) Legal Imagery on the Edge of Symbolism: The Decoration Projects for the Belgian *Cour de Cassation*. In: Manderson D (ed) Law and the visual: transition, transformation and transmission. University of Toronto Press, Toronto, pp 122–140

Laenens C (1953) De geschiedenis van het Antwerps gerecht. P. Van de Velde, Antwerp

Laenens C (1977) Tijdsbeeld en historische herinneringen uit de periode van de oprichting van het Justitiepaleis. In: Van Camp C (ed) Juristen en rechtsleven ten tijde van Rubens. Paul van de Velde, Antwerp, pp 178–212

Le Maitron (2007–2017) Baraquin Edmond, Auguste. In: Le Maitron, dictionnaire biographique. http://maitron-en-ligne.univ-paris1.fr. Accessed 18 June 2017

Monballyu J (2006) Spiegelstraffen in het Brugse strafrecht in de eerste helft van de 16e eeuw. Handelingen van het Genootschap voor geschiedenis te Brugge 143:164–186

Monballyu J (2014) Six centuries of criminal law. History of criminal law in the southern Netherlands and Belgium (1400–2000). Brill Leiden

Monballyu J (2016) Joos de Damhouder. An internationally influential jurist from Bruges. In: Huygebaert S, Martyn G, Paumen V, Van Poucke T (eds) The art of law. Three centuries of justice depicted (exh. cat. Bruges). Lannoo, Tielt, pp 106–119

Ogonovszky-Steffens J (1999) La peinture monumentale d’histoire dans les édifices civils en Belgique (1830–1914). Académie royale de Belgique. Classe des Beaux-Arts, Brussels

(1888) P. Van Ouderaa’s Great Picture “The Last Appeal” at Koekkoek’s Exhibition, Melbourne Athletic Club. Carron, Bird & Co, Melbourne

Persoons G, Buyck J, Bedeer G (1976) Schone Kunsten in Antwerpen: de Koninklijke Vereniging tot Aanmoediging der Schone Kunsten te Antwerpen sinds 1788. Nationaal Hoger Instituut en Koninklijke Academie voor Schone Kunsten, Antwerp

Petkov K (2003) The kiss of peace: ritual, self, and society in the high and late medieval west. Brill, Leiden

Smekens T (1873) Très-humble remontrance d’un ignorant à un savant: lettre à M. Ed. Didron au sujet de ses vitraux d’Anvers. Van Roey, Anvers

Snieders A (1893) Hoe mijn vriend de Archivarius in de Vlaamsche beweging kwam. In: Werken, vol VIII (Dit sijn Snideriën). Maatschappij ‘Voor God en ‘t Volk’, Antwerp, pp 61–73 (1925)

Somers M, van Roey J (1998) Génard, Pieter. In: De Wever B, De Schrijver R (eds) Nieuwe Encyclopedie van de Vlaamse Beweging. Lannoo, Tielt, p 1252

Todts H (1985) Aspecten en tendensen in de laat-19de eeuwse Antwerpse schilderkunst, 1880–1914. In: Buyck J (ed) Antwerpen 1900. Schilderijen en tekeningen 1880–1914. Ministerie van de Vlaamse Gemeenschap, Antwerp

Todts H (1998) Beeldende kunsten. In: De Wever B, De Schrijver R (eds) Nieuwe Encyclopedie van de Vlaamse Beweging. Lannoo, Tielt, pp 413–422

VandenBorre H, Weissenborn H, De Houwer V (1999) De ‘Gotische zaal’ van het Brugse stadhuis; neogotische herinrichting en huidige proefrestauratie. Monumenten & Landschappen 18(5):4–32

Van Caenegem RC (1956) Geschiedenis van het strafprocesrecht in Vlaanderen van de XIe tot de XIVe eeuw. Brussels: Koninklijke Vlaamse Academic voor Wetenschappen, Letteren en Schone Kunsten van België

Van Cleven J (ed) (1994) Neogotiek in België (exh. cat. Ghent). Lannoo, Tielt

Van den Nieuwenhuizen J (2002) Génard, Pieter Marius Nicolaas Johannes. In: National Biografisch Woordenboek, vol XVI. Paleis der Academiën, Brussels, pp 377–385

Van Doorslaer D (1984) Biografie van Pieter Genard, stadsarchivaris van Antwerpen (1830–1899). Katholieke Universiteit Leuven, Leuven

Van Goethem H (1985) De Bond der Vlaamse Rechtsgeleerden (1885–1964). In: Van Goethem H (ed) Honderd jaar Vlaams rechtsleven. Story Scientia, Gent, pp 13–199

Van Huerck E (1919) Notice nécrologique sur M. Pierre Van der Ouderaa. Anvers Secelle, Antwerp

Van Langendonck L (2002) Het hôtel van de Werve de Schilde in het Antwerpse Kipdorp (ca. 1783). Sic transit gloria mundi. In: Grieten S (ed) Vreemd gebouwd: westerse en niet-westerse elementen in onze architectuur. Brepols, Antwerp, pp 199–222
Van Maanen A (2017) Meneer de opsteller: de Antwerpse journalisten in de negentiende eeuw. University Press, Antwerp
Verbruggen C (2009) Schrijverschap in de Belgische belle époque: een sociaal-culturele geschiedenis. Vantilt, Nijmegen
Weber D (1996) Homo criminalis. Belgische parlementsleden over misdaad en strafrecht 1830–1940. VUB Press, Brussels

Stefan Huygebaert is an art historian (Ghent University, 2011). Since October 2012, he is preparing a PhD thesis at the Ghent Legal History Institute/Department of Art History (Ghent University), entitled *Visual Idea(l)s of Law and Justice*. This PhD research analyses the visual language of law & justice in Belgium during the nineteenth century. Since October 2015, he is a Research Foundation—Flanders (FWO) PhD fellow. Both in 2014–2015 and in 2016–2017, Stefan was a pre-doctoral fellow at the Kunsthistorisches Institut in Florenz, within the Minerva Research Group 'The Nomos of Images: Manifestation and Iconology of Law'. He has published on legal and constitutional iconology and nineteenth-century art.

Figures

Fig. 20.1 Pieter Van der Ouderaa, *La punition du parjure*, finished and placed in 1888, Antwerp, *cour d'assises*, photo by author

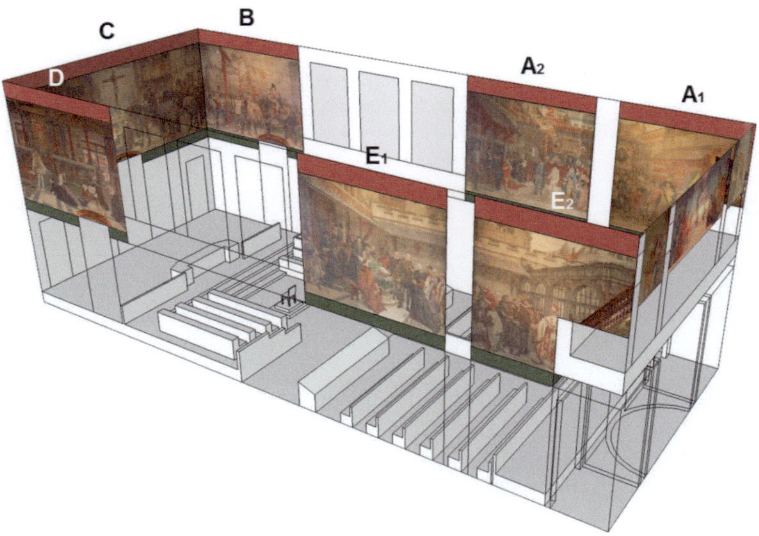

Fig. 20.2 3D reproduction of the Antwerp *cour d'assises*, with paintings and indication of the principles and quotes from costumary law (above the paintings) and summaries (underneath), © Jeroen Van Steenkiste, architect, and author

Fig. 20.3 Pieter Van der Ouderaa, *Baron van de Werve en van Schilde & and his son in the studio of artist P. Van der Ouderaa 1876*, design for a stained glass window, 1876, ϕ 16,7 cm, MoMu Fashion Museum Antwerp, inv.nr. P696, photo by author

Fig. 20.4 Pieter Van der Ouderaa, *The Kiss of Peace* (*De mondzoen/Une réconciliation judiciaire au 16*[e] *siècle*), 1876, Koninklijk Museum voor Schone Kunsten Antwerpen © Lukas—Art in Flanders vzw, photo by Hugo Maertens

Fig. 20.5 Pieter Van der Ouderaa, *En route pour le supplice*, 1880, print from Génard's *Anvers à travers les ages*

Fig. 20.6 Postcard with picture by Edmond Fierlants, *Gevangenisstraat and entry gate to the Steenstraat and the Steen*, 1860, G. Hermans, Antwerp. Author's collection

Chapter 21
Depictions of Justice in the Colonial Courts of British India: The Judicial Iconography of the Bombay High Court

Rahela Khorakiwala

Abstract The Bombay High Court in Mumbai was constructed in 1878 and has its own unique judicial iconography. This contribution investigates the visual narrative of the High Court by analysing the statues of justice and mercy that are placed atop the High Court building, the carvings of the 'monkey judge' and 'fox lawyer' on the pillars of the court, and several other visual representations of justice. The iconography has played a role in the development of popular cultural imagery, and has its own folklore in the court today. This paper is an attempt to document the court in terms of its visual representation and the survival thereof in a colonial construction that is now part of independent India.

21.1 Introduction

As a result of the presence of the British rule in India, there are several buildings that were constructed by the colonial government in order to show its presence in the areas it controlled (Kidambi 2007). The British rule in India started through the East India Company, mainly with the idea of improving trade and commerce. Over the years, however, this situation changed, and the British government eventually assumed direct control over its colony. One of the major ways in which it did this was through the establishment of a British system of judicial administration (Kolsky 2010; Mukherjee 2009). What was particularly relevant, was the establishment of high courts in the erstwhile presidency towns of Calcutta, Bombay and Madras.

The three high courts of Calcutta, Bombay and Madras were established in 1862 when India was still a British colony. Therefore, not only was the administration of justice promulgated in British terms, but the architectural structures from which justice would be dispensed were influenced by British notions of architectural supremacy as well (Baucom 1999). This paper focuses on one such building, which

R. Khorakiwala (✉)
Centre for the Study of Law and Governance, Jawaharlal Nehru University, New Delhi, India
e-mail: rahela.k@gmail.com

S. Huygebaert et al. (eds.), *The Art of Law*, Ius Gentium: Comparative Perspectives on Law and Justice 66, https://doi.org/10.1007/978-3-319-90787-1_21

was built by the British for the administration of justice in the Bombay presidency: the Bombay High Court. While the High Court itself was established in 1862, the building that was supposed to house it was only completed in 1878.

Built by British engineers in a neo-gothic architectural style, the Bombay High Court building stands tall in front of the large *maidan*[1] spaces that line the city. This colonial court disperses its very own images of law and justice—dominated by British ideas as well as being influenced by local narratives. The High Court is unique in that, while it was conceptualised as a colonial construct, it transformed into the legal system as stipulated under the Constitution of India when the country gained independence. In this paper, I will document the judicial iconography of the Bombay High Court, and analyse the statues and carvings seen in and around the court, in an attempt to understand their presence on the walls of the court during colonial times, and their continuing relevance in a post-colonial period.[2]

21.2 A Brief History of the Bombay High Court

The history of the administration of justice in Bombay starts in 1668, when the island of Bombay was transferred from King Charles II to the East India Company (Jain 2012). It changed from being an Admiralty Court in 1684 into the Recorder's Court (1798) and eventually into Supreme Court of Bombay (in 1824).[3]

The political events of 1857[4] triggered changes in the functioning and power structure of the East India Company. As a result, the Government of England assumed direct rule over the territory of British India (Madras High Court 1962). One of the major changes was the introduction of the Indian High Courts Act (1861), which issued Letters Patent under the Great Seal of the United Kingdom that led to the establishment of the high courts of Calcutta, Bombay and Madras (Gopalratnam 1962; Nair 1987). On the 26th of January 1950, the Republic of India was created through the adoption of the Constitution of India, which established the Supreme Court of India as the highest court for the republic. The Bombay High

[1]A large, open field.

[2]The research presented in this paper is part of a larger project wherein I document the representation of law, images and justice in the colonial courts of British India, and how this is seen by contemporaries. While I am a lawyer by training, my work focusses on a legal anthropology of the Bombay High Court, among other courts in India. I have conducted an ethnography of the Bombay High Court, along with interviewing judges, lawyers and court staff. I have also conducted a systematic exploration of the physical space of the court itself and mapped the court building as it stands today. My data-set is a reflection of my observations in the field, along with the idea of law and justice as represented through the oral narrative of the court personnel I interviewed.

[3]See Jain (2012) for a detailed account of the development of the administration of justice in Bombay.

[4]The *sepoy* (Indian soldier) mutiny of 1857 is often considered as the first war for India's independence. The mutiny eventually led to the dissolution of the East India Company.

Court continued to exist under the Constitution of India, and adapted to the change of jurisdiction by placing itself under the final rule of the Supreme Court of India.

21.3 Establishment of the Bombay High Court Building

Designed by Lieutenant-Colonel John Augustus Fuller from the Royal Engineers, the Bombay High Court is a neo-gothic structure built in front of a large stretch of *maidans* in Bombay (Fig. 21.1). Construction of the present building began in April 1871, and was completed in November 1878 (Mehrotra and Dwivedi 2004). The Bombay High Court building was built on a terrain that was once flattened out by the British in fear of an attack by the French in 1772. This land was reserved as an open space in front of the main fort so as to prevent attacks (Mehrotra and Dwivedi 2004). The walls of the fort were demolished in the 1860s, and this vast piece of land was opened up for construction. After gaining some funding from private parties, several public buildings were commissioned. These buildings were all constructed in a neo-gothic style, in order to maintain what the British believed to be an 'imperial image' (Mehrotra and Dwivedi 2004, p. 27).[5] This style is also seen in the adjacent University of Mumbai Library and Convocation Hall, as well as in the iconic Rajabhai Tower (Clock Tower).

Seen from the front, the High Court is a large and daunting structure. The monumentalisation of law through awe-inspiring court buildings is a prominent feature across the world; a large structure is intended to play a symbolic role and to represent the ornate nature of the law (Goodrich 1990; Haldar 1994; Mulcahy 2011). As Haldar (1994, p. 200) writes, '[A]ll courts exist in their architectural representations' and therefore the first impression of a court building is an important signifier of the legitimacy rules and ideas set out by the court for the people who enter its premises. An overwhelming structure plays the role of a dominant figure that indirectly imposes upon the subjects that enter its precincts.[6]

The predominant central tower of the Bombay High Court is flanked by neo-gothic towers with internal spiral staircases. In addition to these staircases, there are spiral staircases at the east and west sides of the building. The roof of the central tower is the building's highest point, and is partially covered with glass, allowing natural light to flood into the court. Under the arches, on each floor, are long corridors that, in the current layout of the court, function as the judge's walkways. Mehrotra and Dwivedi (2004) write of an anonymously authored book

[5]Kidambi (2007, p. 34) argues that the 1870s and 1880s in Bombay witnessed the construction of several buildings specifically designed to 'underscore the imperial character of the city'. As Kidambi lists, these buildings included the Telegraph Office, the General Post Office, the Secretariat, the University Library and Convocation Hall, and the Bombay High Court.

[6]This is seen in structures of all the three presidency town high courts of Calcutta, Bombay and Madras along with the post-independence construction of the Supreme Court of India, amongst other courts in India.

that states that Fuller's design of the High Court building was based on a sketch of one of the castles along the River Rhine in Germany. Hence, the authors compare the central tower block of the court and the turrets to those of a 'medieval citadel' (Mehrotra and Dwivedi 2004, p. 39).

The roof of the High Court is two-thirds of the façade's total height, and extends left and right as two projecting wings along with two grand roofs (Mehrotra and Dwivedi 2004). In line with the neo-gothic style of architecture, there are gothic arched colonnades on each floor. Fuller incorporated these in order to allow the sea breeze to enter the building (as at that point the High Court building was facing the Arabian Sea) for enhanced ventilation (Mehrotra and Dwivedi 2004), yet in such a way that the rain from the southwest monsoon winds would not reach the courtrooms. The judges' chambers were also positioned along these passages.[7]

The walls are covered in *chunam* (lime plaster) with blue basalt and rubble on the exterior. The material for the construction of the High Court building came from local sources. Basalt stone was used across the court building. However, because basalt is a very hard material, it is not used for carvings. Hence, all decorative carvings in the Bombay High Court are done in limestone, which is much softer. There is a set of two private spiral staircases that are only accessible to the judges.

The entire cost of the construction of the building was less than what was originally thought, as is mentioned on a commemorative marble plaque on the first floor landing of the main staircace. The reduced cost of construction has led to its own folklore (*cf. infra*, 4.2) and fascinating judicial iconography in the corridors of the court (Vachha 2011, see the next section).

21.4 Judicial Iconography of the Bombay High Court

The Bombay High Court is a building filled with iconography that represents justice. On a walk around the court, it is impossible not to notice its architectural marvel. The neo-gothic architectural style, along with statues and carvings representing justice in various ways, also including local narratives, generate satire and humour on the walls of the High Court.

21.4.1 The Statue of Justice

When walking towards the High Court, the visitor will notice the statues of mercy and justice placed at the top of the court building. The placement of these two statues can be interpreted as an expression of the way in which law monumentalises

[7]As narrated by Kruti Garg, a conservationist architect, during the guided heritage walking tour of the Bombay High Court on 1 February 2014.

itself in order to impose its legitimacy. While the court includes statues of justice and mercy within the framework of its images, it also conserves its own sacredness by placing these virtues out of the visitor's immediate reach. We can draw a parallel here to Haldar's (1994) analysis of the placement of judicial books at the base of the Supreme Court of Israel. In both instances, direct contact with justice appears to be out of reach—in the case of the Bombay High Court by placing the statues at the top of the building, and in the case of the Supreme Court of Israel by placing the books at the bottom of the building. In their book, Mehrotra and Dwivedi (2004) present the idea that the Bombay High Court statues, at their elevated position, make the allegory of justice and mercy look insignificant. Placed in this way, the motifs of justice and mercy, appear to be out of reach for those entering the court premises on a daily basis. The judicial iconography of this imagery reveals the legal iconology of the position and placement of the statues. Therefore, while the presence of the statues purports to provide the representational meaning of the conveyance of justice and mercy promised by the court of law, their positioning at a distance marks a demarcation made by the law through the creation of both 'blindness and insight' (Douzinas 2000, p. 825; Haldar 1994).

The statue of the virtue Justice atop the Bombay High Court is not blindfolded[8] and holds scales in one hand and a sword in the other (Fig. 21.2). From the physical nature of the statue alone, it is hard to tell whether the personification of justice is male or female. The statue of justice depicted here appears to be the Western interpretation and conception of justice, as it was introduced through the colonial influence over the court. Until the end of the fifteenth century, justice as a virtue was personified as a lady, and she had always been open-eyed. Her blindfold became popular, and even predominant, in the course of the sixteenth century (Huygebaert et al. 2016, 139–157; Jay 2003; Resnik and Curtis 2011).[9] Interestingly, the statue of justice of the Bombay High Court is open-eyed despite the fact that the court was completed in 1878. Furthermore, the statue does not stand alone—it is accompanied on another conical top by a personification of mercy. The building is a remnant of the British rule along with the imperial imposition of laws, rules and procedures, one aspect of which is expressed through the statues of justice and mercy on top of the court building. One also finds an open-eyed statue of justice atop the 1907 Old Bailey courthouse, the central criminal court of justice of England and Wales, located in London (Emsley et al. 2017). The statue of Lady Justice placed atop the sixty-seven feet high dome of the Old Bailey courthouse, sculpted by British artist Frederick William Pomeroy (1856–1924), is a twelve-foot tall gold leaf bronze statue, holding a sword in one hand and the scales of justice in the other (Emsley et al. 2017). In a certain way, the placement of the open-eyed statue of justice in Bombay indicates the way in which

[8]The book by Mehrotra and Dwivedi (2004, p. 47) states that the statue of Justice on top of the Bombay High Court is blindfolded. However, the corresponding image (*ibidem*, p. 49) is open-eyed. During my interviews, I spoke to the editor of the book and he acknowledged that this was an error.

[9]See also the contribution by Valérie Hayaert in this volume.

the colony connected its visual semantics to the metropolis by monumentalising English law as the 'gift' of civilisation (Cohn 1996; Kolsky 2010; Singha 2000) to the colonised other. One can surmise then that imperial rule, in the instance of the Bombay High Court, abandoned the blindfold in order to look at the future of law and its empire in a clear-sighted manner. Furthermore, we can infer that the blindfold was not the dominant signifier of the colonial rule of law during this period. In addition, the placement of the statue of justice adjacent to the statue of mercy on top of the Bombay High Court signifies the benevolent despotism of colonial rule (Cohn 1996; Kolsky 2010; Singha 2000).

Colomb (1992) notes that the visitor's brochure of the Old Bailey courthouse specifically mentions the fact that the statue of Justice does not wear a blindfold. This, the brochure claims, was, 'in defiance of convention, because Justice was originally not blindfolded and because her "maidenly form" is supposed to guarantee her impartiality, thus rendering the blindfold redundant' (Colomb 1992, p. 50). When one looks at the statue of justice in the Supreme Court of India, the absence of the blindfold is vital to our understanding of the post-colonial adaptation of this image.

Several judgments rendered by the courts in India, however, evoke the blindfold. In a 2011 case, the Supreme Court of India stated that, 'justice is only blind or blindfolded to the extent necessary to hold its scales evenly; it is not, and must never be allowed, to become blind to the reality of the situation'.[10] In another case, the court interprets the statue, '(n)ot like Themis, blindfolded, but like Astraea, the Roman [*sic*] Goddess of justice holding a scale without folds on the eyes and occupying the price of place as "Libra" in the Zodiacal constellation'.[11] In both situations, the blindfold is referred to as an obstacle that has to be overcome to achieve a particular ideal of justice. In a case from the Madras High Court, the judges refer to an unplanned action that proved to be a 'blessing in disguise', and describes this occurrence as a case where 'justice has been done even blindfolded by the Appellate Authority'.[12] In this instance justice is deemed to be administered despite the blindfold over the eyes of the statue of Justice. In a parallel drawn by the Supreme Court of India, a judgment writes that, '(t)hough justice is depicted to be blind-folded, as popularly said, it is only a veil not to see who the party before it is while pronouncing judgment', and the veil should not 'turn the mind/attention of the court away from the truth of the cause or lis before it'.[13] This statement from the judgment of the Supreme Court of India has been cited several times by various

[10]*Krishnadevi Malchand Kamathia and Others* v. *Bombay Environmental Action Group and Others*, AIR 2011 SC 1140.

[11]*Kush Sahgal and Others* v. *M.C. Mitter and Others*, AIR 2000 SC 1390.

[12]*C.P. Gopinath* v. *Mrs. Leela Govindan and Another*, Madras High Court, CRP n° 2195 of 1981, decided on 26 February 1982.

[13]*Zahira Habibulla H. Sheikh and Another* v. *State of Gujarat and Others*, AIR 2004 SC 346.

high courts across the country.[14] The blindfold over the eyes of the statue of justice has thus found its way into judgments made by the courts in India.

21.4.2 Carvings

The carvings on the pillars of the Bombay High Court show important symbols of justice. There are similar carvings in the Supreme Court of the United Kingdom, as seen in etchings across its stone walls and on its wooden barricades (Cormack 2010). Both groups of carvings tell similar stories. For the purpose of this paper, the carvings of male faces atop several pillars in the Bombay High Court are important (Fig. 21.3). Each figure is represented with distinctive headwear, which represent the different communities that inhabit Bombay city. Iconographically, the presence of the symbols of the different communities within the premises of the court aims to show that the court is open to persons from all communities, irrespective of caste, colour or creed. The same idea was also present in similar neo-gothic structures that were built around the same time in the vicinity of the High Court. Profiles of men adorning various panels are seen in the Victoria Terminus Railway Station,[15] also built in a neo-gothic architectural style and completed in 1887. As Nicole Vance (2016, p. 18) notes, students of the Bombay School of Art were commissioned to 'sculpt architectural details and reliefs for the railway terminus', and they were told that 'the ornament was to reflect local flowers, plants, animals, and citizens of Bombay'. The architectural reliefs on the Victoria Terminus depict different groups of Indian citizens, ranging from Christians, Hindus, Jains, and Muslims to Parsis, and they are identified by their headwear and facial hairstyle, as depicted in the carvings. These attributes identified various social groups, in the same way as the faces and headwear in the Bombay High Court. Vance (2016, p. 21) also argues that these relief panels gave 'a voice to the many communities who inhabited the city', since '(t)he Indian public who frequently utilised the Grand Peninsular Railway would view these relief panels as a positive representation of their own communities, not the elite society of the British Raj'.

However, the court and the buildings surrounding it remain a predominantly male space.[16] Nevertheless, there are two unexplained carvings of women in saris that are also seen in the Bombay High Court. Since there is no trace of their origin,

[14]This statement has been cited in the High Court of Himachal Pradesh, 2012 (1) Crimes 345; the High Court of Delhi, 205 (2013) DLT 410; the High Court of Jammu and Kashmir, 2008 (1) JKJ 161; and the High Court of Madras, 2016 (3) MLJ (Crl) 641, to list but a few.

[15]The Victoria Terminus Railway Station has been renamed as the Chhatrapati Shivaji Terminus Railway Station since 1996.

[16]See Vance 2016, where the author observes different relief panels across the neo-gothic structures constructed in the same time period. The Legal Practitioners (Women) Act (1923) allowed women to practice as lawyers, but women were already permitted to practice even before this. In practice, however, their number was very limited.

Mehrotra and Dwivedi (2004) argue that they are probably images of women that were related to the artists.

Vance gives us some further details about the origin, establishment and functioning of the Bombay School of Art. Students from this school were often taught to 'both continue in the tradition of Indian decorative art and at the same time be trained in a European academic style' (Vance 2016, p. 30). Therefore, the different reliefs, panels and details were often intended to relate to the people of the city of Bombay. This form of architectural depiction was not limited to the Bombay High Court, but was also seen in the Victoria Terminus, the Gokuldas Tejpal Hospital (Manohar 2016), an 1875 construction, and the University of Bombay buildings. The University, with its clock tower called 'the Rajabhai Clock Tower', completed in 1862, displays full figures of native men of Bombay, along with various carvings of Indian animals (Vance 2016).

Throughout the architectural narrative of the buildings in and around the Bombay High Court in the late 1800s, there is a clear influence from the Bombay School of art on the relief and carving work within these buildings. Two specific carvings that are particularly interesting for the iconography of justice are those of the 'monkey judge' and the 'fox lawyer' seen in the Bombay High Court. The 'monkey' in this carving is holding the scales of justice in one hand and a sword in the other (Fig. 21.4). There is a blindfold across its face, but only one eye is covered. In addition to the carving of the monkey, there is a carving of a 'fox lawyer' (Fig. 21.5). The fox is wearing a band around his neck, which is similar to the white band worn by a lawyer in court.

Legend (or folklore) has it that piqued, the builder who built the court, was not adequately compensated for his work (Mehrotra and Dwivedi 2004; Vachha 2011). He carved images of what he perceived the system of justice to be; judges were like clever pirate-monkeys, with an eye-patch and a sword, while lawyers were cunning foxes who manipulated the system of law in the court (Mehrotra and Dwivedi 2004). However, the monkey with an eye-patch holding scales and a sword can be interpreted in several ways. Vachha (2011) relates it to the Aesop fable of the litigious cats. In the fable, the cats are at dispute with one another, and approach a monkey to be the arbitrator of their issue. Several authors argue that some of Aesop's fables were inspired by the Panchatantra and the Jataka tales, linking them to Indian stories and narratives (Saletore 1970; Walawalkar 1970).

21.4.3 Satire on the Walls of the Bombay High Court

The depiction of the monkey as a judge and the fox as a lawyer is also a form of satire. In an article, Dwivedi (1998, p. 26) describes the Bombay High Court as 'Satire in Stone'. She discusses the presence of a variety of animals that are found carved into the stone structure of the Bombay High Court building. The author argues that these carvings might have been made by Rao Bahadur Mukund Ramchandra, the assistant engineer in the construction of the High Court building. Furthermore, Dwivedi also puts forward the question whether Ramchandra was indeed illustrating the Panchatantra, Jataka or Aesop fables in this building. While the answer is uncertain, Dwivedi (1998, p. 27) states '(t)hat the sculpture is meant to give light relief to sombre business in an imperial court cannot be doubted'. While legal humour was indeed a part of court culture (Galanter 2005; Hoeflich 2012), Dwivedi (1998, p. 27) writes: 'Lampooning the legal community has been a historical tradition but knocking it down a peg or two on its own home turf elevates derision to saucy heights'.

In his collection of postcards, Hoeflich (2012, p. vii) recognises that, while not the largest category, legal themes were still a common theme for postcards, 'but the widespread production of legal-themed postcards also illustrates the extent to which law and lawyers were a dominant part of popular culture'. Hoeflich notes that most of the expressions on these postcards were anti-lawyer sentiments, a theme dating back centuries, and were also found in literature, as has been noted by Galanter (2005). Galanter documents an image from 1692 that depicts the lawyer as a fox, wearing the robe and band. A newspaper image of 1877 frames the actions of a lawyer around the images of a vulture and a fox.

Thus, legal humour as a practice existed previously, and the stone carvings in the Bombay High Court can be understood in this context. Hoeflich (2012, p. viii) also writes that 'the portrayal of lawyers as various types of animals was another common theme of postcards and other paper ephemera', of which '(c)ats, dogs, and monkeys were the most common'. Hence, satirical depictions of the 'monkey judge' and 'fox lawyer' appear everywhere, from etchings in illustrated books or cartoons to the walls of courts. Various people associated with the court have interpreted these images as part of the history of the visual culture of the court, which subsequently influenced representations on postcards, posters, book covers and even mugs (Fig. 21.6). The idea of satire and humour is therefore not alien to the court, and these images of justice could also be a representation of wit as displayed by the artists creating them. A similar idea of humour and satire in stone can be found in the Gokuldas Tejpal Hospital, where caricatures of doctors are seen on the pillars of the building (Manohar 2016). Hence, it is safe to assume that this form of carving was part of the school of art of that time (Vance 2016). The Gokuldas Tejpal Hospital was also designed by Fuller and was completed four years prior to the Bombay High Court, in 1874 (Xenophon 1888).

21.4.4 A Representation of Justice

Along with the depiction of the monkey and the fox, the pillars of the court have carvings of different figures of animals: crocodiles, boars, different breeds of dogs, snakes, lions, and birds among which cranes, owls and eagles, all amidst various plants. Mehrotra and Dwivedi (2004, p. 59) write about the carvings of snakes in grass in different corners of the court. They interpret the snakes as 'maliciously smiling at the humans enacting their various roles in the court'. Again, these carvings are the work of the Bombay School of Art. The carvings of animals, flowers and foliage are fundamental features of the neo-gothic buildings constructed in Bombay city in the late 1800s (Vance 2016).

The numerous symbols and stories embedded in the visual programme of the Bombay High Court give rise to a debate on the scope and sphere of judicial iconography in the Indian legal context. During the course of my observations, various readings on how to interpret court structures have allowed me to see the court space differently. The court therefore presents different stories of its legitimacy, and is a space that showcases a variety of representations of justice that are otherwise hidden behind the everyday routine functioning of the court, and its documented rules and regulations.

The neo-gothic structure of the Bombay High Court displays several instances of legal iconology and semiotics. The High Court ties various allegories of law and justice together into its structure, as well as in its daily practices and procedures. The visual imagery on display through the architectural design and symbolism elucidates the relevance of 'the visual' in understanding the didactic nature of the law. The entire court building, along with its carvings, painted portraits and design, provides an unparalleled visual subject matter that assists in understanding the law and justice that this court space purports.

21.5 Conclusion

The Bombay High Court symbolises and expresses its colonial character in several ways. The statue of Justice atop one tower of the High Court is a depiction that serves as an allegory of justice for this court. The statue has the usual attributes of a sword and scale, but its eyes are not covered. In the interior of the court, there are carvings of a monkey depicted as a judge, which provides satire on the walls of the court. Along with this carving, there is also one of a fox with a lawyer's band, depicting the 'fox lawyer'. These are only a few of the carvings and images that are visible across the court structure.

The purpose of these visual symbols of justice is to depict the law and its forces in a particular way. The large and daunting architectural structure of the Bombay High Court contributes to the majesty and dignity with which the court is viewed, and hence provides the court with a sense of legitimacy. As Haldar (1999, p. 135) explains: 'The elegance of legal architecture provides the background against which justice is seen to be done', and this principle is well exemplified in the Bombay High Court.

The Bombay High Court is an example of a colonial court with a distinct historical lineage. The signs and motifs on display in this court indicate the way in which this court links its historical past with the presence of these images as carried forward in the contemporary times. The visual representations of justice that are on display—through the statue of Justice, carvings of the 'monkey judge' and 'fox lawyer', amongst others—highlight the interplay of colonial architecture with local influences that permeate the Bombay High Court till date. Understanding these images in terms of the satire and humour they bring to the walls of the court opens their visual representations to an array of iconological understandings that reflects on the nature of semiotics of law through the symbols of justice thus created (Kevelson 1987; Panofsky 1982).

Viewing and appreciating these artistic representations of law and justice is imperative in understanding the colonial culture of the High Court and its symbolism during the post-colonial period. When the court is visualised in this way, it helps us appreciate the judicial symbolism and the idea behind its conception and design. The judicial iconography then comes alive for persons to view and understand in their own terms and according to their own appreciation of the motifs and signs that abound the walls of the court.

References

Baucom I (1999) Out of place: englishness, empire, and the locations of identity. Princeton University Press, Princeton (NJ)

Chandrachud DY, Mohta AV, Dalvi RS (2012) A heritage of judging: the Bombay high court through one hundred and fifty years. Maharashtra Judicial Academy and Indian Mediation Centre and Training Institute, Mumbai

Cohn BS (1996) Colonialism and its forms of knowledge: the British in India. Princeton University Press, Princeton (NJ)

Colomb GC (1992) Designs on truth: the poetics of the Augustan mock-epic. Pennsylvania State University Press, University Park (PA)

Cormack P (2010) Gothic 'with a Difference': sculpture and decorative arts at the Supreme Court of the United Kingdom. In: Miele C (ed) The supreme court of the United Kingdom: history, art, architecture. Merrell Publishers, London, pp 98–137

Douzinas C (2000) The legality of the image. Mod Law Rev 63(6):813–830

Dwivedi S (1998) Bombay High Court: satire in stone. The Lawyers Collective February–March: 26–30

Emsley C, Hitchcock T, Shoemaker R (2017) Historical background. History of the old bailey Courthouse (Version 7.0). Old Bailey Proceedings. www.oldbaileyonline.org. Accessed 5 Feb 2017

Galanter M (2005) Lowering the bar: lawyer jokes and legal culture. University of Wisconsin Press, Madison (WI)

Goodrich P (1990) Languages of law: from logics of memory to nomadic masks. In: Goodrich P (ed) Modalities of legal annunciation: a linguistics of courtroom speech, Chapter 6. Weidenfeld and Nicolson, London

Gopalratnam VC (1962) A century completed: a history of the Madras High Court (1862–1962). Madras Law Journal Office, Madras

Haldar P (1994) In and out of court: on topographies of law and the architecture of court buildings (a study of the Supreme Court of the State of Israel). Int J Semiot Law 7(20):185–200

Haldar P (1999) The function of the ornament in Quintilian, Alberti, and court architecture. In: Douzinas C, Nead L (eds) Law and the image: the authority of art and the aesthetics of law. University of Chicago Press, Chicago (IL), pp 117–136

Hoeflich MH (2012) The law in postcards and ephemera. The Lawbook Exchange, Clark (NJ)

Huygebaert S, Martyn G, Paumen V, Van Poucke T (eds) (2016) The art of law. three centuries of justice depicted (exh. cat. Bruges). Lannoo, Tielt

Jain MP (2012) Outlines of indian legal and constitutional history. LexisNexis Butterworths Wadhwa, Nagpur
Jay M (2003) Must justice be blind: the challenge of images to the law. In: Jay M (ed) Refractions of Violence. Routledge, New York (NY), pp 87–102
Kevelson R (1987) Introduction to the first round table on law and semiotics. Law Semiot 1:1–24
Kidambi P (2007) The making of an Indian metropolis: colonial governance and public culture in Bombay, 1890–1920. Ashgate, Aldershot
Kolsky E (2010) Colonial justice in British India. Cambridge University Press, Cambridge
Madras High Court (1962) The Madras High Court: 1862–1962: centenary volume. The Associated Printers, Madras
Manohar S (2016) Doing Justice to Bombay High Court. The Hindu, July 14. http://www.thehindu.com/news/cities/mumbai/news/doing-justice-to-bombay-high-court/article8847019.ece. Accessed 13 Aug 2016
Mehrotra R, Dwivedi S (2004) The Bombay High Court: the story of the building, 1878–2003. Eminence Designs, Mumbai
Mukherjee M (2009) India in the shadows of empire: a legal and political history (1774–1950). Oxford University Press, Oxford
Mulcahy L (2011) Legal architecture: justice, due process and the place of law. Routledge, New York (NY)
Nair PT (ed) (1987) Early history of the calcutta High Court. Banerjee Book Company, Calcutta
Panofsky E (1982) Iconography and iconology: an introduction to the study of Renaissance art. In: Meaning in the visual arts. University of Chicago Press, Chicago (IL), pp 26–54
Resnik J, Curtis D (2011) Representing justice: invention, controversy, and rights in city-states and democratic courtrooms. Yale University Press, New Haven (CT)
Saletore RN (1970) Aesop borrowed from Indian folklore. The times of India, Nov 8:A7
Samant-Gupte K (ed) (2014) Vakilnama: celebrating 150 years of the advocates' association of Western India. Advocates' Association of Western India, Mumbai
Singha R (2000) A despotism of law: crime and justice in early colonial India. Oxford University Press, New Delhi
Vachha PB (2011) Famous judges, lawyers and cases of Bombay. Universal Law Publishing, New Delhi
Vance NA (2016) Integrators of design: parsi patronage of Bombay's architectural ornament. Master of Arts Thesis, Department of Comparative Arts and Letters, Brigham Young University, Provo
Walawalkar RT (1970) Aesop's debt to the Panchatantra. The times of India, Dec 27: A7
Xenophon (1888) Goculdass Tejpal Hospital (Native). Indian Eng 1888:390. https://archive.org/stream/indianengineerin04calcuoft#page/390/mode/1up. Accessed 14 Aug 2017

Rahela Khorakiwala has completed her Ph.D. from Jawaharlal Nehru University, New Delhi, India, where she researched in the field of legal anthropology with a special focus on ethnographic work relating to the visual culture of colonial courts in India. Rahela is a lawyer by profession and has completed her LLM from New York University School of Law, USA, and her graduation in law from Government Law College, Mumbai.

Figures

Fig. 21.1 The Neo-Gothic Styled Bombay High Court, private collection GM

Fig. 21.2 *Justice*, Bombay High Court, from: Samant-Gupte (2014)

Fig. 21.3 Carvings on the pillars of the Bombay High Court, with faces of men with different headgear, from: Chandrachud et al. (2012)

Fig. 21.4 *The Monkey Judge*, from: Chandrachud et al. (2012)

Fig. 21.5 *The Fox Lawyer*, from: Samant-Gupte (2014)

Fig. 21.6 Mug with the image of the monkey judge, sold by *Law Suits and More*, https://lawsuitsandmore.com/. Accessed 14 August 2017

Indexes

I.1 Index of Bible Quotes

The books of the Bible are listed in alphabetical order. Although many authors refer to Biblical persons, facts and stories (e.g. the Last Judgment), the list below only contains the explicit references to Bible verses. The authors' reference can be to a single (or several) verse(s) or to a whole chapter or book. References are copied here as they appear in the contributions. As authors often elaborate on a Biblical quote and come back to the same text twice or several times, the references between brackets refer to the specific sections or sometimes the whole chapter; in the case of Alain Wijffels' contribution, '10a' refers to the annex to chapter "Lawyers and Litigants: The Corrupting Appeal and Effects of Civil Litigation in Hendrick Goltzius' Litis abusus".

S. Huygebaert et al. (eds.), *The Art of Law*, Ius Gentium: Comparative Perspectives on Law and Justice 66, https://doi.org/10.1007/978-3-319-90787-1

I.2 Index of Artists (Incl. Architects)

Many artists are known by abbreviated or alternative names, and particularly before the French Revolution the spelling of the names may vary seriously. The contributors were asked to use the preferential name as registered in the database of the Dutch Institute for Art History, as available on www.rkd.nl. The database was also the main source for the years of birth and death. The numbers in parentheses refer to one or more sections or a whole chapter.

I.3 Index of Authors and Editors

Listed are only literary and legal authors who might have inspired the artworks under scrutiny and are mentioned by the contributors in order to situate the art in its contemporary context, i.e. before the First World War. Not listed are the names of those nineteenth—and twentieth–century (legal and art) historians, whose works are 'secondary' literature, which is referred to in the lists of references at the end of each contribution. The numbers in parentheses refer to one or more sections or a whole chapter.

MIX
Papier aus verantwortungsvollen Quellen
Paper from responsible sources
FSC® C105338

If you have any concerns about our products,
you can contact us on
ProductSafety@springernature.com

In case Publisher is established outside the EU,
the EU authorized representative is:
Springer Nature Customer Service Center GmbH
Europaplatz 3, 69115 Heidelberg, Germany

Printed by Libri Plureos GmbH
in Hamburg, Germany